Moro

THE ROUGH GUIDE

P9-DNW-901

Rough Guide Credits

Text editor:	Mark Ellingham
Editorial:	Martin Dunford, John Fisher, Greg Ward, Jack Holland, Jonathan Buckley, Kate Berens, Jules Brown, Graham Parker
Production:	Susanne Hillen, Andy Hilliard, Gail Jammy, Vivien Antwi, Melissa Flack, Alan Spicer
Finance:	Celia Crowley
Publicity:	Richard Trillo

Dedicated

to Chris Scott, a faithful, amusing and greatly appreciated correspondent.

Contributors

Thanks to: Hamish Brown and Dan Eitzen for the hiking sections; Margaret Hubbard for the piece "From a Woman's Perspective"; Jon Marks for updating the history/politics; Chris Overington for the wildlife section; Jonathan Charteris-Black for his article on *moussems*; Manuel Dominguez and David Muddyman for the section on music; Daniel Goff and Pete Widlinski for the cycling hints; Andrew Davy for help with the maps; Jeanne Muchnick for American travel information; Natania Jansz, for helping through the original edition; and Laghmir Abdelmoula for a lot of help with a lot of things.

Grateful **acknowledgements** to Paul Bowles for the "Moroccan Fictions"; and to Marion Boyars and Peter Owen, respectively, for permission to reprint the pieces by Paul Bowles and Elias Canetti in the "Writers on Morocco" section.

The publishers and authors have done their best to ensure the accuracy and currency of all the information in *The Rough Guide to Morocco*, however, they can accept no responsibility for any loss, injury or inconvenience sustained by any traveller as a result of information or advice contained in the guide.

This fourth edition published October 1993 by Rough Guides Ltd, 1 Mercer St, London WC2H 9QJ. Reprinted February 1994.

Distributed by the Penguin Group:

Penguin Books Ltd, 27 Wrights Lane, London W8 5TZ
Penguin Books USA Inc., 375 Hudson Street, New York 10014, USA
Penguin Books Australia Ltd, 487 Maroondah Highway, PO Box 257, Ringwood, Victoria 3134, Australia
Penguin Books Canada Ltd, 10 Alcorn Avenue, Toronto, Ontario, Canada M4V 1E4
Penguin Books (NZ) Ltd, 182–190 Wairau Road, Auckland 10, New Zealand

Originally published in the UK by Routledge and by Harrap Columbus.
Previous edition published in the United States and Canada as *The Real Guide Morocco*.

Typeset in Linotron Univers and Century Old Style to an original design by Andrew Oliver.
Printed by Cox & Wyman Ltd, Reading.

Illustrations in Part One and Part Three by Edward Briant.
Illustrations on p.1 and p.487 by Henry Iles.

British Library Cataloguing-in-Publication
A catalogue record for this book is available from the British Library.
ISBN 1-85828-040-0.

Morocco

THE ROUGH GUIDE

Written and researched by
**Mark Ellingham, Shaun McVeigh
and Don Grisbrook**

Contributors
Hamish Brown and Dan Eitzen (Atlas mountains),
Jon Marks, Margaret Hubbard, Peter Morris,
Chris Overington and David Muddyman

THE ROUGH GUIDES

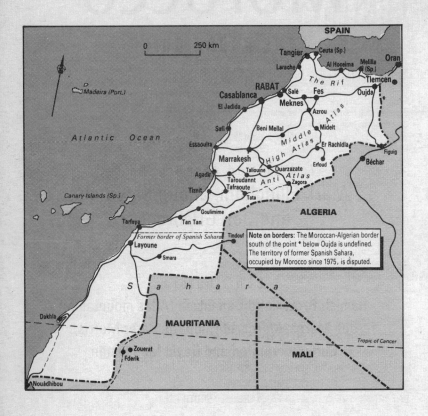

Note on borders: The Moroccan-Algerian border south of the point * below Oujda is undefined. The territory of former Spanish Sahara, occupied by Morocco since 1975, is disputed.

CONTENTS

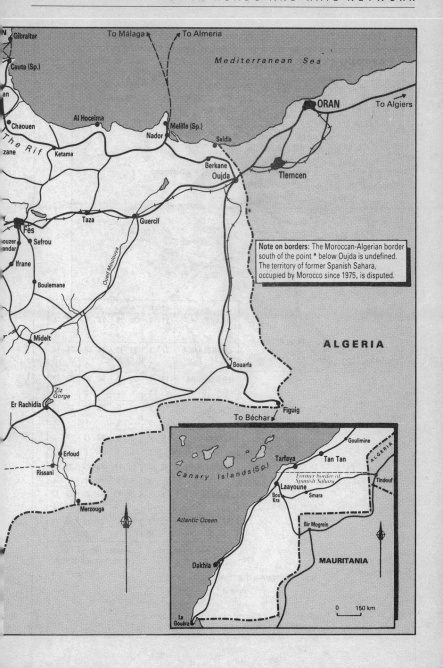

TEMPERATURE CHART

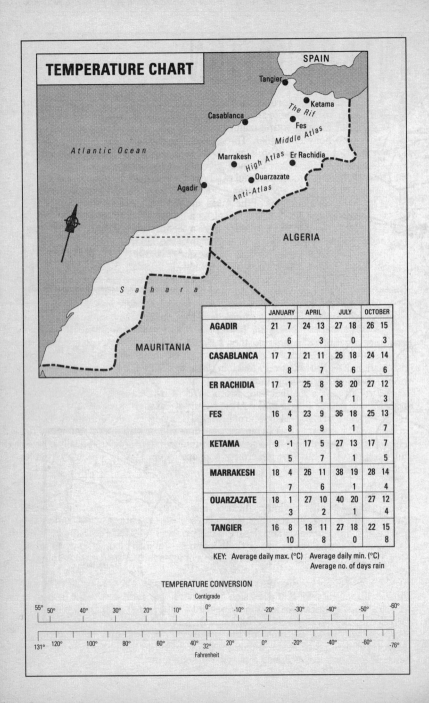

SPAIN

Tangier

Ketama

The Rif

Casablanca

Fes

Middle Atlas

Atlantic Ocean

Marrakesh   *High Atlas*   Er Rachidia

Ouarzazate

Agadir   *Anti-Atlas*

ALGERIA

S a h a r a

MAURITANIA

	JANUARY		APRIL		JULY		OCTOBER	
AGADIR	21	7	24	13	27	18	26	15
	6		3		0		3	
CASABLANCA	17	7	21	11	26	18	24	14
	8		7		6		6	
ER RACHIDIA	17	1	25	8	38	20	27	12
	2		1		1		3	
FES	16	4	23	9	36	18	25	13
	8		9		1		7	
KETAMA	9	-1	17	5	27	13	17	7
	5		7		1		5	
MARRAKESH	18	4	26	11	38	19	28	14
	7		6		1		4	
OUARZAZATE	18	1	27	10	40	20	27	12
	3		2		1		4	
TANGIER	16	8	18	11	27	18	22	15
	10		8		0		8	

KEY: Average daily max. (°C)   Average daily min. (°C)
Average no. of days rain

TEMPERATURE CONVERSION

Centigrade

55° 50° 40° 30° 20° 10° 0° -10° -20° -30° -40° -50° -60°

131° 120° 100° 80° 60° 40° 32° 20° 0° -20° -40° -60° -76°

Fahrenheit

INTRODUCTION

F or Westerners, **Morocco** holds an immediate and enduring fascination. Though just an hour's ride on the ferry from Spain, it seems at once very far from Europe, with a culture – Islamic and deeply traditional – that is almost wholly unfamiliar. Throughout the country, despite the years of French and Spanish colonial rule and the presence of modern and cosmopolitan cities like Rabat or Casablanca, a more distant past constantly makes its presence felt. **Fes**, perhaps the most beautiful of all Arab cities, maintains a life still rooted in medieval times, when a Moroccan empire stretched from Senegal to northern Spain; while in the mountains of the **Atlas** and the **Rif**, it is still possible to draw up tribal maps of the Berber population. As a backdrop to all this, the country's physical make-up is also extraordinary: from a Mediterranean coast, through four mountain ranges, to the empty sand and scrub of the Sahara.

All of which makes **travel** here an intense and rewarding – if not always easy – experience. Certainly, there can be problems in coming to terms with your privileged position as tourist in a nation that, for the most part, would regard such activities as those of another world. And the northern cities especially have a reputation for hustlers: self-appointed guides whose eagerness to offer their services – and whose attitude to tourists as being a justifiable source of income (and to women as something much worse) – can be hard to deal with. If you find this to be too much of a struggle, then it would probably be better to keep to low-key resorts like Essaouira or Asilah, or to the more cosmopolitan holiday destination of Agadir, built very much in the image of its Spanish counterparts, or even a packaged sightseeing tour.

But you'd miss a lot that way. Morocco is at its best well away from such trappings. A week's hiking in the Atlas; a journey through the southern oases or into the pre-Sahara; or leisured strolls around Tangier, Fes or Marrakesh – once you adapt to a different way of life, all your time will be well spent. And it is diffi-cult for any traveller to go for long without running into Morocco's equally power-ful tradition of hospitality, generosity and openness. This is a country people return to again and again.

Regions

Geographically, the country divides into five basic zones: the **coast**, Mediterranean and Atlantic; the great cities of the **plains**; the **Rif** and **Atlas** mountains; and the oases and desert of the **pre-** and fully fledged **Sahara**. With two or three weeks – even two or three months – you can't expect to cover all of this, though it's easy enough (and highly recommended) to take in something of each aspect.

You are unlikely to miss the **mountains**, in any case. The three ranges of the Atlas, with the Rif a kind of extension in the north, cut right across the interior – physical and historical barriers, and inhabited for the most part by the indigenous Moroccan **Berbers**. Contrary to general preconceptions, it is actually the Berbers who make up most of the population; only around ten percent of Moroccans are "pure" Arabs, although with the shift to the industrialised cities, such distinctions are becoming less and less significant.

Morocco's **area** of 710,000 square kilometres is as great as that of France, Spain or Italy. The **population**, over half of which is under 20 years of age, is around 23 million – a dramatic increase compared with just 8 million at independence in 1956.

A more current distinction, perhaps, is the legacy of Morocco's colonial occupation over the fifty-odd years before it reasserted its independence in 1956. The colonised country was divided into **Spanish** and **French** zones – the former contained Tetouan and the Rif, the Mediterranean and the northern Atlantic coasts, and parts of the (now disputed) Western Sahara; the latter comprised the plains and the main cities (Fes, Marrakesh, Casablanca and Rabat), as well as the Atlas. It was the French, who ruled their "protectorate" closely, who had the most lasting effect on Moroccan culture, Europeanising the cities to a strong degree and firmly imposing their language, which is spoken today by all educated Moroccans (after Moroccan Arabic or the local Berber languages).

Highlights

The attractions of the individual regions are discussed in the chapter introductions. Broadly speaking, **the coast** is best enjoyed in the north at **Tangier**, beautiful and still shaped by its old "international" port status; at **Larache**; or at **Saïdia**, below the Rif; in the south at **El Jadida**; at **Essaouira**, perhaps the most easy-going resort; or at remote **Sidi Ifni**. **Agadir**, the main package tour resort, is less worthwhile – but a functional enough base for exploration.

Inland, where the real interest of Morocco lies, the outstanding cities are **Fes** and **Marrakesh**. The great imperial capitals of the country's various dynasties, they are almost unique in the Arab world for the chance they offer to witness some city life that, in patterns and appearance, remains in large part medieval. For monuments, Fes is the highlight, though Marrakesh, the "beginning of the south", is for most visitors the more enjoyable and exciting.

Travel in the **south** – roughly beyond a line drawn between Casablanca and Meknes – is, on the whole, easier and more relaxing than in the sometimes frenetic north. This is certainly true of the **mountain ranges**. The **Rif**, which can feel disturbingly anarchic, is really for hardened travellers; only **Chaouen**, on its periphery, could be counted a "holiday spot". But the **Atlas ranges** (Middle, High and Anti-) are beautiful and accessible.

Hiking in the **High Atlas**, especially around North Africa's highest peak, **Djebel Toubkal**, is in fact something of a growth industry. Even if you are no more than a casual walker, it is worth considering, with summer treks possible at all levels of experience and altitude. And, despite inroads made by commercialisation, it remains essentially "undiscovered" – like the Alps must have been in the last century.

Equally exploratory in mood are the great **southern routes** beyond – and across – the Atlas, amid the **oases** of the pre-Sahara. Major routes here can be travelled by bus; minor ones by rented car or local taxi; the really remote ones by four-wheel drive vehicles or by getting lifts on local *camions* (lorries), sharing space with the market produce and livestock.

The oases, around **Tinerhir**, **Zagora** and **Erfoud**, or (for the committed) **Tata** or **Figuig**, are classic images of the Arab world, vast palmeries stretching into desert horizons. Equally memorable is the architecture that they share with the Atlas – bizarre and fabulous mud (or *pisé*) **kasbahs** and **ksour**, with Gothic-looking turrets and multi-patterned walls.

Climate

As far as the **climate** goes, it would be better to visit the south – or at least the desert routes – outside **midsummer**, when for most of the day it's far too hot for casual exploration, especially if you're dependent on public transport. But July and August, the hottest months, can be wonderful on the coast and in the mountains; there are no set rules.

Spring, which comes late by European standards (around April to May), is perhaps the best overall time, with a summer climate in the south and in the mountains, and water warm enough to swim in on both the Mediterranean and Atlantic coasts. **Winter** can be perfect by day in the south, though be warned that desert nights can get very cold – a major consideration if you're staying in the cheaper hotels, which rarely have heating. If you're planning to **hike** in the **mountains**, it's best to keep to the months from April to October unless you have some experience of snow conditions.

Weather conditions apart, the **Islamic religious calendar**, and its related festivals, will have the most seasonal effect on your travel. The most important factor is **Ramadan**, the month of daytime fasting; this can be a problem for transport, and especially hiking, though the festive evenings do much to compensate. See "Festivals" in the *Basics* section for details of its timing, as well as that of other festivals.

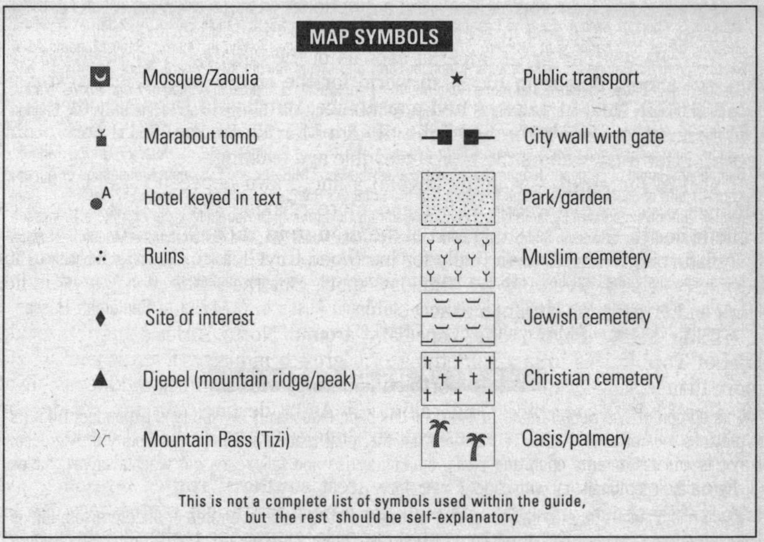

MAP SYMBOLS

�	Mosque/Zaouia	★	Public transport
ᵼ	Marabout tomb	▬■ ■▬	City wall with gate
●ᴬ	Hotel keyed in text		Park/garden
∴	Ruins		Muslim cemetery
◆	Site of interest		Jewish cemetery
▲	Djebel (mountain ridge/peak)		Christian cemetery
)ᴄ	Mountain Pass (Tizi)		Oasis/palmery

This is not a complete list of symbols used within the guide,
but the rest should be self-explanatory

A THOUSAND THANKS

This new edition of *The Rough Guide to Morocco* owes a huge debt to previous **readers and users** who took the trouble to write in with changes and discoveries. A thousand thanks – in no special order – to the following:

Jennifer Fulton; J.D. Nuttall; E.C. Rideal; Andrew Huige; Captain Twalib Mbarak; Bob Azurdia; R. Ennals; Jos van der Akker; Ole Odgaard; Richard Baldwin; Stephen Morris; Tim Bradley; Anton Jansen; Katharine Gwatkin; Nancy Shepherd; Mark Bentinck; D.S. Pain; David Elliott; Patricia Carr; Mio Sato; Kristen Kabasci; Boo Matthews; Duncan Pomeroy; Rachel Hastie; Michael Begg; Angela Wells; Neil Walker; John Kelly; Andrew Maynard; Tiffany Hutt; Jerry van Beers; Martin Webber and Anne-Marie Bradley; Adrian Sanderson; Mark McCrackin; Mike Ivy; Jon Crossland; Bernie Bain; Arjen Tolsma; P. Tugwell; John Peet; Ann Bird; Clare Sayer; Geerdt Magiels; Stephen Goode; Ron Wormald; Alison Coulby, Sam, Angel and Gareth Thomas; Howard B. Caney; Heather Alexander; Charles Fairlie-Cunninghame and Jenni Aldrich; Andy Williams and Katina James; Lucy Redfern; Katrien de Vogelaere & Dirk Verbeke; Philip Le Roux; Stephanie Strøm; Tony Waltham; John Cooper; Dave Driscoll; Clare Ireland; D.L. Wallis; France Selvides; Neil Walker; G.H. Bannister; A. Hill and D. Jeffries; John Brooks; Montagu Curzon;John Hickman; Ross Jones; Anne Raeff and Lori Ostlund; Anna Larsson; Rosemary Palstra; A. Merry; Jan Durekot; Lyn Amami; Albert Neeleman; R. Kramer; Miriam Neuber; Miguel Sanchez; Andrea Colomer; Wim Büys; Håkon Rosendahl; Geoff & Vicki Woollen; Murray Priestman; Richard Ketley; Dhao Wotansen; Anthony B. Keaveny; Tessa Pye; Roy MacLaren; Judith Cantrell; Pierre Flener; Jonathan Ping; Mary Shepherd; Joanna Maude; S. Opacik.

For **help on the ground**, a thousand and one further thanks to the many friends, acquaintances, guides, tourist office staff – everyone in fact – who showed us around and shared knowledge, enthusiasm, expertise and ideas. In particular:

Tali Abdel Aziz and El Aouad Ali of *Tigouga Adventures*, and El Alem Abdessadek, in Taroudannt; Jadid Ahmed and Michelle of the *Auberge Souktana* in Taliouine; Ou Krim Mohammed and Laroussi Housseine in Tafraoute; Jacques Guilbert of *Mehari Tours* in Casablanca; Aârab Mustapha in Rabat; El Mourabite Abdellah in Tiznit for showing us the rock carvings at Aït Herbil; Roger Mimó of the Hôtel de l'Avenir in Tinerhir; Sabir Mohammed of Skoura; Fredéric Damgaard in Essaouira; Menhabi Larbi and Khalid Rachidi of *Menara Tours*, Marrakesh and Casablanca; El Babor Abdelaziz and Annie Guillermont in Beni Mellal; El Kharbachi Ahmed of *Hôtel Khalid*, Nador; Laroussi Ouahabi Abdellah of Larache; El Hannach El Mokhtar in Lixus; Bendriss Bahreddine in Asilah; Baddou Taoufik in Meknes; Sakhi Mohammed and Aboulhassani Abdallah in Safi; Benzianme Saïd of *Golden Tours*, Agadir; Benzakour Amine Anas of *Hôtel Petit Merou*, Cabo Negro; Boufous Saïd of *Hôtel El Farabi*, Tangier; Rahmnouni Hamid of Tetouan; Jeanne Branston of Paris; Abouzerki M'Barek and Oussalam Mohammed of Agadir; Krim Abdeltif of Mohammedia; Sami Mustapha of the Hôtel des Remparts, Essaouira; Serrab El Houssine of Beni Mellal; Zniter Mustapha of El Jadida; Bert Flint in Agadir and Marrakesh; Dr Ronald Messier of Middle Tennessee State University for advice on Sijilmassa; Najim Lahcen of *Hôtel Soleil Bleu*, and Abderrahmane Moubarik of *Hôtel Chems*, Boumalne; Kaddour Horache of Casablanca; Ghaoza Mohammed of El Jadida; Aitoummas Mohammed of Marrakesh; Catherine Campbell and Simon Jordan of *Exodus Expeditions*, and Stephen Brown of Wrexham.

Finally, once again, we are greatly indebted to Annie Austin of *CLM* and to Benlamlih Hassan, Esserghini Hassan and Mike Barnard of the ONMT in London.

HELP US UPDATE

This edition of *The Rough Guide to Morocco* has been extensively revised (and expanded) from its previous incarnations – but . . . facts are not the most readily available commodity in Morocco: hotels and restaurants open and close, standards rise and fall, roads get washed away, buses change their terminals, all with chaotic frequency.

If you find changes (or errors), or feel that there are places we've overrated or underpraised, things we've missed, or covered but which no longer exist, then please write and tell us. Letters about obscure routes through the mountains or desert are as interesting as the low-down on your favourite hotel or restaurant. We'll acknowledge all information used and will send a **free copy**, or any other *Rough Guide* if you prefer, for the most useful (and legible!) letters. Please mark letters "Rough Guide Morocco Update" and send to:

Rough Guides, 1 Mercer St, London WC2H 9QJ, or

Rough Guides, 375 Hudson Street, 4th Floor, New York, NY10014

PART ONE

THE
BASICS

EVITEZ LA FATIGUE
ET LES RISQUES
D'UN LONG VOYAGE

Maroc

FAITES VOS CALCULS ET PRENEZ LE TRAIN.

GETTING THERE FROM BRITAIN AND IRELAND

The simplest way to get to Morocco is, of course, to fly. There are flights from Britain direct to Tangier, Agadir, Casablanca, Marrakesh and other Moroccan airports. Alternatively, you can travel overland (or fly) to France, Spain or Gibraltar and pick up a ferry from there. All-in package deals are worth considering too, either for specialist holidays or off-season bargains.

FLIGHTS FROM BRITAIN

Flying to Morocco from Britain, you have the choice between **direct flights** – scheduled or on charters – or, for the cost-conscious, **flying to Spain** and making your way on from there by ferry. The main problem with **charter flights** is time limitation – most are valid for just one or two weeks. With a **scheduled *APEX* flight** (which must be booked two weeks in advance) you can stay for up to three months and fly to one airport and back from another.

SCHEDULED FLIGHTS

Royal Air Maroc fly more or less daily from London Heathrow to Agadir, Casablanca, Marrakesh and Tangier, and once or twice a week to Ouarzazate; add-on flights from UK regional airports are available. *APEX* fares ex-London cost £170–260 for Tangier, £200–300 for the other destinations, dependent on season; flight times are around three hours (five hours for a flight via Casablanca). For details, contact *Royal Air Maroc*, 205 Regent St, London WI (☎071/439 4361).

The only other scheduled airline with direct flights from Britain to Morocco are *GB Airways*, who fly from London Heathrow to Casablanca (four days a week), Tangier (twice a week) and Marrakesh (once a week), and Gatwick to Tangier (twice a week). Again, add-on flights are available from UK regional airports and fares ex-London £200–300 return. For details, contact *British Airways* (☎081/897 4000 or 0345/222111).

Another alternative is to fly via Paris, which has many more connections with Morocco. *Air France* and *Royal Air Maroc* share services on routes to Casablanca (4–6 flights daily), Marrakesh (1–2 daily), Agadir (daily), Tangier (daily), Oujda and Fes (3–4 weekly). For schedules and fares, which can again include an add-on flight from various regional UK airports, contact *Royal Air Maroc* (see above) or *Air France*, 158 New Bond St, London WI (☎071/499 9511).

CHARTER FLIGHTS

The main Moroccan destinations for British-run charter flights are **Tangier** in the north and **Agadir** in the south, although a few operators also offer **Marrakesh**. The cheapest flights are invariably from London but there are also direct charter flights from Manchester, Birmingham, Newcastle and Glasgow. If you're lucky, outside peak periods (July & Aug, Christmas/New Year and Easter), you might find return flights to Tangier or Agadir for as low as £70–120 return. In peak season you should expect to pay £180–220 return – and you may well have problems finding a seat.

Looking for a charter fare, it is worth keeping an eye out for full **package holidays**. At certain times of the year major operators like *Inspirations* sell off holidays, including accommodation, at prices no greater than the cost of a flight. Lists of tour operators are given on pp.6–7.

VIA SPAIN

Charter flights are usually easier to come by to **Spain** than to Morocco, especially if you want to travel from one of the smaller regional British airports. Fares can drop as low as £60–80 return to Málaga or Almería – the best destinations for travelling on to Morocco.

If you get a flight to **Málaga**, you've a choice of onward travel to Morocco: a ferry direct to

Melilla (see "Ferry Routes and Agents", p.8) or a bus trip down to **Algeciras** and the crossings to Ceuta or Tangier. **Algeciras** is a simple journey by bus (there's no direct train) from Málaga. From the airport, take the train into Málaga train station (Málaga RENFE; every 20–30min), and then a bus from the terminal opposite; the journey takes three to five hours depending on traffic.

If you fly to **Almería**, you'll want to make use of the direct ferry to Melilla.

VIA GIBRALTAR

Gibraltar is another possible starting point for travelling on to Morocco. Scheduled return flights from London on *GB Airways* (handled by British Airways – see previous page) go for around £125 low season, £220 high season, and there are charter flights from major regional British airports. From Gibraltar, there are **ferries** direct to Tangier twice a week, or you can take a local bus to pick up a ferry from Algeciras, just half an hour round the bay (again, see the "Ferry Routes and Agents" box on p.8). There are also flights from Gibraltar on *GB Airways* to Tangier, Casablanca and Marrakesh, though at £85–100, adding on the cost of these to a flight from Britain to Gibraltar makes little sense.

FLIGHT SOURCES AND AGENTS

The best **sources for finding a flight** are the classified advertisements in the travel section of *The Sunday Times* newspaper or (for London) *Time Out*. High street travel agents are also worth a look for reductions on package holidays and charter flights.

Among specialist **agents**, *Alecos Tours* (3a Camden Rd, London NW1 9LG; ☎071/267 2092) offer **discount "SGIT" fares** on scheduled flights to Morocco, while *Gibraltar Travel Ltd* (251 Northfield Ave, London W13 9QU; ☎081/ 579 0307) can be useful for Gibraltar flights. *STA Travel* (86 Old Brompton Rd, London SW7; ☎071/ 937 9921) and *Campus Travel* (52 Grosvenor Gardens, London SW1; ☎071/730 6525) both cater for **student/youth** needs but have a competitive range of fares open to all. Both have offices on campuses throughout Britain and *Campus* operate in Ireland.

Morocco specialists like *CLM*, *Morocco Bound* and *Moroccan Travel Bureau* will all book flight-only holidays, too; see the box on p.6 for their addresses and phone numbers.

If you plan to **overnight** in Gibraltar, beware that there are no hotel rooms available under £50, no youth hostel and no campsite.

FLIGHTS FROM IRELAND

Charter flights direct from Ireland to Morocco are operated by *Sunway Travel*, Blackrock, Dublin 6 (☎01/288 6828). These apart, the cheapest access is either to pay a tag-on fare for a **transit via London or Paris**, or to travel **via Spain** – Málaga (see above) being the obvious airport choice.

For **student/youth** deals, contact *USIT*, who have branches throughout Ireland, including Aston Quay, O'Connell Bridge, Dublin (☎01/778117) and 13b College St, Belfast (☎0232/324073).

BY TRAIN

London to Morocco by **train and ferry** takes the best part of three days, but it's a great trip if you have the time to stop en route and take in something of France and Spain. Paris, the Pyrenees, Madrid, Córdoba and Granada all lie pretty much on the route. Unless you are under 26 (the age qualification for discount *BIGE* tickets or rail passes), however, you will probably end up paying rather more than for a flight.

Train departures are from London's **Victoria Railway Station** (Victoria tube). For schedules contact the **British Railways** International Information Line (☎071/ 834 2345).

TICKETS

Standard rail tickets from London to Casablanca, inclusive of the ferries en route, cost around £320 return. They are available from any *British Rail* travel office, or from *Thomas Cook* and other major travel agents.

BIGE youth tickets – available to anyone under 26 years – discount standard rail fares by 20–35 percent, with a return ticket to Casablanca going for £253. The tickets allow any number of stopovers along a pre-specified route and can be used on all standard European trains (some express services have a surcharge). The period of validity is six months if they have a Moroccan end-destination, two months with a European end-destination.

In Britain, BIGE tickets are marketed as *Eurotrain* by *Campus Travel* (52 Grosvenor Gardens, London SW1; ☎071/730 3402) and are available from any youth/student travel agency.

THE INTERRAIL PASS

Morocco is covered by the European under-26 **InterRail pass** (£249) which buys one month's unlimited travel on trains in Morocco and most of Europe, along with half-price fares on most ferries (including those from Algeciras to Tangier).

Hidden costs are supplements on express trains and fifty percent of the fares on the channel ferries and between the British station you set out from/return to. The pass is available through youth/student travel agencies or from any major *British Rail* station or travel office.

BY COACH

There are regular **coach services from London to Morocco**, via the ferry at Algeciras. Be warned, though, that it is a 50-hour journey to Tangier and another 8 to 12 hours to Marrakesh or Agadir – quite an endurance test.

The coaches are operated jointly by the British and Spanish companies, *Eurolines* and *Iberbus*. The main route (four departures a week, year round) is to Tangier, Rabat, Casablanca, Marrakesh, Tiznit and finally Agadir. The other route (twice a week, year round) runs through Fes, Meknes and Nador to Oujda. Fares from London range from £190 to £220 return, according to destination and season; there are no student/youth reductions on these routes.

For **details** contact *Eurolines* (52 Grosvenor Gardens, London SWI; ☎071/730 0202). **Departures** are from London's **Victoria Coach Station** (Victoria tube).

DRIVING OR HITCHING

If you plan to **drive down to Morocco through Spain and France**, you'll be well advised to set aside a minimum of four days for the journey. The buses detailed above cover the route to Algeciras in 48 hours but they are more or less non-stop, with two drivers and just a few short meal breaks.

There are **car ferries** across to Morocco from Spain at **Almería and Málaga** (to Melilla) and at **Algeciras** (to Ceuta or Tangier). Ferries also sail from **Sète** in France to Tangier (year round) and Nador (June–Sept), and from **Faro** on the Portuguese Algarve to Tangier (June–Aug).

DRIVING ROUTES

Heading through France for the ferries from Spain, there is much to be said for getting off at least some of the main routes. However, if time is all important, the most direct **route** is:

London – Dover/Folkestone (channel ferry to Calais/Boulogne); Calais/Boulogne – Paris – Tours – Poitiers – Bordeaux – Bayonne; San Sebastian – Madrid – Jaen/Córdoba; then Jaen – **Almeria**, Córdoba – **Malaga**, or Córdoba – **Algeciras**.

At quite a significant extra expense, it is possible to cut off the French section of the route by using the **car ferry from Plymouth** to **Santander** in northern Spain. This runs twice weekly most of the year (no sailings in January); for details and prices phone *Brittany Ferries* in Plymouth (☎0752/21321).

VEHICLE RED TAPE

Driving to (and within) Morocco you must take out **Green Card Insurance**; a few insurance companies don't cover Morocco, so you may need to shop around. Entering Morocco, you will need to present the card, along with your **vehicle registration document** – which must be in your name or accompanied by a letter from the registered owner. **Caravans** need temporary importation documents, which are obtainable at the frontier for no charge.

Entering Morocco through the Spanish enclaves of Ceuta or Melilla (the most economic crossings for vehicles), try to avoid, if possible, arriving at the weekend. If there are any problems, you may well be sent back to Ceuta or Melilla to wait until the Monday to sort them out. Some visitors choose to tip at the frontier, leaving a note in their passport, or engage a tout to get them through more quickly.

European, Australasian and North American **driving licences** are recognised and valid in Morocco, though an International Driving Licence, with its French translations (available from the AA or equivalent motoring organisations) is a worthwhile investment. The **minimum age** for driving in Morocco is 21 years. For further details, see the section on "Driving in Morocco", p.26.

HITCHING

Hitching down to Morocco through France and Spain, it's best to buy a bus ticket to cover the first part of the journey. You will, in any case, have to pay for a channel ferry ticket, and buses from London to French cities such as Rouen or Tours don't add significantly to that cost, at around £65 return on *Eurolines* (see above). You could easily spend a lot of time – and money – hitching out of London or the channel ports.

The worst place of all to hitch is Paris; people can wait days on the roads out of the city – don't try it! Once south of Paris, getting rides becomes a little easier but the position deteriorates again as you cross the border into Spain – and Madrid is another terrible city for hitchers. In fact, once at Madrid, you'll probably save money cutting your losses and saving on accommodation by taking the night train down to Algeciras (about 2000ptas, £12). Harassment is also especially overt in southern Spain and hitching there is not recommended for women travelling alone.

Hitching back from Morocco, starting at the car ferry in **Ceuta** is by far your best bet. It's quite possible you'll get a lift the whole way back to Britain from there. Other useful points to ask around are the **campsites** at **Fes**, **Meknes** and **Martil** (near Tetouan), all traditional last stops.

FERRIES TO MOROCCO

Crossing to Morocco by **ferry** – sailing from Europe to Africa – is the most satisfying (and apt) way to arrive in the country. From Spain the trip is just a couple of hours by ferry – or half an hour on the (passenger-only) hydrofoil to Ceuta.

UK SPECIALIST AND PACKAGE OPERATORS

Morocco is covered by a huge variety of UK travel agents and operators, offering everything from straight **package holidays**, through mountain **trekking** or **desert overland "exploration" safaris** in customised trucks and landrovers, to **tailor-made itineraries**, with flights, car rental and hotels booked to your specifications,

MOROCCO SPECIALISTS

CLM (*"Morocco Made to Measure"*), 4a William St, London SW1 (☎071/235 2110). Highly flexible and reliable agency, who will arrange flights and personally planned holidays from a wealth of personal knowledge. Accommodation on offer ranges from modest, out of the way *auberges* to luxury hotels. Upmarket but good value for money.

Best of Morocco, Seend Park, Seend, Wilts SN12 6NZ (☎0380/828533). "Best of" offer a fairly similar service to *CLM*, with accommodation in quality hotels. They also specialise in golfing holidays and (unusually) trekking in style.

Moroccan Sun, Suite 202, Triumph House, 189 Regent St, London W1 (☎071/437 3968).

Morocco Bound, Suite 603, Triumph House, 189 Regent St, London W1 (☎071/734 5307).

Moroccan Travel Bureau, 304 Old Brompton Rd, London SW5 (☎071/373 4411).

These three companies offer tailor-made holidays, though they concentrate more on budget-priced flight and accommodation packages in the main cities and resorts. Note that *Moroccan Sun* and *Morocco Bound* are entirely separate companies, despite sharing the same address.

ACCOMMODATION

CRS, 5 Stilehall Parade, Chiswick High Rd, London W4 3AG (☎081/742 2424). Hotel bookings in major towns, with around 20 percent discount on prices.

TREKKING TOURS

Most trekking companies run High Atlas tours in spring, summer and autumn, which are fine for the averagely fit walker and require no actual climbing. In winter these are areas for experienced hikers only, and south-facing areas such as the Djebel Sarhro, Anti-Atlas (Tafraoute region) and Djebel Sirwa are offered instead.

Sherpa Expeditions, 131a Heston Rd, Hounslow, Middlesex TW5 0RD (☎081/577 2717). Choice of four fifteen-day tours in the High Atlas (Toubkal area and little-explored Mgoun Massif), Djebel Sarhro and Djebel Sirwa.

Exodus Expeditions, 9 Weir Rd, London SW12 0LT (☎081/675 5550). Two- and three-week High Atlas and Djebel Sarhro treks. Highlight is the three-week Atlas Grand Traverse, a crossing of the Middle and High Atlas ranges (summer only). Also truck tours of the country.

Explore Worldwide, 1 Frederick St, Aldershot, Hants (☎0252/344 161). A good range of treks include fifteen days in the High Atlas or Djebel Sarhro, and 8-day Anti-Atlas treks in Djebel Sirwa. Also desert and Imperial City truck tours.

Waymark Holidays, 295 Lillie Rd, London SW6 7LL (☎071/385 5015). Unusual sixteen-day tour of the Western High Atlas/Djebel Sirwa (trekking out from Taroudannt/Taliouine), and fourteen-day truck tour including desert journeys and some hiking in the Todra Gorge.

Routes are covered in the box overpage. Your main choice is in deciding **which port** to head for. Most overland travellers cross (and services are most frequent) on the routes from **Algeciras** to Ceuta (a Spanish enclave) and Tangier. **Ceuta** is the cheaper crossing – with considerable savings for cars – but for pedestrians it is time-consuming, as you need to get a bus to the Moroccan border and another from there to the rather intimidating town of Tetouan.

Tangier is a little easier to get to grips with and is better placed for public transport on into Morocco, being located at the beginning of the railway line.

Among alternatives, the crossings from **Málaga** and **Almería** to **Melilla**, another Spanish enclave, are most useful for drivers heading for Fes or southeast Morocco, while the ferry from **Sète** in southern France to **Tangier** offers a convenient (if expensive) short cut; the ferry from the Portuguese Algarve to Tangier has been scrapped. For passengers, the **hydrofoils** from Algeciras to Ceuta and Tangier cut time off a journey.

It's important to note that for **all ferries from Spain to Morocco** (excepting Ceuta/Melilla) you must collect an exit visa (in Algeciras from a lone official in a passport kiosk) before boarding.

Worldsaway, 101 Eden Vale Rd, Westbury, Wilts (☎0373/827 914). New trekking division of the experienced Guerba overland company (see below), offering High Atlas and Djebel Sarhro trips.

Worldwide Journeys, 8 Comeragh Rd, London W14 9HP (☎071/381 8638). Fairly upmarket operator who run High Atlas and Djebel Sarhro treks, plus desert safaris as part of tailor-made itineraries.

See also Best of Morocco *on the previous page.*

OVERLAND EXPEDITION TOURS

Guerba, 101 Eden Vale Rd, Westbury, Wilts (☎0373/826 611). Two-week tours in customised trucks of the "Moroccan Deserts and Mountains", and "Deep South" (Anti-Atlas region).

Encounter Overland, 267 Old Brompton Rd, London SW5 (☎071/370 6845). Fifteen-day tour of Morocco including a trip up the Todra Gorge and on southern pistes, again in customised trucks.

Top Deck, 64–65 Kenway Rd, London SW5 (☎071/ 373 5095). Tours of Morocco and southern Spain in converted London double-decker buses. Younger clientele than the companies above, and a perennial favourite with Australians in Europe.

Discover, Timbers, Oxted Rd, Godstone, Surrey RA9 8AD (☎0883/744392). Three or four tours each year, taking in some Atlas trekking and overland transit down to Zagora and the desert.

See also listings above for Exodus, Explore Worldwide, Waymark *and* Worldwide Journeys.

CYCLING TOURS (MOUNTAIN BIKES)

Intrepid Trips, Intrepid House, Freefolk, Whitchurch, Hants RG28 7 NJ(☎0256/893 432).

BIRDWATCHING TOURS

Michael Jones, 30b Springfield Rd, Stoneygate, Leicester LE2 3BA (☎0533/700 837).

Naturetrek, Chautara, Bighton, Hants (☎0962/ 733 051).

GENERAL/MAINSTREAM TOUR OPERATORS

The advantage of mainstream operators rests in getting a good value deal on flight plus resort accommodation; some can offer excellent rates, too, on stays at the country's top hotels, like the Mamounia in Marrakesh, El Minzah in Tangier or Palais Jamai in Fes. The best of the operators (some of the majors dropped Morocco from their schedules during the Gulf War) include:

Abercrombie & Kent (☎071/730 9376). Major hotels and "Morocco à la carte". Upmarket.

Cadogan (☎0703/332 551). Tangier, Marrakesh, Agadir. Modest/upmarket

Hayes & Jarvis (☎0703/332 551). Marrakesh, Taroudannt and Agadir; southern and "Imperial City" tours. Recommended by several readers. Modest.

Inspirations (☎0293/822 244). Tangier, Agadir, Marrakesh, Asilah. Cheap/modest.

Kuoni (☎0306/740 888). Agadir, Morocco and tours of the cities and south. Modest.

Meridian (☎071/493 9171). Agadir, Marrakesh, Tangier and tours. Modest.

Prestige (☎0425/480 400). Marrakesh and Agadir. Modest.

Saga (☎0303/875 000). Marrakesh and Agadir, for over 60s only. Modest.

Travelscene (☎081/427 4445). Marrakesh and Casablanca. Modest.

Then, once onboard, you have to complete a **disembarkation form** and have your **passport stamped** at the ship's purser's office. Announcements to this effect are not always made in English, but if you don't have a stamp, you'll have to wait until everyone else has cleared frontier and customs controls before being attended to. **Returning from Morocco to Spain**, you need to collect an embarkation form and departure card and have these stamped by the port police prior to boarding your ferry.

Note that the **ferries to Ceuta, Tangier and Melilla** are **booked solid** for 3–5 days from the beginning of August, and **from those ports** during the last 3–5 days of August: the holiday month for Moroccans working in Northern Europe. Ferries are also packed out at either end of the **Easter** (Semana Santa) week holiday.

FERRY ROUTES AND AGENTS

*All ferry **frequencies** are given below for summer (in general, April to early September) and winter (mid-September to the end of March). **Fares** quoted are for a **regular adult single**; children normally pay half fare.*

*For detailed schedules and prices, contact the UK agent, **Southern Ferries**, 179 Piccadilly, London W1V 0BA (☎071/491 4968), who handle most of the services detailed below.*

*Note: the **ferries** between **Faro and Tangier** and **Sète and Nador**, and the **hydrofoil from Tarifa to Tangier**, have been discontinued.*

ALGECIRAS

● **Algeciras–Tangier ferry** 5–6 crossings daily in summer; 3–4 crossings daily in winter. Passenger £15/$24, medium car from £42/$67; motorbike/bicycle £12.50/$20; 2hr 30min.

● **Algeciras–Ceuta ferry** 12 crossings daily in summer; 6–8 daily in winter. Passenger £10/$16, medium car from £40/$70; 1hr 20min.

● **Algeciras–Ceuta hydrofoil (passenger only)** 4–8 crossings daily, weather permitting, year round. Passenger £15/$25; 30min.

● **Algeciras–Tangier hydrofoil (passenger only)** 1–2 crossings daily, weather permitting, year round. Passenger £15/$25; 1hr.

*The ferries and hydrofoil are operated in Spain by **Transmediterranea** (☎66.52.00) and in Morocco by **Limadet** and **Comarit**. In Algeciras, **tickets** can be bought from any travel agent (there are dozens along the seafront) or at the port gates. It is usually easier to buy from agents (prices are standard), most of which accept credit cards and travellers' cheques.*

● **Algeciras–Ceuta catamaran (passenger only)** 5 crossings daily in summer only, weather permitting. *Operated by **Isnasa**.*

TARIFA

● **Tarifa–Tangier ferry** A new ferry, **Idriss I**, crosses daily except on Sundays, having replaced the old hydrofoil service; 2hr.

*Operated by **Transtour**, this caters mainly for tour groups and is often block-booked.*

GIBRALTAR

● **Gibraltar–Tangier ferry** The *Idriss I* makes the run twice weekly; 3hr.

*Gibraltar agents are **TourAfrica**, ICC (International Commercial Centre), Casemates Square.*

MALAGA/ALMERIA

● **Málaga–Melilla ferry** Daily crossing in summer, daily except Sun in winter, on the *Canjura/Albatross*. Passenger £18/$28 (£35/$55 in 2-berth cabin), medium car from £70; 7hr 30min.

● **Almería–Melilla ferry** 1–2 crossings daily in summer, daily except Mon in winter, on the *Canjura/Albatross*; prices as from Málaga (above); 6hr 30min.

*Operated by **Transmediterranea**, who have offices at c/Juan Diaz 4, Málaga (☎22.43.93) and in Parque José António 26, Almería (☎23.63.56).*

SÈTE

● **Sète–Tangier ferry** The ferry *Marrakesh* runs 3–7 times a month, depending on season, leaving Sète at 7pm, arriving Tangier 9am the following morning; passengers from £130/$200 in 4-berth cabin; medium car from £160/$255; 38hr.

*Bookings well in advance are essential for Sète ferries. The French agent is SNCM, 4 Quai d'Alger (☎74.70.55); in Morocco, book tickets through **COMANAV** offices in Tangier, Casablanca, Marrakesh or Agadir (see local "Listings" sections in the main guide).*

GETTING THERE FROM NORTH AMERICA

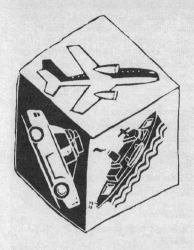

Although there are direct flights from New York and Montréal to Casablanca, most North Americans travel to Morocco via Europe. Flights across the Atlantic to London, Paris or Madrid can be purchased with an add-on connection to a number of Moroccan destinations. Alternatively, if budget rather than time is your main concern, you can simply fly to Europe and buy a low-cost flight for yourself or, best of all, travel overland through Spain and cross over to Morocco on the ferry.

DIRECT FROM THE USA

Royal Air Maroc (*RAM*), the Moroccan national airline, operate direct flights to Casablanca from New York and Montréal. Tickets can be bought in conjunction with one or more add-on flights to other Moroccan airports, or, if you are embarking on a trip across North Africa, with flights east to Tunisia or Egypt. Alternatives to the *RAM* routes include flights on **British Airways**, **Air France**, **KLM** and **Iberia**. These offer a number of Moroccan destinations – Tangier, Casablanca, Marrakesh and Agadir are the most common – routed through the airlines' respective hubs of London, Paris, Amsterdam and Madrid.

Student/youth discount fares are not particularly promising for direct flights, though

STA, **CIEE** and **Nouvelles Frontières** (see boxes for addresses) may turn up the occasional budget fare to Casablanca. All three of these agencies, however, are likely to come up with much better deals on **flights to London, Paris or Madrid**. Given that the cheapest and most frequent flights to Morocco are from France, *Nouvelles Frontières* should probably be your first call if you are planning to holiday purely in Morocco. They should be able to fix up a low-cost add-on fare to one or other of the Moroccan airports. Note that although *STA*, *CIEE* and *Nouvelles Frontières* specialise in the student/youth market, they offer **low-cost fares to all travellers** – irrespective of age or student status.

If you decide to make your own way to **Morocco via Britain**, you will have a wide range of flights to London to choose from. Contact the **discount travel agents** in the box overpage and check Sunday travel supplements of the major newspapers. Reasonable targets for a **return fare to London** are around $550 from the East Coast, $650 from the Midwest, $800 from the West Coast, though at time of writing bargain fares from New York and Miami to London have dropped as low as $400.

Onward travel from **London to Morocco** is covered in the preceding section, "Getting There From Britain".

EAST COAST

Royal Air Maroc operates two flights a week from **New York to Casablanca** – the only regular direct flight from the US to Morocco. Departures from New York are on Tuesdays and Saturdays. APEX return fares vary from $700 (plus tax) in low season, to $825 (plus tax) in high season for the midweek flights; weekend flights are around $50 extra. The high season is from June 1 to August 31 and over the Christmas period.

For anyone under 24, *RAM* issue a **youthpass**, which gives a 10 percent discount on the APEX fares and, perhaps more important, frees you from APEX restrictions, allowing you to buy an open-ended return (6 months' limit) any time up to three days before departure.

At certain times of year, you may find direct **charter flights** to Morocco from the East Coast.

DISCOUNT FLIGHT AGENTS AND CONSOLIDATORS

Council Travel

Head Office

205 E 42nd St, New York, NY 10017; ☎212/661-1450

US regional offices include:

Emory Village, 1561 N Decatur Rd, Atlanta, GA 30307; ☎404/377-9997

2000 Guadalupe St, Suite 6, Austin, TX 78705; ☎512/472-4931

729 Boyleston St, Suite 201, Boston MA 02116; ☎617/266-1926

1138 13th St, Boulder, CO 80302; ☎303/447-8101

1153 N Dearborn St, Chicago, IL 60610; ☎312/951-0585

6923 Snydor Plaza, Suite B, Dallas, TX 75205; ☎214/363-9941

1093 Broxton Ave, Los Angeles, CA 90024; ☎310/208-3551

1501 University Ave SE, Room 300, Minneapolis, MN 55414; ☎612/379-2323

6363 St. Charles Ave, Box 108, New Orleans, LA 70118; ☎504-866-1767

715SW Morrison, Suite 600, Portland OR 97205; ☎503/228-1900

171 Angell St, Suite 212, Providence, RI 02906; ☎401/331-5810

530 Bush St, Suite 700, San Francisco, CA 94108; ☎413/421-3473

1314 Northeast 43rd St, Suite 210, Seattle, WA 98105; ☎206/632-2448

1210 Potomac St NW, Washington, DC 20007; ☎202/337-6464

Nouvelles Frontières

12 E 33rd St, New York, NY 10016; ☎212/779-0600

1001 Sherbrook East, Suite 720, Montréal H2L 1L3; ☎514/526-8444

174 Grande Alée Ouest, Québec, PQ 01R 209; ☎418/525-5255

STA Travel

Head Office

7204 Melrose Ave, Los Angeles, CA90046; ☎213/937-5714

US regional offices include:

48 E 11th St, New York, NY 10003; ☎212/477-7166

166 Geary St, Suite 702, San Francisco, CA 94108; ☎415/391-8407

273 Newbury St, Boston MA 02116; ☎617/266-6014

Encore Short Notice

4501 Forbes Blvd, Lanham, MD 20706; ☎301/459-8020 or 800/638-0830

Moment's Notice

425 Madison Ave, New York, NY 10017; ☎212/486-0503

Stand Buys

311 W Superior St, Chicago, IL 60610; ☎800/548-1116

Travel Avenue

180 North Des Plaines, Suite 201, Chicago, IL 60661; ☎312/876-1116 or ☎800/333-3335

Travel Cuts

Head Office

187 College St, Toronto, ON M5T 1P7; ☎416/979-2406

Canadian regional offices include:

12304 Jasper Ave, Edmonton, T5N 3K5; ☎403/488-8487

6139 South St, Halifax, NS B3H 4JS; ☎902/494-2054

1613 Rue St-Denis, Montréal H2X 3K3; ☎514/843-8511

Place Riel Campus Centre, University of Saskatchewan, Saskatoon, S7N 0W; ☎306/975-5722

1516 Duranleau St, Granville Island, Vancouver, BC V6H 3S4; ☎604/689-2887

University Centre, University of MAnitoba, Winnipeg, MA R3T 2N2; 204/269-9530

Unitravel

1177 N Warson Rd, St Louis, MO 63132; ☎800/325-2222

Check the Sunday travel section of the New York Times and phone around. One company always worth a call for charters is *Access International* (☎800/333-7280).

The major European carriers, *British Airways*, *Air France*, *Iberia* and *KLM* have **scheduled flights to Morocco via Europe**. *British Airways* fly via London to Casablanca, Tangier and Agadir. *Air France* fly to Casablanca via Paris and to Tangier via Madrid. *Iberia* fly to Casablanca via Madrid. *KLM* fly via Amsterdam to Casablanca and Tangiers. APEX return fares from New York cost around $750 high season, $650 low season; for Miami or Orlando departures, add on around $50.

TWA will also fly you scheduled to Madrid to pick up *Iberia* to Casablanca ($685–950) return; and *American* (☎800/433-7300) will fly you to Brussels to pick up *Sabena* to Casablanca ($800–1125 return).

For **London-only flights**, *Virgin Atlantic* offer good service and value fares ($500–600 return) from Newark and Miami.

WEST COAST
Scheduled flights to Morocco via Europe from LA or San Francisco cost around $1000 for high-season APEX, $900 low-season with the main carriers. *Iberia* (☎800/772-4642) are often a bit cheaper than the opposition. Try phoning them, as well as *British Airways* (☎800/247-9297) and *TWA* (☎800/484 9311, or ☎800/864-5731).

Agents worth contacting, in addition to *CIEE*, *STN* and *Nouvelles Frontières*, include *Airkit* in LA (☎213/482-8778) or SF (☎415/764-4933). Check also the travel pages in the *LA Times* or the *San Francisco Chronicle* – either of which may produce the occasional charter or a good deal to London, Paris or Madrid.

MIDWEST
Once again, it is worth spending a Sunday checking the **travel sections** of major newspapers, which can reveal a range of special offers to Europe. On the whole, the cheaper flights involve transiting via New York.

For direct **flights to Europe**, with a **connecting flight to Morocco**, the lowest scheduled fares are *Iberia* from Chicago to Casablanca, via Madrid, or *KLM* from Chicago and Houston to Casablanca or Tangier, via Amsterdam. APEX fares on these cost around $950 high season, $850 low season.

DIRECT FROM CANADA

Royal Air Maroc (☎514/285-1435) have weekly (Saturday) scheduled flights **direct from Montréal to Casablanca**, in the summer only; return APEX return fares are around Can$1100 (plus tax). The rest of the year, passengers connect in New York, but fares dropping as low as Can$710 midweek, $760 weekend (plus tax).

For scheduled flights to **Casablanca via Europe**, *KLM*, *Iberia* and *Air France* are the most promising airlines. *KLM* and *Air France* fly from

TOLL-FREE AIRLINE NUMBERS

American Airlines ☎800/433-7300
British Airways ☎800/247-2747
Continental ☎800/231-0856
Air France ☎800/237-2747
Iberia ☎800/722-4642

KLM ☎800/374-7747
Royal Air Maroc ☎800/892-6726
TWA ☎800/892-4141
Virgin Atlantic ☎800/862-8621

PACKAGE TOUR AGENTS

Adventure Travel Center (☎800/227 8747)). Based in Oakland, California.
Call Step (☎212/308 4249). New York-based.
Les Soleil Tours (☎212/869 1040). New York-based.
Marsans International (☎212/239 3880). New York-based.

Maupintour (☎800/255-6162). Based in Lawrence, Kansas.
Morocco Travel International (☎800/428-5550). Based in Arlington, Virginia.
Royal Air Maroc Tours (☎800/344-6726). New York-based.

Toronto and Vancouver, *Iberia* from Montréal and Toronto. APEX fares from Toronto and Montréal are Can$900–1100 high season, Can$720–850 low season; from Vancouver, add around Can$100 to all these prices.

Shopping round the **travel agencies**, you may be able to get better prices. Good sources include *Travel CUTS* (known as *Voyages CUTS* in Québec) and *Nouvelles Frontières*, which both offer fares in the Can$700–800 range from Montréal. See boxes for addresses.

VIA BRITAIN

If you decide to **transit via Britain**, there is quite a wide range of travel routes available – see the previous section "Getting there from Britain and Ireland". Note that, if you intend to travel by **train**, the *EurRail* pass (available in various permutations for one or two months of travel in Europe – full details from any travel agent) does *not* cover travel in Morocco, although it will get you down to the ferries at Algeciras in Spain. The *InterRail* **pass**, which *does* cover Morocco, is in theory only available to people resident in Europe for six months – though in practice travel agents aren't always too fussy about the regulation.

PACKAGE TOURS

For ease and convenience, **package tours** make a lot of sense: you get to see the country without worrying too much about the hassles of getting to and from. Among available tours, some cover Morocco exclusively, others in combination with Spain and Portugal, or beyond.

Note also that many of the **specialist tours** detailed on pp.6–7 are sold by American travel agents, and if you contact the UK companies direct, they will put you in touch with their North American agent. See boxed listings for recommended North American agencies.

GETTING THERE FROM AUSTRALIA OR NEW ZEALAND

There are no direct flights between **Australia or New Zealand and North Africa**. The most "direct" route is a ticket **via Singapore**, where you can connect with the *Royal Jordanian* flight to Casablanca. Most Australasian travellers, however, make their way to Morocco **via Britain** – and a flight to London, with tag-on flight or overland transport to Tangier or Agadir, usually works out cheapest.

Reliable **agents** to try for flights to London (and connections on to Morocco) are *STA Travel*, who have offices throughout Australia and New Zealand.

Their principal offices are:

● Auckland: 10 High St (☎9/399-995)
● Sydney: 1a Lee St, (☎02/212-1255)
● Melbourne: 256 Flinders St (☎03/347-6911).

RED TAPE AND EXTENDED STAYS

If you hold a full passport from Britain, Ireland, Australia, New Zealand, the Scandinavian countries or North America, you require no visa to enter Morocco for up to ninety days. Among European nations, only Dutch, Belgian and Luxembourg citizens need visas – imposed in response to restrictions placed on visiting Moroccans. In theory (though not, it seems, in practice), entry to Morocco is refused to anyone with an Israeli or South African stamp in their passport. If this applies to you, a replacement passport might be worth obtaining. Note that British Visitors' Passports are not valid for entering Morocco.

CHILDREN AND PASSPORTS

Parents travelling with children should note that photographs of the children must be affixed to the passports of each parent. If this is not done, it is possible that you will be refused entry to Morocco. This is not just a piece of paper bureaucracy: families are regularly refused entry for failing to comply.

When **entering the country**, formalities are fairly straightforward, though you will have to fill in a form stating personal details, purpose of visit and your **profession**. In recent years, Moroccan authorities have shown an occasional reluctance to allow in those who categorise themselves as "journalist"; an alternative profession on the form might be wise. Hippies, too, engender official disfavour; very long hair is best discreetly tied.

Note that items such as **electronic equipment and video cameras** are entered on your passport. If you lose them during your visit, they will be assumed "sold" when you come to leave and (unless you have police documentation of theft) you will have to pay 100 percent duty. All goods on your passport should be "cleared" when leaving to prevent problems on future trips.

To **extend your stay** in Morocco you should – officially – apply to the *Bureau des Étrangers* in the nearest main town for a residence permit (see below). This is, however, a very complicated procedure and it is usually possible to get round the bureaucracy by simply leaving the country for a brief time when your three months are up. If you decide to try this – and it is not foolproof – it is best to make a trip of at least a few days outside

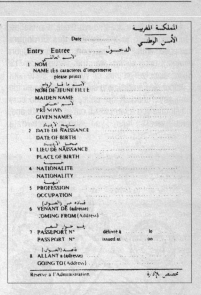

Morocco, to Algeria or Spain. Some people just go to the enclave of Ceuta; the more cautious re-enter the country at a different post. If you are very unlucky, you may be turned back and asked to obtain a **re-entry visa** prior to your return. These can be obtained from any Moroccan consulate abroad (see below).

OFFICIAL BUSINESS

Extending a stay officially involves opening a bank account in Morocco (a couple of days' procedure in itself) and obtaining an *Attestation de Résidence* from your hotel, campsite or landlord. You will need a minimum of 14,000dh (£1100/$1750) deposited in your bank account before making an application.

MOROCCAN CONSULATES ABROAD

Australia: 2 Phillis Lane, North Curl Curl, Sydney NSW (☎649.6019).

Britain: 49 Queens Gate Gardens, London SW7 (☎071/581 5001).

Canada: 38 Range Rd, Ottawa (☎613/236-7391); and 1010 Sherbrook W, Montreal (☎288–8750).

Denmark: Oregarrds Allé 19, 2900 Hellerup, Copenhagen (☎62.45.11).

Netherlands: Oranje Nassaulaan 1-1075, Amsterdam (☎736-215).

Spain: *Embassy*: Serrano 179, Madrid (☎458.0950). *Consulates*: Rambla de Catalunya 78, Barcelona (☎32.99.66); Av. de Andalucia 63, Málaga (☎952/329962); Av. de Francisco 4, Algeciras (☎67.36.98).

Sweden: Kungsholmstorg 16, Stockholm (☎54.43.83).

USA: *Embassy*: 1601 21st St NW, Washington DC (☎202/462-7979). *Consulate*: 10 E 40th St, 24th Floor, New York, NY 10016 (212/758-2625).

Once you have got through these two stages, you need to go to the **Bureau des Étrangers** equipped with: your passport; seven passport photos; two copies of the *Attestation de Résidence*; two copies of your bank statement (*Compte de Banque*); and a 60dh stamp (available from any *Tabac*). If the police are not too busy they'll give you a form to fill out in duplicate and, some weeks later, you should receive a plastic-coated permit with your photo laminated in.

For anyone contemplating this labyrinthine operation, the *Bureau des Étrangers* in **Agadir** is perhaps the simplest place to approach, since a number of expatriates live in the city and banking facilities there (try the *Banque Populaire*) are fairly efficient. The *Bureau is* located behind the fire station on Rue du 18 Novembre.

COSTS AND MONEY

For visitors, Morocco is inexpensive and in most respects excellent value, with costs for food, accommodation and travel low by European or North American standards. If you stay in the cheaper hotels (or camp out), eat local food, and share expenses and rooms with another person, **£60 (US$100) a week** would be enough to survive on. On **£90–120 ($150–200)** you could live pretty well, while with **£300–400 ($500–650) a week** split between two people you would be approaching luxury.

SOME BASIC COSTS

Accommodation costs range from £5/$8 a night for a double room in a basic, unclassified "local" hotel to £150/$250 a night in the country's half-dozen top-range luxury palaces. On a limited budget, you can expect to get a decent double room in a two- or three-star hotel for around £15–25/$25–40 a night, while the occasional splurge in a four-star hotel, with a swimming pool, will set you back around £30–50/$50–80 for a double, depending on season and location.

The price of a **meal** reflects a similar span, but the basic Moroccan staple of soup (usually the bean-based *harira*), brochettes or *tajine* (casserole) can be had in a local café for around £1.50/$2.50. More substantial Moroccan meals can be had for around £3.50/$5.50 and European-style meals in restaurants from around £6/$10. **Drinks** are really the only things that compare unfavourably with European prices: a bottle of Moroccan wine costs upwards of £4/$6.50 and a can of local beer about 80p/$1.25 in the shops, or £2.25/$4 in hotel bars and discos.

Beyond accommodation and food, your major outlay will be for **transport** – expensive if you're hiring a car (£200/$320 a week plus petrol), but reasonable if you use the local trains, buses and collective taxis. The 475-km trip from Fes to Marrakesh, for instance, costs around £10/$16 by bus, or £15/$25 if you use faster collective taxis.

REGIONAL VARIATIONS

To some extent, all of these costs are affected by **where you are and when**. Inevitably, the big **cities** and **resorts** (Agadir especially) prove more expensive, with bottom-line hotel prices from around £10/$16 a night for a double. In more **remote parts** of the country, too, where all goods have to be brought in from some distance away and where transport (often only lorries or landrovers) has to be negotiated, prices can be even steeper; this is particularly true of the popular trekking region of Djebel Toubkal.

HIDDEN COSTS

Hidden costs in Morocco are twofold. The most obvious, perhaps, is that you'll almost certainly end up buying a few things. Moroccan **crafts** are very much a part of the fabric of the towns and cities, with their labyrinthine areas of *souks* (markets). Rugs, blankets, leather and jewellery are all outstanding – and few travellers leave without at least one of these items.

A harder aspect to come to terms with is that you'll be confronting real **poverty**. As a tourist, you're not going to solve any problems, but with a labourer's wages at little more than 5 dirhams (30p/50¢)) an hour, and an unemployment rate in excess of 25 percent, even a small **tip** to a guide can make a lot of difference to individual family life. For Moroccans, giving money and goods is a natural function – and a requirement of Islam. For tourists, rich by definition, local poverty demands at least some response. Do not, however, dispense money indiscriminately to **kids**, which simply promotes a dependence on begging.

CURRENCY

Morocco's basic unit of **currency** is the **dirham** (dh). The dirham is not quoted on international money markets, a rate being set instead by the Moroccan government. The present rates are approximately **£1=12.5dh**, **US$1=8dh**. These reflect a relatively weak pound and dollar price, as of mid-1993; in recent years the pound and dollar have bought up to 15dh and 10dh, respectively.

The dirham is divided into 100 **centimes** (5-, 10-, 20- and 50-centime coins are in circulation), and you may find prices written or expressed in centimes rather than dirhams. Confusingly, centimes may also be referred to as *francs* or, in former Spanish zones of the country, as *pesetas*. You may also hear prices quoted in **rials**, or *reales*. In most parts of the country a dirham is considered to be 20 *rials*, though in Tangier and the Rif there are just 2 *rials* to the dirham. These are forms of expression only: there are no actual physical Moroccan *rials*, *francs* or *pesetas*.

It is possible to buy a small amount of dirhams at the bank exchange desks in the Algeciras ferry terminal or at banks in Gibraltar, but the currency is not easily exchangeable outside Morocco, and there are, in any case, regulations against taking it out of the country. When you're nearing the end of your stay, it's best to get down to as little Moroccan money as possible. To change money back from dirhams, you may be asked to produce exchange receipts – and you can change back only fifty percent of sums detailed on these. At Moroccan banks, you'll be offered re-exchange into French francs only.

CARRYING YOUR MONEY

Arriving in Morocco it is useful to have at least two days' survival money in **cash**, especially as you cannot always count on airport banks/bureau de change offices being open. English pounds, US dollars, French francs or Spanish pesetas are easy to exchange, at banks, hotels and tourist shops; note that both **Irish currency and banknotes** and also **Scottish banknotes** are not recognised or accepted in Moroccan banks. The rest of your money should, ideally, be spread around different forms – Eurocheques, travellers' cheques or Girocheques and plastic – for the sake of security.

Travellers' cheques and cash are easily exchanged at most Moroccan banks, and at the more upmarket hotels, travel agencies and tourist shops; a surcharge of around 3dh per cheque is levied. **Eurocheques** can be cashed at larger banks, though a higher commission – averaging out at around 5 percent – is charged; the limit on each cheque encashment is currently 2000dh (£160/$250). Better value, on the whole, are **International Girocheques** (available through European post offices), which can be changed at any sizeable Moroccan post office.

VISA and **Access/Mastercard** can also be used to obtain cash at some banks (see below), as well as in payment at the more upmarket hotels, restaurants and shops, and for car hire. It's wise to make sure your card is in good condition, as banks will refuse cash advances if machines reject the card.

BANKS AND EXCHANGE

For exchange purposes, by far the most useful and efficient chain of banks is the **BMCE** (*Banque Marocaine du Commerce Exterieur*). There is at least one *BMCE* in all major cities and they are dotted about in smaller towns (see listings in the text of the guide). Their *bureaux de change* (usually located in a separate office to the main bank) are open every day, including weekends, from 8am to 8pm. They handle travellers' cheques and Eurocheques, and give cash advances on *VISA* and *Access*, as well as currency exchange.

The **Banque Credit du Maroc** also handle *VISA*, as does the generally efficient **Citibank**. Most other banks don't often have facilities for credit card transactions, despite the stickers in their windows, though most will exchange cash, Eurocheques and travellers' cheques. If you are travelling in the south, often the **Banque Populaire** alone is represented, and offers limited facilities. Don't expect to be able to use credit cards outside the few principal cities.

Standard banking hours are Monday to Friday, 8.30am to 11.30am and 3pm to 4.30pm in winter; in summer and during Ramadan (see "Festivals") from 8.30am to 2pm. In major resorts there is usually one or more bank that keeps extended hours on *bureau de change* transactions to meet tourist demand.

In most **exchange transactions**, customers fill in forms at one desk, then join a second queue for the cashier. Cheque/cash transactions usually get dealt with in 10 to 15 minutes, but it's wise to allow up to an hour if you need to draw cash on a credit card. Cashing travellers' cheques, you may be asked to produce the receipts for purchase.

AMERICAN EXPRESS

American Express is represented by the *Voyages Schwartz* agencies in Tangier, Casablanca, Marrakesh and Agadir. Their agency in Rabat is at present closed, though it is sched-uled to reopen in the *Hyatt Regency* hotel. At all these offices, not every *American Express* service is available. *Voyages Schwartz* can cash and issue *Amex* travellers' cheques, and hold clients' mail, but they cannot cash personal cheques or receive wired money. Addresses are:

● Tangier: *Voyages Schwartz*, 54 Bd. Pasteur (☎09/93.34.59)

● Casablanca: *Voyages Schwartz*, 102 Av. du Prince Moulay Abdallah (☎02/27.31.33).

● Marrakesh: *Voyages Schwartz*, Rue Mauritania (☎04/43.28.31)

● Agadir: *Voyages Schwartz*, Av. Hassan II (☎08/82.28.94).

Most **offices are open** Monday to Friday 8.30am to 12.30pm and 3pm to 6pm, though banking services are sometimes mornings only.

EMERGENCY CASH

Despite the number of travellers' tales, very few people lose (or are conned out of) all their money in Morocco – but it does happen. Access to an **emergency source** of money – whether it be a credit card or an arrangement with your bank or family to wire you money after a phone call – is reassuring and may prove invaluable.

As a last resort, your **consulate** is duty-bound to offer some assistance – though this will rarely go as far as lending you the money to continue a holiday, or even to fly home unless you accept "repatriation". For addresses, see p.22.

HEALTH AND INSURANCE

For minor health complaints, a visit to a *pharmacie* is likely to be sufficient. Moroccan pharmacists are well trained and dispense a wide range of drugs, including many available only on prescription in Europe or North America. If pharmacists feel you need a full diagnosis, they can recommend a doctor – sometimes working on the premises. Addresses of English- and French-speaking doctors can also be obtained from consulates, large hotels and some tourist offices.

If you need **hospital treatment**, contact your consulate at once and follow their advice. If you are near a major city, reasonable treatment may be available locally. Morocco, however, is no country in which to fall seriously ill.

INOCULATIONS

There are no **inoculations** officially required of travellers, although you should always be up-to-date with polio and tetanus. Typhoid and cholera are widespread, so a jab against these is worthwhile, too – although some doctors doubt the effectiveness of the cholera jab. Some doctors also advise inoculation against hepatitis B, following the recent introduction of effective vaccines. A course of **malaria pills** (preferably weekly *Chloroquin* tablets) is recommended if you intend to travel in the south.

If you haven't had a typhoid jab then buy some *Intétrix* capsules (available from any pharmacy in Morocco). These are excellent anti-bacterial medication – useful for diarrhoea as well as typhoid prevention – and some doctors consider them more effective than inoculation. They are certainly valuable if you are travelling for any length of time in the south.

WATER AND HEALTH HAZARDS

The **tap water** in northern Morocco is generally safe to drink (in Chaouen, for example, it is pumped straight from a well), though in the south it's best to stick to bottled mineral water.

A more serious problem in the south Is that many of the **river valleys and oases** are said to be infected with **bilharzia**, so avoidance of all contact with slow-flowing rivers and oasis water is a wise precaution. Care should be taken, too, in drinking water from **mountain streams**. In areas where there is livestock upstream **giardiasis** is prevalent. Using water purification tablets and boiling any drinking or cooking water would be sensible.

DIARRHOEA

At some stage in your Moroccan travels, it is likely that you will get **diarrhoea**. As a first stage of treatment it's best simply to adapt your diet. Yoghurt is an effective stomach settler and cactus fruit (widely available in summer) are good, too. Steer clear of other fruit and keep up your body fluids by drinking lots of bottled water and tea.

If this course doesn't shake it off in a couple of days, you could obtain **carbosylate capsules** (eg *Carbosylane*) from a chemist, or, if you have an "enteric" type attack (with cramps, for example), **Imodium**. It is important, especially for children, not to exceed the suggested doses; *Imodium* is a morphine-related drug.

OTHER HAZARDS

There are few natural hazards in northern Morocco, whose wildlife is not far different from that of Mediterranean Europe. If you venture into the Sahara, however, be aware of the very real dangers of a bite from a **snake**, **palm rat** or **scorpion**. Several of the Saharan snakes are deadly, as is the palm rat. Bites should be treated as medical emergencies.

A much more common problem for travellers is **heatstroke**. Make sure you are adequately protected against the sun, or you will be extremely vulnerable to attacks – resulting, most commonly, in headaches and nausea.

AIDS

Moroccan cities such as Tangier and Marrakesh have a reputation as gay resorts – diminished these days, but still evident. There is very little awareness of AIDS (or *SIDA*, as it is called in French), although the Moroccan Health Ministry has been represented at recent AIDS conferences. At present, official statistics of AIDS sufferers in Morocco are very low (88 reported cases in 1992), but if the European experience is anything to go by, the reality is likely to be very much higher – and rising.

As throughout the world, the need for extreme caution, and safe sex, cannot be overstressed.

INSURANCE

Travel insurance can buy you peace of mind as well as save you money. Before you purchase any insurance, however, check what you have already. North Americans, in particular, may find themselves covered for medical expenses and loss, and possibly loss of or damage to valuables, while abroad, as part of a family or student policy. Some credit cards, too, now offer insurance benefits if you use them to pay for your holiday tickets.

If you are travelling for any real length of time, however, you are likely to find additional or **specific travel insurance** reassuring. Most of these are pretty comprehensive, anticipating everything from charter companies going bankrupt to delayed (as well as lost) baggage, by way of sundry illnesses and accidents. **Premiums**, however, vary considerably, and it's worth a few phonecalls to see what's on offer. This applies particularly to **North Americans**, who, if transiting via Britain, might consider buying a policy from a British travel agency. British policies tend to be cheaper than American ones, and routinely cover thefts – which are sometimes excluded from the more health-based American policies.

REIMBURSEMENT

All insurance policies work by **reimbursing you** once you return home, so be sure to keep all your receipts from doctors and pharmacists. Any thefts should be reported immediately to the nearest police station and a police report obtained; no report, no refund.

If you have had to undergo serious medical treatment, and incur major hospital bills, contact your consulate. They will normally be able to arrange for an insurance company, or possibly relatives, to cover the fees, pending a claim.

INFORMATION, MAPS AND HIKING BOOKS

Besides this book, the most readily available (and obvious) sources of information on Morocco are the country's tourist board (the ONMT), its *Délégation Régional* offices and *Syndicats d'Initiatives* located throughout Morocco, and local, often self-appointed, guides (see the section following).

TOURIST OFFICES

The **ONMT** maintains general information offices in several European capitals (see box opposite), where you can pick up a limited range of pamphlets and lists.

The most useful of these is the ***Guide des Hôtels***, a complete list of officially rated hotels (as of 1993 – the last publication date). We've included numerous small hotels in this book that aren't classified in the ONMT guide, and many more that are, but there might be times when you'll find it useful as a backup or to check on facilities or booking agents. It is also worth picking up the ONMT's new series of **pamphlets** on the main Moroccan cities and resorts, whose maps sometimes complement our own.

In Morocco itself, there's either a *Syndicat* or **ONMT** office in all towns of any size or interest – often both; their addresses are detailed in the relevant sections of the guide. Occasionally, these offices can supply you with particular local information sheets and they can of course try to help you out with specific questions. Their main use, though, is to get you in touch with an officially recognised guide.

ONMT OFFICES ABROAD

Australia c/o Moroccan Consulate, 11 West St, Sydney NSW 2060 (☎02/9576.717).

Britain 205 Regent St, London W1(☎071/437 0073).

Canada 2001 Rue Université (Suite 1460), Montréal, Québec (☎514/556-2191).

Netherlands 150 Rokin 150, 1012 LE, Amsterdam (☎20/240 025 or 239 089).

Spain C/Quintana 2 (2°e), Madrid (☎01/542 7431).

Sweden Sturegatan 16, Stockholm 11436 (☎08/66099 or 66013).

USA 20 E 46th St (Suite 1201), New York, NY10017 (☎212/557-2520); 421 North Rodeo Drive, Beverly Hills, Los Angeles, CA 90210 (☎271-8939); PO Box 22663, Lake Brunea, Orlando, FL 32830 (☎827–5337).

ROAD MAPS

Maps of Moroccan **cities**, beyond those we've printed and the ones you can get for free from the ONMT, are not particularly worthwhile. The most authoritative local series, the ***Plan-Guides*** published by *Éditions Gauthey*, look impressive but are next to useless once you're trying to find your way round the lanes of a Medina.

What you will probably want, though, is a good **road map**. The best are those published by *Michelin* (1:1,000,000; sheet 969; generally the most accurate), *Kummerley & Frey* (1:1,000,000), and the local *Marcus Carte Routière* (1:1,000,000, with Middle and High Atlas inserts at 1:500,000). The latter is readily available in Morocco.

Note that maps (or guidebooks) which do not show the **former Spanish Sahara (Western Sahara)** as Moroccan territory are liable to confiscation. Even maps showing a reduced-scale version of the territory are frowned upon.

HIKING MAPS AND GUIDES

The Moroccan government periodically clamp down on distribution of **topographic maps** – which are, of course, invaluable to trekkers. At present, however, 1:100,000 sheets covering the popular High Atlas mountain areas are available on the spot (in Imlil), or, on production of a passport, from the Division de la Cartographie, 31 Av. Moulay el Hassan, Rabat (☎07/76.51.92).

In Morocco you can sometimes pick up a map of Toubkal in Imlil, the trailhead for treks in the area. However, if you are planing to go trekking, it is best to try and get maps through a **specialist map outlet** before you leave (see box). Look for 1:100,000 (and if you're lucky 1:50,000) maps of the Atlas and other mountain areas

In addition to the official Moroccan survey maps, *Atlas Maps* (see box) produce very useful, photocopied **map-guides** to the Asni-Toubkal, Western High Atlas (Taroudannt) and Sirwa (Taliouine), Anti-Atlas (Tafraoute), Aklim (Igherm)

and Djebel Bou Iblane/Bou Naceur (Middle Atlas) areas. Written by our High Atlas contributor, Hamish Brown, these are useful complements to the coverage in this guide.

Also well worth acquiring is a new **ONMT pamphlet** entitled *La Grande Traversée des Atlas Marocains*, or *GTAM* – the promotional acronym with which the ONMT is now actively promoting trekking. At present this pamphlet is published in French only (an English version is said to be on the way), but even if your French is patchy the details and tarifs for local trekking guides, and contacts for specialised agencies and four-wheel-drive hire, might be useful. The pamphlet also features a superb pull-out colour panorama of the Atlas. It is available through main ONMT delegation offices in Morocco.

More **detailed trekking guidebooks** are also available in both English and French. The most useful are Michael Peyron's *Grand Atlas Traverse* (West Col, UK; 2 vols; £11.95 each), Robin Collomb's *Atlas Mountains* (West Col, UK: £10.95) and Karl Smith's *Atlas Mountains: A Walker's Guide* (Cicerone Press, UK; £9.95). The two Moroccan walks detailed in Hamish Brown's *Great Walking Adventure* (Oxford Illustrated Press, UK; out of print) are also good background.

If you can get to London en route, you might also want to consult some of the Expedition Reports at the **Royal Geographical Society** (1 Kensington Gore, London SW7); the RGS's *Expeditionary Advisory Centre* (☎071/581 2057) will help locate relevant material, maps and reports.

SPECIALIST MAP SHOPS

Britain

Stanfords, 12–14 Long Acre, London WC2E 9LP (☎071/836 1321). Callers/mail order.

The Map Shop, 15 High St, Upton-upon-Severn, Worcs WR8 0HJ (☎06846/3146). Callers/mail order.

Atlas Maps, 21 Carlin Craig, Kinghorn, Fife, KY3 9RX, Scotland; (sae with all correspondence; closed Feb–May). Mail order only.

USA

Rand McNally: 444 N Michigan Ave, Chicago, IL 60611 (☎312/321-1751); 150 E 52nd St, New York, NY 10022 (☎212/758-7488); 595 Market St, San Francisco, CA 94105 (☎415/777-3131).

Complete Traveller Bookstore: 199 Madison Ave, New York, NY 10016 (☎212/685-9007); 3207 Filmore St, San Francisco CA 92123.

Traveller's Bookstore, 22 W 52nd St, New York, NY 10011 (☎212/664-0995)

Elliott Book Company, 101 South Main St, Seattle, WA 98104 (☎206/624-6600)

Canada

Ulysses Travel Bookshop, 4176 Rue St Denis, Montréal, (☎514/289-0993).

Open Air Books and Maps, 25 Toronto St, Toronto, (☎416/363-0719).

World Wide Books and Maps, 1247 Granville Street, Vancouver.

GUIDES, HUSTLERS, CON-MEN AND KIDS

The question of whether to employ a guide will be one of your first (and most frequent) decisions in Morocco. With tourism so important a part of the economy, guiding has become quite a business – especially in the major cities of Fes and Marrakesh. In addition to the guides trained by the government, there are scores of young Moroccans offering their services to show you round the *souks* (markets) and sights. The "unofficial guides" are not, strictly speaking, legal, and there are occasional crackdowns by the police on offenders. However, they remain very much a factor (and bane) of tourist life.

With all guides, it is important to establish what you want to see. You may well find it useful to agree an itinerary in advance – perhaps showing your guide the points you want to visit on the maps in this book. Do not be pushed into a tour of the craft stores – where your guide will be looking for commission on purchases – or you will see nothing else. If you do want to visit shops, make it clear what kind of goods you are interested in seeing, and equally clear that you do not want to purchase on an initial visit.

OFFICIAL GUIDES

Official guides, engaged through tourist offices (or some of the larger hotels), are paid at a fixed rate of 100dh (£8/$12.50) for a half day. The rate is for the guide's time, and can be shared by a group of people – though the latter would be expected to make some additional tip.

Taking an introductory tour of a new city with an official guide can be a useful exercise in orientation – especially in the vast Medinas (old quarters) of Fes and Marrakesh. Your guide may well be an interesting and entertaining presence, too. Some are highly knowledgeable. There is an advantage also in that, if you are accompanied by an official guide, you won't be approached or hassled by any of their (sometimes less than reputable) unauthorised equivalents.

Official guides can identify themselves by a large, brass "sheriff's badge".

UNOFFICIAL GUIDES AND HUSTLERS

Unofficial guides will approach you in the streets of any sizeable town, offering to find you a hotel, show you the sights, or perhaps, if you look a likely customer, sell you some *kif* (hashish). You will need to develop a strategy to deal with these approaches, otherwise you are unlikely to enjoy urban Morocco.

The most important point to realise is that there are **good** and **bad guides**. Some are genuine students, who may want to earn a small fee, but may equally be interested (as so many claim) in practising their English. Others are out-and-out hustlers, preying on first-visit innocence and paranoia. Your task is to distinguish between offers, to accept (perhaps limited) services from those who seem friendly and enjoyable company, and to deal as humanly as possible with approaches you wish to decline. Politeness is essential, or you'll find things unpleasant, and silence is taken as rudeness; mutual preservation of **dignity** is important.

In general, there is little harm in agreeing to let a guide show you to a **hotel**, though it is best to know which you want to go to – check our listings before arrival. Equally, letting someone guide you to a **café** or **restaurant** won't increase the price of a meal (although waiters will generally make a small tip to the guide).

Offers of a **tour of the town**, however, you may want to avoid. To do so, it is a golden rule to look as if you know where you are going. Never admit to this being your first visit to Morocco. If you feel confident enough, say that you have visited the town before and that you are glad to be back. You will be on your way to setting the parameters of discussion. The most exploitative guides will probably drop you to look elsewhere. If you are unsure of a guide, suggest taking a mint tea together in a café. Don't make any agreement to employ him prior to this, or any suggestion of an agreement. In addition, never allow yourself to be bullied into going with someone with whom you don't feel at ease – there is no shortage of candidates. And if you feel genuinely threatened or harassed, don't hesitate to threaten or indeed to go to the police: hustlers tend to vanish fast at the prospect of police involvement.

If you do decide to hire an unofficial guide, be sure to **fix the rate**, as well as the **itinerary**, in advance. You should make it clear that you know the official rates for guides and should agree on these as a maximum. Many unofficial guides will attempt to charge a rate per person.

CON-MEN AND SCAMS

Hustlers and **con-men** are a distinct minority in Morocco, as anywhere else. Arriving in one of the main hustler cities – Tangier, Fes or Marrakesh – you will, on your first day, encounter just about all those available. On the second and subsequent days, they'll know your face and approaches will notably drop off. However, forewarned is forearmed, so **a few notes on the most common scams**:

● As stressed in the introduction, all guides have an interest in getting you into craft shops, where they can earn commission of 30 to 50 percent. Even if you say you're not interested, they may suggest taking tea with a cousin who owns a shop. Don't be afraid to keep to your agreed itinerary.

● A favourite line is that there is a Berber market taking place – and this is the only day of the week to see it. This is rarely true. You will probably visit everyday shops and *souks*.

● Some of the more exploitative hustlers will guide you into the Medinas, then, when you have no idea where you are, charge a large fee to take you back out and to your hotel. If this happens to you, don't be afraid to appeal to people in the street; your hustler will not want attention.

● A few tales are told each year of people approaching visitors with a letter or package to mail to the USA or Europe when you leave Morocco. Never agree to this; you may be involving yourself in a drugs plant.

● Many more hustlers will simply use the excuse of a letter ("Could you help translate or write one?") as a means of attaching themselves to you; it's best to decline assistance.

● On the trains, especially at Tangier, hustlers sometimes pose as porters or railway staff, demanding an extortionate fee for carrying baggage or payment of supplements. Genuine rail staff wear beige overalls and have ID cards, which, if suspicious, you should ask to see.

● Drivers should beware of hitchhiking-hustlers, who spend all day hitching between a pair of towns and can get highly obnoxious in their demands for money when you approach one or other destination.

● In the south, look out for offers to meet "Blue Men" (desert Touareg nomads) in the "desert". The "nomads" are almost invariably rogues.

● In a number of towns, con-men have been posing as students, working alone or in couples, befriending tourists, and then, after a day or two, telling some sad tale about needing money for getting a passport off a corrupt official, or to look after sick relatives, or some such. You may feel a little foolish if you give money and then meet six other travellers with identical tales to tell.

● Heading for the beach, especially in Tangier, leave most of your money back at your hotel. Thefts and pickpocketing are common, and the odd mugging is not unknown.

● Don't trust anyone who begins their routine with "Where have I seen you before . . . ".

ATTITUDES AND BEHAVIOUR

If you want to get the most from a trip to Morocco, it is vital not to start assuming anyone who approaches or talks to you is a hustler. Too many tourists do, and end up making little contact with what must be one of the most hospitable peoples in the world.

Behaviour and attitude are equally important on your part. If some Moroccans treat tourists with contempt, and exploit them as a simple resource, it has much to do with the way the latter behave. It helps everyone if you can avoid **rudeness** or aggressive behaviour in response to insistent offers from guides. And be aware, too, of the importance of **dress**: shorts are acceptable only on the beach, in resorts; shirts (for both sexes) should cover your arms.

Photography needs to be undertaken with care. If you are obviously taking a photograph of

someone, ask their permission – especially in the more remote, rural regions where you can cause genuine offence. On a more positive front, taking a photograph of someone you've struck up a friendship with and sending it on to them, or exchanging photographs, is often greatly appreciated. In fact, while in Morocco, you may be surprised to find yourself dragged off by new friends or acquaintances to a street or studio photographer for a photo session. This is quite common practice and has no untoward ends.

When **invited to a home**, you normally take your shoes off before entering the reception rooms. It is customary to take a gift: sweet pastries or tea and sugar are always acceptable, and you might even take meat (perhaps by arrangement) to a poorer home. (See also note on "Eating Moroccan style" on p.35).

DEALING WITH KIDS

In the countryside, and especially along the major southern routes, you will find fewer hustlers and guides, but many more kids, eager for a dirham, *un cadeau* (present) or *un stylo* (a pen/pencil). A Dutch correspondent writes: "Dealing with small children is a lot easier than hustlers. All of us have our own odd tricks, like being able to roll one's eyes, imitate bird calls, or wiggle one's earlobes. Ours is to put one finger in our mouth and produce spectacular plopping noises. As soon as a child had asked for a dirham, we performed our trick and the child was usually flabbergasted. Most of the time we ended up teaching the entire villlage youth the trick. Dirhams were a thing of the past, and giggling the universal language."

Working out your own strategy is all part of the game, but, whatever else you do, be sure to keep a good humour: smile and laugh, or kids can make your life hell. Faced with **begging from kids**, we strongly recommend not obliging, as this ties them to a begging mentality.

SECURITY, THE POLICE AND CONSULATES

Keeping your luggage and money secure is an important consideration in Morocco. Even though, for all the tales, the situation is probably no worse than in Spain or Italy, it is obviously wise not to carry large sums of cash or valuables on your person – especially in the main tourist cities like Fes, Marrakesh and Tangier.

Hotels, generally, are secure and useful for depositing money before setting out to explore; larger ones will keep valuables at reception. **Campsites** are considerably less secure, and many campers advise using a **money belt** – to be worn even while sleeping. If you do decide on a money belt (and many people spend time quite happily without!), leather or cotton materials are preferable to nylon, which can irritate in the heat.

If you are **driving**, it almost goes without saying, you should not leave anything you cannot afford to lose visible or accessible in your car.

THE POLICE

There are two main types of **police**: the *Gendarmerie* (who wear grey uniforms and man the checkpoints on roads) and the *Mekhezni* (who wear military-style khaki uniforms).

The *Gendarmes* are the people to approach if you need to report any kind of crime, or if you want assistance; they are based in towns and cities, but also patrol roads. They are sometimes referred to as the *Sûreté* – the overall force which includes them. The *Mekhezni* are of little help to visitors, fulfilling more of a military role,

FOREIGN CONSULATES IN MOROCCO

United Kingdom *Embassy*: 17 Bd. de la Tour Hassan, Rabat (☎07/72.09.05). *Consulates*: 9 Rue Amerique du Sud, Tangier (☎09/93.58.95 or 09/93.58.97); 60 Bd. d'Anfa, Casablanca (☎02/22.16.53); Honorary Consul, c/o Agadir Beach Club Hotel, Chemin du Oued Souss, Agadir (☎08/84.43.43).

USA *Embassy*: 2 Av. de Marrakech, Rabat (☎07/62.265). *Consulates*: 8 Bd. Moulay Youssef, Casablanca (☎02/22.41.49).

Canada *Embassy*: 13 bis Rue Joafar Assadik, Agdal, Rabat (☎07/77.14.76 or 07/77.13.75).

Netherlands *Embassy*: 40 Rue de Tunis (☎07/335.12). *Consulates*: Immeuble Miramonte, 47 Av. Hassan II, Tangier (☎09/93.12.45).

Denmark *Embassy*: 4 Rue de Khemisset, Rabat (☎07/326.84). *Consulates*: 150 Bd. Rahal el Meskini, Casablanca (☎02/31.44.91); 3 Rue Henri Regnault (4th floor), Tangier (☎09/93.81.83).

Sweden *Embassy*: 159 Av. Pres. Kennedy, Souissi, Rabat (☎07/75.47.40). *Consulates*: 3 Rue du Lt. Sylvestre, Casablanca (☎02/30.46.48); 3 Rue de l'Entraide, Agadir (☎08/82.30.48).

Norway *Embassy*: 22 Charia as-Souira, Rabat-Chellah (☎07/76.10.96). *Consulates*: 3 Rue Henri Regnault, Tangier (☎09/93.36.33); Sogep-ONP, Immeuble A, Agadir (☎08/82.17.01).

Irish, Australian and **New Zealand citizens** should use UK consular facilities while in Morocco.

running security from their network of barracks in both urban and rural areas, and operating some of the checkpoints in the south.

If you do need to **report a theft**, try to take along a fluent French-speaker, if your own language is not too hot. You may only be given a scrap of paper with an official stamp to show your insurance company, who then have to apply themselves to a particular police station for a report (in Arabic). If you cannot prove that a theft has taken place, the police may decline to make any report, especially if the theft is of money only. They will always give you a report, however, if you have lost any official document (passport, driving licence, etc).

The **police emergency number** is ☎19.

GETTING AROUND

Moroccan public transport is, on the whole, pretty good. There is an efficient rail network linking the main towns of the north, the coast and Marrakesh, and elsewhere you can travel easily enough by bus or collective taxi. In the mountains and over the more remote desert routes, where roads are often just dirt tracks or pistes, locals maintain a network of market-day lorries — uncomfortable but fun. And for trekkers, the Atlas mountains, in particular, are crossed by a series of beautiful trails, some easy enough to follow by yourself, others best trekked with a guide and mule.

Hiring a car can be a good idea, at least for a part of your trip, opening up routes that are time-consuming or difficult on local transport. Most major companies allow you to hire a car in one city and return it to another.

TRAINS

Trains cover a limited network of routes, but for travel between the major cities they are easily the best option — comfortable, efficient and fairly fast.

The **communications map** at the beginning of this book shows all the train routes in the country, and schedules are listed in the "Travel Details" at the end of each chapter. These change very little from year to year, but it's wise to check times in advance at stations. **Timetables**, printed by *ONCF*, the national railway company, are sporadically available at major train stations and tourist offices.

There are three **classes** of tickets — confusingly, first, second and fourth (*économique*). Fourth class is used only by poorer Moroccans and some railway officials won't sell such tickets to foreigners. **Costs** for a second-class ticket are comparable to what you'd pay for buses; on certain "express" services, which are first and second class only, they are around thirty percent higher. In addition, there are **couchettes** (50dh extra) available on the Tangier–Marrakesh and Tangier–Oujda night trains; these are worth the money for the sake of security, as passengers are locked into a carriage with a guard.

Most of the **stations** are located reasonably close to the modern city centres, in the French-built quarters — the *villes nouvelles*. They generally have **luggage consignment** depots, though these accept only luggage that can be locked

FARES

Fares for train, bus and *grand taxi* journeys follow a reasonably consistent pattern.

For **train** or **bus** journeys, reckon on around 2.5dh for each 10km — 3–3.5dh per 10km for an express service.

Grands taxis charge around 2dh per person for each 10km, if travelling a regular route. Chartering a taxi for yourself or for a group, reckon on 12–15dh per 10km.

(effectively excluding rucksacks). An alternative is usually provided by nearby cafés, who will look after your luggage for a small tip.

GRANDS TAXIS

Collective **grands taxis** are one of the best features of Moroccan transport. They operate on a wide variety of routes, are much quicker than buses (often quicker than trains, too), and fares are very reasonable. They are also a good way of meeting people and having impromptu Arabic lessons.

The taxis are usually big Peugeot or Mercedes cars carrying six passengers (Peugeots have a slightly less cramped seating arrangement). Most business is along specific routes, and the most popular routes have more or less continuous departures throughout the day. Consequently, you don't have to worry about timetables. You just show up at the terminal (locations are detailed, city by city, in the guide) and ask for a *place* to a specific destination. As soon as six (or, if you're willing to pay extra, four or five) people are assembled, the taxi sets off.

Most of the *grands taxis* run over a fairly short route, from one large town to the next. If you want to travel further, you will have to change taxis from time to time. Some routes are covered routinely in **stages** (eg Agadir–Taroudannt, or Agadir–Taliouine) and on others taxi drivers will generally assist you in finding a connecting taxi and in settling the fare with the driver.

On established routes *grands taxis* keep to fixed **fares** for each passenger. Before leaving, ask at your hotel (or around the terminal) what that price is – or, as a general guideline, consult the "Fares" box on the previous page.

If you want to take a **non-standard route**, or an excursion, it is possible to pay for a whole *grand taxi* (*une course*) for yourself or a group. But you'll often have to bargain hard before you get down to a realistic price.

BUSES

Bus travel is marginally cheaper than taking a *grand taxi*, and there are far more **regular routes**. Travelling on public transport for any length of time in Morocco, you are likely to make considerable use of the various networks.

Where you can take a *grand taxi* rather than a bus, however, do so. The difference in **fare** is small, and all except the express buses are very much slower and less comfortable than *grands*

taxis. Bus legroom is extremely limited and long journeys can be torture for anyone approaching six feet or more in height. In summer, it can be worthwhile taking **night buses** on the longer journeys. Though still not very comfortable, many long-distance buses run at night and they are both quicker and cooler.

CTM AND PRIVATE LINES

There are a variety of bus services and companies. In all sizeable towns, you will generally find both *CTM* (the national company) and a number of other companies, privately owned and operated.

The **CTM buses** are faster and more reliable, with numbered seats and fixed departure schedules. Their services are often referred to as the *rapide*, and buses come equipped with videos on the longer routes. Some of the larger **private company** buses, such as *SATAS* (which operates widely in the south) are of a similar standard. By contrast, many other of the private companies are tiny outfits, with a single bus which leaves only when the driver considers it sufficiently full.

In some of the larger cities – Rabat and Marrakesh, for example – *CTM* and the private companies share a single **terminal**, often positioned on the edge of town. You can find out the most useful departure times and routes by asking round at the various windows. In other cities, there might be two or more separate terminals (these are detailed in the guide) and possibly no choice of companies on a particular route.

On the more popular trips (and especially with *CTM* services, which are often just once a day in the south), it is worth trying to buy **tickets in advance**; this may not always be possible on smaller private-line services, but it's always worth enquiring about. You can sometimes experience problems getting tickets at **small towns** along major routes, where buses often arrive and leave already full. It's usually possible to get round this problem by taking a local bus or a *grand taxi* for the next section of the trip (until the bus you want empties a little), or by waiting for a bus that actually starts from the town you're in. Overall, the best policy is simply to arrive early in the day (ideally 5.30–6am) at a bus station.

On private-line buses, you generally have to pay for your **baggage** to be loaded onto the roof (and taken off). Moroccans pay just a small tip for this but tourists are expected to pay 2–3dh (some porters ask as much as 15dh for a rucksack!). If you are asked for more than 2–3dh, try to resist. On *CTM* buses your luggage is weighed and you are issued with a receipt (again about 3dh).

ONCF BUSES

An additional service, on certain major routes, are the express buses run by the train company, **ONCF**. These are fast and very comfortable, connecting Tetouan, Nador, Beni Mellal, Agadir and Laayoune to the main railway lines from, respectively, Tnine Sidi Lyamani (near Asilah), Taourite and Marrakesh (Agadir/Laayoune). They are, however, around fifty percent more expensive than the regular buses and compare, both in terms of time and cost, with the *grands taxis*.

TRUCKS AND HITCHING

In the countryside, where buses may be sporadic or even nonexistent, it is standard practice for **vans** and **lorries** (*camions*), **pick-up trucks** (*camionettes*) and transit-vans (*transits*) to carry and charge passengers. You may be asked to pay a little more than the locals, and you may be expected to bargain over this price – but it's straightforward enough.

In parts of the Atlas, the Berbers run more or less scheduled truck or transit services, generally to coincide with the pattern of local *souks*. If you plan on traversing any of the more ambitious Atlas pistes, you'll probably be dependent on these vehicles, unless you walk. For some general guidelines – above all, about paying at the end – see Dan Richardson's account on pp.406–7.

HITCHING

Hitching is not very big in Morocco. Most people, if they own any form of transport at all, have mopeds – which are said to outnumber cars by something like five hundred to one. However, it is often easy to get rides from other **tourists**, particularly if you ask around at the campsites, and for **women travellers** this can be an effective and positive option for getting round– or at least a useful respite from the generally male preserves of buses and *grands taxis*.

Out on the road, it's inevitably a different matter – and hitching is definitely not advisable for women travelling alone. Hitchers should not be surprised to be asked to **pay for a ride** if picked up by country Moroccans. Local rides can operate in much the same way as truck taxis (see above).

CAR HIRE

Car hire is expensive, from around £180/$290 per week or £30/$50 a day for a basic car with unlimited mileage. Petrol/gas prices are high, too (see box on next page). However, having a car does pays obvious dividends if you are pushed for time, allowing you to explore unusual routes and take in much more in a lot less time. This is especially true in the **south**, where getting around can be quite an effort if you have to rely on local buses. Driving yourself also gives a certain sense of invulnerability, if Morocco's hustling ways are a bit too much for you.

POLICE CHECKS ON TRAVEL

Police checks take place on travellers throughout the country. They come in three forms. One is a check on local transport; European cars, or hire cars, are usually waved through. The second is a routine but simple passport check – most often polite and friendly, with the only delay due to a desire to relieve boredom with a chat.

The third is more prolonged and involves being stopped by police stationed at more or less permanent points on the roads, who will conduct a fairly detailed inquisition into all non-resident travellers. There is a considerable amount of form-filling and delay. In the Deep South these checks may be conducted by the military rather than by the police.

In the **Rif mountains**, especially in the *kif*-(hashish) producing region near Ketama, you may also come across police checks – concerned, obviously enough, with just the one substance.

DRIVING IN MOROCCO

There are few real problems driving in Morocco, but keep in mind that the experience is often very different from that of Europe. Accident rates are high – in large part because much of the population is not yet tuned in to looking out for motorised vehicles. You should treat all pedestrians with the suspicion that they will cross in front of you, and all cyclists with the idea that they may well swerve into the middle of the road.

Daytime driving can, with the caveats stated above, be as good as anywhere. Good road surfaces, long straight roads, very little traffic and fairly long distances between inhabited areas allow for high average speeds. The official **speed limit** outside towns is 100km per hour, which is difficult to keep down to in desert areas, where concepts of speed change. On certain roads the speed limit can be as low as 40km per hour. (There is an on-the-spot fine of 30dh for each offence.) The French rule of giving **priority** to traffic from the right is observed at roundabouts and junctions.

Be very wary about driving **after dark**. It is legal to drive without lights at up to 20km per hour, which allows all cyclists and mopeds to wander at will; donkeys, goats and sheep do not carry lights, either.

By law, drivers and passengers are required to wear seatbelts. Almost no one does, but if you're stopped by the police, you may have a small fine or *cadeau* (present) extracted.

PISTE DRIVING

On the **pistes** (rough, unpaved tracks in the mountains or desert), there are special problems. Here you do need a good deal of driving and mechanical confidence – and if you don't feel your car's up to it, don't drive on these routes. On **mountain roads**, beware of gravel, which can be a real danger on the frequent hairpin bends, and, in spring, **flash-floods** caused by melting snow.

EQUIPMENT

Whether you hire a car or drive your own, always make sure you're carrying a **spare tyre** in good condition (plus a jack and tools). Flat tyres occur very frequently, even on fairly major roads, and you can often be in for a long wait until someone drives along with a possible replacement.

Carrying an emergency windscreen is also useful, especially if you are driving your own car for a long period of time. There are lots of loose stones on the hard shoulders of single-lane roads and they can fly all over the place.

If you're not mechanically minded, make sure to bring a car **maintenance manual** with you – a useful item, too, for anyone planning to hire a vehicle.

PETROL/GAS AND BREAKDOWNS

Petrol/gas stations are to be found in towns of any size but can be few and far between in rural areas: always fill your tank to the limit. *Premium* is the standard brand for cars; lead-free is available at larger stations, including most of the Afriquia branches. Prices are pretty much in line with Western Europe, at 7.5–8dh a litre (which works out at around £2.50/$4 a gallon). Petrol costs for a Renault 4 will work out at around 5dh for every 10km.

Moroccan **mechanics** are usually excellent at coping with breakdowns and all medium-sized towns have garages (most with an extensive range of spare parts for Renaults and other French cars). But be aware that if you break down miles from anywhere you'll probably end up paying a fortune to get a lorry to tow you back.

If you are driving your own vehicle, there is also the problem of having to re-export any car that you bring into the country (even a wreck). You can't just write off a car: you'll have to take it out of Morocco with you.

VEHICLE INSURANCE

Insurance must by law be sold along with all **rental** agreements. **Driving your own vehicle**, you should obtain green card cover from your insurers; this is now valid in Morocco. If you don't have it on arrival, you can buy *Assurance Frontière* for around £25/$40 a month, at any frontier post except for Figuig (the southern entry point from Algeria); to renew it, the main *AF* office is at 197 Av. Hassan II, Casablanca (☎276.142).

PARKING: *GARDIENS* AND HOTELS

In almost every town of at least moderate size, you will find a *gardien de voitures* makes an appearance. *Gardiens* are often licensed by local authorities to look after cars, claiming a few dirhams by way of parking fees.

Most of the larger **hotels** in the *ville nouvelle* quarters of cities have parking space (and occasionally garaging) available.

*Important note: the **minimum age** for driving in Morocco is 21 years.*

Many visitors choose to hire a car in Casablanca, Marrakesh or Agadir, expressly for the southern routes. If you're organised, however, it usually pays to **arrange car rental in Britain**, through the travel agent who arranges your flight. If you have problems, try one of the Morocco specialists detailed on pp. 6–7.

Details of **car rental companies in Morocco** are given where relevant in city listings in the guide. The best-value places are mostly in Casablanca and Agadir. Deals to go for are unlimited mileage and daily/weekly rates; paying by the kilometre invariably works out more expensive. The cheapest car on offer is usually a **Renault 4** – well designed for unsurfaced piste roads, with its high suspension and sturdy frame. If you can't or don't want to drive, car hire companies can usually arrange a **driver** for around 100dh (£8/$12.50) a day, plus meals and accommodation.

Before making a booking, be sure to find out if you can pick the car up in one city and return it to another – freeing yourself for the most interesting routes. Most companies will allow this. Check also, if booking in Morocco, whether you will be charged extra for payment with a credit card; there is often a (negotiable) six percent fee for this. Before setting out, make sure the car comes with spare tyre, tool kit and full documentation – including insurance cover, which is compulsory issue with all rentals.

FLIGHTS

Royal Air Maroc (*RAM*) operate **domestic flights** between all the major cities. If you're very pressed for time, you might want to use the service between **Tangier** and **Marrakesh**; this would cost around £50/$80, well above the bus and train fares but – at two, as opposed to nearly thirteen hours – saves considerable effort. For anyone intrepid enough to explore the **Deep South** of the country, flights can also be worthwhile – for example, returning from the southernmost visitable towns of Ad Dakhla or Laayoune.

Details of *RAM* flights, and addresses of the company's local offices, are given in the main part of the guide and the "Travel Details" at the end of chapters. Remember that you must always confirm flights at a *RAM* office 72 hours before departure. Student and under-26 youth **discounts** of 25 percent are available on all *RAM* domestic flights but only if the ticket is bought in advance from one of their offices.

TRAVELLING BY BIKE

Biking – and particularly **mountain biking** – is becoming an increasingly popular pursuit for Western travellers to Morocco. The country's regular roads are well maintained and by European standards very quiet, while the extensive network of **pistes** – dirt tracks – makes for exciting mountain bike terrain, leading you into areas otherwise accessible only to trekkers or four-wheel drive expeditions. Some of the more intrepid mountain bikers cover footpaths in the High Atlas, too, though for the less than super-fit this can be extremely heavy going. Better, on the whole, to stick to established pistes – many of which are covered by local trucks, which you can pay for a ride if your legs (or your bike) give out.

However you intend to cycle, you will need to go with your eyes wide open. The heat and the long stretches of dead straight road across arid, featureless plains – the main routes to (or beyond) the mountain ranges – can all too easily drain your energy. And a constant backdrop of water-sculpted slopes, all very picturesque by car, is quite another matter if you are cycling through them all day. Even in the mountains, public **water** is very rare – there are very few roadside watering places such as are found in Europe – and **population is sparse**, with towns and villages often a long way apart.

Regular roads are generally well-surfaced but narrow and you will often have to get off the tarmac to make way for traffic. Beware also of open land-drains close to the roadsides, and loose gravel on the bends.

Cycling on the **pistes**, mountain bikes come into their own with their "tractor" tyres and wide, stabilising handlebars. There are few pistes that could be recommended on a regular tourer. Locals refer to surfaced roads as *goudronné* or *revêtue* – and will direct you to these, rather than to pistes.

GETTING YOUR BIKE TO MOROCCO

Most **airlines** – even charters – carry bikes free of charge, so long as they don't push your baggage allowance over the weight limit. When buying a ticket, register your intention of taking your bike and check out the airline's conditions. They will generally require you to invert the handlebars, remove the pedals, and deflate the tyres; some (like *KLM* provide/sell a cardboard **box** to enclose the bike, as protection for other passengers' luggage as much as for the bike; you are, however, unlikely to be offered a box for the return journey. A useful alternative, offering little protection but at least ensuring nothing gets lost, is to customise an industrial nylon sack, adding a drawstring at the neck.

If you plan to fly to Spain and cross over **by ferry to Morocco**, things couldn't be simpler. You ride on with the motor vehicles (thus avoiding the long queues of foot passengers) and the bike is secure during the voyage. At the time of writing, there's a small charge for bikes on the ferries from Algeciras to Ceuta and Tangier, but not on the crossings from Málaga or Almería to Melilla.

GETTING ABOUT: LOCAL TRANSPORT

Once in Morocco, you can make use of local transport to supplement your own wheels. **Buses** will generally carry cycles on the roof. *CTM* usually charge around 10dh per bike – make sure you get a ticket. On other lines it's very much up to you to negotiate with the driver and/or baggage porter (who will expect at least 5dh at each end – don't pay both ends in advance!). If you're riding, and exhausted, you can usually flag down private-line buses (but not usually *CTM* services) on the road.

PETITS TAXIS

Most Moroccan towns are small enough to cover on foot, especially if you stay in a hotel in or near the Medina – where you'll want to spend most of your time. In larger cities, however, local buses can be useful, as can *petits taxis* – usually Fiats or Simcas – which take up to three passengers.

Petits taxis, as opposed to *grands taxis*, are limited to trips within city limits. Officially, all of them should have meters, but in practice you're unlikely to find one that works (at least for tourists) except in Rabat. It is then a matter of bargaining for a price – either before you get in (wise to start off with) or by simply presenting the regular fare when you get out. If you are a lone passenger, your taxi driver may pick up one or two additional passengers en route, each of whom will pay the full fare for their journey, as of course will you. This is standard practice.

Fares vary enormously (in Marrakesh and Agadir, demands can often be excessive), though everywhere it depends to a large extent on what you look like, how you act, and where you're going. Don't be afraid to use *petits taxis* or to argue with the driver if you feel you're being unreasonably overcharged. After 8pm, standard fares rise by 50 percent.

Some *grands taxis* also agree to carry cycles, if they have space on a rack. The fare will be about the same as for a place in the taxi: again, you may well have to bargain! In mountain/desert areas, you can have your bike carried with you on **truck or transit services** (see p.25). Prices for this are highly negotiable, but should not exceed your own passenger fare.

Cycles are carried on **trains** for a modest handling fee, though it's not really worth the hassle. Bikes have to be registered in advance as baggage and they won't necessarily travel on the same train as you (though they will usually turn up within a day!).

ACCOMMODATION

Accommodation doesn't present any special problems. The cheaper **hotels** will almost always let you keep your bike in your room – and others will find a disused basement or office for storage. It is almost essential to do this, as much to deter unwelcome tampering as theft, especially if you have a curiosity-inviting mountain bike. At **campsites**, there's usually a guardian on hand to keep an eye on your bike, or stow it away in his chalet.

ROUTES

Rewarding areas for biking must include:

● **Tizi n'Test** (High Atlas): **Asni to Ijoukak**, and an excursion to Tin Mal.

● **Asni to Setti Fatma** (High Atlas: Ourika Valley) and beyond if you have a mountain bike.

● **Western** (well-watered) **side of the Middle Atlas.**

In summer, at least, it wouldn't be a good idea to go much **beyond the Atlas**, though given cooler winter temperatures **southern oasis routes** – like **Ouarzazate to Zagora** or **Ouarzazate to Tinerhir** – and the **desert routes** down to **Er Rachidia, Erfoud and Rissani** – could be rewarding.

REPAIRS

Most towns reveal a wealth of **general repair shops** in their Medina quarters, well used to servicing local bikes and mopeds. Though they are most unlikely to have the correct spare parts for your make of bike, they can usually sort out some kind of temporary solution.

It is worth bringing with you **spare spokes** (and tool), plus **brake blocks** and **cable**, as the mountain descents can take it out on a bike.

Tyres and tubes can generally be found for tourers, though if you have anything fancy, best bring at least one spare, too.

Obviously, before setting out, you should make sure that your brakes are in good order, renew bearings, etc, and ensure that you have decent quality (and condition) tyres.

PROBLEMS AND REWARDS

All over Morocco, and particularly in rural areas, there are stray, wild and semi-cared-for dogs. A cyclist pedalling past with feet and wheels spinning seems to send at least half of them into a frenzied state. Normally, cycling like the clappers is the best defence, but on steep ascents and off-road this isn't always possible. In these situations, keep the bike between you and the dog, and use your pump or a shower from your water bottle as defence. As insurance against infection, if you do get bitten, a rabies inoculation is advisable.

Another factor to be prepared for is your susceptibility to unwanted attentions of locals. Small children will often stand in the road to hinder your progress, or even chase after you in gangs. This is normally good-natured but it can become intimidating if they start throwing stones. Your attitude is important: be friendly, smile, and maintain strong eye contact. On no account attempt to mete out your own discipline. Small children always have big brothers.

Lastly, the dreaded hustlers – for more on whom see p.20. As a cyclist you will avoid the customary hassle at ports and train stations but you are vulnerable to motorbike hustlers who pull alongside tourists in Fes and Marrakesh. Some of these characters can be pretty unpleasant if you decline their services of guiding you to hotels.

So – as one correspondent put it – after all these warnings, and the extra expense and hassle, *is it worth cycling in Morocco?* His answer was a definite yes: "I felt an extra intimacy with the country by staying close to it, rather than viewing it from car or bus windows. And I experienced unrivalled generosity, from cups of tea offered by policemen at roadside checkpoints to a full-blown breakfast banquet from a farming family whose dog had savaged my leg. People went out of their way to give me advice, food, drink and lifts, and not once did I feel seriously threatened. Lastly, the exhilaration I felt on some of the mountain descents, above all the Tizi n'Test in the High Atlas, will remain with me forever. I was not an experienced cyle tourer when I arrived

in Morocco, but the grandeur of the scenery helped carry me over the passes."

FURTHER INFORMATION

For a fact sheet on conditions for cyclists in Morocco and some suggested routes, it's worth contacting the British Cycle Touring Club, Cotterell House, 69 Meadrow, Godalming, Surrey GU7 3HS (☎04868/7217). The club also arranges good-value insurance, etc, for members.

Inspiration for mountain bikers can be found in Nick Crane's book, *Atlas Biker* (Oxford Illustrated Press, £12.95; UK), an adventurous account of a complete traverse of the High Atlas on – or at times carrying – mountain bikes. For general advice on equipment and clothing, *Bicycle Expeditions* by Paul Vickers (available from the Expedition Advisory Service, Royal Geographical Society, Kensington Gore, London SW7 2AR, UK) is useful.

For details of maps, see p.19.

TREKKING

Trekking is one of the very best things Morocco has to offer. In the High Atlas, the country boasts one of the most rewarding mountain ranges in the world – and one of the least spoilt. If you are used to the Pyrenees or Alps, here you will feel you are moving a century or so back in time.

A number of long-distance Atlas routes can be followed – even a "Grand Traverse" of the full range. Most people, however, limit themselves to shorter treks round the Djebel Toubkal area (best in spring or autumn; conditions can be treacherous in winter). Other promising areas include the Djebel Sirwa, Western High Atlas,

or in winter the **Djebel Sarhro** and **Tafraoute** region of the **Anti-Atlas**. The **Middle Atlas** has some attractive walking, too, around **Azrou** and **Beni Mellal**.

Each of these areas is featured in some detail in this guide. For further information, check the **trekking books** detailed on p.19. And if you haven't had much experience or feel a little daunted by the lack of organised facilities, try one of the **specialist trekking companies** offering Moroccan trips (see box on pp.6–7).

For general **trekking practicalities**, see the Toubkal section in Chapter Five. For details of survey-style **maps**, see p.19.

ACCOMMODATION

Hotels in Morocco are cheap, good value, and usually pretty easy to find. The only times you might have a problem getting a room are in the peak seasons (August, Christmas or Easter), and then only in a handful of main cities and resorts – Fes, Agadir, Tangier and sometimes Tetouan.

There is a basic distinction between **classified hotels** (which are given star-ratings by the tourist board and have fairly regulated standards) and **unclassified hotels** (which do not – and are used more by Moroccans than tourists).

UNCLASSIFIED HOTELS

Unclassified (*non-classé*) hotels are mainly to be found in the older, Arab-built parts of cities – the **Medinas** – and are almost always the cheapest options. They offer the additional advantage of being at the heart of things: where you'll want to spend most of your time, and where all the sights and markets are concentrated. The disadvantages are that the Medinas can at first appear daunting – with their mazes of narrow lanes and blind alleys – and that the hotels themselves can be, at worst, dirty flea traps with tiny, windowless cells and half-washed sheets. At their best, they're fine: traditional "caravanserai" buildings with whitewashed rooms round a central patio.

HOTEL PRICE CODES AND STAR-RATINGS

As of 1993, hotels are no longer obliged to levy set maximum rates, according to their official star-ratings, as had long been the custom. However, **prices** still broadly follow the star-rating system, and this is the basis of our own **hotel price codes** set out below and keyed throughout the guide.

Note that cheaper prices in the lower categories are generally for rooms with just a washbasin – you always pay extra for **en suite** shower and wc – and that double rooms can generally be converted into **triples/family rooms**, with extra beds, for a modest extra charge. Note also that the prices quoted by all hotels are subject to various local and regional **taxes**, which can add 15 to 20 percent to the bill.

Our code	Classification	Single room price	Double room price
ⓤ	Unclassified	25–60dh	40–100dh
①	1*A/1*B	60–105dh	100–125dh
②	2*B/2*A	105–145dh	125–175dh)
③	3*B/3*A	145–225dh	175–275dh
④	4*B/4*A	225–400dh	275–500dh
⑤	5*luxury	Upwards of 400dh	Upwards of 500dh

HAMMAMS

The absence of hot showers in some of the cheaper Medina hotels is not such a disaster. Throughout all the Medina quarters, you'll find local **hammams** – steam baths where you can go in and sweat for as long as you like, get scrubbed down and rigorously massaged, and douse yourself with endless buckets of hot and cold water. Those for women are particularly welcoming and turn out to be a highlight for many women travellers.

Several hammams are detailed in the text, but the best way of finding one is always to ask at the hotel where you're staying. You will often, in fact, need to be led to a hammam, since they are usually unmarked and very hard to find. In some towns, you find separate hammams for women and men; at others there are different hours for each sex – usually 9am–7pm for women, 7pm–1am (and sometimes 5–9am) for men.

For both sexes, however, there's more **modesty** than you might perhaps expect: it's customary for men (always) and women (generally) to bathe in **swimming costume**, and men will undress facing the wall. Women may be surprised to find their Moroccan counterparts completely shaven and may (in good humour) be offered this service; there's no embarrassment in declining.

As part of the Islamic tradition of cleanliness and ablutions, hammams sometimes have a **religious element**, and you may not be welcome in (or allowed in) to those built alongside mosques, particularly on Thursday evenings, before the main weekly service on Friday. On the whole, though, there are no restrictions against *Nisara* ("Nazarenes", or Christians).

Finally, don't forget to bring your own **soap**, **shampoo and towels** along to hammams; the latter are rented but can be a bit dubious. Locals often bring a **plastic mat** to sit on, too, as the floors can get a bit clogged. These can be bought easily enough in any town.

One other minus-point for unclassified Medina hotels is that they often have a problem with **water**. Most of the Medinas remain substantially unmodernised, and in the hotels hot showers are a rarity and the squat toilets sometimes pretty disgusting.

Unclassified hotel **rates** fluctuate widely, according to place, season and demand. The best value rooms are, for some reason, in Chaouen, where hotels charge from around 40dh (£3/$5) a double; in Fes, by contrast, where the quality is a lot worse but rooms in short supply, you would do well to find a double at under 100dh (£8/$12.50). A charge of 30dh per person is pretty standard.

CLASSIFIED HOTELS

Classified (*classé***) hotels** are almost always in a town's *ville nouvelle* – the "new" or administrative quarters, built by the French and usually set slightly apart from the Medina. The **star-ratings** are fairly self-explanatory: starting at the bottom with 1*B, 1*A, 2*B, etc, and going up to 4*B, 4*A, and finally 5*Luxury. **Prices** are pretty reasonable in all but the 5* luxury categories.

At the bottom end of the scale, a **one-star hotel** will offer you a basic double room with a washbasin for around £8/$13, and with a shower and wc for an additional £2/$3. With **two- and three-star hotels**, at the top end of which scale you're paying around £25/$40 for a double with

shower and wc, there's a definite progression in comfort. Indeed, you can find a few elegant, old hotels in these categories which used once to be very grand but have since slipped in competition with the new, purpose-built tourist complexes.

For European/American standards of comfort, however, you need to look, on the whole, at **four-star hotels**. These are used by most foreign tour operators and charge around £30–50/$50–80 for a double. If you can afford the upper end of this scale, you'll be moving into real style, with rooms looking out onto palm-shaded pools and gardens, in buildings that have sometimes been converted from old palace residences. Hotels accorded the **5-star-luxury rating** more or less guarantee a bit of style, either in a historic conversion (the most famous of which are the *Hotel Mamounia* in Marrakesh and the *Palais Jamai* in Fes) or in a modern building with a splendid pool and all the international creature comforts. **Bookings** for the four- or five-star hotels are best made in advance – either by phoning yourself or going through one of the specialist agencies detailed on p.6 and 7.

A SUGGESTED BUDGET COURSE . . .

Ideally, the best course for anyone on a limited budget is to **alternate between the extremes**, spending most nights in basic Medina hotels but going for the occasional blast of grandeur.

At any rate don't limit yourself to the middle categories – these are mostly dull, and staying all the time in the *villes nouvelles* will cut you off from the most interesting aspects of traditional Moroccan life.

YOUTH HOSTELS AND *REFUGES*

Morocco has expanded its **youth hostel** organisation in recent years, and there are now eleven *Auberges de Jeunesse* scattered round the country. Most are clean and reasonably well run, and charges are a modest 15–25dh (£1–1.75/$1.50– 3) per person, per night. The hostels are located at Asni (High Atlas), Azrou (Middle Atlas), Casablanca, Chaouen, Fes, Laayoune, Marrakesh, Meknes, Oujda, Rabat and Tangier. Addresses and details are given for all of these in the relevant sections of the guide. One general attraction is the opportunity for meeting other travellers, including Moroccans on holiday.

REFUGES AND GÎTES

In the **Djebel Toubkal** area of the High Atlas mountains, the French-run *Club Alpin Français* (*CAF*) maintain five huts, or **refuges**, equipped for trekkers. These provide dormitory beds for 10–15dh (80p–£1.20/$1.25–2) per person and sometimes meals and/or cooking facilities. They are detailed in the relevant sections.

Also in trekking areas, a number of locals offer rooms in their houses: an informal scheme which the Moroccan tourist authorities have begun promoting as **gîtes d'étape**. Lists of these

gîtes are to be found in the pamphlet *La Grande Traversée des Atlas Marocains* (see p.19). Current charges are set at 10dh (8p/$1.20) per person, per night, for "non-classé; 30dh (£2.50/ $4) per person, per night, for "2e-classé; breakfast is charged at 12dh and an evening meal at 30dh.

CAMPSITES

Campsites are to be found at intervals along most of the developed Moroccan coast and in most towns or cities of any size. They are inexpensive and often quite informal and makeshift, advertised from season to season on roadside signs. Most sites are very cheap, at around 8dh (60p/$1) per person, plus a similar charge for a motor caravan or campervan; they usually have basic (and sometimes very basic) washing and toilet facilities. A few more upmarket places, in Meknes, Fes or Marrakesh, for example, offer swimming pools and better facilities at around double the cost – sometimes more. Details and addresses are given in relevant sections of the guide.

Note that campsites don't provide total **security**, and you should never leave valuables unattended. When camping **outside official sites**, this obviously applies even more, and if you want to do this, it's wise to ask at a house if you can pitch your tent alongside – you'll usually get a hospitable response. If you're trekking in the Atlas, it is often possible to pay someone to act as a *gardien* for your tent.

EATING AND DRINKING

Like accommodation, food in Morocco falls into two basic categories: ordinary Moroccan meals served in the Medina cafés (or bought from stalls), and French-influenced tourist menus in most of the hotels and *ville nouvelle* restaurants. There are exceptions – cheap local cafés in the new cities and occasional "palace"-style places in the Medina – but, in general, this still holds true. Once again, you'd be advised to stick largely to the Medina places (most are cleaner than they look), with an occasional splurge in the best restaurants you can find.

BASIC CAFÉ FOOD

Basic Moroccan meals generally centre on a thick, very filling soup – most often the spicy, bean-based *harira* (which is a meal in itself, and eaten as such to break the Ramadan fast). To this you might add a plateful of **kebabs** (either *brochettes*, shish kebabs or *kefta*, made from minced meat) and perhaps a **salad** (often very finely chopped, vaguely similar to the Spanish *gazpacho*), together with **dates** bought at a market stall.

Alternatively, you could go for a *tajine*, which is essentially a stew, cooked slowly in an earthenware pot over a charcoal fire. Mopped up with bread, it can be unbelievably delicious.

Either alternative would in all likelihood set you back little more than 20dh (£1.50/$2.50) at one of the hole-in-the-wall places in the Medina, with their two or three tables. You are not expected to bargain for cooked food, but prices can be lower at café-restaurants without menus if you enquire how much things cost before you start eating.

If you're looking for **breakfast or a snack**, you can buy a half-*baguette* – plus butter and jam, cheese or eggs, if you want – from many bread or grocery stores, and take it into a café to order a drink.

RESTAURANT MEALS

More expensive dishes, available in some of the Medina cafés as well as in the dearer restaurants, include **fish**, particularly on the coast, and **chicken** *(poulet)*, either spit-roasted *(rôti)* or with lemon and olives *(poulet aux olives et citron)*.

You will sometimes find *pastilla*, too, a succulent pigeon (in cheaper versions chicken may be used) pie, prepared with filo pastry coated with sugar and cinnamon; it is a particular speciality of Fes.

And, of course, there is *couscous*, perhaps the most famous Moroccan dish, based on a huge bowl of steamed semolina piled high with vegetables and mutton, chicken, or occasionally fish. *Couscous*, however, tends to be

VEGETARIAN/VEGAN OPTIONS

Moroccan cuisine presents pretty limited options for vegetarians – a preference which will meet with little comprehension on your travels. *Tajines* can be requested without meat (and, with some difficulty, without meat stock), but beyond these vegetarian casseroles, and ubiquitous omelettes and sandwiches, the menus don't present very obvious choices. *Harira* (vegetable broth) may or may not be made with meat stock, and most foods are cooked in animal fats.

It's possible, however, to maintain a balanced and reasonably interesting diet, so long as you're not too strict, and are prepared for a few problems outside the cities. If you're vegan, you will really need to come equipped and do a fair bit of cooking for yourself.

Provisions that most vegetarians will feel grateful to have brought include yeast extract, peanut butter, veggie patés/spreads, and stock cubes – which you can present to cafés for preparing your *tajine*. You might also take along a small gas stove and pan – gas is cheap and readily available, and in the cheaper hotels a lot of Moroccan people cook in their rooms.

Locally, there are plenty of beans, grains, seeds and pulses available, basic cheeses, excellent yoghurts, and a great selection of fruit and nuts; dates, figs, almonds and pistachio nuts can all enliven dishes. In the countryside, you may find fresh fruit and vegetables hard to obtain except during the weekly *souk*, but you can often buy from locals, who grow a small stock on their terraces.

In cafés and restaurants, asking for a dish *sans viande ou poisson* (without meat or fish) can still result in your being served chicken or lamb, so you'll need to take the trouble to explain matters very clearly. It often helps to talk of being a vegetarian in terms of religious restrictions or rules: concepts that Moroccans are themselves familiar with.

The most difficult situations are those in which you are invited to eat at someone's house – a common occurrence in the countryside. You may find people give you meat when you have specifically asked for vegetables because they think you can't afford it: a scenario in which you might decide that it's more important not to offend someone showing you kindness than to be dogmatic about your own principles. Picking out vegetables from a meat *tajine* won't offend your hosts; declining the dish altogether, on the other hand, may well end up with the mother/sister/wife in the kitchen getting the flack.

A GLOSSARY OF MOROCCAN FOOD

Note that where food/dishes are commonly available in all kinds of restaurants, both **French** and **Arabic** words are given; in Arabic words, the letters printed in **bold italics** should be stressed.

BASICS

Pain	*l-khobz*	Bread	Sel	*l-melha*	Salt
Oeufs	*l-bayd*	Eggs	Sauce	*l-merga*	Sauce
Poissons	*l-hout*	Fish	Sucre	*soukar*	Sugar
Viande	*l-hem*	Meat		(*sanida* is granulated sugar;
Huile	*zit*	Oil		*soukar*, lump sugar)
Poivre	*lebzar*	Pepper	Légumes	*l-khoudra*	Vegetables
Salade	*shalada*	Salad	Vinaigre	*l-khel*	Vinegar

SOUPS, SALADS AND VEGETABLES

—	*Harira*	Spicy bean soup	Frites	*l'batata*	Fried potatoes
Potage	—	Thick soup	Tomates	*matecha*	Tomatoes
Bouillon	—	Thin soup	Épinards	*salk*	Spinach
Salade Marocaine	—	Mixed salad	Oignons	*l-basla*	Onions

MAIN DISHES

Tajine de viande	*l-hem*	Meat stew
Tajine des poissons	*l-hout*	Fish stew
Couscous (aux sept légumes)	*Couscous bidaoui*	Couscous (with seven vegetables)
Poulet aux olives et citron		Chicken with olives and lemon
—	*Djaja mahamara*	Chicken stuffed with almonds, semolina and raisins
Boulettes de viande	*kefta*	Meatballs
Bifteck	*l-habra*	Steak
Agneau	*Mechoui*	Roast lamb
Pastilla	*B'stilla*	Pigeon pie

MEATS, POULTRY AND FISH

Poulet	*djaj*	Chicken	Sardines	*sardile*	Sardines
Pigeon	*lehmama*	Pigeon	Merlan	*l-mirla*	Whiting
Lapin	*qniya*	Rabbit	Crevettes	—	Shrimps
Mouton	*l-houli*	Mutton	Langouste	—	Lobster

SWEETS AND FRUITS

Cornes de gazelles	*kab l-ghzal*	Marzipan-filled pastry horns	Amandes	*louze*	Almonds
—	*m'hencha*	Coiled, almond-filled pastry	Bananes	*banane*	Bananas
			Fraises	*l-fraise*	Strawberries
Briouats au miel	—	Similar – but covered in honey	Cerises	*hblmluk*	Cherries
			Pêches	*l-khoukh*	Peaches
			Oranges	*limoune*	Oranges
—	*fekkas*	Sweet aniseed biscuits	Melon	*l-battikh*	Melon
			Pasteque	*dellah*	Watermelon
Fromage	*ejben*	Cheese	Raisins	*la'anb*	Grapes
Dattes	*tmer*	Dates	Pommes	*tufaah*	Apples
Figues	*kermous*	Figs	Abricots	*mishmash*	Apricots
			Figues de Bsarbarie	*Kermus d'ensarrah (or Takanareete)*	Cactus fruit (prickly pear)

DRINKS

Eau	*agua, l-**ma***	Water	Bière	*birra*	Beer
(Minerale)	*(**maz**dini)*	(Mineral)	Vin	*sh-**rab***	Wine
Thé	*atay*	Tea	Café	*qahwa*	Coffee
(à la menthe)	*(**dee**yal naanaa)*	(Mint)	(au lait)	*(bi la**h**lib)*	(with milk)

SOME ARABIC PHRASES

What do you have . . .	*Ash**noo kane** . . .*
to eat?	*. . . f'l-**mak**la?*
to drink?	*. . . f'l-mucha**roubat?***
What is this?	*Shnoo **had**a?*
Can you give me	*A**tee**nee . . .*
. . . a knife/fork/spoon?	*. . . moos/for**shet**a/**mal**ka?*
. . . a plate/glass/napkin?	*. . . **t'b**-sil/**kess**/l-**fo**ta?*
Less/without sugar	*Shwee**ya/ble **souk**ar*
Without meat	*Ble l-**hem***
This is not what I asked for!	*Hedee **mesh**ee **hee**a li tlubt!*
This is not fresh/clean!	*Hedee **mesh**ee **tree**a/n'**qee**a!*
This is (not) good!	*Hedee (**mesh**ee) me**zye**na!*
The bill, please.	*L'h'**seb** min**fad**lik.*
Please write it down.	*Min**fad**lik, k'**tib'h**.*

EATING MOROCCAN STYLE

Eating in local cafés, or if **invited to a home**, you may find yourself using your hands rather than a knife and fork. Muslims eat only with the **right hand** (the left is used in toilet), and you should do likewise. Hold the bread between the fingers and use your thumb as a scoop.

Eating from a **communal plate** at someone's home, it is polite to take only what is immediately in front of you, unless specifically offered a piece of meat by the host.

disappointing. There is no real tradition of going out to eat in Morocco, and this is a dish that's traditionally prepared at home for a special occasion (on Friday, the holy day, in richer households; perhaps for a festival in poorer ones). As a general rule, you'll need to give two or three hours' notice for it to be cooked.

At festivals, which are always good for interesting food, and at the most expensive tourist restaurants, you may also come across **mechoui** – a whole sheep roasted on a spit.

To supplement these standard offerings, most tourist restaurants add a few **French dishes** – steak, liver, various fish and fowl, etc – and the ubiquitous **salade marocaine**, actually very different from the Moroccan idea of salad, since it's based on a few tomatoes, cucumbers and other greens. Together with a dessert consisting either of fruit or pastry, these meals usually come to around 75–100dh (£6–8/$10–12.50) per person.

CAKES, DESSERTS AND FRUIT

Cakes and desserts are also available in some Moroccan cafés, though you'll find them more often at pastry shops or street stalls. They can be excellent. The most common are *cornes de gazelles*, sugar-coated pastries filled with a kind of marzipan, but there are infinite variations, like *m'hencha* – almond-filled pastry coils which sometimes appear covered in honey.

Yoghurt (*yaourt*) is also delicious, and Morocco is surprisingly rich in seasonal **fruits**. In addition to the various kinds of **dates** – sold all year but at their best fresh from the October harvests – there are grapes, melons, strawberries, peaches and figs, all advisably washed before eaten. Or for a real thirst-quencher (and a good cure for a bad stomach), you can have quantities of **prickly pear**, cactus fruit, peeled for you in the street for a couple of dirhams.

TEA AND OTHER DRINKS

The national drink is **thé à la menthe** – green tea ("Whisky Marocain" or "Whisky Berber") flavoured with sprigs of mint and a minimum of four cubes of sugar per cup. It tastes a little sickly at first but is worth getting used to – perfect in the summer heat and a ritual if you're invited into anyone's home or if you're doing any serious bargaining in a shop. In cafés, it is usually cheaper to ask for a pot (*une théière*) for two or three people. You can also occasionally get red or **amber** tea – more expensive and rarely available, but delicious when you can find it – and tea with **aniseed** (*anis*) and **verbena** (*verveine*). **"English style" tea** is usually referred to as *thé Lipton* – after the ubiquitous brand of teabags.

Also common at cafés and street stalls are a range of wonderful fresh-squeezed **juices**: *jus d'orange*, *jus d'amande* (almond), *jus des bananes* and *jus de pomme* (apple), the last three milk-based and served chilled. *Leben* – yoghurt and water – is often sold at train and bus stations and does wonders for an upset stomach.

Other **soft drinks** inevitably include Coke, along with Fanta and other fizzy lemonades – all pretty inexpensive and sold in large bottles. **Mineral water**, which is a worthwhile investment throughout the country, is usually referred to by brand name, ubiquitously *Sidi Harazem* or *Sidi Ali* (the latter is preferable), or the naturally sparkling *Oulmès*.

Coffee (*café*) is best in French-style cafés – either *noir* (black), *cassé* (with a drop of milk), or *au lait* (made with milk). Instant coffee is known, like tea, after its brand – in this case *Nescafé*.

Lastly, do not take risks with **milk**: buy it fresh and drink it fresh. If it smells remotely off, don't touch it.

WINE AND BEER

As an Islamic nation, Morocco gives **drinking alcohol** a low profile. It is, in fact, not generally possible to buy any alcohol at all in the Medinas, and for beer or wine you always have to go to a tourist restaurant or hotel, or a bar in the *ville nouvelle*. Outside of tourist hotels, **bars** – which are often called *brasseries*, though they serve no food – are very much **all-male preserves**, in which women travellers may feel uneasy.

On the drinks front, Moroccan **wines** can be palatable enough, if a little heavy for drinking without a meal. The best to be found is the pinkish red *Clairet de Meknès*, made purposefully light in

EAU MINÉRALE NATURELLE
sidi harazem

French claret style. Other varieties worth trying include the strong red *Cabernet*, the rosé *Gris de Boulaoune* and the dry, white *Spécial Coquillages*.

Those Moroccans who drink in bars tend to stick to **beer**, usually the local *Stork* or *Flag*, which are about 50 percent cheaper than imported European brands.

KIF (HASHISH)

The smoking of **kif** (hashish, *chocolaté*) has for a long time been a regular pastime of Moroccans and tourists alike. Indeed, in the 1960s and 1970s (or further back, in the 1930s), its ready availability, good quality and low cost made *kif* a major tourist attraction. It is, however, illegal, or, as the ONMT puts it:

> Tourists coming to Morocco are warned that the first article in the Dahir of April 24th 1954 prohibits the POSSESSION, the OFFER, the DISTRIBUTION, the PURCHASE, the SALE and the TRANSPORTATION as well as the EXPORTATION of CANNABIS IN WHATEVER FORM. The Dahir allows for a penalty of IMPRISONMENT from three months to five years and a fine of 2400 to 240,000 dirhams, or only one of these. Moreover the law court may ordain the SEIZURE of the means of transport and the things used to cover up the smuggling as well as the toxic products themselves.

What this means in practice is slightly different. There is no real effort to stop Moroccans from using *kif*, but as a tourist you are peculiarly vulnerable. Not so much because of the **police**, as because of the **dealers**. Many have developed aggressive tactics, selling people hash (or, occasionally, even planting it) and then returning or sending friends to threaten to turn you in to the police; or occasionally they themselves may even be actual informers, and turn you in to the police. Either way, it can all become pretty paranoiac and unpleasant – and large fines (plus prison sentences for substantial amounts) do get levied.

What can you do to avoid all this? Most obviously, keep well clear – above all, of the *kif*-growing areas of the **Rif mountains** and the processing centre in **Ketama** – and always reply to hustlers by saying you don't smoke. If you *are* coming to Morocco to indulge, don't buy anything in the first few days (definitely not in Tangier and Tetouan), and only smoke* where you feel thoroughly confident and in control.

Above all, **do not try to take any out** by air (*Midnight Express* could equally have been about Morocco), or bring any out of the Rif area. And don't even think of taking any into Algeria or over to Spain. Penalties in **Algeria** are amazingly harsh (a life sentence is theoretically possible), and there's nearly always a prison sentence in **Spain**, too, for anyone caught importing.

If you do find yourself in trouble there are **consulates** for most nationalities in Rabat/Casablanca and, to a lesser extent, in Tangier (see lists on p.22). All of the consulates are notoriously unsympathetic to drug offenders – the British one in Rabat has an old French poster on the wall, "*Le kif détruit l'esprit*" – but they can help with technical problems and find you legal representation.

---

*Kif is not necessarily what's smoked in Morocco – a traditional speciality is *majoun*, a kind of fudge made with the pounded flowers and seeds of the plant. As James Jackson wrote in his *An Account of the Empire of Morocco, 1814*, "a piece of this as big as a walnut will for a time entirely deprive a man of all reason and intellect". It is also reputed to be good for settling your stomach.

COMMUNICATIONS: POST, PHONES AND MEDIA

MAIL AND POSTE RESTANTE

Letters between Western Europe and Morocco generally take around a week to ten days, around two weeks to North America or Australasia. There are postboxes at the **PTT** (post office) and on the wayside; they seem to get emptied fairly efficiently, even in out-of-the-way places.

Stamps can often be bought alongside postcards, or from any *Tabac*, as well as at the PTT, where there is usually a dedicated window or counter (labelled "timbres"). There is always a separate window for parcels, where the officials will want to examine the goods you are sending. Always take them unwrapped; alongside the parcels counter, there is someone (on a franchise) to supply wrapping paper, string and all the trimmings, or wrap your parcel, if you want.

Post office hours are Monday to Friday, 8am to noon and 3 to 6pm in winter, 8am to 3pm in summer; closed Saturday and Sunday.

POSTE RESTANTE

Receiving letters **poste restante** can be a bit of a lottery, as Moroccan post office workers don't always file letters under the name you might expect. Ask for all your initials to be checked (including *M* for Ms, etc), and, if you're half-expecting anything, suggest other letters as well.

To pick up your mail you need your passport. To have mail sent to you, it should be addressed (preferably with your surname underlined) to *Poste Restante* at the *PTT Centrale* of any major city (Marrakesh is notoriously inefficient).

Alternatives to sending *poste restante* to post offices are to pick a big **hotel** (anything with three or more stars should be reliable) or have things sent *c/o American Express* – represented in Morocco by *Voyages Schwartz* in Tangier, Fes, Casablanca, Agadir and Marrakesh (see the section in "Costs and Money" for addresses).

PHONES

The **public telephone section** is usually housed in a city's main post office (*PTT Centrale*), though it often has a separate entrance and stays open longer hours – 24 hours a day in some of the main cities. Since **international direct dialling** reached Morocco it's been possible to place calls with little problem, and in most major towns you can also make international calls from centrally placed **phone boxes** (*cabines*). In large cities you can now use phonecards in some *cabines*; they are usually on sale at a nearby kiosk. Alternatively, you can **make calls through a hotel**. Even fairly small places will normally do this; however, be sure to ask in advance both of possible surcharges and the chargeable rate.

To **make a call from a *cabine***, you place the phonecard – or coins – into the slot on the phoneset and then dial. Using coins, a few dirhams are enough for a call within Morocco; for international calls you need at least four of the larger 5dh coins for Europe and eight or more for North America or Australia.

Note that international calls are charged for each **three-minute period**. If you go one second over, you're charged for the next period. If phoning from a PTT, you can request the operator to cut you off after a three-minute period.

MOROCCAN CALLS AND NUMBERS

The Moroccan phone system has recently been rationalised, with all numbers prefixed by one of eight **area zones**:

02 Casablanca	03 Settat
04 Marrakesh	05 Fes
06 Oujda	07 Rabat
08 Laayoune	09 Tangier

To call a number in another zone, you use the prefix; if you are calling from within the same zone, you omit it. The full number will always have **eight digits** (including the zone prefix), unless it's incredibly out-of-the-way, in which case it may still just have a village name and **two-digit** number, which you have to dial through the operator.

When dialling, the **ringing tone** consists of one-and-a-half-second bursts of tone, separated by a three-and-a-half-second silence. The **engaged tone** is similar to the one used in Britain. A series of rapid pips may also be heard, indicating that your call is being connected.

Phoning Morocco from abroad, you dial the international code (010 from Britain), then the country code (212) and the full eight-digit number (omitting the initial zero of the zone code).

INTERNATIONAL CALLS

For an international call, dial 00 and wait for a musical-sounding dialling tone, which is the signal that you can put in an international call. First, dial the country code:

Australia 61	Britain 44
Canada 1	Netherlands 31
Spain 34	USA 1

Then dial the individual number, leaving out the initial 0 of its local code. If you are successfully connected you will hear the local tones for your number. If not, you will hear either a busy signal, a recording in Arabic and then French informing that lines are "saturated", or silence. Persevere: it may well take three or four attempts to get through.

The **rate for international calls** is currently around 18dh (£1.50) a minute to Britain and Western Europe, 60dh (US$7) a minute to the US and Canada. A good policy is to phone someone briefly and get them to ring you back. Actual reverse charge calls are hard to arrange.

THE MEDIA

As for other means of staying in touch, various British and French **newspapers** and the *International Herald Tribune* are available in all the main cities. *Le Monde* is the most common.

If you take a short-wave radio, you can pick up the **BBC World Service**, which is broadcast on various frequencies through the day, from 6am to midnight local time. The most consistent evening reception is generally on 9.41 and 5.975 mHz (31.88m and 50.21m bands); full programme listings are available from the BBC or the British Council in Rabat. You can also pick up the **Voice of America**.

Some of the pricier hotels these days can receive **satellite TV** – occasionally *Sky* and more commonly the French *TV5* channel. In the north of the country you can also receive Spanish stations and, in Tangier, the English-language **Gibraltar** TV and radio broadcasts. **Morocco's own two TV channels** broadcast in Arabic, but include some French programmes – and news bulletins in both French and Spanish.

THE MOROCCAN PRESS

The **Moroccan press** encompasses a reasonable range of papers, published in French and Arabic. Of the **French-language** papers, the most accessible is the official – and somewhat rigorously pro-government – French-language daily, *Le Matin du Sahara* (circulation 70,000). Others include *L'Opinion* (conservative opposition) and *Al-Bayannne* (communist).

In **Arabic**, there are *Al Alam* (circ. 50,000), which is supportive of the Istiqlal party, and *Al Muharnir* (circ. 17,000), which supports the socialist USFP party. There is also a fundamentalist paper, *Al Djemaa* (circ. 3000).

FESTIVALS: RAMADAN, HOLIDAYS AND *MOUSSEMS*

If the popular image of Islam is somewhat puritanical and ascetic, Morocco's festivals – the *moussems* and *amouggars* – do their best to contradict it. The country abounds in holidays and festivals of all kinds, both national and local, and coming across one can be the most enjoyable experience of travel in Morocco – with the chance to witness music and dance, as well as special regional foods and market *souks*.

Perhaps surprisingly, there are rewards, too, in coinciding with one of the major Islamic celebrations – above all *Ramadan*, when all Muslims (which in effect means all Moroccans) observe a total fast from sunrise to sunset for a month. This can pose some problems for travelling but the celebratory evenings are again good times to hear music and to share in hospitality.

RAMADAN

Ramadan, in a sense, parallels the Christian Lent. The ninth month of the Islamic calendar, it commemorates the time in which the Koran was revealed to Muhammad. In contrast to the Christian West, though, the Muslim world observes the fast extremely rigorously – indeed Moroccans are forbidden by law from "public disrespect" of the fast, and a few are jailed for this each year.

The Ramadan fast involves abstention from food, drink, smoking and sex during daylight hours throughout the month. With most local cafés and restaurants closing during the day, and people getting on edge towards the month's end, it is in some respects a disastrous time to travel. It is certainly no time to try and hire a guide in the mountains – nobody will undertake the work – and it is probably safer to travel by bus during the mornings only, as drivers will be fasting, too. (Airline pilots are forbidden from observing the fast). But there is a compensation in witnessing and becoming absorbed into the pattern of the fast. At sunset, signalled by the sounding of a siren and the lighting of lamps on the minarets, an amazing calm and sense of wellbeing fall on the streets, as everyone drinks a bowl of *harira* and, in the cities at least, gets down to a night of celebration and entertainment.

The **entertainment** takes different forms. If you can spend some time in Marrakesh during the month, you'll find the Djemaa el Fna square there at its most active, with troupes of musicians, dancers and acrobats coming into the city for the occasion. In Rabat and Fes, there seem to be continuous promenades, with cafés and stalls all open up to 3am. Urban cafés provide venues for live music and singing, too, and in the southern towns and Berber villages, you will often come across the ritualised *ahouaches* and *haidus* – circular, trance-like dances often involving whole communities.

If you are a **non-Muslim** outsider you are not expected to observe Ramadan, but it is good to be sensitive about not breaking the fast (particularly smoking) in public. In fact, the best way to experience Ramadan – and to benefit from its naturally purifying rhythms – is to enter into it. You may not be able to last without an occasional glass of water, and you'll probably have breakfast later than sunrise, but it is worth an attempt.

OTHER ISLAMIC HOLIDAYS

At the end of Ramadan comes the feast of **Aïd es Seghir**, a climax to the festivities in Marrakesh, though observed more privately in the villages. Equally important to the Muslim calendar is **Aïd el Kebir**, which celebrates the willingness of Abraham to obey God and to sacrifice Isaac. The Aïd el Kebir is followed, about three weeks later, by **Moharem**, the Muslim new year.

Both *aïds* are traditional family gatherings. At the Aïd el Kebir every household that can afford it will slaughter a sheep. You see them tethered everywhere, often on rooftops, for weeks prior to the event; after the feast, their skins are to be seen, being cured on the streets. Note that, on both *aïd* days, shops and restaurants close and buses don't run; on the following day, all transport is packed, as people return to the cities from their family homes.

The fourth main religious holiday is the **Mouloud**, the Prophet's birthday. This is widely observed, with a large number of *moussems* (see next page) timed to take place in the weeks around it.

PUBLIC HOLIDAYS

Nowadays each of the big **religious feasts** is usually marked by **two days off**. These are announced or ratified by the king, each time, on TV and radio the preceding day.

On these public holidays, and on the secular *Fêtes Nationales* (see box below), all **banks**, **post offices** and most **shops** are closed; **transport** is reduced, too, but never stops completely.

MOUSSEMS AND AMMOUGARS

Moussems – or *ammouggars* – are held in honour of saints or *marabouts*. They are basically local, and predominantly rural, affairs. Besides the Aïd es Seghir and Aïd el Kebir, however, they form the main religious and social celebrations of the year for most Moroccans, especially for the country Berbers.

Some of the smaller *moussems* amount to little more than a market day with religious overtones; others are essentially harvest festivals, celebrating a pause in agricultural labour after a crop has been successfully brought in. Quite a number, however, have developed into substantial occasions – similar in some respects to Spanish fiestas – and a few have acquired national significance. If you are lucky enough to

---

RAMADAN AND ISLAMIC HOLIDAYS

Islamic religious holidays are calculated on the **lunar calendar**, so their dates rotate throughout the seasons (as does Ramadan's). Exact dates in the lunar calendar are impossible to predict – they are set by the Islamic authorities in Fes – but approximate dates for the next three years are:

	1994	**1995**	**1996**
Ramadan	Feb 11	Jan 31	Jan 21
Aïd es Seghir	March 12	March 1	Feb 19
Aïd el Kebir	May 21	May 10	April 30
Moharem	July 16	July 5	June 24
Mouloud	August 29	August 18	August 7

FÊTES NATIONALES

Fêtes Nationales, all celebrated to some extent, are tied to Western calendar dates:

January 1	New Year's Day	August 14	Allegiance Day
March 3	Feast of the Throne	November 6	Green March
May 1	Labour Day	November 18	Independence Day
July 9	King's Birthday		

The **Feast of the Throne** is the largest secular holiday, a very colourful affair, celebrated throughout Morocco, over two to three days, with fireworks, parades, dancing and music.

be here for one of the major events, you'll get the chance to witness Moroccan popular culture at its richest, with horse-riding, music, singing and dancing, and of course eating and drinking.

AIMS AND FUNCTIONS

The ostensible aim of the *moussem* is religious: to obtain blessing, or *baraka*, from the saint and/or to thank God for the harvest. But the social and cultural dimensions are equally important. *Moussems* provide an opportunity for country people to escape the monotony of their hard working lives in several days of festivities. They may provide the year's single opportunity for friends or families from different villages to meet. Harvest and farming problems are discussed, as well as family matters – marriage in particular – as people get the chance to sing, dance, eat and pray together.

Music and singing are always major components of a *moussem* and locals will often bring tape recorders to provide sounds for the rest of the year. The different religious brotherhoods, some of whom may be present at larger *moussems*, each have their own distinct styles of music, dancing and dress.

Moussems also operate as **fairs**, or markets, with artisans offering their produce to a wider market than is available at the weekly *souk*. Buyers in turn can inform themselves about new products and regional price differences, as the *moussem* attracts people from a much wider area than the *souk*. There is a welcome injection of cash into the local economy, too, with traders and entertainers doing good business, and householders renting out rooms.

At the **spiritual level**, people seek to improve their standing with God through prayer, as well as the less orthodox channels of popular belief. Central to this is *baraka*, good fortune, which can be obtained by intercession of the saint. Financial contributions are made and these are used to buy a gift, or *hedia*, usually a large carpet, which is then taken in procession to the saint's tomb; it is deposited there for the local *shereefian* families, the descendants of the saint, to dispose of as they wish. Country people may seek to obtain *baraka* by attaching a garment or tissue to the saint's tomb and leaving it overnight to take home after the festival.

The procession which takes the gift to the tomb is the high point of the more **religious** *moussems*, such as that of **Moulay Idriss**, where an enormous carpet is carried above the heads of the religious **brotherhoods**. Each of these brotherhoods will be playing its own music, hypnotic in its rhythms; spectators and participants may go into trance, giving themselves up to the music. If you witness such events, it is best to keep a low profile (and certainly don't take photographs); the presence of foreigners or non-Muslims at these times is sometimes considered to impede trance.

Release through trance probably has a therapeutic aspect, and indeed some *moussems* are specifically concerned with **cures** of physical and psychiatric disorders. The saint's tomb is usually located near a freshwater spring, and the cure can simply be bathing in and drinking the water. Those suffering from physical ailments may also be treated at the *moussem* with herbal remedies, or by recitation of verses from the Koran. Koranic verses may also be written and placed in tiny receptacles fastened near the affected parts. The whole is reminiscent of the popular remedies found at European pilgrimage centres like Lourdes.

PRACTICALITIES

There are enormous numbers of *moussems*. An idea of quite how many can be gathered from the frequency with which, travelling about the countryside, you see *koubbas* – the square, white-domed buildings covering a saint's tomb. Each of these is a potential focal point of a *moussem*, and any one region or town may have twenty to thirty separate annual *moussems*. Establishing when they take place, however, can be difficult for outsiders; most local people find out by word of mouth at the weekly *souks*.

Many *moussems* are held around religious occasions such as the **Mouloud**, which change date each year according to the lunar calendar (see box opposite). Others, concerned with celebrating the **harvest**, have their date decided at a local level according to when the harvest is ready. *Moussems* of this type are obviously more difficult to plan a visit around than those which occur at points in the Islamic year. **August** and **September** are the most promising months overall, with dozens of *moussems* held after the grain harvest when there is a lull in the agricultural year before sowing starts prior to the first rains in October or November.

The **lists** below give an approximate idea (sometimes an exact one) of when the *moussems* are, but you will generally need to ask at a local level for information. Sometimes tourist offices may be able to help, though often not.

The **accommodation** situation will depend on whether the *moussem* is in the town or countryside. In the country, the simplest solution is to take a tent and camp – there is no real objection to anyone camping wherever they please during a *moussem*. In small towns there may be hotels – and locals will rent out rooms in their houses. **Food** is never a problem, with dozens of traders setting up stalls, though it is perhaps best to stick to the grills, as stalls may not have access to running water for cleaning.

MOULOUD *MOUSSEMS*

Meknes: Ben Aissa *Moussem*

The largest of all the *moussems*, this includes a spectacular **fantasia** (a charge of horses with riders firing guns at full gallop) if weather conditions permit, held near Place El Hedim. With this, the enormous conical tents, and crowds of country people in white djellabahs, beneath the city walls, it has the appearance of a medieval tournament. At least, that is, until you see the adjoining fairground, which is itself fun, with its illusionists and riders of death.

In the past, this *moussem* was the principal gathering of the **Aissoua** brotherhood, and the occasion for them to display their extraordinary powers of endurance under trance – cutting themselves with daggers, swallowing glass and the like. Their activities today are more subdued, though they still include going into trance, and of course playing music. Their focus is the *marabout* tomb of Ben Aissa, near the road in from Rabat.

Accommodation in Meknes is a problem at this time unless you arrive two or three days in advance. However, you could quite easily visit on a day trip from Fes.

Salé: Wax Candle *Moussem*

As the name suggests, this festival centres on a procession of wax candles – enormous lantern-like creations, carried from Bab El Rih to the Grand Mosque on the eve of the Mouloud. The candle bearers (a hereditary position) are followed by various brotherhoods, dancing and playing music.

The **procession** starts about 3pm and goes on for three or four hours; the best place to see it is at Bab Bou Hadja, where the candles are presented to local dignitaries.

OTHER POPULAR *MOUSSEMS*

May	**Moulay Bousselham**. *Moussem of Sidi Ahmed Ben Mansour.*
June	**Goulimine**. Traditionally a camel traders' fair, elements of which remain.
	Tan Tan. *Moussem of Sidi Mohammed Ma el Ainin*. Large-scale religious and commercial *moussem*. Saharan "Guedra" dance may be seen performed.
July	**Tetouan**. *Moussem of Moulay Abdessalem*. A very religious, traditional occasion with a big turnout of local tribesmen. Impressive location on a flat mountain top south of the town.
August	**Setti Fatma**. Large and popular *moussem* in the Ourika valley, southeast of Marrakesh.
	El Jadida. *Moussem of Moulay Abdallah*. Located about 9km west of the city at a village named after the saint. Features displays of horse-riding, or *fantasias*.
	Tiznit. *Moussem of Sidi Ahmed ou Moussa*. Primarily religious.
September	**Chaouen**. *Moussem of Sidi Allal Al Hadh*. Located in the hills out of the town.
	Moulay Idriss Zerhoun. *Moussem of Moulay Idriss*. The largest religious *moussem*, but visitable only for the day as a non-Muslim. Impressive display by brotherhoods, and a highly charged procession of gifts to the saint's tomb. Also a large *fantasia* above the town.
	Imilchil. *Marriage Moussem*. Set in the heart of the Atlas mountains, this is the most celebrated Berber *moussem* – traditionally the occasion of all marriages in the region, though today also a tourist event. In fact there now seem to be two *moussems*, with one laid on specifically for package tours from Marrakesh and Agadir; the real event is held in the last week in September or the first in October.
	Fes. *Moussem of Moulay Idriss II*. The largest of the *moussems* held inside a major city, and involving a long procession to the saint's tomb. The Medina is packed out, however, and you will need to line the route early in order to see anything.

HARVEST *MOUSSEMS*

February	Tafraoute (almonds)
March	Beni Mellal (cotton)
April	Immouzer des Ida Outanane (honey)
May	Berkane (clementines)
	El Kelâa des Mgouna (roses)
June	Sefrou (cherries)
July	Al Hoceima (sea produce)
August	Immouzer du Kandar (apples/pears)
November	Erfoud (dates)
	Rhafsaï (olives)

CULTURAL FESTIVALS

The big cultural highlights are the **Marrakesh Festival** (usually September – but subject to variation), which brings together musicians and dancers from throughout the country, and the **Asilah International Festival** (last two weeks of July). The latter features a mixed bag of the arts, with exhibitions of Moroccan and Egyptian artworks and whole sequence of concerts from performances by Egyptian and Lebanese singing stars to American college enembles. For more details, see, respectively, p.326 and p.82.

SPORTS AND ACTIVITIES

Morocco is doing much to keep up with the increasing interest in activity and sporting holidays. In addition to its magnificent trekking opportunities (for information on which see p.29), the country offers impressive golf and tennis facilities, a couple of ski resorts (plus some adventurous off-piste skiing) and excellent fishing. The national sporting obsession, however, is football; enthusiasts can join in any number of beach kick-about games, or watch local league and cup matches.

FOOTBALL

Football is important in Morocco. When the national team gained a place in the 1986 World Cup quarter finals (their finest hour to date), the squad were rewarded with villas, cars and small businesses. On their return, they were taken to a massive victory celebration in Casablanca, parading through the streets on a float with a giant football – out of whose hatch stepped King Hassan to shake hands with each player.

Although Morocco failed to qualify for the 1990 championships and its bid to host the 1994 championship was narrowly (many would say unjustly) defeated by the USA, enthusiasm remains high, with teams competing at the top level in the various **African Cup** club and country championships.

Domestically, there is an annual **league** and a knock-out competition, the **Throne Cup**. For a long time there was just one full-time professional team, **FAR** (the army), but recent seasons have seen the introduction of sponsorship and other semi-professional sides, the best of which are **WIDAD** and **RAJA**, the two big Casablanca teams, **MAS** from Fes and **KAC** from Kenitra.

The league games have a tendency towards defensive play – the points system gives two points for a draw and three for a win – but there is always the potential for displays of individual dynamism and inspiration, a parallel, so Moroccans would have it, with the Brazilian style of play. Brazilian comparisons could certainly be made with the social background of Moroccan football, players developing their game in unstructured kick-arounds on the beach, street or patches of wasteland. The lack of a team strip in these games (and hence easy recognition of team mates) discourages long balls and intricate passing, and encourages individual possession and quick one-twos. The same conditions produced Pelé and Maradona.

SKIING

Morocco isn't immediately thought of as a skiing destination, but the High Atlas mountains are reliably snow-covered from February to early April, and occasionally the Middle Atlas, too, has sufficient snows for the sport.

In the High Atlas, the main resort is **Oukaïmeden**, two hours' drive from Marrakesh. It is quiet, well appointed and inexpensive, with pleasant chalet hotels, seven piste runs, a ski lift, local instructors, and equipment for hire. In the Middle Atlas, **Mischliffen** – a volcanic crater – has rather more limited facilities, with three lifts, a shorter and unreliable season, and very old-fashioned equipment rental. A third prospective ski centre is the high-altitude resort of **Bou Iblane** in the Anti-Atlas, which offers little more than an approach road (not always covered by the snowplough) and a single ski lift.

Off-piste skiing is increasingly popular in the High Atlas, in particular around the famed Toubkal massif (see p.342), where groups often combine skiing with mountaineering to the summits. At present, in the absence of organised facilities, this is an area of the sport best limited to those with considerable experience and expertise.

RIDING

The established base for **riding holidays** is *La Roseraie* hotel at **Ouirgane** on the Tizi n'Test road. The hotel runs trekking tours into the **High Atlas**, offering anything from one-day excursions to extended trips staying at villages en route. In addition, it has tennis courts, a swimming pool and is developing a health centre – all at quite reasonable cost.

Stays or packages at *La Roseraie* can be arranged through most of the Moroccan specialist agents detailed on pp.6–7.

FISHING

French visitors to Morocco have long appreciated the possibilities for fishing. The country offers an immense Atlantic (and small Mediterranean) **coastline**, with opportunities to arrange boat trips at Safi, Essaouira, Moulay Bousselham (near Asilah) and elsewhere.

Inland, the **Middle Atlas** shelters beautiful **lakes** and **rivers**, many of them well stocked with trout. Good bases could include **Azrou** (near the Aghmas lakes), **Ifrane** (near Zerrrouka), **Khenifra** (the Oum er Rbia River) and **Ouirgane** (the Nfis River). Pike are also to be found in some Middle Atlas lakes (such as Aguelmame Azizgza, near Khenifra), and a few of the huge artificial **barrages**, like **Bin el Ouidaine** (near Beni Mellal), are said to contain huge bass.

For the really determined and adventurous, the most exciting Moroccan fishing is reputed to be along the coast of the **Western Sahara**, where catches weigh in regularly at 20–30 kilos. The regional capital of Laayoune is the only feasible base at present, unless you're totally self-reliant.

For all fishing in the country, you need to take your own **equipment**. For coarse or fly fishing you need a **permit** from the *Administration des Eaux et Fôrets* (11 Rue Revoil, Rabat). For trout fishing, you are limited to the hours between 6am and noon; the season starts on March 31.

WATER SPORTS AND SWIMMING

Agadir has **sailing**, **yachting**, **windsurfing** and **diving** on offer, with **Tarhazoute**, just north of the resort, developing a growing reputation among **windsurfers**. The biggest windsurfing destination, however, is **Essaouira**, more or less west of Marrakesh, which draws European devotees of the sport all year round. Anywhere on the Atlantic coast, be aware of strong undertows.

Inland, most towns of any size have a municipal **swimming pool** – they're always very cheap and addresses are given in the guide. In the south, you'll be dependent on campsite pools or on those at the luxury hotels (who often allow outsiders to swim, either for a charge or if you buy drinks or a meal).

GOLF AND TENNIS

The British opened a golf course in Tangier as far back as 1917 – a rather more refined alternative to their then-favoured sport of pig-sticking in the hills. Today the country has an international-level course at **Rabat** (*Royal Dar-es-Salam*), further 18-hole courses at **Mohammedia** (*Royal Golf*), **Marrakesh** (*Royal Golf*) and **Tangier** (*Royal Country Club*), and nine-hole courses at **Casablanca** (*Royal Anfa*), **Agadir** (*Royal Golf*), **Cabo Negro** (*Royal Golf*) and **Meknes** (*Royal Golf* – actually within the confines of the Royal Palace gardens).

For a **golf-centred holiday** package, or details (and photos) of the courses, consult the golf brochure issued by *Best of Morocco* (100 Week St, Maidstone, Kent ME14 1RG; ☎0622/692278). *CLM* (4a William St, London SW1; ☎071/235 2110) also arrange golfing holidays.

Tennis courts are now to be found at virtually all of Morocco's 4* and 5* hotels, especially those in Agadir (which now has a total of over 120 courts) and Marrakesh. To check on the presence or otherwise of courts consult the ONMT's *Guide des Hôtels*.

Equipment can often be loaned from hotels but it is rarely of a quality to satisfy serious enthusiasts: you'd be advised to take rackets and balls.

SOUKS AND MOROCCAN CRAFTS

Souks – markets – are a major feature of Moroccan life, and among the country's greatest attractions. They are to be found everywhere: each town has its special *souk* quarter, large cities like Fes and Marrakesh have labyrinths of individual *souks* (each filling a street or square and devoted to one particular craft), and in the countryside there is a moveable network, shifting between the various villages of a region.

SOUK DAYS

Some of the villages, or areas between villages, are in fact named after **their market days**, so it's easy to see when they're held.

The *souk* days are:

Souk el Had – Sunday (literally, "first market")

Souk el Tnine – Monday market

Souk el Tleta – Tuesday market

Souk el Arba – Wednesday market

Souk el Khamees – Thursday market

Souk es Sebt – Saturday market

There are no village markets on **Friday** (*el Djemaa* – the "assembly", when the main prayers are held in the mosques), and even in the cities, *souks* are largely closed on Friday mornings and very subdued for the rest of the day.

In general, village *souks* begin on the afternoon preceding the *souk* day, as people arrive from all over the region.

CRAFT TRADITIONS

Moroccan **craft**, or *artesanie*, traditions are still highly active, and even goods mass-produced for tourists are surprisingly untacky. To find pieces of real quality, however, is not that easy – some crafts have become dulled by centuries of repetition and others have been corrupted by modern techniques and chemical dyes.

In general, if you're planning on buying anything, it's always worth getting as close to the source of the goods as possible, and to steer clear of the main tourist centres. **Fes** might have the richest traditions, but you can often find better work at much cheaper prices elsewhere; **Tangier** and **Agadir**, neither of which has imaginative workshops of their own, are certainly best avoided. As stressed throughout the guide, the best way to get an idea of standards and quality is to visit the various **traditional crafts museums** spread round the country: there are good ones in Fes, Meknes, Tangier, Rabat and Marrakesh.

CARPETS, RUGS AND BLANKETS

Moroccan **carpets** are not cheap – you can pay £1000 and more for the finer Arab designs in Fes or Rabat. However, it is possible to find **rugs** or **kellims** (which are woven rather than knotted) at more reasonable prices, with a range of strong, well-designed weaves from £30–50 ($50–80).

Most of these kellims will be of Berber origin and the most interesting ones usually come from the High and Middle Atlas; if you're looking seriously, try to get to the town *souk* in **Midelt** or the weekly markets in **Azrou** and other villages around **Marrakesh**. The chain of *Maison Berbère* shops in Ouarzazate, Tinerhir and Rissani are good hunting grounds, too.

On a simpler and cheaper level, the **Berber blankets** (*foutahs*, or *couvertures*) are imaginative, and often very striking with bands of reds and blacks; for these, **Tetouan** and **Chaouen**, on the edge of the Rif, are promising.

JEWELLERY

Silver jewellery went into decline with the loss to Israel of Morocco's Jewish population, the country's traditional workers in precious metals and crafts in general; in the **south**, however, you can pick up some fabulous Berber necklaces and bracelets, always very chunky, with bold combi-

nations of semiprecious (and sometimes plastic) stones and beads. There's a particularly good jewellery *souk* in Essaouira.

SEMI-PRECIOUS STONES

You'll see a variety of semi-precious stones on sale throughout Morocco, and in the High Atlas they are often aggressively hawked on the roadsides. If you're lucky enough to be offered genuine **amethyst** or **quartz**, prices can be bargained to very tempting levels. Be warned, however, that all that glitters is not necessarily the real thing. Too often, if you wet the stone and rub, you'll find telltale traces of dye on your fingers . . .

WOOD AND POTTERY

Marquetry is one of the few crafts where you'll see genuinely old pieces – inlaid tables and shelves – though the most easily exportable objects are boxes and chess sets, beautifully inlaid in *thuya* and cedar woods in **Essaouira**.

Pottery on the whole is disappointing, but tourist produce though it is, the blue-and-white designs of **Fes** and the multicoloured pots of **Chaouen** are highly attractive. The essentially domestic pottery of **Safi** – Morocco's major pottery centre – is worth a look, too, with its crude but effective plates and garden pots. Best of all, perhaps, are the works produced by the Oulja pottery at **Salé**, near Rabat.

CLOTHING AND LEATHER

Moroccan clothes are easy to purchase, and though Westerners – men at least – who try to imitate Moroccan styles by wearing the cotton or wool *djellaba* (a kind of cloak) tend to look a little silly, there are some highly desirable items. Some of the cloth is exquisite in itself, and walking down the dyers' *souks* is an inspiration.

Leather is also excellent, and here you can buy and wear goods with perhaps greater confidence. The classic Moroccan shoes are **babouches**, open at the heel, immensely comfortable, and produced in yellow (the usual colour), white, red (for women) and occasionally grey or (for the truly fetishistic) black; a good pair – and quality varies enormously – can cost £6–15 ($10–25).

BARGAINING

Whatever you buy, and wherever you buy it, you will want (and be expected) to **bargain**. There are no hard and fast rules – it is really a question of paying what something is worth to you – but there are a few general points to keep in mind.

First, **bargaining is entirely natural** in Morocco. If you ask the price in a market, the answer, as likely as not, will come in one breath – "Twenty; how much will you pay?"

Second, don't pay any attention to **initial prices**. These are simply a device to test the limits of a particular deal or situation. Don't think, for example, in terms of paying one-third of the asking price (as some guides suggest) – it might well turn out to be a tenth or even a twentieth. Equally, though, it might not – some sellers actually start near the price they have in mind and will bustle you out of their shop for offering an "insulting" price. Don't feel intimidated by either tactic; if you return the following day for some coveted item, you will most likely be welcomed as an old friend. Take your chances!

Third, **don't ever let a figure pass your lips** that you aren't prepared to pay – nor start bargaining for something you have absolutely no intention of buying – there's no better way to create bad feelings.

Fourth, take your time. If the deal is a serious one (for a rug, say), you'll probably want to sit down over tea with the vendor, and for two cups you'll talk about anything but the rug and the price. If negotiations do not seem to be going well, it often helps to have a friend on hand who seems a little less interested in the purchase than you – as they may well become, given the protracted experiences involved . . .

The final and most golden rule of them all is never to go shopping with a **guide** or a hustler, even "just to look" – the pressures will be either too great or it'll be too boring, depending on how long you've been in the country and how you've learned to cope with these people.

In the villages – and with beach traders – you might find **bartering goods** to be more satisfactory than bargaining over a price. This way you know the value of what you're offering better than your partner (though he'll have a pretty good idea, too), and in a sense you're giving a fairer exchange. Items particularly sought after are training shoes (even if they're well worn), printed T-shirts (rock designs – especially Prince – are favourites), football shirts (British or American) and other sports clothes, basic medicines (in country areas), and Western department-store clothes (*Marks & Spencer* has particularly good currency).

An approximate idea of what you should be paying for handicrafts can be gained from checking the **fixed prices** in the state- or co-operative-run *Ensembles Artisanals*. Even here, though, there is sometimes room for bargaining as prices are slightly higher than elsewhere.

MOSQUES AND MONUMENTS

Without a doubt, the major disappointment of travelling in Morocco is not being allowed into its mosques: all non-Muslims are excluded and the rule is strictly observed. However, there is much architecture to be admired in the form of *medersas* – medieval "colleges" attached as teaching institutions to urban mosques – and in the numerous, elaborately decorated gateways (*babs*) to be found in any well-preserved city walls. Cities also reveal some beautiful *fondouks* – caravanersais – and the occasional palace. There is a scattering of remains, too, from Morocco's ancient civilisations under Roman and even Phoenician rule. Most public monuments, including *medersas*, museums and archaeological sites, levy a standard 10dh admission fee and operate standard civil service hours (9am–noon & 3–6pm).

MOSQUES AND KOUBBAS

The only "mosques" that non-Muslims *are* allowed to visit are the ruined Almohad structure of **Tin Mal** in the High Atlas, the courtyard of the sanctuary-mosque of Moulay Ismail in **Meknes**, the sanctuary of Mohammed V in **Rabat**, and the Bou Inania *medersa* in **Fes**. Elsewhere, you'll have to be content with an occasional glimpse through open doors, and even in this you should be sensitive: people don't seem to mind tourists peering into the Kairaouine Mosque in Fes (the country's most important religious building), but in the country you should never approach a shrine too closely.

This rule applies equally to the numerous domed and whitewashed *koubbas* – the tombs of *marabouts*, or local saints – and the "monastic" *zaouias* of the various Sufi brotherhoods. It is a good idea, too, to avoid walking through **graveyards**, as these also are regarded as sacred places.

OTHER ISLAMIC MONUMENTS

As some compensation, many of the most beautiful and architecturally interesting of Morocco's monuments are open to public view – the great imperial gateways, or *babs*, of the main cities, for example, and, of course, the **minarets** (towers from which the call to prayer is made) attached to the mosques.

Of buildings that can be visited, highlights must include the **Berber Kasbahs** (fortified castle residences) of the south; a series of city **palaces** and **mansions** – many of them converted into hotels, restaurants or craft shops – in Fes and Marrakesh; and the intricate *medersas* of Fes, Meknes, Salé, and Marrakesh.

The *medersas*, many of them dating from the thirteenth and fourteenth centuries, are perhaps the most startling – and certainly the most "monumental" – of all Moroccan buildings, each displaying elaborate decoration and designs in stucco (gypsum or plaster), cedar and tile mosaics (known in Morocco as *zellij*). Originally, these buildings served as religious universities or student residences for a neighbouring mosque school, but by the turn of the century they had largely fallen into decay and disuse. Today, they have almost all become secularised. Their role is discussed in the chapter on **Fes**, which is where you'll find the richest and most varied examples.

ANCIENT REMAINS

Unlike Tunisia and Algeria, Morocco never saw extensive **Roman** colonisation – and indeed, the south of the country remained unconquered by any outside force until the French invasion of the 1920s. Ancient sites are, therefore, limited. The most interesting, and really the only one worth going out of your way to visit, is **Volubilis**, close to Meknes. For enthusiasts, **Lixus** (near Larache) is worthwhile, and there are good bronze collections and statuary at **Rabat**.

A number of **prehistoric sites**, with well-preserved **rock paintings** (*gravures rupestres* in French), survive in the south of the country, though most are extremely difficult to reach – and find. The most rewarding and easily accessible ones are around **Oukaïmeden**, near Marrakesh. More significant, but remote, sites are scattered among the hills near the desert town of **Foum El Hassan**.

FROM A WOMAN'S PERSPECTIVE

● **Margaret Hubbard spent one month travelling on her own around Morocco:**

I knew that there were likely to be difficulties in travelling as a woman alone around Morocco. I'd been warned by numerous sources (this book's previous edition included) about hustling and harassment and I was already well aware of the constraints imposed on women travellers within Islamic cultures. But above and beyond this, I knew I'd be fascinated by the country. I had picked up a smattering of Arabic and the impetus to study Islamic religion and culture during trips to Damascus and Amman (both times with a male companion). Also, I already had enough experience of travelling alone to know that I could live with myself should I meet up with no one else.

So, a little apprehensive, but very much more determined and excited, I arrived in Tangier, took the first train out to Casablanca, and found a room for the night. It was not until I emerged the next morning into the bright daylight of Casablanca that I experienced my first reaction to Morocco.

BEGINNINGS

Nothing could have prepared me for it. Almost instantly, I was assailed by a barrage of: "*Voulez-vous coucher avec moi?*" "*Avez-vous jamais fait l'amour au Maroc?*" "*Venez avec moi, madame*" "*Viens, m'selle*". Whatever I had to say was ignored at will, and wherever I went, I felt that I was being constantly scrutinised by men.

Fighting off the panic, I headed for the bus station, where, after a lot of frantic rushing to and fro (I couldn't decipher the Arabic signs), I climbed onto a bus for Marrakesh.

Marrakesh proved to me that I was right in coming to Morocco. It wasn't that the harassment was any less – in fact, it was almost as constant as in Tangier. But wandering through the Djemaa el Fna (the main square and centre of all life in Marrakesh), among the snake charmers, kebab vendors, blanket weavers, water sellers, monkey trainers, and merchants of everything from false teeth to handwoven rugs, I became ensnared to such an extent that my response to the men who approached me was no longer one of fear but rather a feeling of irrelevance.

There was too much to be learned to shut out contact with people, and I heard myself utter, as if it were the most normal reply in the world: "*Non, monsieur, je ne veux pas coucher avec vous, mais pouvez-vous me dire pourquoi ils vendent* false teeth/*combien d'années il faut pour faire des tapis à main/pourquoi les singes* (monkeys). . . ?*" That first night, I returned to my room at 2am more alive than I had felt for months.

STRATEGIES

I'd also stumbled upon a possible strategy for pre-empting, perhaps even preventing, harassment. Moroccan hustlers know a lot about tourists and have reason to expect one of two reactions from them: fear or a sort of resigned acceptance.

What they don't expect is for you to move quickly through the opening gambits and launch into a serious conversation about Moroccan life. Using a mixture of French and Arabic, I developed the persona of a "serious woman" and, from Marrakesh to Figuig, discussed the politics of the Maghreb, maternity rights, housing costs, or the Koran with almost anyone who wanted my attention.

It became exhausting, but any attempt at more desultory chat was treated as an open invitation and seemed to make any harassment more determined. That isn't to say that it's impossible to have a more relaxed relationship with Moroccan men — I made good friends on two occasions with Arab men and I'm still corresponding with one of them. But I think this was made easier by my defining the terms of our friendship fairly early on in the conversation. (As a general rule, whenever I arranged to meet up with someone I didn't know very well, I chose well-lit public places. I was also careful about my clothes — I found it really did help to look as inconspicuous as possible, and I almost always wore loose-fitting blouses, longish skirts, and, occasionally, also a head scarf.)

CONTACT: THE HAMMAM

After exploring Marrakesh for five days, I took a bus out over the Atlas mountain range to Zagora. The journey took twelve hours and the bus was hot and cramped, but wedged between a group of Moroccan mothers, jostling their babies on my lap and sharing whatever food and drink was going around, I felt reassured, more a participant than an outsider.

This was also one of the few occasions that I'd had any sort of meaningful contact with Moroccan women. For the most part, women tend to have a low profile in public, moving in very separate spheres from the tourists. There are some women's cafés but they're well hidden and not for foreigners.

For me, the most likely meeting place was the hammam, or steam bath, which I habitually sought out in each stopping place. Apart from the undoubted pleasures of plentiful hot water, these became a place of refuge for me. It was a relief to be surrounded by women, and to be an object of curiosity without any element of threat. Any ideas about Western status I might have had were lost in the face of explaining in French, Arabic, and sign language to an old Moroccan woman with 24 grandchildren the sexual practices and methods of contraception used in the West. "Is it true that women are opened up by machine?" is a question that worries me still.

FESTIVITIES

I arrived in Zagora on the last night of the festival of the king's birthday. It was pure chance. The town was packed with Moroccans who had travelled in from nearby oases. Oddly, though, I met just one other tourist — a German man. We were both swept along, as insignificant as any other single people in the crowd, dancing and singing in time to the echoing African sounds.

At the main event of the night, the crowd was divided by a long rope with women on one side and men on the other, with only the German and me standing side by side. I felt overwhelmed with a feeling of excitement and wellbeing, simply because I was there.

INTO THE DESERT

From Zagora I headed for Figuig and the desert, stopping overnight en route in Tinerhir. It's possible that I chose a bad hotel for that stop, but it was about the worst night that I had spent in the entire trip. The men in and around the hotel jeered, even spat, at me when I politely refused to accompany them, and throughout the night I had men banging on the door shutters of my room. For twelve hours I stood guard, tense,

afraid, and stifled by the locked-in heat of that dismal hotel room. I escaped on the first bus out*.

Further south I met up with a Danish man in a Land Rover and travelled on with him to spend four days in the desert. It was a simple business arrangement – he wanted someone to look after the van while he slept and I wanted someone to look out for me while I slept. I can find no terms that will sufficiently describe the effect the desert had on me. It was awesome and inspiring and it silenced me. I also found that the more recent preoccupations that I had about my life, work, and relationships had entirely slipped from my mind. Yet strangely, I could recall with absolute clarity images from over ten years ago. I remain convinced that the desert, with its simplicity, its expansiveness, and its power changed me in some way.

At Figuig I parted company with the Dane and made it in various stages to Fes. I tended to find myself becoming dissatisfied after travelling for a while with a male companion. This was not because I didn't enjoy the company, which was, more often than not, a luxury for me, but I used to feel cheated that I was no longer at the forefront and that any contact with Moroccans would have to be made through him. This is often the case in Islamic countries, where any approaches or offers of hospitality are proffered man to man, with the woman treated more or less as an appendage. I was prepared to go on alone however uncomfortable it might become, so long as I was treated as a person in my own right.

[*Editor's note: Individual experiences of Moroccan towns obviously differ enormously. A correspondent recently wrote in to say that, although she agreed with the tenor of this piece, she had spent a lot of time in Tinerhir and in her experience it was the friendliest town she has visited in the country .]

JOGGING

In Fes I discovered yet another, perhaps even more effective, strategy for changing my status with Moroccan men. I am a runner and compete regularly in marathons, and I'm used to keeping up with my training in almost any conditions. Up until Fes, I'd held back, uncertain as to the effect of dashing out of a hotel in only a tracksuit bottom and a T-shirt. My usual outfit, the long skirt and blouse, was hardly suitable for the exercise I had in mind. After seriously considering confining myself to laps around the hotel bedroom, I recovered my sanity and my sense of adventure, changed my clothes, and set off.

The harassment and the hustling all melted away. I found that the Moroccans have such a high regard for sport that the very men who had hassled me in the morning were looking on with a respectful interest, offering encouragement and advice as I hurtled by in the cool of the evening. From then on, I became known as "the runner" and was left more or less in peace for the rest of my stay.

After this, I made it a rule to train in all the villages and towns I stayed in on my way back to Tangier. Now when I run, I conjure up the image of pacing out of Chaouen towards the shrine on the hillside, keeping time with the chants of the *muezzin* at dawn.

RETURN TO TANGIER

Returning to Tangier, I felt as far removed as it is possible to feel from the apprehensive new arrival of the month before. I felt less intimidated and more stoic about my status as an inferior and an outsider, and I had long since come to accept that I was a source of income to many people whose options for earning money are severely limited.

Walking out of the bus station, I was surrounded by a group of hustlers. I listened in

---

OTHER READERS' ADVICE

● Don't be afraid to **express outrage**. Public harassment of women is never something that would be accepted within the community. If you are harassed in the street, or a public place, a loud expression of outrage, or an attempt to involve passers by, should immediately result in public anger against the man and a very uncomfortable situation for him. This works in Morocco in a way that it wouldn't, for example, in Spain or Italy, where macho male attitudes mean that public harassment is a fact of life for Spanish or Italian women.

● **Dress** is all-important. Modest skirts and tops covering your arms are recommended but the single greatest improvement comes through wearing a **headscarf**. Moroccan women go out in public with a headscarf and doing likewise greatly influences the way people behave towards you. A wide selection of headscarves is available practically everywhere in Morocco.

silence and then said, in the fairly decent Arabic that I had picked up along the journey from Figuig to Fes, that I had been in the Sahara and hadn't got lost so I didn't think I needed a guide in Tangier, and furthermore, that I had talked with some Touaregs in Zagora who told me that it is a lie that Moroccans buy their women with camels; would they please excuse me, I had arrangements?

I spent the next few days wandering freely around the town, totally immersed in plotting how to return.

DIRECTORY

ADDRESSES Arabic names – *Derb, Zankat*, etc – are gradually replacing French ones. The main street or square of any town, though, is still invariably *Avenue* or *Place* Hassan II (the present king) or Mohammed V (his father); see pp.554–6. Street signs are usually in French and Arabic lettering.

ANIMAL WELFARE Animals – and especially pack animals – have a tough life in Morocco. The **Society for the Protection of Animals in North Africa** (SPANA) works throughout North Africa to improve conditions, replacing painful, old-style bits on donkeys and horses, employing vets, and runing animal clinics and refuges. They have centres in Rabat, Marrakesh, Meknes, Khemisset, Chemaia and Tangier – all of which can be contacted or visited if you are interested or are concerned about animals you've come across. The best initial contact address in Morocco is SPANA's administrative office in Temara (☎07/74.04.93). The Society also has a British office at 15 Buckingham Gate, London SW1E 6LB (☎071/828 0997).

CONSULATES AND EMBASSIES are in Rabat, Tangier and Casablanca; see p.22 for lists.

CONTRACEPTIVES Somewhat poor quality and unreliable condoms can be bought in most chemists, and so can the pill (officially by prescription, but this isn't essential). If you're suffering from diarrhoea, the pill (or any other drug) may not be in your system long enough to be absorbed, and consequently may become ineffective.

CULTURAL SOCIETIES OVERSEAS Anyone interested in Morocco is recommended to join the **Society for Moroccan Studies** (c/o School of African and Oriental Studies, Thornhaugh St, Russell Square, London WC1H 0XG); the society publishes an interesting bi-annual journal and hosts a series of lectures. Also of interest, for British residents, is the older-established **British Moroccan Society** (c/o Embassy of Morocco, 49 Queens Gate Gdns, London SW7 5NE), which organises various Moroccan-orientated events and discussions, usually in London.

CUSTOMS ALLOWANCES You're allowed to bring a litre of spirits into Morocco, which is well worth doing. Up to 200 cigarettes are also permitted, which saves money on American brands.

ELECTRICAL VOLTAGE Most of the country runs on 220v but some towns still have 110v sockets and it's not uncommon to have both in the same building. Note that electric shavers work okay but heat-producing items like hairdryers need converters to function properly.

GAY ATTITUDES Male homosexuality is common in Morocco, although attitudes towards it are a little schizophrenic. No Moroccan will declare himself gay – which has connotations of femininity and weakness; the idea of being a passive partner is virtually taboo, while a dominant partner may well not consider himself to be indulging in a homosexual act. Private realities, however, are rather different from public show. (On which subject, note that Moroccan men often walk hand-in-hand in public – a habit which has nothing to do with homosexuality and is simply a sign of friendship).

If you are visiting Morocco specifically as a "gay destination" be warned that the legendary Joe Orton days of Tangier – and Marrakesh – as gay resorts are over, the Moroccan government having instituted a major crackdown (and wholesale closure of brothels) following independence. Gay sex is, of course, still available, and men travelling alone or together will certainly be propositioned. But attitudes are tending increasingly towards hustling and exploitation on all sides. It is, in addition, officially illegal under Moroccan law. Article 489 of the Moroccan penal code prohibits any "shameless or unnatural act" with a person of the same sex and allows for imprisonment of six months to three years, plus a fine. There are also various provisions in the penal code for more serious offences, with correspondingly higher penalties in cases involving, for example, corruption of minors.

As emphasised under "Health", AIDS is a real threat in Morocco, despite a lack of reported cases. There is some awareness of AIDS among Moroccans but most are steadfast in seeing it as a "disease for foreigners" and the concept, let alone practice, of "safe sex" is yet to emerge.

There is no public perception of lesbianism.

HOSPITAL EMERGENCIES ☎15.

LAUNDRIES in the larger towns will take in clothes and wash them overnight, but you'll usually find it easier to ask at hotels – even basic places will be able to offer the service.

OPENING HOURS follow a farily consistent pattern: **banks** (Mon–Fri 8.15–11.30am & 2.15–4.30pm); **shops** (Mon–Sat 8.30am–noon & 2–6.30pm); **offices** (Mon–Thurs 8.30am–noon & 2.30–6.30pm; Fri 8.30–11.30am & 3–6.30pm).

RELATIONSHIPS Following clampdowns on "unofficial guides", there are laws in effect that can make relationships with Moroccans problematic. In theory, any Moroccan – without a guide's permit – seen "accompanying" a tourist can be arrested and imprisoned. In practice this is rarely enforced but friendships, especially with young Moroccans in tourist cities like Tangier, Agadir or Marrakesh, should be discreet. On the whole, once invited to a home, and having met a family, you are unlikely to encounter problems, and your hosts will deal effectively with any enquiries from curious local policemen.

TAMPONS can be bought at general stores, not chemists, in most Moroccan cities. Don't expect to find them in country or mountain areas.

TIME Morocco keeps Greenwich Mean Time the whole year. It is therefore one hour (two hours in summertime) behind Spain – something to keep in mind when catching ferries.

TIPPING You're expected to tip – among others – waiters in cafés (1dh per person) and restaurants (5dh or so); museum and monument curators (3dh); *gardiens de voitures* (4–5dh; see "Driving"); petrol pump attendants (2–3dh); and bus porters (3–4dh; see "Buses").

WORK Your only chance of paid work in Morocco is **teaching English**. For information, try the following schools: *The British Council* (6 Av. Moulay Youssef, Rabat; or 10 Spring Gdns, London SW1; ☎071/930 8466), *The American Language Centre* (1 Place de la Fraternité, Casablanca; also in Rabat, Kenitra, Tangier, Tetouan, Meknes, Fes and Marrakesh) or *The American School* (Rue Al Amir Abdelkader, Agdal, Rabat; also in Casablanca and Tangier). Reasonable spoken French is normally required by all of these.

WORK CAMPS If you are interested in taking part in a work camp, a number of possibilities exist. The *United Nations Association* (UK head office: 3 Whitehall Court, London SW1; ☎071/930 2931) recruit international teams to work on manual and community projects for two or three weeks in the summer; applicants pay their own travel costs but are provided with accommodation. Alternatively, there are three Moroccan organisations: *Les Amis des Chantiers Inter-nationaux de Meknes* (PO Box 8, Meknes), whose projects generally involve agricultural or construction work around Meknes – three weeks in July and August, accommodation and food provided; *Chanteuse Jeunesse Maroc* (PO Box 566, Rabat), who offer some inspired work camps – recently, creating green spaces at Asilah, and constructing lanes and alleyways in shanty towns near Mohammedia; or *Pensés et Chantiers* (26 Rue de Pakistan, BP 1423, Rabat), involving community schemes – painting, restoration and gardening. Most of the work camps are open to all-comers over 17 years of age; travel costs have to be paid by the participant, but you generally receive free accommodation (take a sleeping bag) and meals.

USEFUL THINGS TO BRING

● **Alarm clock**. Vital for early-morning buses.

● **Bags** should be lockable. Left-luggage depots at train stations will only accept locked bags.

● **Bartering gifts**. If you want to bargain for hand-icrafts, bring things to barter with (see "Bargaining"); hiking in the Atlas, spare gear is always appreciated by local guides.

● **Camping gear**. If you are planning on a lot of camping, a sleeping bag and foam pad are invalua-ble, but it is worth considering whether you will make enough use of campsites to justify the weight, as hotels are remarkably cheap. A good compromise is to pack a **sheet sleeping bag** – reassuring in those hotels that don't relentlessly pursue cleanliness awards. **Camping gas** is widely available in larger towns (but not *Epigas*).

● **Clothes**. Keep both practicality and sensitivity in mind. As emphasised in the piece "From a Woman's Perspective", Morocco is a deeply conservative nation: the more modest your dress the less hassle you will attract.

On the practicalities front, keep in mind that the mountain areas and Sahara alike can get distinctly **chilly** at night, even in spring and autumn. A warm sweater is invaluable. So, too, in winter and spring, is some kind of waterproof clothing and a solid pair of shoes: storms (and resulting flash floods) are commonplace and wandering round a muddy Medina in sodden sandals is a miserable experi-ence. For advice on **hiking gear**, see pp.346–7.

● **Film**. Kodak and Fuji film is available in most towns and major resorts, but it's relatively expen-sive and may well be pretty old stock. It's best to bring adequate supplies. For photography in the Medinas – all dark alleyways and hidden corners – fast film (400–800 ASA) is useful. If you're look-ing for good landscape photographs, especially in the south, slow film (and/or early rising) is a must. See notes on behaviour.

● **Medicines**. Salt tablets, some insect repellent, water purifying tablets, anti-diarrhoea tablets, aspirin and plasters are all useful. You may also find yourself dispensing them to locals, especially in mountain areas, where they are in very short supply.

● **Plug**. If you like your water to fill a basin, it is worth packing an omnisize plug: few hotels (even relatively upmarket ones) supply such equipment.

● **Toiletries** and (rough!) **toilet paper** are easy enough to obtain in all but the most remote parts of the country.

PART TWO

THE

GUIDE

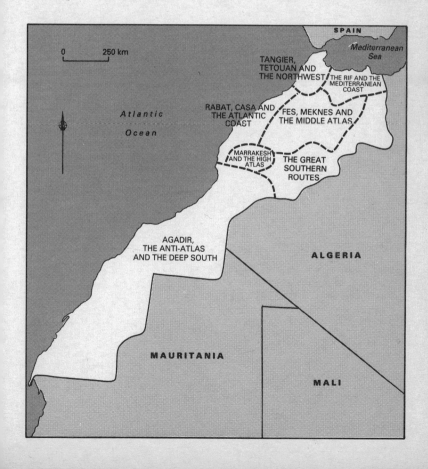

CHAPTER ONE

TANGIER, TETOUAN AND THE NORTHWEST

he northwest can be an intense introduction to Morocco. Its two chief cities, Tangier and Tetouan, are by reputation difficult, with guides and hustlers preying on first-time travellers. However, once clear of the points of arrival, and having set your bags down in a hotel, it doesn't take long to get the measure of them – and to enjoy the experience. **Tangier**, hybridised and slightly seedy from its long European contact, has a culture distinct from any other Moroccan city, and a setting and skyline the equal of any Mediterranean resort. Difficult it may be, but it is compelling, too, in its age-old role as meeting point of Europe and Africa. **Tetouan**, in the shadow of the wild Rif mountains, feels more Moroccan – its Medina a glorious labyrinth, dotted with squares, *souks* and buildings from its seventeenth-century founding by refugees from Spanish Andalusia.

Moving on from either city, the most popular destination is the mountain town of **Chaouen** – a small-scale and enjoyably laid-back place to come to terms with being in Morocco. It is most easily reached via Tetouan. Heading south from Tangier – which stands at the beginning of the railway lines to Fes, Rabat, Casablanca and Marrakesh – the best places to get acclimatised are the seaside resorts of Asilah and Larache. **Asilah** is a low-key, though growing tourist resort, and in August hosts an **International Festival** – northern Morocco's major cultural event of the year. **Larache** is less well known and perhaps more enjoyable, with its relaxed feel, fine beach and proximity to the ancient Carthaginian-Roman site of **Lixus**.

International zones – and language

Northern Morocco has an especially quirky **colonial history**, having been divided into three separate zones. Tetouan was the administrative capital of the **Spanish zone**, which encompassed Chaouen (and the Rif) and spread south through Asilah and Larache – itself a provincial centre. The **French zone** began at Souk El Arba du Rharb, the edge of rich agricultural plains sprawling south towards the French Protectorate's capital, Rabat. **Tangier**, meanwhile, experienced **"International Rule"** under a group of European embassies.

One modern consequence of this past is that, although French is the official second **language** (after Arabic) throughout Morocco, most people in the northwest are equally, or more, fluent in **Spanish** – a basic knowledge of which can prove extremely useful. Adding to and perpetuating the colonial legacy is the fact that Spanish TV and radio can be received (and attracts enthusiastic audiences) throughout much of northern Morocco.

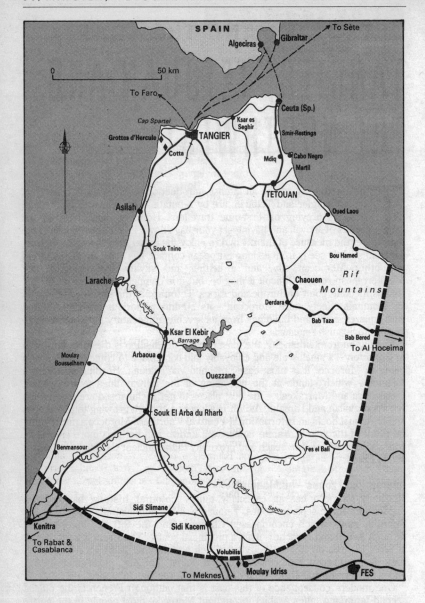

SPAIN

To Sète

Algeciras   Gibraltar

0   50 km

To Faro

Ceuta (Sp.)

Cap Spartel

Ksar es Seghir

Smir-Restinga

Grottes d'Hercule

TANGIER

Cotta

Mdiq   Cabo Negro

Martil

TETOUAN

Asilah

Oued Laou

Souk Tnine

Bou Hamed

D j e b a l a

Rif Mountains

Larache

Oued Loukos

Chaouen

Derdara

Bab Taza

Ksar El Kebir
Barrage

Bab Bered
To Al Hoceima

Moulay Bousselham

Arbaoua

Ouezzane

Souk El Arba du Rharb

Benmansour

Fes el Bali

Sidi Slimane

Oued Sebou

Kenitra
To Rabat & Casablanca

Sidi Kacem

Volubilis

To Meknes   Moulay Idriss

FES

TRAIN NETWORK ROUTE

ONCF, the Moroccan rail company, operates connecting buses twice daily between **Tetouan** and the station at **Sidi Tnine Lyamani**, just south of Asilah.

TANGIER AND THE COAST

Tangier has an international airport and ferry connections with Algeciras, Gibraltar and the French port of Sète. Unless you are bringing a car over from Spain, it's a preferable crossing to Ceuta: both for the town, in its own right, and for the convenience in moving straight on into Morocco. Asilah is a mere forty minutes' ride on the train; Meknes, Fes, Rabat and Casablanca are all comfortably reached within the day, while if you are in a hurry to get south, there is a night express train for Marrakesh.

The **coast** detailed in this section is the **Atlantic** stretch south towards Rabat. **Asilah**, on the train line, is the easiest destination; **Larache** can be reached by bus or *grand taxi* only, either from Tangier or (simpler) from Asilah. A more distinctively Moroccan resort is **Moulay Bousselham**, south of Larache and accessible by bus or *grand taxi* via Souk El Arba du Rharb.

Tangier (Tanja, Tanger, Tangiers)

For the first five decades of this century **TANGIER** was one of the stylish resorts of the Mediterranean – an "International City" with its own laws and administration, plus an eclectic community of exiles, expatriates and refugees. It was home, at various times, to Spanish and Central European refugees; to Moroccan nationalists; and – drawn by loose tax laws and free-port status – to over seventy banks and 4000 companies, many of them dealing in currency transactions forbidden in their own countries. Writers also were attracted to the city: the American novelist Paul Bowles has lived in Tangier since the war, William Burroughs spent most of the 1950s here, and most of the Beats – Jack Kerouac, Allen Ginsberg, Brion Gysin and the rest – all passed through. Tangier was also the world's first and most famous gay resort, a role it maintains to a smaller degree.

When Moroccan independence was gained in 1956, however, Tangier's special status was removed. Almost overnight, the finance and banking businesses shifted their operations to Spain and Switzerland. The expatriate colony* dwindled, too, as the new national government imposed bureaucratic controls and instituted a "clean-up" of the city. Brothels – previously numbering almost a hundred – were banned, and in the early 1960s "The Great Scandal" erupted, sparked by a handful of paedophilia convictions and escalating into a wholesale closure of the once outrageous gay bars.

These ghosts have left a slight air of decay about the city, still tangible in the older hotels and bars, despite a recent flurry of development and, especially, apartment building. There seems, too, a somewhat uncertain overall identity: a city that seems halfway to becoming a mainstream tourist resort – and an increasingly popular destination for holidaying Moroccans – yet which still retains hints of its dubious past amid the shambling 1930s architecture and style. It is, as already noted, a tricky place for first-time arrivals – hustling and mugging stories here should not be underestimated – but once you get the hang of it, Tangier is lively and very likeable, highly individual and with an enduring eccentricity.

---

*At the international colony's peak in the early 1950s, Tangier's ex-pats numbered some 60,000 – nearly half the then-population. Today there are under 2000 (including 800 Spanish, 600 French, and around 150 Britons and Americans) in a city population of 315,000.

Orientation

After the initial confusion of an unfamiliar Arab city, Tangier is surprisingly easy to find your way around. As with all the larger Moroccan towns, it's made up of two parts: the **Medina**, the original Moroccan town, and the **Ville Nouvelle**, built by its European colonisers. Inside the Medina, a classic web of alleyways and stepped passages, is the old fortified quarter of the **Kasbah**, with the former Sultanate's palace at its centre.

Together with the **beach** and the seafront **Avenue d'Espagne**, the easiest reference points are the city's three main squares – the Grand Socco, Petit Socco and Place de France. **Place de France** is a conventional, French-looking square at the heart of the Ville Nouvelle, flanked by elegant cafés and a **terrace-belvedere** looking out over the straits to Spain (Tarifa is usually visible). From here, **Boulevard Pasteur** (the main city street) leads off past an ONMT **tourist office**, a couple of blocks up, towards the main **PTT** (post office).

In the other direction from Place de France, **Rue de la Liberté** runs down to the **Grand Socco**, an amorphous open space in front of the Medina. The north side of the square opens onto the Medina's principal street, **Rue es Siaghin**, which culminates in the **Petit Socco**, a tiny square of old cafés and cheap hotels.

Guides and hustlers

Be prepared on arrival for unofficial **"guides"** – or hustlers – who can be incredibly persistent around the port entrance. They will tell you some fairly amazing

---

STREET-NAME CHANGES

Tangier **street-name signs** are the most confusing in the country, with the old French and Spanish colonial names still in use alongside their Arabicised successors. In addition *Rue* and *Calle* are sometimes replaced by *Zankat*, and *Avenue* and *Boulevard* by *Charih*.

Local maps tend to use the new Arabic versions, though not all of the street signs have been changed. In the text and maps of this guide, we have used new names only when firmly established. Among the main street-name changes, note:

Main squares
Place de France – Place de Faro
Grand Socco – Place du 19 Avril 1947
Petit Socco – Place Souk Dakhil

Ville Nouvelle
Avenue Louis (sic) van Beethoven – Avenue Yacoub El Mansour
Avenue d'Espagne – Avenue des FAR (Forces Armées Royales)
Rue Dante – Rue El Farabi
Rue Dickens – Rue Ibn Albanna
Rue Goya – Rue Moulay Al Abdallah
Rue de la Liberté – Rue El Houria

Rue Murillo – Rue Ahmed Choukri
Rue de la Plage – Rue Salah Eddine El Ayoubi
Rue Rembrandt – Rue El Jaba El Quatania
Rue Sanlucar – Rue El Moutanabi
Rue Shakespeare – Avenue El Hadj Mohammed Tazi

Medina
Rue des Chrétiens – Rue des Almouahidines
Rue de la Marine – Rue Djemaa Kebir
Rue des Postes – Rue Mokhtar Ahardane

tales: the hotels are full, the Medina is dangerous, the trains and buses are on strike. Don't take too much of this at face value, and don't feel in any way duty bound to employ anyone's services – you don't need a guide in Tangier and you certainly don't want one of the port hustlers.

POINTS OF ARRIVAL AND CITY TRANSPORT

BY FERRY

Disembarking at Tangier can be a slow process, with long queues for passport control and customs: be prepared. Most importantly, make sure that you have your **passport stamped** (and departure card collected) while *on board the ferry*; announcements to this effect are not always made in English, so make your way to the purser's office during the journey. If you miss out on this, you'll be left until last by the officials in Tangier.

Once ashore, and through customs, you pass into the **ferry terminal building**. There's a **bureau de change** here which sells dirhams at standard rates for most currencies and travellers' cheques (for credit card exchange you need a bank in the city, see "Directory"). Also within the building is an **ONCF** office for **train tickets**, worth queuing for immediately if you're going straight on to Asilah, Rabat, Meknes or Fes; for details of departures, see p.78. **Hydrofoils** dock just in front of the ferry terminal building, where there's an individual passport office.

The Gare du Port is sited almost directly below the ferry terminal; you can't miss it as you come out. Nearby – and still inside the port enclosure – there are ranks for **grand and petit taxis** (see below for practicalities); they are best engaged here, before you get outside the enclosure to the hustling of the port gates.

BY AIR

Tangier's **airport** is 15km outside the city. If you arrive on a package tour you'll be met by a hotel shuttle (try to get a transfer with your ticket, if you're on flight only). If you're on your own, either bargain with the **taxi** drivers, who *should* charge 60–70dh for up to six passengers (get a group together before leaving the terminal building, or they will charge each person 60–70dh), or walk the two kilometres to the main road, where you can pick up the #17 or #70 **buses** to the Grand Socco (see "Orientation", opposite).

The **bank** at the airport exchanges cash only and is often closed.

CITY TAXIS AND BUSES

Grands taxis (large cream/beige Mercedes) are permitted to carry up to six passengers. The price for a ride should be fixed in advance – 10dh per person is standard for any trip within the city, including tip. Small blue/green **petits taxis** (which carry just three passengers) can be flagged down around the town. Most of these are metered – standard rate for a city trip is 5dh per person. On the streets you can **hail a taxi**, whether it has passengers or not; if it is going in your direction it will generally take you. If you join a taxi with passengers, you pay the full fare, as if it were empty. Both *grand* and *petit taxi* rates increase by fifty percent **after 9pm**.

Minibuses operated by the private company, *Bourghaz*, run to a number of useful destinations – including the bus station and Cap Spartel; there is a stop just outside the port gate. Regular city bus services are less useful.

For details on the bus and taxi terminals for journeys out of Tangier, see "Leaving Tangier", on pp.78–79.

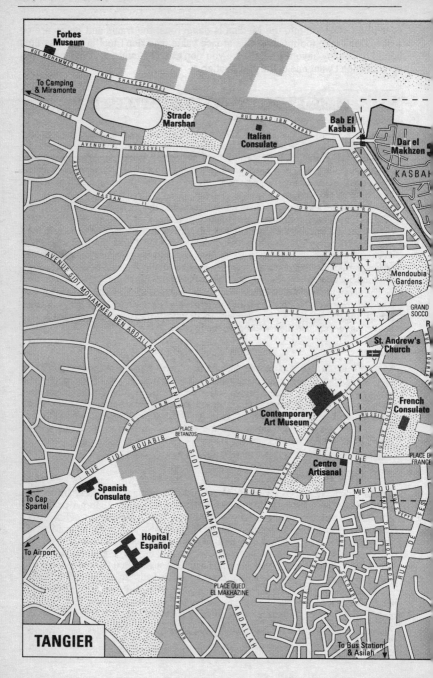

Forbes Museum

RUE MOHAMMED TAXI

To Camping & Miramonte

TRUE SHAKESPEARE

RUE DE

RUE DE

U.S.A.

AVENUE F ROOSEVELT

Strade Marshan

RUE ASAD IBN FARRAT

Italian Consulate

Bab El Kasbah

Dar el Makhzen

KASBAH

AVENUE

HASSAN II

AVENUE DU DR. CENARRO

AVENUE SIDI MOHAMMED BEN ABDALLAH

AVENUE HASSAN I

RUE DE LA KASBAH

Mendoubia Gardens

RUE ARRAKIA

GRAND SOCCO

AVENUE HASSAN II

RUE BOUARIE

St. Andrew's Church

IBN LAIDOUN

Contemporary Art Museum

RUE D'ANGLETERRE

RUE DE RUSSIE

French Consulate

PLACE BETANZOS

RUE DE BELGIQUE

RUE D'OUJDA

PLACE DE FRANCE

RUE SIDI BOUABIB

RUE DE

Centre Artisanal

Spanish Consulate

SIDI MOHAMMED BEN

RUE DU MEXIQUE

RUE DE FES

To Cap Spartel

To Airport

Hôpital Español

RUE D'ANGLETERRE

RUE MAHATMA GANDHI

ABDALLAH

PLACE OUED EL MAKHAZINE

RUE DE

To Bus Station & Asilah

TANGIER

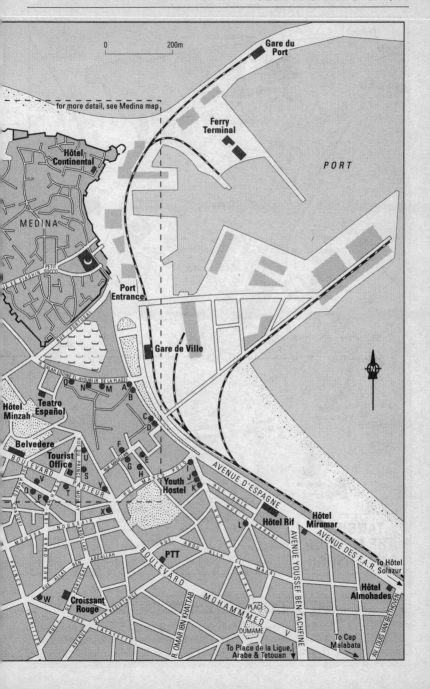

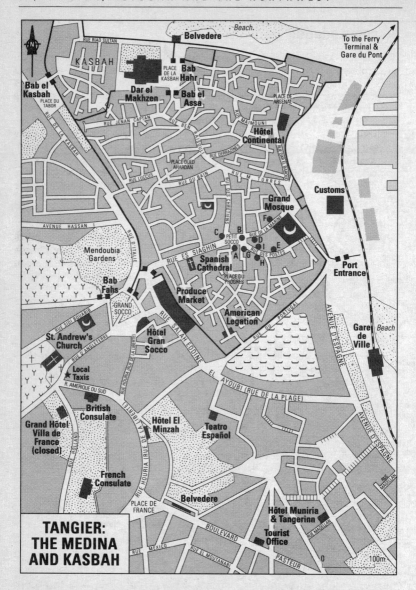

TANGIER:
THE MEDINA
AND KASBAH

HOTEL KEYS ON TANGIER MAPS

All hotels in our listings are either **labelled or keyed** on the **main city map** on the previous page (in the case of Seafront/Ville Nouvelle hotels) or on the **Medina map** above (for Medina hotels).

Accommodation

Tangier has dozens of **hotels and pensions**, and finding a room is never much of a problem: if the first place you try is full, ask them to phone and reserve you a place elsewhere – most will be happy to do so. The city does, however, get crowded during July and August, with some of the unclassified places doubling their prices. If you want a cheap bed at this time of year, you'll often do best by going for one of the officially classified hotels.

Of the **hotels** listed below, a few of the Moderate places are detailed simply just they are regular package choices (which you may find yourself booked into); the rest, however, are all to some extent recommended. As always, there is a choice between the **Medina** or **Ville Nouvelle**. Hotels in the Ville Nouvelle, including the seafront area, have a virtual monopoly on comfort (and regular running water), as well as an easier, more familiar feel.

Seafront hotels

All the places below are along or just off the seafront **Avenue d'Espagne** and its continuation **Av. des F.A.R.** (Av. des Forces Armées Royales); the name change takes place, it seems, after the Hôtel Rif, though maps differ. Several hotels are in Rue Magellan, which is easy to miss: it zigzags up from the seafront between the hotels *Biarritz* and *Cecil* towards Bd. Pasteur in the Ville Nouvelle.

For ease of reference, the listings in this section are in order of appearance (rather than by price, as elsewhere in the guide), moving around the bay from the port and train stations. They are all within walkable distance of the port and train stations, though you may prefer to take a *petit taxi* for the further ones.

Hôtel Valencia [A], 72 Av. d'Espagne (☎09/93.07.70). A decent hotel in a useful situation – almost opposite the city train station – but a bit overpriced for what's on offer. ③

Hôtel L'Marsa [B], 92 Av. d'Espagne (☎09/93.23.39). Clean and inexpensive pension with a handful of rooms and a good café-restaurant. ⓪

HOTEL PRICE CODES AND STAR-RATINGS

As of 1993, hotels are no longer obliged to levy set maximum rates, according to their official star-ratings, as had long been the custom. However, **prices** still broadly follow the star-rating system, and this is the basis of our own **hotel price codes** set out below and keyed throughout the guide.

Our code	Official classification	Single room price	Double room price
⓪	Unclassified	25–60dh	40–100dh
①	1*A/1*B	60–105dh	100–125dh
②	2*B/2*A	105–145dh	125–175dh
③	3*B/3*A	145–225dh	175–275dh
④	4*B/4*A	225–400dh	275–500dh
⑤	5*luxury	Upwards of 400dh	Upwards of 500dh

TELEPHONE CODES

All telephone numbers in the Tangier/Tetouan region are prefixed 09. When making a call within the region you omit this prefix. For more explanation of phone codes and making calls within (or to) Morocco, see pp.37–38.

Hôtel Biarritz [C], 102–104 Av. d'Espagne (☎09/93.24.73). Old hotel, renovated of late, and with a decent restaurant below. ①

Hôtel Cecil [D], 112 Av. d'Espagne (☎09/93.10.87). This is one of the town's oldest hotels but had lapsed into one of the city's seediest by its centenary in the 1980s. A new owner has worked wonders and it's today a highly attractive pension-style place. ③

Hôtel Magellan [E], 16 Rue Magellan(☎09/93.87.26). Well kept, inexpensive pension, with reliable hot showers. ⑩

Hôtel El Muniria [F], 1 Rue Magellan(☎09/93.53.37). Old established ex-pat-owned hotel that remains friendly and good value, and has a late-night bar (the *Tanger-Inn*) that can be amusing. Burroughs, Kerouac and Ginsberg all stayed here when they first came to Tangier, Burroughs writing *The Naked Lunch* in room 9. ①

Hôtel Ibn Batouta [G], 8 Rue Magellan (☎09/94.72.12). Another pleasant, well-run pension, just across the street from the *El Muniria*. ①

Hôtel Panoramic Massilia [H], 11 Rue Targha (☎09/93.50.11). Another good alternative, of similar standard, on the street that runs between the top end of Rue Magellan and Rue Marco Polo; has a restaurant and bar. ①

Hôtel Marco Polo [I], corner of Av. d'Espagne/Rue El Antaki – aka Rue Grotius (☎09/93.82.13). Comfortable German-run hotel, with a fair restaurant-bar. ②

Hôtel El Djenina [J], Rue El Antaki (☎09/93.60.75). A bit drab, though well maintained, with hot baths in all rooms. ②

Hôtel Bristol [K], Rue El Antaki (☎09/93.10.70). A little fancier than any of the preceding, with en suite baths, plus a bar and restaurant. ③

Auberge de Jeunesse/Youth Hostel [label], 8 Rue El Antaki (☎09/94.01.27). A brand new hostel – clean and well run. ⑩

Hôtel El Farabi [L], 8 Rue Saidia/corner Rue El Farabi (☎09/93.45.66). A friendly and comfortable hotel, well maintained by a family from Tafraoute. ②

Hôtel Rif [label], 152 Av. des FAR (☎09/93.59.10). Long-established upmarket beach hotel, now looking a touch old-fashioned, and perhaps all the more pleasant for it. ④

Hôtel Miramar [label], Av. des FAR (☎09/93.89.48). By far the best budget hotel on the seafront – very 1930s, with big rooms and hot showers, and a fine restaurant and bar. ②

Hôtel Almohades [label], Av. des FAR (☎09/94.00.26). Large package hotel recently downgraded from five-star luxury status; not very impressive. ④

Hôtel Solazur [label], Av. des FAR (☎09/93.36.37). This is arguably the best of the upmarket beach hotels and was requisitioned by Malcolm Forbes for his seventieth birthday bash (see p.73); they complained of the lack of air conditioning, to which Forbes retorted "What did they expect me to do – build them a hotel?". Quite. ④

Central Ville Nouvelle hotels

Most of these recommendations are within a few blocks of Place de France/Place de Faro and the central Boulevard Pasteur; coming up from the port, if you've got much luggage, a taxi could be a useful investment.

Rue Salah Eddine El Ayoubi (aka Rue de la Plage). This street runs up from the town train station to the Grand Socco and is lined with small pensions. Many of them charge outrageous prices to new arrivals sent over by port hustlers, and all inflate their prices in the summer months. **Pension Madrid** (no. 140; ☎09/93.16.93; M), **Pension Miami** (no. 126; ☎09/93.29.00; N) and **Pension Talavera** (no. 124; ☎09/93.14.74; O) are reasonable bets if rooms seem a problem elsewhere. ⑩

Rue El Moutanabi (aka Rue Sanlucar). This street, parallel to Bd. Pasteur, has a couple of better-value unclassified options: **Hotel Al Hoceima** (no. 2; ☎09/93.30.63; P) and **Pension Atlal** (no. 4; ☎09/93.72.99; Q). ⑩

Hôtel Grand Socco [R], Grand Socco (no phone). Not the most salubrious rooms but an interesting location, poised on the edge of the Medina, and extremely easy to find; has a number of large rooms that offer good value for three to five people. ⑩

Maroc Hôtel [S], 1 Av. du Prince Moulay Abdallah (☎09/93.18.31). This hotel is literally falling apart, but it's a nice place in its own way, and with a fine restaurant on the ground floor. ①

Hôtel de Paris [T], 42 Bd. Pasteur (☎09/93.81.26). A pleasant, functional hotel right at the heart of things. Recently renovated. ①

Hôtel Lutetia [U], 3 Av. Prince Moulay Abdallah (☎09/93.18.66). Excellent value for its two-star category and well located – a block below Bd. Pasteur. Has a bar, too. ②

Africa Hôtel [V], 17 Rue Moussa Ibn Noussair (☎09/93.55.11). Attractive and quite stylish, with a swimming pool on the roof, and accorded four stars in the not-too-distant past. ③

Hôtel Chellah [W], Rue Allal Ben Abdallah (☎09/94.33.88). Regular tour group hotel, with a small pool and garden. ③

Hôtel Tanjah Flandria [X], 6 Bd. Mohammed V (☎09/93.32.79). Slightly superior package tour hotel, with a pool on the roof, disco and sauna. ④

Hôtel Rembrandt [Y], corner of Bd. Pasteur/Bd. Mohammed V (☎09/93.78.70). Another large package tour hotel, with a pool, restaurant and good views of the port. ④

Hôtel El Minzah [label], 85 Rue El Houria (aka Rue de la Liberté) (☎09/93.58.85). Tangier's finest, with a wonderful garden and pool overlooking the sea and town. ⑤

Note: The old **Grand Hôtel Villa de France** on Rue de Hollande is, at present, closed. It was once among the country's most elegant hotels – Matisse stayed in, and painted the view from, room 35 – but it fell on hard times in the late 1980s and has been acquired for as yet unspecified "redevelopment".

Medina hotels

With the exception of the *Continental* and the *Mamora,* these listings – the best of a number of Medina hotels – are unclassified and fairly basic; they are safe enough, though, so long as you have the initial confidence for the area, and have distinct character. To reach the Medina from the port or train station, there's a choice of routes: either up Rue du Portugal to the Grand Socco, or up the steps behind the port entrance, round to the Grand Mosque and the junction of Rue des Postes/Rue Dar El Baroud. If you're unsure of yourself – and the Medina can be intimidating if this is your first visit to Morocco – it's best to take a taxi.

Hôtel Fuentes [a], 9 Place Petit Socco, at the heart of the Medina (☎09/93.44.69). A scruffy but friendly little place, above a café, this was one of the first hotels in Tangier and boasted Camille Saint-Saens among its nineteenth-century residents. ①

Pension Becerra [b], 8 Place Petit Socco (☎09/93.23.69). Basic, with showers in summer only, but rooms as cheap as they come. ①

Hôtel Mauretania [c], 2 Rue des Chrétiens – aka Rue des Almouahidines, just off the Petit Socco (no phone). Cold showers, but otherwise fairly well kept. ①

Pension Amal [d], 5 Rue des Postes – aka Rue Mokhtar Ahardane (☎09/93.36.00). Very low prices, okay rooms and hot showers. ①

Pension Marhaba [e], 14 Rue des Postes, on an alley to the left just before reaching the Grand Mosque (☎09/93.88.02). Decent rooms with views of town and sea; cold showers. ①

Pension Laraiche [f], 74 Rue de la Marine (no phone). A very well-maintained hotel, with decent rooms and cold showers. ①

Hôtel Palace [g], 2 Rue des Postes (☎09/93.61.28). A touch of past splendours – balconies and a central court with fountain – led Bertolucci to adopt this as a location in his film of Paul Bowles's novel, *The Sheltering Sky.* Rooms are quite pleasant, including a few en suite. ①

Hôtel Olid [h], 12 Rue des Postes (☎09/93.13.10). A hotel that maintains an official one-star classification, as befits slightly better facilities than in any of the preceding options. ①

Hôtel Mamora [i], 19 Rue des Postes (☎09/93.41.05). A further step up: slightly overpriced, perhaps, but offering a bit more security and comfort at the heart of the Medina. ②

Hôtel Continental [label], Rue Dar El Baroud (☎09/93.10.24). This is by far the best choice in the Medina. Founded in 1888, it was once the most fashionable hotel in Tangier, and had

Queen Victoria's son Alfred as its first official guest. It is well run (the staff, Abdessalam and Tifou, are institutions), and it still has style, with a grand piano and huge parrot cage in the hall and a beautiful terrace overlooking the port – and it was another of Bertolucci's locations for *The Sheltering Sky*. To reach the hotel, either take a taxi from by the port entrance, or walk up to the Petit Socco and take Rue de la Marine to the left of Rue des Postes; follow this around past the Grand Mosque and a terrace, and you'll come to the hotel gates. As the hotel is offered by several package companies (including British operator, *Inspirations*), bookings are strongly recommended; ask for rooms 108 or 208, which are a *fin-de-siècle* treat – or, if they're gone, for any first- or second-floor seafront room; "back" rooms are not so good. ③

Campsites

Tangier's campsites are sited well outside the city, and worth considering mainly if you are travelling in a campervan or with a caravan; for those with a tent, security is not great, and costs (especially if you have no transport) the equal of a reasonable budget hotel. Choices are:

Camping Miramonte (☎09/93.71.33). The closest and most popular campsite, 3km from the centre, with a reasonable restaurant and facilities. It's a bit tricky to find, due to lack of signs. Driving, leave the city on the road to the west of the Kasbah; on public transport, take local buses #2, # 21, or preferably #1 from the Grand Socco.

Camping-Caravaning Tingis (☎09/94.01.91). This large complex is 6km east of the city, out towards Cap Malabata (see p.81), beside the Oued Moghoga lagoon. The site is well-equipped with tennis court, shops and swimming pool, but it's a 2km walk from the beach (which, with the nearby woods, is highly unsafe at night), overpriced, and plagued by mosquitoes. To get there, take bus #15 from the Grand Socco. Open summer only.

Robinson Plage Camping, 8km from town, towards Cap Spartel and close to the Caves of Hercules (see p.80); take the *Bourghaz* minibus from the port; a *grand taxi* is pricey, unless you have a group to share costs. A pleasant, well-wooded site with showers (but no swimming pool), café, restaurant and shop.

The beach and Ville Nouvelle

Tangier's interest and attraction lies in the city as a whole: its café life, beach, and the tumbling streets of the Medina. The handful of "monuments", with the notable exception of the Dar El Makhzen palace, are best viewed as adding direction to your wanderings, rather than as unmissable sights.

The town beach

It was the beach and mild climate which drew in Tangier's first expatriates, the Victorian British, who used to amuse themselves with afternoon rides along the sands and weekends of "pig-sticking" in the wooded hills behind. Today's pleasures come a little more packaged on the **town beach**, with camel rides and a string of club-like beach bars. However, by day the sands are diverting and fun, with Moroccans entertaining themselves in acrobatics and football.

It is compulsory to change in a cabin, so when you arrive you may feel like attaching yourself to one of the **beach bars**, most of which offer showers and deck chairs, as well as food and drink. Some of these are institutions, like *Emma's BBC Bar* (still serving up bacon-and-egg breakfasts), *The Sun Beach*, where Tennessee Williams reputedly wrote a first draft of *Cat on a Hot Tin Roof* or *The Windmill*, where Joe Orton knocked about. Others, like *The Macumba*, retain a predominantly gay clientele. Perhaps the most lively and pleasant is *Miami Beach*, with its gardens to laze around in, but the scenes change each year, so look around and take your pick. All are open in summer only.

By day, it more or less goes without saying, don't leave anything on the beach unattended. By night, limit your exploration to the beach bars (a few of which offer evening cabarets – if Arabic Country & Western appeals), as the beach itself becomes a dangerous venue for rough trade.

The Grand Socco and Place de France

The **Grand Socco** is the obvious place to start a ramble around the town. Its name, like so many in Tangier, is a French–Spanish hybrid, proclaiming its origins as the main market square. The markets have long gone, but the square remains a meeting place and its cafés are good points to sit around and absorb the city's life. The Grand Socco's official but little-used name, **Place du 9 Avril 1947**, commemorates the visit of Sultan Mohammed V to the city on that date – an occasion when, for the first time, he identified himself with the struggle for Moroccan independence.

A memorial to this event (in Arabic) is to be found amid the luxuriant **Mendoubia Gardens**, flanking the square. These were originally the residence of the Mendoub – the Sultan's representative during the international years – but are nowadays part of the grounds of the city's law courts, and in general closed to the public. At weekends, though, when the courts are closed, the caretaker can sometimes be persuaded to give a brief tour; knock at the low green gate in the wall. The gardens include a spectacular Banyan tree, said to be 800 years old.

The old **markets** of the Grand Socco were moved out in the 1970s, onto the Rue de Portugal (running down to the port) and to some cramped terraces beside the Rue d'Angleterre, southwest of the square. More interesting, however, is the little **Fondouk Market**, which is to be found by following **Rue de la Liberté** from the Grand Socco towards Place de France, then turning left down a series of steps, past the *El Minzah* hotel. The stalls here offer everything from pottery to spectacle repairs, from fruit and vegetables to junk.

Over in the **Place de France**, the cafés are the main attraction – and at their best in the late afternoon and early evening, when an interesting mix of local and expatriate regulars turn out to watch and be watched. The seats to choose are outside the *Café de Paris*, a legendary rendezvous throughout the years of the International Zone. During World War II, this was notorious as a centre of deal making and intrigue between agents from Britain, America, Germany, Italy and Japan; later the emphasis shifted to Morocco's own politics: the first nationalist paper, *La Voix du Maroc*, surfaced at the café, and the nationalist leader Allal El Fassi, exiled in Tangier from the French-occupied zone, set up his Istiqlal party headquarters nearby.

Saint Andrew's church and the Modern Art museum

Just south of the Grand Socco, on Rue d'Angleterre, is the Anglican church of **Saint Andrew**, one of the city's odder sights in its fusion of Moorish decoration and English country churchyard. The caretaker, Mustapha, is generally around to show off the church, whose interior is notable for its rendition of the Lord's Prayer in Arabic script around the chancel arch.

In the graveyard, among the laments of early deaths from malaria, you come upon the tomb of **Walter Harris** (see *Contexts*), the most brilliant of the chroniclers of "Old Morocco" in the closing decades of the nineteenth century and the beginning of the twentieth. Another eccentric Briton, **Emily Keane**, is also commemorated. A contemporary of Harris, she lived a very different life, marrying in 1873 the Shereef of Ouezzane – at the time one of the most holy towns of the country (see p.112). Other graves reveal epitaphs to **Caid Sir Harry MacClean**, the Scottish military adviser to Sultan Moulay Abd El Aziz at the turn of the century, and to **Dean** of *Dean's Bar* ("Missed by all and sundry").

The church is still used for a Sunday morning service (11am), though the congregation has fallen to around twenty, and drinks afterwards in the church-yard – for many years an institution of Tangier British life and presided over by the colony's social chief, the Hon. David Herbert, brother of the Earl of Pembroke, and author of a couple of Tangier reminiscences – has been forsaken of late.

A little further down the Rue d'Angleterre is a large white-walled villa, formerly the British Consulate and now the **Musée d'Art Contemporain de Tanger** (daily except Tues 9am–noon & 3–6pm; 10dh). Devoted exclusively to contemporary Moroccan artists, it often has interesting exhibitions.

The American Legation and Spanish Theatre

If you follow Rue de la Plage out of the Grand Socco, then turn left down towards the port on the Rue du Portugal, you come to a small gate in the Medina wall, opposite the Jewish Cemetery. Just through the gate is the **Old American Legation** (open daily 10am–5pm; free), a fascinating former palace given to the US government by the Sultan Moulay Slimane, and preserved today as an American Historic Landmark. Morocco was the first overseas power to recognise an independent United States and this was the first American ambassadorial residence, established in 1777. A three-storey palace, bridging an alleyway below, it houses excellent historical exhibits on the city's history – including the correspondence between Sultan Moulay Ben Abdallah and George Washington – and displays of Moroccan-resident American artists.

Over to the southeast of the Grand Socco, off the Rue de la Plage, is another interesting relic of Tangier's international past, the **Gran Teatro Cervantes** – the old Spanish theatre. Located on a side street still labelled in Spanish as Calle Esperanza, it is an unmistakeable buiding, with its tiled, art deco front, and, save for the conversion of one bay on the ground floor into a garage, stands much as it must have done in its heyday. You can usually look around inside, where the glass dome, stage and balcony remain intact.

The Medina

The Grand Socco offers the most straightforward **approach to the Medina**. The arch at the northwest corner of the square opens onto Rue d'Italie, which becomes Rue de la Kasbah, the northern entrance to the Kasbah quarter. To the right, there is an opening onto Rue es Siaghin, off which are most of the *souks* (markets) and at the end of which is the Petit Socco, the Medina's principal landmark and square. An alternative approach to the Medina is from the seafront: follow the steps up, walk round by the Grand Mosque, and Rue des Postes (aka Rue Mokhtar Ahardane) will lead you into the Petit Socco.

Rue es Siaghin

Rue es Siaghin – Silversmiths' Street – was Tangier's main thoroughfare into the 1930s, and remains an active one today, with a series of fruit, grain and cloth markets opening off to its sides. Halfway up, locked and decaying, is the old **Spanish Cathedral** and **Mission**; to the right, just before it, was formerly the

Mellah, or Jewish quarter, centred around Rue des Synagogues. Moroccan Jews traditionally controlled the silver and jewellery trade – the "Siaghin" of the street name – but few remain in Tangier, having left at independence for Gibraltar, France and Israel. The street itself has long been taken over by tourist stalls.

The Petit Socco

The **Petit Socco** (Little Market) seems too small ever to have served such a purpose. Old photographs, in fact, show it almost twice its present size: it was only at the turn of the century that the hotels and cafés were built. These, however, give the place its atmosphere: seedy and slightly conspiratorial, and the location for many of the Moroccan stories of Mohammed Mrabet (see *Contexts*).

In the heyday of the "International City", with easily exploited Arab and Spanish sexuality a major attraction, it was in the alleys behind the Socco that the straight and boy brothels were concentrated. William Burroughs used to hang out around the square: "I get averages of ten very attractive propositions a day," he wrote to Alan Ginsberg, ". . . no stasis horrors here." However, the Socco cafés (the *Central* was the prime Beat location) lost much of their allure at independence, when the sale of alcohol was banned in the Medina, but they remain a good place to sit around, talk and get some measure of the town.

Towards the Kasbah

It is beyond the Petit Socco that the Medina proper seems to start, "its topography", to quote Paul Bowles, "rich in prototypal dream scenes: covered streets like corridors with doors opening into rooms on either side, hidden terraces high above the sea, streets consisting only of steps, dark impasses, small squares built on sloping terrain so that they looked like ballet sets designed in false perspective, with alleys leading off in several directions; as well as the classical dream equipment of tunnels, ramparts, ruins, dungeons and cliffs".

Walking up from the Petit Socco, you can follow **Rue des Chrétiens** (aka Rue des Almohades) and its continuation **Rue Ben Raisouli** and emerge, with luck, around the lower gate to the Kasbah. Heading past the Socco towards the sea walls are two small streets straddled by the Grand Mosque. If you want to get out and down to the beach, follow **Rue des Postes** and you'll hit a flight of steps. If you feel like wandering, take the other one, **Rue de la Marine**, which curls into **Rue Dar El Baroud** and the entrance to the old *Hôtel Continental* – another fine place to sit and drink tea. From here it's relatively simple to find your way across to the square below the Kasbah Gate.

The **Grand Mosque** itself is screened from public view – and, as throughout Morocco, entrance is strictly forbidden to non-Muslims. Enlarged in the early nineteenth century, the mosque was originally constructed by the sultan Moulay Ismail in celebration of the return of Tangier to Moroccan control in 1685. Prior to this, the city had seen some two centuries of European rule: it was first conquered by the Portuguese in the aftermath of the Moors' expulsion from Andalusia and the Algarve, and in 1663 it passed to the British as part of the dowry of Catherine of Braganza, bride to Charles II.

It was the British – in just 22 years of occupation – who destroyed the city's medieval fortifications, including a great upper castle which covered the entire site of the present-day Kasbah. Under virtually constant siege, they found it an expensive and unrewarding possession: "an excrescence of the earth", according to Samuel Pepys, who oversaw the garrison's withdrawal, shocked at the women of the town ("generally whores") and at the governor ("with his whores at the little bathing house which he has furnished with jade a-purpose for that use"). Dining alone with the chaplain, Pepys had "a great deal of discourse upon the viciousness of this place and its being time for God Almighty to destroy it".

The Kasbah and beyond

The **Kasbah**, walled off from the Medina on the highest rise of the coast, has been the palace and administrative quarter since Roman times. It is a strange, somewhat sparse area of walled compounds, occasional colonnades, and a number of luxurious villas built in the 1920s, when this became one of the Mediterranean's most chic residential sites. Richard Hughes, author of *A High Wind in Jamaica* (and of a book of Moroccan tales), was the first European to take a house here – his address fabulously titled "Numéro Zero, Le Kasbah, Tangier". Among those who followed was the eccentric Woolworth's heiress, Barbara Hutton, who reputedly outbid General Franco for her palace. Her parties were legendary – including a ball where thirty Reguibat racing camels and their drivers were brought 1000 miles from the Sahara to form a guard of honour.

Local guides point with some pride to these locations, but the main point of interest here is the former **Sultanate Palace**, or **Dar El Makhzen**, now converted to an excellent museum of crafts and antiquities (open, in theory at least, daily except Tuesdays, from around 9.30am to noon, and again from 3 to 6pm). It stands near the main gateway to the Medina, the **Bab El Assa**, to the rear of a formal court, or *mechouar*, where the town's pashas held public audience and gave judgement well into the present century. The entrance to the palace, a modest-looking porch, is in the left-hand corner of the court as you enter from the Medina – scores of children will probably direct you.

The Dar El Makhzen and Café Detroit

The **Dar El Makhzen** – built, like the Grand Mosque, by Moulay Ismail – last saw royal use as recently as 1912, with the residence of the Sultan Moulay Hafid, who was exiled to Tangier after his forced abdication by the French. The extraordinary negotiations which then took place are chronicled in Walter Harris' *Morocco That Was*. According to Harris, the ex-Sultan found it "an uncomfortable, out-of-date, and out-of-repair old castle, and it formed by no means a satisfactory place of residence, for it was not easy to install 168 people within its crumbling walls with any comfort or pleasure". Most of the 168 seem to have been members of the royal harem and well able to defend their limited privileges. Moulay Hafid himself ended up with "only a couple of very shabby rooms over the entrance", where he apologetically received visitors and played bridge with a small circle of Americans and Europeans.

However out of date and uncomfortable the palace may have been, it is by no means a poor example of Moroccan craftsmanship and architecture. The design is centred on two interior courtyards, each with rich arabesques, painted wooden ceilings and marble fountains. Some of the flanking columns are of Roman origin, particularly well suited to the small display of **mosaics and finds from Volubilis** (see Chapter Three). The main part of the museum, however, is devoted to **Moroccan arts**, laid out according to region and including an exceptional collection of ceramics from Meknes and Fes.

At the entrance to the main part of the palace is the **Bit El Mal**, the old treasury, and adjoining is a small private **mosque**, near to which is the entrance to the herb- and shrub-lined palace **gardens**, shaded by jacaranda trees. If you leave this way, you will come out by the stairway to the **Café-Restaurant Detroit**, set up in the early 1960s by Beat writer Brion Gysin. Gysin created the place partly as a venue for the Musicians of Jajouka, drummers and pipe-players from a village close to Tangier who achieved cult fame through an LP recorded by his friend, Rolling Stone Brian Jones, and who resurfaced on the Stones' 1990 *Steel Wheels* album. The café is now an overpriced tourist spot but worth the price of a mint tea for the views. Its main entrance is on Rue Riad Sultan, the street running alongside the outer walls of the Kasbah to the main gate and Rue de la Kasbah/ Rue d'Italie.

The Forbes Museum and Jews' Beach

Leaving the Medina by the Kasbah gate, a ten- to fifteen-minute walk will bring you to the quarter known as the *marshan*, an exclusive residential quarter with a number of villas and consulates. The finest of the residences is the **Palais Mendoub** on Rue Mohammed Tazi (aka Rue Shakespeare), Tangerine residence of the millionaire publisher Malcolm Forbes (see below), until his death in 1990, and home of the **Forbes Museum of Military Miniatures** (9am–5pm daily except Thurs & festivals; free), for which he left an endowment.

The centrepiece of the museum is – as it proclaims – the largest collection of toy soldiers in the world. This is actually more interesting than you might expect, focusing on a series of battle tableaux, including the 1578 *Battle of the Three*

MALCOLM FORBES: TANGIER'S LAST TYCOON?

The American publishing tycoon, **Malcolm Forbes** bought the **Palais Mendoub** (see above) in 1970. His reason, ostensibly at least, was the acquisition of a base for launching and publishing an Arab-language version of *Forbes Magazine* – the "millionaires' journal". For the next two decades, until his death in 1990, he was a regular visitor to the city, and it was at the Tangier palace that he decided to host his last great extravagance, his **seventieth birthday party**, in 1989.

This was the grandest social occasion Tangier had seen since the days of Woolworth-heiress Barbara Hutton (see facing page), whose scale and spectacle Forbes presumably intended to emulate and exceed. Spending an estimated $2.5m, he brought in his friend Elizabeth Taylor as co-host and chartered a 747, a DC–8 and Concorde to fly in 800 of the world's rich and famous from New York and London. The party entertainment was on an equally imperial scale, including 600 drummers, acrobats and dancers, and a *fantasia* – a cavalry charge which ends with the firing of muskets into the air – by 300 Berber horsemen.

In the media, Malcolm's party was a mixed public relations exercise, with even the gossip press feeling qualms about such a display of American affluence in a country like Morocco, and, despite Liz Taylor's presence at Forbes's side, using the choice of location to hint at the tycoon's sexual preferences (a story that broke in full cry after Forbes's death). However, Forbes most likely considered the party a success, for his guests included not just the celebrity rich – Gianni Agnelli, Robert Maxwell, Barbara Walters, Henry Kissinger – but half a dozen US state governors and the chief executives or presidents of scores of multinational corporations likely to advertise in his magazine. And, of course, it was tax deductible.

Kings at Ksar El Kebir (in which virtually the entire Portuguese nobility was killed or imprisoned), and the 1975 *Marche Verte*, when 350,000 unarmed Moroccans, led by King Hassan, "reclaimed" the former Spanish Sahara. Along with the model soldiers, the museum has a fascinating display of wartime propaganda posters, and you also get the chance to visit the gorgeous **palace gardens** – and possibly part of Forbes's private wing (which includes a remarkable private gym and an intriguing "Throne Room").

Rue Shakespeare runs on west from the museum, eventually giving out into a track that leads down to the **Jews' Beach** – so called from its role as the landing stage for Spanish Jews fleeing the Inquisition. There is a congenial **beach café** here in summer.

Eating, drinking and nightlife

Tangier is not really a night-time city, and if you're looking for international resort-style action, or the Tangier of sin-city legend, you'll be disappointed. There are nevertheless good and generally inexpensive **restaurants**, a fair scattering of **bars** and **discos**, and possibilities for films and the occasional concert.

Restaurants below are rated as: **inexpensive** (£2–5/$3–8 a head); **moderate** (£5–10/$8–16); and **expensive** (over £10/$16).

Restaurants

As with most Moroccan cities, the cheapest places to eat are in the **Medina**, though note that alcoholic drinks are not served in this quarter. For fancier meals – and drinks – you'll need to try the **Ville Nouvelle** or the **seafront**; for late-night snacks, several of the cafés around the Grand Socco stay open all night. All of our **"out of town"** recommendations will require use of a car.

MEDINA

Restaurant Andaluz, 7 Rue de Commerce. The best of the hole-in-the-wall cafés on this street – the first alley to the left off Rue de la Marine (the street running from the Petit Socco to the Grand Mosque). With a trio of tables, it is about as simple as it's possible to be – and excellent, serving impeccably fried swordfish and grilled brochettes. Very cheap.

Restaurant Ibn Batouta, Rue es Siaghin. Small, unpretentious restaurant on the main street of the Medina. Cheap.

Sandwich Salam, 1 Place Petit Socco. Upstairs café snackbar that's clean and friendly. Cheap.

Hammadi's, 2 Rue d'Italie. This is actually just outside the west wall of the Medina: a rather kitsch salon, where traditional Moroccan dishes are served to entertainment from a worthwhile band of Andalusian musicians. Moderate.

Restaurant Marhaba, 67 Palais Ahannar, off Rue de la Kasbah (inside the Kasbah Gate, take the first small alley to the left). A splendid old palace, stacked with antiques, and with good music and food. Moderate.

VILLE NOUVELLE

Restaurant Africa and **Cleopatra's**, 83 and 152 Rue Salah Eddine El Ayoubi (aka Rue de la Plage). The two best places among many on this street, which leads down from the Grand Socco. Both are crowded, local eateries, serving up no-nonsense Moroccan dishes. Cheap.

Restaurant Agadir, 21 Rue Prince Heritier, off Place de France. A personal favourite, with accomplished French and Moroccan cooking. Moderate.

El Dorado, 21 Rue Allal Ben Abdallah (by the *Hôtel Chellah*). Dependable Jewish-Moroccan/Spanish cooking. Moderate.

Guitta's, 110 Sidi Bouabid. Simple European dishes, cooked by an Italian family but with British roasts on Sunday: quintessential International Zone Tangier. Moderate.

Restaurant Osso Buco, on the ground floor of the *Maroc Hôtel*, 1 Av. du Prince Moulay Abdallah. Italian cooking from an extensive menu. Moderate.

Romero's, 12 Av. du Prince Moulay Abdallah – off Bd. Pasteur (☎09/93.22.77). Spanish seafood, including a fine *paella*, served in vast portions. Moderate.

Raihani's, 10 Rue Ahmed Chaoki – opposite the terrace-belvedere on Bd. Pasteur (☎09/93.48.66). Excellent traditional Moroccan food – worth at least one meal for the superb *couscous* and *pastilla* (pigeon pie); also a good French-based menu. Moderate.

Las Conchas, Rue Ahmed Chaouki. Good French menu, presided over by an English woman manager. Moderate.

La Grenouille, Rue Rembrandt – by the *Hotel Rembrandt*, off Bd. Pasteur (☎09/93.62.42). Old-established French restaurant; unreliable quality. Expensive.

Damascus, 2 Av. de Prince Moulay Abdallah – off Bd. Pasteur (☎09/93.22.77). Fancy Moroccan decor and cuisine – *couscous*, *tajines* and even *bastilla*. Expensive.

Hôtel El Minzah, 85 Rue de la Liberté (☎09/93.58.85). The hotel's Moroccan restaurant, *El Korsan*, has a reputation as one of the country's very best, serving authentic and traditional specialities – including a superb *mechoui* (roast lamb), if ordered ahead – to the accompaniment of good Moroccan musicians. *El Korsan*, the French restaurant, is impressive, too. Both are very expensive. The *Patio Wine Bar*, which serves French *brasserie*-style meals, is a little more modest.

SEAFRONT

Hôtel-Restaurant L'Marsa, Av. d'Espagne. Superb pizzas, and home-made ice cream to follow, served on a roof terrace, open-air patio or inside. Moderate.

Hôtels Miramar, **Panoramic Massilia**, **Biarritz**, **Marco Polo**, and **Charf**, all along or just off the Av. d'Espagne – see pp.62–63 for a key. All feature good-value set meals. Moderate.

Emma's BBC Bar, on the beach. This is the only one of the beach-cafés where food is a genuine attraction. Open summer only. Moderate.

OUT OF TOWN

Sol Beach Restaurant-Bar, 4km along the coast road towards Cap Spartel. A rewarding lunchtime trip for grilled fish and beers. Open year round, 9am to 9pm. Moderate.

Le Mirage, Cap Spartel. This offers horse and camel rides, fishing, a couple of resident apes, and some of the best cooking anywhere in or around Tangier. Moderate.

Restaurant Marbel, near the Hôtel Tarik at Cap Malabata. Right on the beach and owned by an Italian married to a Moroccan. Fine seafood and fish. Moderate.

Chez Abdou, 17km out of town, on the coastroad leading north towards Asilah, in the so-called Fôret Diplomatique. Again recommended for seafood. Expensive.

Cafés

All the following are good for breakfast.

Hôtel-Restaurant L'Marsa, Av. d'Espagne. Recommended above for its pizzas, this serves equally delicious croissants, *pains chocolats* and cakes for breakfast or tea.

Patisserie Venise, Rue Allal Ben Abdallah. Excellent pastries.

Café Metropole, Bd. Pasteur. The best *café-au-lait* in town. Pastries can be bought across the road at *Patisserie Le Petit Prince* and consumed at your table.

For **late-night snacks**, *Café Atlas*, by the *Hôtel Rembrandt*, stays open till 4am, and the cafés in the Grand Socco more or less all night.

Bars

Tangier **bars** have been much depleted over the last few years.*The Parade*, the most legendary, died with its owner in 1987, and most of the others have fallen into a not very interesting seediness. Possibilities include:

Tanger Inn, 16 Rue Magellan – below the *Hôtel Muniria*. Deadpan imitation of a Brighton pub, and quite an institution, run by an ex-Household Cavalry trooper and his friend for the last twenty years. Open 9pm–2am.

Dean's Bar, Rue Amerique du Sud – opposite the British Consulate. The closest bar to the Medina – a tiny shop-room that was once the haunt of people like Tennessee Williams, Francis Bacon and Ian Fleming. It is now frequented more or less exclusively by Moroccans, and serves inexpensive beers with Spanish *tapas*.

Carousel Bar, off Rue Prince Heritier. Comfortable British-run wine bar.

Le Pub, Rue Sorolla – behind the *Hôtel Tanjah Flandria*, off Bd. Mohammed V. British-run pub, with hunting scenes on the walls and bar food. Open 9pm–1am.

Hôtel Miramar, 168 Av. des F.A.R. The *Miramar*'s bar is one of the more pleasant of those in the seafront hotels; other hotel bars include the *Panoramic Massilia*, *Marco Polo* and *Rif*.

Hôtel Chellah, Rue Allal Ben Abdallah. Lively, with occasional bands, and a happy hour from 6–7pm daily.

Caid's Bar in the *Hôtel Minzah*, 85 Rue de la Liberté. Long the chi-chi place to meet – ritzy decor and very pricey drinks. Over the bar is a painting of Caid Harry Maclean (see p.70).

In summer, the **beach bars** (see p.75) also stay open until 1am or 2am.

Discos and clubs

The principal area for **discos** is a grid of streets off Place de France, in particular Rue Sanlucar (aka Zankat Moutanabi) and Rue Méxique, and Rue du Prince Moulay Abdallah (off Bd. Pasteur); drinks are two or three times regular bar prices.

Scott's, Rue El Moutanabi (aka Rue Sanlucar). Traditionally (though not exclusively) a gay disco, this is worth a look if only for its very particular choice of paintings – Berber boys in Highland military uniform. Take care if leaving late at night, as the street is none too safe; the best idea is to tip the doorman 5dh to order you a taxi.

Regine's, Rue El Mansour Dahbi (opposite the Roxy Cinema); **Borsalino's**, Rue du Prince Moulay Abdalah; **Hôtel Chellah**, Rue Allal Ben Abdallah. Mainstream discos.

Radio Club, Rue du Prince Moulay Abdallah. Attractively sleazy club which sometimes puts on Moroccan bands.

Morocco Palace, Rue du Prince Moulay Abdallah. A clear winner among Tangier's night-spots, this strange, sometimes slightly manic place puts on traditional Moroccan music and dance (plus a couple of Egyptian belly-dancing sets) each night from around 9pm until 4am. Customers are predominantly Moroccan and expect – and get – a good show.

Concerts and films

Music concerts – traditional and popular – are sporadic events in Tangier. The old Spanish bullring, out near the bus station in the Ville Nouvelle, has had a recent major refurbishment as an open-air concert hall, so it might be worth asking about events there at the tourist office. Cultural events are also hosted by the **Old American Legation** (see p.70) and the **Centre Cultural Français** (pick up a programme from *Galerie Delacroix*, 86 Rue de la Liberté).

There are a dozen or so **cinemas** scattered about the Ville Nouvelle, in the grid around Boulevard Pasteur. Films are frequently shown in their original language, with Arabic subtitles, though some are dubbed into French. The *Cinema Rif* on the Grand Socco shows an exclusive and entertaining diet of Indian and Kung Fu films.

Shops and stalls

Many of the Tangier **market stalls and stores** are eminently avoidable, geared to selling tourist goods that wouldn't pass muster elsewhere. But a few are worthwhile, unique, or both; a half-hour preliminary browse at the more "fixed price" outlets on Boulevard Pasteur is useful for establishing roughly what you should pay for things.

Crafts and antiques

Ensemble Artisanal, Rue Belgique; left-hand side, going up from Place de France). Modern Moroccan crafts are displayed in this government-run store, as in other major cities. They are rarely the best or the cheapest available, but prices are (more or less) fixed, so this is a good first call if you feel you need to get an idea of quality and costs before bargaining elsewhere.

Bazaar Tindouf, 64 Rue de la Liberté, opposite the *Hôtel Minzah*. One of the better quality junk-antique shops, with a good array of cushion-carpets and old postcards. Bargaining is difficult but essential.

Khaliq Al Arabi, 22 Rue de Hollande (sign is in Arabic only). Another good junk/antique shop for browsing. The **Fes Market**, adjoining, is a lively area for fruit and vegetables.

Volubilis Boutique, 15 Place Petit Socco. A more than usually interesting mix of traditional Moroccan and Western fashion.

Perfumerie Madini, 14 Rue Sebou, in the Medina; from the Petit Socco take the alley between the *Tingis* and *Centrale* cafés, which leads into Rue Sebou, and look for the shop on your left. Madini makes inspired copies of brand-name perfumes from natural oils, which he sells at a fraction of the "real" price, as well as musk and traditional fragrances. Given a couple of days and a sample, he will reproduce any scent you like. Closed 1–4pm and Friday.

Rue Touahin – first right off Rue Saighin, entering the Medina from the Grand Socco. This line of jewellery stalls may turn up something appealing, though don't take silver, gold or most stones at face value: judge on aesthetics.

See also the details on markets on p.69.

Directory

Airlines *GB Airways,* 83 Rue de la Liberté (☎09/93.34.59) have flights to Gibraltar and London. For domestic flights (and some international destinations) contact *Royal Air Maroc* at 1 Place de France (☎09/93.47.22). For flights to Spain (cheapest departures are from Melilla) try *Iberia* at 35 Bd. Pasteur (☎09/93.61.779). *Air France,* 7 Rue du Mexique (☎09/93.64.77), may have good deals, too.

American Express Represented by *Voyages Schwartz*, 54 Bd. Pasteur (☎09/93.34.59). Open Mon–Fri 9am–noon and 3–7pm, Sat 9am–12.30pm only.

Banks Most are grouped along Bd. Pasteur/Bd. Mohammed V. The *BMCE bureau de change* on Bd. Pasteur is the most efficient, changing cash and travellers' cheques, and handling cash advances on *Visa* and *Access*; it's open 8am–2pm and 4–8pm every day of the week. The *SGMB* (opposite the main post office at 58 Mohammed V) takes some bank cheques backed by credit cards. *Crédit du Maroc,* Bd. Pasteur, also handles *Visa* transactions.

Beer and wine is sold by supermarkets in the Ville Nouvelle.

Books The long-established *Librairie des Colonnes* at 54 Bd. Pasteur has a fair selection of English-language books, including some of Paul Bowles's Moroccan translations. *Alfarabi*, 4 Fernando de Portugal, stocks second-hand books in English and French.

Car parking The *Hôtel Tanjah Flandria* (labelled T on the main plan) has an underground garage: 10dh for 24hr.

Car hire Most of the big companies have offices along Bd. Pasteur/Bd. Mohammed V – *Avis* at no. 54 (☎09/93.89.60), *Hertz* at no. 36 (☎09/93.33.22), *Europcar/InterRent* at no. 87

(☎09/93.82.71), among them. Cheaper and fairly reliable are *Leasing Cars*, 24 Rue Henri Regnault, and at the airport. Discounts are sometimes available if you arrange car hire through one of the package holiday representatives – contact them at any of the larger hotels (like the *Rif* on the seafront).

Car repairs Garages can be recommended by the *Royal Automobile Club de Maroc* at 8 Av. Prince Héritier. For Renaults, try *Tanjah-Auto*, 2 Av. de Rabat (☎09/93.69.38); for Citroëns try 33 Rue Victor Hugo (aka Rue Abou Alla Mari), one block behind the main post office; Garage Peugeot, 37 Rue Quevedo (☎09/93.50.93) has also been recommended.

Chemists There are several English-speaking chemists in the Place de France (try the Paris, opposite the *Café de Paris*) and along Bd. Pasteur.

Consulates include: **Britain**, 9 Rue Amérique du Sud (☎09/93.58.97; Mon–Fri 9am–12.30pm & 1–3.30pm); **France**, Place de France (☎09/93.20.39); **Spain**, Rue Sidi Bouadid (☎09/93.70.00) The **US** consulate has closed and the nearest diplomatic representation is in Rabat, see p.255).

LEAVING TANGIER

Travelling on **into Morocco** from Tangier is simplest either by **train** (the lines run to Meknes/Fes/Oujda or to Rabat/Casablanca/Marrakesh; all trains stop at Asilah en route), or, if you are heading east to Tetouan, by **bus** or shared **grand taxi**. Leaving the country, **ferries** run to Algeciras, Tarifa, Gibraltar and Sète (France).

TRAINS

There are two stations: the **Gare du Port** (by the port) and **Gare de Ville** (400 metres along the seafront from the port). At present the 4pm (Rabat/Casablanca; connection at Sidi Slimane for Meknes/Fes) and 11.30pm (Rabat/Casablanca/Marrakesh) trains leave from the Port station, calling at the Ville station ten minutes later. All other departures are from the Ville station only. There is a **baggage consigne** at the Ville train station, but it will accept locked luggage only; cafés across the road will oblige for a small fee.

If you **arrive in Tangier by ferry and plan to travel straight on**, the **4pm train** is likely to be the most convenient departure. The **11.30pm** departure is essentially a **night train to Marrakesh**. There is also a **12.30am** departure from the Ville station which is essentially a **night train to Oujda**. Neither of these trains runs in winter (Oct–June). They save losing a couple of days' travel (and a night's hotel bill), but if you take them, try to book a couchette, available as a supplement, which gives you a guaranteed booking and a separate carriage with an attendant – useful for baggage security. You're given bedding; take your own toilet paper.

Beware of hustlers saying you need to change at Asilah: you don't. It's simply a ruse to sell you carpets in their shop while you wait for the next train.

BUSES AND GRANDS TAXIS

Until recently, most of Tangier's **buses** left from down by the port entrance, but a recent shift has moved all departures to a **new terminal by the Syrian Mosque** at the end of Rue de Fes. This is around 2km from the centre of town, reached by following Rue de Fes to the Rue de Lisbonne roundabout where the road to the airport separates from that to Tetouan. It's a long walk, so either get a *petit taxi* (12dh) or one of the *Bourghaz* minibuses from the port entrance. Useful departures include **Tetouan** and **Chaouen** (the latter doesn't involve a change of bus, though you stop in Tetouan for 20 min; don't pay extra to hustlers there who might just suggest your ticket includes only a "reservation fare" for the Chaouen stage!).

English-language newspapers are sold outside the post office, in various stores along Bd. Pasteur, and by news dealers around the *Café de France*.

Medical treatment The **Croissant Rouge** on Rue El Mansour Dahbi (opposite the Roxy Cinema and next door to *Regine's* club) have a 24-hour English-speaking medical service.

Motorbike hire Bikes are available for short-term lease from the garage on Av. Youssef Ibn Tachfine.

Photographic developing *Studio Farah*, opposite the *Hôtel Minzah* on Rue de la Liberté, offers a good quality two-hour service.

Police Main station is on Rue Ibn Toumert. Emergency ☎19.

Post, Phones, Poste Restante All available at the main PTT, 33 Bd. Mohammed V; open Mon–Sat 8.30am–noon & 2.30–6.30pm; phone section is open 24hr. As Tangier has direct dialling you can phone (internationally) from any phone box or from one of the smaller PTTs; by day the PTT at the junction of Rue El Msala and Rue Belgique, opposite the Artisan Centre, is a quieter place to make phone calls – and, oddly, cheaper than at the main PTT.

There are **grands taxis** leaving through the day to **Tetouan**, again from the bus station by the Syrian Mosque. To get a place in a taxi, just announce yourself to the driver at the head of the rank. You will then be crammed (with five other passengers) into the car. The cost is only slightly more than going by bus and journey time is considerably less. Taxis can also be chartered here for expeditions further afield, direct to **Chaouen** or **Asilah** for example, and work out relatively economical shared between a group. On your own, heading for Chaouen, it's a lot cheaper to get a bus on from Tetouan. The cost of a place to Tetouan is a standard tariff (currently 20dh); all other destinations are negotiable.

For destinations in the immediate **vicinity of Tangier**, such as the Caves of Hercules or Cap Malabata, you need to negotiate a *grand taxi* at the rank by the old *Grand Hôtel Villa de France* on Rue de Hollande.

FERRIES AND HYDROFOILS

Details of **ferry/hydrofoil routes** are to be found in the "Basics" section of this book (see p.8). Tickets and timetables can be obtained from any travel agent in Tangier (there are several on Bd. Pasteur), or direct from the main agents:

Transmediterranea/Intercona, 31 Av. de la Resistance (☎09/93.67.45). Algeciras.

Limadet, 13 Rue du Prince Moulay Abdallah (☎09/93.36.21). Algeciras.

Comavit, 7 Rue du Mexique (☎09/93.12.20). Algeciras.

Comanav, 43 Av. Abou Alla El Maari (☎09/93.26.49). Algeciras.

Transtour, 4 Rue Jabha Al Ouatania (☎09/93.40.04). Tarifa/Gibraltar.

Transmediterranea/Intercona, 31 Av. de la Resistance (☎09/93.67.45). Sète.

Although **ferries** invariably depart an hour or so late, you should **check in** at the port at least one hour before official sailing time to get through the chaos of official business. At the ferry terminal, you have to get an embarkation card and departure card from the *depart* desk of the ferry companies, then you must take this, along with your passport, to the police *visa de passeport* desk on the same floor (opposite the bar), and have your passport stamped before going through customs to the boat. Arrive later than an hour before official departure time and you may find the visa police have knocked off – which means waiting for the next ferry. **Hydrofoils** have a separate *visa de passeport* desk and departures are normally on time.

Two **periods to avoid** the ferries from Tangier are the end of the **Easter week** (Semana Santa) holiday, and the **last week of August,** when the ferries can be full for days on end with Moroccan workers returning to northern Europe.

Tour companies *Nat Tours* (☎09/93.20.68) is a reliable company which can arrange hotel bookings and most aspects of travel in Tangier and elsewhere in Morocco.

Tourist office There's an ONMT office at 29 Bd. Pasteur (☎09/93.82.39), just down from Place de France and open Mon–Sat 8am–2pm. English speaking and helpful; ask for their free maps of Fes, Rabat-Salé and Marrakesh, all useful supplements to the ones we've printed.

Around Tangier: capes, caves and coast

The **Bay of Tangier** curves around to a pair of capes – Malabata to the east, Spartel to the west. Either make a pleasant detour or afternoon's trip, if you have a day to fill waiting for a ferry or flight.

West: the Caves of Hercules and "Atlantic Beach"

The **Caves of Hercules** is something of a symbol for Tangier, with its strange sea window, shaped (a little) like a map of Africa. The name, like Hercules' legendary founding of Tangier, is purely fanciful, but the caves, 18km outside the city and above the "Atlantic Beach", make an attractive excursion, together with the minor Roman site of Cotta. If you feel like staying for a few days by the sea, the beach can be an attractive base, too; even in midsummer only stray groups of visitors share the long surf beaches. Take care with currents, however, which can be very dangerous even near the shore.

Getting to the cape and caves, the cheapest access is on the local *Bourghaz* **minibus** service; this runs throughout the day from near the port gates. An alternative is to charter a **grand taxi** (from outside the old *Grand Hôtel Villa de France*, or by the port gates); this should cost around 120dh for the 36-km return trip – for which price most drivers can be persuaded to drop you in the morning and pick you up in the late afternoon; pay at the end. If you have your own transport, you can make a round trip by continuing from the caves along the S701 and then taking either the minor S702 or the faster P2 back to Tangier.

La Montagne, the Cape and the Caves

The most interesting route to the caves and cape runs around and above the coast via the quarter known as La Montagne. From Place de France, take Rue Belgique to the beginning of Rue de la Montagne. **"The Mountain"**, less imposing than its name suggests, was a rebel base against the British and Portuguese occupations of Tangier, but is now thoroughly tamed; its cork and pine woods shield the city's most exclusive villas. Among them are two vast royal palaces. The first, built by the Victorian British consul Sir John Hay, was (until her recent death), the residence of King Hassan's mother; the other, heavily guarded, is among the numerous retreats of the Saudi royal family.

After 14km from Tangier, you reach a short turnoff to the lighthouse at **Cap Spartel** – a dramatic and fertile point, known to the Greeks and Romans as the "Cape of the Vines"; the small *Café-Restaurant Sol*, nearby serves seafood meals, especially sardines and squid. Beyond and to the south begins the vast and wild "Atlantic Beach", known locally as **Robinson Plage**, broken only by a rocky spit – 4km from the Cape – and then rambling off for as far as you can see.

The **Caves of Hercules** are located on this spit. Natural formations, occupied in prehistoric times, they are most striking for a man-made addition – thousands of disc-shaped erosions created by centuries of quarrying for millstones. There were still Moors cutting stones here for a living until the 1920s, but by that time their place was beginning to be taken by professional guides and discreet sex hustlers; it must have made an exotic brothel. Today, there's a standard admission charge (9am–sunset), though you're unlikely to get away without a guide, too, whose descriptive abilities tend to be somewhat dwarfed by the utter obviousness of all there is to see ("wet cave", "dark cave", "sea", etc).

Ancient Cotta

Five minutes' walk past the caves, a track turns inland from the beach and leads you to the rather scant ruins of **Ancient Cotta**, a small Roman town, founded in the second century AD and occupied for 200 years or so. Like Lixus to the south (see pp.88–89), the town produced *garum* (a kind of anchovy paste) for export. Parts of the factory, and of a temple and baths complex, can be made out, while nearby have been found the ruins of several Roman farms which cultivated olives for oil. Even before the Romans, and certainly afterwards, this was a well-populated and prosperous area.

Accommodation

Close by the caves, on the same rocky spit, is a **hotel**, the *Hôtel Robinson* (☎09/ 93.87.65; ③), a pleasant old-established place, and a **restaurant**, *Le Mirage*, with a fine terrace overlooking the sea, and a group of apes (to rival those of Gibraltar, across the straits). On the wooded, landward side of the restaurant there is also a **campsite**, *Camping Robinson* (see p.68). The *Mirage* has a **swimming pool**, open to anyone having a meal, and a bar; at its shop you can hire fishing tackle, or arrange for a horse (or, under supervision, camel) for a ride along the beach.

East: Cap Malabata and Ksar es Seghir

The best beaches in the immediate vicinity of Tangier are to be found at **Cap Malabata**, where much wealthy villa development has been taking place. Beyond, here, if you have transport, **Ksar es Seghir**, offers a pleasant stop on the coast road to Ceuta.

Cap Malabata and Villa Harris

The bay east of Tangier is flanked by an almost continuous chain of villas and apartments up until the "complexe touristique" of **Cap Malabata**, a resort strip dominated by a *Club Méditerranée*. This encompasses – and, sadly, restricts access to – the splendid turn-of-the-century **Villa Harris** and its gardens, built by the writer Walter Harris (see p.69) and given by him to the people of Tangier. Harris's wife rather decently cited his obsession with the garden (rather than his predilection for boys) in her case for divorce. Notwithstanding the Villa, and some indeterminate ruins said to be either Roman Tingis or a Portuguese fort, the best reason for a trip to the Cape is for a swim and lunch at the excellent *Restaurant Mar-bel*, owned by an Italian and right on the beach.

You can get to Cap Malabata on bus #15 from the Grand Socco, or by local taxi, but once **around the cape** the buses give out (save for a single daily bus from Tangier to Ksar es Seghir), along with the hotels and villas. There is in fact virtually no development the whole way down the coast to Ceuta: just a beautiful road winding above enticing stretches of beach in the north.

Ksar es Seghir and Djebel Moussa

If you can overcome the transport problem, **KSAR ES SEGHIR** is as relaxed and picturesque a base as could be imagined, still largely enclosed by twenty-foot-high Portuguese walls. A small fishing port, it attracts a fair number of Moroccan summer campers, but few Europeans. There's a friendly café-restaurant on a terrace above the sea and there may be **rooms** for rent if you ask around.

South of Ksar es Seghir the road to Fnideq climbs around the **Djebel Moussa** – the mountain which, with Gibraltar, forms the so-called Pillars of Hercules, gateway to the Classical world. Mythologies aside, the twin pillars effect remarkable thermal currents, speeding passage for **migratory birds** at this, the shortest crossing between Africa and Europe. A spring or autumn visit will almost guarantee sightings, as up to 200 species make their way across the Straits.

Asilah

The first town beyond Tangier – and the first stop on the railway – **ASILAH** is one of the most elegant of the old Portuguese Atlantic ports, ranking with El Jadida and Essaouira to the south. First impressions are of wonderful square stone ramparts, flanked by palms, and an outstanding beach – an immense sweep of sand stretching halfway to Tangier. Further exploration reveals the Medina, which is one of the most attractive in the country, colour-washed at every turn, and with a series of murals painted for the town's annual International Festival. In addition, the town itself is small, easy to manage, and very clean – perhaps due in part to the fact that the country's Minister of Culture maintains a residence here.

The minister is also closely involved in the **International Festival**, a month-long event encompassing art exhibitions and a series of performances – ranging from Lebanese singers to European jazz, Moroccan folk musicians to American university choirs. It is followed by a three-day **horse fair**, with a *fantasia* (cavalry charge with muskets) display on each of the days.

Arriving and accommodation

The **train station** is 2km north of the town – an easy enough walk if you miss the connecting bus. Arriving by **grand taxi** (1hr from Tangier), or by **bus**, you're dropped in or around **Place Mohammed V**, a small square at the edge of the Medina, a short walk from the ramparts and a prominent gate, **Bab El Kasaba**.

Hotels

Asilah can be packed full during the International Festival, but most of the year accommodation is easy to find and inexpensive. The following recommendations are in ascending order of price.

Hôtel Nasr, Place Mohammed V, facing the ramparts and the sea. A pretty basic place, but pleasantly run and with the cheapest accommodation around. ①

Hotel Al-Karam, Rue Allal Ben Abdallah. Straw-hut rooftop room, by the beachs. ①

Hôtel Marhaba, 9 Rue Zellaca (☎09/91.71.44). Slightly more comfortable and expensive – and crazily decorated. ①

Hôtel Asilah, 79 Av. Hassan II (☎09/91.72.86). Not very welcoming, though rooms on a terrace above the ramparts, overlooking the daily vegetable market, are quite attractive. ①

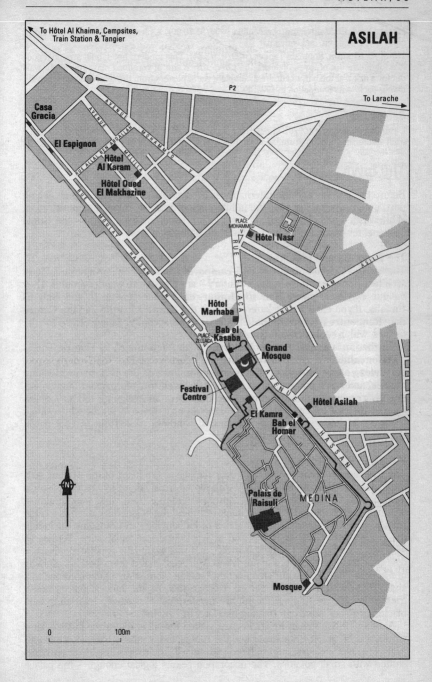

ASILAH

To Hôtel Al Khaima, Campsites,
Train Station & Tangier

P2

To Larache

Casa
Gracia

El Espignon

Hôtel
Al Karam

Hôtel Oued
El Makhazine

PLACE
MOHAMMED
V

Hôtel Nasr

Hôtel
Marhaba

Bab el
Kasaba

PLACE
ZELLACA

Grand
Mosque

Festival
Centre

El Kamra

Bab el
Homar

Hôtel Asilah

Palais de
Raisuli

MEDINA

Mosque

0   100m

Hôtel Oued El Makhazine, Av. Melilla (☎09/91.70.90). A pleasant and comfortable hotel, close to the seafront, and with a bar. ②

Hôtel Al Khaima, Route de Tanger (☎09/91.72.34). This modern hotel, built around a pool, is a kilometre out of town, opposite the *Camp Africa* site. If you don't stay, you might walk out for a drink at the bar, to admire a complete set of posters from the International Festivals, dating back to its foundation in 1975. ③

Campsites

Camping Echrigui (☎09/91.71.82). This is the closest of a string of campsites south of the train station, about 500m from the town. It is well maintained and as good a choice as any.

The town

Before the tourists and the International Festival, Asilah was just a small fishing port, quietly stagnating after the indifference of Spanish colonial administration. Whitewashed and cleaned up, it now has a prosperous feeling to it – the Grand Mosque, for example, has been rebuilt and doubled in size.

The ramparts and Medina

The Medina's circuit of **towers and ramparts** – built by the Portuguese military architect Botacca in the sixteenth century – are pleasant to wander around. They include two main gates: **Bab El Homar**, on Avenue Hassan II, and **Bab El Kasaba**. If you enter by the latter, you pass the **Grand Mosque** and the **Centre des Rencontres Internationales**, a venue and accommodation centre for the festival, with a cool open courtyard.

Further on is a small square overlooked by the "red tower", **El Hamra**. This is used for exhibitions, particularly during the International Festival. Turn right past here, along a tiny network of streets, and down towards the platform overlooking the sea, and you'll come upon at least a half-dozen **murals** painted (and subsequently repainted) during the festivals; they form an intriguing mix of fantasy-representational art and geometric designs. In turn, these offset the white-wahed walls of the houses, with their doors and windows picked out in cool pastel shades. It's quite an entrancing quarter.

Palais de Raisuli

The town's focal sight – stretching over the sea at the heart of the Medina – is the **Palais de Raisuli**, built in 1909 with forced tribal labour by one Er Raisuli, a local bandit. One of the strangest figures to emerge from what was an almost routinely bizarre period of Moroccan government, he began his career as a cattle rustler, achieved notoriety with a series of kidnappings and ransoms (including the British writer Walter Harris and a Greek-American millionaire, Perdicaris, who was bailed out by Teddy Roosevelt), and was eventually appointed governor over practically all the tribes of northwest Morocco. Harris described his captivity in *Morocco That Was* as an "anxious time", made more so by being confined in a small room with a headless corpse. Despite this, captor and captive formed a friendship, Harris finding Raisuli a "mysterious personage, half-saint, half-blackguard", and often entertaining him later in Tangier.

Another British writer, Rosita Forbes, visited Raisuli at his palace in 1924, later writing his biography. She described the rooms, today mostly bare, as hung with rugs "of violent colours, embroidered with tinsel", their walls lined with cushions stuffed with small potatoes. The decoration seems logical enough – the palace today still looks more like a glittering Hollywood set than anything real. The great reception room, a long glass terrace above the sea, even has dialogue to match: Raisuli told Forbes that he made murderers walk to their death from its windows – a ninety-foot drop to the rocks. One man, he said, had turned back to him, saying, "Thy justice is great, Sidi, but these stones are more merciful".

The palace overhangs the sea ramparts towards the far end of the Medina (away from the beach). It is used in August for the International Festival but is difficult to obtain entry to at other times. If you're interested (and the interior is worth seeing), knock or ask around and you may strike lucky with the caretaker. He may refuse entry on the grounds that the building (which is also known as the Palais de la Culture) is being prepared for the next International festival – albeit six months off. And then, during the festival, entry is often restricted to official guests. If you are really determined, enlist the help of a local, or visit the Hôtel de Ville beforehand and ask them to give you a note in Arabic for the caretaker.

Restaurants, cafés, the market and hammam

The town's most prominent **restaurants** are *El Oceano* and *La Alcazaba*, facing each other in the Place Zellaca, just outside the ramparts. Both have outdoor tables and Spanish-style fried fish; *La Alcazaba* scores for its site, with tables shaded by palms, across the road, and a roof terrace overlooking the ramparts and harbour; *El Oceano* has, alas, acquired a microwave. Further north along the seafront are a couple of similar restaurants, *Casa Gracia* and *El Espignon*, again specialising in fish and seafood; the latter is convenient for the campsites.

Asilah's other diversions include a fine **music café**, *Café Haddou*, by the *Hôtel Azilah*, and a **disco**, in season, at the *Hôtel Al Khaima* (there are other summer discos at the campsites, such as *Club Solataire* and *Safari Club*, north of town) There's a Djebali villagers' **market**, at its liveliest on Thursday and Sunday, held on the far side of the Tangier–Rabat road. Ask directions to the town's small **hammam**, tucked down an alleyway in the north of the Medina. Unusually, the keeper charges Westerners a group rate and gives you the place to yourselves.

The beaches

As with Tangier, the **beach** is the main focus of life. The most popular stretches are to the north of the town, past the building works for a new marina and port complex and out towards the campsites. For more isolation, walk south, past the Medina ramparts, for about fifteen minutes.

Mzoura

If you have an interest in ancient sites, you might devote a half-day to explore the prehistoric **stone circle of Mzoura**, south of Asilah. The site, whose name means "Holy Place" in Arabic, originally comprised a tumulus, assumed to be the tomb of some early Mauritanian king, enclosed by an elliptical circle of some 167 standing stones. It was excavated in 1935 and the mound is now reduced to a series of watery hollows. To the north of the circle, there still stands a tall, upright stone known as El Uted, where, legend has it, Sebastian, the young king of Portugal, picnicked on his way from Asilah, where he had landed, to his death the following day at the cataclysmic Battle of the Three Kings at Ksar El Kebir (see pp.90 and 494–95). There is a model of Mzoura, pre-excavation, in the archaeological museum in Tetouan.

To reach Mzoura, follow the P12 south of Asilah for 16km, then turn left along the P37 towards Tetouan. After crossing the railway line, and 4km from the junction with the P2, turn left by a petrol station and onto a side road signposted Sidi El Yamina and Mzoura. From here the site is 5km northeast, across a confusing network of sandy tracks; it would be wise to take a guide from Sidi El Yamina.

Larache

LARACHE is a relaxed, easy-going resort, its summer visitors primarily Moroccan tourists. In consequence it is one of the best towns of the north in which to spend a few days by the sea: the local beach to the north is superb and for once is very mixed, with as many women around as men – a reassuring feeling for women travellers looking for a low-key spot to bathe. Nearby, too, are the ruins of **ancient Lixus**, legendary site of the Gardens of the Hesperides.

Physically, the town looks like an amalgam of Tangier and Tetouan – an attractive place, if not spectacularly so. It was the main port of the northern Spanish zone and – though the central Plaza de España has become Place de la Libération – still bears much of its former stamp. There are faded old Spanish hotels, Spanish-run restaurants and Spanish bars, even an active Spanish cathedral for the small colony who still work at the docks. In its heyday it was quite a metropolis, publishing its own Spanish newspaper and journal, and drawing a cosmopolitan population that included the French writer Jean Genet, who spent the last decade or so of his life here.

Before the Spanish colonisation in 1911, Larache was a small trading port, its activities limited by dangerous offshore sand bars. Without these, it might have rivalled Tangier, for it is better positioned as a trade route to Fes. Instead, it eked out a living by building pirate ships made of wood from the nearby Forest of Mamora for the "Barbary Corsairs" of Salé and Rabat. There had been an earlier period of Spanish occupation in the seventeenth century, before it was reclaimed and repopulated by Moulay Ismail.

Accommodation

Larache has some decent accommodation but there's not a lot of choice. In summer, you'd be well advised to book ahead.

Hôtel Saada [C], 16 Av. Moulay Mohammed Ben Abdallah (☎09/91.36.41). Basic but cheap and clean. ①

Pension Amal [D], Rue Abdallah Ben Yasin (☎09/91.27.88). Clean, quiet and friendly, this is signposted – off to the left down an alleyway – on the street from the bus station to the Place de la Libération. ①

Pension Atlas [E], in the Medina. The only hotel in the tiny Medina – it is just to the right as you go in through the gate. Nothing much to recommend it. ①

Hôtel Cervantes [B], Place de la Libération. Somewhat grim. ①.

Hôtel España [A], Place de la Libération/entrance on Av. Hassan II (☎09/91.31.95). The Grand Hotel in Spanish days – much decayed but retaining a touch (and no more!) of elegance. ①

Hôtel Riad [F], Av. Moulay Mohammed Ben Abdallah (☎09/91.26.26). The town's "smart" hotel looks grand enough – it was the former mansion of the Duchesse de Guise, mother of the current pretender to the French throne – but it is in dire need of an overhaul and has a distinctly musty feel to its bedrooms. It does, however, have quite a fine restaurant-bar. ③

The town and beach

The town's circular main square, the **Place de la Libération** – originally, of course, the Plaza de España – is a striking piece of Spanish colonial architecture. It is set just back from the sea and a straightforward 400-metre walk from the (combined) bus station and *grand taxi* stand.

A high archway, **Bab El Khemis**, at the centre of the *place* leads into the **Medina**, a surprisingly compact wedge of alleys and stairways leading down towards the port. It is now the poorest area of Larache – better-off families have moved out to the new parts of town, leaving their houses here to the elderly – but it doesn't seem so bad a place to live, artfully shaded and airy in its design. The colonnaded market square, just inside the archway, was again built by the seventeenth-century Spanish.

If you carry on through the Medina, you can reach the small Place de Makhsen, below the **Château de la Cigogne** (Stork's Castle), a hulking, three-sided fortress compound from the original Spanish occupation. Standing back from here, to the right, is a bizarre Andalucian palace, built by the Spanish in 1915 and now used as a music school. Opposite, overlooking the Oued Loukos and across to Lixus, is a fine esplanade and a small **museum**, converted from a prison (and complete with dungeon), containing a few Roman coins and other relics from Lixus.

The beach and coastline

If you walk from the Place de la Libération, directly to the seafront, you find yourself on another and longer promenade, Avenue Moulay Ismail. The shore below here is wild and rocky, but cross its estuary of the Oued Loukos and there are miles of fine sandy **beach** sheltered by trees and flanked by a handful of café-restaurants. You can get there by bus (#4 from the port, every 20min – some buses start from the *place*), a circuitous seven-kilometre route, or, more fun, from the port in a flotilla of small **fishing boats** (1.5dh per person fare) which shuttle across from the base of a flight of stone steps and help you out in the shallows on the other side. From the *place*, the quickest route down to the **port** is along the promenade and under the crumbling ruins of the **Fort Kebibat** (Little Domes), built by Portuguese merchants in the sixteenth century.

In summer, an oddity on the beach is the variety of foreign languages you hear – yet with so few foreigners around. The explanation is the number of migrant families, scattered about Europe, who return to the town for the holiday. As well as communities in Barcelona, Naples and Paris, Larache accounts for most of the Moroccan community in London, and on the beach you're likely to come upon kids with disarming English accents. Almost all of the London Moroccans come from the Bayswater area.

For an alternative walk, head to the south of the town, **along the cliffs** to the **lighthouse** and past the jail, and you will eventually come to the neglected Spanish Christian cemetery, where **Jean Genet** is said to be buried. Another version has it that Genet made a deathbed conversion to Islam and is buried in the main Muslim cemetery.

Eating and drinking

Meals in Larache, except at the Medina cafés, or the sardine grills down by the port, remain resolutely Spanish. The cheapest cafés are in the Place de la Libération, around the entrance archway of the Medina. For seafood, try *Restaurant Larache* at 18 Av. Moulay Mohammed Ben Abdallah, next door to the *Hôtel Saada*, or the Estrella del Mar at the end of Ave. Mohammed Zerktouni. Take a look, too, at the restaurant at the *Hôtel Riad*, which is a lot better standard than the accommodation there.

The *Hôtel Riad* also has a good **bar**. Another is to be found on Rue Abdallah Ben Yasin, close by the *Hôtel Amal*; this looks a dive but it is friendly enough – and prices are half those in the *Riad*.

Ancient Lixus

Ancient Lixus is one of the oldest – and most continuously – inhabited sites in Morocco. It had been settled in prehistoric times, long before the arrival of Phoenician colonists around 1000 BC, under whom it is thought to have become the first trading post of North Africa. Later, it was in turn an important Carthaginian and Roman city, and was deserted only in the fifth century AD, two hundred years after Diocletian had withdrawn the empire's patronage. There are remains of a church from this period, and Arabic coins have also been found.

As an archaeological site, then, Lixus is certainly significant, and its legendary associations with Hercules (see box below), are rich soil for the imagination. It has to be said, though, that the visible ruins are not especially impressive, and only around a quarter of the site has ever been excavated. Even so, if you're spending any amount of time in Larache, or passing through by car, the Lixus ruins are good for an hour or two's exploration. They lie upon and below the summit of a low hill on the far side of the estuary leading south from the town, at the crossroads of the main Larache–Tangier road and the narrow lane to Larache beach. It's a four- to five-kilometre walk to the ruins from either the beach or town, or you can use the bus which runs between the two; alternatively, for about 75dh you could charter one of the boats to row you over from Larache, wait an hour or so, and then row you back to the town or beach. The site is not effectively enclosed, so there are no real opening hours.

The site

The site's **Lower Town**, spreading back from the modern road, consists largely of the ruins of factories for the production of salt – still being panned nearby – and, as at Cotta, anchovy-paste *garum*. The factories seem to have been developed in the early years of the first century AD by the Carthaginians, and they remained in operation until the Roman withdrawal.

A track, some 100m down the road to Tangier, leads up to the Acropolis (upper town), passing on its way eight rows of the Roman **theatre** and **amphitheatre**, unusually combined into a single structure. Its deep, circular arena was adapted for circus games and the gladiatorial slaughter of animals. Morocco, which Herodotus knew as "the wild-beast country", was the major source for these Roman *venationes*, and local colonists must have grown rich from the trade. Amid **baths** built into the side of the theatre, a mosaic remains in situ, depicting Neptune and the Oceans.

Climbing above the baths and theatre, you pass through ramparts to the main enceinte (fortifications) of the **Acropolis** – a somewhat confused network of walls and foundations – and **temple sanctuaries**, including an early **Christian basilica** and a number of **pre-Roman buildings**. The most considerable of the sanctuaries, with their underground cisterns and porticoed priests' quarters, were apparently rebuilt in the first century AD, but even then retained Phoenician elements in their design.

LIXUS AND HERCULES

The **legendary associations** of Lixus – and the site's mystique – centre on the Labours of Hercules. For here, on an island in the estuary, Pliny and Strabo record reports of the palace of the "Libyan" (by which they meant African) King Antaeus. Behind the palace stretched the **Garden of the Hesperides**, to which Hercules, as his penultimate labour, was dispatched.

In the object of Hercules' quest – the **Golden Apples** – it is not difficult to imagine the tangerines of northern Morocco, raised to mythic status by travellers' tales. The site, too, seems to offer reinforcement to conjectures of a mythic pre-Phoenician past. Megalithic stones have been found on the Acropolis – they may have been linked astronomically with those of Mzoura (see pp.85–86) – and the site was known to the Phoenicians as Makom Shemesh (City of the Sun).

Heading south towards Fes or Rabat

Heading **south from Larache**, the main road and most of the buses bypass **Ksar El Kebir** on their way towards Meknes, Fes or Kenitra/Rabat. You'll probably do likewise, though the town does have one of the largest weekly markets in the region on Sundays). Just past here, you cross the old border between Spanish and French colonial zones. Beyond, Roman enthusiasts may want to explore the minor sites at **Banassa** and **Thamusidia**, while **birdwatchers** should head for the lagoon and local bathing resort of **Moulay Boussleham**.

Ksar El Kebir

As its name – in Arabic, "the Great Enclosure" – suggests, **KSAR EL KEBIR** was once a place of some importance. Founded in the eleventh century, it became an early Arab power base and was enlarged and endowed by both Almohads and Merenids, and perennially coveted by the Spanish and Portuguese of Asilah and Larache. It was close by here that, in 1578, the Portuguese fought the disastrous **Battle of the Three Kings**, the most dramatic and disastrous in their nation's history – a crusading expedition which saw the death or capture of virtually the entire nobility; for the Moroccans it resulted in the fortuitous accession to power of Ahmed El Mansour, the greatest of all Merenid sultans.

The town fell into decline in the seventeenth century, after a local chief incurred the wrath of Moulay Ismail, causing him to destroy the walls. Neglect followed, although its fortunes revived to some extent under the Spanish protectorate, when it served as a major barracks.

Practicalities

The **Sunday souk** is held right by the bus and *grand taxi* terminals. On any morning of the week, however, there are lively **souks** around the main **kissaria** (covered market) of the old town – in the quarter known as *Bab El Oued* (the Gate of the River). There is also an active **tannery** on the south side of the Medina and a handful of minor Islamic monuments scattered about. With time to spare, there would probably be some reward in engaging a local to show you around.

If you want to stay, ask directions to the *Café-Hôtel Andaluz* (⓪), which has clean **rooms** and a fair bit of charm.

Arbaoua and Souk El Arba du Rharb

Beyond Ksar El Kebir, a decaying customs post at **ARBAOUA** marks the old colonial frontier between the Spanish and French zones. There is a row of worthwhile **pottery stalls** at the border post, while close by, on the wooded hill, is a group of French-built hunting lodges and a **hotel**, the *Hostellerie Route de France* (☎09/90.26.29; ②), which does highly recommended French meals and has a friendly bar. Adjoining it is a **campsite**, though beware that the land to the west of here is a hunting reserve.

South again, **SOUK EL ARBA DU RHARB** is the first settlement of any size, though it is little more than its name suggests (Wednesday Market of the Plain), a roadside sprawl, with some grill-cafés and a couple of **hotels**, the unwelcoming

Grand (☎07/90.20.20; ⑩) and the *Gharb* (☎07/90.22.03; ⑦; under restoration at last check). The town is not, in any case, a very compelling place to stay, though you may want to head here for transport connections to Ouezzane (a standard *grand taxi* run, or infrequent buses) or Moulay Bousselham (regular *grands taxis* and buses).

Moulay Bousselham

MOULAY BOUSSELHAM is a very low-key resort, popular almost exclusively with Moroccans. It comprises little more than a single street, crowded with grill-cafés and sloping down to the sea at the side of a broad lagoon and wetland area, known as **Merdja Zerga**. This is one of northern Morocco's prime **birdwatching** locations (see below), and any foreign visitor will be enouraged to see the lagoon's flamingo and other bird colonies in one of the locals' fishing boats.

The **beach** itself is sheltered by cliffs – rare along the Atlantic – and has an abrupt drop-off, which creates a continual thrash of breaking waves. While a lot of fun for swimming, the currents can be highly dangerous and the beach is strictly patrolled by lifeguards. Take care.

Accommodation, food and a festival

Most Moroccan visitors to Moulay Bousselham stay at the lagoon **campsite**, which is beautifully positioned but is very run down and plagued by mosquitoes; it is also open in summer only. If you don't want to camp, the alternatives are distinctly limited: you might get a **room** above one of the cafés (or even a house if you stay a week or more: ask around). Otherwise there are just two small **hotels**. The best of these is a new, family-run villa, the *Villanova Club* (③), on the seafront, which comes highly recommended. The other is the older *Le Lagon* (☎28; open June–Sept only; ③), which also has the only **bar** in the place, along with a somewhat ritzy nightclub.

WETLAND WILDLIFE: MERDJA ZERGA

Adjoining the Moulay Bousselham lagoon is a large wetland area – recently given protected wildlife status – known as **Merdja Zerga** (or Merdja Lerga). This open barren space is used for grazing by nomadic herds of sheep, cattle and goats, while around the periphery are lines of dwarf palm and the giant succulent agave.

This diversity of habitat, and the huge extent of the site, ensures rewarding **birdwatching** at all times of year. There are large numbers of waders, including a large colony of flamingoes, plus little ringed plovers, black-winged stilts and black-tailed godwits. These can be seen most easily by taking a boat trip – though make sure that you arrange to set off at least an hour before high tide, though, or you will run aground a tantalising distance from the birds – and, of course, need to rent the boat again the next day.

For serious birdwatchers, it is the **gulls and terns** that roost on the central islands which are worthy of the closest inspection, as among the flocks of lesser black-backed gull and black tern, it is possible to find rarer species such as **Caspian tern**. Sunset is a time for vigilance as the site also boasts several pairs of North African **marsh owl** which hunt over the adjacent grassland after dusk.

If you're after food, any of the grill-cafés will fix you a mixed platter of fish – served in copious quantity and at very reasonable prices.

The saint from which the village takes its name, the **Marabout Moulay Bousselham**, was a tenth-century Egyptian, whose remains are housed in a *koubba* prominently positioned above the settlement. In July this sees one of the largest **moussems** – or religious festivals – in the region.

Banasa and Thamusida

This pair of minor Roman sites is really of specialist interest – and for those with transport. **Banasa** lies south of Souk El Arba, and **Thamusida** just west of the main P2 road to Kenitra.

Banasa

BANASA was settled from around 250BC, but later enlarged by Octavian (the future Emperor Augustus) as a colony for veterans. It was linked by both land and water with Lixus (see pp.88–89) and prospered into the second and third centuries AD, the period from which most of the visible ruins date. Within the traces of the city walls, the central feature is a forum, around which stood the capitol, a basilica (or law courts) and municipal buildings. In the town, among the houses and shops, were two public baths.

The custodian, who lives nearby, will probably notice your arrival and add a little life to the stones. He can point out a few mosaics, though most, he claims, have been removed to museums.

The site is easy to find. Leave Souk El Arba by the main road (P2) to Kenitra, then, just after Souk Tleta, turn left onto a minor road, crossing the Oued Sebou by a bridge. After 2km you reach a T-junction with the S210: turn left and, after another 2km, look for a track on the left (better signposted coming the other way). This leads to the ruins, which are overlooked by a *koubba*.

Thamusida

THAMUSIDA is more or less contemporary with Banasa, some 45km to the north. A Roman camp and small town, it was occupied from around 200BC, fortified fifty years later, and abandoned by 250AD, after fire damage. You can trace the walls of the camp and barracks, and make out a temple and baths, though the site as a whole is less extensive – and less interesting than Banasa; its setting, however, closer to the Oued Sebou, is impressive.

There are two possible **approaches** to the site, which is quite tricky to find. Neither approach is signposted and both are along tracks impassable in wet weather. The **first** approaches the site from the east. Leave the Souk El Arba road 13km north of Kenitra by a petrol station on the right hand side and near a few houses known as Souk El Khemis. After a couple of kilometres, the track splits three ways: follow the central track. The **second**, possibly easier to find, approaches from the southwest. Continue on the P2, under the railway bridge, and 8km from Kenitra turn right along a track signposted Nkhakhsa (2476); there is a level crossing and then the village of Ahmed Taleb. Once again, the track divides several times.

In both cases, look (and ask) for a prominent *koubba*, dedicated to Sidi Ali Ben Ahmed, and a favourite picnic spot for locals. The site lies between this *koubba* and the river.

CEUTA, TETOUAN AND CHAOUEN

The Spanish enclave of **Ceuta** is a slightly frustrating port of entry. Although in Africa, you are not yet in Morocco, and you must make your way to the border at Fnideq, then on from there to **Tetouan**, the first Moroccan town. It can be a time-consuming business. However, if you are making for **Chaouen**, Tetouan has the advantage of regular bus connections.

An alternative, seasonal, port of entry is the village of **Mdiq**, north of Tetouan, which has a weekly (currently Thursday) catamaran connection with Gibraltar. This could be the gentlest of all introductions to Morocco. Mdiq apart, the **Mediterranean** here has few resorts of note, though **Martil** is pleasant enough, as (in its own, basic way) is the "travellers' resort" of **Oued Laou**, in the shadow of the Rif. All are easily reached from Tetouan.

Ceuta (Sebta)

A Spanish enclave since the sixteenth century, **CEUTA** (SEBTA in Arabic) is a curious political anomaly. Along with Melilla, east along the coast, it was retained by Spain after Moroccan independence in 1956 and today functions largely as a military base, its economy bolstered by a limited duty-free status. It is something of an embarassment for the Spanish government, in the light of its own claims to Gibraltar, visible just a few sea miles across the straits. They would find it hard politically to return the colony to Morocco, and, in many ways, nobody is much interested in their so doing. Large numbers of Moroccans live and/or work in Ceuta and the economies on both sides of the border seem to benefit.

Currency, incidentally, is relaxed, with both dirhams and pesetas used and accepted in shops and restaurants.

The town

Ceuta has a long and eventful history, with occupation by Phoenicians, Romans, Visigoths and Byzantines, prior to the Moors, who from the eighth century onwards used it as a springboard for invasions of Andalucia. The Europeans only regained pre-eminence in the fifteenth century, with Portugal first taking control, and ownership passing to Spain in 1580. In 1936, the port was used by Franco to launch his revolt against the Spanish Republic, igniting the Spanish Civil War.

All of this notwithstanding, there's not a great deal to see – or to do. The town is modern, functional and provincial in the dullest Spanish manner, and its most attractive part is within a couple of hundred metres of the ferry dock, where the **Plaza de Africa** is flanked by a pair of Baroque churches, **Nossa Senhora de Africa** (Our Lady of Africa) and the **Cathedral**. Bordering the square, to the west, is the **Foso de San Felipe**, a walled moat that is all that survives of the town's fortress. Beyond here is a one-room **Museu Arqueologico** (Tues–Sun 9am–1pm & 5–7pm), which is scarcely worth the time of day. Its only possible appeal would be to visit the subterranean galleries below but these are at present closed to visitors.

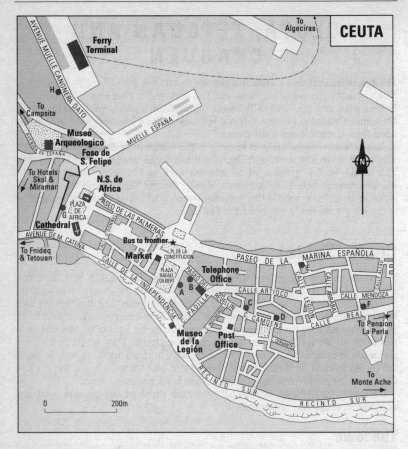

Over to the east of the Plaza de Africa, an oldish quarter rambles up from the end of the long **Paseo del Revellin**. To the south, the **Museu de la Legión** (Sat & Sun only 11am–2pm & 4–6pm), on the Paseo de Colón, offers an intriguing glimpse of Spanish-African military history, crammed with uniforms, weapons and paraphernalia of the infamous Spanish Foreign Legion.

If you walk to the end of the Paseo del Revellin, you can continue along a circuit of the peninsula, which is known as **Monte Acho**, in little over an hour. As the buildings, three to a dozen blocks in width, gradually disappear from view, the land swells into a rounded, pine-covered slope, offering fine views out to the Rock of Gibraltar. Around midway, signs direct you to the **Ermida de San Antonio**, an old convent rebuilt during the 1960s and dominated by a monument to Franco.

And that's about it, as far as diversions go. The local authorities plan to create a town beach, but at present there are no sands to speak of – locals go by bus to **Playa Benzou**, some way out of town. The duty-free status of the port draws many of the Tangier expatriates on day trips to buy cheap spirits, and Spanish day-trippers to buy radios and cameras, but neither are very compelling pursuits for casual visitors. If you do want a cheap bottle for Moroccan travels, check the *Roma* supermarket on Paseo del Revellin.

Accommodation and food

If you plan to stay overnight in Ceuta, be warned that it isn't easy to find a room – and not cheap when you do; with its large garrison and its consumer goods, the town has a constant flow of Spanish families. Accommodation problems are compounded at **festival times**, the main events being Carnival (February), Holy Week, the Fiesta de Nuestra Señora de Monte Carmel (July 16), and the Fiesta de Nuestra Señora de Africa on August 5.

Note that, **phoning Ceuta** from Morocco (or anywhere else outside Spain), you must prefix phone numbers with the international code (☎0034). Dialling numbers within Ceuta, omit the local code (☎56).

Accommodation

Most of the town's dozen or so hotels and *hostales*, and cheaper *pensiones*, *casas de huespedes* and *fondas* are to be found along the main thoroughfare, Paseo del Revellin, or its extensions, Calle Camoens and Calle Real. Available options include:

Pousada de Juventud/Youth Hostel [A], Plaza Rafael Gilbert 27. Dormitory beds and rooms for two to six people, but open during July and August only. IYHFA cards are required.

Casa de Huespedes Revellin [B], Paseo del Revellin 2, 2nd floor (☎56/51.67.62). Okay. ①

Pension Rosi 2 [C], Calle Camoens (☎56/51.97.56). Again, adequate. ①

Pension Marina [E], Calle Marina Española 26 – 3rd floor (☎56/51.32.06). Fairly basic – and tiny. ①

Pension Los Angelos [F], Calle Real (☎56/51.38.92). Adequate. ①

Pension La Perla, Calle Real (☎56/51.58.28). Off our map – about 100m further along from the *Gran Hôtel Ulises* . Reasonable. ①

Hôtel-Residencia Africa [H], 9 Avda. Muelle Canonero Dato (☎56/50.94.70). A useful new hotel, sited right opposite the ferry terminal. ②

Hôtel Skol (☎56/51.41.48), **Hôtel Miramar** (☎56/51.41.46), Avda. Reyes Catolicos 6 and 23. A pair of reliable, two-star hotels, 1km out from the centre; off our map. ③

Gran Hôtel Ulises [D], Calle Camoens 5 (☎56/51.45.40). Comfortable but pricey. ④

Gran Hôtel La Muralla [G], Plaza de Africa 15 (☎56/51.49.40). The local *parador*. Ceuta's prime choice if you can afford it. ④

Camping Marguerita (☎56/50.38.40). Ceuta's only campsite – 4km out of town to the west. If you're travelling by car, take the Avda. de España and follow the signs; after 3km, look for a signpost and a steep sideroad up to the left. There are hot showers and a restaurant; no shop.

Food and drink

Ceuta's main concentration of restaurants is around the Plaza de la Constitucion and includes a couple of Indian restaurants (Indians also run many of the duty-free shops). Possibilities include:

Gran Muralla, Plaza de la Constitución 4. Popular Chinese restaurant.

Delfin Verde, Avda. Muelle Cananero Dato, opposite the ferry terminal.

Casa Silva, Calle Real 87. Fish and seafood specialities. Moderate to expensive.

Meson de Serafin, Monte Hacho. Good views as well as cooking, on the peninsula. Moderate to expensive.

Regina, Calle Independencia. Multitudes of *tapas* and *raciones*.

Pub Bo-Go, Pasaje Cervantes. All-night bar.

Restaurant La Torre, in the Gran Hôtel La Muralla, Plaza de Africa (☎56/51.49.40). Generally reckoned to be the best restaurant in town, serving Andalucian classics. Expensive.

ENTERING MOROCCO FROM CEUTA: FNIDEQ

Since the Algeciras–Ceuta ferries and hydrofoils are quicker than those to Tangier (and the ferries significantly cheaper for cars), Ceuta is a popular **point of entry**. Coming over on a first visit to Morocco, however, try to arrive early in the day so that you have plenty of time to move on to Tetouan – and possibly beyond. There is no customs/passport check at the port. You don't officially enter Morocco until the border at **FNIDEQ**, 3km out of town. This can be reached by local bus from the centre of Ceuta (turn left as you come off the ferry or hydrofoil and it is about 800m away, in Plaza de la Constitución).

At **the border**, formalities are brief on the **Spanish side** (at least, if you are leaving Spain: searches are common for those coming back – and there are long tailbacks of cars on Sunday evenings). On the **Moroccan side**, they are often rather convoluted and time-consuming, especially for drivers. What you need to obtain to get across is a registration form (yellow or white) for yourself, and, if you have a car, an additional green form; these are available – if you ask for them – from the security *chefs* outside the frontier post. The car form requires inconvenient details such as chassis number and date of registration. If you despair of getting a form and having it processed, you can always enlist an official porter (they have badges – ask to see them) for a 10dh tip. The whole business can take ten minutes on a good day, an hour on a bad one.

Once across and into Morocco proper, the easiest transport is a shared **grand taxi** to **Tetouan** (20dh per person) or **Chaouen** (60dh per person); buses also run infrequently to Tetouan. There are **exchange facilities**, which accept cash and travellers' cheques, at the frontier.

Drivers should note that **petrol/gas** in Ceuta is about 40 percent cheaper than in Morocco, so stock up as best you can.

FERRIES TO SPAIN

Leaving Ceuta **by ferry** for Algeciras, you can normally turn up at the port, buy tickets, and board a ferry within a couple of hours. The two periods to avoid, as at Tangier, are the end of the **Easter week** (Semana Santa) holiday and the **last week of August**, when the ferries can be full for days on end with Moroccan workers returning to northern Europe.

If you plan to use the quicker **hydrofoil service** to Algeciras, it's best to book the previous day – though you should be okay outside the high season; details and tickets are available from the agents at Avenida Muelle Caõnero Dato 6 (☎56/51.60.41), by the ferry terminal.

For details of ferry services, see p.8.

Be aware that all arrivals from Ceuta need to go through customs at Algeciras – and drug suspects are very thoroughly searched.

Tetouan

If you're a first-time Moroccan visitor coming from Ceuta, **TETOUAN** will be your introductory experience to a Moroccan city: a disadvantage that you'll quickly be made aware of. The Medina here seems – initially – overwhelming and totally unfamiliar, and the hustlers, often dealing large quantities of *kif* from the nearby Rif mountains, have the worst reputation in Morocco. On the positive side, the city is home to a large university (based at Martil), so people you meet are just as likely to be genuine students – but you do need to keep your wits about you for the first few hours, especially at the bus station.

Physically, Tetouan is strikingly beautiful, poised atop the slope of an enormous valley against a dark mass of rock. Its name (pronounced *Tet-tá-wan*) means "open your eyes" in Berber, an apparent reference to the town's hasty construction by Andalusian refugees in the fifteenth century. The refugees, both Muslims and Jews, brought with them the most refined sophistication of Moorish Andalusia – an aristocratic tradition that is still reflected in the architecture of the Medina. Their houses, full of extravagant detail, are quite unlike those of other Moroccan towns; indeed, with their tiled lintels and wrought-iron balconies, they seem much more akin to the old Arab quarters of Córdoba and Seville.

Orientation, accommodation and meals

Despite first impressions (particularly if you arrive at the chaotic bus station), and the "guides" and "students" who lay claim to new arrivals, Tetouan is not too hard a city in which to get your bearings – or to find your own way around. If you arrive by bus, or by *grand taxi*, you'll find yourself on the edge of the **Ville Nouvelle** – slightly left of centre near the bottom of our town map. Built by the Spanish as the capital of their colonial zone, this quarter of town follows a straightforward grid. At its centre is **Place Moulay El Mehdi**, with the PTT (post/telephone office) and main banks, and from there the grid stretches east towards the Medina, still partially walled and entered from a gateway onto the town's main square, the ever-busy **Place Hassan II**.

The **Medina** is not as large as it appears and, by day at least, you won't get lost for long without coming to an outer wall or gate – beyond which you can loop back to the Ville Nouvelle. Specific points of interest are detailed in the section following and are not too hard to find on your own. If this is your first foray into Morocco, however, you might want to consider arranging an **official guide** at the **tourist office**, a few metres down Bd. Mohammed V from Place El Mehdi. The office (Mon–Fri 8am–2pm & 3–6pm, Sat & sometimes Sun 8am–2pm) will also **change money** when the banks are closed.

If you run into trouble, the main **police station** is on Rue de Prince Sidi Mohammed (the former Bd. General Franco – as some signs still proclaim).

Accommodation

Try to ignore all offers from touts and head for one of the recommendations below and keyed on the map on the previous page. You're likely to get the best deal at the **classified hotels**; most **unclassified pensions** (including those we've listed) raise their prices well above basic rates in summer. This is partly because newly arrived tourists will pay whatever they're asked, but it also reflects

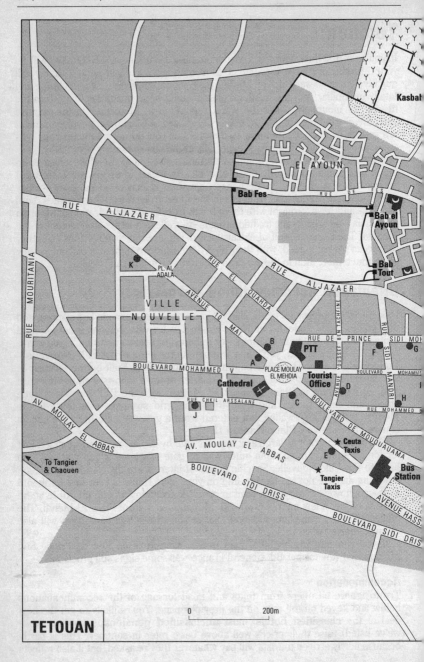

TETOUAN

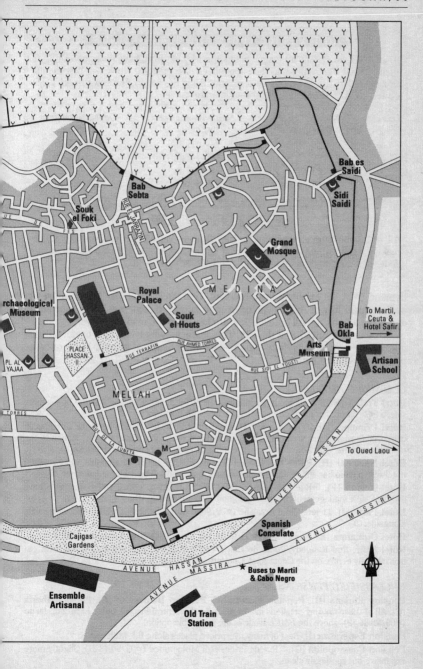

Bab es
Saidi

Sidi
Saidi

Bab
Sebta

Souk
el Foki

Grand
Mosque

M E D I N A

rchaeological
Museum

Royal
Palace

Souk
el Houts

To Martil,
Ceuta &
Hotel Safir

Bab
Okla

Arts
Museum

PLACE
HASSAN
II.

RUE TERRAFIN

RUE AHMED TORRES

RUE SIDI EL YOUSTI

Artisan
School

PL. AL
YAJAA

MELLAH

TORRES

RUE DE LA LUNETA

To Oued Laou

AVENUE HASSAN II

AVENUE MASSIRA

Spanish
Consulate

Cajigas
Gardens

★ Buses to Martil
& Cabo Negro

Ensemble
Artisanal

AVENUE HASSAN II MASSIRA

AVENUE HASSAN II

Old Train
Station

N

HOTEL PRICE CODES AND STAR-RATINGS

As of 1993, hotels are no longer obliged to levy set maximum rates, according to their official star-ratings, as had long been the custom. However, **prices** still broadly follow the star-rating system, and this is the basis of our own **hotel price codes** set out below and keyed throughout the guide.

Our code	Official classification	Single room price	Double room price
⓪	Unclassified	25–60dh	40–100dh
①	1*A/1*B	60–105dh	100–125dh
②	2*B/2*A	105–145dh	125–175dh
③	3*B/3*A	145–225dh	175–275dh
④	4*B/4*A	225–400dh	275–500dh
⑤	5*luxury	Upwards of 400dh	Upwards of 500dh

TELEPHONE CODES

All telephone numbers in the Tangier/Tetouan region are prefixed 09. When making a call within the region you omit this prefix. For more explanation of phone codes and making calls within (or to) Morocco, see pp.37–38.

---

demand. With its excellent local beaches, Tetouan is a popular Moroccan resort and rooms in July or August can be in short supply. If at all possible, phone ahead and make a booking. All hotels below are keyed on the map overpage.

There is no **campsite** in the city. The nearest – which can be a useful fallback if you have problems finding a room – is on the beach at **Martil**, 11km out (see p.104 for transport details).

CLASSIFIED HOTELS

Hôtel Trebol [E], 3 Av. Yacoub El Mansour (☎09/96.20.18). Right behind the bus station; safe, a little damp, but more or less adequate and with hot showers. ①

Hôtel Principe [D], 20 Av. Youssef Tachfine (☎09/96.27.95). Much better in all respects: comfortable rooms and showers that function. Sited midway up from the bus station to the main *place* of the Ville Nouvelle. Has a ground-floor café for breakfast and snacks. ①

Hôtel Nacional [H], 8 Rue Mohammed Torres (☎09/96.32.90). Reasonable, old-fashioned hotel with a patio bar and restaurant; sometimes insists on full board in midsummer. ①

Hôtel Regina [F], 5 Rue Sidi Mandri (☎09/96.21.13). After a spell when standards have dropped, new management now ensures good value for money. ①

Hôtel Paris [J], 11 Rue Chkil Arsalane (☎09/96.67.50). Adequate if a little dull, with a café alongside. ②

Hôtel Oumaima [K], Rue 10 Mai (☎09/96.34.73). Central, clean and functional. ②

Hôtel Safir, Rue Kennedy/Route de Ceuta (☎09/96.70.44). Package tour hotel, 3km out from the city centre on the Ceuta road. Comfortable but hardly worth the extra. ④

UNCLASSIFIED PENSIONS

Pension Riojana [B], **Pension Florida [A]**, **Pension Bienvenito [A]**, **Pension Iberia [C]**. All of these are tiny pensions in – or just off – the central Place Moulay El Mehdi. *Iberia* (☎09/96.36.79), above the *BMCE* bank, is the preferable option.

Pension Esperanza [I]. Best of many overpriced places along Bd. Mohammed V.

Pension Cosmopolita [G], 5 Rue de Prince Sidi Mohammed (☎09/96.48.21). Slightly more expensive but spotlessly clean.

Pension Camas [L], Pension Suiza (M), Rue Luneta. Both very basic – on a narrow street at the edge of the Medina, reached from the corner of Place Hassan II.

There are some thirty or so other pensions, a few of them within the Medina itself – most around its periphery. The highest concentration is in **Place Hassan II**, which separates the Ville Nouvelle and Medina. These, the favourite choice of bus station hustlers, are to be avoided; if a guide brings you here, he'll have virtual access to your room as long as you stay, and he's *not* going to believe that you don't want to buy *kif*, or anything else on offer. The **Hôtel Dersa** – which used to be the city's best hotel – is also not recommended, having dropped all three of its stars and become a very seedy den of dealers and prostitutes.

Restaurants

As ever, the cheapest food is to be found in the **Medina**, particularly the stalls inside Bab El Rouah and along Rue Luneta in the Mellah. For variety, try one of the many places on or around **Bd. Mohammed V** or **Rue Mohammed Ben Larbi Torres** in the Ville Nouvelle. Good choices include:

Restaurant Moderne, Pasaje Achaach, off Rue Mohammed Ben Larbi Torres (to find it, go through the arcades opposite *Cinema Español* on Place Hassan II). One of the best budget restaurants in town; extensive menu with fast, friendly service; no alcohol. Open 9am–9pm.

Restaurant Zarhoun, 7 Rue Mohammed Ben Larbi Torres. A little pricier but with an attractive traditional salon, *tapas* in the licensed bar, and Spanish clientele from Ceuta – a recommendation in itself. Open noon to midnight; closed Sun.

Restaurant Saigon, Rue Mohammed Ben Larbi Torres. Cheap.

Bar Italiano, Rue Mohammed Ben Larbi Torres. Beer and free *tapas*.

The Medina

Tetouan has been occupied twice by the Spanish. It was seized, briefly, as a supposed threat to Ceuta, from 1859 to 1862, a period which saw the Medina converted to a town of almost European appearance, complete with street lighting. Then in 1913 a more serious, colonial occupation began. Tetouan served first as a military garrison for the subjugation of the Rif, later as the capital of the **Spanish Protectorate Zone**, and as such almost doubled in size to handle the region's trade and administration.

"Native tradition" was respected to the extent of leaving the Medina intact, and even restoring its finer mansions, but in social terms there was very little progress. Spanish administration retained a purely military character, and only a handful of schools was opened throughout the entire zone. This legacy had effects well beyond independence in 1956, and the town, alongside its Rif hinterland, adapted with difficulty to the new nation, dominated by the old French zone. Its relationship with the central government continues to be uneasy, and it was at the centre of the 1984 riots.

Place Hassan II and the Mellah

Looking around Tetouan, the place to orientate yourself is **Place Hassan II**, the old meeting place and market square. This used to have a very Spanish character, formal gardens at its heart and a Mauresque Spanish Consulate taking up the east side, but in 1988 it was completely remodelled, with a pavement of Islamic motifs replacing the gardens, minaret-like floodlights at each corner and a brand new Royal Palace – replacing the Spanish Consulate and incorporating parts of an old nineteenth-century Caliphal Palace that stood beside it. It's all quite a shock if you've visited in the past.

The usual approach to the Medina is through **Bab El Rouah** (Gate of the Winds), the archway just south of the Royal Palace. The next lane south of this opens on to the main street of the **Mellah**, which was built as late as 1807, when the Jews were moved from an area around the Grand Mosque. Very few of the population remain today, although if you ask around someone will probably point out the old synagogues.

Into the Medina: the souks

Entering the Medina proper, at Bab El Rouah, you find yourself on **Rue Terrafin**, a relatively wide lane which (with its continuations) cuts straight across to the east gate, Bab El Oqla. To the left of Rue Terrafin, a series of alleys give access to most of the town's food and craft *souks*. The **Souk El Houts**, a small shaded square directly behind the grounds of the Royal Palace, is one of the most active: devoted to fish in the mornings, meat in the afternoons, and with an all-day smattering of local pottery stalls.

From the north side of the square, two lanes wind up through a mass of alleys, *souks* and passageways towards Bab Sebta. Following the one on the left for about twenty metres you'll see an opening (on the right) to another small square. This is the **Guersa El Kebira**, essentially a cloth and textile *souk*, where a number of stalls sell the town's exceptional *foutahs* – strong and brilliantly striped lengths of rug-like cotton, worn as a cloak and skirt by the Djebali and Riffian women.

Leaving the Guersa at its top right-hand corner, you should emerge more or less on **Place de l'Oussa**, another beautiful little square, easily recognised by an ornate, tiled fountain and trellis of vines. Along one of its sides is an imposing nineteenth-century **Xharia**, or almshouse; on another is an *artesania* shop, elegantly tiled and with good views over the quarter from its roof.

Beyond the square, still heading up towards Bab Sebta, are most of the specific **craft souks** – among them copper and brass workers, renowned makers of *babouches* (thick leather slippers), and carpenters specialising in elaborately carved and painted wood. Most of the shops along the central lane here – **Rue El Jarrazin** – focus on the tourist trade, but this goes much less for the *souks* themselves.

So, too, with the nearby *souks* around **Rue de Fes**, which is reached most easily by following the lane beside the Royal Palace from Place Hassan II. This is the main thoroughfare of a much more mundane area selling ordinary everyday goods, with the occasional villagers' **Joutia**, or flea market. At its main intersection – just to the right as you come out on to the lane up from Place Hassan II – is **Souk El Foki**, once the town's main business sector, though it's little more than a wide alleyway. Following this past a small perfume *souk* and two sizeable mosques, you meet up with Rue El Jarrazin just below **Bab Sebta**.

Walk out this way, passing (on your left) the superb portal of the **Derkaoua Zaouia** (no admission to non-Muslims), and you enter a huge **cemetery**, in use since at least the fifteenth century and containing unusually elaborate Andalusian tombs. Fridays excluded, non-Muslims are tolerated in most Moroccan cemeteries, and walking here you get illuminating views over the Medina and across the valley to the beginning of the Rif.

Had you proceeded along the main drag of Rue Terrafin/Rue Ahmed Torres/ Rue Sidi El Yousti, you would have reached the eastern edge of the Medina at **Bab Okla**. The quarter to the north of here, below the Grand Mosque, was the Medina's most exclusive residential area and contains some of its finest mansions. Walking towards the gate you see signs for a *Palais*, one of the best of the buildings, but converted into a carpet and crafts warehouse aimed at tourists.

The Museum of Moroccan Arts and the Crafts School

Considerably more authentic, and an interesting comparison for quality, is the **Museum of Moroccan Arts** (*Musée d'Art Marocain*), whose entrance is just outside Bab Okla. A former arms bastion, the museum has one of the more impressive collections around of traditional crafts and ethnographic objects. Take a look particularly at the *zellij* – enamelled tile mosaics – and then cross the road to the **Crafts School** (*École de Métiers*), where you can see craftsmen working at new designs in the old ways, essentially unmodified since the fourteenth century. Perhaps owing to its Andalusian heritage, Tetouan actually has a slightly different *zellij* technique to other Moroccan cities – the tiles are cut before rather than after being fired. A slightly easier process, this is frowned upon by the craftsmen of Fes, whose own pieces are more brittle but brighter in colour and closer fitting.

Both school and museum are open 9am–noon and 2.30–5.30pm on Monday, Wednesday, Thursday and Friday; 9am–noon only on Saturday; closed Tuesday and Sunday; the school closes down for most of August.

Centre Artisanal and Archaeological Museum

Outside the Medina the most interesting sight is the **Centre Artisanal** on the main road below the town. The regular exhibits on the ground floor are well worth a check if you're planning to make purchases in the *souks* and want to assess prices and quality first. But where it scores most highly is in the displays of craftworking. Go up the stairs, at either the front or back of the main building, and you come to a fascinating array of carpet and embroidery workshops, while outside the building there are metalwork, basketry and musical instrument artisans at work.

If time needs filling, there is also a pleasant, if rather unmemorable, **Archaeological Museum** (same hours as Museum of Moroccan Arts, above). This was assembled during the Spanish protectorate, so it features exhibits from throughout their zone: prehistoric stones from the Western Sahara among them. Highlights, as so often in North Africa, are the Roman mosaics, mostly gathered from Lixus and the oft-plundered Volubilis.

Leaving Tetouan: transport

From the main **bus station** there are regular departures to Chaouen, Meknes, Fes and Tangier; ask around for times at the various windows, as both *CTM* and private companies operate on each of these routes, and, if it's convenient, take the *CTM*. Beware of con-men at the station. Tales abound of youths posing as bus officials and demanding "supplements" or "booking fees" on top of your ticket – often on the bus itself; resist and, if needs be, appeal to your fellow passengers.

Heading for **Tangier** or **Ceuta** it's easiest to travel by **grand taxi**; these are routine runs – just go along to the ranks (see map) and get a place (currently 25dh and 15dh, respectively); it's also possible to negotiate a price for Chaouen (around 250dh – for up to six passengers). Ceuta taxis (or buses) will drop you at the border; once there, you can walk across and pick up a Spanish bus for the 3km into town.

For the **beaches** at Martil, Cabo Negro and Mdiq – each easy day trips – buses leave frequently through the day in summer from behind the old train station on the road to Ceuta, or from the bus station in winter. For **Oued Laou**, there are two buses daily from the main station (7am and 5pm), or – considerably easier – you can share a *grand taxi* (from the Oued Laou road junction).

If you prefer to travel on by **train**, make your way to the **ONCF office** on Avenue 10 Mail, alongside Place El Adala and facing the *Avenida* cinema – three blocks northwest of Place El Mehdia in the Ville Nouvelle. This sells through tickets to Fes, Rabat, Marrkesh, etc, including a connecting bus service (leaving at 6.50am and 3.55pm) to the station of Tnine Sidi Lyamani, just south of Asilah.

The Tetouan beaches: Mdiq to Oued Laou

Despite the numbers of tourists passing through, Tetouan is above all a resort for Moroccans, rich and poor alike – a character very much in evidence on the extensive beaches to the east of the town. Throughout the summer, and particularly after Ramadan, whole villages of family tents appear at **Martil**, **Mdiq** and, further down the coast, particularly around **Restinga-Smir** and on towards the frontier with Ceuta at Fnideq. At **Oued Laou**, 40km southeast of Tetouan, there's a younger and slightly alternative atmosphere – something which is attracting small but growing groups of German, French and, to a lesser extent, British and American travellers.

West: Martil, Cabo Negro and Mdiq

MARTIL, essentially Tetouan's city beach, was its port as well until the river between the two silted up. From the fifteenth to eighteenth centuries, it maintained an active corsair fleet, twice provoking Spanish raids to block the harbour. Today it is a small but active fishing village with a slightly ramshackle appearance, owing to unmade roads and the rows of tourist huts along the seafront. The beach, stretching all the way around to the fashionable villas of Cabo Negro, is superb – a stretch of fine, yellow sand that is long enough (at 8km!) to remain uncrowded, despite its summer popularity.

There are various options for accommodation. For a simple pension **room**, try the *Hôtel Nuzha* (①; open in summer only), on Rue Miramar, or the nearby *Pension Rif* (①; open all year) on Boulevard Tetouan; both of these are on the east side of town, by the signposted *Camping Martil*, and if they don't have room, they may be able to find you a private room. More expensive, but value for money, is the *Hôtel de l'Étoile de la Mer* (☎09/96.92.76; ②), on the seafront by the *grands taxis* stand; known locally as the *Nejuna El Bahr*, it has a café and restaurant. The *Restaurant Rio Martil*, opposite, competes with good seafood meals.

Of the two **campsites**, *Camping Martil*, set just back from the beach, is friendly and cheap, though not a place to leave bags unattended. *Camping Oued El Mellah* (signposted out of town) has similarly limited security and facilities; it does, however, have shade and access to the beach through a wood.

Cabo Negro

Most of the Martil buses go on to **CABO NEGRO**, at the far end of the beach. This is an attractive alternative for lying about on the sands, with a jetty and rocks to explore, though the only accommodation available is at the rather upmarket *Hôtel Petit Merou* (☎09/96.81.15; ③). It would be wise to book ahead for this, or, in summer, for a meal at the *Restaurant La Ferma* (☎09/96.80.75), which is known for its lobster. The restaurant also runs stables, where **horses** can be hired for rides along the beach.

Mdiq

MDIQ is a lovely coastal village and fishing port, which can be approached via Martil and Cabo Nero, or direct from Tetouan (18km on the P28). Though it is getting a little overdeveloped, its beach is superb and there are some nice places to stay. The best of these is the *Residence Jbel Zem Zem* (☎09/97.32.19; ③), eighteen self-contained flatlets, with a café on the ground floor and wonderful views. A cheaper alternative is the *Hôtel Plaza* (☎09/97.51.66; ①), which has a bar and a good restaurant. Nearby, but at the other extreme, is a major resort hotel, the *Golden Beach* (☎09/97.50.96; ④). There is no campsite.

Restinga-Smir and Fnideq

RESTINGA-SMIR is more a collective name for a length of beach than for an actual place or village: an attractive strip of the Mediterranean, but a little too dominated by package hotels and "holiday villages". Nevertheless, many Moroccan families still camp in the woods between here and Fnideq. The rather spartan but inexpensive *Al Fraia* **campsite**, here, opposite the *El Andalouz* tourist complex and 15km from Fnideq, makes a good first or last stop in the country in summer; in winter it's open but deserted and not so secure.

In addition, there is a new **hotel** in **FNIDEQ**, just 2km from the border: the *Hôtel Ceuta* (☎09/97.61.40; ①), on Avenue Mohammed V. Fnideq, however, has little to recommend it, except a busy market for cheap Spanish goods.

Southeast: in the shadow of the Rif

Southeast of Tetouan the coastline is almost immediately distinct. For a few kilometres, the road (S608) follows the sea and the still more or less continuous beach, dotted with communities of tents. But very soon it begins to climb into the foothills of the Rif, a first taste of the crazily zigzagging Moroccan mountain roads, though in this case always with the sea down below, and including the occasional swoop down to cross the estuary of a fast mountain stream. Alongside one such stream, the **Oued Amsa**, is *Camping Amsa* (18km from Tetouan); in winter the river often sweeps away the bridge to the campsite but in summer all is tranquility and the site is nicely shaded.

Tetouan is connected to Oued Laou by **bus** and **grand taxi** (see p.104).

Oued Laou

When you finally emerge at **OUED LAOU** (44km from Tetouan), you're unlikely to want to return too immediately. A stay, in any case, is a positive option. Oued Laou is not an especially pretty place – Riffian villages tend to look spread out and lack any core. However, it has a terrific, near-deserted beach, which extends for miles on each side, particularly to the southeast, where the river has created a wide, fertile bay down to Kaaseras, 8km distant. Equally important, Oued Laou is a very easy-going sort of place and one of the best parts of the Rif to meet and talk with local people. Hustlers have nothing to hustle except *kif* and rooms, and aren't too bothered about either; having come out here, off the tourist track, it is assumed that you're not completely innocent.

There are two small **hotels** and a campsite. The *Hôtel-Café Oued Laou* (⑨) is open all year round and has hot showers in winter; the *Hôtel-Restaurant Laayoune* opens from mid-June to mid-September only and has no showers. They are to be found side by side, one block from the beach on Boulevard Massira. If they are full, or if you want to pay a bit less, they'll find you **rooms** elsewhere – everyone knows everyone here. Camping Oued Laou (open year round) is a secure site, a hundred metres back from the beach. A new café is being built here, to add to a small cluster of restaurants. On Saturdays, there is a **souk**, held 3km inland of the beachside settlement, which draws in villagers from all over the valley; look for the terracotta pottery, fired locally.

East: Kâaseras, El Jebha and the roads to Chaouen

Heading east from Oued Laou is quite complicated without your own transport. The coast road is now paved all the way to **El Jebha** (see below), but just one bus a day, leaving Tetouan at 7am, travels the full six-hour-plus, 120-km, route, via Oued Laou, Kaaseras, Targa and Bou Hamed.

It's little problem to get a taxi as far as **KÂASERAS**, however, just twenty minutes from Oued Laou – and in similar mould. A tiny resort, it is geared towards Moroccans camping on the beach, though there are usually a few rooms to be had, if you ask around. If you are heading from Oued Laou to Chaouen, it's possible to drive (or get a bus connection) via Kâaseras, and continue along the minor road (8304) up the Oued Laou valley – which includes some impressive gorge sections. At present, a bus from Kâaseras leaves for Chaouen at 6am, and returns in the afternoon, leaving Chaouen at 5pm.

It's also possible to make a circuit to Chaouen via **EL JEBHA** (see p.119), though just two buses a week do the run, up through the Rif. In addition, this village is not the most appealing of destinations – a shabby sort of place, with little beyond a group of fishermen's cottages and a strip of not-terribly-clean beach.

Chaouen (Chefchaouen, Xaouen)

Shut in by a fold of mountains, **CHAOUEN** becomes visible only once you have arrived – a dramatic approach to a town which, until the arrival of Spanish troops in 1920, had been visited by just three Europeans. Two of these were missionary explorers: Charles de Foucauld, who spent just an hour in the town, disguised as a rabbi, in 1883, and William Summers, an American who was poisoned by the townsfolk here in 1892. The third, in 1889, was the British journalist Walter Harris, whose main impulse, as described in his book, *Land of an African Sultan*, was "the very fact that there existed within thirty hours' ride of Tangier a city in which it was considered an utter impossibility for a Christian to enter".

This impossibility – and Harris very nearly lost his life when the town was alerted to the presence of "a Christian dog" – had its origins in the foundation of the town in 1471. The region hereabouts was already sacred to Muslims due to the presence of the tomb of Moulay Abdessalam Ben Mchich – patron saint of the Djebali tribesmen and one of the "four poles of Islam" – and over the centuries acquired a considerable reputation for pilgrimage and *marabouts* – "saints", believed to hold supernatural powers. The town was actually established by one of Moulay Abdessalam's *shereefian* (descendant of the Prophet) followers, Moulay Rachid, as a secret base from which to attack the Portuguese in Ceuta and Ksar es Seghir. In the ensuing decades, as the population was boosted by Muslim and Jewish refugees from Spain, Chaouen grew increasingly anti-European and autonomous. For a time, it was the centre of a semi-independent Emirate, exerting control over much of the northwest, in alliance with the Wattasid sultans of Fes. Later, however, it became an almost completely isolated backwater. When the Spanish arrived in 1920, they were astonished to find the Jews here speaking, and in some cases writing, medieval Castilian – a language extinct in Spain for nearly four hundred years.

These days, Chaouen is well established on the excursion routes and indeed becoming a little over-concerned with tourism. There are the inevitable *souks* and stalls for the tour groups, a monstrous hotel that has been allowed to disfigure the twin peaks (*ech-Chaoua*: the horns) from which the town takes its name, and hustlers, sadly, are on the increase. But local attitudes towards tourists, and to the predominantly backpacking travellers who stop over, remain relaxed; pensions are among the friendliest and cheapest around, and to stay here a few days and walk in the hills remains one of the best possible introductions to Morocco.

Orientation and rooms

With a population of around 20,000 – a tenth of Tetouan's – Chaouen is more like a large village in size and feel, and confusing only on arrival. **Buses** and **grands taxis** drop you on one or other side of the marketplace, outside the walls of the town in a vague straggle of new buildings grouped about the Mosque of Moulay Rachid. There are a couple of **banks** here for money exchange: the *Banque Marocaine* and *Banque Populaire*.

To reach the Medina, walk up across the marketplace to the tiny arched entrance, **Bab El Ain**, just beyond the prominent *Hôtel Magou*. Through the gate a clearly dominant lane winds up through the town to the main square, **Place Outa El Hammam** (flanked by the gardens and ruined towers of the **Kasbah**) and, beyond, to a second, smaller square, **Place El Makhzen**.

Both along and just off this main route in the Medina are a series of small, **unclassified pensions**, converted from private houses. These are the places to stay for anyone wanting to meet and mix with fellow travellers – rooms can be a bit cell-like, but most are exceptionally clean and remarkably inexpensive. For more comfort (and less "community life"), several of the **classified hotels** in the adjoining Ville Nouvelle quarters are good value, too.

Unclassified pensions

As these are all so close together in the Medina, and prices all very similar (a very low 25–40dh for a double room), they are listed in descending order of recommendation.

Pension Abi Khancha (A), 57 Rue Lala El Hora (☎09/98.68.79). An excellent new pension, 30m up on the right from the Bab El Ain. A converted house, it has an open courtyard, salon and a high terrace. ①

Pension Znika (H), Rue Znika (☎09/98.66.24). Another new, excellent-value pension, with welcoming management, and plans to add a café-restaurant on its panoramic terrace. ①

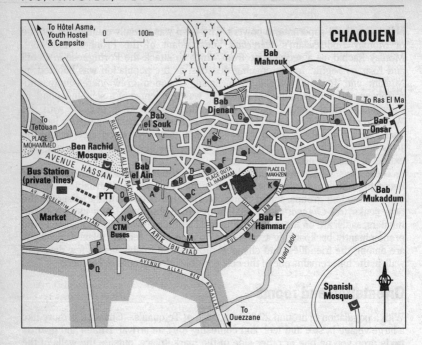

Pension Castellana (E), 4 Rue Bouhali (☎09/98.62.95). Just to the left at the near end of Place Outa El Hammam – follow the signs. Aficionados return loyally to the *Castellana* each year, creating a distinctly laid-back and youthful atmosphere; others take one look and leave! The manager often arranges communal meals. ⑩

Pension Valencia (G), Rue Hassan I (☎09/98.60.88). Clean, well-maintained travellers' hostel, a shade hippy; opposite is the excellent *Restaurant Granada*. ⑩

Hôtel Andaluz (D), 1 Rue Sidi Salem (☎09/98.60.34). Small, basic pension, whose rooms face an inner courtyard – not too airy, but otherwise okay, and with a very nice manager. It is signposted off to the left at the near end of Place Outa El Hammam. ⑩

Pension Al Hamra (J), Rue Ibn Askar Hay (☎09/98.63.62). A good new pension, slightly out of the way, in the higher quarter of the Medina, going up towards Bab Onsar. ⑩

Pension Cordoba (I), Rue Granada. And yet another new pension, converted from a traditional, turn-of-the-century Berber house. Good value for money, as is the *Restaurant Tissemal* next door. ⑩

Pension Ibn Batouta (B), Rue Sidi Boukhancha (☎09/98.60.44). One of the quietest of the pensions, with less feel of a "travellers' hang-out"; located in an alley to the left, about 70m along from Bab El Ain. Cold showers only. ⑩

Hôtel Mauretania (C), 15 Hadi Alami (☎09/98.61.84). For the participatory: communal dormitories, as well as individual rooms, awash with rock music and international bonhomie. Located down a network of alleys to the southeast of Place Outa El Hammam. ⑩

Hôtel El Kasabah (F), 15 Hadi Alami (☎09/98.62.26). Just off Place Outa El Hammam – but not so clean as the rest, cold showers only, and hardly recommended. ⑩

Classified hotels

Hôtel Bonsai (P), 12 Rue Sidi Srif (☎09/98.69.80). A new hotel in a converted house, with scented orange trees in the garden. A pleasant owner, who has returned from Casablanca. ①

Hôtel Sahara (N), 9 Rue Zarktune (☎09/98.66.15). Close to Bab El Ain and the market. Lacks atmosphere but is functional and good value. ①

Hôtel Salam (L), 39 Rue Tarik Ibn Ziad (☎09/98.62.39). Just below Bab El Hamman and long a favourite with individuals and groups. Back rooms and a shady roof terrace overlook the valley. Meals are served in a salon or on the terrace. Highly recommended. ①

Hôtel Rif (M), 29 Rue Tarik Ibn Ziad (☎09/98.69.82). Attracts a mainly youthful clientele, with its well-stocked sound system, bar, restaurant, and low rates for long stays. Opinions differ on the management; women travelling alone have, in the past, cautioned others not to stay here. ②

Hôtel Panorama (Q), 33 Rue Moulay Abderrahmane Chrif (☎09/98.66.15). Friendly new hotel near the CTM bus station. Quiet, with fantastic views from the roof terrace of the Medina and valley below. ①

Hôtel Magou (O), 23 Rue Moulay Idriss (☎09/98.62.75). Overlooking the market. Well established, comfortable but a bit dull. ②

Hôtel Parador de Chaouen (K), Place El Makhzen (☎09/98.61.36). The former Spanish "grand hotel", once part of the parador chain, recently reconstructed for the package trade. The bar and swimming pool help justify the expense. ④

Hôtel Asma (off map), (☎09/98.60.02). An ugly modern building on the site of an old fort, half an hour's walk above the town. Comfortable rooms geared for package trade. ④

The campsite and youth hostel

Chaouen's **campsite** is on the hill above the town, by the *Hôtel Asma* (see above), whose signs you can follow along the road; on foot, there is a shortcut through the cemetery. It is shaded and inexpensive but can be crowded in summer. The **youth hostel** (*auberge de jeunesse*), adjoining, has dormitory beds – but you'd be better off in a Medina pension.

The town and river

Like Tetouan, Chaouen's architecture has a strong Andalusian character: less elaborate (and less grand), perhaps, but often equally inventive. It is a town of extraordinary light and colour, its whitewash tinted with blue and edged by soft, golden, stone walls – and it is a place which, for all its present popularity, still seems redolent of the years of isolation. The roofs of its houses, tiled and with eaves, are an obvious physical assertion, in contrast to the flat ones found everywhere else in Morocco. But it is something you can sense about life in general here, even about the people themselves – inbred over many generations.

The souks and Mellah

Since the Medina is so small, it is more than ever a place to explore at random: the things which draw your attention are not so much "sights" as unexpected strands of detail. At some point, though, head for the two main squares, and for the **souks** – just below Place Outa El Hammam.

There are basic town *souks* held on Mondays and Thursdays in the market square, so these, to some degree, have been set up for, or at least geared to, the tourist industry. But both the quality and variety are surprising. When the Spanish arrived – just seven decades ago – Chaouen craftsmen were still working leather in the manner of twelfth-century Córdoba, tanning with bark, and hammering silver to old Andalusian designs. Although you won't see any of this today, the town's carpet and weaving workshops remain active and many of their designs unchanged. Vendors are well used to haggling with travellers, and if you're staying for a few days, prices can fall dramatically.

It's interesting, too, to observe the contrasts in feel between the main, Arab part of Chaouen and the still modestly populated Jewish quarter of the **Mellah**. This is to be found behind the jewellers' *souk*, between the Bab El Ain and the Kasbah.

Place Outa El Hammam and the Kasbah

The elongated **Place Outa El Hammam** is where most of the town's evening life takes place. It's a pretty square, with its cafés overhung by upper rooms (some the preserve of *kif* smokers), though by day, alas, it's virtually obscured by massed ranks of tour buses. On one side of the square is the town's **Kasbah**, a quiet ruin with shady gardens, and a little museum of crafts and old photos; it was built, like so many others in northern Morocco, by Moulay Ismail. Inside, and immediately to the right, in the first of its compounds, are the old town prison cells, where Abd El Krim (see pp.118–19) was imprisoned after his surrender in 1926. Five years earlier, he had himself driven the Spanish from the town, a retreat which saw the loss of nearly 20,000 of their troops.

The *place* was once the main market square, and off to its sides are a number of small **fondouks**; one of the more visible is at the beginning of the lane opposite the Kasbah (no. 34). The local Djebala tribesmen, who form most of the town's population, have a particular tradition of homosexuality, and there were boy markets held here until as recently as 1937, when they were officially banned by the Spanish administration.

Place El Makhzen and Ras El Ma

Place El Makhzen – the old "government square" – is in some ways a continuation of the marketplace, an elegant clearing with an old fountain, and pottery stalls set up for the package tourists.

If you leave the Medina at this point, it's possible to follow **the river** around the outside of the walls, and up above Bab Onsar. Here, past a couple of traditional flour-mills, you reach **Ras El Ma** (the water-head), a small cascade in the mountainside with water so clear and cold that, in the local phrase, "it knocks your teeth out to drink it". It has long been a favourite picnic spot – and is to an extent a holy place, due to the nearby *marabout's* tomb of Sidi Abdallah Habti. There are a couple of **cafés** close by to while away the midday hours.

Over to the south of the town, an enjoyable walk is to the ruined **"Spanish Mosque"**. Set on a hilltop, its interior is covered in graffiti, but nevertheless it gives a good sense of the layout of a mosque – normally off-limits in Morocco. Nobody seems to mind you looking around.

Up into the hills

Further afield, a good **day's hike** is to head east, up over the mountains behind Chaouen. As you look at the "two horns" from town, there is a path winding along the side of the mountain on your left. A four-hour (or more) hike will take you up to the other side, where a vast valley opens up, and if you walk further, you'll see the sea. The valley, as even casual exploration will show, is full of small farms cultivating *kif* – as they have done for years. Walking here, you may occasionally be stopped by the military, who are cracking down on foreign involvement in the crop. For more ambitious hikes – and there are some wonderful paths in the area – ask at the pensions about hiring a **guide**. Someone knowledgeable can usually be found to accompany you, for around 50 to 100dh a day. (The harder the climb, the more it costs!)

CHAOUEN'S HAMMAMS

The uncertain showers in some of the pensions are mitigated by the ease of visiting the local **hammams**. The town, unusually, has separate hammams for men and women. The male one is next door to the *Pension Castellana,* off Place Outa El Hammam; the one for women, which is older and much more elaborate, is in the quarter of the *souks* – ask someone to show you the way because it totally defies written directions.

In recent years, entrance to the hammams for tourists has been limited, and sometimes refused unless you have a group and book the hammam together. Ask your pension/hotel for advice, or for someone to accompany you.

Food, transport and other practicalities

Compared with the hotels, Chaouen **restaurants** offer surprisingly little choice. In the **Place Outa El Hammam** a few of the cafés – *Restaurant Kasbah* is the best – serve up regular Moroccan meals. Elsewhere in the **Medina**, look for the *Restaurant Tissemal*, alongside the *Pension Cordoba*; the *Restaurant Granada*, near the *Pension Valencia*; or the *Restaurant Assaada* – a tiny, three-table joint on a nameless lane just north of Bab El Ain. All three are recommended.

In the **Ville Nouvelle**, many of the classified hotels have restaurants open to non-residents – the *Hôtel Rif* and *Hôtel Salam* are two of the more promising. Alternatively, there are a couple of okay restaurants outside the Medina, up from the Bab El Ain on Rue Moulay Ali Ben Rachid: *Restaurant Ben Rachid* and, further up, *Restaurant Zouar*.

If you want beer or wine with your meal, you'll need to try the restaurants at the *Hôtel Parador de Chaouen* or *Hôtel Asma*, or the *Restaurant-bar Omo Rabi*, on Rue Tarik Ibn Ziad.

Swimming

The *Hôtel Parador de Chaouen* has a pool, open to non-residents for 25dh a day. Alternatively, you can join the locals, by sharing a taxi to a **pool in the river** a few kilometres downstream – an excellent alternative for which any of the pension managers will give full instructions.

Festivals

As the centre of so much *maraboutism*, Chaouen and its neighbouring villages have a particularly large number of **moussems**. The big events are those in Moulay Abdessalam Ben Mchich (40km away: usually in May) and Sidi Allal El Hadj (August 9). There are dozens of others, however – ask around and you should come upon something.

Buses and grands taxis

Leaving Chaouen by **bus** can be difficult. Departures to Fes, and to a lesser degree, Meknes, are often full: try to get tickets the day before. At present, there are departures to Fes at around 6.30am and 10am; to Meknes at noon. If you can't get on any of these direct buses, an alternative is to take a *grand taxi* or local bus to Ouezzane and another from there, or to return to Tetouan (where most of the buses originate). For Tetouan, buses leave at least four times a day – much less of a problem – or you can share a *grand taxi*. Buses also run daily to the Ceuta border at Fnideq (11am; 2hr) and to Oued Laou (5pm; 1hr 30min), and twice weekly through the Rif to El Djebha (see p.119).

For the more affluent, or anyone who can get a group of people together, **grands taxis** can be **chartered** – a stylish way to travel to Tangier or to Fes. The cost for either trip should be around 450dh, for up to six passengers.

Ouezzane (Wazzan)

OUEZZANE, like Chaouen, has a fine, mountainous site, looping around an outreach of the Djebala mountains. It stands virtually at the edge of the Rif and formed the old traditional border between the *Bled es-Makhzen* (the governed territories) and the *Bled es-Siba* (those of the lawless tribes). As such, the town was an important power base, and particularly so under the last nineteenth-century sultans, when its local sheikhs became among the most powerful in Morocco.

The Ouezzani

The sheikhs – the *Ouezzani* – were the spiritual leaders of the influential **Tabiya brotherhood**. They were *shereefs* (descendants of the Prophet) and came in a direct line from the Idrissids, the first and founding dynasty of Morocco. This, however, seems to have given them little significance until the eighteenth century, when Moulay Abdallah es-Shereef established a *zaouia* (religious cult centre) at Ouezzane. It acquired a huge following, becoming one of the great places of pilgrimage and an inviolable sanctuary. Unlike Chaouen, the town that grew up around this centre was not itself sacred, but until the turn of this century Jews and Christians were allowed to take only temporary residence in one of the *fondouks* set aside for this purpose. Walter Harris, who became a close friend of the Ouezzani *shereefs* in the late nineteenth century, found the town "the most fanatical that Europeans may visit" and the *zaouia* a virtually autonomous religious court. Strange to relate, however, an Englishwoman, Emily Keane, married in 1877 the principal *shereef*, Si Abdesslem, whom she had met while out riding. For several decades she lived in the town, openly as a Christian, dispensing medical care to the locals. Her *Life Story*, written after her husband's death, ends with the balanced summing up: "I do not advise anyone to follow in my footsteps, at the same time I have not a single regret." She is buried in the Anglican church in Tangier.

The Zaouia, town and souks

The **Zaouia**, distinguished by an unusual octagonal minaret, is the most striking building in the town, and though the Tabiya brotherhood now maintain their main base elsewhere, it continues to function and is the site of a lively spring **moussem**, or pilgrimage festival. (As in the rest of Morocco, however, entrance to the *zaouia* area is forbidden to non-Muslims.)

The older quarters of Ouezzane – many of their buildings tiled, gabled and sporting elaborate doors – enclose and rise above the *Zaouia*, newer suburbs sprawling into the hills on each side. It's an attractive enough place, and if of little specific interest, has a definite grandeur in its site.

The souks

The main **souks** climb up from an archway on the main square, Place de l'Indépendance, behind the *Grand Hôtel*. Ouezzane has a local reputation for its woollen rugs – most evident in the weavers' *souk*, around Place Rouida near the top end of the town. Also rewarding is the metalworkers' *souk*, a covered lane under the Mosque of Moulay Abdallah Shereef; to find it, ask directions for the pleasant (and adjacent) *Café Bellevue*. The town also has a couple of Centres Artesanal – one facing Place de l'Indépendance, the other on Av. Hassan II.

There is a large **Thursday souk** on the Place de l'Indépendance.

Rooms and transport

Few tourists stay in Ouezzane, as it is only a couple of hours out of Chaouen, but there are worse places to be stranded. The bus and *grand taxi* terminal is about 50m below the **Place de l'Indépendance**, where you'll also find three reasonable, basic **hotels**, the *Marhaba*, *Horloge* and *El Elam* (all ⑩). There is little to choose between these, though all are preferable to the *Grand Hôtel* or *Hôtel de la Poste* (again, both ⑩), just off the square on Av. Mohammed V. There is a **hammam** opposite the *Hôtel de la Poste*, and numerous grill-cafés on the square.

Buses

Ouezzane provides a useful link if you're travelling by public **transport** (bus or *grand taxi*) between **Chaouen and the Atlantic coast**, or vice versa. There are a fair number of **buses** also to Meknes and Fes, but if you're stopping or staying, buy onward tickets well in advance; as with Chaouen it's not unusual for them to arrive and leave full.

travel details

Trains

Five trains a day leave Tangier, all running through either SIDI KACEM or SIDI SLIMANE, where you may need to get a connection to the Meknes/Fes/Oujda or Rabat/Casablanca/ Marrakesh lines. The following timetable is current as of publication, and, though there may be small changes, its pattern should remain very similar.

Tangier (12.30am), Asilah (1.17am), Meknes (5.14am), Fes (6.19am). Continues to Taza/Oujda (8.45am/12.26pm). *This train has couchettes but runs from July 1–Sept 30 only.*

Tangier (7.15am), Asilah (7.58am), Sidi Slimane (10.26am: change for Meknes/Fes/Oujda, arriving 11.59am/12.53pm/6.30pm), Rabat (11.25am), Casablanca Port (12.55pm).

Tangier (11.28am), Asilah (12.21pm), Sidi Kacem (2.54pm: change for Rabat/Casablanca Voyageurs, arriving 5.17pm/6.41pm), Meknes (4.32pm), Fes (5.33pm), Taza (8.06pm) and Oujda (midnight).

Tangier (4.20pm), Asilah (5.05pm), Sidi Slimane (7.41pm: change for Meknes/Fes, arriving 9.15pm/10.12pm), Rabat (9.12pm), Casablanca Port (10.27pm). From Fes, there is a 1.49am connection to Taza (3.45am) and Oujda (7am). From Casablanca Port, there is a 1am connection to Marrakesh (6am).

Tangier (11.40pm), Asilah (12.25am), Rabat (4.40am), Casablanca Voyageurs (5.54am) and Marrakesh (9.40am). *This train has couchettes, but runs from July 1–Sept 30 only.*

Note: *ONCF* run connecting bus services to/from **Tetouan** from/to Tnine Sidi Lyamani, near Asilah.

Buses

From Tangier Asilah (7 daily; 1hr); Larache (6; 1hr 40min); Tetouan (12; 1hr 30min); Rabat (2; 5hr); Meknes (2; 7hr); Fes (2; 8hr).

From Asilah Larache (5 daily; 1hr).

From Larache Ksar El Kebir (3 daily; 40min); Souk El Arba (5; 1hr); Rabat (4; 3hr 30min); Meknes (2; 5hr 30min).

From Souk El Arba Moulay Bousselham (5 daily; 35min); Ouezzane (3; 1hr 30min).

From Ouezzane Meknes (2 daily; 4hr); Fes (2; 5hr 30min); Chaouen (4; 1hr 20min).

From Tetouan Tangier (12; 1hr 30min); Chaouen (10; 3hr); Fnideq (24; 25min); Oued Laou (2; 2hr).

From Chaouen Tetouan (10 daily; 3hr); Ketama/ Al Hoceima (2 ; 5hr/8hr); Meknes (1; 5hr 30min); Fes (2; 7hr); El Jebha (2 a week; 7hr).

Grands Taxis

From Tangier Regularly to Tetouan (1hr); less frequently to Larache, Rabat, and occasionally Fes.

From Ouezzane Regularly to Souk El Arba (1hr) and Chaouen (1hr 15min).

From Tetouan Regularly to Tangier (1hr), Oued Laou (1hr 20min) and Fnideq (Ceuta border) (20min).

From Souk El Arba Regularly to Moulay Bousselham (30min) and Larache (50min).

Ferries

See p.8 for details of ferries, hydrofoils and catamarans from Tangier and Ceuta.

Flights

From Tangier Daily flights on RAM to Casablanca (and from there on to Marrakesh, etc); there are also direct flights to Agadir (3 a week), Fes (1 a week) and Marrakesh (1 a week). International flights most days to Gibraltar, Madrid, London, etc.

CHAPTER TWO

THE RIF AND THE MEDITERRANEAN COAST

A nyone who has heard of the **Rif mountains** at all has usually done so in connection with Ketama, and the sale of **kif**, or hashish. There are towns enough in Morocco where you'll be offered *kif* for sale, but at Ketama it is simply assumed that this is why you are here. "How many kilos?" they ask. *Kif* and Ketama are big business.

Talking about the Rif you have to state this first, since *kif* dominates so much of the region's character. Even where uncultivated, the plants grow wild around the stoney slopes. The cultivation itself is legal, but Moroccan laws forbid its sale, purchase and even possession outside the region. Don't be blinded by the local ways: police roadblocks are frequent, informers legion. An additional hazard are the drug industry's local mafiosi, cruising around the hills in their black Mercedes and not above a bit of traditional banditry, stopping tourists and forcing *kif* purchases upon them. If you're driving and cautious, it's wise to avoid the whole area around **Ketama** – bounded to the south by Had-Ikauen, to the east and west by Targuist and Bab Berred. If you're not driving and cautious, simply stay on the bus – it's a fine scenic trip.

The **Rif mountain range** itself is a vast, limestone mass, over 300km long, up to 2500m in height, and with dense upland forests of cedars. The whole impression is one of enormity, a grandiose place full of faintly outrageous views, and with a very real sense of isolation. The Rif is, in fact, the natural boundary between Europe and Africa, and with the Sahara it cuts off central Morocco from Algeria and the rest of the Maghreb. In the past this was a powerful barrier – it took the first recorded European traveller three months to travel from Al Hoceima to Melilla – and it is sustained today by a strong spirit of independence and age-old xenophobia among the tribes. There is no other part of Morocco where you feel so completely incidental to ordinary local life.

Things are very different, however, with the **towns** to the east of the range. **Taza** and **Oujda**, important and historic posts on the "corridor" into Algeria, are among the most easy-going in the country – Oujda, in particular, with its large university population and proximity to Algeria's most liberal city, Oran. And there are relaxed times to be had, too, on those few points where the Rif gives way to the **Mediterranean coast**. Contrary to its daunting appearance from the great "backbone" roads, the Rif does have **beaches** – though they're few and far between, and virtually undeveloped east of Tetouan.

The only real beach resort in this chapter – the Mediterranean coast around Tetouan is covered in Chapter One – is **Al Hoceima**, and even here the hotels

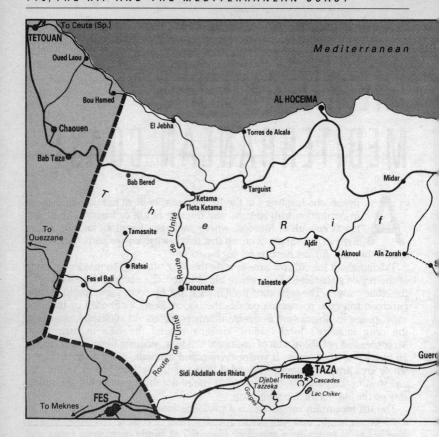

TRAIN NETWORK ROUTE

ONCF, the Moroccan rail company, operates connecting buses twice daily between **Nador** and the station at **Taourirt**, midway between Taza and Oujda.

spread for less than half a kilometre. Elsewhere it's a question of a few sporadic campsites, the liveliest being at **Saïdia**, on the border with Algeria, where many Moroccan families spend their summer holidays; few tourists join them, though they are easy-going and good points for meeting people, without any hustling.

Note that the region has useful **ferry connections** between Melilla – which, like Ceuta, is Spanish territory – and the Spanish ports of Málaga and Almería. If you are bringing a car across from Spain, these are well worth considering. Fes is easily reached, either through the Rif, or by cutting down to the Taza road, and from Oujda there is a grand desert route **south to Figuig** and beyond to the oases of the Tafilalt (see Chapter Seven). Note also that the **route into Algeria at Oujda** is now fairly straightforward, following improved Moroccan-Algerian relations, and even has possibilities for linking up between train services.

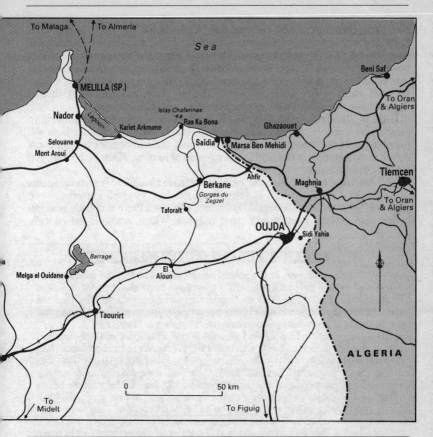

On top of the Rif: the road from Chaouen to Ketama and Al Hoceima

There are very few journeys in Morocco as spectacular as that from **Chaouen to Al Hoceima**. The road literally – and perversely – follows the backbone of the Western Rif, the highest peaks in the north of the country. You can look down on one side to the Mediterranean coast, and on the other across the southern range; "big mountains and more big mountains" – as Paul Bowles put it in a wonderful travel piece, "The Rif, to Music", in *Their Heads are Green* – "mountains covered with olive trees, with oak trees, with bushes, and finally with giant cedars".

Even without the caution on *kif*, this is not a route to be undertaken by inexperienced drivers; although in good condition, it seems constructed entirely of zigzags and hairpin turns. Once beyond Bab Taza, you wind around the tops of ridges, sheer drops on either side to deep and isolated valleys. Going by bus the Riffians sleep or talk through it – a fact that seems almost as remarkable as the surrounding scenery.

Bab Taza, Bab Berred and Ketama: the *kif* heartland

BAB TAZA, 23km out of Chaouen, is the first village of any size – an attractive place surrounded by rolling, green, flower-strewn countryside and slopes of brown and outcrops of claret thyme. It has a Wednesday *souk* and a café. Ten kilometres further on is CHEFERAT, a small hamlet with a noted spring and a small waterfall which rushes under the road. Like Bab Taza, it has no hotel, though there are two cafés, one on the roadside serving grilled brochettes.

BAB BERRED, a smallish market village and former Spanish administrative centre, has a couple of reasonable pensions, the *Tizirane* and *Saada* (both ⑨), near the *grand taxi* stand. The village also signals the real beginning of *kif* country – it is surrounded, in fact, by the plants – and at Ketama, 30km to the east, you arrive at the epicentre.

KETAMA, even in transit, is an initiation because absolutely everybody seems to be involved in "Business". If you get off the bus, you will immediately be offered *kif* – immense, unbelievable quantities of it – and there is nobody who will believe that you are here for any other purpose. Which, really, is fair enough.

ABD EL KRIM AND THE REPUBLIC OF THE RIF

Up until the establishment of the Spanish protectorate in 1912, the **tribes of the Rif** existed outside government control – a northern heartland of the *Bled es-Siba*. They were subdued temporarily by *harkas*, the burning-raids with which sultans asserted their authority, and for a longer period under Emperor Moulay Ismail; but for the most part, bore out their own name of *Imazighen*, or "Free Ones".

Closed to outside influence, the tribes developed an isolated and self-contained way of life. The Riffian soil, stony and infertile, produced constant problems with food supplies, and it was only through a complex system of alliances (*liffs*) that outright wars were avoided. Blood feuds, however, were endemic, and a major contributor to maintaining a viably small population. Unique in Morocco, the Riffian villages are scattered communities, their houses hedged and set apart, and each family maintained a pillbox tower to spy on and fight off enemies. They were different, too, in their religion: the *Ulema*, the prayer said five times daily – one of the central tenets of Islam – was not observed. *Djinns*, supernatural spirits from pagan nature cults, were widely accredited, and great reliance was placed on the intercession of local marabouts.

It was an unlikely ground for significant and organised rebellion; yet, for over five years (between 1921 and 1927), the tribes forced the Spanish to withdraw from the mountains. Twice they defeated whole armies – bringing down the Madrid monarchy in the process – and it was only through the added intervention of France, and nearly half a million troops, that the Europeans won eventual victory. In the intervening years, the leaders of the revolt, the brothers **Mohammed and M'hamid Abd El Krim**, were able to declare a Republic of the Rif and to establish much of the apparatus of a modern state.

Well educated, and confident of the Rif's mineral reserves, they manipulated the *liff* system to forge an extraordinary unity among the tribes, negotiated mining rights in return for arms with Germany and South America, and even set up a Riffian State Bank. Still more impressive, they managed to impose a series of social reforms – including the destruction of family pillboxes and the banning of *kif* – which allowed the operation of a fairly broad administrative system. In their success, however, was the inevitability of defeat. It was the first nationalist move-

Anywhere in Morocco, if people introduce themselves as "from Ketama", there is no ambiguity about what they are offering. Dealers here are likely to try and get you to **stay at their farms** – something not be recommended, even if you've got an insatiable appetite and curiosity for *kif* production. Tales abound of travellers who have lost everything, often at knife-point, after taking up one of these offers.

The only **hotel** in Ketama itself is the old Spanish *parador*, the *Hôtel Tidighine* (☎16; ③). Before *kif* took such a hold, it was popular with French tourists intent on the nearby skiing and boar hunting on **Djebel Tidirhine**, but it's been best avoided for the last thirty or so years. The Chaouen–Al Hoceima buses actually drop you outside the hotel, a confusing stop since there's virtually nothing else in sight. The main village, is, in fact, 8km down the road to Fes at **TLETA KETAMA**. There are a couple of basic hotels here – the *California* and *Saada* (both ⑩), though neither exactly invites a stay.

Roads to the coast lead off 23km before and 12km beyond Ketama to EL JEBHA (see p.106). This is a good trip but there are much better resorts at Torres de Alcala and Kalah Iris, reachable from the next junction (see overpage).

---

ment in colonial North Africa, and although the Spanish were ready to quit the zone in 1925, it was politically impossible that the French would allow them to do so.

Defeat for the Riffians – and the exile of Mohammed Abd El Krim – brought a virtual halt to social progress and reform. **The Spanish** took over the administration en bloc, governing through local *caids* (district administrators), and although they exploited some mineral deposits there was no road-building programme or any of the other "civilising benefits" introduced in the French zone. There were, however, two important changes: migration of labour (particularly to French Algeria) replaced the blood feud as a form of population control, and the Riffian warriors were recruited into Spain's own armies. The latter had immense consequences, allowing General Franco to build up a power base in Morocco. It was with **Riffian troops** that he invaded Andalusia in 1936, and it was probably their contribution which ensured the fascist victory in the Spanish Civil War.

Abd El Krim was a powerful inspiration to later nationalists, and the Riffians themselves played an important guerrilla role in the 1955–56 **struggle for independence**. When, in April 1957, the Spanish finally surrendered their protectorate, however, the Berber/Spanish-speaking tribes found themselves largely excluded from government. Administrators were imposed on them from Fes and Casablanca, and in October 1958, the Rif's most important tribe, the Beni Urriaguel, rose in open **rebellion**. The mutiny was soon put down, but necessitated the landing at Al Hoceima of then-Crown Prince Hassan and some two-thirds of the Moroccan army.

A quarter of a century later, the Rif is still perhaps the most unstable part of Morocco, remaining conscious of its under-representation in government and its underdevelopment, despite substantial school-building programmes, improved road communications and a large, new, agricultural project in the plains south of Nador and Al Hoceima. Labour **emigration**, too, remains high – with Western Europe replacing Algeria as the main market – and (as in the rest of Morocco) there is widespread resentment at the difficulty of obtaining a passport for this outlet. With the growth of more sophisticated government systems, and a sizeable hierarchy of local administration, further tribal dissidence now seems unlikely. It is interesting to note, though, that it was in the Rif – above all in the towns of Nador, Al Hoceima and Tetouan – that the 1984 riots began, and it was here that the most serious disturbances were reported.

THE TRADITIONS OF *KIF* . . .

Smoking (and eating) *kif* – or hashish – is an age-old tradition in the Rif and northern Morocco. Its effects were enthusiastically described by James Grey Jackson in *An Account of the Empire of Marocco* , published in 1809:

The plant called Hashisha *is the African hemp plant; it grows in all the gardens and is reared in the plains of Marocco for the manufacture of string, but in most parts of the country it is cultivated for the extraordinary and pleasing voluptuous vacuity of mind which it produces in those who smoke it; unlike the intoxication from wine, a fascinating stupour pervades the mind, and the dreams are agreeable. The* kief, *which is the flower and seeds of the plant, is the strongest, and a pipe of it half the size of a common English tobacco pipe, is sufficient to intoxicate. The infatuation of those who use it is such that they cannot exist without it.*

The Kief *is usually pounded, and mixed with an invigorating confection which is sold at an enormous price; a piece of this as big as a walnut will for a time entirely deprive a man of all reason and intellect: they prefer it to opium from the voluptuous sensations which it never fails to produce. Wine or brandy, they say, does not stand in competition with it.*

The Habisha, *or leaves of the plant, are dried and cut like tobacco, and are smoked in very small pipes; but when the person wishes to indulge in the sensual stupour it occasions, he smokes the* Hashisha *pure, and in less than half an hour it operates: the person under its influence is said to experience pleasing images: he*

Continuing east from Ketama, with the cedar forests giving way to barren, stony slopes, you reach the town of **TARGUIST**, Abd El Krim's last stronghold (see box on previous page) and the site of his surrender to the French. Paul Bowles described the place, thirty years ago, in "The Rif, to Music", as "a monstrous excrescence with long dirty streets, the wind blowing along them, whipping clouds of dust and filth against the face, stinging the skin". It has not improved and despite a trio of **pensions** (all ⑩) would be a perverse place to stay. It does, however, have a large **Saturday souk**, which draws villagers from the dozens of tiny communities in the neighbouring hills, and at the junction on the main road, next to a petrol station, is a modest but good **restaurant**, the *Targuist*, favoured by long-distance buses.

Torres de Alcala and Kalah Iris

A pair of temptingly low-key beach resorts, **Torres de Alcala** and **Kalah Iris**, can be reached by a road (signposted Beni Boufrah and Torres de Alcala) 5km west of Targuist. They can be reached by grand taxi from Targuist or Al Hoceima, or by a daily bus; the bus leaves Targuist at 6am, arrives at Torres de Alcala at 7.30am and Al Hoceima at 9am, then turns round from Al Hoceima at 3pm, arriving at Torres de Alcala at 4.30pm and Targuist at 6pm.

Torres de Alcala
TORRES DE ALCALA is a simple, whitewashed fishing village, 250m from a small, pebbly beach. Cliffs frame beach and village, and on the western headland is a deserted fort, probably Spanish, with stunning views along the

fancies himself in company with beautiful women; he dreams that he is an emperor, or a bashaw, and that the world is at his nod. There are other plants which possess a similar exhilarating quality, amongst which is a species of the Palma Christi, the nuts of which, mixed with any kind of food, affect a person for three hours, and then pass off. These they often use when they wish to discover the mind of a person, or what occupies his thoughts.

. . . AND THE MODERN INDUSTRY

Although many of the Riffian tribes in the mountains had always smoked *hashish*, it was the Spanish who really encouraged its cultivation – probably as an effort to keep them placid. This situation was apparently accepted when Mohammed V came to power, though the reasons for his doing so are obscure. There is a story, probably apocryphal, that when he visited Ketama in 1957, he accepted a bouquet of *kif* as a symbolic gift; the Riffis add that this was because he feared their power, though this seems to have been swiftly forgotten amid the following year's rebellion.

Whatever, Ketama continued to supply the bulk of the country's *kif*, and in the early 1970s it became the centre of a significant drug industry, exporting to Europe and America. This sudden growth was accounted for, apparently, by a single factor: the introduction, by an American dealer, of techniques for producing hash resin. Overnight, the Riffians had a compact and easily exportable product and, inevitably, big business was quick to follow.

Mediterranean coast. It's a perfect resort-in-embryo, with, as yet, no hotel (though a few rooms are rented in summer), no campsite (camping is actually forbidden here) and no electricity. Just a bakery and, on the beach, a small café.

Along a rocky cliff-path, 5km to the east, are the **ruins of Badis**, which from the fourteenth to the early sixteenth century was the main port of Fes, and used for trade with the Western Mediterranean states, in particular Venice. A once-considerable caravan route ran across the Rif, following the course of the modern S302 road, the so-called Route de l'Unité (see overpage)

Offshore from Badis is a small island, the **Peñon de Velez de la Gomera**, which, like the islands of Al Hoceima and Chafarinas downcoast, remains Spanish territory. It was this that caused the port's downfall. The Spaniards occupied it in 1508, then in 1522 it passed to the Turks, who used it as a base for raids along the Spanish coast. Philip II of Spain attempted to regain it, failed to do so, but destroyed Badis in the process. Subsequently, the island was used by Turkish and other pirates before, in this century, the Spanish took possession, using it until recent years as a penitentiary (*peñon*).

Kalah Iris

At **KALAH IRIS**, 4km east of Torres de Alcala, along a paved road, there's a longer beach, with a natural breakwater, formed by a sandspit which runs out to one of two islets in the bay. There is no village as such here but a few resort facilities: a **campsite** (open year round, and with 20 **bungalows**, sleeping up to six people, for rent), a restaurant, café and a shop with fresh food. The resort is not totally undiscovered, with excursions being offered to European holidaymakers in Al Hoceima, but it's still a delightful spot.

The Route de L'Unité: Ketama to Fes

At the end of the Spanish Protectorate in 1957, there was no north–south route across the Rif, a marked symbol both of its isolation and of the separateness of the old French and Spanish zones. It was in order to counteract these aspects – and to provide working contact between the Riffian tribes and the French-colonised Moroccans – that the great **Route de l'Unité** was planned, cutting right across the range from Ketama south to Fes.

The Route, completed in 1963, was built with volunteer labour from all over the country – Hassan II himself worked on it at the outset. It was the brainchild of Mehdi Ben Barka, first President of the National Assembly and the most outstanding figure of the nationalist Left before his exile and subsequent "disappearance" in Paris in 1965. Ben Barka's volunteers, 15,000-strong for much of the project, formed a kind of labour university, working through the mornings and attending lectures in the afternoons.

Today the Route de l'Unité sees little traffic – travelling from Fes to Al Hoceima, it's quicker to go via Taza; from Fes to Tetouan, via Ouezzane. Nevertheless, it's an impressive and very beautiful road, certainly as dramatic an approach to Fes as you could hope for.

Taounate and Tissa

Going by bus, the village which most tempts a halt is **TAOUNATE**. The largest community along the Route, it stands on a hill above the valley of the Oued Sra (soon to be dammed up to form a vast, 35-kilometre-long lake). If you can make it for the huge **Friday market** here, you should be able to get a lift out to any number of villages in the region. There is nowhere to eat or to stay in the village, but there are roadside grill-cafés 10km to the south at ÂIN-AÏCHA.

Continuing south along the Route, there is a turning, 33km from Taounate, to **TISSA**. At the **stables** here, which can be visited, horses and riders (who are paired for life) are trained to take part in **fantasias** – the traditional charge, culminating in firing of muskets in the air, that is put on these days largely for tourists. There is a **horsefair** at the village in early October.

West: Rafsaï and Fes El Bali

To the west of Taounate, the S304 leads in fifty kilometres to Fes El Bali (daily bus), by way of **RAFSAÏ**, the last village of the Rif to be overrun by the Spanish and the site of a December **Olive Festival**. If you're into scenic roads and have the transport, a forty-kilometre dirt road extends out from here to the **Djebel Lalla Outka**, the peak reputed to offer the best view of the whole Rif range. The road is reasonable as far as the village of TAMESNITE but thereafter is very rough piste – accessible only in summer.

FES EL BALI itself is a useful connecting point with buses to the city of Fes and to Ouezzane. The village takes its name, *El Bali* (The Old), from an eleventh-century Almoravid fort, little of which remains. If you're stuck here, there's a cheap and basic **hotel**.

South of the town rises the **Djebel Amergou** (681m), which is capped by the ruins of another, more substantial **Almoravid fort**. It can be reached in a couple of hours' hiking from the roadside village of ET TNINE, about 15km south on the P26 to Fes.

East: Aknoul

Going **east from Taounate**, an attractive though less spectacular route heads through cork and holm oak forests towards the scattered and rather grim village of **AKNOUL**. From here you can pick up a bus or *grand taxi* down to Taza, or sporadic buses over to Nador or Al Hoceima.

Taza and the Djebel Tazzeka

TAZA was once a place of great importance: the capital of Morocco during parts of the Almohad, Merenid and Alaouite dynasties, and controlling the only practicable pass to the east. This, the Taza Gap, forms a wide passage between the Rif and Middle Atlas. It was the route into the country taken by Moulay Idriss and the first Moroccan Arabs, and the Almohads and Merenids both successfully invaded Fes from here. Each of these dynasties fortified and endowed Taza, but as a defensive position it was never very effective: the local Zenatta tribe were always willing to join an attack and, in the nineteenth century, they managed to overrun it completely, with centralised control returning only with the French occupation of 1914.

Modern Taza seems little haunted by this past, its monuments sparse and mostly inaccessible to non-Muslims. It is, however, a pleasant market town – an easy place to get acclimatised if you have arrived in Morocco at Oujda or Melilla – and its Medina is saved from anonymity by a magnificent hilltop terrace site, flanked by crumbling Almohad walls. In addition, there is a considerable attraction in the surrounding countryside – the national park of **Djebel Tazzeka**, with its circuit of waterfalls, caves and schist gorges.

Orientation and practicalities

Taza splits into two parts, the **Medina** and the French-built **Ville Nouvelle**; the quarters are separated by nearly 3km of road and, to all intents, completely distinct. A shuttle bus runs between them, and another connects the Ville Nouvelle with the train station and adjacent bus and *grands taxis* terminal, 3km further out along the Av. de la Gare (also known as Av. Prince Heretier). *Petits taxis* are also available for rides between the stations, Ville Nouvelle and Medina.

The **Ville Nouvelle** was an important military garrison in the Riffian war and retains much of the barrack-grid character. Its centre, **Place de l'Indépendance**, actually serves a population of 40,000, but it's so quiet you'd hardly know it. There is a small, helpful **tourist office** on Av. de Tetouan. Most of the **restaurants** are grouped round the Place de l'Indépendance, or along Av. de Tetouan. The *Restaurant Majestic*, 26 Av. Mohammed V, has reasonable-value set meals.

Accommodation

Hôtel de la Poste, Place de l'Indépendance (☎05/67.25.89). The best-value hotel in town, opened in 1990, and well managed. ①

Grand Hôtel du Dauphine, Place de l'Indépendance (☎05/67.35.67). Once grand as the name proclaims, though now pretty down-at-heel and a bit grubby. Nonetheless, it's a fine Art Deco building and the rooms are decent-sized. ②

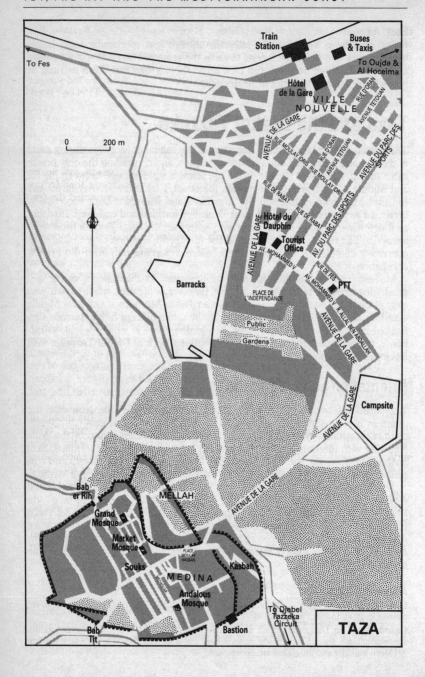

TAZA

Hôtel Guillaume Tell, Place de l'Indépéndance. More or less opposite the *Dauphine*, this fifth-floor lodging house is a cheaper but grim alternative. ⑩

Hôtel Friouato-Salam, Av. de la Gare (☎05/67.25.93). A concrete outpost in scrubland, between the campsite and Medina. Only the presence of a pool is a temptation. ③

Hôtel de la Gare, opposite the train station (☎05/67.24.48). Basic but not too bad – rooms off a small courtyard with a banana tree in the middle. A useful location, too, if you have to get a dawn bus to Nador or across the Rif. ⑩

The town **campsite** seems to have disappeared.

The Medina

Buses from Place de l'Indépendance stop at **Place Moulay Hassan**, just below the **Mechouar** – the main street of the Medina. A modernised area, the Medina is compact and easy enough, though to locate and find your way round the few scattered sights it might be worthwhile to enlist a guide.

The most prominent building in the south section of the Medina is the **Andalous Mosque**, though its courtyards are characteristically well concealed from public view. Close by, just off to the west of the Mechouar, is the **Bou Abul Hassan Medersa**. A somewhat inconspicuous Merenid building, it is hard to find and usually kept closed. If you can locate the *gardien*, there are rewards to be had in a classic court and beautiful *mihrab*.

The Palais Bou Hamra

To the rear of the Andalous Mosque is the **Palais Bou Hamra**, the largely ruined residence of the *Rogui* Bou Hamra, pretender to the throne in the early years of this century. There is little to see today, but for a decade or so this was a power base controlling much of eastern Morocco. Like most protagonists of the immediate pre-colonial period, Bou Hamra was an extraordinary figure: a former forger, conjurer and saint, who claimed to be the legitimate Shereefian heir and had himself proclaimed Sultan at Taza in 1902.

The name *Bou Hamra* – "man on the she-donkey" – recalled his means of travel round the countryside, where he won his followers by performing "miracles". One of these involved talking to the dead, which he perfected by the timely burying of a disciple, who would then communicate through a concealed straw; the pronouncements over, Bou Hamra flattened the straw with his foot (presumably not part of the original deal) and allowed the amazed villagers to dig up the by-then-dead witness.

Bou Hamra's own death – after his capture by Sultan Moulay Hafid – was no less melodramatic. He was brought to Fes in a small cage on the back of a camel, fed to the court lions (who refused to eat him), and was eventually shot and burned. Both Gavin Maxwell and Walter Harris give graphic accounts (see "Books" in *Contexts*).

The souks and Grand Mosque

Taza's **souks** branch off to either side of the Mechouar, midway between the Andalous and Grand Mosques. Since there are few and sporadic tourists, these are very much working markets, free of the artificial "craft" goods so often found. In fact, one of the most memorable is a *souk* for used European clothing – a frequent feature of country and provincial markets, the more fortunate dealers having gained access to the supplies of international charities. The **granary** and the covered stalls of the **kissaria** are also worth a look, in the shadow of the Djemaa es Souk or Market Mosque.

The **Grand Mosque**, at the end of the Mechouar, is historically one of the most interesting buildings in the country – but, like that of the Andalous, so discreetly screened that it's difficult to gain any glimpse of the interior. Even the outside is elusive: shielded by a net of buildings, you have to walk up towards Bab er Rih for a reasonable impression of its ground plan. Founded by the Almohad sultan Abd El Moumen, it is probably the oldest Almohad structure in existence, predating even the partially ruined mosque at Tin Mal (see Chapter Five), with which it shares most stylistic features.

Bab er Rih and the bastions

Above the Medina, at **Bab er Rih** (Gate of the Winds), it is possible to get some feeling for Taza's historic and strategic significance. You can see up the valley towards the Taza Gap, Djebel Tazzeka and the Middle Atlas on one side, the reddish earth of the Rif behind, on the other.

The actual gate now leads nowhere and looks somewhat lost below the road, but it is Almohad in origin and design. So, too, is most of the circuit of walls, which you can follow round by way of a **bastion** (added by Moulay Ismail, in Spanish style) back to Place Moulay Hassan.

Transport connections from Taza

Taza is quite a transport junction, with good connections west to Fes, east to Oujda and north to Nador and Al Hoceima.

For **Fes** there's a wide choice of options. *Grands taxis* run throughout the day (just ask and wait for a place) from by the train station, arriving in Fes at Bab Ftouh (where you'll need to pick up a city taxi or bus to get to the hotels at Bab Boujeloud or the Ville Nouvelle). Fes is also served by four daily trains, plus a number of buses. **Oujda** is easiest reached by train – a quick route across the eastern steppes, through Guercif and Taourirt (see section following).

For the **Rif**, most buses leave very early in the morning. There are currently two to **Nador** (at 4.30 and 5am): one going via **Aknoul**, the other over a new and more direct road to the east of Taourirt (on the P1). There are also one or two buses each morning to **Al Hoceima**, via Aknoul. **From Aknoul** you can catch sporadic, local buses across the southern slopes of the Rif to Taounate on the Route de l'Unité.

All the **buses** leave from by the train station – whatever anyone may tell you about stops in the Ville Nouvelle!

The Djebel Tazzeka . . . and beyond

A loop of some 123km around Taza, the **Cirque du Djebel Tazzeka** is really a car-driver's route, with its succession of mountain views, marking a transition between the Rif and Middle Atlas. However, it has a specific "sight" in the immense **Friouato Cave** (*Gouffre du Friouato*), 22km from Taza. This is a feasible hitch (stand at the turnoff just below the Medina) or a reasonable shared *grand taxi* ride (negotiate at the rank by the train station).

The cirque: cascades, a lake and Friouato

The **Tazzeka road** curls around below the Medina before climbing to a narrow valley of almond and cherry orchards. About 10km out of Taza you reach the **Cascades de Ras El Oued**, a series of small waterfalls reduced to a trickle in the dry summer months. Beyond this point, you loop up towards the first pass (at 1198m) and emerge beside the **Chiker Lake**, again pretty dry in midsummer.

The **Gouffre du Friouato** lies near the far end of this depression, along a short, signposted track to the right. Explored down to 180m, the cave complex is said to be the deepest in North Africa, and its entrance – over 30m wide – must certainly be the most impressive. The complex has not been developed as an attraction, but there is a guard around for most of the year who will steer you to some of the more spectacular caverns. You'll need a torch – if you don't have one, wait to see if some other tourists turn up.

Beyond Friouato, the cirque route runs through the dark schist **gorges of the Oued Zireg**. But the most dramatic and scenic stretch is undoubtedly the **ascent of the Djebel** itself. This is passable by car in dry weather but very dangerous at other times: a very rough, seven-kilometre road cuts its way up some 15km beyond Friouato, leading to a TV broadcasting tower near the summit. The view from the top, encased in forests of cedars, stretches to the Rif, to the mountains around Fes and to much of the eastern Middle Atlas.

Completing the cirque, you can rejoin the Fes–Taza road at SIDI ABDALLAH DES RHIATA.

A route to Midelt

For anyone with a car, there is an adventurous route from near the Chiker lake, leading off **through the Middle Atlas to Midelt**. This begins as a fairly reasonable paved road to MEGHRAOUA, where a dirt road (very rough) takes over to TALZEMT, eventually joining the P20 to Midelt at ENJIL DES IKHATARN.

Taza to Oujda

The route from **Taza to Oujda** is as bare as it looks on the map: a semi-desert plain, broken by little more than the odd roadside town.

Msoun and Guercif

MSOUN, 3km north of the main road, 29km east of Taza, is a rare point of interest. The village, inhabited by around 300 members of the semi-nomadic Haoura, is built within a **kasbah**, dating to the reign of Moulay Ismail (1672–1727), and still turreted and complete on three sides. You can see the original rainwater cistern and grain silos, alongside the settlement's shop, post office and mosque. Visitors are a curiosity here and you're likely to be guided around and possibly taken off to meet the *mukhtar* (headman).

Further along the route, past the agricultural centre of **GUERCIF**, another brief detour from the road will bring you to the hamlet of **GOUTTITIR**, constructed around a hot spring, in a rocky, steep-sided gully, whose waters are pumped up to supply a hammam (used by men during the day; women after dusk). There are very basic **rooms** (no beds!) and **meals** to be had nearby at the *Café Sidi Chaffi*.

Taourirt

TAOURIRT, the largest town along the route, was the crossroads between the old north–south caravan route linking Melilla and the ancient kingdom of Sijilmassa (see p.421), as well as the Taza corridor between Morocco and Algeria. The presence of the army (who occupy the old Kasbah) and of prominent radio aerials confirms its continuing strategic importance, and for travellers it is a useful train and road junction, with buses north to Nador connecting reasonably well with train arrivals from Oujda or Fes. The town itself is of little interest, however, save for its large **Sunday souk**. There are two **hotels**, much the better of which is the *El Mansour* (☎06/69.40.03; ①), with a good café, on the road leading south out of the town towards Debdou.

If you have transport, a more tempting overnight stay would be to camp out beside the **Cascades** – and natural swimming pool – northwest of Taourirt. To reach them, drive west along the P1 back towards Taza, then turn north along the road to the MELGA EL OUIDANE barrage; they are 9km up this road.

Al Hoceima

Coming from the Rif, **AL HOCEIMA** can be a bit of a shock. It may not be quite the "exclusive international resort" the tourist board claim, but it is truly Mediterranean and has developed enough to have little in common with the farming villages and tribal markets of the mountains around.

If you're travelling through the Rif, you will probably want to stop here and rest a couple of days – maybe for longer. It is a relaxing place, with none of the hassle of Tangier or Fes or Tetouan, and the cafés and streets full of people going about their business or pleasure. In late spring, or September, when the beaches are quiet, it's near idyllic. In midsummer, though, be warned that the town and its beaches get pretty crowded under the weight of Moroccan families and French and German package tourists, and rooms can be difficult to find. It is, after all, a small town and not geared to tourism on the scale of, say, Tangier or Agadir.

This size is one of its charms. It has wide boulevards, fringed with occasional palms on familiar Spanish lines, and yet, at every turn, you can see either the wooded hills behind the town, or the sea. From some vantage points, you also get

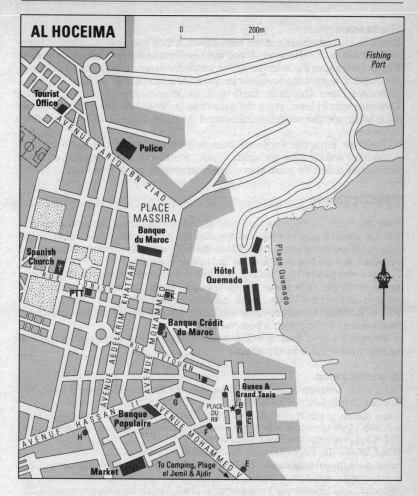

a view of the **Peñon de Alhucemas**, another of the trio of Spanish-owned islands (and another former penitentiary), over in the bay to the east of town. It's a pretty focal point, topped with sugar-white houses, a church and tower. The Spanish took it in 1673 and have held it ever since – a perennnial source of dispute between Morocco and Spain. Some Moroccan patriots refer to it as the *Ile de N'Kor*, after the Oued Nakor, which flows into the bay.

There seems, however, no lobby for a change of name for Al Hoceima itself, which was developed only after the Spanish invasion of the Rif (see p.118) in 1926, and was known by them as **Villa Sanjuro** (a name still occasionally used for the old part of town). It was in the bay here that the Spanish landed in their original invasion – and here, too, that the then-Crown Prince Hassan led Moroccan forces to quell the Riffians' revolt in 1958, following independence.

The beaches

Swimming – and walking in the olive-groved hills if you want a change – is the main attraction of Al Hoceima. If you wake early enough it is worth going down to **Plage Quemado**, the town beach, to watch the *lamparo* fishermen coming in; they work at night using acetylene lamps to attract and dazzle the fish.

Besides Plage Quemado, there is a far less crowded beach at Asfiha, a kilometre west of town, along the Ajdir road (a cheap *petit taxi* ride, if you don't fancy walking). This stretches right round the bay to Djebel Hadid, the headland to the east.

There are further beach possibilities at Torres de Alcala and Kalah Iris (see p.120–21), which, although 60km away, are nevertheless thought of as Al Hoceima beaches. They can be reached from town by bus or *grand taxi*.

Practicalities

Until the 1950s, Al Hoceima consisted of just a small fishing port to the north of the bay, and a fringe of white houses atop the barren cliffs to the south. At the heart of this older quarter is the **Place du Rif**, enclosed by café-restaurants and pensions, and the terminal for CTM and private-line buses.

The newer part of town, with its neat grid of boulevards, occupies the land sloping down to the cliffs above the town beach, **Plage Quemado** – between the harbour and original village. If this quarter can be said to have a heart, it is the **Place Massira**, a squeaky-clean square on the cliff top, at the top end of **Av. Mohammed V**, the principal boulevard.

There is a helpful **tourist office** on Av. Tariq Ibn Ziad, beyond the Provincial offices and the police headquarters.

Accommodation

Most of the pensions in and around the Place du Rif are reasonable, if basic. The following are in order of preference:

Hôtel Florido [A], 40 Place du Rif (☎09/98.22.35). The top choice: an ornate Spanish building, with a café (decorated with Abd El Krim's truncated Star of David emblem) open all hours, and a restaurant open noon to midnight. ④

Hôtel Afrique [B], Rue de Tahnaout. Another old pension with good rooms. ③

Hôtel Nord/Hôtel Casablanca [C], 20 Rue Imzouren (☎09/98.30.79). Adjacent pensions under the same management. ④

Hôtel Rif [G], 13 Rue Moulay Youssef (☎09/98.22.68). Last choice when others are full. ④

Hôtel Populaire [F], 27 Place du Rif. Cold showers only. ③

Hôtel Assalam [D], 10 Place du Rif.(☎09/98.20.90). Above a café and summer restaurant. ④

Hôtel Bilboa [E], 28 Av. Mohammed V. A little further out – and only worth the walk if all the others are full. ④

CLASSIFIED HOTELS

The town's smartest hotel, the four-star *Hôtel Mohammed V* on Place Massira, has been closed since 1989 and there is no indication of when it will be revived. Meanwhile, the other hotels, in ascending order of price, are:

Hôtel Marrakesh [K], 2 Rue Abdallah Hammou (☎09/98.30.25). A good one-star hotel, recently redecorated and with reliable hot showers. ①

Hôtel Karim [H], 27 Av. Hassan II (☎09/98.21.84). A large hotel, with more comfort and a bar – but a long way from the beach. ②

Hôtel National [I], 23 Rue du Tetouan (☎09/98.26.81). Okay rooms and central location. ②

Hôtel Quemado, Plage de Quemado (☎09/98.23.71). Four ugly barrack blocks on the beach constitute this package hotel, used by German and French tour groups in summer and in winter by Spanish ones on weekend breaks. Includes a bar, restaurant and disco. In summer, booking in advance is essential, through *Maroc-Tourist* (☎07/76.39.15) in Rabat. ③

Hôtel Maghreb El Jadida [J], 56 Av. Mohammed V (☎09/98.25.04). The best upmarket choice: a central, newly refurbished hotel, with a top-floor restaurant and bar. ③

CAMPSITES

There are two campsites, as different from each other as they could possibly be:

Camping Plage El Jamil , 500m east of town along the Ajdir road (☎09/98.40.26). A small, friendly site backing onto a stoney beach, where pedalos and water ski-ing are on offer. Also known by its old Spanish name, *Camping Cala Bonita*.

Club Mediterranée, 4km out of town, past Ajdir, off the Ketama–Nador road (☎09/98.20.20). The largest *Club* in Morocco, with space for 1250 campers, sleeping two to a straw-roofed, concrete-based, unlit hut. Extensive facilities. Very French atmosphere. In season, you generally have to book ahead, and for at least a week, through the *Club* office in Casablanca (☎02/31.19.06).

Note that *Camping Plage Kalah Iris*, listed in some guides under Al Hoceima, is actually 60km west, near Torres de Alcala (see pp.120–21).

Restaurants and nightlife

In addition to the hotel resaurants at the Florido and Maghreb El Jadida – both of which are recommended – there are five other good choices for meals:

Restaurant Belle Vue, Av. Mohammed V. A café all year – with snacks available – and a fully fledged restaurant each summer.

Restaurant Snack-Saada, 24 Av. Hassan II. Small but wide-ranging menu. Open late.

Restaurant Merhaba, Place du Rif.

Restaurant Temsamen, Av. de Tetouan – close to the Place du Rif.

Restaurant de Paris, Av. Mohammed V. Good-value meals, though opening hours are at the whim of the cosmopolitan owner.

For **nightlife**, you have a choice of the *Jupiter Disco* at the main beach, or discreet **bars** on the top floors of the hotels *Quemado* and *El Maghreb El Jadida*.

Transport

As in the rest of the Rif, most **buses** leave Al Hoceima early – to Taza at 4am; to Fes (via the Route de l'Unité), Chaouen and Tetouan slightly later. The **tourist office** can give information and times.

If you need to get anywhere in a hurry, there are plenty of **grands taxis**, negotiable even for Rabat and Casablanca. It should be possible to find fellow passengers to share the expense of a taxi to Chaouen, Fes or the Melilla border.

The local **airport**, *Aeroport de Côte du Rif*, is 17km east of Al Hoceima on the Nador road (P39), just before the village of Imzouen. It caters largely for charter flights from France and Germany – used as much by Moroccan workers as tourists – although *RAM* have a couple of flights each week to Casablanca.

East to Nador and Melilla

There is little of apparent interest to slow your progress over the 164km stretch of the P39 from **Al Hoceima to Nador**. For anyone who has read about the events of the Rif War, however, the names of the villages will be familiar. This was the territory of Abd El Krim's first, dramatic rising – the so-called **Rout of Annoual** – of July–August 1921. In those two months, the Spanish were forced back to Melilla, losing over 18,000 of their troops along the way.

The occasional lookout post and barrack remain to be seen, if you follow the tracks off the P39 at MIDAR or DRIOUCH. At Driouch there are basic rooms to be had at the *Hôtel Essalem* (①).

Mont Araoui

MONT ARAOUI, where the road crosses the Oued Moulouya, marked the border of the old Spanish and French zones, a position still guarded by Moroccan sentries. A large and wonderful **Sunday souk** takes place here, with storytellers, dentists and a sort of roulette wheel ("spin the live rat in the pail"). There are also numerous café-restaurants and a single **hotel**, *A Chabab* (①), which is a little better than the hotel at Driouch (above).

Selouane

SELOUANE, 9km further east (and 11km short of Nador), at a rather complex junction of the roads to Al Hoceima and Oujda, has a Saturday *souk*, but is worth a couple of hours' visit on any day of the week. It boasts an interesting Kasbah, built by Moulay Ismail, used as a base by the bizarre pretender to the throne, Bou Hamra (see p.497), and now adapted as a storehouse.

The main reason for a visit, however, is for a **meal** at the *Restaurant Brabo*, 110 Av. Mohammed V (☎06/60.90.33; closed Mon; accepts credit cards). This is, in our opinion, the best **place to eat** in this entire chapter: a superlative restaurant, run by a Belgian and his Moroccan wife, who plan to add accommodation in the near future.

South to Guercif

The road **south to Guercif**, heading off between Mont Araoui and Tiztoutine, is narrow and paved. It makes an interesting alternative to Taza or Oujda, with its vistas of palms and scrub, and the occasional wandering camel.

Nador

Entering or leaving Morocco at the Spanish enclave of Melilla you will have to pass through **NADOR**. If you're a birdwatcher, the marshes and dunes of Kariet Arkmane and Ras El Ma, 30–40km east of the town, may well entice a stay of several days (see "Wildlife" box overpage). If not, you will probably want to move straight out and on. Nador itself, fringed by a shallow lagoon, is earmarked as a centre for economic development and has little to offer conventional tourists.

When the Spanish left in 1957, Nador was just an ordinary Riffian village, given work and some impetus by the port of Melilla. Its later choice as a provincial capital was perhaps unfortunate. There was little to do for the local university students, while the iron foundry proposed to fuel the Rif's mining industry, never materialised: two reasons that explain why the 1984 riots started in this town. However, the past decade has seen some attempt to address these problems, and much new building is in progress.

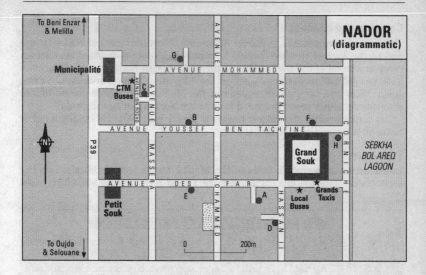

Orientation, hotels and restaurants

The bulk of Nador lies between the **Selouane–Melilla road** (P39), to the west, and the **lagoon** of **Sebkha bou Areq** (or Mar Chica), to the east. It is grouped about a grid of six major avenues and focused on a marketplace, the two-storey **Grand Souk**, down by the lagoon corniche.

There is a wide choice of **hotels**, many of them built recently as the town has been promoted for business and industry. The following is just a selection:

Hôtel Al Mahatta [A], 38 Av. Abbas Mohammed Akkad (☎06/60.27.77). The town's largest hotel, with 200 rooms on three floors, often full with Algerian and Tunisian visitors. A good restaurant stays open all day and until midnight. ③

Hôtel Maghreb [B], 72 Av. Youssef Ben Tachfine (☎06/60.46.64). Good value but very often full. ①

Hôtel Ibn Khaldoun [C], 91 Av. Ibn Rochd (☎06/60.70.42). Another reasonable pension, with hot showers in the evenings. ①

Hôtel Annoual [D], 16 Rue No. 20, Hay Khattabi (☎06/60.27.77). Cheap one-star hotel, opposite the bus station, with a restaurant and café. ①

Hôtel Khalid [E], 129 Av. des F.A.R. (☎06/60.67.26). An excellent, modern hotel, with a good-quality restaurant, managed by a local who spent several years in Holland; accepts credit cards. ②

Hôtel Mediterranée [F], 2/4 Rue Youssef Ibn Tachfine (☎06/60.64.95). Reasonable, modest hotel, opposite the prominant *Hôtel Rif.* ②

Hôtel Mansour Ed Dahabi [G], 105 Rue de Marrakech (☎06/60.65.83). Another new hotel, with a restaurant and bar. ②

Hôtel Rif [H], Rue Youssef Ibn Tachfine (☎06/60.47.73). An outpost of the *Maroc-Tourist* chain, overlooking the lagoon. Equipped with a swimming pool, restaurant and bar, but with a rather sad, empty air about proceedings. ④

For **meals**, beside the hotel-restaurants, *Romero's*, 48/50 Av. Youssef Ben Tachfine, overloking the Grand Souk, is recommended. If you have your own transport, you should definitely take the opportunity to try *Restaurant Brabo* at Selouane (see previous page).

Camping and beaches

The nearest **campsite** is at **Kariet-Arkmane**, 30km southeast of Nador, at the end of the lagoon (see overpage). In summer, Moroccan families also set up camp at several of the the the beaches to the northwest of Nador, especially around BOUYAFAR (30km northeast) and at the **Cap des Trois Forches**, the cape, again 30km out, on the continuation of the Melilla road. There are no official campsites at either resort but you'd have no problem in joining the locals.

For a quick swim, the closest **beach** to Nador is at BOUKANA, 10km out of town, on the road towards Melilla.

Transport

Local buses and **grands taxis** to the Melilla border (see p.139) and beaches leave Nador from the bus station near the Grand Souk and lagoon. **CTM** buses

---

BIRDS AND DUNES: EAST OF NADOR

The coast east of Nador (described above) offers compelling sites for birdwatching – and plant wildlife – with a series of highly frequented freshwater and saline sites.

At **KARIET ARKMANE** a path leads out, opposite the village mosque, past salt pans and a pumping station (right-hand side) to an **extensive area of salt marsh**. This is covered by the fleshy-stemmed **marsh glasswort** or *salicornia*: a characteristic "salt plant" or *halophyte*, it can survive the saline conditions through the use of glands which excrete the salt. The **insect life** of the salt marsh is abundant, including damselflies, brightly-coloured grasshoppers and various ants and sand spiders. The **birds** are even more impressive, with black-winged stilt, greater flamingo, coot, great-crested grebe, and various gulls and terns wheeling overhead.

Further along the coast, a walk east of the resort of **RAS-EL-MAR** demonstrates the means by which plants invade **sand dunes**: a sequential colonisation is known as **"succession"**, where one plant community gradually cedes to the next as a result of its own alteration of the environment. Typical early colonisers are marram grass and sea couch, which are eventually ousted by sea holly and sea spurge and finally by large, "woodier" species such as pistacihu, juniper and cistus *sp*. Whole sequences can be seen occurring over time along the beach. The area attracts a variety of interesting **sea birds** as well, including two internationally rare species: **Audouin's gull** (thought to breed on the adjacent offshore Chafarinas Islands) and **slender-billed curlew**. Other more familiar birds include dunlin, Kentish plover and oystercatcher.

Even further along the coast is the freshwater lagoon system which marks the mouth of the **OUED MOULOUYA**. The lagoons here are separated from the sea by a remarkable series of sand spits, no more than fifty metres across, and the **birdlife** is outstanding. Secluded among the reedbeds, it is possible to locate grey heron, white stork and little egret while the water's surface is constantly patrolled by the ever-alert black terns and kingfishers. Other varieties which you should manage to spot, wading in the shallows, are redshank, spotted redshank (in summer) and black-tailed godwit.

The Spanish-owned **Islas Chafarinas**, incidentally, are another important wildlife site, which Spanish ecologists are attempting to have declared a nature park. The three small islets support the Mediterranean's largest seabird colonies, and are home to the only known pair of **monk seals** surviving anywhere in Spanish waters. These are strictly protected as only about 500 pairs exist in the world.

leave from the opposite side of town, near the Municipalité and *Hôtel Ryad* at the top end of Av. Mohammed V. For Tetouan or Chaouen, it's best to break the trip in Al Hoceima (3hr 30min): from there, they are still an eight-hours-plus journey.

If you are heading for **Fes**, **Taza** or **Oujda**, the best course is to take the buses run by **ONCF**, the rail company, to **Taourirt**, on the Fes–Oujda train line. They leave from outside the *ONCF* office on Av. Sidi Mohammed.

Note that the **ferry** which used to run from Nador to Sète no longer operates.

The coast east to Ras-el-Ma

The coast to the east of Nador has some of the most interesting **wildlife** sites in Morocco (see box opposite), and good beaches in addition. To get the most out of this area, a car would be a great help. However, you can make use of the *grands taxis*, or the daily bus from Nador (which runs along road 8101 to Kariet Arkmane and Ras-el-Ma, then turns round and heads back to town).

Kariet Arkmane

The village of **KARIET ARKMANE**, 30km from Nador, gives access to a sand and shell-packed **road along the spit of the lagoon**. This is a desolate area but picturesque in its own way, with saltmarshes that provide manifold attractions for birdwatchers. The road out follows the edge of the lagoon from Kariet, passing an old Spanish lookout post en route to a shell-beach – a popular weekend spot with Spaniards from Melilla – before giving out at a tiny fishing village. There is a **campsite**, *Camping Karia Plage*, right on the beach, and a youth hostel nearby.

Ras-el-Ma and the Oued Mouloya

The road **east of Kariet** is a pleasant drive, too, twisting into the hills, never far from the sea, and eventually bringing you to **RAS-EL-MA** (or Raz-ka-Bona, as it is also known), 70km from Nador – and closer to Saïdia and Berkane (see p.140). Facing another of Spain's offshore island possessions on this coast, the three tiny **Islas Chafarinas**, this is a mix of resort and fishing village, with a good **beach**, a smattering of cafés and street vendors, and a makeshift summer campsite. Beyond the resort, dunes run virtually undisturbed to the Algerian border.

If you have your own transport, you could complete a loop back towards Nador from Ras-el-Ma, trailing the **Oued Moulouya** on road 8100 – or take the road across the river to the beaches around Saïdia (see p.141).

Melilla (Mlilya)

There ought to be an eccentric appeal to Spanish-occupied **MELILLA**, and in part there is: if you're curious what provincial Spanish towns looked like in the late 1950s, there is no better place to come to find out. More conventional tourist pleasures are to be found, too, in an exploration of the walled old town, **Medina Sidonia**, with its stunning views out across the Mediterranean.

Together with Ceuta, Melilla is the last of Spain's Moroccan enclaves on Moroccan soil – a former penal colony which saw its most prosperous days under the protectorate, when it was the main port for the Riffian mining industry. Since Moroccan independence in 1956, the city's population has halved to a little over

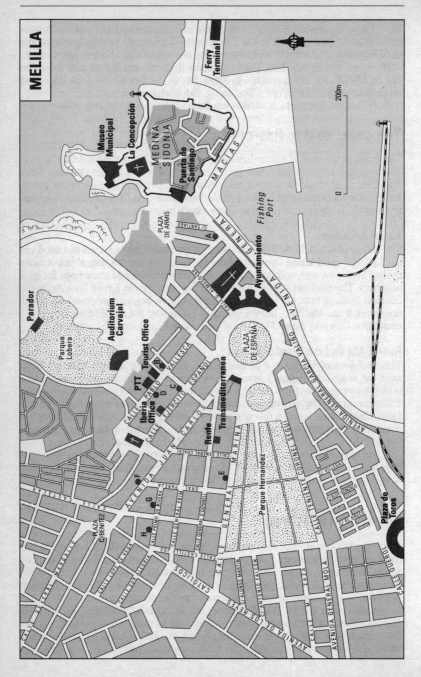

MELILLA

Ferry Terminal

Museo Municipal

La Concepción

MEDINA SIDONIA

Puerta de Santiago

MACIAS

Fishing Port

PLAZA DE ARMIS

C/ SANTIAGO

AVENIDA GENERAL

Ayuntamiento

Parador

Auditorium Carvajal

Parque Lobera

PTT

Tourist Office

Iberia Office

CALLE PABLO VALLESGA

PLAZA DE ESPAÑA

Renfe

Transmediterranea

CALLE PABLO VALLESGA

CALLE EJERCITO ESPANOL

CALLE CARLOS 5

CALLE GENERAL CHACEL

CALLE MARINA

Parque Hernandez

AVENIDA GENERAL GARCIA VALINO

CALLE TENIENTE CORONEL SEGUI

AVDA. GRAL. PAREJA

AVENIDA GENERAL

CALLE PRIMO DE RIVERA

CALLE GRAL. PRIM

CALLE GENERAL O'DONNELL

CALLE CASTELAR

C/ VILLEGAS

PELIG GONZALO

C/EL GRECO

Plaza de Toros

PLAZA C. BENITEZ

CALLE GENERAL MARINA

CALLE CATOLICOS

AVENIDA DE LOS REYES

AVENIDA GENERAL MOLA

CALLE QUEROL

CALLE M

PLAZA

CALLE ANTONIO FALCON

CALLE ALFONSO MARIN

CALLE LOPE DE VEGA

CALLE COLOMBIA

MARGALLO

200m

0

N

60,000, split two-to-one between Christians and Muslims, along with 3000 Jews and a few hundred Indian Hindus. Many of the Christians are gypsies, who, like the other communities, are well integrated, despite an episode of rioting in 1986, after the enactment of Spain's first real "Aliens Law" threatened to deprive certain Muslim families of their residence rights. Melilla is no "little Spain", for all its reputation on the mainland as traditional and fascist, and, like Ceuta, it actually wants – and has for a decade been promised – autonomous status: a plea which seems permanently lost in the Madrid government in-tray, for fear of offending Morocco. Meanwhile, the mainstay of the economy, as at Ceuta, remains the double anomaly of an army garrison plus the duty-free status of the port.

The town

Melilla centres on the **Plaza de España**, overlooking the port, and the **Avenida del Juan Carlos I**, leading inland off it. This is the most animated part of town, especially during the evening *paseo*, when everyone promenades up and down, or strolls through the neighbouring **Parque Hernandez**.

To the northeast, occupying a walled promontory, and adjacent to the ferry terminal, is the old part of town, **Medina Sidonia**. It is here that you should head, if you have time to fill waiting for a ferry – or you want to avoid queueing at the border after disembarking (see p.139).

Medina Sidonia

Until the beginning of this century, the walled "Old Town" of **Medina Sidonia**, wedged in above the port, was all there was of Melilla. The enclave's security was always vulnerable, and at various periods of expansionist Moroccan rule – it was blockaded throughout the reign of Moulay Ismail – the Spanish population was limited to their fortress promontory and its sea approaches. The settlement was founded in 1497, a kind of epilogue to the expulsion of the Moors from Spain in the year that saw the fall of Granada.

The quarter's cramped, whitewashed streets suggest the Andalusian Medinas of Tetouan or Chaouen, though inside, the design is much more formal; it was in fact laid out along the lines of a Castilian fort, following a major earthquake in the sixteenth century.

Steps near the harbour lead up to its main square, **Plaza Maestranza**, entered by the Gothic **Puerta de Santiago**, a gate flanked by a chapel to Saint James the Apostle – known to Spaniards, of course, as *Matamoros*, "the Moor-Slayer". Beyond the square, you come to an old barracks and armoury, and, if you follow the fortifications round from here, you'll come to a small fort, housing a somewhat miscellaneous **Museo Municipal** (Mon–Fri 9am–1pm & 3–6pm). Below this is the church of **La Concepción**, crowded with baroque decoration, including a revered statue of *Nuestra Señora de Victoria* (Our Lady of Victory), the city's patroness.

The new town: Modernista

In the new town, many of the buildings around the **Plaza de España** were designed by **Enrique Nieto**, a *modernista* contemporary of the renowned Catalan architect, Gaudí. His 1930s tile and stucco facades are a quiet delight of the New Town, though, sadly, often masked by the rows of duty-free shops.

Practicalities

Like Ceuta, Melilla is not an easy place in which to stay. Rooms are in short supply – and expensive by Moroccan standards. If you have problems, the **tourist office** (*turismo*; Mon–Fri 9am–2pm, Sat 10am–noon) in the Edificio de Correos, c/Pablo Vallesca, next to the **post office** (PTT), might be able to suggest alternatives.

There are a number of **banks** on or near Avda. Juan Carlos which will change cheques, sterling, dollars or dirhams. Banco Central is at c/del Ejercito Español 1 and Banco de España is on the Plaza de España itself.

Accommodation

Most of the budget *hostales* and *pensiones* are down towards the port, in the side streets off the Paseo del Generál Macias. Others are scattered about the grid of streets radiating from the Plaza de España. The following are listed in ascending order of price; codes approximate to those used for Moroccan hotels elsewhere in the guide (see p.30).

Pension El Porto [A], c/Santiago 1 (☎68.12.70). New and Moroccan-run, near the port. ①

Hostal-Residencia Rioja [C], c/Ejercito Español 6 (☎68.27.09). Old but good value, with friendly and helpful staff. ①

Hostal-Residencia Parque [E], Avda. Generál Marina 15 (☎68.21.43). Comfortable hotel facing the Parque Hernandez. ①

Hôtel Nacional [H], Avda. Primo de Rivera 10 (☎68.45.40). Good value. ②

Hostal-Residencia Cazaza [G], Avda. Primo de Rivera 6 (☎68.46.48). Good value. ②

Hostal-Residencia Anfora [B], c/Pablo Vallesca 8 (☎68.33.40). ②

Hôtel Avenida [F], Avda. Juan Carlos I 24 (☎68.49.49). ②

Hôtel Rusadir San Miguel [D], c/Pablo Vallesca 5 (☎68.12.40). A more upmarket place with a reasonable restaurant. ③

Parador de Melilla [labelled], Avda. de Candido Lobera (☎68.49.40). The town's top choice – closed at time of writing for refurbishment, so phone ahead. ③

Note that, **phoning Melilla** from Morocco, you must prefix phone numbers with the international (☎0034) and local (952) codes.

Restaurants and bars

The two best **places to eat** in central Melilla are in Medina Sidonia. For homely Spanish cooking and ambience, look for *Meson de la Tortilla/Casa El Marco*, c/San Miguel 2. For more expensive, but excellent value, meals, and with views of the coast to the north, try *Babacao La Muralla*, c/Fiorentina 1, in the south corner of the ramparts. Both are licensed.

Down by the port on Avenida Generál Macios, is a new snack bar, *La Pergola*, where the town's youth hang out of an evening. That apart, there's not a lot on, though the **bars** at the *Metropol* on Plaza de España and at the *Bodegas Madrid* on c/de Castelar are usually busy.

There is also a **flamenco club**, the *Peña Francisco*, near the *Babacoa La Muralla* restaurant in Medina Sidonia.

Ferries and flights

The **ferries** *Canguro* and *Albatros* run three to five times a week between Melilla and **Málaga** and **Almería** (see p.8). Making advance bookings is critical in

THE MELILLA–NADOR BORDER

On a good day you can cross the **Melilla–Nador border** in ten or fifteen minutes. At other times, you may need considerable time and patience. During the summer it's often extremely crowded, with Moroccans returning from (or going to) jobs in Europe, as well as travellers off the ferry. If you want to avoid the queues, it is a good idea to spend a couple of hours in Melilla after arriving off a ferry, to let the main traffic get through.

If you are **driving**, be aware that smuggling goes on at the border, with periodic police crackdowns; in recent years, the main trade has been a human one, with Moroccans attempting to cross illegally into mainland Spain. Driving at night, keep an eye out for road checks – not always well lit but usually accompanied by tyre-puncturing blockades.

Hire cars, incidentally, are not allowed across the border.

MELILLA–NADOR

To get to the main Melilla border post at **Beni Enzar**, there are buses to and from the Plaza de España (every 15min; takes 20min). At the border post, on the Moroccan side, you should be prepared to show evidence of 3500dh in foreign currency or cheques (about £260); this seems to be the one frontier where such evidence is (sometimes) requested. If you have any problems, don't argue but instead return later in the day for the next shift.

NADOR–MELILLA

From Nador, there is a local bus and numerous *grands taxis* to the border. Delays at the post are mainly on the Moroccan side, where officials can take a while collecting passports, passing them round and eventually stamping them. Leave up to two hours if you have a ferry connection to make. If you are just planning on a day trip to Melilla, it is better not to admit to it.

CURRENCY EXCHANGE

The frontier **currency exchange**, on both sides, is for cash only. However, you can use dirhams and pesetas quite widely in Melilla and Nador, and banks in both towns have exchange facilities between the two currencies.

August – with waits of up to three days possible if you just turn up for a boat – and the period at the end of Semana Santa (Easter week) is also best avoided. For information and tickets, contact *Transmediterranea*, Plaza de España 6 (☎68.12.45; Mon–Fri 9am–noon & 2–6pm; Sat 9am–noon). *Transmediterranea* is also experimenting with a faster catamaran service, possibly from Melilla to Málaga and/or Almería, but it is not yet in service.

Alternatively, for much the same cost, there are *Iberia* **flights** to **Málaga** (45min); up to eight a day in season, three to five daily out of season. Again, reserve ahead of time if possible, and be warned that flights don't leave in bad weather. The *Iberia* office is at the corner of Avda. Juan Carlos I and Avda. de Candido Lobera (☎68.24.34 or 68.15.07; Mon–Fri 9am–noon & 2–6pm). To call the **airport** direct, phone ☎68.99.47 or ☎68.99.48.

A helpful travel agency for information and reservations is *Andalucia Travel*, Teneinte Coronel Segui 10, facing the Parque Hernandez (☎67.07.30; Mon–Fri 9am–noon & 2–6pm; Sat 9am–noon).

The Zegzel Gorge, Berkane and Saïdia

The **route east from Nador to Oujda** is fast, efficient and well served by both buses and *grands taxis*. It holds little of interest along the way, but if you've got the time (or ideally a car), there's an attractive detour around Berkane into the **Zegzel gorge**, a dark limestone fault in the Beni Snassen mountains – the last outcrops of the Rif. And on the coast there is the considerable attraction of **Saïdia**, one of the country's most pleasant and relaxed seaside resorts.

The Gorge Route

The **Oued Zegzel** is a tributary of the Moulouya, which as it runs south of Berkane has carved out a fertile shaft of mountain valleys. These for centuries marked the limits of the Shereefian empire.

The route through these valleys is easily accessible today, though still forbiddingly steep: all traffic goes *down* (south from Berkane), climbing up again from the main road to Taforalt and winding from there to Berkane. If you've got a car, this is the route to follow. If not, stay on the bus to Berkane, where you can get a seat in a *grand taxi* to Taforalt and there negotiate another one back, via the gorge road. Neither is an expensive operation because the routes are used locally (and are popular with tourists).

Taforalt, the Grotte du Chameau and the gorge

TAFORALT is a quiet mountain village, active (or as active as it ever gets) only for the **Wednesday souk**. It does, though, have a reliable supply of *grands taxis*, and you should be able to move on rapidly towards the Zegzel.

Before setting on a price, get the driver to agree to stop off for a while at the **Grotte du Chameau** (15km), a cavern of vast stalactites – one of them remarkably camel-like in shape. The cave, with various tunnels leading off, is completely uncommercialised, so bring a torch if possible. Near the entrance is a hot stream, which locals use for bathing.

The gorge, or rather **gorges**, begin about a kilometre beyond the cave, scrupulously terraced and cultivated with all kinds of citrus and fruit trees. As the road crisscrosses the riverbed, they progressively narrow, drawing your eye to the cedars and dwarf oaks at the summit, until you eventually emerge (28km from Taforalt) on to the plain of Berkane.

Berkane

BERKANE is a strategic little market town, French-built and prosperous, set amid an extensive region of orchards and vineyards. If you stay, you're likely to be the only European in the town – in consequence there are no hustlers and people may even buy *you* a coffee. Good eating places are to be found in the long, unpaved street running uphill from Av. Hassan II, along with lots of very dark, tented *souks*. The best **place to stay** is the *Hôtel Ennajah* (☎06/61.29.14; ⑩), on the corner of Bd. Hassan II and Bd. Moulay Youssef, near the bus station. The hotel also has a good restaurant, the owner having worked some time in Belgium. **Moving on** is straightforward, with frequent buses and *grands taxis* both to Oujda and Saïdia.

Saïdia

Sited right on the Algerian border, **SAÏDIA** is a good choice for staying put for a few days. Despite a superb stretch of beach (which from time to time attracts international development plans), it remains a resort as low-key and relaxed as it's possible to imagine – a one-street sort of place, rambling back from the sea in the shadow of an old and still occupied nineteenth-century Kasbah.

Saïdia's **beach** really is special: an immense, sandy strand, stretching west to face the tiny Chafarinas islands at Ras-el-Ma (see p.135), and east, across the Oued Kiss, into Algeria. Moroccans proclaim that at Saïdia "we swim together with Algerians", which isn't exactly true, though there's a very similar resort over on the Algerian side.

Saïdia makes a good base for **birdwatchers**, too, with marshes and woodland stretching behind the beach towards the Oued Moulouya (see box on p.134).

Practicalities

In the summer months, Saïdia is very lively and a lot of fun; from mid-September through to May, in contrast, it becomes virtually deserted, with variable, rather windy weather.

There are three small **hotels**, the *Al Kalaa* (☎06/61.51.23; ②), *Hannour* (☎06/61.51.15; ②) and *Select* (☎06/61.51.10; ①) – the latter two closed out of season – and an expensive bungalow holiday complex. In summer, if you don't book a room in advance, you'll probably need to camp. In classic, local-resort fashion, Saïdia has two **campsites**, one for families only (off the main street), another (towards the Kasbah) for single people – pick your category.

Liveliest of the town's **café-restaurants** are a group by the market, past the Kasbah and looking across into Algeria. At night, the *Hôtel Hannour* is the centre of life, with its **bar**, restaurant and occasional entertainment.

There are regular **buses** and **grands taxis** between Saïdia and Oujda.

Oujda

Open and easy-going, with a large and active university, **OUJDA** has that rare quality in Moroccan cities – nobody makes demands on your instinct for self-preservation. After the Rif, it is a surprise, too, to see women in public again, and to re-enter a Gallic atmosphere – as you move out of what used to be Spanish Morocco into the old French Protectorate zone. Morocco's easternmost town, Oujda was the capital of French *Maroc Orient* and an important trading centre. It remains today a lively and prosperous place, strikingly modern by Moroccan standards, and with a population approaching half a million.

With its strategic location at the crossroads of eastern and southern routes across Morocco-Algeria, Oujda, like Taza, was always vulnerable to invasion and has frequently been the focus of territorial claims. In the thirteenth and fourteenth centuries, there were periods of occupation by the Algerian Ziyanids of Tlemcen, and from 1727 until the early nineteenth century Oujda was under Turkish rule – the only town in present-day Morocco to have been part of the Ottoman Empire. Following the French defeat of the Ottomans in Algeria, France twice occupied the town, prior to its incorporation within the Moroccan

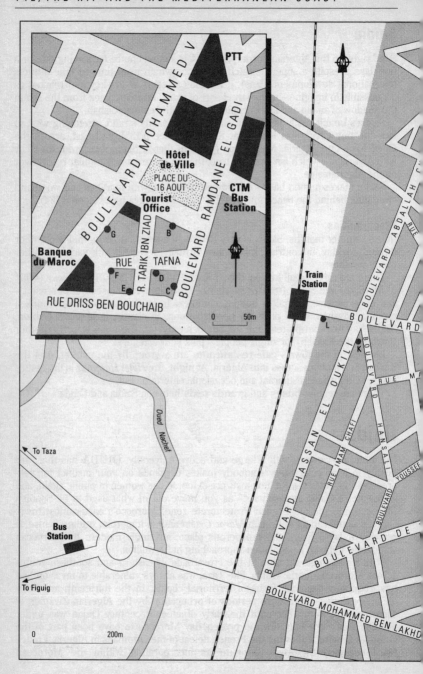

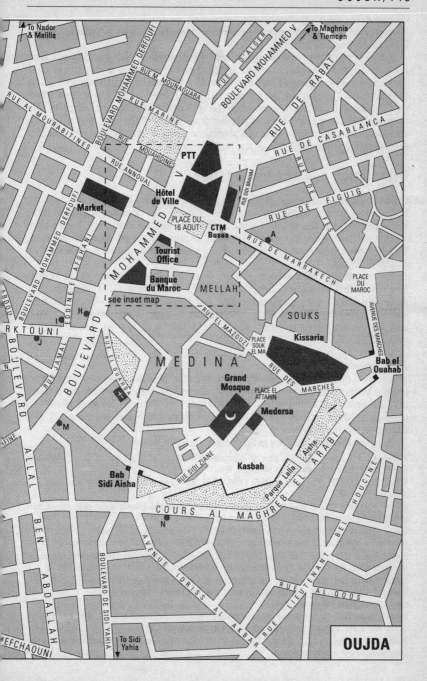

To Nador
& Melilla

To Maghnia
& Tlemcen

RUE M. MOUNAQUARA

RUE D'ALGER

BOULEVARD MOHAMMED V

RUE DE RABAT

RUE AL MOURABITINES

RUE MARINE

BOULEVARD MOHAMMED V

RUE DE CASABLANCA

RUE
MOUAHIDINES

RUE ANNOUAL

PTT

RUE SIDI BRAHIM

RUE DE FIGUIG

BOULEVARD MOHAMMED DERFOUFI

Market

Hôtel
de Ville

PLACE DU
16 AOUT

CTM
Buses

RUE DE FES

RUE DE MARRAKECH

A

MOHAMMED V

Tourist
Office

Banque
du Maroc

MELLAH

PLACE DU
MAROC

BOULEVARD MOHAMMED DERFOUFI

see inset map

RUE EL MAZOUZI

SOUKS

AVENUE DES MARCHES

RBDOU

EDDINE E AFGHANI

H

RKTOUNI

BOULEVARD

RUE EL OUAHAB

PLACE
SOUK
EL MA

Kissaria

Bab el
Ouahab

J

RUE JAMAL

M E D I N A

RUE DES

BOULEVARD

Grand
Mosque

PLACE EL
ATTARIN

MARCHES

FINE

M

Medersa

Aisha

RUE B. EL ARABI

ALLAL

RUE SIDI ZIANE

Kasbah

Parque Laila

HOUCINE

BEL

Bab
Sidi Aisha

BEN

N

COURS   AL   MAGHREB

ABDALLAH

AVENUE IDRISS AL AKBAR

BOULEVARD DE SIDI YAHIA

RUE LIEUTENANT BEL

RUE   AL QODS

EFCHAOUNI

To Sidi
Yahia

OUJDA

Protectorate in 1912: an early and prolonged association, which remains tangible in the streets and attitudes.

In recent years, the town's proximity to the Algerian border and distance from the government in Rabat has led to something of a reputation as a centre of dissidence and unrest. This was particularly evident during the Algerian border war in the early 1960s, and again, over recent years, in a series of student strikes. Much more striking, however, at least since the restoration of Moroccan-Algerian relations in 1988, is the upbeat and international tempo of the city, with Algerians coming in to shop, and Moroccans sharing in some of the cultural dynamism of neighbouring Oran, the home of *Raï* music.

Orientation and accommodation

Oujda consists of the usual **Medina** and **Ville Nouvelle**, the latter highly linear in its layout, having started out as a military camp. The Medina, walled on three sides, lies right in the heart of town, with **Place du 16 Août**, the town's main square, at its northwest corner. Around this square are grouped the Hôtel de Ville, the **post office**, several **banks**, and a **tourist office** (open daily 8am–noon & 2.30–6.30pm).

Arriving at the **train station** you are in easy walking distance of the centre. The new **bus station**, which handles virtually all services, CTM and private, is more of a walk (or an inexpensive *petit taxi* ride), 500m southwest of the train station, across the Oued Nachef. The **airport** is 15km north, off the P27; *RAM* and *Air France* share an office inside the *Hôtel Oujda* on Bd. Mohammed V (☎06/68.39.63).

Accommodation

There are a number of **unclassified hotels** in the **Medina**; many are poor value, but the better choices are detailed below. Around the **Ville Nouvelle** are a range of much better, classified hotels, many of them recently built. Booking ahead is a good idea, wherever you plan to stay, as all classes of hotels are often full with Algerians on shopping sprees.

The closest **campsites** are in Saïdia (see previous page).

Hôtel du 16 Août [A], 128 Rue de Marrakech (☎06/68.41.97). Best of the unclassified hotels, with clean rooms and hot showers. ⓪

Hôtel Zegzgel [B], Place du 16 Août (☎06/68.31.58). Central but a bit noisy, and with cold showers only. ⓪

Hôtel Majestic [F], 8 Rue Neggai (☎06/68.29.48). Old hotel, in a quiet side street, just inside the Medina; washbasins in the rooms but no showers. ⓪

Hôtel Ziri [H], Bd. Mohammed V (☎06/68.45.40). Occupies the third, fourth and fifth floors of an office block; reception is on the ground floor. A little noisy and cold showers only. ①

Royal Hôtel [J], 13 Bd. Zerktouni (☎06/68.22.84). Much better: clean rooms with hot showers; next door, the *Café Les Pyramides*, provides breakfast and is lively in the evenings. ①

Hôtel Simon [E], corner of Bd. Tariq Ibn Ziad and Idriss Ben Bouchaib (☎06/68.63.03). Just inside the Medina, this was the first French hotel in Oujda – opened in 1910. A nice place, with a restaurant, café and bar. ①

Hôtel Afrah [D], 15 Rue Tafna (☎06/68.65.33). New hotel, opened in 1991, with imaginative decor and a fine view across the Medina from its rooftop café. ②

Hôtel Lutetia [K], 44 Bd. Hassan Loukili (☎06/68.33.65). Convenient position right by the train station, but a little seedy. ②

Hôtel Angad [**C**], Bd. Ramdane El Gadi (☎06/68.14.51). Another new hotel, on a pedestrianised street just inside the Medina. ②

Hôtel des Lilas [**I**], Rue Jamal Eddine El Afghani (☎06/68.08.41). Another decent, new hotel – with a restaurant but no bar. ③

Hôtel Concorde [**G**], 57 Bd. Mohammed V (☎06/68.23.28). Yet another new hotel, run by the prestigious *Concorde* chain. Has a restaurant and bar. ③

Hôtel Al Massira [**N**], Bd. Maghreb El Arabi (☎06/68.53.01). Modern hotel, with a pool and tennis court, run by the reliable *Salam* chain. ④

Hôtel Oujda [**M**], Bd. Mohammed V (☎06/68.40.93). A bit undistinguished but has a bar and small swimming pool. ④

Hôtel Terminus [**L**], Place de l'Unité Africaine (☎06/68.32.11). The best upmarket choice, facing the train station, with a characterful bar, pretentious restaurant, gardens, and a fine swimming pool. Part of the *Concorde* chain. ④

The town

Oujda's **Medina** is largely a French reconstruction – obvious by the ease with which you can find your way around. Unusually, though, it has retained much of the city's commercial functions and has an enjoyably active air.

Entering from **Bab El Ouahab**, the principal gate, you'll be struck by the amazing variety of food – both on café and market stalls – and it's well worth a look for this alone. Olives are Oujda specialities, and especially wonderful if you're about after the September harvest. In the old days, more or less up until the French occupation, Bab El Ouahab was the gate where the heads of criminals were displayed. In the evenings it is still a square where storytellers and musicians come to entertain, an increasing rarity in post-independence Morocco.

Exploring the quarter, a good route to follow from the gate is straight down the main street towards **Place d'Attarine**, flanked by a *kissaria* and a grand *fondouk*. At the far end of the *souks* you come upon **Souk El Ma**, the irrigation *souk*, where the supply of water used to be regulated and sold by the hour. Walking on from here, you'll arrive back at Place du 16 Août 1953.

Running along the outside of the Medina walls, the **Parc Lalla Aisha** is a pleasant area to seek midday shade. Following it round to the west, you arrive at the Bab Sidi Aicha, from which the Rue El Ouahda runs north to the old **French Cathedral**. This is an evocative place. Its present congregation numbers about ten, the fonts are dry, and the statue niches empty, but there is a beautiful chapel. It is usually kept locked; for admission, ring at the door of the presbytery at the back.

Food, music and moussems

Oujda has a strong life of its own, and is one of the most enjoyable Moroccan cities to while away an evening. Hustlers don't really feature here – though there are plenty of people looking to change dirhams for dinars, or vice versa – and the bars and restaurants are sociable and open places.

Restaurants

The focus of evening activity is **Bab El Ouahab**, around which you can get all kinds of grilled food from stalls. On the other side of the Medina, too, there are plenty of good eating places on, or just off, **Bd. Zerktouni**.

CROSSING INTO ALGERIA – AND SOUTH TO FIGUIG

The state of Moroccan–Algerian relations has undergone a dramatic improvement over recent years, making a border crossing at **Oujda–Maghnia** (or, 369km to the south, at Figuig) a relatively routine matter. There are still no **trains** running across the frontier, however. Instead, the line terminates at Oujda and restarts inside Algeria at Maghnia. For the missing 27km (15km in Morocco, 12km in Algeria), those without a car are dependent on hitching, taxis, or the somewhat sporadic local buses. It remains a time-consuming business.

VISAS AND CURRENCY EXCHANGE

Citizens of the UK, Ireland, USA, Canada, Australia, New Zealand and The Netherlands must obtain a **visa in advance** to enter Algeria; Scandinavian citizens can currently enter with a routine stamp at the border.

You can get a visa at any overseas Algerian consulate, including **Rabat** (where they are issued on the same day; see Chapter Four). The Algerian consulate in **Oujda** (11 Bd. de Taza; ☎06/68.37.40 or ☎06/68.37.41) can issue visas, too, but they take about a week to do so, as they have to send all the details to Rabat. If you are in Oujda without a visa, and in a hurry to cross into Algeria, it would be easier and quicker to get the night train up to Rabat and back.

Formalities at both borders are relatively quick and straightforward, at least for pedestrians, though there are random checks on the Algerian side for illegal importation of currency, etc. Car-drivers should allow three to four hours for registration. While in Algeria, you must **change** the equivalent of 1000 dinars (about £80) at the official government rate (currently 13 dinar to £1; 8 dinars to $1). This can be at any time during your stay – you don't have to do it at the border – and should last for a week's travel. Staying beyond that, many travellers pay for items in foreign currency or use the thriving black market (which can be up to four times the official exchange rate). Note that **petrol/gas** is much cheaper in Algeria.

THE OUJDA–MAGHNIA BORDER

Heading for the Oujda–Maghnia border, there are frequent *grands taxis*, leaving from the fountain at the end of Rue de Marrakech (5dh a place), and buses (no fixed timetable) from the main bus station. Better still, try and hitch a ride with other travellers – you can usually arrange this the night before by going round the better hotels (the *Terminus, Al Massira* and *Oujda*), and it should take you through to TLEMCEN, the first Algerian town of any size and a place well worth spending some time in (see "Onwards" in *Contexts*).

SOUTH TO THE FIGUIG BORDER

Crossing over at FIGUIG (see p.424) is by no means a bad option, though it's an unbelievably hot trip in the summer months. Despite its uncertain appearance on some maps, there is a fast new road down from Oujda – a 369km trek, but no more than seven hours by bus. Try and get the early morning departure (currently at 6am); there are two later on, but by noon things can be pretty stifling. All of these buses leave from the main *Gare Routière*.

En route, there are a few roadside settlements and mining towns – for coal and zinc. If you are driving, **AÏT BENIMATHAR**, 83km from Oujda, is a good point to break the journey: the village has a group of kasbahs, an important (and ancient) **Monday souk**, and, about 4km to the west, a small oasis, **Ras El Aïn**, with a highly seasonal waterfall. **TENDRARA**, 198km from Oujda, has a **Thursday souk** for the nomadic Beni M'Guil.

In the Ville Nouvelle, in addition to the hotel restaurants mentioned above, recommended restaurants include:

Restaurant Marios, La Mamounia, Restaurant Dauphin, all on or just off Bd. Mohammed Derfoufi. A trio of good restaurants; the Dauphin specialises in fish.

China Town, corner of Bd. Zerktouni and Bd. Mohammed V. Chinese restaurant, on the first floor.

Restaurant de France, 87 Bd. Mohammed V. Dependable French and Moroccan cooking.

Raï music

Since the development of more open relations with Algeria, and Oujda's increasingly close links with Oran, across the border, the city has become a promising place to catch performances of **Raï music** – a wild blend of traditional songs and rock, with a swirling funky beat, whose chief exponents include Oran-residents such as Cheb Khalaed (*the* superstar), Cheb Fadhela, Cheb Sahraoui and Chaba Fadhela. The music has taken recent hold in Morocco, and especially Oujda, where it is always worth asking about **concerts**. You may well catch a local Moroccan Raï group, or even one of the big Algerian stars, who occasionally give concerts at the Oujda football stadium.

The Sidi Yahia moussems

SIDI YAHIA, 6km south of Oujda, is a rather unimpressive little oasis for most of the year, with a "cascade" that is switched on at weekends. However, it's a place of some veneration, housing as it does the tomb of the *marabout* **Sidi Yahia**, a holy man identified by local tradition with John the Baptist. Nobody is quite sure where the saint is buried – several of the cafés stake an optimistic claim – but at the **moussems** held here in August and September almost every shrub and tree in the oasis, is festooned with little pieces of cloth, a ritual as lavish and extraordinary as anything in the Mediterranean church.

travel details

Trains

From Taza 4–5 trains daily to Oujda (3hr 30min), and in the other direction to Fes (2hr).

From Oujda 5–6 trains daily to Taza (3hr 30min) and Fes (5hr 30min–6hr). Also, on Saturday night, there's a weekly train (mainly for freight) to Bouarfa (8hr).

Note: *ONCF* runs connecting bus services to Nador from Taourirt, midway between Taza and Oujda.

Buses

From Al Hoceima Nador (2 daily; 3hr 30min); Fes (1; 7hr).

From Chaouen Ketama/Al Hoceima (2 daily; 5hr/8hr); El Jebha (2; 7hr).

From Ketama Fes (2 daily; 3hr 30min).

From Fes El Bali Daily to Taounate and Aknoul.

From Taza Fes (3 daily; 2hr 30min); Al Hoceima (2; 4hr 30min); Nador (2; 5–5hr 30min).

From Nador Berkane/Oujda (5 daily; 2hr/3hr); Melilla (local buses to the border); Fes (3; 8hr).

From Berkane Oujda (6 daily; 1hr); Saïdia (4; 1hr).

From Oujda Saïdia (6 daily, 1hr); Figuig (3; 7hr); Midelt (1; 13hr).

Grands Taxis

From Taza Regularly to Fes (1hr 30min) and Oujda (2hr 30min). Occasionally to Al Hoceima.

From Al Hoceima Regularly to Nador (3hr). Infrequently to Fes and Taza.

From Nador Regularly to Oujda (2hr 30min) and Al Hoceima (3hr).

From Oujda Regularly to Saïdia (50min) and Taza (2hr 30min). Negotiable for the Algerian border.

Flights

From Oujda Casablanca (most days; 1hr), on *RAM*.

From Melilla Málaga (7 daily; 35–40min); Almería (daily, except Thurs; 30min). Both on *Iberia*.

Ferries

For details of ferry routes, see p.138.

CHAPTER THREE

FES, MEKNES AND THE MIDDLE ATLAS

The imperial capital of the Merenid, Wattasid and Alouite dynasties, **Fes** has for ten centuries been at the heart of Moroccan history – and for five hundred years was one of the major intellectual and cultural centres of the West, rivalling the university cities of Europe. It is today unique in the Arab world, preserving the appearance and much of the life of a medieval Islamic city. In terms of monuments, above all the intricate university *medersas*, or colleges, Fes has as much as the other Moroccan imperial capitals together, while the city's *souks*, extending for over a mile, maintain the whole tradition of urban crafts.

In all of this – and equally in the everyday aspects of the city's life – there is enormous fascination and, for the outsider, a real feeling of privilege. But inevitably, it is at a cost. Declared a historical monument by the French, and subsequently deprived of its political and cultural significance, Fes retains its beauty but is now in drastic and evident decline. Its university faculties have been dispersed around the country, with the most important departments in Rabat; the Fassi business elite have mostly left for Casablanca; and, for survival, the city depends increasingly on the tourist trade.

Fes's claims are well known, and, after Tangier, it is by far the most touristed city of the north. **Meknes**, in contrast, sees comparatively few visitors, despite being an easy and convenient stopover en route by train from Tangier or Rabat, or by bus from Chaouen. The megalomaniac creation of Moulay Ismail, most tyrannical of all Moroccan sultans, it is once again a city of lost ages, its enduring impression being that of an endless series of walls. But Meknes is also an important modern market centre and its *souks*, though smaller and less secretive than those of Fes, are almost as varied and generally more authentic. There are, too, the local attractions of **Volubilis**, the best preserved of the country's Roman sites, and the hilltop town of **Moulay Idriss**, the most important Moroccan shrine, forbidden to non-Muslims and hidden from Europeans until 1916.

South of the two imperial cities stretch the cedar-covered slopes of the **Middle Atlas**, which in turn gradually give way to the High Atlas. Across and around this region, often beautiful and for the most part remote, there are three main routes. The most popular, a day's journey by bus, skirts the range beyond the market town of **Azrou** to emerge via **Beni Mellal** at Marrakesh. A second one climbs southeastward from Azrou towards **Midelt**, an excellent carpet centre, before passing through great gorges to Er Rachidia and the vast date palm oasis of Tafilalt – the beginning of a tremendous southern circuit (see Chapter Six). The third route, running between these two, is much more adventurous and is

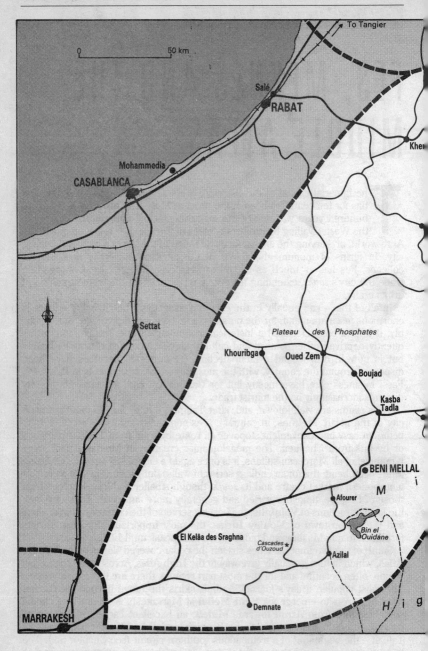

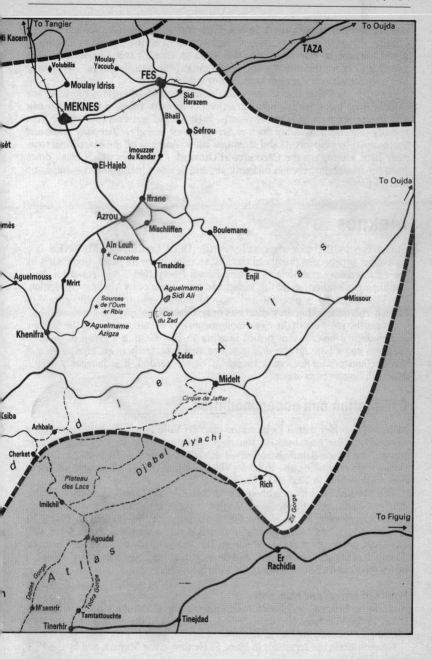

described (in reverse order) in the High Atlas section (see Chapter Five). Leaving the main Azrou–Marrakesh highway at **El Ksiba**, it follows a series of pistes (dirt roads) directly **across the Atlas** to Tinerhir (see Chapter Six). It is possible to cover this route – one of the great Moroccan journeys – by getting lifts over the various stages in local Berber lorries,

If you're travelling one of the main highways, and you've got the time, the Middle Atlas has other, definite attractions of its own. Close to Fes, **Immouzer** and **Ifrane** are popular summer resorts, their air and waters a cool escape from the city. The Berber market town of **Azrou** is host to a great **Tuesday souk** and surrounded by pine forests and mountain lakes. And just off the Marrakesh road, near Beni Mellal, are the **Cascades d'Ouzoud** – waterfalls which crash down from the mountains, even in midsummer, and beside which you can swim, camp and hike.

Meknes

Cut in two by the wide river valley of the Oued Boufekrane, **MEKNES** is a sprawling, prosperous provincial city. Monuments from its past – dominated by the extraordinary creations of Moulay Ismail (see p.158) – well reward a day's rambling exploration, as do the varied and busy *souks* of its Medina. In addition, the Ville Nouvelle is pleasant and easy to handle, and there is the appeal of Roman Volubilis, within easy short bus or taxi distance.

To get the most out of the city's monuments and the atmosphere of the Medina and *souks*, it's best to visit before heading to Fes. Getting a grasp of Meknes prepares you a little for the drama of Fes, and it certainly helps give an idea of quality (and prices) for crafts shopping; visited second, it is inevitably a little disappointing by comparison.

Orientation and accommodation

Meknes is simpler than it looks on the map. Its **Ville Nouvelle** stretches along a slope above the east bank of the river, radiating from an impressive public square, the **Place Administrative** – a stretch of garden and a fountain, flanked by the main post office, the Hôtel de Ville, a helpful ONMT office, and a block of flats on stilts built in 1953 by Le Corbusier.

The **Medina**, and its neighbouring Mellah (the old Jewish quarter), occupies the west bank, with the walls of Moulay Ismail's **Imperial City** edging away, seemingly forever, to its south. The focal point of the Medina is **Place El Hedim**, which has been recently remodelled into a vast pedestrian plaza with fountains, decorated arcades and shops. This is a good place to fix your bearings: downhill, *petits taxis*, *grands taxis* and buses run to local destinations, while uphill buses #5, #7 and #9 head towards the Ville Nouvelle.

Points of arrival and transport
Arriving by **bus** you will be dropped either at the CTM bus station on Av. des F.A.R. in the Ville Nouvelle, or at a new bus terminal on the north side of the New Mellah, just outside the Bab El Khemis.

Grands taxis use terminals in Place El Hedim, in the Medina, and by the PTT in the Ville Nouvelle.

There are two **train stations**, both in the Ville Nouvelle on the east bank. The **main station** is a kilometre away from the central area; a smaller, more convenient one, the **Gare El Amir Abdelkader**, is a couple of blocks from the centre (behind the *Hôtel Majestic*); all trains stop at both.

Leaving Meknes

Leaving Meknes for **Fes**, you have the choice of either taking a *CTM* bus, train or, quickest of all, *grand taxi*; the latter leave Meknes at Place El Hedim and set down in Fes at the train station.

CTM have at least daily departures, too, for **Azrou**, **Midelt**, **Rabat** and **Marrakesh**. Heading for **Chaouen**, check times with the tourist office, and try to buy a ticket in advance.

Hotels

Hotels are concentrated in the **Ville Nouvelle**, and if you want anything like comfort, or proximity to bars and restaurants, this is the place to stay. It's only a fifteen-minute walk from there to the **Medina**, monuments and *souks*.

MEDINA HOTELS
These are all keyed on the **Medina map** on p.156.

Maroc Hôtel [A], Rue Rouamazine (☎05/53.00.75). This is by far the cleanest and quietest of the Medina hotels. It has cold showers only but next door is a hammam for women and douche for men (with ample hot water). ⑩

Hôtel de Paris [B], 58 Rue Rouamazine (no phone). Just up the street from the *Maroc* – and the best fallback if you find it full. ⑩

Hôtel Agadir [C], 9 Rue Dar Smen (☎05/52.01.41). Friendly and with a bit of character but very basic rooms and no showers. ⑩

Hôtel Regina [D], 19 Rue Dar Smen (☎05/53.02.80). Simple but clean rooms off an open courtyard; cold showers. ⑩

Hôtel Nouveau [E], 65 Rue Dar Smen (☎05/53.31.39). Basic and undistinguished. ⑩

HOTEL PRICE CODES AND STAR-RATINGS

Hotels are no longer obliged to levy set maximum rates, according to their official star-ratings, as had long been the custom. However, their **prices** still broadly follow the star-rating system, and this is the basis of our own **hotel price codes** set out below and keyed throughout the guide.

Our code	*Official classification*	*Single room price*	Double room price
⑩	Unclassified	25–60dh	40–100dh
①	1*A/1*B	60–105dh	100–125dh
②	2*B/2*A	105–145dh	125–175dh
③	3*B/3*A	145–225dh	175–275dh
④	4*B/4*A	225–400dh	275–500dh
⑤	5*luxury	Upwards of 400dh	Upwards of 500dh

TELEPHONE CODES

All telephone numbers in the Meknes/Fes region are prefixed 05. When making a call within the region you omit this prefix. For more explanation of phone codes and making calls within (or to) Morocco, see pp.37–38.

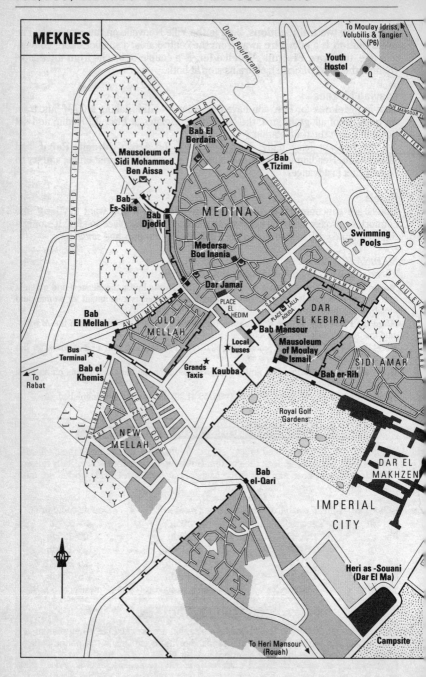

MEKNES

To Moulay Idriss,
Volubilis & Tangier
(P6)

Youth
Hostel

Oued Boufekrane

BOULEVARD CIRCULAIRE

Bab El
Berdaïn

Mausoleum of
Sidi Mohammed
Ben Aissa

Bab
Tizimi

Bab
Es-Siba

Bab
Djedid

MEDINA

Swimming
Pools

Medersa
Bou Inania

Dar Jamaï

PLACE
EL
HEDIM

DAR
EL KEBIRA

Bab
El Mellah

OLD
MELLAH

Bab Mansour

SIDI AMAR

Bus
Terminal

Bab el
Khemis

Local
buses

Mausoleum
of Moulay
Ismaïl

Bab er-Rih

Grands
Taxis

Kaubba

To
Rabat

NEW
MELLAH

Royal Golf
Gardens

DAR EL
MAKHZEN

Bab
el-Qari

IMPERIAL

CITY

N

Heri as -Souani
(Dar El Ma)

To Heri Mansour
(Rouah)

Campsite

0   200m

OMAR ABDELAZIZ

AV. EL MOUQAOUAMA

AV. EL AMIR MOULAY ABDELLAH

AV. PLACE
IFRIQUIA

RUE   OUJDA

AVENUE   HASSAN I

To Fes
(P1)

AVENUE HASSAN II

AV. PLACE
IFRIQUIA

P

M

RUE ACCRA

L

Gare El Amir
Abdelkader

VILLE

RUE   ALGER

AVENUE DE FES

ONMT

N

PTT

Hôtel
de Ville

I H

AVENUE DE LA GARE

S.I.

PLACE
ADMINISTRATIVE

J

C D B

E

ROYALES

A

e Corbusier
Flats

Tribunal

DRISS II

ARMÉES

F

NOUVELLE

Main
Train Station

AVENUE   DES   FORCES

G

BENDOUNGA

AVENUE   BENGAL

Hospital

RUE   DJERARI

Stadium

AVENUE

BIR   ANZARANE

DERRAHMAN   IBN   ZIDANE

Oued Boufekrane

Bab en
Naoura

Kasbah
Hadrache

To
Azrou
(P21)

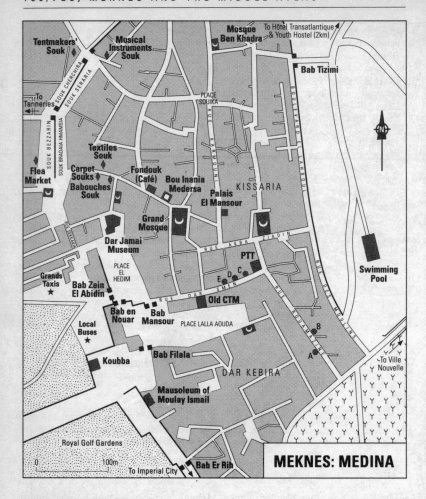

MEKNES: MEDINA

VILLE NOUVELLE HOTELS

Hotels below are all keyed on the **main map** on p.154 and are listed in ascending order of price.

Auberge de Jeunesse [labelled], Av. Okba Ibn Nafi (☎05/52.17.43). The city youth hostel is a bit out of the way (follow signs to the luxury *Hôtel Transatlantique*), but well maintained, with rooms around a court. No curfew; closed 10am–noon & 4–7pm. IYHF cards are required but can be purchased here – as the building also houses the Moroccan YHA.

Hôtel Guillaume Tell [D], 51 Rue de la Voûte (☎05/52.12.03). A rather basic hotel, on a small side street, opposite the *Volubilis Nightclub* on Av. des F.A.R. ⓤ

Hôtel du Marché [P], 1 Av. Hassan Lamri (no phone). Also rather basic. ⓤ

Hôtel Central [I], 35 Av. Mohammed V (☎05/52.02.48). A rambling building with dark rooms and cold showers. ⓤ

Hôtel Toubkal [C], 49 Av. Mohammed V (☎05/52.22.18). Okay but cold showers only. ⓤ

Hôtel Bordeaux [A], 64 Av. de la Gare (☎05/52.25.63). Handy for the main train station, better rooms and a good atmosphere, helped by the bar in an adjoining building. ⑩

Hôtel Touring [K], 34 Av. Allal Ben Abdallah (☎05/52.23.51). A step up in quality: hot showers, central heating and a good atmosphere. ①

Hôtel Excelsior [B], 57 Av. des F.A.R. (☎05/52.19.00). Recently renovated and good value for money; again, handy for the main train station. ①

Hôtel Majestic [L], 19 Av. Mohammed V (☎05/52.20.35). An old but comfortable hotel with friendly management and clean, balconied rooms. Probably the best mid-priced choice in the Ville Nouvelle. ②

Hôtel Panorama [G], 9 Av. des F.A.R. (☎05/52.27.43). Decent-sized rooms but the hotel also has a reputation as a brothel. ②

Hôtel Moderne [J], 54 Bd. Allal Ben Abdallah (☎05/52.17.43). Modest and overpriced hotel, opposite the Watania building. ③

Hôtel Continental [F], 42 Av. des F.A.R. (☎05/52.54.71). This has lately become a bit of a roach-trap – and the very noisy bar may not be to all tastes, either. ③

Hôtel Palace [N], 11 Rue du Ghana (☎05/52.57.77). A much better, if slightly pricier, choice, with respectable rooms and a pleasant bar. ③

Hôtel de Nice [M], 10 Rue Accra (☎05/52.03.18). Reasonable old hotel with a decent restaurant and bar. ③

Hôtel Volubilis [E], 45 Av. des F.A.R. (☎05/52.01.02). Under the same ownership as the *Hôtel Nice*, this has a lively bar which serves snacks and breakfast. ③

Hôtel Bab Mansour [H], 38 Rue Emir Abdelkader (☎05/52.52.39). A modern hotel which recommends itself as the choice "pour hommes d'affaires". Has a covered garage, a bar, nightclub and a restaurant that touts its fish specialities. ③

Hôtel Rif [O], Rue Accra (☎05/52.25.91). An upmarket 1950s hotel in the centre, used by tour groups. Bar, restaurant and a small swiming pool. ④

Hôtel Transatlantique [Q], Rue El Meriniyine (☎05/52.00.02). The city's finest, owned by the ONCF, like the Palais Jamai in Fes. This one is a modern hotel and not in the same class, though comfortable enough, and with two restaurants and a good-size swimming pool. ④

Camping

The city's **campsite**, *Camping Aguedal*, is a twenty-minute walk from Place El Hedim (or a 10dh *petit taxi* ride), sited opposite the Heri as-Souani. It is a pleasant, shaded site (*aguedal*, or *agdal*, means "garden"), with reasonable facilities.

The Imperial City

More than any other Moroccan town, Meknes is associated with a single figure, the **Sultan Moulay Ismail** (see box on next page), in whose 55-year reign (1672–1727) the city was built up from a provincial centre to a spectacular capital with twenty gates, over fifty palaces and some fifteen miles of exterior walls.

The principal remains of Ismail's creation – the **Ville Imperiale** of palaces and gardens, barracks, granaries and stables – sprawl below the Medina, amid a confusingly manic array of walled enclosures. If you intend to take in everything, it's a long morning's walk. Starting out from the Ville Nouvelle, make your way down to the main street at the edge of the Medina (**Rue Rouamazine/Rue Dar Smen**), and along to **Place El Hedim** and its immense gateway, **Bab Mansour**. There are usually **guides** hanging around here if you want to use one; you don't need to, but if you can find someone entertaining, he'll probably elaborate on the story of the walls with some superbly convoluted local legend.

THE SULTAN MOULAY ISMAIL (1672–1727)

"The Sultan Moulay Ismail," wrote his chronicler, Ezziani, "loved Mequinez, and he would have liked never to leave it." But leave it he did, ceaselessly campaigning against the rebel Berber chiefs of the south, and the Europeans entrenched in Tangier, Asilah and Larache, until the entire country – for the first time in five centuries – lay completely under government control. His reign saw the creation of Morocco's strongest ever – and most coherent – army, which included a crack negro guard, the Abid regiment, and, it is reckoned, a garrison force of one in twenty of the male population. The period was, in a very real sense, Morocco's last golden age, though the ruthless centralisation of all decisions, and the fear with which the sultan reigned, led, perhaps inevitably, to a subsequent slide into anarchy and weak, inward-looking rule.

Ismail's achievements were matched by his tyrannies, which, even by the standards of the time – and contemporary Europeans were burning their enemies and torturing them on the rack – were judged extreme. His reign began with the display at Fes of 700 heads, most of them of captured chiefs, and over the next five decades, apart from battles, it is estimated that he was responsible for over 30,000 deaths. Many of these killings were quite arbitrary. Mounting a horse, Ismail might slash the head off the eunuch holding his stirrup; inspecting the work on his buildings, he would carry a weighted lance, with which to batter skulls in order to "encourage" the others. "My subjects are like rats in a basket," he used to say, "and if I do not keep shaking the basket they will gnaw their way through."

Throughout Morocco, the sultan was a tireless builder, constructing towns and ports, and a multitude of defensive Kasbahs, palaces and bridges. By far his greatest efforts, however, were directed at Meknes, where he sustained an obsessive building programme, often acting as architect and sometimes even working alongside the slaves and labourers. Ironically, in Meknes itself, the passing of time has not been easy on his constructions. Built mainly of *tabia*, a mixture of earth and lime, they were severely damaged by a hurricane even in his lifetime, and thereafter, with subsequent Alaouite sultans shifting their capitals back to Fes and Marrakesh, were left to decay. Walter Harris, writing only 150 years after Ismail's death, found Meknes "a city of the dead . . . strewn with marble columns, and surrounded by great masses of ruin". In recent years, however, the city authorities have set about restoring the main monuments with some energy.

Bab Mansour and around

Place El Hedim ("square of demolition and renewal") immediately recalls the reign of Moulay Ismail. Originally, it formed the western corner of the Medina, but the sultan demolished the houses here in order to form a grand approach to his palace quarter, the *Dar Kebira*. He used it, too, as a depot for marble columns and other construction material he had gathered from sites and cities throughout Morocco, including Roman Volubilis.

The centrepiece of the city's whole ensemble of walls and gateways is the great **Bab Mansour**, startlingly rich in its ceremonial intent, and almost perfectly preserved. Its name comes from its architect – one of a number of Christian renegades who converted to Islam and rose to high position at Ismail's court; there is a tale that when the sultan inspected the gate, he asked El Mansour whether he could do better – a classic catch-22, whose response ("yes") led to immediate and enraged execution. The story may be apocryphal, however, for the gate was actually completed under Ismail's son, Moulay Abdallah.

Whatever, the gate is the finest in Meknes and an interesting adaptation of the classic Almohad design, flanked by unusual inset and fairly squat bastions, which are purely decorative, their marble columns having been brought here from Volubilis. The decorative patterns on both gate and bastions are basically elaborations of the *darj w ktarf* (a cheek-and-shoulder pattern, begun by the Almohads), the space between each motif filled out with a brilliant array of *zellij* created by a layer of cut-away black tiles, just like the ornamental inscription above, which extols the triumph of Ismail and, even more, that of Abdallah, adding that there is no gate in Damascus or Alexandria its equal. Alongside Bab Mansour is a smaller gateway in the same style, **Bab Djemaa en Nouar**.

Through Bab Mansour, and a further gate, Bab Filala, beyond, you will find yourself in a large open square, on the right of which is a domed **Koubba** (10dh admission). This was once a reception hall for ambassadors to the imperial court. Below it, a stairway descends into a vast series of subterranean vaults, known in popular tradition as the **Prison of Christian Slaves**. This was probably, in fact, a storehouse or granary, although there were certainly several thousand Christian captives at Ismail's court. Most were captured by the Sallee Rovers (see "Rabat") and brought here as slave labour for the interminable construction projects; reputedly any of them who died while at work were simply buried in the walls they were building.

Ahead of the *koubba*, set within the long wall and at right angles to it, are two very modest **gates**. The one on the right is generally closed and is at all times flanked by soldiers from the royal guard; within, landscaped across a lake and the sunken garden of Ismail's last and finest palace, are the **Royal Golf Gardens** – private and generally *interdit*. The gate on the left opens on to an apparently endless corridor of walls and, a few metres down, the entrance to the **Mausoleum of Moulay Ismail**.

The Mausoleum

Together with the tomb of Mohammed V in Rabat, and the Medersa Bou Inania in Fes, **Moulay Ismail's Mausoleum** (Mon–Fri: July 1–Sept 16 9am–5pm; rest of the year 8.30am–noon & 3–6pm) is the only active Moroccan shrine that non-Muslims may visit. Modest dress, for both women and men, is required.

The mausoleum has been a point of reverence since Ismail's death (it was constructed in his own lifetime) and continues in high esteem. This may be puzzling to Westerners, given the tales of the ruler's excesses, but in Morocco he is remembered for his achievements: bringing peace and prosperity after a period of anarchy, and driving out the Spanish from Larache and the British from Tangier. His extreme observance of orthodox Islamic form and ritual also conferred a kind of magic on him, as, of course, does his part in the foundation of the ruling Alaouite dynasty. Although technically the dynasty began with his brother, Moulay Rachid, Ismail is generally regarded as the founder.

Entering the mausoleum, you are allowed to approach the **sanctuary** in which the sultan is buried – though you cannot go beyond this annexe. Decorated in bright *zellij* and spiralling stuccowork, it is a fine if unspectacular series of courts and chambers. But what is most interesting, perhaps, is that the shrine was thoroughly renovated in the 1950s at the expense of Mohammed V, and also that the sarcophagus is still the object of veneration. You will almost invariably see country people here, especially women, seeking *baraka* (charismatic blessing) and intercession from the saintly sultan's remains.

The Dar El Makhzen and Heri as-Souani

Past the mausoleum, a gate to your left gives access to the dilapidated quarter of **Dar El Kebira**, Ismail's great palace complex. The imperial structures – the legendary fifty palaces – can still be made out between and above the houses here: ogre-like creations, whose scale is hard to believe. They were completed in 1677 and dedicated at an astonishing midnight celebration, when, the chronicles record, the sultan personally slaughtered a wolf so that its head might be displayed at the centre of the gateway.

In the grandeur of the plan there is sometimes claimed a conscious echo of Versailles – its contemporary rival – though, in fact, it was another decade until the first reports of the French building reached the imperial court. When they did, Ismail was certainly interested, and in 1699 he even sent an ambassador to Paris with the task of negotiating the addition of Louis XIV's daughter, Princess Conti, to his harem. He returned without success.

On the opposite side of the long-walled corridor, beyond the Royal Golf Gardens, more immense buildings are spread out, making up Ismail's last great palace, the **Dar El Makhzen**. Unlike the Kebira, which was broken up by Moulay Abdallah in 1733, this is still a minor royal residence – though Hassan II rarely visits Meknes. The most you can get are a few brief glimpses over the heads of the guards posted by occasional gates in the crumbling, twenty-foot-high wall.

The corridor itself, which eventually turns a corner to bring you out by the campsite and the Heri as-Souani, may perhaps be the **"strangee"** which eighteenth-century travellers recorded. A mile-long terrace wall, shaded with vines, it was a favourite drive of the sultan, who, according to several sources, was driven around in a bizarre chariot drawn by his women or eunuchs.

At the corridor's end is the chief sight of the imperial city, the **Heri as-Souani** (or Dar el-Ma), which is often introduced by local guides as "Ismail's stables". The stables, in fact, are further south (see below), and the startling series of high vaulted chambers to be seen here were again a series of storerooms and granaries, filled with provisions for siege or drought. A twenty-minute walk from Bab Mansour, they give a powerful impression of the complexity of seventeenth-century Moroccan engineering. Ismail's palaces each had underground plumbing (well in advance of Europe), and here you find a remarkable system, with chain-bucket wells built between each of the storerooms. One on the right, near the back, has been restored; there are lights you can switch on for a closer look.

Equally worthwhile is the view from the **roof** of the as-Souani, approached through the second entrance on the right (10dh admission). From the roof garden, which in summer has a **café**, you can gaze out over the Dar El Makhzen and the wonderfully still **Agdal Basin** – built as an irrigation reservoir and pleasure lake. Over to the southwest, in the distance, you can make out another seventeenth-century royal palace, the **Dar al-Baida** (the "White House"), now a military academy, and beyond it (to the right), the **Rouah**, or stables.

The Rouah

Known locally as the **Heri Mansour** (Mansour's Granary), Moulay Ismail's stables, the **Rouah**, are a further twenty- to thirty-minute walk from the Heri as-Souani. They are officially closed to visitors, though if you hang around for a while a guide will probably turn up with keys. To find the site, follow the road diagonally behind the campsite and Heri as-Souani for half a kilometre; when you reach a junction, turn right and you reach the **Djemaa Rouah** (Stable Mosque), a large, heavily restored building preceded by a well-kept gravel courtyard. Walk round behind the mosque and you will see the stables off to your right – a massive complex perhaps twice as large as the as-Souani.

In contemporary accounts the **Rouah** was often singled out as the greatest feature of all Ismail's building projects: some three miles in length, traversed by a long canal, with flooring built over vaults used for storing grain, and space for over 12,000 horses. Today, the province of a few scrambling goats, it's a conclusive ruin – piles of rubble and *zellij* tiles lining the walls and high arched aisles of crumbling *pisé* extending out in each direction. As such, it perhaps recalls more than anything else in Meknes the scale and madness of Moulay Ismail's vision. The sultan once decreed that a wall should be built from here all the way to Marrakesh – a convenient access for his carriage and a useful guide for the blind beggars to find their way.

The Medina

The Medina, although taking much of its present form and size under Moulay Ismail, bears less of his stamp. Its main sights, in addition to the **souks**, are a Merenid *medersa* or "college" – the **Bou Inania** – and a nineteenth-century palace museum, the **Dar Jamai**; both are rewarding and easy to find.

The Dar Jamai

The **Dar Jamai** (Mon–Fri July 1–Sept 16 9am–5pm; rest of the year 8.30am–noon & 3–6pm; 10dh) stands at the back of Place El Hedim, from which it is reached down a stairway. One of the best examples of a nineteenth-century Moroccan palace, it was built by the same family of viziers (high government officials) who put up the Palais Jamai in Fes.

Its exhibits, some of which have been incorporated to recreate reception rooms, are predominantly of the same age, though some of the pieces of **Fes** and **Meknes pottery** date back more or less to Ismail's reign. These ceramics, elaborate polychrome designs from Meknes and strong blue and white patterns from Fes, make for an interesting comparison, and the superiority of Fes's handicrafts tradition is evident. The best display, however, is of **Middle Atlas carpets**, and in particular the bold geometric designs of the Beni Mguild tribe.

The souks

To reach the *souks* from Place El Hedim, follow the lane immediately behind the Dar Jamai. You will come out in the middle of the Medina's major market street; on your right, leading to the Grand Mosque and Bou Inania Medersa, is **Souk es Sebbat**; on your left is **Souk en Nejjarin**.

Turning first to the left, you enter an area of textile stalls, which later give way to the carpenters' (*nejjarin*) workshops from which the *souk* takes its name. Shortly after this, you pass a mosque on your left, beyond which is an entrance to a parallel arcade. The **carpet market**, or **Souk Joutiya as-Zerabi**, is just off here to the left. Quality can be very high (and prices, too), though without the constant stream of tourists of Fes or Marrakesh, dealers are much more willing to bargain. Don't be afraid to start too low.

Out at the end of Souk en Nejjarin you come to another *souk*, the **Bezzarin**, which runs up at right angles to the Nejjarin, on either side of the city wall. This looks like a ramshackle, run-down neighbourhood, but if you follow the outer side of the wall, you'll come across an interesting assortment of craftsworkers, grouped together in their own trading guilds and often with an old *fondouk* or warehouse to the front of them. As you proceed, there are **basketmakers**, **ironsmiths** and **saddlers**, while near **Bab El Djedid**, at the top, you'll find **tent makers** and a couple of **musical instrument workshops**.

Had you turned right beyond the Dar Jamai, onto **Souk es Sebbat**, you would have entered a classier section of the market – starting off with the *babouche* vendors, and then moving on to the fancier goods aimed at tourists near the *medersa*, finally exiting into the covered **kissaria**, dominated by caftan sellers. From here it is easy enough to find your way to the Bou Inania Medersa, whose imposing portal is visible on the left-hand side of the street. If you want a tea break before doing that, there's a nineteenth-century **fondouk** a short way back, which now doubles as a café and carpet/crafts emporium – look for its open courtyard. Meknes mint, incidentally, is reputed to be the best in Morocco.

Bou Inania Medersa

The **Bou Inania Medersa** (Mon–Fri July 1–Sept 16 9am–5pm; rest of the year 8.30am–noon & 3–6pm; 10dh) was built around 1340–50, and is therefore more or less contemporary with the great *medersas* of Fes. It takes its name from the notorious Sultan Abou Inan (see p.187), despite the fact that it was actually founded by his predecessor, Abou El Hassan, the great Merenid builder of Chellah in Rabat.

A modest and functional building, the *medersa* follows the plan of Hassan's other principal works in Rabat (the Chellah *zaouia* and Salé *medersa*), in that it has a single **courtyard** opening on to a narrow **prayer hall**, and is encircled on each floor by the students' **cells**, with exquisite screens in carved cedar. It has a much lighter feel to it than the Salé *medersa*, and in its balance of wood, stucco and *zellij* achieves a remarkable combination of intricacy – no area is left uncovered – and restraint. Architecturally, the most unusual feature is a ribbed dome over the **entrance hall**, an impressive piece of craftsmanship which extends right out into the *souk*.

From **the roof**, to which there's usually access, you can look out (and you feel as if you could climb across) to the tiled pyramids of the Grand Mosque. The *souk* is mainly obscured from view, but you can get a good, general panorama of the town and the mosques of each quarter. Inlaid with bands of green tiles, the minarets of these distinctive mosques are characteristic of Meknes; those of Fes or Marrakesh tend to be more elaborate and multicoloured.

North from Bou Inania

North of the *medersa* and Grand Mosque, the Medina is for the most part residential, dotted with the occasional fruit and vegetable market, or (up past the mosque of Ben Khadra) a carpenters' *souk*, for the supply of wood. If you continue this way, you'll eventually come out in a long, open square which culminates in the monumental **Bab El Berdaïn** (The Gate of the Saddlers). This was another of Ismail's creations, and echoes, in a much more rugged and genuinely defensive structure, the central section of Bab Mansour.

Outside, the city walls continue to extend up along the main road to Rabat, and past – about 1500m out – the **Bab El Khemis** (or Bab Lakhmis), another very fine gate with a frieze containing a monumental inscription etched in black tiles on the brickwork. Between the two gates, inside the wall on your left, you will catch occasional glimpses of an enormous **cemetery** – almost half the size of the Medina in extent. Non-Muslims are not permitted to enter this enclosure, near the centre of which lies the *zaouia* and shrine of one of the country's most famous and curious saints, **Sidi Ben Aissa**.

Reputedly a contemporary of Moulay Ismail, Ben Aissa conferred on his followers the power to eat anything, even poison or broken glass, without suffering any ill effects. His cult, the *Aissaoua*, became one of the most important in Morocco, and certainly the most violent and fanatical. Until prohibited by the French, some 50,000 devotees regularly attended the saint's annual *moussem* on the eve of Mouloud. Entering into a trance, they were known to pierce their tongues and cheeks with daggers, eat serpents and scorpions, or devour live sheep and goats. The only other confraternity to approach such frenzy was the *Hamacha* of Moulay Idriss, whose rites included cutting each other's heads with hatchets and tossing heavy stones or cannonballs into the air, allowing them to fall down on their skulls. Both cults continue to hold *moussems*, though successive Moroccan governments have effectively outlawed their more extreme activities.

Restaurants, bars and nightlife

For most practical needs, beyond a basic bed and meal, you'll need to cross the river to the Ville Nouvelle. Most things you might want in this quarter are grouped within a few blocks of the central Place Administrative: Meknes is a small town compared to Fes or even Tangier.

Cafés and restaurants

As ever, you have a choice between the Medina – where most places are basic café-grills – or the Ville Nouvelle – where you'll find a dozen or so restaurants, mostly serving French-style menus. Good choices include:

MEDINA

Restaurant Economique, 123 Rue Dar Smen – opposite Bab Djemaa en Nouar. This is one of the better of the Medina's café-restaurants.

Restaurant Zitouna, 44 Rue Djemaa Zituna. A bit fancier, with good traditional food.

One place to avoid, despite its handbills at the *Maroc Hôtel*, is the *Rôtisserie Oumnia*.

VILLE NOUVELLE

Restaurant Novelty, 12 Rue de Paris. Generous helpings and fast service. Cheap.

Pizzeria Le Four, 1 Rue Atlas – near the *Hôtel Majestic*, off Av. Mohammed V. Pizzas and pasta. Moderate.

Restaurant Montana, 4 Rue Atlas – opposite *Le Four* (above). There is a bar on the ground floor; upstairs is a restaurant decorated to imitate a tent. Moderate.

Annexe Metropole, 11 Rue Charif Idrissi, near the junction with Av. Hassan II. Excellent cooking and well worth the (little) extra. Moderate.

Restaurant Cuisin'Or, 3 Rue Antsirabé, near the *Hôtel de Nice*. Again, highly recommended, and open to midnight. Moderate.

La Coupole, corner of Av. Hassan II and Rue du Ghana. Reasonably priced Moroccan and European food. Also a bar and nightclub.

Restaurant Dauphin, Rue de Paris. Reliable French cooking, with a reputation for seafood dishes. Moderate to expensive.

Hôtel Transatlantique, Rue El Meriniyine (☎05/52.00.02). The Moroccan restaurant is very well thought of – and pretty reasonable, given the hotel's five-star status.

Bars

There are bars in many of the Ville Nouvelle hotels (see p.156), most of which are quite lively of an evening. For a really sedate drink, the *Hôtel Transatlantique* would be your best bet. In addition, the following can be worth a try:

Club de Nuit, corner of Av. Hassan II and Av. des F.A.R. Remember bars with swing doors and sawdust on the floors? This will take you back. Noisy and mixed.

Bar Continental, more or less opposite the *Club de Nuit*.

Cabaret Oriental, Av. Hassan II. Occasionally hosts bands into the small hours.

Directory

Animal welfare *SPANA* representative: M. Mzioud, 72 Bab El Kari (☎05/53.01.66).

Banks are concentrated around Place Administrative, and along Av. Mohammed V (the *Crédit du Maroc* is at no. 33) and Av. des F.A.R. (*BMCE* at no. 98). In the Medina, the *Banque Populaire* on Rue Dar Smen, near Bab Mansour, has exchange facilities. The *Hôtel Rif* will exchange cash outside banking hours.

Car hire Try either *Zeit*, 4 Rue Anserabi (☎05/52.59.18), or *Stop Car*, 3 Rue Essaoira (☎05/52.50.61). None of the major companies has offices in Meknes.

Car repairs *Renault* garages are to be found on Rue Charif and out on the Route de Fes. For *VW* try *Maroc-France*, Av. Hassan II (☎05/52.28.58); for *Opel*, *Central Garage*, 7 Rue de Nice (☎05/52.15.10).

Chemist/pharmacist *Pharmacie Central*, Av. Mohammed V (☎05/52.11.81; open daily). *Pharmacie d'urgence de nuit*, next to the Hôtel de Ville on Place Administrative (☎05/52.33.75; open 8.30pm–8.30am).

Cinemas Central ones include the *Empire* on Av. Mohammed V (near Hôtel Majestic); *Camera*, on Place Ifriquia; and *Régine*, near the *Hôtel Bab Mansour*.

Festivals The city's *Ben Aïssa Moussem* (held over the Mouloud; see p.40) is one of the country's most impressive. Also worth planning for are the *Beni Rached Moussem* (seven days after Mouloud; at the village of Beni Rached, out of town on the Moulay Idriss road) and the *Moulay Idriss Moussem* (September).

Hammam If you're staying in the Medina, the *Maroc Hôtel* should be able to steer you towards a hammam; in the Ville Nouvelle, you'll find a good one off Av. Hassan II, at 4 Rue Patrice Lumumba, with separate sections for women and men (both 7am–9pm).

Police The local HQ is at the bottom end of Place Administrative, near the junction of Av. Hassan II and Av. Moulay Ismail (☎19).

Post Office The **PTT** is just off Place de France (summer Mon–Fri 8am–2pm; winter 8.30am–noon & 2.30–6pm); the **telephone** section stays open until 9pm, but there are public callboxes by the entrance.

Royal Air Maroc have an office at 7 Av. Mohammed V (☎05/52.09.63); the nearest airport is at Saïs, south of Fes.

Swimming Pools There are two public pools down by the river, reached along a lane from Bd. El Haboul or from the intersection of Av. Hassan II and Av. Moulay Ismail. The first you encounter is very cheap; a little further down there's another – classier, less crowded, and three or four times the price. The pool at the *Hôtel Rif* is open to non-residents for a 30dh day-fee.

Volubilis and Moulay Idriss

An easy excursion from Meknes, **Volubilis** and **Moulay Idriss** embody much of Morocco's early history: Volubilis as its Roman provincial capital, Moulay Idriss in the creation of the country's first Arab dynasty. Their sites stand 4km apart, at either side of a deep and very fertile valley, about 30km north of Meknes.

Transport and accommodation

You can take in both sites on a leisurely day trip from Meknes. **Grands taxis** make regular runs to **Moulay Idriss** (10dh a place) from the bus terminal area by Bab El Khemis in the Medina and from near the PTT in the Ville Nouvelle. For **Volubilis**, you can take a Ouezzane bus and ask to be set down by the site (which is a 500m walk downhill from the P28 road), or you could charter a *grand taxi* at Place El Hedim. The whole taxi (un course) costs around 50dh, which can be split between up to six passengers; if you pay a little more, the taxi driver will wait at Volubilis and take you on to Moulay Idriss, where you can look round at leisure and then get a regular place in a *grand taxi* back to Meknes.

You can also, of course, walk between Volubilis and Moulay Idriss, which are only around 4km apart.

Non-Muslims are not permitted to stay overnight in the town of Moulay Idriss – the only place in Morocco to keep this religious prohibition. However, there is a shaded **campsite**, *Camping Zerhoun*, 11km along the direct road from Volubilis to Meknes; this has a small café with a few rooms to let. Note that roads around this area are somewhat confusing; for the campsite, it's easiest to ask directions to the nearby *Refuge Zerhoun*.

Volubilis

A striking site, visible for miles from the various bends in the approach road, **VOLUBILIS** occupies the ledge of a long, high plateau. Below its walls, towards Moulay Idriss, stretches a rich river valley; beyond lie dark, outlying ridges of the Zerhoun mountains. The drama of this scene – and the scope of the ruins – may well seem familiar. It was the key location for Martin Scorsese's film, *The Last Temptation of Christ*.

Some history

Except for a small trading post on the island off Essaouira, Volubilis was the Roman Empire's most remote and far-flung base. The imperial roads stopped here, having reached across France and Spain and then down from Tangier, and despite successive emperors' dreams of "penetrating the Atlas", the southern Berber tribes were never effectively subdued.

Direct Roman rule here, in fact, lasted little over two centuries – the garrison withdrew early, in 285 AD, to ease pressure elsewhere. But the town must have taken much of its present form well before the official annexation of North African Mauretania by Emperor Claudius in 45 AD. Tablets found on the site, inscribed in Punic, show a significant Carthaginian trading presence in the third century BC, and prior to colonisation it was the western capital of a heavily Romanised but semi-autonomous Berber kingdom, which reached into northern Algeria and Tunisia. After the Romans left, Volubilis saw very gradual change.

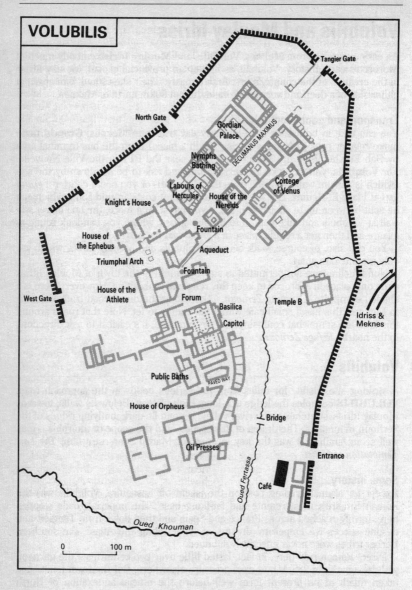

VOLUBILIS

Tangier Gate

North Gate

Gordian Palace

DECUMANUS MAXIMUS

Nymphs Bathing

Labours of Hercules

Cortege of Venus

Knight's House

House of the Nereids

House of the Ephebus

Fountain

Aqueduct

Triumphal Arch

Fountain

West Gate

House of the Athlete

Forum

Basilica

Temple B

Capitol

Idriss & Meknes

Public Baths

PAVED WAY

House of Orpheus

Bridge

Oil Presses

Entrance

Oued Fertassa

Café

Oued Khouman

0   100 m

Latin was still spoken in the seventh century by the local population of Berbers, Greeks, Syrians and Jews; Christian churches survived until the coming of Islam; and the city itself remained alive and active well into the eighteenth century, when its marble was carried away by slaves for the building of Moulay Ismail's Meknes.

What you see today, well excavated and maintained, are largely the ruins of second- and third-century AD buildings – impressive and affluent creations from its period as a colonial provincial capital. The land around here is some of the most fertile in North Africa, and the city exported wheat and olives in considerable quantities to Rome, as it did wild animals from the surrounding hills. Roman games, memorable for the sheer scale of their slaughter (9000 beasts were killed for the dedication of Rome's Colosseum alone), could not have happened without the African provinces, and Volubilis was a chief source of their lions. Within just two hundred years, along with Barbary bears and elephants, they became virtually extinct.

The site

Open daily, sunrise–sunset; 20dh admission.

The entrance to the site is through a minor gate in the city wall, built along with a number of outer camps in 168 AD, following a prolonged series of Berber insurrections. Just inside are the **ticket office**, a shaded **café-bar** and a small, open-air **museum** , with remains of many altars and other sculptural fragments.

The best of the finds made here – which include a superb collection of bronzes – have all been taken to the Rabat museum. Volubilis, however, has retained in situ the great majority of its **mosaics**, some thirty or so in a good state of preservation. You leave with a real sense of Roman city life and its provincial prosperity, while in the layout of the site it is not hard to recognise the essentials of a medieval Arab town.

Following the path up from the museum and across a bridge over the Fertassa stream, you come out on a mixed area of housing and industry, each of its buildings containing the clear remains of at least one **olive press**. The extent and number of these presses, built into even the grandest mansions, reflect the olive's absolute importance to the city and indicate perhaps why Volubilis remained unchanged for so long after the Romans' departure. A significant proportion of its 20,000 population must have been involved in some capacity in the oil's production and export.

Somewhat isolated in this suburban quarter is the **House of Orpheus**, an enormous complex of rooms just beside the start of a paved way. Although substantially in ruins, it offers a strong impression of its former luxury – an opulent mansion for perhaps one of the town's richest merchants. It is divided into two main sections – public and private – each with its separate entrance and interior court. The private rooms, which you come to first, are grouped around a small patio which is decorated with a more or less intact **dolphin mosaic**. You can also make out the furnace and heating system (just by the entrance), the kitchen with its niche for the household gods, and the **baths** – an extensive system of hot, cold and steam rooms.

The house's public apartments, a little further inside, are dominated by a large **atrium**, half reception hall, half central court, and again preserving a very fine mosaic, **The Chariot of Amphitrite drawn by a Seahorse**. The best example here, however, and the mosaic from which the house takes its name, is that of the **Orpheus Myth**, located to the south in a room which was probably the *tablinium*, or archives.

Above the Orpheus House, a broad, paved street leads up towards the main group of public buildings – the Capitol and Basilica, whose sand-coloured ruins

MOULAY IDRISS AND THE FOUNDATION OF MOROCCO

Moulay Idriss El Akhbar (The Elder) was a great-grandson of the Prophet Muhammad; his grandparents were Muhammad's daughter Fatima, and cousin and first follower, Ali. Heir to the Caliphate in Damascus, he fled to Morocco around 787, following the Ommayad victory in the great civil war which split the Muslim world into Shia and Sunni* sects.

In Volubilis, then still the main centre of the north, Idriss seems to have been welcomed as an *imam* (a spiritual and political leader), and within five years had succeeded in carving out a considerable kingdom. At this new town site, more easily defended than Volubilis, he built his capital, and he also began the construction of Fes, later continued and considerably extended by his son Idriss II, that city's patron saint. News of his growing power, however, filtered back to the East, and in 792, the Ommayads had Idriss poisoned, doubtless assuming that his kingdom would likewise disappear.

In this they were mistaken. Idriss had instilled with the faith of Islam the region's previously pagan (and sometimes Christian or Jewish) Berber tribes and had been joined in this prototypical Moroccan state by increasing numbers of Arab Shiites loyal to the succession of his *Alid* line. After his assassination, Rashid, the servant who had travelled with Idriss to Morocco, took over as regent until 807, when the founder's son, Idriss II, was old enough to assume the throne.

*Although of Shiite origin, the Moroccan tribes soon adopted the Sunni (or Malekite) system, in line with the powerful Andalusian Caliphate of Córdoba. Present-day Morocco remains orthodox Sunni.

dominate the site. Taking the approach on the left, you pass first through the remains of the city's main **Public Baths**. Restored by the Emperor Gallienus in the second century AD, these are clearly monumental in their intent, though sadly the mosaics are only fragmentary. The arrangement of the **Forum** is typical of a major Roman town: built on the highest rise of the city and flanked by a triumphal arch, market, capitol and basilica.

The **Capitol**, the smaller and lower of the two main buildings, has been dated from inscriptions to 217 AD – a time at which this whole public nucleus seems to have been rebuilt by the African-born Severian emperors. Adjoined by small forum **baths**, it is an essentially simple building, with a porticoed court giving access to a small temple and altar. Its dedication – standard throughout the Roman world – was to the official state cult of Capitoline Jove, Juno and Minerva. The large five-aisled **Basilica** to its side served as the courthouse, while immediately across the forum were the small court and stalls of the central **market**.

The **Triumphal Arch**, right in the middle of the town, had no particular purpose other than creating a ceremonial function for the principal street, the Decumanus Maximus – on whose side it is more substantially ornamented. Erected in honour of the Severian emperor, Caracalla, its inscription records that it was originally surmounted by a bronze chariot. This, and the nymphs which once shot water into its basins below, are gone, though with its tall Corinthian columns (of imported marble), it is still an impressive monument. The medallions on either side, heavily eroded, presumably depict Caracalla and his mother, Julia Donna, who is also named in the inscription.

MANSIONS AND MOSAICS

The finest of Volubilis's mansions – and its mosaics – line the **Decumanus Maximus**, fronted in traditional Roman and Italian fashion by the shops built in tiny cubicles. Before you reach this point, however, take a look at the remains of an **aqueduct** and **fountains** across from the triumphal arch; these once supplied yet another complex of public baths. Opposite them is a small group of **houses**, mostly ruined but retaining an impressive **Mosaic of an Athlete** or "chariot jumper" – depicted receiving the winner's cup for a *desultor* race, a display of great skill which entailed leaping on and off a horse in full gallop.

First of the Decumanus Maximus mansions, the **House of the Ephebus** takes its name from the bronze of a youth found in its ruins (and today displayed in Rabat). In general plan it is very similar to the House of Orpheus, once again containing an olive press in its rear section, though this building is on a far grander scale – almost twice the size of the other – with pictorial mosaics in most of its public rooms and an ornamental pool in its central court. Finest of the mosaics is a representation of **Bacchus Being Drawn in a Chariot by Panthers** – a suitable scene for the *cenacula*, or banquet hall, in which it is placed.

Separated from the Ephebus House by a narrow lane is a mosaic-less mansion, known after its facade as the **House of Columns**, and adjoining this, the **Knight's House** with an incomplete mosaic of **Dionysos Discovering Ariadne** asleep on the beach at Naxos; both houses are themselves largely ruined. More illuminating is the large mansion which begins the next block, similar again in its plan, but featuring a very complete mosaic of the **Labours of Hercules**. Almost comic caricatures, these give a good idea of typical provincial Roman mosaics – immediate contrasts to the stylish **Orpheus and Bacchus** and **Nymphs Bathing** of the second house down.

Beyond this area, approaching the partially reconstructed **Tangier Gate**, stands the **Palace of the Gordians**, former residence of the procurators who administered the city and the province. Despite its size, however, even with a huge **bath house** and pooled courtyards, it is an unmemorable ruin. Stripped of most of its columns, and lacking any mosaics, its grandeur and scale may have made it an all too obvious target for Ismail's building mania. Indeed, how much of Volubilis remained standing before his reign began is an open question; Walter Harris, writing at the turn of the twentieth century, found the road between here and Meknes littered with ancient marbles, left as they fell following the announcement of the sultan's death.

Back on the Decumanus, cross to the other side of the road and walk down a block to a smaller lane below the street. Here, in the third house you come to, is the most exceptional ensemble of mosaics of the entire site – the **Cortege of Venus**. You cannot enter the house but most of the fine mosaics can be seen by walking round the outside of the ruins. If you imagine walking into the main section of the house, a central court is preceded by a paved vestibule and opens on to another, smaller patio, around which are grouped the main reception halls (and mosaics). From the entrance, the **baths** are off to the left, flanked by the private quarters, while immediately around the central court is a small group of mosaics, including an odd, very worn representation of a **Chariot Race** – with birds instead of horses.

The villa's most outstanding mosaics lie beyond, in the "public" sections. On the left, in the corner, is a geometrical design, with medallions of **Bacchus**

Surrounded by the Four Seasons; off to the right are **Diana Bathing** (and surprised by the huntsman Actaeon) and the **Abduction of Hylas by Nymphs**. Each of these scenes – especially the last two – is superbly handled in stylised but very fluid animation. They date, like that of the **Nereids** (two houses further down), from the late second or early third century AD, and were obviously a serious commission. It is not known for whom this house was built, but its owner must have been among the city's most successful patrons; here were found the bronze busts of Cato and Juba II which are now the centrepiece of Rabat's museum.

Leaving the site by a path below the forum, you pass close by the ruins of a **temple** on the opposite side of the stream. This was dedicated by the Romans to Saturn, but seeems to have previously involved the worship of a Carthaginian god; several hundred votive offerings were discovered during its excavation.

Moulay Idriss

MOULAY IDRISS takes its name from its founder, Morocco's most venerated saint and the creator of its first Arab dynasty. His tomb and *zaouia* lie right at the heart of the town, the reason for its sacred status and the object of constant pilgrimage – and an important September **moussem**. For non-Muslims, barred from the shrines, there is little specific that can be seen, and nothing that may be visited, but wandering the hilly lanes with their delightful window-views, or just sitting in a café absorbing the holiday-pilgrim atmosphere, is pleasant enough.

The town

Arriving in Moulay Idriss, you find yourself below an enlongated *place* near the base of the town; above you, almost directly ahead, stand the green-tiled pyramids of the shrine and *zaouia*, on either side of which rise the two conical quarters of Khiber and Tasga.

The **souks**, such as they are, line the streets of the Khiber (the taller hill) above the *zaouia*. They offer a variety of religious artefacts for Muslim visitors, together with excellent local nougat – which is produced and sold here in great quantities – and, in autumn, *arbutus* (strawberry tree) berries.

Moulay Idriss' shrine and zaouia, rebuilt by Moulay Ismail, stands cordoned off from the street by a low, wooden bar placed to keep out Christians and beasts of burden. To get a true sense of it, you have to climb up towards one of the vantage points near the pinnacle of each quarter – ideally, the **Terrasse Sidi Abdallah El Hajjam** right above the Khiber. It's not easy to find your way up through the winding streets (most end in abrupt blind alleys), and, unless you're into the challenge of it all, you'd do better to enlist the help of a young guide down in the *place*.

Moving on from Meknes

Heading **north** from Meknes, towards Larache, Tangier or Chaouen, Volubilis (see preceding pages) provides by far the most interesting excursion; heading **east to Fes**, there is little to delay you on the hour-long journey. Covered below are the routes **west to Rabat** and **south to Azrou**, both of which offer a few points of interest along the way. For details on the trains, buses and *grands taxis* from Meknes, see pp.152–53, 230–31.

West: Khemissèt and Lake Roumi

The road **west of Meknes** (P1) is a pleasant drive, running at first through a rich, cultivated landscape, then cutting across low, forested hills, with lavender (planted for scent) on the lower slopes. Above a bend in the road, 30km from Meknes, is a model village (labelled "Village Pilote" on the *Michelin* map) built in 1965 as the first of a planned rehousing programme.

KHEMISSÈT, 46km from Meknes, is a small market town, created by the French to encourage settlement of the scattered Zemmour Berbers of the region. It hosts a Tuesday *souk* which is known for its carpets and wood carvings, and has a fairly pleasant **hotel**, the *Diouri* (☎05/55.26.45; ②), on the eastern outskirts of town. Driving from Meknes to Rabat, the hotel is about midway, and its restaurant makes a good stop for lunch.

If you're in no hurry, a diversion to the **Dayet er Roumi** – Lake Roumi – is highly recommended. This lies 15km southwest of Khemissèt, just off the S106, and it's a gorgeous place: shimmering water, lots of birdsong, woodsmoke from the fires of shepherds – every inch the pastoral idyll. In summer, a **campsite** (10dh per person and per tent) and **café** operate by the water's edge, and rent out pedalos to while away the afternoon. Swimming here is also fine, and you can fish, if you come equipped with a permit (see p.44).

To reach the café and campsite, you need to turn left, off the S106, on a rough road by a cactus field with five trees; the signposted road to the lake, 1500m beyond, leads only to a group of lakeside houses. If you don't have a car, it's possible to charter a *grand taxi* at Khemissèt.

South: Agouraï, El Hajeb and the Paysage d'Ito

South of Meknes is one of Morocco's few remaining **wine-growing areas**. Under French rule, Morocco and Algeria produced up to a third of the table wine consumed in France – and had a few quite respectable vintages. Since independence, inevitably, the profile and the marketplace dropped, as, alas, has the quality, which is very hit-and-miss.

Nonetheless, some decent reds – marketed as *Toulal* – are produced at **AÏT-SOUALA**, on the minor S3065 road, west of the main Azrou road, and if you're curious, the vineyards can be visited. Continuing along the 3065 brings you out at the **kasbah** of **AGOURAÏ**, built by Moulay Ismail and now enclosing a small Berber village. It's an interesting spot, with water sluicing down the main street, and a buzzing Thursday **souk**. There is a café but no rooms or meals to be had.

Back on the main road to Azrou, the P21, the cultivation changes to wheat, planted in the *poljes* or depressions of this classic karst countryside. The small town of **El HAJEB** ("eyebrow" in Arabic) occupies a high, cliffside site, alongside a ruined nineteenth-century fort. It has a Monday **souk**, a bank, several cafés, and a simple but adequate **campsite**, the *Yasmina*.

Just south of the town, the road divides, with a minor route, the S309, leading through cedar forests to Ifrane (see p.213). The P21 to Azrou, though, is the road to take, for after 18km (17km north of Azrou) you reach the remarkable **Paysage d'Ito** – a natural roadside balcony on the edge of a volcanic plateau, with a really stunning panorama, stretching for perhaps seventy kilometres. The landscape is wonderfully bizarre, with outcrops of extinct volcanoes, and was used as the backdrop for many of the early science fiction films of the 1950s and 1960s.

Fes

The history of Fes is composed of wars and murders, triumphs of arts and sciences, and a good deal of imagination.

Walter Harris: *Land of an African Sultan*

The most ancient of the imperial capitals, and the most complete medieval city of the Arab world, **FES** is – for the moment at least – unique. It is a place that stimulates your senses, with haunting and beautiful sounds, infinite visual details and unfiltered odours, and it seems to exist suspended in time somewhere between the Middle Ages and the modern world. As is usual, the city has a French-built Ville Nouvelle, but some 200,000 of the city's approximately half-million inhabitants continue to live in the extraordinary Medina-city of **Fes El Bali** – which owes little to the West besides its electricity and its tourists.

As a spectacle, this is unmissable, and it's difficult to imagine a city whose external forms (all you can really hope to penetrate) could be so constant a source of interest. But stay in Fes a few days and it's equally hard to avoid the paradox of the place. Like much of "traditional" Morocco, the city was "saved" and then re-created by the French – under the auspices of General Lyautey, the Protectorate's first Resident-General. Lyautey took the philanthropic and startling move of declaring the city a historical monument; philanthropic because he was certainly saving Fes El Bali from destruction (albeit from less benevolent Frenchmen), and startling because until then many Moroccans were under the impression that Fes was still a living city – the imperial capital of the Moroccan empire rather than a preservable part of the nation's heritage. In fact, this paternalistic protection conveniently helped to disguise the dismantling of the old culture. By building a new European city nearby – the Ville Nouvelle – and then transferring Fes's economic and political functions to Rabat and the west coast, Lyautey successfully ensured the city's eclipse along with its preservation.

To appreciate the significance of this demise, you only have to look at the Arab chronicles or old histories of Morocco, every one of which takes Fes as its central focus. The city had dominated Moroccan trade, culture and religious life – and usually its politics, too – since the end of the tenth century. It was closely and symbolically linked with the birth of an "Arabic" Moroccan state due to their mutual foundation by Moulay Idriss I, and was regarded, after Mecca and Medina, as one of the holiest cities of the Islamic world. Medieval European travellers wrote of it with a mixture of awe and respect – as a "citadel of fanaticism" and yet the most advanced seat of learning in mathematics, philosophy and medicine.

The decline of the city notwithstanding, **Fassis** – the people of Fes – have a reputation throughout Morocco as being successful and sophisticated. Just as the city is situated at the centre of the country, so are its inhabitants placed at the heart of government, and most government ministries are headed by Fassis. What is undeniable is that they have the most developed Moroccan city culture, with an intellectual tradition, and their own cuisine (sadly not at its best in the modern city restaurants), dress and way of life.

The development of Fes

When the city's founder, Moulay Idriss I, died in 792, Fes was little more than a village on the east bank of the river. It was his son, **Idriss II**, who really began the city's development, at the beginning of the ninth century, by making it his capital and allowing in refugees from Andalusian Córdoba and from Kairouan in Tunisia – at the time, the two most important cities of western Islam. The impact on Fes of these refugees was immediate and lasting: they established separate, walled towns (still distinct quarters today) on either riverbank, and provided the superior craftsmanship and mercantile experience for Fes's industrial and commercial growth. It was at this time, too, that the city gained its intellectual reputation. The tenth-century Pope Silvester II studied here at the Kairouine University, and from this source he is said to have introduced Arabic mathematics to Europe.

The seat of government – and impetus of patronage – shifted south to Marrakesh under the Berber dynasties of the **Almoravides** (1068–1145) and **Almohads** (1145–1250). But with the conquest of Fes by the **Merenids** in 1248, and their subsequent consolidation of power across Morocco, the city regained its preeminence and moved into something of a "golden age". Alongside the old Medina, the Merenids built a massive royal city – **Fes El Djedid**, literally "Fes the New" – which reflected both the wealth and confidence of their rule. They enlarged and decorated the Kairaouine mosque, added a network of *fondouks* (inns) for the burgeoning commercial activity, and greatly developed the Kairaouine University – building the series of magnificent **medersas**, or colleges, to accommodate its students. Once again this expansion was based on an influx of refugees, this time from the Spanish reconquest of Andalusia, and it helped to establish the city's reputation as "the Baghdad of the West".

It is essentially Merenid Fes which you witness today in the form of the city and its monuments. From the fall of the dynasty in the mid-sixteenth century, there was decline as both Fes and Morocco itself became isolated from the main currents of Western culture. The new rulers – the **Saadians** – in any case preferred Marrakesh, and although Fes re-emerged as the capital under the **Alaouites,** it had begun to lose its international stature. Moulay Ismail, whose hatred of the Fassis was legendary, almost managed to tax the city out of existence, and the principal building concerns of his successors lay in restoring and enlarging the vast domains of the royal palace.

Under **French colonial rule,** there were positive achievements in the preservation of the old city and relative prosperity of the Ville Nouvelle, but little actual progress. As a thoroughly conservative and bourgeois city, Fes became merely provincial. Even so, it remained a symbol of Moroccan pride and aspirations, playing a crucial role in the **struggle for independence** – events marvellously brought to life in Paul Bowles's novel *The Spider's House*.

Since **independence**, the city's position has been less than happy. The first sultan, Mohammed V, retained the French capital of Rabat, and with this signalled the final decline of the Fassi political and financial elites. In 1956, too, the city lost most of its Jewish community to France and Israel. In their place, the Medina population now has a predominance of first-generation rural migrants, often poorly housed in mansions designed for single families but now accommodating four or five, while the city as a whole is increasingly dependent on handicrafts and the tourist trade. If UNESCO had not moved in over the last decades with its Cultural Heritage plan for the city's preservation, it seems likely that its physical collapse would have become even more widespread.

Socially, too, the city has had major problems. It was a focus of the riots of December 1990 (see p.501), in which the disaffected urban poor and the students

POINTS OF ARRIVAL/DEPARTURE

● **By train**. The train station is in the Ville Nouvelle, ten minutes' walk from the concentration of hotels around Place Mohammed V. If you prefer to stay in Fes El Bali, either take a *petit taxi*, or walk down to Av. Hassan II, where you can pick up the #9 or #10 bus to Dar Batha (pronounced *dar ba-t-ha*), near Bab Boujeloud.

Beware of unofficial taxi drivers who wait at the station and charge very unofficial rates for the trip into town; the standard fare for Bab Boujeloud should be no more than 6dh per person. Be prepared, too, for hustlers: Fes is possibly the worst city in Morocco in this respect, and the station is a key locale.

Leaving Fes, if heading for **Nador/Melilla**, note that *ONCF* run connecting buses from Taorirt on the Oujda line; you can buy tickets straight through.

● **By bus**. Coming in by bus can be confusing, since there are terminals in both the Ville Nouvelle and by the various gates to the Medina. However, coming from most destinations, you will more than likely arrive at the main **gare routière** (a kind of "bus yard") adjoining **Place Baghdadi**, by **Bab Boujeloud**, the western gate to Fes El Bali, or at the **CTM** on Av. Mohammed V in the Ville Nouvelle.

The main exception is if you're coming from, or departing for, **Taza and the east**, for which buses use a terminal by the Medina's southeast gate, **Bab Ftouh**. Note also that convenient **night buses** cover routes to the south – to Marrakesh and Rissani, for example.

● **Grands taxis**, like buses, tend to operate in and out of **Place Baghdadi**, though they're tucked around the corner, downhill from Bab Boujeloud. Exceptions are those from/for **Azrou/Sefrou**, which use ranks on Rue de Normandes (between Place de l'Atlas and Bd. Mohammed V in the Ville Nouvelle) and at Bab Ftouh.

● **By air**. Fes's tiny **airport** is 11km south of the city at Saïs, off the P24 to Immouzer (☎05/62.47.12 or 05/62.47.99); it is easiest reached by *grand taxi* (30dh for the taxi; 5dh a place). There are various internal flight services – including Marrakesh and Er Rachidia – and a useful, weekly flight to Oran in Algeria. Details from the *RAM/Air France* office at 54 Av. Hassan II (☎05/62.55.16).

● **Driving**. Be prepared for "motorbike guides" – Morocco's most annoying hustlers – who haunt the approach roads to Fes, attach themselves to tourist cars

vented their frustrations on government buildings. A particular casualty of the riots was the luxury *Hôtel des Merenides*, above the Medina, which was completely burnt out.

Orientation, maps and guides

Even if you'd felt you were getting accustomed to Moroccan cities, Fes is likely to prove bewildering. The basic layout is simple enough, with a Moroccan **Medina** and French-built **Ville Nouvelle**, but here the Medina comprises two separate cities: **Fes El Bali** (Old Fes), down in the bowl of the Sebou valley, and **Fes El Djedid** (New Fes), established on the edge of the valley during the thirteenth century.

Fes El Djedid, dominated by a vast enclosure of royal palaces and gardens, is relatively straightforward. **Fes El Bali**, however, where you'll want to spend most of your time, is an incredibly intricate web of lanes, blind alleys and *souks*. It

and insist on escorting you to a hotel. They can be deeply unpleasant and are not best countered by aggression; on the whole, it's easier just to tell them where you're going (book your hotel in advance) and give them a small tip on arrival. Make it clear you do not want a subsequent tour of the city.

PETITS TAXIS AND CITY BUSES

● **Petits taxis** in Fes generally use their meters, so they're very good value; after 9.30pm, there's a fifty-percent surcharge on top of the meter price.

Useful *petit taxi* ranks include:

Place Mohammed V (Ville Nouvelle).

Main PTT on Av. Hassan II (Ville Nouvelle).

Place des Alaouites (Fes El Djedid).

Place Baghdadi (north of Bab Boujeloud, Fes El Bali).

Dar Batha (south of Bab Boujeloud, Fes El Bali).

Bab Guissa (north gate, by Palais Jamai, Fes El Bali).

Bab er Rsif (central gate, south of the Kairaouine Mosque, Fes El Bali).

Bab Ftouh (southeast gate, Fes El Bali).

● **City buses** Useful city bus routes are detailed, where relevant, in the text. As a general guide these are the ones you're most likely to want to use:

#1: Place des Alaouites–Dar Batha (by Bab Boujeloud).

#2: Rue Escalier (below the post office)–Bab Semmarine.

#3: Place des Alaouites–Place de la Résistance (Ville Nouvelle).

#9: Place de la Résistance–Dar Batha.

#10: Bab Guissa–Place des Alaouites.

#18: Place de la Résistance–Bab Ftouh (via Rsif Mosque square).

#19: Train station–Place des Alaouites.

Note: These numbers are marked on the sides of the buses; there are completely different numbers on the backs.

takes two or three days before you even start to feel confident in where you're going, and on an initial visit you may well want to pay for a guide (see below) to show you the main sights and layout. The learning process is not helped, either, by the fact that most of the streetsigns are in Arabic only.

Maps

The **maps** in this guide are as functional as any available. Overpage is a plan of the Ville Nouvelle, showing the outline of Fes El Djedid and edge of Fes El Bali; on the following pages is a general plan of Fes El Bali (with enlargements of the Bab Boujeloud area on p.181 and the Kairaouine Mosque area on p.191). An additional map of Fes El Djedid is on p.203. Inevitably, all maps of Fes El Bali – including our own – are heavily simplified: more than any other Medina in Morocco, it is composed of an impenetrable maze of lanes and blind alleys, whose precise orientation and localised names do not exactly lend themselves to cartography.

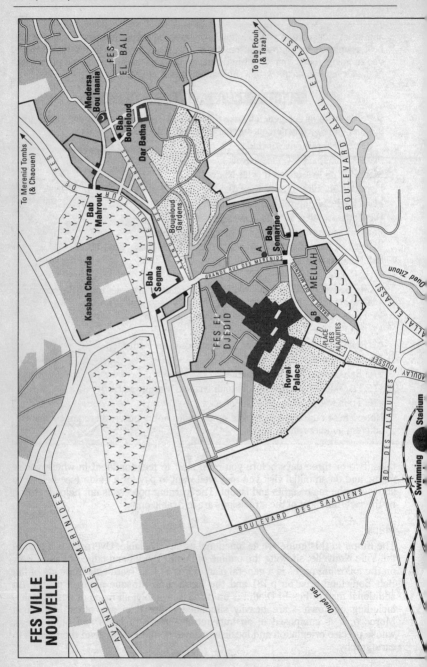

FES VILLE
NOUVELLE

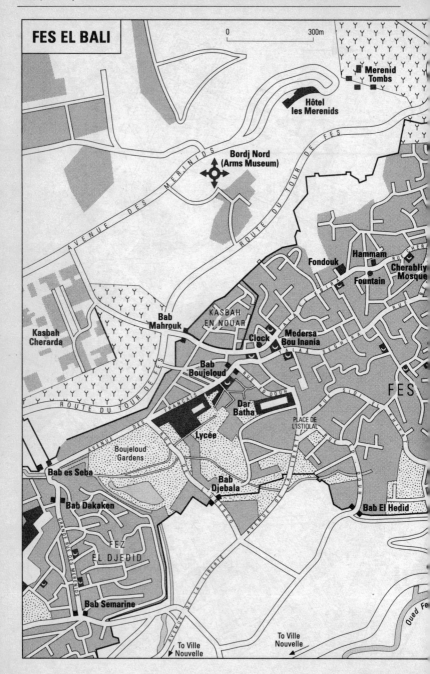

FES EL BALI

0   300m

Merenid
Tombs

Hôtel
les Merenids

Bordj Nord
(Arms Museum)

AVENUE DES MERINIDS

ROUTE DU TOUR DE FES

Fondouk

Hammam

Cherabliy
Mosque

Fountain

Bab
Mahrouk

KASBAH
EN NOUAR

Medersa
Bou Inania

Clock

Kasbah
Cherarda

FES

Bab
Boujeloud

ROUTE DU TOUR DE FES

Dar
Batha

PLACE DE
L'ISTIQLAL

Lycée

Boujeloud
Gardens

Bab es Seba

Bab
Djebala

Bab Dakaken

Bab El Hedid

FEZ
EL DJEDID

Bab Semarine

AVENUE DE LA LIBERTE

To Ville
Nouvelle

To Ville
Nouvelle

Oued Fe

Guides

A half-day tour from an **official guide** is a useful introduction to Fes El Bali; the fee is 100dh for a half day, no matter how many people are in your group. Official guides can identify themselves by round gold medallions and can be engaged at the *Syndicats d'Initiative* **tourist offices** (at Bab Boujeloud, the main entrance to Fes El Bali, or Place Mohammed V in the Ville Nouvelle; Mon–Sat 8am–7pm), or outside the more upmarket hotels, or at the youth hostel.

Anywhere else, guides who tout their services are likely to be **unofficial** and technically illegal. This doesn't necessarily mean they're to be avoided – some of those who are genuine students (as all guides claim to be) can be excellent. But you have to choose carefully, ideally by drinking a tea together before settling a rate or declaring interest. An unpleasant trick, employed by the more disreputable, is to take you into Fes El Bali and, once you're disorientated, maybe with dusk descending, demand rather more than the agreed fee to take you back to your hotel. Don't allow yourself to be intimidated.

Whether you get an official or unofficial guide, it's essential to work out in advance the **main points you want to see**: a useful exercise would be to mark them on the map of Fes El Bali in this book and show this to your guide. At all events, make it absolutely clear that you're not interested in **shopping**; you can buy goods much more effectively, and much cheaper, on your own; see "Shopping for Crafts" on p.207 for some ideas on this.

Finding a place to stay

Staying in Fes, you have the usual choice between comfort (and reliable water supply) in the modern **Ville Nouvelle** hotels or lack of facilities in the basic, unclassified Medina hotels in **Fes El Bali** and **Fes El Djedid**. There is often a shortage of hotel space in all categories, so be prepared for higher than usual prices and – if at all possible – phone ahead for a room.

If you are not overly concerned about the size and cleanliness of your room, or if you can get a room at the *Hôtel Batha* (or afford one at the luxury *Hôtel Palais Jamaï*), then **Fes El Bali/Fes El Djedid** is definitely the place to be. You will be at the heart of the city's *souks* and traditional life, well placed to explore the monuments, and witness to the amazing sounds of the early morning calls of muezzins from the hundreds of mosques. For any degree of comfort, however, you will need to stay in the **Ville Nouvelle**, where there is a wide choice of classified hotels – most of them adequate if unexciting – and a youth hostel. A few of the better hotels have swimming pools, which can be worth a bit of a splurge in midsummer, when the heat of this flat site can be overwhelming. The Ville Nouvelle hotels also offer advantages in their proximity to restaurants and bars, and to the train station.

Fes El Bali

With two notable exceptions – the upmarket *Hôtel Batha* and *Palais Jamaï* – all of the hotels in Fes El Bali are basic, unclassified dives, which could do with more regular cleaning and plumbing. They are also greatly overpriced, with some places charging the equivalent of two-star prices when they can get away with it in the summer months. However, so long as your expectations are low, they're adequate – and the group around Bab Boujeloud are in a great position, poised for exploration of the old city's sights and *souks*. The problem of water – or, rather, lack of it – in many of these cheap hotels can be overcome by taking a **hammam** or steam bath.

BAB BOUJELOUD PENSIONS

Bab Boujeloud is the western gateway to Fes El Bali and offers pedestrian access to Fes El Djedid. In the nearby **Place de l'Istiqlal** there are bus and *petit taxi* ranks for getting to and from the Ville Nouvelle.

The hotels below are listed in order of preference and are keyed on the map below.

Hôtel Jardin Public du Pacha [B], signposted down a short lane by the Boujeloud Mosque (☎05/63.30.86). This is is a friendly place and on the whole a bit cleaner than the other Bab Boujeloud hotels; rooms are mainly grouped around a courtyard, though a few have external windows. Cold showers. ①

Hôtel Cascade [E], 26 Rue Serajine (☎05/63.54.68). Small, shabby rooms are compensated by a roof terrace – and an old hammam on the second floor. ①

Hôtel Erraha [B], Place Boujeloud (☎05/63.32.26). Noisy and nothing to write home about, but there are no roaches – and the staff keep out hustlers. ①

Hôtel National [A], Place Boujeloud (☎05/63.32.48). Marginally less salubrious than the *Erraha*, opposite. ①

Hôtel Mauretania [D], Rue Serajine (☎05/63.35.18). Small, unenticing cells. ①

Hôtel Lamrani [F], Talâa Seghira (☎05/63.44.11). Again, not for the claustrophobic, nor for hygiene enthusiasts. ①

Through Bab Boujeloud, on the Talâa Seghira are two **hammams**, known as the new and old *Hammam Bildi*; these are open to foreigners, though it is best (especially for women) to ask someone at your hotel to escort you. Hours are 1pm to midnight for women, midnight to 1pm for men; bring a towel, shampoo and swimsuit.

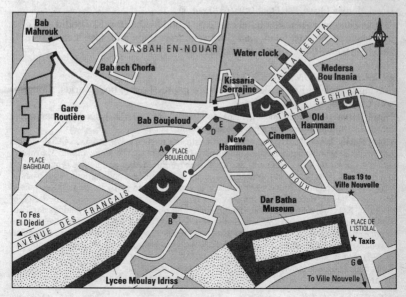

HOTEL PRICE CODES AND STAR-RATINGS

Hotels are no longer obliged to levy set maximum rates, according to their official
star-ratings, as had long been the custom. However, their **prices** still broadly follow
the star-rating system, and this is the basis of our own **hotel price codes** set out
below and keyed throughout the guide.

Our code	Official classification	Single room price	Double room price
⓪	Unclassified	25–60dh	40–100dh
①	1*A/1*B	60–105dh	100–125dh
②	2*B/2*A	105–145dh	125–175dh
③	3*B/3*A	145–225dh	175–275dh
④	4*B/4*A	225–400dh	275–500dh
⑤	5*luxury	Upwards of 400dh	Upwards of 500dh

TELEPHONE CODES

All telephone numbers in the Fes/Meknes region are prefixed 05. When making a
call within the region you omit this prefix. For more explanation of phone codes
and making calls within (or to) Morocco, see p.37.

BAB FTOUH AND BAB El DJEDID PENSIONS
An alternative trio of pensions is to be found by **Bab Ftouh** – a gate at the
bottom right hand corner of our map on p.181; this is an untouristed area and all
of the hotels listed are used more or less exclusively by Moroccans.
Hôtel Bahia, Bab Ftouh(☎05/64.92.01). ⓪
Hôtel Andalous, Bab Ftouh(☎05/63.39.91). ⓪
Hôtel Moulay Idriss, Bab Ftouh(☎05/63.81.86). ⓪

A fourth and more pleasant hotel can to be found by the **Bab El Djedid**, the next
gate along to the west (ie moving clockwise) from Bab Ftouh (see map on p.181).
Hôtel El Hamra, Bab El Djedid (☎05/64.90.20). ⓪

UPMARKET OPTIONS IN FES El BALI
Staying in style in Fes El Bali would be to get the best of both worlds, though it
won't come cheap.
Hôtel Batha [G on map above], Place de l'Istiqlal (☎05/63.64.37). Excellent new hotel,
facing the Dar Batha museum. Very pleasant en suite rooms. ④
Hôtel Palais Jamai, Bab Guissa – the north gate, see map on p.179. (☎05/63.43.31). This is
one of the three most famous hotels in Morocco (the others are the *Mamounia* in Marrakesh
and the *Gazelle d'Or* in Taroudant) and its site above the Medina justifies its reputation – if
not its prices. The beauty of the hotel lies partly in the building and gardens – the basis of
which is a nineteenth-century vizier's palace (see p.198) – and partly in the position, poised
just above Fes El Bali, with panoramic views (and sounds) of the city below. The hotel, in
addition, has a rare literary fame, having served as one of the principal settings for Paul
Bowles's novel, *The Spider's House*. Sadly, you do have to pay for the experience and the
service and maintenance aren't always what you might expect of a five-star palace. Rooms on
a weekly rate are offered for around £250/$380 per person through British travel agents (see
pp.6–7), but if you book independently expect to pay upwards of £80/$125 per night for a
basic double – more for views over the Medina, and a staggering £350/$530 if you want one
of the original (and admittedly breathtaking) palace suites in the old part of the hotel. ⑤

Hôtel Les Merenides, Bordj Nord – on the road above Fes El Bali, see the map on p.176. This was one of the city's prestige hotels until the Fes riots of 1990, when it was left burnt out by the mobs. At time of writing, it remains closed.

Fes El Djedid

Fes El Djedid is quite a good alternative to the Boujeloud area hotels: still within a ten- to fifteen-minute walk of Fes El Bali, and a bit less frequented by tourists (and hustlers). Keyed letters refer to the Ville Nouvelle/Fes El Djedid map on p.176.

Hôtel du Commerce [B], Place des Alaouites (☎05/62.22.31). Better than most of the Medina hotels, though summer puts a strain on the plumbing – and the lighting isn't exactly generous. The hotel does, however, face the royal palace. ①

Hôtel du Croissant [A], Grand Rue des Merenides (☎05/62.56.37). Reasonable-value alternative, though it gets very mixed reports on cleanliness. ①

The other two hotels in Fes El Djedid – the **Hôtel du Parc** and **Hôtel Moulay Al Cherif**, both on Grand Rue des Merenides – are pretty squalid and not recommended.

The Ville Nouvelle

As rooms can be tricky to obtain in Fes, all the Ville Nouvelle hotels are listed below. As usual, they are in ascending order of price, and keyed letters again refer to the main Ville Nouvelle/Fes El Djedid map on p.176.

Auberge de Jeunesse (youth hostel), 18 Rue Abdeslam Serghini (☎05/62.40.85). An easygoing, friendly hostel, which rents out space on the roof if the dormitories are full, and provides its own guides for exploring Fes El Bali. If travelling on your own, you won't get a cheaper bed. Opening hours are strictly adhered to: 8–9am, noon–3pm and 6–10pm.

Hôtel Rex [Z], 32 Place de l'Atlas (☎05/64.21.33). A bit out of the way – 1km from the centre of the Ville Nouvelle – but well maintained and very good value. ①

Hôtel Savoy [V], just off Bd. Chefchaouni (☎05/62.06.08). Not very glamorous but again good value. ①

Hôtel Volubilis [J], 42 Bd. Chefchaouni (☎05/62.04.63). Adequate second choice to the *Savoy*, next door. Not to be confused with the four-star *PLM Volubilis*. ①

Hôtel Regina [K], 21 Rue du 16 Novembre (☎05/62.24.27). Very ordinary; cold showers. ①

Hôtel Jeanne d'Arc [P], 36 Av. Mohammed es Slaoui (☎05/62.12.33). Sepulchral but clean. It is a little tricky to find, with a small sign obscured by trees. ①

Hôtel du Maghreb [L], 25 Av. Mohammed es Slaoui (☎05/62.59.99). Another rather discreet hotel, nearby; reception is at the top of the stairs. Nothing special. ①

Hôtel Renaissance [Q], 29 Rue Abdelkarim El Kattabi (☎05/62.21.93). Grim murals but friendly, clean and quiet – above a pedestrianised strip of this street. ①

Hôtel Central [M], corner of Rue Nador and Bd. Mohammed V (☎05/62.23.33). Cheapest of the classified hotels – and for that reason often full; no single rooms. There is an outstanding hammam nearby, hidden on a lane off Bd. Mohammed V: ask to be taken there. ①

Hôtel Excelsior [R], corner of Rue Roland Frejus and Bd. Mohammed V (☎05/62.56.02). A bit spartan, with hot water in winter only, and not too clean; also a noisy location. ①

Hôtel CTM [X], Rue Ksar El Kebir/Av. Mohammed V (☎05/62..28.11). A pleasant 1930s building, with decent-sized rooms. Very good value. ①

Hôtel Kairouan [D], 84 Rue du Soudan (☎05/62.35.90). Well-kept and decorated hotel with a superb tea room next door. ①

Hôtel Royal [E], 36 Rue du Soudan (☎05/62.46.56). A welcoming hotel with decent rooms – all with showers. ①

Hôtel Amor [G], 31 Rue du Pakistan (☎05/62.33.04/05/62.27.24). A bit of a jump in quality, with an attractive tiled frontage and a small bar. ②

Hôtel Lamdaghri [O], 10 Kabbour El Mangad (☎05/62.03.10). Bigger rooms and better service than the *Amor* makes this perhaps the best of the two-star hotels. ②

Hôtel Olympic [T], Rue Houmam Fetouaki (☎05/62.45.29). A clean, reliable and functional hotel, near the market, with reasonable prices for its class. Used by tour groups. ③

Hôtel de la Paix [P], 44 Av. Hassan II (☎05/62.50.72). An old established tour group hotel, often full but well worth a call, as it's a lot more comfortable than any of the above. ③

Hôtel Splendid [N], 9 Rue Abdelkrim (☎05/62.21.48). A good, modern hotel with a garden, bar and swimming pool; it relies a bit too much on tour groups to bother with individuals. ③

Hôtel Mounia [Y], 60 Rue Asilah (☎05/62.48.38). New hotel with very helpful management; also has a bar, restaurant and disco. ③

Grand Hôtel [S], Bd. Abdallah Chefchaouni (☎05/62.55.11). Old colonial hotel, opposite the sunken gardens on Place Mohammed V, with good rooms and a bar. ③

Moussafir Hôtel [C], Place de la Gare (☎05/65.19.02). New hotel that's part of an imaginative chain of hotels built beside train stations. Like the others, it has distinct and tasteful blue-and-white decor, a small but neatly designed pool, and a decent bar and restaurant. ④

Hôtel Zalagh [U], Rue Mohammed Diouri (☎05/62.28.10). A four-star hotel that's not quite what it was, with dodgy air conditioning, and rather gloomy decor. However, it retains fine views across the valley to Fes El Djedid and a touch of art deco style. Its pool and bar are a favourite hangout for young locals – and effectively public. ①

Hôtel Sofia [H], 3 Rue du Pakistan (☎05/62.42.65). Modern chain hotel with pool and the works, frequented almost exclusively by tour groups. ④

Hôtel PLM Volubilis [W], Av. Allal Ben Abdallah (☎05/62.11.25). Similar to the above, at the top end of town. Not terribly impressive. ④

Hôtel de Fes [I], Av. des F.A.R. (☎05/62.30.06). Again, a large and not tremendously distinguished tour group hotel, on the fringe of the Ville Nouvelle. ④

Camping

Camping Diamant Vert (☎05/64.08.10), Aïn Chkeff. This is the nearest campsite to Fes – 5km west of the city. It's a pleasant, spacious site and staying here ensures free entry to the adjoining leisure complex – which includes a swimming pool, sports facilities, a playground, a mini-zoo (camels, monkeys and peacocks), a large restaurant and a disco. There is a very much better restaurant nearby, the *Étoile de Fes*, alongside the four-star *Hôtel Reda*. Bus #17 runs from Place de Florence in Fes Ville Nouvelle past the campsite.

Note that the **old campsite in the Ville Nouvelle** closed in 1989, although it is still marked on many maps of the city (including the current *ONMT* pamphlet).

Fes El Bali

With its mosques, *medersas* and *fondouks*, combined with a mile-long network of *souks,* there are enough "sights" in **Fes El Bali** to fill three or four days just trying to locate them. And even then, you'd still be unlikely to stumble across some of them except by chance or through the whim of a guide. In this – the apparently wilful secretiveness – lies part of the fascination, and there is much to be said for Paul Bowles's somewhat lofty advice to "lose oneself in the crowd – to be pulled along by it – not knowing where to and for how long . . . to see beauty where it is least likely to appear". If you do the same, be prepared to really get lost. However, despite what hustlers may tell you, the Medina is not a dangerous place, and you can always ask a boy to lead you out towards one of its landmarks: Bab Boujeloud, Talâa Kebira, the Kairaouine Mosque, Bab er Rsif or Bab Ftouh.

Making your own way in purposeful quest for the *souks* and monuments, you should be able to find everything detailed in the following pages – with a little patience. As a prelude it's not a bad idea to head up to the **Merenid tombs** on the rim of the valley (see box overpage), where you can get a spectacular overview of the city and try to make out its shape. For a break or escape from the intensity of the Medina, head to the **Boujeloud Gardens** (officially retitled "Jardins de la Marche Verte"; open 9am–6pm), a real haven and with a pleasant open-air café, to the west of Bab Boujeoud.

There are four principal entrances and exits to Fes El Bali:

● **Bab Boujeloud**. The western gate, easily identified by its bright polychrome decoration and the hotels and cafés grouped on either side.

● **Bab Er Rsif**. A central gate, by the square (and car park) beside the Mosque er Rsif, this is a convenient entrance, just a few blocks below the Kairaouine Mosque. Bus #19 runs between the square and Av. Mohammed V in the Ville Nouvelle.

● **Bab Ftouh**. The southeast gate at the bottom of the Andalous quarter, with cemeteries extending to the south. Bus #18 runs between here and Place de l'Istiqlal (near Bab Boujeloud) and there is also a *petit taxi* rank.

● **Bab Guissa**. The north gate, up at the top of the city by the *Hôtel Palais Jamai*: a convenient point to enter (or leave) the city from (or heading to) the Merenid tombs. *Petits taxis* are available by the gate.

Into the Medina: Bab Boujeloud and Dar Batha

The area around **Bab Boujeloud** is today the principal entrance to Fes El Bali: a place with a great concentration of cafés, stalls and activity where people come to talk and stare. Provincial buses leave throughout the day from **Place Baghdadi** (just west of the gate), while in the early evening there are occasional entertainers and a flea market spreading out towards the old Mechouar (the former assembly point and government square) and to **Bab El Mahrouk**, an exit onto the road to the Merenid tombs.

This focus and importance is all comparatively recent, since it was only at the end of the last century that the walls were joined up between Fes El Bali and Fes El Djedid and the subsequently enclosed area was developed. Nearly all the buildings here date from this period, including those of the elegant **Dar Batha** palace, designed for the reception of foreign ambassadors and now a very fine **Museum of Moroccan Arts and Crafts**. Bab Boujeloud itself is comparatively modern, too, constructed only in 1913. Its tiled facades are blue (the traditional colour of Fes) on the outside, facing the ramparts, and green (the colour of Islam) on the interior, facing into the Medina.

DAR BATHA

The **Dar Batha** (open daily except Tues 9–11.30am & 3–6pm; 10dh) is worth a visit both for its collections and for its courtyards and gardens, which offer useful respite from the general exhaustion of the Medina. The museum entrance is 30m up the narrow lane separating it from the *Hôtel Batha*.

The art and crafts collections concentrate on local artesan traditions. There are stunning examples of **carved wood,** much of it rescued from the Misbahiya and other *medersas;* another magnificent room of **Middle Atlas carpets**; and excellent examples of **zellij-work**, **calligraphy** and **embroidery**.

Above all, though, it is the **pottery** rooms which stand out. The pieces, dating from the sixteenth century to the 1930s, are beautiful and show the preservation of technique long after the end of any form of innovation. This timeless quality is constantly asserted as you wander around Fes. There is no concept here of the "antique" – something is either new or it is old, and if the latter, its age could be anything from thirty years to three centuries.

THE MERENID TOMBS AND A VIEW OF FES

A crumbling and fairly obscure group of ruins, the **Merenid tombs** are not of great interest in themselves. People no longer know which of the dynasty's sultans had them erected and there is not a trace remaining of the "beautiful white marbles' vividly coloured epitaphs" which so struck Leo Africanus in his sixteenth-century description of Fes. Poised at the city's skyline, however, they are a picturesque focus and a superb vantage point. All round you are spread the Muslim cemeteries which ring the hills on each side of the city, while looking down you can delineate the more prominent among Fes's reputed 365 mosque minarets.

Getting up to the tombs is no problem. You can walk it in about twenty minutes from Bab Boujeloud, or take a taxi (around 10dh from the Ville Nouvelle). From the Boujeloud area, leave by **Bab El Mahrouk**, above the bus terminus, and once outside the walls, turn immediately to the right. After a while you come to a network of paths, climbing up towards the stolid fortress of **Borj Nord**. Despite its French garrison-like appearance, this and its southern counterpart across the valley were actually built in the seventeenth century by the Saadians. The dynasty's only endowment to the city, they were used to *control* the Fassis rather than to *defend* them. Carefully maintained, the Borj now houses the country's **arms museum** – an interminable display of row upon row of muskets, most of them confiscated from the Riffians in the 1958 rebellion.

Clambering across the hillside from Borj Nord – or following (by road) Route de Tour du Fes past the burnt-out and boarded-up *Hôtel des Merenides* – you soon emerge at **the tombs** and an expectant cluster of guides. Wandering round here, you will probably be standing on the city's original foundations, before its rapid expansion under Moulay Idriss II. But it is **the view** across the deep bowl of the

INTO THE MEDINA: THE TALÂA SEGHIRA AND TALÂA KEBIRA

Until you get a grasp of Fes El Bali, it's useful to stick with **Bab Boujeloud** as a point of entry and reference. With its polychrome tiled facades, it is a pretty unmistakeable landmark, and once inside, things are initially straightforward. You will find yourself in a small square (see map on p.181), flanked by the *Hôtel Cascade* (on your right) and with a couple of minarets almost directly ahead. Just beyond the *Hôtel Cascade,* the square splits into two main lanes, traversed by dozens of alleys but running parallel for much of the Medina's length.

The lower (righthand) fork is the **Talâa Seghira** (also known, in its French translation, as Rue du Petit Talâa), a street which begins with a handful of small foodstalls, where you can buy chunks of *pastilla,* the great Fassi delicacy of pigeon-pie; further down, the lane, renamed Rue Ben Safi, has little of specific interest until it loops up to rejoins the upper lane at the Souk El Attarin.

The upper lane, **Talâa Kebira** (aka Rue du Grand Talâa), through an arched gateway labelled "Kissariat Serajine", is the major artery of the Medina, and with its continuations runs right through to the Kairaouine Mosque. For virtually its whole length it is lined with shops and stalls, and, about a hundred metres down, it is host to the most brilliant of all the city's monuments, the **Medersa Bou Inania**. You can see the entrance to this *medersa*, down a step on your right, just before you come to a whitewashed arch-bridge over the road.

● **Access** Bus #18 from the Ville Nouvelle has a stop more or less outside Dar Batha in Place de l'Istiqlal, two minutes' walk below Bab Boujeloud. Here, and around the gate, you'll be pestered with offers of a **guide**. If you don't want one, be firm and explain that you're only

valley below which holds everyone's attention – Fes El Bali neatly wedged within it, white and diamond shaped, and buzzing with activity.

Immediately below is Adourat el-Kairaouine, or the Kairaouine quarter: the main stretch of the Medina, where Idriss settled the first Tunisian refugees. At its heart, towards the river, stands the green-tiled courtyard of the **Kairaouine Mosque**, the country's most important religious building, preceded and partially screened by its two minarets. The main one has a dome on top and is whitewashed, which is an unusual Moroccan (though characteristically Tunisian) design; the slightly lower one to its right (square, with a narrower upper floor) is *Borj en Naffara* (The Trumpeter's Tower), from which the beginning and end of Ramadan are proclaimed. Over to the right of this, and very easily recognised, are the tall pyramid-shaped roof and slender, decoratively faced minaret of the city's second great religious building, the **Zaouia of Moulay Idriss II**.

The **Andalous quarter**, the other area settled by ninth-century refugees, lies some way over to the left of this trio of minarets – divided from the Kairaouine by the appropriately named **Bou Khareb** (The River Carrying Garbage), whose path is marked out by a series of minarets. **Djemaa El-Andalous**, the principal mosque of this quarter, is distinguished by a massive, tile-porched, monumental gateway, behind which you can make out the roofs enclosing its great courtyard.

Orientation aside, there is a definite magic if you're up here in the early evening or, best of all, at dawn. The sounds of the city, the stillness and the contained disorder below all seem to make manifest the mystical significance which Islam places on urban life as the most perfect expression of culture and society.

From the tombs you can enter Fes El Bali either through **Bab Guissa** (which brings you out at the Souk El Attarin), or by returning to **Bab Boujeloud.** There is a *petit taxi* stand by Bab Guissa.

going down to Bou Inania – which will probably be your first move anyway. Most hustlers give up after about fifty metres or so. If you do want a guide, arrange an official one at the tourist post by Bab Boujeloud. To get a **petit taxi** in the Bab Boujeloud area, walk up to Place Baghdad by the Boujeloud bus terminal.

The Bou Inania medersa and clock

If there is just one building you actively seek out in Fes – or, not to put too fine a point on it, in Morocco – it should be the **Medersa Bou Inania**. The most elaborate, extravagant and beautiful of all Merenid monuments, it comes close to perfection in every aspect of its construction – its dark cedar is fabulously carved, the *zellij* tilework classic, and the stucco a revelation.

In addition, the *medersa* is the city's only building still in religious use that non-Muslims are permitted to enter. Non-believers cannot, of course, enter the prayer hall – which is divided from the main body of the *medersa* by a small canal – but are allowed to sit in a corner of the marble courtyard and gaze across to it. The **admission hours** are daily from around 8am until 5pm, with the exception of Friday mornings (closed) and times of prayer (when tourists may be asked to leave); as with all the Fes *medersas*, there is a standard 10dh admission fee.

Set somewhat apart from the other *medersas* of Fes, the Bou Inania was the last and grandest built by a Merenid sultan. It shares its name with the one in Meknes, which was completed (though not initiated) by the same patron, **Sultan Abou Inan** (1351–58). But the Fes version is infinitely more splendid. Its cost alone was legendary, and Abou Inan is said to have thrown the accounts into the river on its completion, claiming that "a thing of beauty is beyond reckoning".

At first glance, Abou Inan doesn't seem the kind of sultan to have wanted a *medersa* – his mania for building aside, he was most noted for having 325 sons in ten years, deposing his father, and committing unusually atrocious murders. The *Ulema*, the religious leaders of the Kairaouine Mosque, certainly thought him an unlikely candidate and advised him to build his *medersa* on the city's garbage dump, on the basis that piety and good works can cure anything. Whether it was this, or merely the desire for a lasting monument, which inspired him, he set up the *medersa* as a rival to the Kairaouine itself, and for a while it became the most important religious building in the city. A long campaign to have the announcement of the time of prayer transferred here failed in the face of the Kairaouine's powerful opposition; but the *medersa* was granted the status of a Grand Mosque – unique in Morocco – and retains the right to say the Friday *khotbeh* prayer.

THE MEDERSA

The basic **layout** of the *medersa* is quite simple – a single large courtyard flanked by two sizeable halls and opening onto an oratory – and is essentially the same design as that of the wealthier Fassi mansions. For its effect it relies on the mass of decoration and the light and space held within. You enter the **courtyard** – the *medersa's* outstanding feature – through a stalactite-domed entrance chamber, a feature adapted from Andalusian architecture.

Off to each side of the courtyard are stairs to the upper storey, lined with student cells, and to the roof. Depending on the progress of restoration work, you may or may not be able to go up; if you can, head straight for the roof to get an excellent (and very useful) overview of this part of the city. The cells, as is usual in *medersas*, are bare and monkish except for their windows and decorated ceilings.

In the courtyard, the **decoration**, startlingly well-preserved, covers every possible surface. Perhaps most striking in terms of craftsmanship are the wood carving and joinery, an unrivalled example of the Moorish art of *laceria*, "the carpentry of knots". The elegant, black Kufic script that rings three sides of the courtyard and divides the *zellij* (ceramic tilework) from the stucco adds a further dimension; unusually, it is largely a list of the properties whose incomes were given as an endowment, rather than the standard Koranic inscriptions. Abou Inan, too, is bountifully praised amid the inscriptions, and on the foundation stone he is credited with the title *caliph*, an emotive claim to leadership of the Islamic world pursued by none of his successors.

THE WATER CLOCK AND LATRINES

More or less opposite the *medersa*, just across the Talâa Kebira, Bou Inania's property continues with an extraordinary **water clock**, built above the stalls in the road (but at time of writing removed for restoration). An enduring curiosity, this consists of a row of thirteen windows and platforms, seven of which retain their original brass bowls. Nobody has been able to discover exactly how it functioned, though a contemporary account detailed how at every hour one of its windows would open, dropping a weight down into the respective bowl.

Clocks had great religious significance during the Middle Ages in establishing the time of prayer, and it seems probable that this one was bought by Abou Inan as part of his campaign to assert the *medersa's* preeminence; there are accounts of similar constructions in Tlemcen, just across the border in Algeria. As to its destruction, Fassi conspiracy tales are classically involved – most of them revolve round the miscarriage of a Jewess passing below at the time of its striking and a Jewish sorcerer casting the evil eye on the whole device. The building to which

THE FUNCTION OF MEDERSAS

Medersas – student colleges and residence halls – were by no means unique to Fes and, in fact, originated in Khorassan in Iran, gradually spreading west through Baghdad and Cairo. They seem to have reached Morocco under the Almohads, though the earliest ones still surviving in Fes are Merenid, dating from the early fourteenth century.

The word *medersa* means "place of study", and there may have been lectures delivered in some of the prayer halls. In general, however, the *medersas* served as little more than dormitories, providing room and board to poor (male) students from the countryside and hence allowing them to attend lessons at the mosques. In Fes, where students might attend the Kairaouine University for ten years or more, rooms were always in great demand and "key money" was often paid by the new occupant. Although *medersas* had largely disappeared from the Islamic world by the late Middle Ages, most of those in Fes remained in use right up to the 1950s, and a few are still occupied by students today.

the clock is fixed, which was, in fact, once owned by a rabbi, is popularly known as "The House of the Magician".

Completing the *medersa* complex, and immediately adjacent to the clock, are the original **public latrines** built for Friday worshippers. These have recently been closed, though it is possible that this will be temporary. Predating their use in the West by some four centuries, the "Turkish-style" toilets here were at last look very functional, flushed by quantities of running water. If they have re-opened – and you're male – take a look inside at the large central patio with its ablutions pool and unexpectedly rich stucco ceiling.

Further down Talâa Kebira

Making your way down the **Talâa Kebira** – a straightforward route to follow – you will eventually emerge at the labryinth of lanes round the Kairaouine Mosque and Zaouia Moulay Idriss II. It's interesting less for any specific "sights" than for the general accumulated stimuli to your senses. The diarist Anaïs Nin expressed her reaction in terms of odours: ". . . of excrement, saffron, leather being cured, sandalwood, olive oil being fried, nut oil so strong at first that you cannot swallow". To which might be added sound – the shouts of muleteers (*balak!* means "look out!"), mantric cries from the beggars, the bells of water vendors – and, above all, the sight of the people, seen in shafts of light filtered through the rush roofings which cover much of the Talâa's length.

Along the first (upward) stretch watch out for a very large **fondouk** on your left, just after a row of blacksmiths' shops, about 300m beyond the Medersa Bou Inania. This was originally a **Merenid prison**, fitted out with solid colonnades and arches; it is now home to people selling butter and honey out of large vats.

Before the advent in Morocco of French-style cafés, at the beginning of this century, the *fondouks* – or *caravanserais* as they're called in the East – formed the heart of social life outside the home. They provided rooms for traders and richer students, and frequently became centres of vice, intrigue and entertainment. There were once some two hundred in Fes El Bali, but although many still survive, often with beautiful fourteenth- and fifteenth-century decorations, they tend now to serve as small factories or warehouses. Another **fondouk**, about 100m further down, is today used for curing animal skins (and smells awful).

RUE ECH CHERABLIYIN

A little way down from this latter *fondouk*, the street changes name – to **Rue Ech Cherabliyin** – and, past the oldest **hammam** still in use in Fes, you find yourself in a district of **leather stalls and shoemakers**. The Fassi *babouches*, leather slippers, are reputed to be the best in the country, and here, unusually, you'll find sophisticated-looking grey and black pairs in addition to the classic yellow and white. If you want to buy a good pair, you'll have to spend some time examining the different qualities; for the best, be prepared to bargain hard until you're down to around 150dh.

The **Cherabliyin** (Slippermakers') **mosque**, in the midst of the quarter, was endowed by the Merenid sultan, Abou El Hassan, builder of the Chellah complex in Rabat. It has been substantially restored, though the minaret is original. If you've gazed at the Koutoubia in Marrakesh, or the great Almohad monuments of Rabat, you'll recognise the familiar *darj w ktarf* motifs of its decoration.

SOUK EL ATTARIN

Continuing, Rue ech Cherabliyin is flanked by a forgettable sequence of "typical" handicraft shops before reaching, at the bottom of the hill, an arched gateway marked **Souk El Attarin** – the "Souk of the Spice Vendors". This was the formal heart of the old city, and its richest and most sophisticated shopping district. It was traditionally around the grand mosque of a city that the most expensive commodities were sold and kept, and, approaching the Kairaouine, this pattern is more or less maintained. Spices themselves are still sold here, as well as Egyptian and Japanese imports, while in the web of little squares off to the left, you'll find all kinds of manufactured goods.

There are a few small cafés inside the spice *souk*, and on the main street is the **Dar Saada**, a nineteenth-century mansion now housing an expensive carpet shop and restaurant; you can look in or drink a cup of tea feeling only moderate pressure to buy something.

Just beyond the Dar Saada, this time on the right of the street, is the principal **kissaria**, or covered market, again dominated by textiles and modern goods; totally rebuilt after a fire in the 1950s, it lacks any particular character.

● **Access.** Reaching the end of Souk El Attarin you come to a **crossroads of lanes** lying slightly askew from the direction of the street. On your right (and ahead of you) are the walls of the **Kairaouine Mosque;** to your left, and entered a few yards up the lane, is the magnificent **Attarin Medersa** (see below). First, however, it seems logical to take a look at the area below the Souk El Attarin – dominated, as it has been for five centuries, by the **shrine and zaouia of Moulay Idriss II,** the city's patron saint.

The Zaouia of Moulay Idriss II and around

The principal landmark to the south of the Souk El Attarin is the **Zaouia Moulay Idriss II**, one of the holiest buildings in the city. Although enclosed by a highly confusing web of lanes, it is not difficult to find: take the first lane to the right – Rue Mjadliyin – as soon as you have passed through the arch into the Attarin and you will find yourself in front of a wooden bar which marks the beginning of its *horm*, or sanctuary precinct. Until the French occupation of the city in 1911, this was as far as Christians, Jews or mules, could go, and beyond it any Muslim had the right to claim asylum from prosecution or arrest. These days non-Muslims are allowed to walk round the outside of the *zaouia*, and although you are not permitted to enter, it is possible to get a glimpse inside the shrine and even see the saint's tomb.

Passing to the right of the bar, and making your way round a narrow alleyway, you emerge on the far side of the *zaouia* at the **women's entrance.** Looking in from the doorway, the **tomb** of Moulay Idriss II is over on the left, and a scene of intense and apparently high-baroque devotion is usually going on all round it. The women, who are Idriss's principal devotees, burn candles and incense here and then proceed around the corner of the precinct to touch, or make offerings at, a round brass grille which opens directly onto the tomb. A curious feature, common to many *zaouias* but rarely within view, are the numerous European clocks – prestigious gifts and very popular in the last century, when many Fassi merchant families had them shipped over from Manchester (their main export base for the cotton trade).

There is no particular evidence that Moulay Idriss II was a very saintly *marabout*, but as the effective founder of Fes and the son of the founder of the Moroccan state, he obviously has considerable *baraka*, the magical blessing which Moroccans invoke. Originally it was assumed that Idriss, like his father, had been buried near Volubilis, but in 1308 an incorrupted body was found on this spot and the cult was launched. Presumably, it was an immediate success, since in addition to his role as the city's patron saint, Idriss has an impressive roster of supplicants. This is the place to visit for poor strangers arriving in the city, for boys before being circumcised, and for women wanting to facilitate childbirth; also, for some unexplained reason, Idriss is a national protector of sweetmeat vendors. The shrine itself was rebuilt in the eighteenth century by Sultan Moulay Ismail – his only act of pious endowment in this city.

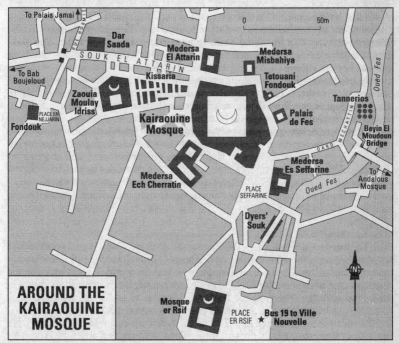

AROUND THE KAIRAOUINE MOSQUE

PLACE EN NEJJARIN

Standing at the women's entrance to the *zaouia,* you'll see a lane off to the left – **Rue du Bab Moulay Ismail** – full of stalls selling candles and silverware for devotional offerings. If you follow this lane round to the wooden bar, go under the bar (turning to the right), and then, keeping to your left, you should come out in the picturesque square of **Place En Nejjarin** (Carpenters' Square).

Here is the very imposing **Nejjarin Fondouk**, built in the early eighteenth century along with a beautiful canopied fountain on one side of the square. The *fondouk,* crumbling all round its courtyard, is at present closed for restoration, though it was in use up until a few years ago as a hostel for students at the nearby Kariaouine university.

In the alleys that lead off the square, you'll find the **Nejjarin souk**, easiest located by the sounds and smells of the carpenters chiselling away at sweet-smelling cedar wood. They produce mainly stools and tables – three-legged so they don't wobble on uneven ground – along with various implements for winding yarn, wooden boxes for storage and coffins. If there's a wedding coming up, you may see them making special ornamented tables, with edges, used for parading the bride and groom at shoulder level – a Fassi custom. Parallel to this lane is a **metalworkers' souk**, where the men hammer patterns onto large iron tubs and implements.

To return to the Souk El Attarin, turn left at the point where you entered the Place en Nejjarin.

SOUK El HENNA

A similar arrangement of buildings characterises the **Souk El Henna**, a quiet, tree-shaded square adjoining what was once the largest madhouse in the Merenid empire – an imposing building now in use as a storehouse. The stalls here continue to sell henna and the usual cosmetics (kohl, antimony, etc.); on one side of the square there is a huge pair of scales used for weighing the larger deliveries. In addition, several outlets here offer the more esoteric ingredients required for medical cures, aphrodisiacs and magical spells. If you get talking to the stallkeepers, you'll be shown an amazing collection of plant and animal (often insect) derivatives.

Pottery stalls are gradually encroaching on this traditional pharmacological business. Cheap but often striking in design, the pieces include Fassi pots, which are usually blue and white or very simple black on earthenware; and others from Safi, the pottery most commonly exported from Morocco, distinguished by heavy green or blue glazes; and Salé, often elaborate modern designs on a white glaze.

To get down to the square, take the lane to the right immediately in front of the entrance arch to Souk El Attarin.

The Kairaouine Mosque

The **Djemaa El Kairaouine** – the Kairaouine Mosque – was the largest mosque in Morocco until the construction of the new Hassan II Mosque in Casablanca – and it is one of the oldest universities anywhere in the world. It remains today the fountainhead of the country's religious life, governing, for example, the timings of Ramadan and the other Islamic festivals. There is an old Fassi saying that all roads in Fes lead to the Kairaouine – a claim which retains some truth.

The mosque was founded in 857 by a Tunisian woman, a wealthy refugee from the city of Kairouan, but its present dimensions, with sixteen aisles and room for

20,000 worshippers, are essentially the product of tenth- and twelfth-century reconstructions: first by the great Caliph of Cordoba, Abd er Rahman III, and later under the Almoravids.

For non-Muslims, who cannot enter the mosque's courts and prayer halls, the Kairaouine is a rather elusive sight. The building is so thoroughly enmeshed in the surrounding houses and shops that it is impossible to get any clear sense of its shape, and at most you can get only partial views of it from the adjoining roof-tops or through the four great entrances to its main courtyard. Nobody seems to object to tourists gaping through the gates, though inevitably the centrepieces that would give order to all the separate parts – the main aisle and the *mihrab* – remain hidden from view.

The overall effect of this obscurity is compounded by the considerable amount of time you're likely to spend getting lost around this area. The best **point of reference** round the Kairaouine – and the building most worth visiting in its own right – is the Medersa El Attarin, whose entrance is at the far end of the Souk El Attarin, at the northwest corner of the Kairaouine Mosque. From here you can make your way round the mosque to a succession of other *medersas* and *fondouks*, picking up glimpses of the Kairaouine's interior as you go.

The Attarin Medersa

The **Medersa El Attarin** (daily 9am–noon & 2–6pm, closed Friday mornings; 10dh admission) is, after the Bou Inania, the finest of the city's medieval colleges. It has an incredible profusion and variety of patterning – equally startling in the *zellij,* wood and stucco. Remarkably, each aspect of the decoration seems accomplished with an apparent ease, and the building's elegant proportions are never under threat of being overwhelmed.

The *medersa* was completed in 1325 by the Merenid sultan, Abou Saïd, and is thus one of the earliest in Fes. Interestingly, its general lightness of feel is achieved by the relatively simple device of using pairs of symmetrical arches to join the pillars to a single weight-bearing lintel – a design repeated in the upper storeys and mirrored in the courtyard basin. The later Merenid design, as employed in the Bou Inania, was to have much heavier lintels (the timbers above the doors and windows) supported by shorter projecting beams; this produces a more solid, step-like effect, losing the Attarin's fluid movement.

The basic ground plan, however, is more or less standard: an entrance hall opening onto a courtyard with a fountain, off which to the left are the latrines, and directly ahead the prayer hall. On your way in, stop a while in the **entrance hall,** whose *zellij* decoration is perhaps the most complex in Fes. A circular pattern, based on an interlace of pentagons and five-pointed stars, this perfectly demonstrates the intricate science – and the philosophy – employed by the craftsmen. As Titus Burckhardt explains (in his *Moorish Art in Spain*), this lies in direct opposition to the Western arts of pictorial representation:

> . . . *with its rhythmic repetitions, [it] does not seek to capture the eye to lead it into an imagined world, but, on the contrary, liberates it from all the pre-occupations of the mind. It does not transmit specific ideas, but a state of being, which is at once repose and inner rhythm.*

Burckhardt adds that the way the patterns radiate from a single point serves as a pure simile for the belief in the oneness of God, manifested as the centre of every form or being.

In the **courtyard** you'll notice a change in the *zellij* base to a combination of eight- and ten-pointed stars. This probably signifies the hand of a different *maallem* (master craftsman), most of whom had a single mathematical base which they worked and reworked with infinite variation on all commissions. In comparison with these outer rooms, the actual **prayer hall** is very bare and meditative, focusing on its *mihrab* (or prayer niche) flanked by marble pillars and lit by a series of small *zellij*-glass windows.

If you are allowed to go up the stairs in the entrance hall, do so. Around the second floor are **cells** for over sixty students, and these operated as an annexe to the Kairaouine University until the 1950s. Budgett Meakin (in 1899) estimated that there were some 1500 students in the city's various *medersas* – a figure which may have been overestimated since it was based not on an actual count of the students themselves but on how many loaves of bread were prepared for them each day. Non-Muslims were not allowed into the *medersas* until the French undertook their repair at the beginning of the protectorate, and were banned again (this time by the colonial authorities) when the Kairaouine students became active in the struggle for independence.

VIEWS OF THE KAIRAOUINE

From the roof of the Attarin Medersa (not always open to visitors) you can get one of the most complete views possible of the **Kairaouine Mosque**.

Looking out across the mosque's green roof tiles three **minarets** are visible. The square one on the left belongs to the Zaouia Moulay Idriss. To its right are the Kairaouine's Burj an-Naffara (Trumpeter's Tower) and original minaret. The latter, slightly thinner in its silhouette than usual – most minarets are built to an exact 5 : 1 (width : height) ratio – is the oldest Islamic monument in the city, built in the year 956. Below it, you can also make out a considerable section of the central courtyard of the mosque – the **sahn**.

For a closer glimpse of the *sahn* at ground level, the best vantage point is the Bab El Wad gate: 20m down from the Attarin entrance (turn left as you step out, then immediately left again). At the end of the courtyard, a pair of magnificent pavilions are visible – the last additions to the structure of the mosque, added by the Saadians in the sixteenth century. They are modelled on the Court of the Lions in Granada's Alhambra palace, and were perhaps constructed by Spanish Muslim craftsmen.

Around the Kairaouine and Place Seffarine

There is a further new angle on to the *sahn* of the Kairaouine from the **Bab Medersa**, a gate near the end of this first stretch of the mosque wall. Opposite, as you'd expect, is another college – the semiderelict (but occasionally open) **Misbahiya Medersa**. It has some fine details, though much of its best wood carving is now displayed at the Dar Batha museum. The elegant central basin was brought over by the Saadians from Almeria in Spain; the marble floor in which it is set level came from Italy. Surprisingly large, with courtyards (and two latrines) at each corner, it was built a couple of years before Bou Inania, again by the Merenid sultan, Abou El Hassan.

THE TETOUANI FONDOUK AND PALAIS DE FES

Moving on around the corner of the Kairaouine, you pass the **Tetouani** (or *Istroihani*) **fondouk**, a well-preserved Merenid building where the traders from

Tetouan used to stay. Now partially occupied by a carpet store, you can look inside without any obligation and you'll probably be shown the huge, ancient door lock which draws across its gateway.

A few doors down, past another, much smaller *fondouk,* is the so-called **Palais de Fes**, a grand nineteenth-century mansion converted to a series of restaurants and a fine carpet shop. You can walk in and look round without pressure to buy, and if you ask you'll be allowed up to the **roof** to get a different view of the Kairaouine and an interesting exercise in orientation concerning the immediate area. There is a café-restaurant on the roof, which will serve tea and pastries outside meal times – highly recommended.

PLACE SEFFARINE AND THE KAIRAOUINE LIBRARY

Another gate to the Kairaouine, essentially of Almoravid construction, stands right opposite the Palais de Fes; it is one of the ten which are opened only for Friday prayers. Alongside, notice the cedar panelling, placed to guide the blind towards the mosque.

If you follow this round, through a tight-wedged alley, you soon emerge into a very distinctive open square, metalworkers hammering away on each of its sides, surrounded by immense iron and copper cauldrons and pans for weddings and festivals. This is **Place Seffarine** – almost wilfully picturesque, with its faience fountain and gnarled old fig trees.

On the near side of the square a tall and very simple entrance in the white-washed walls leads into the **Kairaouine Library**, again a building frustratingly denied to non-Muslims. Established by the Kairouan refugees in the ninth century, and bolstered by virtually the entire contents of Córdoba's medieval library, it once held the greatest collection of Islamic, mathematical and scholarly books outside Baghdad. Amazingly, and somewhat pointedly marking Fes's decline, much of the library was lost or dissipated in the seventeenth century. Now restored and in use, it is one of the most important in the Arab world.

The **university** here has had its function largely usurped by the modern departments established around Fes El Djedid and the Ville Nouvelle, and dispersed throughout Morocco. However, until recent decades it was the only source of Moroccan higher education. Entirely traditional in character, studies comprised courses on Koranic law, astrology, mathematics, logic, rhetoric and poetry – very much as the medieval universities of Europe. Teaching was informal, with professors gathering a group of students round them in a corner of the mosque, the students contriving to absorb and memorise the body of the professors' knowledge. It was, of course, an entirely male preserve.

A good spot to get your bearings, Place Seffarine offers a number of possible routes. You can continue round the mosque by taking the first lane to the right as you enter the square – **Sma't El Adoul** (The Street of the Notaries). The notaries, professional scribes, are sadly out of business, but before looping back to reach the Attarin *medersa*, you will be able to peek through a number of gates revealing the Kairaouine's rush-matted and round-arched interior. If you don't take this turning but continue straight ahead, you enter an area of *souks* specialising in **gold and silver jewellery** and used metal goods – a magnificent range of **pewter teapots** among them. As this road begins to veer left down the hill, a right turn will lead you up to the **Cherratin Medersa** (and eventually to Zaouia Moulay Idriss).

First, though, it is worth taking a look at the **Seffarine Medersa**, right on Place Seffarine.

THE MEDERSA ES-SEFFARINE

The **Medersa Es-Seffarine** (same hours as Attarin; 10dh) is the earliest of these Fes colleges. Its entrance is fairly inconspicuous, and you might need it pointed out to you: leaving the Seffarine square at the bottom lefthand corner you follow a short lane down to the left and then briefly to the right – the door (studded and with an overhanging portico) is on your left.

Built around 1285 – twenty years before the Attarin, 42 before the Bou Inania – the Seffarine is unlike all the other *medersas* in that it takes the exact form of a traditional Fassi house, with an arched balcony above its courtyard. It is heavily decayed, though still with suggestions of former grandeur in the lofty prayer hall. Elsewhere, the wandering vine and delicate ablutions pool give it a domestic air; in the far left-hand corner are wash basins and latrines.

For a small tip, the custodian will unlock the door to the **roof**, an atmospheric place where you can look down on the Seffarine square and listen to the individual rhythms of the metalworkers. Next door to the building are two newer *medersas*, still used for housing groups of students from the Lycée.

THE MEDERSA ECH-CHERRATIN

Very different from the Seffarine, and indeed all the previous *medersas*, the **Medersa Ech-Cherratin** (see directions from Place Seffarine, above) dates from 1670 and the reign of Moulay er Rachid, founder of the Alaouite dynasty.

The whole design represents a shift in scope and wealth – to an essentially functional style, with student cells grouped round three corner courtyards and a latrine round the fourth. Comprising some 120 rooms (each with space for two students), the *medersa* was in use until very recently and the cells are still partitioned and occasionally provided with electric light. The craftsmanship here represents a significant decline, though there is some impressive woodwork round the individual courtyards. It is interesting, too, in a general way as a rare surviving building from this period.

This *medersa* has recently been closed for restoration: knock for admission and you might be able to tip a workman to let you look around.

● **Access.** Continuing down the lane **beyond the entrance to Medersa es-Seffarine**, swinging down the hill to the right, you reach **Rue des Teinturiers** (The Dyers' *Souk*: see the following section) and a **bridge** over the Oued Fes, below which you can leave the Medina by the *place* beside the **Mosque er Rsif**.

South of the Kairaouine: The Dyers' Souk and tanneries

If you're beginning to find the medieval prettiness of the central *souks* and *medersas* slightly unreal, then this region, just below the Kairaouine, should provide the antidote. That's because the dyers' and tanners' *souks* – basis of the city's commercial wealth from the tenth to the nineteenth century – represent the nauseating underside of everything you've seen until now.

THE DYERS' SOUK

The **dyers' street** – **Souk Sabbighin** (or Rue des Teinturiers, in French) – is directly below the Seffarine Medersa. Continue down past the *medersa* to your left, and then turn right immediately before the bridge ahead.

The *souk* is short and very weird, draped with fantastically coloured yarn and cloth drying in the heat. Below, workers in grey, chimney-sweep-looking clothes toil over ancient cauldrons of multicoloured dyes. The atmosphere is thick and mysterious, and not a little disconcerting so close to one of the city's main entrances.

● **Access.** At the end of the dyers' *souk* you come to a second bridge, the humpbacked **Qantrat Sidi El Aouad** – almost disguised by the shops built on and around it. Walking across, you'll find yourself in the **Andalous quarter** (see overpage), and if you follow the main lane up to the left, Rue Sidi Youssef, you'll come out at the Andalous Mosque. Staying on the Kairaouine side of the river and taking the lane down to your right at the end of the *souk*, you should emerge at the open **square by the Rsif Mosque**; from here, if you want to return to the Ville Nouvelle, you can get a #19 bus, or a *petit taxi*.

THE TANNERIES

For the tanneries quarter – the **Souk Dabbaghin** – return to Place Seffarine and take the right-hand lane at the top of the square (the second lane on your left if you're coming from the Palais de Fes). This lane is known as **Darb Mechattin** (Combmakers' Lane), and runs more or less parallel to the river for 150m or so, eventually reaching a fork. The right-hand branch goes down to the river and **Beyin El Moudoun Bridge** – another approach to the Andalous Mosque. The left branch winds up amid a maze of eighteenth-century streets for another 150 to 200m until you see the tanneries on your right; it sounds a convoluted route but is in fact a well-trodden one.

The most physically striking sight in Fes, the **tanneries** are constantly being visited by groups of tourists, with whom you could discreetly tag along for a while if you get lost. Otherwise, follow your nose or accept a guide up from Place Seffarine. The best time to visit is in the morning, when there is most activity. You will be asked to pay a small fee – 10dh is usual – to one of the local *gardiens*.

There is a compulsive fascination about the tanneries. Cascades of water pour through holes that were once the windows of houses; hundreds of skins lie spread out to dry on the rooftops; while amid the vats of dye and pigeon dung (used to treat the leather) an unbelievably gothic fantasy is enacted. The rotation of colours in the enormous honeycombed vats follows a traditional sequence – yellow (saffron), red (poppy), blue (indigo), green (mint) and black (antimony) – though vegetable dyes have mostly been replaced by chemicals, with worrying effects on the health of the workers involved.

This innovation and the occasional rinsing machine aside, there can have been little change here since the sixteenth century, when Fes took over from Cordoba as the pre-eminent city of leather production. As befits such an ancient system, the ownership is also intricately feudal: the foremen run a hereditary guild and the workers pass down their specific jobs from generation to generation.

The processes can best be seen from surrounding terrace rooftops, where you'll be directed along with the other tourists. There is, oddly enough, a kind of sensuous beauty about it – for all the stench and voyeurism involved. Sniffing the mint that you are handed as you enter (to alleviate the nausea) and looking across at the others doing the same, however, there could hardly be a more pointed exercise in the nature of comparative wealth. Like it or not, this is tourism at its most extreme.

North to Bab Guissa and the Palais Jamai

This region – **north from Souk El Attarin** towards Bab Guissa and the Palais Jamai Hôtel – is something of a tailpiece to the Kairaouine quarter of Fes El Bali. It is not a route which many tourists take, scattered as it is with curiosities rather than monuments, but in this itself there's a distinct attraction. Additionally, leaving the city at Bab Guissa you can walk out and round to the **Merenid Tombs**, a beautiful walk as the sun is going down on the city.

A ROUTE TO BAB GUISSA – AND THE JEWELLERS' SOUK

From **Souk El Attarin,** there are dozens of lanes climbing up in the general direction of Bab Guissa, many of them blind alleys which send you scuttling back to retrace your steps. One of the more interesting and unproblematic approaches is to take the first lane to your left just inside the entrance arch to the *souk* (that is, about 15m before you come to the *Dar Saada* palace restaurant). Following this as directly as you can, you will soon emerge at the **Joutia**, the ancient fish and salt market.

Spreading out above here is the **Sagha** – the **jewellers' quarter** – which curves round to the right into a small square flanked by the eighteenth-century **Fondouk Sagha** and a small fountain. The *fondouk* is now used as a wool store-house, though you can wander in to take a look at the elegant cedar woodwork and (heavily restored) stucco.

Back at the main lane – Place Sagha and its *fondouk* are about 20m off to the right – you pass a series of small café-restaurants and a cinema near **Place Achabin**, the herbalists' square, where remedies and charms are still sold. The **café-restaurants** in this area are among the best value in Fes El Bali, serving good solid meals, and many double as *pâtisseries*, good for a mint tea or some fresh orange while rambling round the Attarin/Kairaouine area. Most of them are located in Rue Hormis.

Beyond Place Achabin, the road continues uphill, through an area filled with carpenters' workshops, towards Bab Guissa. On your way, look out for the **Fondouk Guissa** – or *Fondouk El Ihoudi* (The Jews' Fondouk) – on the left-hand side of the road. This dates back to the thirteenth century and was at the centre of the city's Jewish community until their removal to the Mellah in Fes El Djedid. It is used today for the sorting and storing of skins brought up from the tanneries: not a building for the queasy.

BAB GUISSA AND THE HÔTEL PALAIS JAMAI

The **Bab Guissa** and **Mosque Bab Guissa**, at the top of the hill, are of little interest, rebuilt in the nineteenth century to replace a string of predecessors which have occupied this site for 800 years.

A quick right just before the gate, however, takes you up to the **Hôtel Palais Jamai** – a building whose luxury comes as quite a shock after a day's rambling through the Medina below. It was built towards the end of the last century by the Jamai brothers, viziers to Sultan Moulay Hassan and, in effect, the most powerful men in the country. Fabulously rapacious, the brothers eventually fell from power amid spectacular intrigues at the accession of Abdul Aziz in 1894. Walter Harris records the full story in *Morocco That Was*, dwelling in great detail on the brothers' ignominious fate – "perhaps the blackest page of Moulay Abdul Aziz's reign".

> *They were sent in fetters to Tetouan, and confined, chained and fettered, in a dungeon. In the course of time – and how long those ten years must have been – Hadj Amaati (The Elder) died. The governor of Tetouan was afraid to bury the body, lest he should be accused of having allowed his prisoner to escape. He wrote*

to the court for instructions. It was summer, and even the dungeon was hot. The answer did not come for eleven days, and all that time Si Mohammed remained chained to his brother's corpse! The brother survived. In 1908 he was released after fourteen years of incarceration, a hopeless, broken, ruined man. Everything he had possessed had been confiscated, his wives and children had died; the result of want and persecution. He emerged from his dark dungeon nearly blind, and lame from the cruel fetters he had worn. In his days of power he had been cruel, it is said – but what a price he paid!

In overt and dramatic contrast to this tale, you can wander into the hotel for a drink. Ask to do so on the terrace beside the old palace, now dwarfed by a huge modern extension. An hour in the gardens here, with their box-hedge courtyards and fountains, really does merit the bar prices. The palace quarters themselves are used as special suites and conference rooms, but if they're unoccupied you may be able to look round one or two – ask at reception if a porter can show you the "Royal Suites"; a tip will be expected.

● **Access.** From **Bab Guissa** you can take a shortcut across through the hill cemetery to the Merenid tombs, or you can follow the road up and around. At **Bab Ferdaous**, just outside the *Palais Jamai*, there's a *petit taxi* stand, and from here **bus #10** runs to Place des Alaouites in Fes El Djedid.

The Andalous Quarter

Coming across the **Bou Khareb** River from the Kairaouine to the **Andalous bank** is not quite the adventure it once was. For the first three centuries of their existence, the two quarters were entirely separate walled cities and the intense rivalry between them often resulted in factional strife. The rivalry still lingers enough to give each a distinct identity, though since the thirteenth century this has been a somewhat one-sided affair: as the Fassis tell it, the Andalusians are known for the beauty of their women and the bravery of their soldiers, while the Kairaouinis have always had the money.

Whatever the reasons, the most famous Andalusian scholars and craftsmen have nearly all lived and worked on the other side of the river and as a result the atmosphere has a somewhat provincial character. Monuments are few and comparatively modest, and the streets are quieter and predominantly residential. As such, it can be a pleasant quarter to spend the early evening – and to get caught up in the ordinary, daily life of Fes El Bali. Street trading here (and in the southern quarters of the Kairouine side, too) tends to revolve round daily necessities, providing a link between the "medieval" town and continuing urban life. And your relationship with the city changes alongside, as you cease for a while to be a consuming tourist – a factor reflected also in the near-total absence of "guides" and hustlers.

There are four principal **approaches to the quarter**, all providing more or less direct access to the area round the Andalous Mosque.

● **Cross the river at the El Aouad Bridge**. From here, take **Rue Sidi Youssef** up the hill to the right, and keep going straight to the top, where you'll come into line with the minaret of the Andalous Mosque. At this point, veer left, and you will see (on your right) the elaborate facade of the **Sahrija Medersa**.

● **Cross the river to the north, near the tanneries, on the Bein El Moudoun Bridge** (The Bridge Between the Cities). Then follow the main street, **Rue Seftah,** all the way up the hill as it winds round to the Andalous Mosque.

● **Start at the square by Mosque Er Rsif**. From here you can get to **Rue Sidi Youssef** by going through the gate opposite the mosque entrance, then taking a first left by the first mosque (Sidi Lemlili) you come to, followed by a right turn up the hill. The square can be reached (somewhat circuitously) from the area around the Kairaouine Mosque, or you can get a **bus** to it (#19) from the Ville Nouvelle.

● Start at **Bab Ftouh, at the bottom of the quarter, and head north to the Andalous Mosque.** Bab Ftouh is connected by **bus** #18 to the Place de l'Istiqlal, by the Dar Batha; a handy point from which to leave Fes El Bali.

THE SAHRIJA MEDERSA AND ANDALOUS MOSQUE

If you are seeking direction for your wanderings in the Andalous Quarter, the **Medersa Es-Sahrija** is the quarter's most interesting monument and is generally rated the third finest *medersa* in the city, after the Attarin and Bou Inania. Anywhere else but Fes it would be a major sight, though here, perhaps because of its state of dilapidation, it fails to stand out as much as it should.

Still, it is currently undergoing restoration, and there's a considerable range and variety of original decoration. The *zellij* is among the oldest in the country, while the wood carving harkens back to Almohad and Almoravid motifs with its palmettes and pine cones. Built around 1321 by Sultan Abou El Hassan, it is slightly earlier than the Attarin and a more or less exact contemporary of the *medersa* in Meknes – which it in many ways resembles.

There is frustratingly little to be seen of the nearby **Andalous Mosque**, other than its monumental entrance gates, as it is built right at the highest point of the valley. Like the Kairaouine, it was founded in the late ninth century and saw considerable enlargements under the Almoravids and Merenids. The Sahrija Medersa originally served as a dormitory annexe for those studying at the mosque's library and under its individual professors.

A last medersa, the **Sebbayin**, or **Medressa El Oued**, is located just southwest of the Sahrija. It, too, was once an Andalous Mosque student annexe, and it remains in use, as a residence for Lycée students.

TOWARDS BAB FTOUH AND THE POTTERS' QUARTER

South from the Andalous Mosque – out towards **Bab Ftouh** – you emerge into a kind of flea market: clothes sellers at first, then all variety of household and general goods and odds and ends. At the top of the hill, on the edge of a cemetery area, there are often entertainers – clowns, storytellers, the occasional musician, all performing to large audiences.

This region of the city, a strange no-man's land of **cemeteries** and run-down houses, was once a leper colony, and traditionally a quarter of necromancers, thieves, madmen and saints. At its heart, close by Bab Ftouh, is the whitewashed **koubba of Sidi Harazem**, a twelfth-century mystic who has been adopted as the patron saint of students and the mentally ill. The saint's *moussem*, held in the spring, is one of the city's most colourful; in past centuries it was often the cue for riots and popular insurrections. The **potters' quarter** used to be located by Bab Ftouh, though they have recently been moved out some three kilometres along the Taza road. If you're interested in the techniques – the moulding, drying and decorating of the pots and tiles – it's possible to look around the workshops. Although the quarter is new, the designs and workmanship remain traditional.

● **Access.** At **Bab Ftouh** you can pick up a *petit taxi* to any part of town (the route up to the Merenid tombs is good for its views), or you can catch bus #18 back to the Ville Nouvelle.

Fes El Djedid

Unlike Fes El Bali, whose development and growth seems to have been almost organic, **Fes El Djedid** – "Fes the New" – was an entirely planned city, built by the Merenids at the beginning of their rule, as both a practical and a symbolic seat of government. The work was begun around 1273 by the dynasty's second ruling sultan, Abou Youssef, and in a manic feat of building was completed within three years. The capital for much of its construction came from taxes levied on the Meknes olive presses; the Jews were also taxed to build a new grand mosque; and the labour, at least in part, was supplied by Spanish Christian slaves.

The site which the Merenids chose for their city lies some distance from Fes El Bali. In the chronicles this is presented as a strategic move for the defence of the city, though it is hard to escape the conclusion that its main function was as a defence of the new dynasty against the Fassis themselves. It was not an extension for the people, in any real sense, being occupied largely by the **Dar El Makhzen,** a vast royal palace, and by a series of army garrisons. With the addition of the **Mellah** – the Jewish ghetto – at the beginning of the fourteenth century, this process was continued. Forced out of Fes El Bali following one of the periodic pogroms, the Jews could provide an extra barrier (and scapegoat) between the sultan and his Muslim faithful, as well as a useful and close to hand source of income.

Over the centuries, Fes El Djedid's fortunes have generally followed those of the city as a whole. It was extremely prosperous under the Merenids and Wattasids, fell into decline under the Saadians, lapsed into virtual ruin during Moulay Ismail's long reign in Meknes, but revived with the commercial expansion of the nineteenth century – at which point the walls between the old and new cities were finally joined.

Events this century, largely generated by the French Protectorate, have left Fes El Djedid greatly changed and somewhat moribund. As a "government city", it had no obvious role after the transfer of power to Rabat – a vacuum which the French filled by establishing a huge *quartier reservé* (red-light district) in the area around the Grand Mosque. This can have done little for the city's identity, but it was not so radical or disastrous as the immediate aftermath of independence in 1956. Concerned about their future status, and with their position made untenable by the Arab-Israeli war, virtually all of the Mellah's 17,000 **Jewish population** emigrated to Israel, Paris or Casablanca; today only a few Jewish families remain in the Mellah, though there is still a small community in the Ville Nouvelle.

● **Access.** You can reach Fes El Djedid in a ten-minute walk from **Bab Boujeloud** (the route outlined below), or from the Ville Nouvelle by walking up or taking a **bus** (#3 from Place de la Résistance) to **Place des Alaouites** beside the Mellah.

West from Boujeloud

Walking down to Fes El Djedid from **Bab Boujeloud** involves a shift in scale. Gone are the labyrinthine alleyways and *souks* of the Medina, to be replaced by a massive expanse of walls. Within them, to your left, are a series of gardens: the private **Jardins Beida**, behind the Lycée, and then the public **Jardins de Boujeloud** with their pools diverted from the Oued Fes. The latter have an entrance towards the end of the long Av. des Français, and are a vital lung for the

FES EL DJEDID

old city. If everything gets too much, wander in, lounge about on the grass, and spend an hour or two at the tranquil **café**, by an old waterwheel, at their west corner.

THE PETIT MECHOUAR

Moving on, near the end of the gardens, you pass through twin arches to reach a kind of square, the **Petit Mechouar**, which was once the focus of city life and still sees the occcasional juggler or storyteller during Ramadan evenings. To its left, entered through another double archway, begins the main street of Fes El Djedid proper – the **Grande Rue.**

To the right is the monumental **Bab Dekakin** (Gate of the Benches), a Merenid structure which was, until King Hassan realigned the site in 1967–71, the main approach to the Royal Palace and Fes El Bali. It was on this gate that the Infante Ferdinand of Portugal was hanged, head down, for four days in 1437. He had been captured in an unsuccessful raid on Tangier and his country had failed to raise the ransom required. As a further, salutary warning, when his corpse was taken down from the Bab, it was stuffed and displayed beside the gate, where it remained for the next three decades.

THE VIEUX MECHOUAR

Through the three great arches you will find yourself in another, much larger courtyard, the **Vieux Mechouar**. Laid out in the eighteenth century, this is flanked along the whole of one side by the Makina, an Italian-built arms factory, which is today partially occupied by a rug factory and various local clubs.

A smaller gate, the nineteenth-century **Bab as Smen**, stands at the far end of the court, forcing you into an immediate turn as you leave the city through the Merenid outer gateway of **Bab Segma**, whose twin octagonal towers slightly resemble the contemporary Chellah in Rabat.

If you are walking to the **Merenid tombs** from here, you can either turn sharp right (and scramble up the hillside, after the Bordj Nord – see p.186), or go straight ahead along the longer Route du Tour de Fes. The latter route takes you past the huge **Kasbah Cherada**, a fort built by Sultan Moulay Rashid in 1670 to house – and keep at a distance – the Berber tribes of his garrison. The partially walled compound is now the site of a hospital, a school and an annexe of the Kairaouine University.

QUARTIER MOULAY ABDALLAH AND THE SOUKS

Back at the Petit Mechouar – and before turning through the double arch onto the Grande Rue des Merenides – a smaller gateway leads off to the right at the bottom of the square. This gives entrance to the old *quartier reservé* of **Moulay Abdallah**, where the French built cafés, dance halls and brothels. The prostitutes were mostly young Berber girls, drawn by a rare chance of quick money, and usually returning to their villages when they had earned enough to marry or keep their families. The quarter today has a slightly solemn, empty feel about it, with the main street twisting down to Fes El Djedid's **Great Mosque**.

Through the main gateway, the **Grand Rue** zigzags slightly before leading straight down to the Mellah. There are **souks**, mainly for textiles and produce, along the way but nothing very much to detain you too long. Just by the entrance, though, immediately to the left after you go through the arch, a narrow **lane** curves off into an attractive little area on the periphery of the Boujeloud gardens. There's an old **water wheel** here which used to supply the gardens, and the small café (mentioned above) in the gardens nearby. On the way down, you pass a handful of stalls; among them are, traditionally, the *kif* and *sebsi* (kif pipe) vendors.

The Mellah and Royal Palace

With fewer than a dozen Jewish families still remaining, the **Mellah** is a rather melancholic place, largely resettled by poor Muslim emigrants from the country-side. The quarter's name – *mellah*, "salt" in Arabic – came to be used for Jewish ghettos throughout Morocco, though it was originally applied only to this one in Fes. In derivation it seems to be a reference to the job given to the Fassi Jews of salting the heads of criminals before they were hung on the gates.

The enclosed and partly protected position of the Mellah represents fairly accurately the Moroccan Jews' historically ambivalent position. Arriving for the most part with compatriot Muslim refugees from Spain and Portugal, they were never fully accepted into the nation's life. Nor, however, were they quite the rejected people of other Arab countries. Inside the Mellah they were under the direct protection of the sultan (or the local *caid*) and maintained their own laws and governors.

THE EVENING ROOST AT FES

The evening roost at Fes makes a spectacular sight. The performance begins with the frenzied activities of the resident starlings (including spotless starlings) but these are soon eclipsed by the overhead passage of dozens of little egret, gracefully returning to their roost sites in the Middle Atlas and environs. The skies soon appear to swarm with the appearance of literally thousands of alpine swift, wheeling on crescent-shaped wings in search of insects. To complete the spectacle, it is worth casting an eye along the rooftop silhouette as the light begins to fade. With a little perseverence it is possible to locate the characteristic body profiles of white stork on their rooftop nests along the perimeter walls which line Fes El Djedid.

Whether the creation of a ghetto ensured the actual need for one is, of course, debatable. Certainly, it was greatly to the benefit of the reigning sultan, who could both depend on Jewish loyalties and manipulate the international trade and finance which came increasingly to be dominated by them in the nineteenth century. For all this importance to the sultan, however, even the richest Jews had to lead extremely circumscribed lives. In Fes before the French Protectorate, no Jew was allowed to ride or even to wear shoes outside the Mellah, and they were severely restricted in their travels elsewhere.

HOUSES, SYNAGOGUES AND CEMETERIES

Since the end of the Protectorate, when many of the poorer Jews here left to take up an equally ambivalent place at the bottom of Israeli society (though this time above the Arabs), memories of their presence have faded rapidly. What still remain are their eighteenth- and nineteenth-century **houses** – immediately and conspicuously un-Arabic, with their tiny windows and elaborate ironwork. Cramped even closer together than the houses in Fes El Bali, they are interestingly designed if you are offered a look inside.

It is worth weaving your way down towards the **Hebrew cemetery**, too, with its neat, white, rounded gravestones restored to pristine condition as part of the UNESCO plan. There are also two surviving **synagogues**: the *Fassiyin* (which is now a carpet workshop) and the *Serfati*, slightly grander but currently occupied by a Muslim family. If you hire a guide, offer him a few dirhams and you may be able to see them both.

THE ROYAL PALACE

At the far end of the Mellah's main street – Grand Rue des Merenides (or Grand Rue de Mellah) – you come into **Place des Alaouites**, fronted by the new ceremonial gateway to the **Royal Palace**. The palace, which has been constantly rebuilt and expanded over the centuries, is one of the most sumptuous complexes in Morocco, set amid vast gardens, with numerous pavilions and guest wings.

In the 1970s, it was sometimes possible to gain a permit to visit part of the palace grounds, which were described in Christopher Kininmonth's *Traveller's Guide* as "the finest single sight Morocco has to offer . . . many acres in size and of a beauty to take the breath away". Today, the palace complex is strictly off limits to all except official guests, though it is reputedly little used by Hassan II, the present king, who divides most of his time between his palaces in Ifrane, Rabat and Marrakesh.

Food and drink

By day at least, there's little to keep you in the **Ville Nouvelle**, the new city established by Lyautey at the beginning of the Protectorate. Unlike Casa or Rabat, where the French adapted Moroccan forms to create their own showplaces, this is a pretty lacklustre European grid. The Ville Nouvelle is, however, home to most of the faculties of the city's university, and is very much the city's business and commercial centre. If you want to talk with Fassis on a basis other than that of guide to tourist, you'll stand the most chance in the cafés here, and it's more likely that the students you meet are exactly that. The quarter is also the centre for most of the city's restaurants, cafés, bars and other facilities.

Fes El Bali and **Fes El Djedid** are quieter at night, except during Ramadan (when shops and stalls stay open till two or three in the morning). They have, as with all Medina quarters throughout Morocco, no bars, and with the exception of a few touristic "Palace-Restaurants", their eating places are on the basic side.

Eating and drinking in the Ville Nouvelle

The Ville Nouvelle has quite a selection of restaurants, though few go any way towards justifying the city's reputation as home of the country's finest cuisine. Cafés, at least, are plentiful – and there are a few bars.

RESTAURANTS

The better possibilities, in ascending order of price, include:

Restaurant Chamonix, 5 Rue Moukhtar Soussi, off Bd. Mohammed V, behind the *Grand Hôtel*. Reliable Moroccan and European (pizza, paella, etc) dishes. Open to midnight.

Restaurant du Centre, 105 Bd. Mohammed V. Copious portions of Moroccan/French food

Restaurant Chawarma, 42 Rue Tetouan (off Place de l'Atlas). Modern and unatmospheric, but very friendly; serves good Moroccan dishes and sandwiches at low prices.

Restaurant Marrakech, 11 Rue Abes Tazi (opposite *Hôtel CTM*). Again good and cheap.

Chez Vittoria, 21 Rue Nador (near *Hôtel Central*). Filling and inexpensive pizzas attract a young crowd of Fassi students and the like.

Oued de la Bière, 59 Bd. Mohammed V. An old-style French restaurant, still recommended for meals though, despite the name, it is now unlicensed to sell beer or wine.

Le Cheminée, 6 Rue de l'Indonésie (near the train station). Solid French fare.

Restaurant Le Mounia, 11 Bd. Mohammed Zerktouni (near *Hôtel Splendid*). A small, welcoming restaurant with an extensive, modest-priced menu. They will also change money and cheques for customers.

Restaurant Courria, 29 Rue Tetouan (off Place de l'Atlas). The only fish restaurant in Fes, so the patronne claims – and it is fresh and very well cooked. Egyptian decor and music.

CAFÉS AND BARS

Cafés and **patisseries** are scattered throughout the Ville Nouvelle, with some of the most popular around Place Mohammed V – the *Café de la Renaissance* here was an old Foreign Legion hangout – and along Av. Mohammed es Slaoui, Av. Hassan II and Bd. Mohammed V. One of the most popular of these, boasting excellent croissants (and very clean toilets), is the *Café Floria*, beside the PTT on Av. Hassan II. Another very pleasant café is located in the sunken gardens alongside Bd. Mohammed V.

For **bars**, you have to look a little harder. There are a couple along the Av. Slaoui (the *Es Saada* here is usually lively) and the pretty seedy, but cheap, *Dalila* at 17 Bd. Mohammed V, its upstairs bar a place for serious Moroccan drinking; amother quite amusing bar, with 1960s decor, is just opposite the Municipal Market on Bd. Mohammed V. Beyond these, you're down to the handful of **hotel bars**: in the *Zalagh* (outdoors, by the swimming pool), *Moussafir*, *Mounia*, *Lamdaghri*, *Splendid* and *Grand*, and the upmarket and rather dull *Hôtel de Fes*, *PLM Volubilis* and *Sofia*.

Eating and drinking in Fes El Bali

Fes El Bali has possibilities for budget meals and, at greater cost, for sampling (relatively) traditional cuisine in some splendid old palaces. **Fes El Djedid** also has some basic café-restaurants, though none worth specially recommending.

BUDGET MEALS

The two main areas for budget eating in Fes El Bali are around Bab Boujeloud and along Rue Hormis (which runs up from Souk El Attarin towards Bab Guissa and has a good three-store restaurant plus some hole-in-the-wall places). Other cheapish café-restaurants are to be found near Bab Ftouh. If your money doesn't allow a full meal, you can get a range of **snacks** around Bab Boujeloud, including chunks of *pastilla* from the stalls near the beginning of Talâa Seghira.

Restaurant Bouayad, Place Boujeloud – next to the Hôtel Cascade. This is about the best of the Bab Boujeloud café-restaurants – clean, honest and with a decent *tajine* and *pastilla*; it's also open pretty much through the night.

La Baraka, 33 Talâa Seghira – on the left walking down from Bab Boujeloud. Good food, nice decor and all spotlessly clean – even the toilets.

Palais Tariana, 25 Talâa Seghira. A step upmarket – but not greatly so – with meals from a traditional Moroccan menu for about 70dh. Housed in an old Andalusian-style palace.

FANCIER MEALS

For a Fassi banquet, in an appropriate palace setting, most places charge around 150–200dh a head. If you're interested, phone ahead for a table at one or other of the following:

Palais M'Nebhi, off Talâa Seghira – not easy to find, so you may need to be guided from Bab Boujeloud (☎05/63.38.93). A beautiful palace built in the 1840s and used by General Lyautey. The *couscous* is recommended.

Palais de Fes, 16 Rue Boutouil-Kairaouine (☎05/63.47.07). Caters largely for tour groups, but the rooftop setting is as good as any in the city. Located by the Kairaouine Mosque and labelled on our map on p.178. Open at lunchtime only.

Dar Saada, 21 Souk El Attarin (☎05/63.33.43). Wonderful *pastilla* or (ordered a day in advance) *mechoui*. All their portions are vast, and two people can do well by ordering one main dish and a plate of vegetables. Located in the Souk El Attarin, in another century-old palace, and labelled on our map on p.178.

Restaurant Al Firdaous, 10 Rue Jenjifour, Bab Guissa – just down from the *Hôtel Palais Jamai* (☎05/63.43.43). A rich merchant's house of the 1920, decked out to look like a tent. Meals, with music and belly dancing, from 150dh. Open noon to 3pm and 8.30 to 11.30pm.

Restaurant les Remparts, 2 Arset Jiar, Bab Guissa – 20m from the *Hôtel Palais Jamai* (☎05/63.74.15). A brand new restaurant in a meticulously renovated, breathtakingly beautiful mansion. The meals are as good as any in the country, too; there are superior folklore shows; and prices are reasonable for the standard. Highly recommended.

Restaurant Al Fassia, in the *Hôtel Palais Jamai* (☎05/63.43.31). A distinguished Moroccan cuisine restaurant, with a terrace overlooking the Medina. There are few more stylish ways to spend an evening, but count on at least 250dh each, and considerably more if you get the full courses. The hotel also has a distinguished French restaurant.

Shopping for crafts

Fes has a rightful reputation as the centre of Moroccan traditional crafts but if you're buying rather than looking, bear in mind that it also sees more tourists than any of its rivals. Rugs and carpets, however much you bargain, will probably be cheaper in Meknes, Midelt or Azrou; and although the brass, leather and cloth here are the best you'll find, you will need plenty of energy, a good sense of humour and a lot of patience to get them at a reasonable price. Fassi dealers are expert hagglers – making you feel like an idiot for suggesting such a low price, jumping up out of their seats and pushing you out of the shop, or lulling you with mint tea and elaborate displays.

All of this can be fun, but you do need a certain confidence and to have some idea of what you're buying and how much you should be paying for it. For some guidelines on **quality**, take a look around the **Dar Batha** museum – keeping in mind, of course, that exhibits here are the best available.

If you want to check on the prices of more modest artefacts, have a browse through the various shops along Av. Mohammed V in the **Ville Nouvelle**, which tend to have fairly fixed prices (and are easy to leave!), and, especially, at the government-run and strictly fixed-price Centre Artisanal, out past the Hôtel Sofia on Av. Allal Ben Abdallah.

TWO NEARBY SPAS: MOULAY YACOUB AND SIDI HARAZEM

The spa villages of **Moulay Yacoub** and **Sidi Harazem**, respectively 20km northwest and 15km southeast of Fes, are largely medicinal centres, offering – as for many centuries past – cures for the afflicted. They are not by any stretch of the imagination mainstream tourist attractions but Moulay Yacoub, in particular, makes a pleasant day-trip for a swim and hot bath. Either site can be reached by *grand taxi* for around 10dh a place; taxis leave for Moulay Yacoub from Bab Boujeloud and to Sidi Harazem from Bab Ftouh.

Moulay Yacoub

The trip to **MOULAY YACOUB** takes you across pleasant, rolling countryside, with wonderful views south across the plain of Saïss, with the Middle Atlas beyond. The village itself tumbles down a steep hillside, with a **swimming pool** and large **hammam** (with separate sections for women and men) around midway down. At the foot of the hill, in the "basin", are new and more scientific thermal baths used for serious medical treatment. Cars and taxis park at the top of the village, leaving you to descend flights of steps, flanked with some attractive little restaurants and cafés. There are also four unclassified hotels – one is an annexe of the *Grand Hôtel* in Fes and can be booked through them – and numerous rooms to let in private houses.

Sidi Harazem

The eucalyptus-covered shrine of **SIDI HARAZEM** was established by Sultan Moulay er-Rachid in the seventeenth century, though the centre owes its current fame to its best-selling mineral water. The oasis is today heavily orientated towards its health industry; the old **thermal baths** tend to be crowded and the swimming pool not always full. The main point of a visit, for those not seeking a cure, would be for the April *moussem* – one of the Fes region's biggest.

Directory

Banks Most of the banks are grouped along Bd. Mohammed V. As always, the *BMCE* (on Place Mohammed V) is best for exchange and handles *VISA/Access* transactions, as well as travellers' cheques. Others include: *Banque Populaire* (Av. Mohammed V; quick service for currency and travellers' cheques), *Crédit du Maroc* (Av. Mohammed V; also handles *VISA*) *SGMB* (at the intersection of Rue de la Liberté and Rue Soudan; again, handles *VISA*). *Crédit du Maroc* also has a branch in Fes El Bali (currency exchange only), in the street above the Medersa ech-Cherratin. Outside banking hours, most of the four- or five-star hotels will change money and cheques.

Books The *English Bookshop*, 68 Av. Hassan II (by Place de la Résistance), has a great selection of English novels, stocked for the city's students, and a fair number of North African writers. The *Librairie du Centre*, 134 Bd. Mohammed V (near the post office), is also worth trying.

Car hire Fes has quite a number of hire companies, though none are as cheap as the best deals in Casa. Call around the following, which all allow return delivery to a different centre: *Avis*, 50 Bd. Chefchaouni (☎05/62.67.46); *Budget*, corner of Rue BAhrein and Av. HAssan II (☎05/62.09.19); *Europcar/InterRent*, 41 Av. Hassan II (☎05/62.65.45); *Hertz*, inside the *Hôtel de Fes*, Av. des F.A.R. (☎05/62.28.12); *Tourvilles*, 15 Rue Houmam Fetouaki, off Bd. Mohammed V (☎05/62.66.35); and *Zeit*, 35 Av. Mohammed es Slaoui (☎05/62.55.10).

Car repairs *Mécanique Générale*, 22 Av. Cameroun, in the Ville Nouvelle, is highly recommended, with excellent mechanics and fair prices. Try also *Source Pièce Auto*, 50 Rue Zambia, again in the Ville Nouvelle, for parts and advice; *Auto Maroc*, Av. Mohammed V (☎05/62.34.35) for Fiat repairs; and the garage on Rue Soudan (☎05/62.22.32) for Renault repairs.

Chemist/pharmacist There are numerous *pharmacies* throughout the Ville Nouvelle. The *Pharmacie du Municipalité*, just up from Place de la Résistance, on Av. Abdelkrim El Khattabi, stays open all night.

Cinemas Several in the Ville Nouvelle show foreign films – mainly dubbed into French. The one by Bab Boujeloud is entertaining, showing an Indian and a Kung Fu film each day.

Festivals and cultural events The big local festivals are the students' *Moussem of Sidi Harazem* (held outside the city at Sidi Harazem – see above – at the end of April) and the *Moulay Idriss II Moussem* (held in the city, in September). There are other *moussems* held locally – ask at the tourist office for details – and some good events a little further out, like the *Fête des Cerises* at Sefrou (see p.209) in June, and the *Fête du Cheval* at Tissa (see p.122) in early October. **Cultural events** in the city are relatively frequent, both Moroccan- and French-sponsored. Again, ask for details at the *ONMT* office.

Filling stations Several are to be found on the Place de l'Atlas, near the beginning of the road to Sefrou/Midelt.

Newspapers British papers and the *International Herald Tribune* are sold at the boutique in the *Hôtel de Fes*; at a news-stand at the foot of Rue Abdelkrim El Khattabi, one block from Place Mohammed V; and another good news-stand on nearby Rue de Edouard Escalier, facing the space used as a car park.

Photographic The boutique at the *Hôtel de Fes* does good quality film/photo work.

Police *Commissariat Central* is on Av. Mohammed V; ☎19.

Post office The main **PTT** is on the corner of Bd. Mohammed V/Av. Hassan II in the Ville Nouvelle (open summer 8am–2pm; winter 8.30am–noon & 2.30–6pm); the **poste restante** section is next door to the main building; the **phones section** (open until 9pm) has a separate side entrance when the rest is closed.

Royal Air Maroc have an office at 54 Av. Hassan II (☎05/62.04.56). The Fes airport is 15km south of the city at Saïs.

Swimming pools There is a **Municipal Pool** (open mid-June to mid-Sept) on Av. des Sports, just west of the train station. You can also pay a small fee to use the pool at the *Hôtel Zalagh* (open year round).

Tourist office The main *ONMT* office is at the Av. des Etats Unis corner of the Place de la Résistance – unmarked and set slightly back from the road.

THE MIDDLE ATLAS

Heading south from Fes, most people take a bus straight to **Marrakesh** or to **Er Rachidia**, the start of the great desert and *ksour* routes. Both journeys, however, involve at least ten to twelve hours of continuous travel, which, in the summer at least, is reason enough to stop off along the way.

The second, stronger reason, if you have the time (or, ideally, a car), is to get off the main routes and up into the mountains. Covered in forests of oak, cork and giant cedar, the **Middle Atlas** is beautiful and relatively little visited. The brown-black tents of nomadic Berber encampments immediately establish a shift from the European north, the plateaux are pockmarked by dark volcanic lakes, and, at **Ouzoud** and **Oum er Rbia,** there are some magnificent waterfalls. If you just want a day trip from Fes, the Middle Atlas is most easily accessible at **Sefrou**, a relaxed market town, 28km southeast.

On the practical front, **bus** travellers may find a few problems stopping en route between Fes and Marrakesh, as many of the buses arrive and depart full. However, by taking the occasional *grand taxi*, or stopping for a night to catch a dawn bus, you shouldn't find yourself stuck for long. Along the Fes–Azrou–Midelt–Er Rachidia route, buses are no problem.

Sefrou and around

SEFROU, 30km south of Fes, is a very ancient walled town at the foothills of the Middle Atlas. The first stop on the caravan routes to the Tafilalt, it marked, until the Protectorate, the mountain limits of the *Bled El Makhzen* – the governed lands. It actually predates Fes as a city and might well have grown into a regional or imperial capital, if Moulay Idriss I and II had not acted differently. Into the 1950s, at least a third of the then 18,000 population was Jewish; there seems to have been a Jewish-Berber population here long before the coming of Islam and, although most of them subsequently converted, a large number of Jews from the south again settled in the town under the Merenids.

From Fes, the town can be reached in an hour by **bus** or **grand taxi**; the latter leave from just below Place de la Résistance in the Ville Nouvelle. In summer it makes a cool daytrip, as it is situated some 2900ft above sea level; in winter, it can often be covered in snow; it is a relaxed place which sees few tourists (or hustlers). The only times that the town draws crowds are during the annual **Fête des Cerises**, a cherry festival in June, accompanied by various music and folklore events, and the August **Moussem of Sidi Lahcen Lyoussi**, an eighteenth-century saint whose tomb is in the Medina.

Accommodation and other practicalities

Following the closure of the old *Hôtel des Cerises*, which stands empty on the bend of Bd. Mohammed V, Sefrou has a very sparse choice of **hotels**. The best, if you can afford it, is the *Hôtel Sidi Lahcen Lyoussi* (☎05/66.04.97; ②), which has an alpine chalet feel, a good restaurant, a bar (residents only after 8pm) and an intermittently full swimming pool. The *Café Lafarine*, just north of the Medina on the Fes road, also rents out a few rooms.

Alternatively, you can stay up above town. A couple of kilometres to the west, by the *koubba* mentioned overpage, there is a **campsite** (☎05/67.33.40), with a

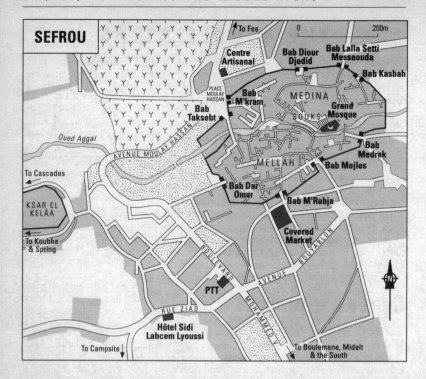

swimming pool and (cold) showers, and the basic *Hôtel-Café Boualserhin* (⑩).
There is also another cheap hotel, the *Hôtel-Bar Cascades* (⑩), by the waterfall
west of the bridge (again see overpage).

For **food and drink**, in addition to the hotels, you could try the *Café-
Restaurant Oumnia*, on Bd. Mohammed V, for inexpensive meals; there is also
the *Bar La Poste*, by the PTT, for drinks.

Note that there is often **no water** in Sefrou from 6pm to 6am, so if you want a
shower, arrive early! Note also that the town's two **banks** are not very wised up
to cashing cheques, though they have no problems with cash exchange.

The town

Although Sefrou is not a large place – the population today is only 40,000 – its
general layout is a little confusing. If you are coming in by bus or grand taxi, you
are usually dropped in **Place Moulay Hassan**, off which is the main entrance to
the Medina. Beyond, the road and most of the buses continue round a loop above
the town and valley, crossing the river and straightening out onto **Bd.
Mohammed V**, the principal street of the Ville Nouvelle.

The Medina

In many ways it's a pity that Sefrou is so close to Fes, in comparison with which
its Medina inevitably feels rather low-key. It is, however, on its own modest scale,

equally well-preserved, and the untouristy atmosphere makes it a very pleasant place to explore. The **Thursday souk**, for example, remains very much a local affair, drawing Berbers from the neighbouring villages to sell their garden produce and buy basic goods.

Enclosed by its nineteenth-century ramparts and split in two by the river, the Medina isn't difficult to find your way around. Coming from the PTT on Bd. Mohammed V, you can take a shortcut down on the right of the road straight into the Mellah; if you were to turn up to the left, this would eventually lead you to Place Moulay Hassan. The most straightforward approach, though, is through **Bab M'Kram** in Place Moulay Hassan – on your left as you face the walls.

Entering at Bab M'Kram, you find yourself on the main street of the old Arab city, which winds down to the river, passing through a region of **souks**, to emerge at the **Grand Mosque**. The *souks* include some impressive ironwork stalls and, reflecting the traditional Jewish heritage, a number of silversmiths.

The Mellah

The **Mellah**, a dark, cramped conglomeration of tall, shuttered houses and tunnel-like streets, lies across the river from the Grand Mosque. It is today occupied largely by Muslims, though many of Sefrou's Jews only left for Israel after the June 1967 Six-Day War, and the quarter still seems distinct.

Over the years of the French Protectorate, the Sefrou Jewish community had become quite well off, owning good agricultural land in the environs. But when most of the houses here were built, in the mid-nineteenth century, the people's living conditions must have been pretty miserable. Edith Wharton, visiting in 1917, found "ragged figures . . . in black gabardines and skull-caps" living one family to a room in most of the mansions, and the alleys were lit even at midday by oil lamps. "No wonder", she concluded rather sanctimoniously, "[that] the babies of the Moroccan ghettoes are nursed on date-brandy, and their elders doze away to death under its consoling spell."

Into the hills

High enough into the Middle Atlas to avoid the dry summer heat, Sefrou is a place where you might actually want to do some walking. There are dozens of **springs** in the hills above the town and, for part of the year, active waterfalls.

For a relatively easy target, take the road up behind the post office, which will divide into a fork after about a kilometre. The left branch goes up past the campsite; the right leads to a small, French-built fort, known as the **Prioux** and still in military use, and to the **koubba**, or tomb, of one Sidi Bou Ali Serghin.

Another good walk is to go up in the hills above the **Oued Aggaï**, a path followed by **Rue de la Kelâa** (just before the bridge, coming from the post office). There are gorges, coves and waterfalls in this direction (for which you may want to engage a local guide).

Bhalil

BHALIL, 7km northwest of Sefrou (signposted off the Fes road), claims pre-Islamic Christian origins and, more visibly, retains a number of troglodyte (cave) dwellings. If you have a car, this is worth a brief detour on your way from Fes; it is signposted to the right 5km before Sefrou. The **cave houses** are to the rear of the village, reached by a dirt road; ask directions to Mohammed Chraibi (BP 42, Bhalil), the official guide, who will show you his own cave home.

The village itself – or at least the old part of it – is charming, its whitewashed houses tumbling down a hillside, and connected by innumerable bridges.

South and east of Sefrou

South and east of Sefrou are some of the most attractive swathes of the Middle Atlas: dense, wooded mountains, with great scope for hiking or piste driving, and not a hint of tourism. Immediately south of the town is the Massif du Kandar, which loops round to Imouzzer du Kandar. To the west, further afield, are the Bou Iblane mountains – an exploration of which could be combined by drivers with the Djebel Tazzeka circuit, near Taza (see p.126).

If you are simply intending to head south from Sefrou, there is a daily bus to **Midelt**, via the unremarkable roadside town of BOULEMANE, but none to Ifrane or Azrou on the Fes–Marrakesh road. To cross over to this route on local transport, it would be simplest to return to Fes.

The Massif du Kandar
The P4620 route over the Massif du Kandar leaves the P20 Sefrou–Midelt road 14km south of Sefrou. It has some rough stretches of track but is passable in summer with a Renault 4; in winter, you need to check conditions locally. For those without transport, it would be possible to charter a *grand taxi* in Sefrou (or, travelling west–east, in Immouzer du Kandar) for the the 34-km route.

Shortly after the piste turns off from the Sefrou–Midelt road, it begins to climb up into the hills around the **Djebel Abad** (1768m). If you reckon your car can make it – or you feel like walking – you can follow a rocky four-kilometre track almost to the summit of the mountain; this leads off, to the right of the road, 10km down the P4620, coming from the Sefrou direction.

The Djebel Bou Iblane
East of Sefrou – and southeast of Fes – is a huge area of high country, culminating in the two mountains of **Djebel Bou Iblane** (3190m) and **Djebel Bou Nacceur** (3340m). It is an extraordinarily varied landscape: the northern aspects rise from the cedar forests, while the south is stark and waterless, although demarcated by the great Oued Moulouya. The whole area is sparsely populated, and trekkers are almost unknown, yet it's rewarding and has relatively easily access. From either Sefrou or Fes, you could arrange a *grand taxi* to take you to the centre of the range – dropping you either at the forestry hut of TAFFERTE or at the abandoned ski resort under Djebel Bou Iblane. From here, a web of pistes radiate throughout the area, and a circular trek with a mule would be memorable.

Imouzzer du Kandar, Ifrane and Mischliffen

The first hills you see of the Middle Atlas, heading directly south from the plains around Fes, seem strangely un-Moroccan. At the "hill station" resort of **Ifrane**, where the French colonial chiefs retreated from the heat, the king now has an important summer palace, and at **Mischliffen** there's a ski centre. The road up to these two resorts is almost ceremonial. En route, and a little more mundane, is another small French-built hill station, **Immouzer du Kandar**, and a gorgeous freshwater lake, the **Dayet Aaoua**.

Imouzzer du Kandar

IMOUZZER DU KANDAR, 78km south of Fes, is a one-road, one-square kind of place, where Fassis come up to swim, picnic and spend a few days. There are a handful of hotels if you feel like doing the same, and some good restaurants, too: it's a relaxed place, with a pleasant atmosphere.

A small Monday **souk** is held within the ruined Kasbah, and a **festival**, the *Fête des Pommes*, takes place in June, with a number of music and dance events. The municipal **swimming pool**, near the centre, is open from mid-June to mid-September and filled, like everything here, with natural spa water.

Accommodation and meals

There are two unclassified and three classified hotels:

Hôtel du Centre, right beside the bus stop on the main road (☎05/56.30.03). Good-value hotel, run by the same family as the *des Truites*, below. ①

Hôtel Belle Vue (☎05/56.31.27). Again, reasonable rooms, plus a small bar and café. ①

Pension-Restaurant La Vallée Heureuse (☎05/56.37.70). A pleasant new pension with fine views; follow the signs as you come into town from Fes. ①

Hôtel des Truites, on the left of the road in from Fes (☎05/56.30.02). The best choice: a delightful place with a bar and (unpredictable) restaurant, and more great views. ②

Hôtel Royal, Bd. Mohammed V (☎05/56.30.80). Central hotel with a reliable restaurant, but facing a small lake devoid of water for the past few years. ③

The town **campsite** is closed at present.

Dayet Aaoua

A good excursion from Immouzer, or an alternative place to break the journey south, is the beautiful freshwater lake of **Dayet Aouwa**; it is sited just to the left of the P24, 9km south of Immouzer. You can camp round the lakeside or – if you find it open – stay at the *Chalet du Lac* (☎05/60 for Ifrane PTT, who connect calls). This an old-style French-run hunting lodge with erratic seasonal openings, a restaurant, a bar and rowing boats for hire. Like other lakes in the Ifrane area, Aaoua is a rewarding **birdlife habitat** – see box overleaf.

The P24 continues past the lake to Ifrane, climbing through ever more dense shafts of forest. If you are driving, it's possible to reach Ifrane by a longer and more scenic route, following a piste (P4627) up behind the Dayet Aaoua, then looping to the right, past another (sometimes dry) lake, **Dayet Hachlef**, on piste P3325, before joining the last section of the road in from Boulemane (P21).

Ifrane

IFRANE was created in 1929 as a self-conscious *"poche de France"*, and its pseudo-Alpine villas and broad suburban streets have a distinctly peculiar feel in their Moroccan setting. After independence, they were absorbed by Moroccan government ministries and the wealthier bourgeoisie, and in recent years they have been granted additional prestige by the addition of a **Royal Palace**, whose characteristic green tiles (a royal prerogative) can be seen on the descent into the valley. In 1991 King Hassan announced a project to set up, under the joint sponsorship of the US, Saudi Arabia and Morocco, an **American University**: an institution that would have a large science complex, and a mosque, church and

BIRDLIFE IN THE DAYET AAOUA AND MIDDLE ATLAS LAKES

Dayet Aaoua, like other freshwater lakes in the Middle Atlas, has a good mosaic of habitat types and supports a wide variety of animals. Green frogs take refuge from the summer drought within the lake's protective shallows, and a multitude of dragonflies and damselflies patrol the water's surface in their resplendent red, blues and greens.

The **birdlife** is similarly diverse, attracting all kinds of waders and wildfowl. Waders include black-winged stilt, green sandpiper, redshank and **avocet** (one of Morocco's most elegant birds), and the deeper waters provide food for flocks of grebes (great-crested, black-necked and little varieties), and in the spring the magnificent **crested coot** (which has spectacular bright red knobs on either side of its white facial shield, when in breeding condition). The reedbeds provide cover for **grey heron** and **cattle egret** and ring out with the sound of hidden **reed-** and **fantailed warbler**.

The water's edge is traced by passage grey and yellow wagtails and in the summer the skies are filled with migrating swallows and martins – the sand martin especially. This abundance of life proves an irresistible draw for resident and migrant birds of prey and Aaoua offers regular sightings of the acrobatic **red kite** circling overhead. You may also see flocks of collared pratincole, whose darting flight is spectacular, and quartering overhead, the characteristic form of **Montagu's harrier**, ever alert for any unsuspecting duck on the lake below.

synagogue to provide, as he put it, "a meeting place for the sons of Abraham". As yet, there are no signs of the university, though, as befits a royal resort, the town is quite impressive in itself – squeaky clean and brilliantly lit by streetlamps and iluminated globes. It is, however, expensive (for accommodation, meals and even provisions in the shops) and is somewhat lacking in the human touch. A policeman is on permanent duty to stop anyone posing for photographs on the resort's landmark **stone lion** – carved apparently by an Italian prisoner of war – and when the court is in residence in summer, security is very tight.

A walk by the river, below the royal palace, is pleasant, as is the cool summer air, and the excellent municipal swimming pool. There is little else to detain you, though, and unless you're camping – there is a muncipal **campsite** (☎05/56.61.56), out on road to Meknes – accommodation is expensive and not always easy to obtain. For the record, the three **hotels** are:

Grand Hôtel, Av. de la Marche Verte (☎05/56.64.07). An unexciting, chalet-style hotel. ②

Hôtel les Tilleuls (☎05/56.65.58). A more comfortable choice – recently refurbished, and with a restaurant. ③

Hôtel Mischliffen (☎05/56.64.16). Superb views and facilities – for which you pay dearly. ⑤

The *Hôtel Perce Neige*, listed in the ONMT hotel guide, has been taken over by La Samir, a petrol company, for its employees and is not open to the public.

As for other details, the *Restaurant de la Rose* does decent, modest-priced set meals; and **CTM** buses operate from outside the *Grand Hôtel*.

The Mischliffen

The Mischliffen is simply a shallow bowl in the mountains – the crater of an extinct volcano – enclosed on all sides by cedar forests. There's no village here and few buildings, and it's of interest, really, just for the skiiing, which can be somewhat unpredictable.

In the skiing season (Jan–March: but snow cover is often patchy) there are taxis from Ifrane up to its **refuge-club** (restaurant and bar, but no accommodation) and to the rather ancient **ski lifts**. You can **rent ski equipment** in Ifrane at the *Café-Restaurant Chamonix*, though like the ski lifts, it is about thirty years old.

Azrou

AZROU, the first real town of the Middle Atlas, stands at a major junction of routes – north to Meknes and Fes, south to Khenifra and Midelt. As might be expected, it's an important market centre (the main *souk* is held on Tuesday), and it has long held a strategic role in controlling the mountain Berbers. Moulay Ismail built a Kasbah here, the remains of which still survive, while more recently the French established the prestigious **Collège Berbère** – part of their attempt to split the country's Berbers from the urban Arabs. The *collège*, renamed the Lycée Tarik Ibn Ziad, and still a dominant building in the town, provided many of the Protectorate's interpreters, local administrators and military officers, but in spite of its ban on using Arabic and any manifestation of Islam, the policy was a failure. Azrou graduates played a significant role in the nationalist movement – and were uniquely placed to do so, as a new French-created elite. Since independence, however, their influence has been slight outside of the army, many Berber student activists having followed Mehdi Ben Barka's ill-fated socialist UNEP party (see *Contexts*).

The town and its souk

Arriving in the town, you immediately notice a massive outcrop of rock – the *azrou* ("rock" in Berber) from which the town takes its name. Adjoining it is the main square, **Place Mohammed V**, with an impressive new Grand Mosque. On the other side of the rock is a public swimming pool, which in summer is almost reason enough to stop over in town.

The most compelling reason for a visit to Azrou, however, is provided by its **Tuesday souk**, which draws Berbers from all the surrounding mountain villages. It is held a little below the rock – just follow the crowds down and across the valley. The fruit and vegetable stalls sprinkled all over this area seem at first to be all there is; look further, though, and you'll see a stretch of wasteland – often with a few musicians and storytellers performing – beyond which is a smaller section for carpets, textiles and general goods. The **carpet stalls**, not particularly geared towards tourists, can turn up some beautiful items; reasonably priced if not exactly bargains.

For a further selection of rugs and carpets take a look at the **Cooperative artesanale** (daily 8.30am–noon & 2.30–6pm), on the Khenifra road; this has seen better days – it's a bit sleepy compared with other co-operatives – but some decent modern rugs, plus stone and cedar carvings, are still produced. Also worth an hour or so are some of the permanent stalls near the new bus station and in the old quarter of town off Place Saouika (aka Place Moulay Hachem Ben Salah). Most of the rugs you are shown have bright, geometric designs, based on the traditional patterns of the Beni M'Guild tribe.

There is little else to do in the town, though you can spend most of the day climbing through the hills roundabout – there are many seasonal springs – or wandering down to the river, which is reputedly well stocked with trout. Further afield – see box on p.218 – there are also extensive cedar forests.

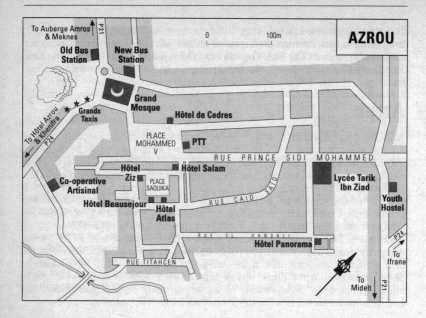

Rooms and food

There is a fair spread of accommodation, with rooms – albeit not very good at the cheaper end of the scale – easy enough to find. Choices are:

Auberge de Jeunesse (✆ 05/56.83.82). A reasonable youth hostel, on the outskirts of town; it's about a kilometre walk out from the centre, towards the roads to Fes and Midelt.

Hôtel Beauséjour, 45 Place Saouika (no phone). Good central site and with a fine roof terrace; cold showers; next door is a café under the same, enthusiastic ownership. ⑩

Hôtel Salame, off Place Souika (✆05/56.25.62). Okay rooms and hot showers; its entrance is just behind Place Souika. ⑩

Hôtel Ziz, 83 Place Souika (✆05/56.23.62). Not too impressive; cold showers. ⑩

Hôtel Atlas, 61 Place Souika (no phone). Very cramped rooms – and no showers at all. ⑩

Hôtel des Cèdres, Place Mohammed V (✆05/56.23.26). The best of the cheap hotels, with a long balcony overlooking the square; the restaurant, however, is poor value. ①

Hôtel Azrou, Route du Khenifra (✆05/56.21.16). A kilometre or so out from the centre – downhill to the southwest of Place Mohammed V. Reasonable rooms, a restaurant and bar. ②

Hôtel Panorama, Rue El Hansali (✆05/56.20.10). A friendly, family-run enterprise, with a pleasant restaurant and bar, and good views; a short walk from the town centre. ③

Auberge Amros, 3km out on the Meknes road (✆05/56.20.05). This is a wonderful little auberge, out in the forested countryside; it has a terrific restaurant, which draws many locals from Azrou, and a pleasant bar. ①

There is at present no campsite, though the owner of the *Hôtel Panorama* is considering developing one near his hotel.

As for **food**, in addition to the hotels above, there is a decent bar-restaurant, the Relais Forestier, next door to the *Hôtel Cedres*, and an excellent, unnamed *café-patisserie* on the corner of the main square, with great coffee and croissants. Around the bus station, there are also various inexpensive grills and foodstalls.

Two **banks** (*BMCE* and *Banque Populaire*) are located in Place Mohammed V.

Buses and grands taxis

Azrou has two **bus stations**, both adjoining Place Mohammed V. Between them, you can choose from five buses per day to Midelt, Er Rachidia and Rissani, and it's not usually a problem to get a bus to Fes (or, less frequently, Meknes). For Marrakesh, you should ask around and try to buy tickets the night before you plan to leave; several of the buses arrive full, though there is one (currently departing at 4am, arriving in Marrakesh at 10.30–11am) which starts at Azrou.

Around the other side of the rock is a **grand taxi** stand, with regular runs to Ifrane and Fes, and sporadic (but possible) ones for Khenifra.

Aïn Leuh and the waterfalls of Oum er Rbia

South of Azrou lies some of the most remote and beautiful country of the Middle Atlas: a region of cedar forests, limestone plateaus and *polje* lakes, that is home to some superb wildlife (see box overleaf), including Barbary apes.

It makes rewarding countryside for a few days' exploration, either by car or on foot. At the heart of the region – an obvious focus for a trip – are the **waterfalls of Oum er Rbia**, the source of Morocco's largest river. If you don't have transport, you can get a daily **bus** from Azrou to **Aïn Leuh**, 30km along the route (and with some minor falls of its own), or, if you have the money, or get a group together, you could always charter a **grand taxi** from Azrou.

Aïn Leuh

AÏN LEUH (17km from Azrou along the main Khenifra road, then 13km up the S303) is a large Berber village, typical of the Middle Atlas, with its flat-rooted houses tiered above the valley. As at Azrou, there are ruins of a Kasbah built by Moulay Ismail; and in the hills behind the town there are **springs** and a more or less year-round waterfall.

Aïn Leuh's **souk** is held on Wednesday (a good day to hitch), though it can extend a day in either direction. It is the weekly gathering point of the **Beni M'Guild** tribe – still semi-nomadic in this region, and to be seen camping out beside their flocks in heavy, dark tents. As a colonial *zone d'insécurité*, this part of the Atlas was relatively undisturbed by French settlers, and the traditional balance between pasture and forest has remained largely intact.

The Oum er Rbia sources and Aguelmane Azigza

The road to the **Oum er Rbia waterfalls** begins just south of Aïn Leuh and is signposted "Aguelmane Azigza/Khenifra". It has recently been paved along its entire course, and several new bridges constructed over the Rbia; in winter, however, it can still get waterlogged and impassable, so ask about conditions in Azrou or Khenifra before setting out. For the most part it runs through mountain forest, where you're almost certain to come across apes.

About 20km south of Aïn Leuh, to the left of the road, there's a small lake, **Lac Ouiouane**, adjoining a couple of farms and a large *maison forestière*. A stretch of more open country, with grazing sheep and odd pitched-roof farmsteads, leads to the descent to the Oum er Rbia valley. The road twists down, bends through a side valley and round to a concrete bridge over the Rbia, with a small parking

---

BARBARY APES AND OTHER CEDAR FOREST WILDLIFE

The **cedar forests** which lie to the **south of Azrou** are a unique habitat in Morocco, their verdant atmosphere contrasting starkly with the surrounding aridity and barrenness of the Middle Atlas range. They shelter several troupes of **Barbary apes**, a glimpse of which is one of the wildlife highlights of a visit to Morocco. They can be found feeding along the forest margins – sometimes on the outskirts of Azrou itself – but they are shy animals and any excessive intrusion is likely to be met with a retreat to the lofty sanctuary of the treetops.

Almost as exhilarating is the forest **birdlife**, whose possibilities include the two species of Moroccan woodpecker, the pied and red great spotted and green and yellow Levaillant's varieties. Other overhead highlights include the splendid **booted eagle**, often seen soaring on outstretched wings in an attempt to evade the unwanted attentions of resident ravens. Kestrels nest in the Oum er Rbia gorge, near the falls (see below) in spring.

The cedars also provide shelter for a vibrant carpet of flowers – pink peonies, scarlet dianthus, blue germander, golden compositae and a variety of orchids – which makes an ideal haven for a host of **butterflies** (from April onwards), among them the brilliant sulphur cleopatra, large tortoiseshell and cardinal.

See also Aguelmane Azigza, below.

---

area by the river. (Coming from the south, the descent to the Oum er Rbia is unmistakeable – around 45km from Khenifra).

Guides will offer their services here for the **walk to the falls** but they are unnecessary as a clear path leads up to the gorge – a ten- to fifteen-minute walk. At the end of the path is a small waterfall, down petrified limestone deposits. All the water comes out in forty or more springs (sources), a little further down the gorge. Many have rough café-shelters built beside them, along the river edge.

The natural basin below the falls seems like a tempting place to swim, though beware that the currents here are extremely strong; there are smaller pools nearby. The water, full of salt sediments, is not drinkable.

Aguelmane Azigza and beyond

On past the bridges, the main road heads off to the west, crossed by a confusing array of pistes. After 18km, a turnoff on the left leads to the **Aguelmane Azigza**, a dark and very deep lake, secluded among the cedar trees. You can camp and swim here, as many Moroccans do. There's also a **lodge-café**, relatively new, though closed up, for some reason, recently.

Azigza has terrific **wildlife**. The wooded slopes of the lake throng with insect life, including the brilliant red and black grasshopper and the beautiful small Amanda's blue butterfly, while the forest provides nesting and feeding areas for woodland finches and titmice, including the elusive hawfinch with its diagnostic heavy bill. There's more birdlife in the waters, too, including diving duck (mainly grebes and coot) and marbled teal in autumn and winter.

From the Azigza turnoff, it's a further 24km to Khenifra. Alternatively, for the exploration-minded, the P3404 piste (poor but being improved) leads off east into the Djebel Irhoud mountains to ITZER and, finally, ZEIDA on the P20. A rather better road, the P3485, which is being surfaced, runs off from this to join the P21 at KIA AÏT OUTFELLA, just south of the Col du Zad.

South to Midelt and Er Rachidia

If you're travelling the southern circuits of the *ksour* and Kasbahs of the south, you're almost certain to take this route in one direction or the other. It's 125km from **Azrou to Midelt** and a further 154km to **Er Rachidia** – quite feasible distances for a single bus trip or a day's driving, but more satisfying taken in a couple of stages. You cross passes over both Middle and High Atlas ranges, catch a first glimpse of the south's fabulous *pisé* architecture and end up in the desert.

Azrou to Midelt

Climbing up from Azrou, the Midelt road (P21) follows a magnificent stretch of the Middle Atlas, winding through the forests to emerge at the **valley of the Oued Gigou**, the view ahead taking in some of the range's highest peaks. By bus you have little alternative but to head straight to Midelt, reached in around two hours, via the market village of TIMADHITE (large **Thursday souk**). With a car, there are two very brief and worthwhile detours.

The first of these comes 52km from Azrou, as the road levels out on a strange volcanic plateau littered with dark pumice rock. A turnoff here, to the left, is signposted to **Aguelmane Sidi Ali**, the largest of many mountain lakes formed in the extinct craters of this region. It's only a kilometre from the road: long, still and eerily beautiful. Besides an occasional shepherd's tent and flock, there is unlikely to be anything or anyone in sight; if you can improvise a fishing rod, there are reputed to be plenty of trout, pike and perch.

The other point where you might want to leave the road is 24km further down, past the Col du Zad, a 2178-metre pass across the Middle Atlas, and just before the junction with the old road (and caravan route) from Sefrou and Boulemane. Here, a road leads right in for 6km to the small village of **ITZER**, whose **market** is one of the most important in the region. Held on Mondays and Thursdays, it can be a good source of Berber rugs and carpets.

Back on the main road, you pass road junctions at BOULÔJUL (where the P20 from Boulemane joins) and ZEIDA (the P33 from Khenifra). A little beyond the latter is a good new little tourist complex, the *Centre Timnay*, including a shop, café-restaurant and a rocky **campsite**. The owner, Aït Lemkaden Driss, hopes to develop this as a base for **landrover and walking expeditions** in the region.

Midelt

At **MIDELT**, approached through a bleak plain of scrub and desert, you have left the Middle Atlas behind. Suddenly, through the haze, appear the much greater peaks of the High Atlas, which rise sheer behind the town to a massive range, the **Djebel Ayachi**, at over 3700m.

The drama of this site, tremendous in the clear, cool evenings, is the most compelling reason to stop over, for the town itself initially looks very drab – one street with a couple of cafés and hotels and a small *souk*. In fact, it's a pleasant place to stay – partly because so few people do, partly because it's the first place where you become aware of the much more relaxed (and predominantly Berber) atmosphere of the south. The best time to be here is for the huge **Sunday souk**, which spreads back along the road towards Azrou.

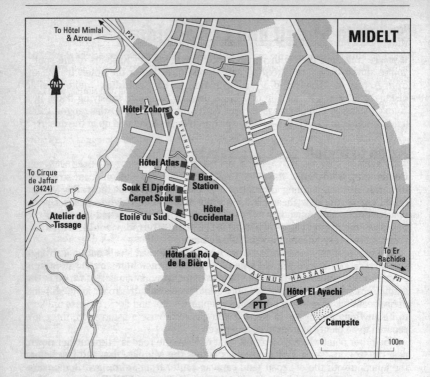

MIDELT

To Hôtel Mimlal & Azrou

P21

Hôtel Zohors

To Cirque de Jaffar (3424)

Hôtel Atlas

Souk El Djedid
Carpet Souk

Bus Station

Atelier de Tissage

Etoile du Sud

Hôtel Occidental

Hôtel au Roi de la Bière

To Er Rachidia

P21

AVENUE HASSAN II

Hôtel El Ayachi

PTT

Campsite

0   100m

The town: carpet shopping

The most interesting section of town, meriting at least a stop between buses, is the area around the old *souk* – **Souk Djedid**, behind the stalls facing the bus station. Just to the south of the main *souk*, which is a daily fruit and vegetable market, is an arcaded **carpet souk**, its wares slung out in rotation in the sunlight (for natural bleaching) and piled up in bewildering layers of pattern and colour in the various shops to the rear. This is a relaxed place for shopping and the rugs are superb – mostly local, geometric designs from tribes of the Middle Atlas. Ask to see the "antique" ones, few of which will be more than ten or twenty years old, but they are usually the most idiosyncratic and inventive. Good examples can also be seen at the **Etoile du Sud** carpet shop, just south of the *souk*, behind the *Hôtel Occidental*.

More carpets – and traditional-styled blankets and textiles – can be seen or bought at the **Atelier de Tissage**, part of a convent run by a group of French Franciscan nuns. It is located just off to the left on the road to **Tattiouine** (signposted "Cirque Jaffar"; first right after the bus station). Many of the nuns have been living here for years, and will quite happily talk about their time in Morocco.

If you follow the Tattiouine road a few kilometres further, you find yourself in countryside very different from that around Midelt, with eagles soaring above the hills and mule tracks leading down to the valleys, and an occasional Kasbah. For more on this area – and the Cirque du Jaffar beyond – see below.

Practicalities

Midelt has a reasonable choice of hotels, and a campsite:

Camping Midelt, 2km out on the road to Er Rachidia. Cheap but lacking facilities; you'd be better off camping in the gardens of the nearby *Hôtel Ayachi* (see below), who will often allow this if you are going to eat at their restaurant.

Hôtel Occidental [B], Av. Mohammed V (☎05/58.20.07). Central, old and simple, with cold showers. Very clean and welcoming, however, and recommended. ②

Hôtel au Roi de la Bière [C], corner of Av. Hassan II and Av. des F.A.R. (☎05/58.26.75). Similarly basic but not so good. ②

Hôtel Zohors [A], 15 Rue Mohammed Amraoui (☎05/58.20.28). Simple rooms off a court-yard. Again, not very good, though convenient for the CTM bus stop. ②

Hôtel Atlas, 3 Rue Mohammed Amraoui (☎05/58.29.38). A spotless new pension; family run and serving a good breakfast. ②

Hôtel Mimlal, Route de Fes (☎05/58.27.66). New hotel, 1km out on the road to Fes. ①

Hôtel Ayachi [D], Av. Mohammed V (☎05/58.21.61). The town's most upmarket hotel, favoured by tour groups and often full. Despite a 1990 *International Gastronomy Award*, on proud display, the restaurant and service are not terribly brilliant. ③

There are small **hammams** in the town for men and women – ask directions.

For **meals**, try Café-*Restaurant Fes*, signposted on Rue des Esserghin, which does a very generous *menu du jour* (it likes advance warning in the evening). Other decent restaurants include the *Brasserie Chez Aziz*, on the Er Rachidia road, and *Café-Restaurant Le Sapin*, on Av. Moulay Abdallah, by a small park where the locals play *boules* on warm evenings.

The Cirque Jaffar, Djebel Ayachi and beyond

The classic route around Midelt is the **Cirque Jaffar**, a very poor piste, practicable only in dry weather, which leaves the Midelt–Tattiouine road to edge its way through a kind of hollow in the foothills of the **Djebel Ayachi** (see below). This runs round the *cirque*, then loops back to the Midelt–Azrou road after 34km (turn right, on to the 3426, near the *Maison Forestière de Mitkane*); it is only 79km in all back to Midelt, though it takes a good half a day to get around.

Djebel Ayachi and Tounfite

Djebel Ayachi can be climbed from Midelt, either returning to the town, or as part of a through-trek to Tounfite. From Midelt, a taxi or pick-up can be arranged to the springs 2km beyond Tattiouine, and the long **Ikkis valley** followed, with a bivouac at its head (the col at the end leads to the Cirque du Jaffar). An easy ascent leads to the many summits of this huge range, which was long thought to be the highest in Morocco (it is 3700m – compared to Toubkal at 4167m). A descent south to the Oued Taarart valley brings you to several villages and a Wednesday truck out to Tounfite.

At TOUNFITE, rooms are available and buses and taxis link it with Boumia (with a Thursday *souk*), Zeïda and Midelt. The village also gives access to the Djebel Masker – a long day's climb, rising from cedar forests.

Across the Atlas

An exciting and intrepid route is to continue along the *Cirque Jaffar* road across the Atlas, eventually reaching Arhbala and El Ksiba, or Imilchil up in the High Atlas. This can be done by vehicle or trekking. For the latter, consult Michael

Peyron's *Grand Atlas Traverse* guide, which details the whole zone between Midelt and the Toukbal massif.

Renault 4s make it over the Atlas from Midelt to Tinerhir in summer, though it's a lot easier with four-wheel-drive vehicles; everyone needs a pick and spade for the occasional very rough detour (beware of scorpions, by the way, when shifting rocks), as well as some warm clothes and a tent for sleeping out at night (Atlas nights are cold). If you don't have a vehicle, you can use Berber lorries over the various stages, though beware that you'll be largely dependent on the patterns of local markets, and reckon on up to three days for the journey to Imilchil, and a similar number from there down to the fabulous Todra Gorge and Tinerhir (see pp.405–9). For some guidelines on trucking it over the Atlas, see the travellers' account on pp.406–7.

South towards Er Rachidia

There's less adventure in continuing **south from Midelt to Er Rachidia**, though the route is a striking one, marking the transition to the south and the desert. The area was long notorious for raids upon caravans and travellers carried out by the Aït Haddidou, a nomadic Berber tribe, fear of whom led the main spring along this route to be known as *Ain Khrob ou Hrob* – "Drink and Flee". The tribe were pacified with great difficulty by the French, as late as the 1930s, and in consequence, the traditional *ksour* (fortified villages; the singular is *ksar*) are often shadowed by old Foreign Legion posts.

The Tizi n'Talrhmeht and Rich

Around 30km south of Midelt, you cross one of the lower passes of the High Atlas, the **Tizi n'Talrhmeht** (Pass of the She-Camel), before descending to what is essentially a desert plain. At AÏT MESSAOUD, just beyond the pass, there's a distinctly Beau Geste-like Foreign Legion fort, and a few kilometres further down, you come across the first southern *ksar*, AÏT KHERROU, a river oasis at the entrance to a small gorge. After this, the *ksour* begin to dot the landscape as the road follows the path of the great Ziz River.

The main settlement in these parts is **RICH**, a market town and administrative centre, approached from the main road (P21) along a rather bizarre red-washed esplanade. Enclosed by palms watered by a *sequia* (irrigation channel) from the Oued Ziz, the town developed around a *ksar* and was an important fort during the Protectorate. It has a lively **souk** (Sundays), at the entrance to which are two cheap, unclassified **hotels**, the *Es Salama* (☎05/58.93.43; ①) and marginally preferable El *Massira* (☎05/58.39.40; ①).

A route over the Atlas

West of Rich, the Atlas mountains stretch desolately into the distance, skirted by a road up behind the town which trails the last section of the Oued Ziz. The road begins as the P3442 and is surfaced as far as AMOUGUER, where the rough P3443 piste takes over **to Imilchil** (see pp.406–8 for a map and account), by way of OUTERBATE and SOUNTAT: a wonderful trip through great gorges, valleys and passes.

The route is passable (just) in a Renault 4, though only in the dry summer months, and it can also be travelled in stages by **Berber lorries** (*camionettes*), paying as you go. Going on the lorries, the most promising day to set out from

Rich is Friday, when you might get a ride the whole way to Imilchil, for its Saturday *souk*; make enquiries at the Rich hotels.

The Ziz Gorges

The scenic highlight of the regular Midelt–Er Rachidia route are the dramatic **Ziz Gorges**, tremendous erosions of rock which carve a passage through the Atlas. The route follows the Ziz valley from AÏT KROJMANE (7km from Rich) on, just past the *Ziz* ("gazelle" in Berber) filling station. You enter the gorges proper, around 25km from Rich, shortly after the **Tunnel du Légionnaire**, built by the French in 1930 to open up the route to the south, and still guarded by drowsy soldiers. The gorges are truly majestic, especially in late afternoon, cut by great swathes of sunlight, and the incredible mountain landscape is accompanied by sudden vistas of brilliant green oasis and red-brown *ksour*.

You emerge from the gorges near the vast **Barrage Hassan Addakhil**, built in 1971 to irrigate the valley of the Tafilalt beyond, and to supply electricity for ER RACHIDIA (see p.411). The dam also regulates the flow of the Oued Ziz, preventing the serious flooding which occurred frequently before it was built, as witnessed by the deserted *ksour* in the gorges above and below the lake.

Azrou to Kasba Tadla

The **main route from Azrou to Marrakesh** – the P24 – skirts well clear of the Atlas ranges, its interest lying in the subtle changes of land, cultivation and architecture on the plains as you move into the south. The towns along the way are hot, dusty, functional market centres, unlikely to tempt you to linger. However, once again, contact with the Middle Atlas is close at hand, if you leave the main road and take to the pistes. A great network of them spreads out behind the small town of **El Ksiba**, itself 8km off the P24 but easily hitched to from the turnoff or reached by bus from Kasba Tadla.

Khenifra

It's unlikely that you'll get stranded in **KHENIFRA** and it's equally difficult to imagine any other reason to stay there. It is a dull-looking market town and provincial centre, whose reputation for providing some of the best Moroccan musicians (including Rouisha, one of the biggest stars) seems hard to credit. From an outsider's perspective, the only bit of life to be seen is at the twice-weekly **souks** (Wed & Sun) or the Saturday afternoon rug auction, put on by Berber women just across the bridge from the highway which bypasses the town. Historically, the town's chief claim to fame is as a focus of resistance, as the fiefdom of one Moha ou Hammou, in the early years of the Protectorate. The French suffered one of their worst military defeats here, losing 600 men when they took the town in 1914.

If you're following this chapter in reverse (from Marrakesh) note that you can approach the Cascades of Oum er Rbia (see p.217–18) from Khenifra. If you've just done this, or plan to do so, you might just want to use the local **accommodation**: a particularly gloomy unclassified hotel by the *CTM* station at the end of town, or a couple of slightly more enticing ones, the *Voyageurs* and the *France* (each with a restaurant), down by the river. The only classified hotel is the *Hôtel Hamou* (☎05/58.60.20; ④), over in the hillside Ville Nouvelle.

SOUTH OF BENI MELLAL: ATLAS HIKES AND *PISTES*

The Middle Atlas to the south and southeast of Beni Mellal is ideal hiking and land-rover expedition territory. Below are suggestions for four- or five-day expeditions in the region; they are impracticable outside the summer months.

Djebel Tassemit (2248m) towers like a high wall behind Beni Mellal. Despite its height, it is a relatively easy climb, by way of Aïn Asserdoun and the ruined Kasbah de ras El Aïn, to the south of town. **Djebel R'Nim** (2411m) and **Djebel Tazerkount** (1730m) continue the wall to the southwest. For the energetic, they are not hard to climb, but two lower tracks cut between them from north to south. One of these runs southeast from Beni Mellal itself, and then swings southwest to **Ouaouizarht**, at the top end of the Bin El Ouidane lake (see p.227). The other runs south from **Oulad M'Barek** on the P24 and then swings southeast to Ouaouizarht.

South of **Bin El Ouidane**, the lower slopes of the High Atlas are appealing. A track from Ouaouizarht skirts the lake until it strikes southeast through forests towards Tilouggite (it is by this stage an extremely rough track, practicable only by jeep or lorry). This winds through the mountains for some 70km before reaching ZAOUIA AHANESAL, passing en route ZAOUIA TEMGAL (40km), above which are some strange rock formations shaped like a Gothic cathedral and known as such: **La Cathédrale des Rochers**. It would be possible to cover this route in stages, using local Berber lorries or jeeps.

Southeast of Azilal a dirt-track leads to the village of AÏT MEHAMMED and then on to TAMDA, before joining the *piste* running south from ZAOUIA AHANESAL. Continuing up into the Central Atlas from Aït Mehammed, another difficult *piste* leads to the **Bou Goumez valley**, a possible hiking/climbing base for the 4000m peaks of the **Irhil M'Goun** – the highest in Morocco outside the Toubkal massif.

MAPS AND ASSISTANCE
If you haven't obtained a large-scale survey **map** (see p.19), a good substitute is the *Michelin* map, which has an insert covering this area at 1:600,000.

If you want **assistance**, two mountain guides are available in Beni Mellal or Azilal. Contact either: **Serrab El Houssine** (21 Bloc 1 Foughol, Av. Hassan II, Beni Mellal; ℅03/48.13.26), who will accompany groups or, if you wish, just help you plan routes; or **Mohammed Achari** (Imelghas, Aït Bou Goumez, Azilal), who will guide groups in the Irhil M'Goun and also has mules for hire. Both charge around 200–300dh a day. More expensive landrover expeditions are arranged by **Imilchil Voyages**, 416 Bd. Mohammed V, Beni Mellal (☎03/48.90.60).

Oulmès

Northwest of Khenifra, a road leads through the Djebel Mouchchene, a forested outcrop of the Middle Atlas, towards Rabat. This is an attractive route through countryside cut by rivers and ravines, and with wild boar in the hills. There is a major **souk** at the crossroads settlement of AGUELMOUSS each Saturday.

Midway along the route is the small town of **OULMES** and – some 4km distant – the spa-hamlet of **OULMÈS-TARMILATE**, home of Morocco's most popular fizzy mineral water. The spa makes a good stop, if you can afford the *Hôtel les Thermes* (☎03/55.09.01; closed July & Aug; ③). Below the hotel you can walk down to a spring known as **Lalla Haya**, where Oulmès water cascades out from the rocks.

El Ksiba, Arhbala and across the Atlas

EL KSIBA is a sizeable and busy Berber village with a **Sunday souk**, enclosed by apricot, olive and orange groves. It has one small **hotel**, the *Hostelerie Henri IV* (☎03/41.50.02; ②), on a loop road which bypasses the main part of the village; this is a pleasant place, French-run, with a good restaurant and bar, and accepts credit cards. There is also a **campsite**, *Camping Taghbalout*, on the edge of the village, and others hidden in the wooded Atlas slopes, along the Arhbala road.

South of the town, a reasonable piste (P1909, then P1901) heads off into the Atlas, across **towards Imilchil and the Plateau of the Lacs** (see the map and reverse description of this route on p.406–8). This is more or less practicable by Renault 4, weather permitting. If you are relying on local transport, you should be able to get a bus or lorry along the newly surfaced road to the market village of ARHBALA (or AGHBALA), where a rough piste heads off towards Midelt. Local lorries shuttle passengers to Imilchil via CHERKET and TASSENT; connections are easiest early in the morning on Wednesday, when Arhbala has its *souk,* or on Thursday, the day before the *souk* at Imilchil.

Another, recently surfaced road, the P1805, leads southwest from the P1909 to the reservoir of **Bin El Ouidane** (see overleaf), via BEN CHERRO, TAGUELFT (where there is a very basic hotel, without electricity or running water) and OUAOUIAZARHT. The road itself is a wonderful single track through rugged, sparsely vegetated Middle Atlas countryside, over several 1500m passes.

Kasba Tadla

KASBA TADLA was created by Moulay Ismail, and takes its name from a fortress he built here, strategically positioned beside the Oum er Rbia River. It remains a military town, with all the life that that entails, and is scarcely a place to linger. However, if you have a car, or are between buses, you might as well take the odd hour to look round. The **Kasbah** is only a few blocks from the bus station – a massive, crumbling quarter, whose palace and even mosque have lapsed into dereliction, their shells occupied by small farmholdings and cottages. The town has a sizeable **souk** on Mondays.

For anyone stranded, there are two cheap and very basic **hotels** near the bus station: the *Hôtel Atlas*, 46 Bd. El Majjata Obad (☎03/41.87.31; ⑩), and, round the corner, the *Hôtel des Alliés* at 38 Av. Mohammed V (☎03/41.81.72; ⑩). The only other option is the *Hôtel Bellevue* (☎03/41.81.72; ④), out at the Kasba Tadla turn-off on the Khenifra–Beni Mellal road; it is functional enough, but modern and unexciting.

Beni Mellal

BENI MELLAL is one of Morocco's fastest-growing towns, with a population of some 250,000. It has few specific sights – and few tourists – and makes an easy, restful stop en route to Marrakesh. As a market centre for the broad, prosperous flatlands to the south, it hosts a large **Tuesday souk** – good for woollen blankets, which feature unusual Berber designs. It is also useful for its transport links, with a regular bus towards the wonderful Cacades d'Ouzoud (see overleaf).

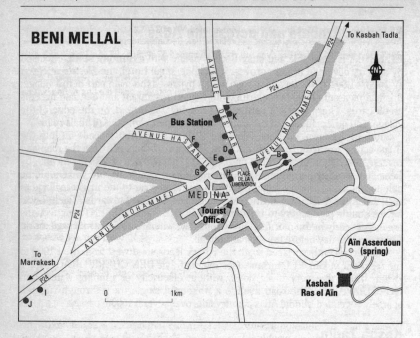

As far as sights go, the town's **Kasbah**, again built by Moulay Ismail, has been often restored and is of no great interest. Time would be better spent by walking up to the smaller, ruined **Kasbah de Ras El Aïn**, set above gardens, and to the spring of **Aïn Asserdoun**, to the south of town. The latter (signposted on a Circuit Touristique from town) is especially pleasant, feeding a series of artificial falls (Moroccans love waterfalls) amid well-tended gardens.

Practicalities

The main road from Fes to Marrakesh (the P24) now skirts the suburbs of Beni Mellal, as so often, the **bus station** has been implanted here, and to reach the centre from there you may want to get a *petit taxi* to save a long uphill walk. The old Fes–Marrakesh road still runs through the core of the town, as the **Av. Mohammed V**, and midway along it is the cream-and-white arcaded **Place de la Libération**, focus of the old **Medina** quarter, which climbs up the lower slopes of the Djebel Tassemit. The **Ville Nouvelle** sprawls down into the plain to the south, towards the ring road.

There are a dozen or so **hotels** scattered in and around the town, many of them newly built:

Hôtel El Amria [D], Av. des F.A.R. (☎03/48.35.31). Best of the unclassified hotels: clean rooms, hot showers and sympathetically run. ①

Hôtel Es Saada [C], 129 Rue Tarik Ibn Ziad (☎03/48.29.91). A good second choice – recently renovated and again with hot showers. ①

Hôtel El Fath [H], 15 Place de la Libération (no phone). Quiet, clean and newly decorated, with fabulous views from the roof terrace; cold showers only. ①

Hôtel des Voyageurs [G], Av. Mohammed V (☎03/48.24.72). On the edge of the Medina, with another fine roof terrace overlooking the plain; cold showers only. ①

Auberge du Vieux Moulin [B], Av. Mohammed V (☎03/48.27.88). A pleasant, old-style French hotel, with a good restaurant and relaxed bar. Recommended. ①

Hôtel de Paris [A], Hay Ibn Syna, off Av. Mohammed V (☎03/48.22.45). Less good, with cold showers only. ①

Hôtel Aïn Asserdoun [A], Av. des F.A.R. (☎03/48.34.93). New, with a small restaurant. ①

Hôtel Zidania [L], Av. des F.A.R. (☎03/48.18.98). New hotel opposite the bus station, with a fast-food restaurant. ①

Hôtel Sharaf [K], corner of Av. des F.A.R. and Av. 20 Août (☎03/48.12.21). Another one, nearby, with a restaurant. ①

Hôtel Gharnata [E], Av. Mohammed V (☎03/48.34.82). Another good new hotel which accepts credit cards; reasonable restaurant. ②

Hôtel Beni Mellal Atlas [F], corner of Av. Hassan II and Ruc Chaouki (☎03/48.92.11). And yet another new hotel – with a recommended restaurant. ②

Hôtel Al Bassatine, Route de Fkish Ben Salah (☎03/48.22.47). On the northwest edge of town, alongside the orange and olive groves. Comfortable rooms and the best restaurant in the neighbourhood – French-run until recently. ③

Hôtel Ouzoud (☎03/48.37.52; I); **Hôtel Chems** (☎03/48.34.60; J). Two indistinguishable and largely undistinguished modern hotels on the Fes–Marrakesh road, built for groups on the Imperial Cities tour. ④

For **meals**, in addition to the above, the *Restaurant Dounia Day* on Av. Mohammed V is excellent value. Next door to it is the *Café Basma*, which is a good spot for coffee and watching the world go by.

Oulad Nemâa: a Saturday souk

If you're in Beni Mellal on a Saturday, it's worth a trip to what is traditionally the Middle Atlas's largest weekly **market**, held 35km southwest of the town at **SOUK SEBT DES OULAD NEMÂA**. There are regular buses.

The Cascades d'Ouzoud

The **Cascades d'Ouzoud** are a fairly long detour from the Beni Mellal–Marrakesh road – taking at least half a day's journey to reach if you're going by local bus and taxi. However, there are few places in Morocco so enjoyable and easy-going as these fallls, with their seasonal campsites, and in midsummer it's incredible to encounter the cool air here, with the water crashing down onto a great drop of rocks amid thickets of lush green trees and vegetation.

Getting to Ouzoud is simplest from Beni Mellal; there's a regular bus to Azilal (a winding 63km), where you can usually get a place in a *grand taxi* to the springs (10dh a place or 50dh for the *taxi*). There is also a bus twice a day from Marrakesh along the S508 road, which passes by Azilal. Getting back to Azilal is generally no problem, with *grands taxis* regularly shuttling from the Cascades.

Bin El Ouidane and Azilal

On the way from Beni Mellal to Azilal, the road climbs almost straight up from the plain, zigzagging through the hills and crossing the immense **Bin El Ouidane reservoir**. This was one of the earliest (1948–55) and most ambitious of the country's irrigation schemes and it has changed much of the land around Beni Mellal – formerly as dry and barren as the phosphate plains to the west. It supplies much of central Morocco's electricity.

There's a small **hotel** beside the barrage, the *Auberge du Lac* (year round; ☎Bin El Ouidane 5 or ☎Afourer 76 – through the operator; ②), which offers the choice of rooms in its main building, bungalow rooms by the lake, or camping. It also has a bar, a good restaurant, boats for hire, and fishing; swimming is prohibited. In winter, be warned, it is very cold up here – and although the hotel has hot water it has no room heating.

AZILAL, 27km further on, is just a small village, with a garrison, banks, a Thursday *souk* and transport links; somewhat inexplicably, it has a tourist office (on Av. Hassan II; ☎48.83.34) and even an ONMT pamphlet devoted to it. If by any chance you find yourself stranded here, there is a recently refurbished **hotel**, the *Tanout* (☎03/45.82.81; ②), on the road in from Beni Mellal. Note that the **buses** from Azilal to Marrakesh run twice daily, currently at 7am and 2pm.

The Cascades

The **Cascades d'Ouzoud** are a very popular place to camp in the summer, with both Moroccan and foreign tourists attracted by the falls and cool, high air. They are, as yet, refreshingly uncommercialised. At the roadside, there is a small **hotel-café**, variously called *Mohammed's* or *Dar Essalam* (☎Ouzoud 1 – through the operator; ①). This has an open courtyard, with orange tree, off which are some large dormitory rooms. They are often used by *Club Med* groups, though individuals are welcome; in summer, it is wise to book ahead.

Alongside the hotel is a **campsite**, shaded by fruit trees and bordered by a stream, which also has a few rooms; it is run by a local Berber, T'Hami Abassi, who cooks good meals on request. Several further **cafés** are located on terraces along the way down to the falls, and most offer camping for a few tents, either for a small fee, or free if you eat and drink at them during your stay. They tend to have a fairly youthful, international clientele.

From the campsites, a series of signposted paths wind down to the valley and the great basins below the **cascades**. You can swim in one of these – a fabulous natural pool – and might spot the the occasional Barbary ape under the oak and pomegranate trees. Your best chance of a sighting is at daybreak or an hour or so before dusk, when they come out to drink in the river. On terraces just above the falls (and best reached from T'Hami Abassi's campsite) are a group of eleven tiny and very ancient **watermills**, some still in operation for grinding corn.

A memorable short hike is to go beyond the lower pools to the so-called "**Mexican Village**", a fascinating place connected by semi-underground passages. To get there, follow the path down to the lower pools and you will see a path climbing up on the left, past a farmhouse and up to the top of the plain. Follow this path west. The village is sited on the slopes of the wooded hills, about 1km along the path (which drops to a small stream before climbing up to the houses). Tourists are very much a novelty.

On from Ouzoud – and into the High Atlas

Continuing south to Marrakesh from Ouzoud, it's easiest to backtrack to Azilal, picking up a bus there to Beni Mellal or (if you time it right) direct to Marrakesh. If you have transport, however, you could drive down to KHEMIS-DES-OULAD on the Beni Mellal–Marrakesh road (P24); 17km of this 51km route is poor piste, passable only in dry weather.

Alternatively, if you're into a spot of High Atlas exploration, you might be tempted by one of the **pistes south from the S508**. These lead into the Bou Goumez valley – an increasingly popular trekking destination – and to the **Irhil M'Goun** mountains, often described as the "Moroccan Dolomites", due to their sheer rockfaces. It is a remote region, populated in part by transhumant shepherds who bring their flocks up here in summer from the oases beyond the Atlas.

Bou Goumez valley and the Irhil M'Goun

A **dirt track southeast of Azilal** leads to the village of AÏT MEHAMMED and from there into the **Bou Goumez valley**, a possible trekking/climbing base for the 4000m peaks of the **Irhil M'Goun** – the highest in Morocco outside the Toubkal massif – and some astonishing gorges. It is possible to continue south through the mountains to exit via El Kelaa de M'Gouna.

From Azilal you can get a taxi up to Aït Mehammed, from whence lorries or landrover taxis run on Wednesday, Friday and Sunday to TABANT/SOUK EL HAD, the administrative centre of the Bou Goumez, which has a large Sunday *souk*. Alternatively, you could make a two-day trek from Aït Mehammed with an overnight stop at the pretty hamlet of SREMPT (Sabre Brahim offers rooms) and the crossing of the Tizi n'Aït Ourit (2606m) with its vast view of the mountain ranges. Another possible approach is via Demnate (see below) from where trucks go on to the road-end at Imi n'Wakka (Tabat n'Tirsal) under the bulk of Djebel Rhat. There is a spectacular trek of several days down the Bou Willi valley to connect with the Bou Goumez. On the Tizi n'Tirghyst (2390m) are prehistoric rock-carved pictures.

Several of the valley villages have *gîte* accommodation, meals and mule hire (see lists in the ONMT Atlas guide). Mohammed Achari (Imelghas, Aït Bou Goumez, Bureau Tabant, par Azilal) is a **mountain guide** of wide experience.

Across the Atlas via Zaouia Ahanesal

From Bin El Ouidane, a minor road turns off to OUAOUIZARNT, crosses to the south of the lake and then turns into an extremely rough track, practicable only by jeep or lorry. This winds through the mountains for some 70km before reaching ZAOUIA AHANESAL, passing en route ZAOUIA TEMGAL (40km), above which are some strange rock formations shaped like a Gothic cathedral and known as such: **La Cathédrale des Rochers**. It would be possible to cover this route in stages, using local transport resources. First get yourself a lift to Ouaouizarnt, then ask around the marketplace for a jeep going to TILOUGGITE, then ask around and wait for lorries (*camions*) going to TEMGA and beyond.

Azilal to Marrakesh: Demnate

Having come as far as Azilal and the cascades, it is easier to continue along the S508 road to Marrakesh rather than try and cut back on to the main road from Beni Mellal. It is in any case the more interesting route.

Demnate

You'll probably have to change buses along the way at **DEMNATE**, a walled market town, with a Glaoui-era Kasbah, and a **Sunday souk**. The *souk* is by far the largest in the region and an interesting, unaffected event that is well worth trying to coincide with. It is held just outside the ramparts, the stalls spreading out into the town streets with their used clothes and other goods, together with enormous stacks of fresh produce.

Demnate has a small **hotel**, the *Iminifri* (①), which is basic but friendly, and if you have the time and the transport, a road up above the town climbs after 6.5km to a curious-looking natural bridge – **Imi n'Ifri**. Close to a series of springs, which account for the Demnate valley's prosperous and intense cultivation, this is the site of a large *moussem* held two weeks after the Aïd El Kebir.

Demnate to Marrakesh

The land between Demnate and Marrakesh is generally poor and rocky, distinguished only by sporadic clusters of farmhouses or shepherds' huts. If you take the bus, it might follow either of the routes to Marrakesh – via Tamelelt (where you rejoin the P24) or a perfectly well-paved road via Tazzerte and Sidi Rahhal.

Given the choice, go for the latter. An old Glaoui village, **TAZZERTE** is fronted by four crumbling Kasbahs, from which the clan (see "Telouet" for its history) used to control the region and the caravan routes to the north. There is a small Monday market held here, and a larger one on Fridays at Sidi Rahhal, 7km further down.

SIDI RAHHAL, named after a fifteenth-century *marabout*, is also a point of significant local pilgrimage and host to an important, week-long *moussem* (flexible date in the summer). The saint, in whose honour the festivities take place, has an unusual Judeo-Muslim tradition, and a multitude of stories told about him. All are timeless in their evocations of magic and legend. The most popular ones recount how he had the power to conduct himself and other creatures through the air – a "talent" which led to a minor incident involving the Koutoubia minaret in Marrakesh, whose upper storey one of his followers is supposed to have knocked down with his knee.

Coming into Marrakesh from either Demnate or Beni Mellal, you skirt part of the huge **palmery** which encloses the northern walls of the city. Arriving by bus, you will almost certainly find yourself at the main **bus station** by Bab Doukkala – a ten-minute walk from the centre of Gueliz (or the Ville Nouvelle), or twenty minutes (or an 8–10dh taxi ride) from Place Djemaa El Fna and the Medina.

travel details

Trains

Fes–Meknes Nine daily in each direction (45min–1hr).

Fes–Rabat/Casablanca Seven daily (Rabat 3hr 30min–4hr 30min/Casa 5hr–6hr); all via Meknes, Sidi Kacem (2hr 30min), Kenitra (3hr 30min) and Salé (4hr).

Fes–Taza/Oujda Five to six daily (2–2hr 15min/ 5hr 45min–6hr).

Fes–Tangier Five daily. Two are direct (leaving Fes at 4.55am and 2.58, arriving at Tangier at 10.29am and 9.10pm, respectively. Others all go via Meknes, Sidi Kacem (3hr 30min) and Asilah (5hr), reaching Tangier in around 6hr.

Fes/Meknes–Marrakesh Four daily (8–10hr from Fes) via Sidi Kacem and Casablanca.

Buses

From Meknes Fes (hourly; 50min); Larache/ Tangier (2 daily; 5hr 30min/7hr); Rabat (3; 4hr); Ouezzane (2; 4hr); Chaouen (1; 5hr 30min); Azrou (4; 1hr 30min); Midelt (1; 5hr 30min); Beni Mellal/ Marrakesh (1; 6hr/9hr).

From Fes Chaouen (2; 5hr); Mdiq (1; 5hr); Larache/Tangier (2; 4hr 30min/6hr); Rabat (6; 5hr 30min); Casa (8; 7hr); Taza (3; 2hr 30min); Al Hoceima (1; 11hr 30min); Sefrou (3; 1hr 30min); Immouzer/Ifrane (5; 1hr/1hr 30min); Azrou (5; 2hr 30min); Midelt/Er Rachidia (3; 5hr 30min/8hr 30min); Beni Mellal/Marrakesh (3; 8hr 30min/ 11hr).

From Sefrou Boulemane/Midelt (2hr/5hr).

From Azrou Ifrane/Immouzer (4 daily; 1hr/1hr 30min); Midelt/Er Rachidia (5; 2hr/5hr); Khenifra/ Kasba Tadla/Beni Mellal/Marrakesh (3; 3hr/4hr/ 4hr 30min/7hr).

From Midelt Er Rachidia (2; 3hr), Oujda (1; 13hr).

From Kasbah Tadla El Ksiba (3 daily; 20min); Beni Mellal (4; 1hr).

From Beni Mellal Demnate (4 daily; 3hr); Marrakesh (6; 6hr).

Grands Taxis

From Meknes Regularly to Fes (40min) and Volubilis/Moulay Idriss (35min).

From Fes Regularly to Meknes, Sefrou (1hr), Immouzer/Ifrane (1hr 20min/1hr 40min) and Taza (1hr 40min).

Other **local and Middle Atlas** routes are specified in the text.

Flights

From Fes *RAM* flights to Casablanca (daily), Agadir and Marrakesh (both twice a week), and to Er Rachidia, Oujda and Tangier (all once weekly). Three flights a week to London (two via Casablanca; one via Tangier).

CHAPTER FOUR

THE WEST COAST: FROM RABAT TO ESSAOUIRA

This chapter takes in almost five hundred kilometres of Atlantic coastline, from Kenitra in the north down to Essaouira in the south. It is, inevitably, a mix of influences, characters and landscapes, ranging through long stretches of scarcely developed lagoons and sands to Morocco's urban heartland. This latter comprises the cities of **Rabat** and **Casablanca** – the respective seats of government and of industry and commerce – and the neighbouring **Salé**, **Kenitra** and **Mohammedia**. Together, this conurbation has a population of over four million – over a fifth of the country's total. It is an astonishingly recent growth to pre-eminence in what was, until the French Protectorate, a largely neglected strip of coast. At the turn of this century, Rabat was a straggling port with a population of 30,000 (today it is 518,000), while Casablanca (modern population 2,140,000), was a minor harbour town of 20,000 inhabitants.

Inevitably, given this development, it is French and post-colonial influences that are dominant. Don't go to **Casa** – as Casablanca is popularly known – expecting some exotic movie location; it is a modern city that looks very much like Marseilles. **Rabat**, too, which the French developed as an administrative capital to replace the old imperial centres of Fes and Marrakesh, looks markedly European, with its cafés and boulevards. Still, if you want to get an idea of what Morocco is all about, these, at some stage, are places to spend time. Casa is perhaps best visited after spending a while in the country, when you'll appreciate both its differences and its fundamentally Moroccan character. Rabat, on the other hand, is one of the best places to make for as soon as you arrive. Well connected by train with Tangier, Fes and Marrakesh, it makes an easy cultural shift in which to gain some initial confidence, and, along with the old port of **Salé**, across its estuary, it also has some of Morocco's finest and oldest monuments, dating from the Almohad and Merenid dynasties.

South along the coast, populations and towns thin out, as the road skirts a series of beaches and dunes, with the odd detour inland when cliffs take hold. **Essaouira**, which is also easily accessible from Marrakesh, is a long-established backpackers' resort, and more recently a major centre for windsurfers. For most independent travellers, it is Morocco's coastal highlight, blending as it does a slightly alternative feel with the air of a traditional provincial town. **El Jadida**, established as a beach resort by the French, is more the preserve of people from Casablanca; it sees fewer foreign visitors and, oddly, is more expensive and exclusive. **Oualidia**, to its south, has a similar, though more relaxed and small-scale, style. **Safi**, between El Jadida and Essaouira, is a predominantly industrial town, but a friendly place, and with excellent beaches nearby.

Kenitra and the coast to Rabat

Travelling to Rabat from Tangier or Fes, you will bypass the stretch of coast around Kenitra – which for the most part is no great loss. **Kenitra** itself is a dull, scruffy little town, as is its beach and port at **Mehdiya**. Drivers can make pleasant detours, however, further south, to the **Plage des Nations** – Rabat's local beach resort – and to the botanical extravagance of the **Jardins Exotiques**. (If you don't have transport, they are easiest visited as a day trip from the capital). **Birdwatchers** may also want to explore the **Lac de Sidi Bourhaba**, near Mehdiya, which has protected status due to its notable birds of prey.

Kenitra and Mehdiya

KENITRA was established by the French as Port Lyautey – named after the Resident General – with the intention of channelling trade from Fes and Meknes. It never quite took off, however, losing out in industry and port activities to Casablanca, despite the rich farming areas of its hinterland. It has a population today of around 300,000, employed mainly in paper mills and a large fish cannery. Until recently, additional income was provided by a large naval and military base, shared with the US, but the Americans left around the time of the Gulf War, and the Moroccans have scaled down their own operations (the fact that it was from Kenitra that the 1972 coup attempt was launched did not help secure its future). A rather sad array of bars, pizza joints and discos struggle along in their wake.

Orientation is straightforward, with a long main street, **Bd. Mohammed V/ Av. Mohammed Diouri** – running from the Gare de Ville (at one end of town) to the bus station (at the other) by way of the central **Place Administrative**. It is about fifteen minutes' walk from the square to either bus or train station.

The town has a dozen or so **hotels** and a good campsite:

Hôtel de la Poste, 307 Bd. Mohammed V (☎07/36.41.89). Basic but cheap, with hot showers in the rooms. ①

Hôtel La Rotonde, 60 Av. Mohammed Diouri (☎07/37.14.01). Decent rooms, plus a café, restaurant and bar. ②

Hôtel Ambassy, Av. Hassan II (☎07/36.29.26). A bit more comfort and very central; again has a restaurant (modestly priced and recommended), plus two bars. ②

Hôtel Mamora, Av. Hassan II (☎07/37.17.75). Another step up, with a swimming pool. ③

Hôtel Safir, Place Administrative (☎07/37.19.21). A large *Safir*-chain hotel on the main square. All facilities and a large swimming pool. ④

Camping La Chenaie, just out of town – follow signs for the Club Equestre (☎07/36.30.01). An excellent, inexpensive and secure site, with grassy pitches, cold showers, a restaurant and swimming pool. ③

Mehdiya

MEHDIYA PLAGE, Kenitra's beach, 11km to the west, is a dull, greyish strip with a few houses and chalets, intermittent beach cafés and plenty of summer crowds. It is reached easily enough by *grand taxi* (these leave Kenitra from Rue Mohammed Diouri), but if you're after a spot to break a journey and swim, you'd be better off at the more relaxed Plage des Nations, to the south. The only **hotel**, the *Atlantique* (☎116 through the operator; ②), is open in summer only and a bit grim, although its bar has a reputation for putting on good local musicians; the *Auberge de la Fôret*, still listed by some guides, has closed.

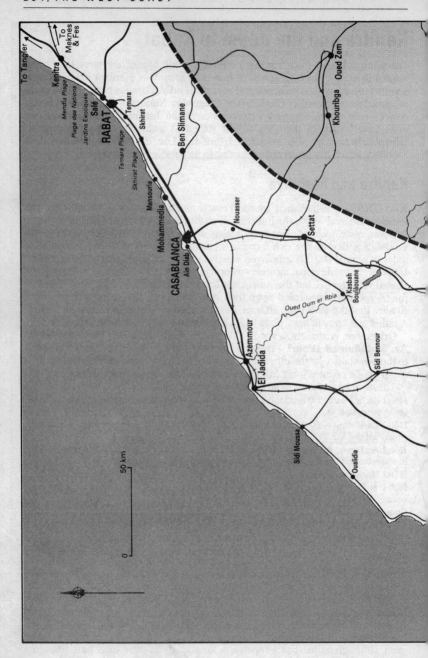

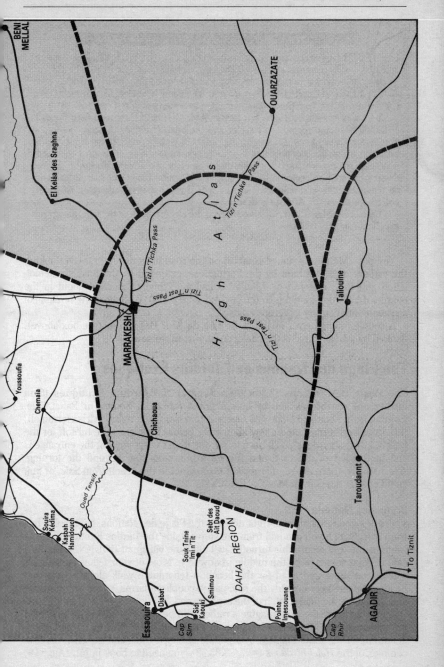

BIRDWATCHING AT LAC SIDI BOURHABA

Lac de Sidi Bourhaba, just inland from Mehdiya (see p.233), is a large freshwater lake, divided by a central causeway. The best viewing points for its rich birdlife are on the causeway, where the ever-present damselflies and dragonflies provide a spectacular display of flight and colour. Marsh frogs and Berber toad also make their vocal contribution from the sanctuary of the northern reedbeds.

The **birds** of Sidi Bourhaba are outstanding; the reedbeds throng with the calls of flitting reed and melodious warbler and the open stretches of water hold good numbers of crested coot (in spring) and marbled teal (in autumn and winter). It is, however, for its birds of prey that the site is best known. Circling almost constantly overhead are **marsh harriers**, with their characteristic low quartering flight, and these are joined on occasion by the smaller and whiter black-shouldered **kite** with its diagnostic black shoulders (and red eyes if you get close enough!). At sunset you may also see the **African marsh owl**.

There is a wildlife *Centre d'Education* on the eastern bank of the lake, along with excellent camping facilities.

You pass Mehdiya's ruined **Kasbah** on the road in from Kenitra. Overlooking the estuary, this was built by the Portuguese, extended by the Spanish, demolished and then restored by Moulay Ismail and, finally, knocked about in the course of US troop landings in the last war (see p.273); it shelters the remains of a seventeenth-century governor's palace.

A couple of kilometres inland is the **Lac de Sidi Bourhaba** (see box above), flanked by a *koubba* that is the site of an August **moussem**.

The Plage des Nations and Jardins Exotiques

The **Plage des Nations** (22km from Kenitra) and **Jardins Exotiques** (6km further on) can be reached by bus or *grand taxi* from Kenitra or Rabat/Salé. Coming from Rabat, take bus #28 (every 20min from Salé Bab El Mrisa terminal); this stops and turns round a few kilometres before it reaches the turnoff for the beach. For the gardens you'll have to ask the driver to let you off: the entrance is just to the left of the road and there's a bus stop 20m beyond the turning. Alternatively, there are regular *grands taxis* direct to the beach from Salé, or you could charter a taxi from Rabat or Kenitra.

Plage des Nations

There is a good asphalt road right down to the Plage des Nations, but the #28 bus from Salé (which you can hail from the stop outside the Jardins Exotiques) turns round some way before this turnoff – just after the village of BOUKNADEL, by a café in what seems to be the middle of nowhere. Most of your fellow passengers will get out here and head for the beach: a ten-minute walk along a path that heads off diagonally towards the sea, past a couple of farms, round some woods and then joins the final stretch of the asphalt road.

After this approach, you imagine a rather wild beach, with battered cliffs and a few picnic groups. **Plage des Nations**, or SIDI BOUKNADEL as it's also known, is nothing of the kind. Flanked by a couple of beach cafés and the slick modern complex of the *Hôtel Firdaous* (☎07/73.83.32 – you need to book in July/Aug; ④), it seems more Westernised than Rabat itself. Certainly, unlike the capital's Kasbah or Salé beaches, it's a resort where young Moroccan women feel able to come out for the day, rather than suffer the uncontestedly male domination of the city's beaches. And with everyone here to take a day's holiday, it's a very relaxed and friendly sort of place. The beach itself is excellent, with big, exciting waves – but dangerous currents, so it is patrolled by lifeguards along the central strip. The hotel has a freshwater swimming pool which is open to all for a small charge, plus a snackbar and restaurant.

Jardins Exotiques

The **Jardins Exotiques** were laid out by one M. François in the early 1950s, in what contemporary French guidebooks called "une manière remarquable". They fell into something of a decline in the 1980s but have recently been taken over by the Ministry of the Interior, whose twenty-strong staff of gardeners have been assiduously renovating the various original creations. If you can visit the gardens in spring or early summer, they are a delight.

Entering the gardens (open daily from sunrise to sunset; 10dh admission), you find yourself directed across a series of precarious bamboo bridges and dot-directed routes through a sequence of brilliant regional creations. There is a **Brazilian rain forest**, dense with water and orchids; a formal **Japanese garden**; and then suddenly a great shaft of **French Polynesia**, with rickety summer-houses set amid long pools, turtles paddling past, palm trees all round and terrific flashes of bright-red flowers. The last of the series, returning to a more local level, is an **Andalusian garden** with a fine collection of Moroccan plants.

The gardens, in addition, have a little **zoo**, with Barbary apes from the Middle Atlas, and a rather half-hearted children's playground. There is, as yet, no café.

Rabat

Capital of the nation since independence – and, before that, from 1912 to 1956, of the French Protectorate – **RABAT** is in many ways the city you'd expect: elegant in its spacious European grid, slightly self-conscious in its civilised modern ways, and, as an administrative centre, a little bit dull. If you arrive during Ramadan, you'll find the main boulevards an astonishing night-long promenade – at other times, it's hard to find a café open past ten at night. Rabat, as they tell you in Casa, is *provincial*.

None of this makes any difference to the considerable historic and architectural interest in the city – and across the estuary in Salé – which include some of the finest and oldest Arab monuments in the country, dating from the Almohad and Merenid dynasties. You can spend an enjoyable few days looking round these, and out on the local beaches, and there is a major plus in that, unlike Fes or Marrakesh, you can get round the place quite happily without a guide, and talk in cafés with people who do not depend on tourist money.

Some history

Rabat's **monuments** punctuate the span of Moroccan history. The plains inland, designated *Maroc Utile* by the French, have been occupied and cultivated since Paleolithic times, and both Phoenicians and Carthaginians established trading posts on modern-day Rabat's estuary site.

The earliest known settlement, *Sala*, occupied the citadel known today as **Chellah**. Here, after the demise of the Carthaginians, the **Romans** created their southernmost colony. It lasted well beyond the breakup of the empire in Africa and eventually formed the basis of an independent Berber state, which reached its peak of influence in the eighth century, developing a code of government inspired by the Koran but adapted to Berber customs and needs. It represented a challenge to the Islamic orthodoxy of the **Arab** rulers of the interior, however, and to stamp out the heresy, a *ribat* – the fortified monastery from which the city takes its name – was founded on the site of the present-day Kasbah.

The *ribat's* activities led to Chellah's decline – a process hastened in the eleventh century by the founding of a new town, **Salé**, across the estuary. But with the arrival of the **Almohads** in the twelfth century, the Rabat Kasbah was rebuilt and a city again took shape around it. The Almohad fort, renamed **Ribat El Fathi** (Stronghold of Victory), served as a launching point for the dynasty's campaigns in Spain, which by 1170 had returned virtually all of Andalusia to Muslim rule.

Under the Almohad Caliph **Yacoub El Mansour,** a new imperial capital was created. Its legacy includes the superb **Oudaïa Gate** of the Kasbah, **Bab er Rouah** at the southwest edge of town, and the early stages of the **Hassan Mosque.** Until recent years, this was the largest ever undertaken in Morocco and its minaret, standing high above the river, is still the city's great landmark. Mansour also erected over five kilometres of fortifications – but neither his vision nor his success in maintaining a Spanish empire was to be lasting. He left the Hassan Mosque unfinished, and only in the last sixty years has the city expanded to fill his dark circuit of *pisé* walls.

After Mansour's death, Rabat's significance was dwarfed by the imperial cities of Fes, Meknes and Marrakesh, and the city fell into neglect. Sacked by the Portuguese, it was little more than a village when, as New Salé, it was resettled by seventeenth-century Andalusian refugees. In this revived form, however, it entered into an extraordinary period of international piracy and local autonomy. Its corsair fleets, the **"Sallee Rovers",** specialised in the plunder of merchant ships returning to Europe from West Africa and the Spanish Americas, but on occasion raided as far afield as Plymouth and the Irish coast – Defoe's Robinson Crusoe began his captivity "carry'd prisoner into Sallee, a Moorish port".

The Andalusians, owing no loyalty to the Moorish sultans and practically impregnable within their Kasbah perched high on a rocky bluff above the river, established their own pirate state, the **Republic of the Bou Regreg**. They rebuilt the Medina below the Kasbah in a style reminiscent of their homes in Spanish Badajoz, dealt in arms with the English and French, and even accepted European consuls, before, under Moulay Rashid, and his successor, Moulay Ismail, the town finallly reverted to government control.

Arriving, orientation and hotels

With its **Medina** and **Ville Nouvelle** bounded by the river and Almohad walls, central Rabat never feels like a big city, and indeed all the city's points of interest are within easy walking distance. Our **maps** (a general one is on the next page; an enlargement of the Kasbah des Oudaïas appears on p.246; and Salé is covered in a separate map on p.257) are adequate for most purposes. If you can find one, it is well worth picking up the *ONMT* pamphlet on Rabat in advance; it has a less

POINTS OF ARRIVAL

BY TRAIN
By far the easiest way to arrive. The **Rabat Ville** station (don't get off at *Rabat-Salé*, across the estuary in Salé, or at *Rabat-Agdal*, over to the west) is at the heart of the Ville Nouvelle, with most hotels within a few minutes' walk. Unusually, there are luggage lockers.

BY BUS
The main bus terminal is located in Place Zerktouni – 3km out from the centre by the road junction for Casa and Beni Mellal. To get into town from here (or vice versa), you'll have to take a local bus (#30 and others stop along Bd. Hassan II by the *Hôtel Majestic*) or compete for a *petit taxi* (6dh or so – usually metered – for up to three people). Easier, if you are coming by bus from the north, is to get off in Salé (see p.256) and take a *grand taxi* from there into Rabat; the distance is no greater.

BY GRAND TAXI
Grands taxis for non-local destinations operate from outside the main bus station (see above). Those from/to Casa cost only a couple of dirhams more than the bus and leave more or less continuously through the day. *Grands taxis* to Skhirat, Bouknadel and other local destinations leave from the lengthy and chaotic stand on Bd. Hassan II.

BY AIR
From the **Mohammed V Airport** (out towards Casablanca), buses run to the square outside the *Hôtel Terminus* (by the train station); journey time is approximately 90 minutes. Departures **to the airport** from Rabat are (currently) at 5am, 6.30am, 8.30am, 10am, 12.30pm, 3.30pm, 6.30pm; tickets are sold at a kiosk by the departure point, immediately before the bus leaves. In both directions, specify *le prochain depart* (the next service). *Grands taxis* are an expensive alternative (400dh), unless you can split the fare; the airport is also connected by train with Casablanca (see p.268).

CITY BUSES AND TAXIS

Local bus services radiate out from Bd. Hassan II. Buses #1, #2 and #4 run from here (via Allal Ben Abdallah) to Bab Zaer, by way of Chellah; #6 and #12 cross the bridge to Salé; and #17 heads south to Temara Beach.

Petits and **grands taxis** can also be found on Bd. Hassan II. Note that *petits taxis* are not allowed to run between Rabat and Salé.

detailed plan but shows the location of the bus station, plus the main roads into the city.

Accommodation

Hotel space can be tight in midsummer, and especially in July, when budget-priced rooms, in particular, are at a premium. It's best, if at all possible, to make an advance reservation by phone, and to go for one of the classified hotels, which offer more comfort, for not much more, than the Medina places.

The nearest **campsite** is across the river at **Salé**; it has recently been revamped and is pleasant and well equipped. An alternative, if you have transport, is at **Temara Plage**, 15km south (see p.260).

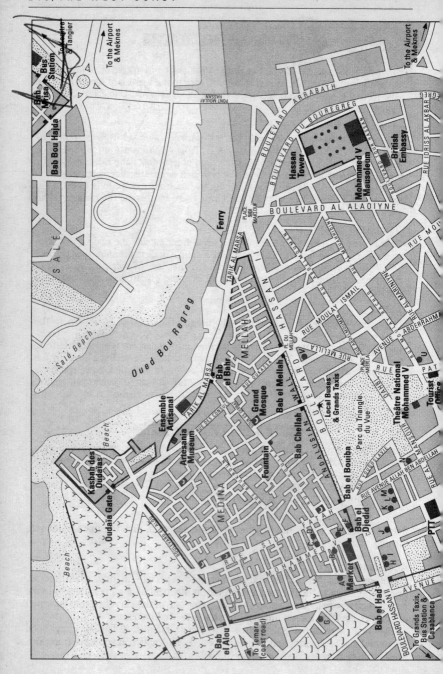

RABAT

Chellah

Bab Zeers

BOULEVARD MOUSSA IBN NOSSAIR

French Embassy

U.S. Embassy

BOULEVARD TARIK IBN ZIAD

Algerian
Embassy

PLACE
LINCOLN

ONMT

RUE AL JAZAIR

AV. DE OUARZAZATE

AVENUE MOHAMMED V

American
Bookstore

British
Council

Archeological
Museum

AVENUE YACOUB AL MANSOUR

RUE MOULAY

HASSAN

LUMUMBA

Cathedral

Flower
Market

American
Embassy

AVENUE

Grand
Mosque

PLACE DE LA MOSQUÉE

AVENUE ALLAL BEN ABDALLAH

RUE ABDOU FARIS EL MARINI

MECHOUAR

RAM
Airport
bus

PLACE DES
ALAOUITES

Rabat ville
Train Station

AVENUE MOHAMMED V

AVENUE MOULAY HASSAN

English
Bookshop

Bab er
Rouah

PLACE
AN NASR

Royal
Palace

AV. IBN TOUMERT

TOUMERT

AVENUE JEAN JAURÈS

AVENUE AN NASR

To Casablanca

200m

0

HOTEL PRICE CODES AND STAR-RATINGS

As of 1993, hotels are no longer obliged to levy set maximum rates, according to their official star-ratings, as had long been the custom. However, **prices** still broadly follow the star-rating system, and this is the basis of our own **hotel price codes** set out below and keyed throughout the guide.

Our code	Official classification	Single room price	Double room price
⓪	Unclassified	25–60dh	40–100dh
①	1*A/1*B	60–105dh	100–125dh
②	2*B/2*A	105–145dh	125–175dh
③	3*B/3*A	145–225dh	175–275dh
④	4*B/4*A	225–400dh	275–500dh
⑤	5*luxury	Upwards of 400dh	Upwards of 500dh

TELEPHONE CODES

All telephone numbers in the Rabat/Kenitra region are prefixed 07. When making a call within the region you omit this prefix. For more explanation of phone codes and making calls within (or to) Morocco, see p.37.

MEDINA HOTELS

These are the pick of the Medina's fourteen hotels; see map p.240.

Hôtel Marrakesh (D), 10 Rue Sebbahi (☎07/72.77.03). One of the better Medina hotels. Basic, with cold showers, but reasonable-sized rooms, and friendly staff. ⓪

Hôtel Maghreb (C), 2 Rue Sebbahi (☎07/73.22.07). A reasonable alternative. ⓪

Hôtel France (A), 46 Souk Semarine (☎07/72.34.57). Has a bit of character, with a banana tree patio and terrace. Basic facilities but excellent public showers in the lane behind. ⓪

Hôtel les Voyageurs (B), 8 Souk Semarine (☎07/72.37.20). A cut above the other Medina hotels – and slightly dearer. Worth booking, as it's a popular choice. ⓪

Hôtel du Centre (E), 1 Rue Nouail (no phone). Clean and decently furnished. ⓪

Hôtel Dorhmi (F), 313 Rue Mohammed V (☎07/72.38.98). Immediately on the right, inside Bab Djedid. A decent hotel with a pleasant café, the *Essalam*, at street level. ⓪

VILLE NOUVELLE HOTELS

Recommendations below are in roughly ascending order of price and are once again keyed on the map (on p.240). Anything much upmarket of the *Hôtel Balima* is not especially worth your money; Rabat's four- and five-star hotels are standard international chain efforts, and there are better places elsewhere if you want to splurge.

Auberge de Jeunesse (G), 34 Rue Marrassa (☎07/72.57.69). Rabat's youth hostel is conveniently sited, just outside the Medina walls. Standards have improved of late and it's now clean, well furnished and to be recommended. IYHF card required, however full it is.

Petit Hôtel Vatel (I), 13 Bd. Hassan II (☎07/72.30.95). Small indeed – just seven rooms – but conveniently sited, and with rooms overlooking a quiet courtyard, and with hot shower. It is not easy to find: look for the *Café-Restaurant Shahrazade*, and go through the arch. ⓪

Hôtel Berlin (K), 261 Av. Mohammed V (☎07/72.34.35). Another good, small hotel (nine rooms), with hot showers; located above a Vietnamese restaurant. ⓪

Hôtel Central (O), 2 Rue Al Basra (☎☎07/70.73.56). A good budget choice, and, with 34 rooms, likely to have space. Nice location by the *Hôtel Balima*, near the train station. ①

Hôtel Gaulois (J), corner of Rue Hims and Av. Mohammed V (☎07/72.30.22). One of a cluster of budget hotels at the bottom end of Av. Mohammed V; reasonable for the price. ①

Hôtel Majestic (H), 121 Bd. Hassan II (☎07/72.29.97). A nice old hotel with a faded charm, though prices are a bit high for its class. It's often full – you'd be lucky to find a room much after midday. The café opposite will serve food and drink in the hotel garden. ①

Hôtel Velleda (Q), 106 Av. Allal Ben Abdallah (☎07/76.95.31). A decent hotel near the train station; it's not very easy to find, being tucked away on the fourth floor (there is a lift) above a dry cleaners. ②

Hôtel de la Paix (M), 2 Rue Ghazza (☎07/72.29.26). A reasonably pleasant downtown standby; especially useful for single rooms. ②

Splendid Hôtel (L), 24 Rue Ghazza (☎07/72.32.83). A nice old hotel that has a sense of better days; the best of its large rooms overlook a garden courtyard. Opposite is the *Café-Restaurant Ghazza*, good for a meal at most times of day or night. ②

Royal Hôtel (N), corner of Rue Amman and Av. Allal Ben Abdallah (☎07/72.11.71). Reasonable rooms, close to the Parc du Triangle de Vue. ②

Grand Hôtel (U), 19 Rue Patrice Lumumba (☎07/72.72.85). Quiet, old established hotel with a bar and restaurant. ②

Hôtel Bouregreg (V), corner of Rue Nador/Bd. Hassan II (☎07/72.41.10). The former *Hôtel Rex*, renovated and under new management; faces the Medina walls. Recommended. ②

Hôtel Balima (P), corner of Rue Jakarta and Av. Mohammed V (☎07/70.86.25). This was once Rabat's top hotel, and, though long superseded, it retains a deco grandeur – as well as moderate-priced *suites*! Thami El Glaoui, Pasha of Marrakesh, stayed in one on his visits to the city in the 1950s, and if you can afford it, you could do no better than to do the same. ③

Hôtel d'Orsay (R), 11 Av. Moulay Youssef, on Place de la Gare (☎07/76.13.19). Conveniently located by the station. A bit pricey but friendly, helpful and efficient, and a good mid-range alternative if the *Balima* is full. ③

Hôtel Belère (S), 33 Av. Moulay Youssef (☎07/76.99.01). Comfortable, air-conditioned tour group hotel. ④

Hôtel Chellah (T), 2 Rue d'Infi (☎07/76.54.54). A rather characterless block, but has a good grill-restaurant, *Le Kanoun*. ④

The Medina and souks

Rabat's **Medina** – all that there was of the city until the French arrived in 1912 – is a compact quarter, wedged on two sides by the sea and the river, on the others by the twelfth-century Almohad and seventeenth-century Andalusian walls. It is not the most interesting Medina in the country – open and orderly in comparison to those of Fes or Marrakesh, for example – but coming here from the adjacent avenues of the modern capital it remains a surprise. In appearance, the quarter is still essentially the town created by Andalusian Muslim refugees from Badajoz in Spain, and with these external features intact, its way of life seems remarkably at odds with the government business and cosmopolitanism of the Ville Nouvelle.

That this is possible – here and throughout the old cities of Morocco – is largely due to **Marshal Lyautey**, the first, and certainly the most sympathetic to the indigenous culture, of France's Resident Generals. Colonising Algeria over the previous century, the French had destroyed most of the Arab towns, replacing their traditional structures (evolved through the needs of Islamic customs) with completely European plans. In Rabat, Lyautey found this system already underway, the builders tearing down parts of the Medina for the construction of a new town and administrative quarters. Realising the aesthetic loss – and the inappropriateness of wholesale "Europeanisation" – he ordered work to be halted and the Ville Nouvelle built outside the walls.

It was a precedent accepted throughout the French and Spanish zones of the colony, a policy which inevitably created "native quarters", but one which also preserved continuity, maintained the nation's past and, at least so Lyautey believed, showed the special relationship of the Protectorate.

Into the Medina

The basic grid-like regularity of the Medina, cut by a number of long main streets, makes this a good place to get to grips with the feel of a Moroccan city. In plan it is typical, with a main market street – **Rue Souika** and its continuation **Souk es Sebbat** – running beside the Grand Mosque, and behind it a residential area scattered with smaller *souks* and "parish" mosques. The buildings, characteristically Andalusian, in the style of Tetouan or Chaouen, are part stone and part whitewash, with splashes of yellow and turquoise and great, dark-wood studded doors.

From **Bd. Hassan II**, a series of streets give access to the Medina, all of them leading more or less directly through the quarter, to emerge near the Kasbah and the old, hillside cemetery. On the west side, the two main streets – **Rue Mohammed V** and **Rue Sidi Fatah** – are really continuations of Ville Nouvelle avenues, though, flanked by working-class café-restaurants and cell-like hotels, their character is immediately different. Entering along either, past a modern food market and a handful of stalls selling fruit, orange juice and snacks, you can turn very shortly to the right and come out on the cubicle shops of **Rue Souika**. Dominated by textiles and silverware along the street's initial stretch, these give way to a concentration of *babouche* and other shoe stalls as you approach the Grand Mosque. They are all fairly everyday – though quite high quality – shops, not for the most part geared to tourists.

Stalls selling cheaper goods, and the *joutia* (flea market), are off towards the river, round the old Jewish quarter of the Mellah (see below). Along the way are few buildings of particular interest, as most of the medieval city – which predated that of the Andalusians on this site – was been destroyed by Portuguese raids in the sixteenth century.

The **Grand Mosque**, founded by the Merenids in the fourteenth century, is a partial exception, though it has been considerably rebuilt – its minaret, for example, was only completed in 1939. Entry to the mosque is, as throughout Morocco, forbidden to non-Muslims. Opposite, there is a small example of Merenid decoration in the stone facade of a public **fountain**, which now forms the front of an Arabic bookshop.

The Mellah and Joutia

The most direct approach from Bd. Hassan II to the Grand Mosque section of the Medina is through **Bab Chellah**, which gives way onto a broad, tree-lined, pedestrian way. Alternatively, continuing a couple of blocks (past the *Hôtel Bou Regreg*), you can go in by the **Bab El Mellah**, which gives onto Rue Oukassa.

To the east of this street is the **Mellah**, the old Jewish quarter, and still the poorest and most rundown area of the city. It no longer has a significant Jewish population, though some of its seventeen synagogues survive in various forms. (The only one synagogue functioning in Rabat today is in a modern building, a block away in the Ville Nouvelle). The quarter itself, where all of the city's Jews were once required to live, was created only in 1808; Jews previously owned several of the mansions along Rue des Consuls, a bit further to the north.

With its meat and produce markets, the Mellah looks a somewhat uninviting and impenetrable area, but it is worth walking through towards the river. The **Joutia**, or **flea market**, spreads out here along the streets below Souk es Sebbat, down to Bab El Bahr. There are clothes, pieces of machinery whose parts can no longer be replaced and (something you don't see too often) a number of vendors touting wonderful old movie posters, garishly illustrating titles like *Police Militaire* and *La Fille du Désert*.

Towards the Kasbah: Rue des Consuls

Beyond the Mellah, heading towards the Kasbah, you can walk out by **Bab El Bahr** and follow an avenue near the riverside up to the Oudaïa Gate; to the left of this road is a small **Artesania Museum** (officially open 9am–noon & 3–6pm but often closed), to the right a run of the mill **Centre Artesanal.**

Rue des Consuls, a block inland, is a more interesting approach; like the Mellah, this, too, used to be a reserved quarter – the only street of the nineteenth-century city where European consuls were permitted to live. Many of the residency buildings survive, as do a number of impressive merchants' *fondouks* – most in the alleys off to the left. The main street, particularly at its upper end, is largely a centre for **rug and carpet shops** and on Tuesday and Thursday mornings becomes a **souk,** with locals bringing carpets – new and old – to sell. Rabat carpets, woven with very bright dyes (which, if vegetable-based, will fade), are a traditional cottage industry in the Medina, though they're now often made in factories, one of which you can see on the Kasbah's *platforme* (see p.247).

The Kasbah des Oudaïas

The site of the original *ribat* and citadel of the Almohad, Merenid and Andalusian towns, the **Kasbah des Oudaïas** is a striking and evocative quarter. Its principal gateway, the **Bab Oudaïa**, is perhaps the most beautiful in the Moorish world, and within the Kasbah walls is one of the country's best craft museums and a perfect Andalusian garden.

The Bab Oudaïa

The **Bab Oudaïa**, like so many of the great external monuments of Morocco, is of Almohad foundation. Built around 1195, concurrently with the Hassan Tower, it was inserted by Yacoub El Mansour within a line of walls already built by his grandfather, Abd El Moumen. The walls in fact extended well to its west, leading down to the sea at the edge of the Medina, and the gate cannot have been designed for any real defensive purpose – its function and importance must have been purely ceremonial. It was to be the heart of the Kasbah, its chambers acting as a courthouse and staterooms, with everything of importance taking place within its immediate confines. The **Souk El Ghezel** – the main commercial centre of the medieval town with its wool and slave markets – was located just outside, while the original sultanate's palace stood immediately inside it.

The effect of the gate is startling. It doesn't impress so much by its size, which is not unusual for an Almohad structure, as by the visual strength and simplicity of its decoration. This is based on a typically Islamic rhythm, establishing a tension between the exuberant, outward expansion of the arches and the heavy, enclosing rectangle of the gate itself. Looking at the two for a few minutes, you begin to sense a kind of optical illusion – the shapes appear suspended by the

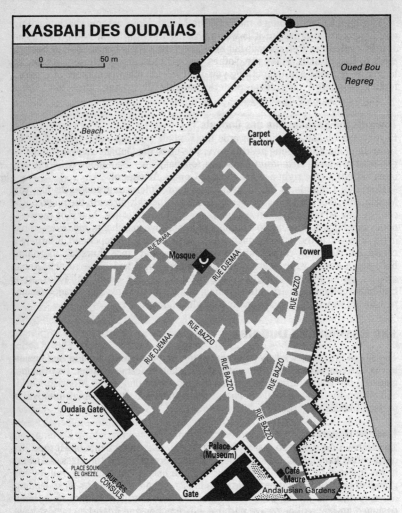

KASBAH DES OUDAÏAS

0 50 m

Oued Bou Regreg

Beach

Carpet Factory

RUE ZIRARA

Mosque

RUE DJEMAA

Tower

RUE BAZZO

RUE DJEMAA

RUE BAZZO

RUE BAZZO

RUE BAZZO

Beach

RUE DJEMAA

RUE BAZZO

Oudaïa Gate

Palace (Museum)

PLACE SOUK EL GHEZEL

RUE DES CONSULS

Café Maure

Gate

Andalusian Gardens

great rush of movement from the centre of the arch. The basic feature is, of course, the arch, which here is a sequence of three, progressively more elaborate: first, the basic horseshoe; then, two "filled" or decorated ones, the latter with the distinctive Almohad *darj w ktarf* patterning, a cheek-and-shoulder design somewhat like a fleur-de-lis. At the top, framing the design, is a band of geometric ornamentation, cut off in what seems to be an arbitrary manner but which again creates the impression of movement and continuation outside the gate.

The dominant motifs – scallop-shell-looking palm fronds – are also characteristically Almohad, though without any symbolic importance; in fact, there's very little that's symbolic in the European sense in any Islamic decoration, the object being merely to distract the eye sufficiently to allow contemplation.

Around the Kasbah

You can enter the **Kasbah** proper through the Oudaïa Gate (or, if it's closed, through the small gateway on its right), or by a lower, horseshoe arch at the base of the ceremonial stairway. This latter approach leads directly to the **Andalusian gardens** and **palace museum**, which can also be reached fairly easily after a brief loop through the Kasbah.

An airy, village-like part of the city, the Kasbah is a pleasant quarter in which to wander – and not remotely dangerous or "closed to visitors", as the hustlers round the gate may try to suggest. Hardly more than 150m from one end to the other, it's not a place where you really need a guide; but if you're approached, talk to the hustlers, be easygoing and explain you're only wandering down to *le platforme*.

Once inside the Oudaïa Gate, it would actually be hard not to find the way down to the *platforme* since there's just one main street, **Rue Djemaa** (Street of the Mosque), which runs straight down to a broad belvedere/terrace commanding views of the river and sea. Along the way, you pass by the **Kasbah Mosque**, the city's oldest, founded in 1050, though rebuilt in the eighteenth century by an English renegade known as Ahmed El Inglise – one of a number of European pirates who joined up with the Sallee Rovers.

El Inglisi was also responsible for several of the forts built below and round the **Platforme**, their gun positions echoed across the estuary in Salé. The Bou Regreg ("Father of Reflection") River is quite open at this point and it would appear to have left the corsair fleets vulnerable, harboured a little downstream, where the fishing boats today ferry people across to Salé. In fact, a long sandbank lies submerged across the mouth of the estuary – a feature much exploited by the shallow-keeled pirate ships, which would draw the merchant ships in pursuit, only to leave them stranded within the sights of the city's cannon. This is action which you can imagine, up here amid the low-lying alleys and the sea towers, though, as so often in Morocco, it is hard to come to terms with just how recent a past it is.

From the *platforme*, it is possible to climb down towards the *Caravelle Restaurant* – a good lunch stop – and the **beach**, crowded with locals throughout the summer, as is the Salé strip across the water. Neither of these beaches is very inviting, in fact, and if you're more interested in swimming than in keeping your head above the polluted water, you'd be better off at the more relaxed (and less exclusively male) sands at the Plage des Nations or Temara (see pp.236 and 260).

The Palace Museum and Gardens

Getting down to the **Palace Museum** and gardens is fairly straightforward: from the main Kasbah street, Rue Gazzo zigzags down towards them.

Depending on which fork you take, you'll come out either by the entrance to the palace or at the **Café Mauré** – beside the gardens. Oddly enough, the café is not at all "Moorish" but it's a fine place to retreat: high on a terrace overlooking the river, serving mint tea, brewed up on an ancient brazier, and trays of pastries. It is used as much by Moroccans as tourists, and is ordinarily priced.

The **Palace** itself is seventeenth-century, one of many built by Moulay Ismail, the first sultan since Almohad times to force a unified control over the country. Ismail, whose base was at Meknes, gave Rabat – or New Salé, as it was then known – a relatively high priority. Having subdued the pirates' republic, he took over the Kasbah as a garrison for the Oudaïas – Saharan tribesmen who accepted military service in return for tax exemption, and who formed an important part of his mercenary army. This move was in part because they proved uncontrollable in Fes or Meknes, but it was also an effective way of ensuring that the pirates kept up their tribute with a constant supply of slaves and booty.

An interesting building in its own right, the palace today houses a fine **Museum of Moroccan Arts** (open mid–June to mid–Sept 9am–3pm; rest of the year 8.30am–noon & 2.30–6pm; closed Tues; 10dh). The design of the building is classic: a series of reception rooms grouped round a central court, giving access to the private quarters where you can take a look at the small hammam – a feature of all noble mansions. Within the main building, there are displays of Berber and Arab jewellery from most of the regions of Morocco, while the main reception hall has been furnished in the styles of nineteenth-century Rabat and Fes. A room just off to the left as you leave is often kept shut, though opened on request; once the palace mosque, it houses a very fine display of local carpets.

The museum collections – including groups of traditional costumes, which again reveal the startling closeness of a medieval past – are continued in a series of rooms bordering on the beautiful "**Andalusian Garden**". Occupying the old palace grounds, this was actually constructed by the French in the present century – though true to Spanish-Andalusian tradition, with deep, sunken beds of shrubs and flowering annuals. If you're familiar with Granada, it is illuminating to compare this (the authentic Moorish concept) with the neat box hedges with which the Alhambra has been restored. But historical authenticity aside, it is a delightful place, full of the scent of datura, bougainvillea and a multitude of herbs and flowers. It has a definite modern role, too, as a meeting place for women, who gather here in dozens of small groups on a Friday or Sunday afternoon.

The Hassan Mosque and Mohammed V Mausoleum

The most ambitious of all Almohad buildings, the **Hassan Mosque** and its vast minaret dominates almost every view of the capital – a majestic sight from the Kasbah, from Salé, or glimpsed as you arrive across the river by train. If it had been completed, it would (in its time) have been the second largest mosque in the Islamic world, outflanked only by the one in Smarra, Iraq. Even today its size seems a novelty.

There is also the poignancy of its ruin. Designed by El Mansour as the centre-piece of the new capital and as a celebration of his great victory over the Spanish kings at Alarcos, the mosque's construction seems to have been more or less abandoned at his death in 1199. The tower was probably left much as it appears today; the mosque's hall, roofed in cedar, was used until the Great Earthquake of 1755 (which destroyed central Lisbon) brought down its central columns. Its extent, however, must always have seemed an elaborate folly. Morocco's most important mosque, the Kairaouine in Fes, is less than half the Hassan's size, but served a much greater population, with adequate space for 20,000 worshippers. Bearing in mind that it is only men who gather for the weekly Friday prayer – when a town traditionally comes together in its Grand Mosque – Rabat would have needed a population of well over 100,000 to make adequate use of the Hassan's capacity. As it was, the city never really took off under the later Almohads and Merenids, and when Leo Africanus came here in 1600, he found no more than a hundred households, gathered for security within the Kasbah.

The **tower**, or minaret, was begun by Yacoub El Mansour in 1195 – at the same time as the Koutoubia in Marrakesh and the Giralda in Seville – and it is one of the few Moroccan buildings which approach the European idea of monumentality. This is due in part to its site, on a level above the river and most of the city, but perhaps equally to its unfinished solidity. The other great Moroccan minarets, perfectly balanced by their platform decoration and lanterns, are left "hanging" as if with no particular weight or height. The Hassan Tower, with no such movement, stands firmly rooted in the ground.

The minaret is unusually positioned at the centre rather than the northern corner of the rear of the mosque. Some 50m tall in its present state, it would probably have been around 80m if finished to normal proportions – a third again the height of Marrakesh's Koutoubia. Despite its apparent simplicity, it is perhaps the most complex of all Almohad structures. Each facade is different, with a distinct combination of patterning, yet the whole intricacy of blind arcades and interlacing curves is based on just two formal designs. On the south and west faces these are the *darj w ktarf* of the Oudaïa Gate; on the north and east are the *shabka* (net) motif, an extremely popular form adapted by the Almohads from the lobed arches of the Cordoba Grand Mosque – and still in modern use.

The Mohammed V Mausoleum

Facing the tower – in an assertion of Morocco's historical independence and continuity – are the **Mosque and Mausoleum of Mohammed V**, begun on the sultan's death in 1961 and inaugurated six years later. The **Mosque**, extending between a stark pair of pavillions, gives a somewhat foreshortened idea of how the Hassan Mosque must once have appeared, roofed in its traditional green tiles.

The **Mausoleum**, designed by a Vietnamese architect, Vo Toan, was one of the great prestige projects of modern Morocco. Its brilliantly surfaced marbles and spiralling designs, however, seem to pay homage to traditional Moroccan techniques, while failing to capture their rhythms and unity. It is, nevertheless, an important shrine for Moroccans – and one which, unusually, non-Muslims are permitted to visit. You file past fabulously costumed royal guards to an interior balcony; the tomb, carved from white onyx, lies below, groups of old men squatting beside it, reading from the Koran.

Around the Ville Nouvelle

French in construction, style and feel, the **Ville Nouvelle** provides the main focus of Rabat's life, above all in the cafés and promenades of the broad, tree-lined Av. Mohammed V, and in the pleasant **Parque du Triangle de Vue**, opposite the south wall of the Medina – popular afternoon meeting places (they close around 6pm). Another attractive and colourful spot is the **Flower Market**, held in a sunken garden just to the north of Av. Moulay Hassan.

There's a certain grandeur in some of the old, *Mauresque* public buildings around the main boulevards, too, which were built with as much desire to impress as any earlier epoch. However, it is the **Almohad walls and gates**, the **citadel of Chellah** (see the following section) and the excellent **Archaeological Museum** which hold most of interest in the quarter.

The walls and gates

More-or-less complete sections of the **Almohad walls** run right down from the Kasbah to the Royal Palace and beyond – an extraordinary monument to Yacoub El Mansour's vision. Along their course four of the original **gates** survive. Three

– **Bab El Alou, Bab Zaer** and **Bab El Had** – are very modest. The fourth, **Bab er Rouah** (Gate of the Wind), is on an entirely different scale, recalling and in many ways rivalling the Oudaïa.

Contained within a massive stone bastion, **Bab er Rouah** again achieves the tension of movement – with its sunlike arches contained within a square of Koranic inscription – and a similar balance between simplicity and ornament. The east side, approached from outside the walls, is the main facade, and must have been designed as a monumental approach to the city; the shallow-cut, floral relief between arch and square is arguably the finest anywhere in Morocco. Inside, you can appreciate the gate's archetypal defensive structure – the three domed chambers aligned to force a sharp double turn. They are used for exhibitions and usually open.

From Bab er Rouah, it's a fifteen-minute walk down towards the last Almohad gate, the much-restored **Bab Zaer**, and the entrance to the **Necropolis of Chellah**. On the way, you pass a series of modern gates leading off to the vast enclosures of the **Royal Palace** – which is really more a collection of palaces, built mainly in the nineteenth century and decidedly off-limits to casual visitors – and, off to the left (opposite the *Hôtel Chellah*), the Archaeological Museum.

The Archaeological Museum

Rabat's Archaeological Museum (open mid–June to mid–Sept 9am–3pm; rest of the year 8.30am–noon & 2.30–6pm; closed Tues; 10dh) is by far the most important in Morocco. Although small – surprisingly so in a country which saw substantial Phoenician and Carthaginian settlement and three centuries of Roman rule – it houses a small but exceptional collection of Roman era bronzes.

The bronzes, displayed in a special annexe, date from the first and second centuries AD and were found mainly at the provincial capital of Volubilis (see p.139), together with a few pieces from Chellah and the colonies of Banasa and Thamusida. Highlights include superb figures of a guard dog and a rider, and two magnificent portrait heads, reputedly those of Cato the Younger (Caton d'Utique) and Juba II – the last significant ruler of the Romanised Berber kingdoms of Mauretania and Numidia before the assertion of direct imperial rule. Both of these busts were found in the House of Venus at Volubilis.

The Chellah Necropolis

The most beautiful of Moroccan ruins, **Chellah** (open sunrise to sunset; 10dh) is a startling sight as you emerge from the long avenues of the Ville Nouvelle. Walled and towered, it seems a much larger enclosure than the map suggests, and it feels for a moment as if you've come upon a second Medina. The site is, in fact, long uninhabited – since 1154, when it was abandoned in favour of Salé across the Bou Regreg. But for almost a thousand years prior to that, Chellah (or *Sala Colonia*, as it was known) had been a thriving city and port, one of the last to sever links with the Roman Empire and the first to proclaim Moulay Idriss founder of Morocco's original Arab dynasty. An apocryphal local tradition maintains that the Prophet himself also prayed at a shrine here.

Under the Almohads, the site was already a royal burial ground, but most of what you see today, including the gates and enclosing wall, is the legacy of the Merenid sultan, **Abou El Hassan** (1331–51). The greatest of Merenid rulers,

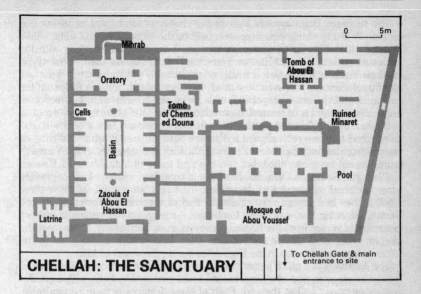

CHELLAH: THE SANCTUARY

↓ To Chellah Gate & main entrance to site

conquering and controlling the Maghreb as far east as Tunis, Abou El Hassan, "The Black Sultan", was also their most prolific builder. In addition to Chellah, he was responsible for important mosques in Fes and Tlemcen, as well as the beautiful *medersas* of Salé and Meknes.

The **main gate** here is the most surprising of Merenid monuments, its turreted bastions creating an almost Gothic appearance. Its base is recognisably Almohad, but each element has become inflated, and the combination of simplicity and solidity has gone. In its original state, with bright-coloured marble and tile decoration, the effect must have been incredibly gaudy – a bit like the nineteenth-century palaces you see today in Fes and Marrakesh. An interesting technical innovation, however, are the stalactite (or "honeycomb") corbels which form the transition from the bastion's semi-octagonal towers to their square platforms; these were to become a feature of Merenid building. The Kufic inscription above the gate is from the Koran and begins with the invocation: "I take refuge in Allah, against Satan, the stoned one ... "

The Sanctuary

There are usually a number of guides hanging around the gate, but hiring them is not mandatory – once inside, things are clear enough. Off to your left, in a state of long-suspended excavation, are the main **Roman ruins** (closed off for many years past), including the visible outlines of a forum, temple and craftsmen's quarter. The **Islamic ruins** are down to the right, within a second inner sanctuary approached along a broad path through half-wild gardens of banana, orange and ancient fig trees, sunflowers, dahlias and datura plants.

Their most prominent and picturesque feature is a tall stone-and-tile minaret, a ludicrously oversized stork's nest perched invariably on its summit. Storks, along with swallows and crows, have a certain sanctity in Morocco, and their presence on minarets is a sign of good fortune.

The sanctuary itself appears a confusing cluster of tombs and ruins, but it is essentially just two buildings: a mosque, built by the second Merenid sultan, Abou Youssef (1258–86), and a *zaouia*, or mosque-monastery, added along with the enclosure walls by Abou El Hassan. You enter directly into the *sahn*, or courtyard, of **Abou Youssef's Mosque**, a small and presumably private structure built as a funerary dedication. It is now very much in ruins, though you can make out the colonnades of the inner prayer hall with its *mihrab* to indicate the direction of prayer. To the right is its minaret, now reduced to the level of the mosque's roof.

Behind, both within and outside the sanctuary enclosure, are a series of scattered **royal tombs** – each aligned so that the dead, dressed in white and lying on their right sides, may face Mecca to await the Call of Judgement. Abou Youssef's tomb has not been identified, but you can find those of both **Abou El Hassan** and his wife **Shams ed Douna**. Hassan's is contained within a kind of pavilion whose external wall retains its decoration, the *darj w ktarf* motif set above three small arches in a design very similar to that of the Hassan Tower. Shams ed Douna, (Morning Sun) has only a tombstone – a long, pointed rectangle covered in a mass of verses from the Koran. A convert from Christianity, Shams was the mother of Abou El Hassan's rebel son, Abou Inan, whose uprising led to the sultan's death as a fugitive in the High Atlas during the winter of 1352.

The **Zaouia** is in a much better state of preservation, its structure, like Abou El Hassan's *medersas,* that of a long, central court enclosed by cells, with a smaller oratory or prayer hall at the end. Each of these features is quite recognisable, along with those of the latrine, preceding the main court, for the worshippers' purification. There are fragments of *zellij* (mosaic tilework) on some of the colonnades and on the minaret, which again give an idea of its original brightness, and there are traces, too, of the *mihrab's* elaborate stucco decoration. Five-sided, the **mihrab** has a narrow passageway (now blocked with brambles) leading to the rear – built so that pilgrims might make seven circuits round it. This was once believed to give the equivalent merit of the *hadj*, the trip to Mecca: a tradition, with that of Muhammad's visit, probably invented and propagated by the *zaouia's* keepers to increase their revenue.

Off to the right and above the sanctuary enclosure are a group of **koubbas** – the domed tombs of local saints or *marabouts* – and beyond them a **spring pool**, enclosed by low, vaulted buildings. This is held sacred, along with the eels which swim in its waters, and women still bring hard-boiled eggs to invoke assistance in fertility and childbirth.

Eating and drinking

For a capital city, Rabat is pretty quiet. By 9.30 at night, the restaurants are closing up and most of the population home. Nonetheless, the city's café life is pleasant, and it has one of the country's best collections of restaurants – many of them inexpensive.

Medina café-restaurants

As ever, the cheapest places to eat are to be found in the **Medina**. Just on the edge of the quarter, down Rue Mohammed V and along Rue Souika, there are a string of good everyday **café-restaurants** – clean enough and serving regular Moroccan fare. They are excellent value, especially at lunchtime, when many have fixed-price meals for the office and shop workers. Alternatively, for only a few dirhams, you can pick up a range of snacks and juices just inside the Medina walls (by the market shown on our map).

Ville Nouvelle restaurants

In the **Ville Nouvelle** you can pick from a fine selection of Moroccan and French restaurants, plus a few Oriental places, if you want a change of cuisine. Worthwhile choices, in roughly ascending order of price, include:

Café-Restaurant El Bahia, Bd. Hassan II (built into the Andalusian wall, close by the junction with Av. Mohammed V). Reasonably priced *tajines*, kebabs and salads, served in a pleasant courtyard. Cheap to moderate.

Café-Restaurant Shahrazade, 119 Bd. Hassan II, near the *Petit Hôtel Vatel*. Quick, friendly service, in or out of doors. Cheap to moderate.

Café-Restaurant Mona Lisa, Passage Derby – a small square at 258 Av. Mohammed V. Good place for an early evening meal; leisurely and a yound crowd. Cheap to moderate.

Le Clef, Rue Hatim – a narrow sidestreet just off Av. Moulay Youssef, next to the *Hôtel d'Orsay*. Downstairs in the bar serious drinking goes on, but the restaurant upstairs is quiet and does good French and Moroccan dishes. Moderate.

Café-Restaurant de la Paix, 1 Av. Moulay Youssef, just off Place de la Gare. Again, some heavy drinking in the ground floor bar, but you can eat well outside (in an old French-style glass corridor) or outside. Moderate.

Café-Restaurant Français, 3 Av. Moulay Youssef, just off Place de la Gare. Another upstairs restaurant – arguably the best around the train station. Moderate.

Restaurant Hong Kong, 261 Av. Mohammed V (on the first floor, entry through a tourist shop). A Vietnamese restaurant – despite the name – and very good. Moderate.

Restaurant La Pagode, 13 Rue Baghdad – parallel to (and south of) the train station. Small restaurant serving Vietnamese and Chinese dishes. Moderate.

Le Fouquet's, 285 Av. Mohammed V. Fish and seafood restaurant which receives mixed reports. On good days, it's good, but it doesn't always get the catch in. Moderate.

Restaurant l'Oasis, 7 Rue Al Osquofiah. Well-prepared and generous Moroccan dishes, including a delicious chicken in honey. Moderate.

Restaurant Saïdoune, in the mall at 467 Av. Mohammed V, opposite the *Hôtel Terminus*. A good Lebanese restaurant run by an Iraqi; also a bar. Moderate.

Café-Restaurant Saadi, 81 bis Av. Allal Ben Abdallah, on the corner with Rue El Kahira. The café is on the street, with a restaurant part in the arcade at the side. Fine *couscous* and *tajines*; beer and wine. Moderate.

La Bamba, 3 Rue Tanta – a small sidestreet behind the *Hôtel Balima*. Spanish-style fish and seafood. Moderate.

La Mamma, 6 Rue Tanta. *La Bamba*'s Italian-style rival. Pizzas and grills. Moderate.

Hôtel Balima, Av. Mohammed V. Inexpensive dishes in the snackbar; pricier ones in the main restaurant (open from 8.30pm), but they're nothing special – the bar and café terrace under the trees is the thing here. Moderate.

Le Mandarin, 100 Av. Abdel Krim Al Kattabi (☎07/72.46.99; closed Wed). Popular business restaurant in L'Ocean quarter, southwest of the Bab Oudaïa. The best Oriental food in the city. Moderate to expensive.

Koutoubia, 10 Rue Pierre Pavent (☎07/72.01.25). An upmarket bar and restaurant, which claims King Hassan among past clientele, and a patron who knew his father, Mohammed V. Excellent cooking. Expensive (but not cripplingly so).

Cafés, bars and nightlife

Avenues Mohammed V and Allal Ben Abdallah have some excellent **cafés**, for coffee, soft drinks and pastries. Particularly pleasant spots include the **Hôtel Balima** terrace café (very popular with locals – and a bit cruisy), the **Café Mauré** in the Kasbah, and the café in the shady **Parc du Triangle de Vue**, just south of Bd. Hassan II, which is usually full of students working or arguing over a mint tea.

Bars – outside the main hotels – are few and far between. The one inside the *Hôtel Balima* is as good a place as any; it tends to stay open late, if there are customers, and it is popular with Moroccans – many of whom come to watch Sky Channel on its TV, especially if there's football on. Other bars are to be found at the restaurants *Le Clef, de la Paix, Saïdoune* and *Koutoubia* (see p.253), and there are a couple of places – the *Baghdad Bar* and *Dolce Vita* – on Rue Tanta, behind the *Hôtel Balima*.

After these have closed, about the only **late-night options** are a string of **disco-bars** around Place de Melilla (east of the Parc du Triangle de Vue), and on Rue Patrice Lumumba – where you'll find the *Biba* and *Jefferson* discos. Another popular dance-club is *5th Avenue*, located in the Agdal quarter, south of the centre, and easiest reached by *petit taxi*.

Directory

Airlines *Royal Air Maroc* is just across from the train station on Av. Mohammed V (☎07/70.97.66); *Air France* (☎07/70.72.28) is on the same avenue at no. 281, and *Iberia* at no. 104, 2nd floor. *British Airways* have no Rabat office.

American Express have no agent in Rabat; their nearest office is in Casablanca.

Animal welfare *SPANA* have an animal refuge in Rabat, located at 1 Bd. de l'Océan (☎07/79.00.43).

Banks Most are along Av. Allal Ben Abdallah and Av. Mohammed V. The *BMCE* (change facilities open Mon–Fri 8am–8pm, Sat & Sun 10am–2pm & 4–8pm) have offices at 260 Av. Mohammed V and at the train station; they handle *VISA/Mastercard*, travellers' cheques and cash.

Beaches Nearest options are the Kasbah and Salé beaches, with the latter best reached by one of the ferryboats which cross from below the Mellah. For clearer waters, head by bus to either Plage des Nations (see p.236) or Temara (see p.260).

Books The *American Bookstore*, Rue Tanja (marked on our map) has a good selection of Penguin novels, etc, along with an enterprising shelf on Moroccan architecture, Islam and some of Paul Bowles's translations of Moroccan fiction. The *English Bookshop*, 7 Rue Alyamama (again marked on our map), stocks and exchanges a wide selection of second-hand paperbacks. You can get coffee-table books on Morocco and phrasebooks from several of the bookshops along Av. Mohammed V.

Car hire Cheaper deals tend to be available in Casablanca, but if you want a car in Rabat, there are twenty or so hire agencies to choose from. A full list of these is available from the ONMT tourist office (see below). Main companies include: *Avis*, 7 Rue Abou Faris Al Mairini (☎07/76.97.59); *Hertz*, 467 Av. Mohammed V (☎07/73.44.75); *InterRent*, 25 bis Rue Patrice Lumumba (☎07/72.23.21); and *Tourist Car*, 12 Rue Hassan II (1st floor; ☎07/72.62.31).

Car repairs Try *Concorde* (6 Av. Allal Ben Abdallah) or, particularly for Renaults, the garage at 14 Av. Misr.

Cinemas There are several cinemas on Av. Mohammed V; *Cinema Martignan*, below *Le Fouquet's* restaurant has the latest US and French films. Near the *Hotel Royal*, is the *Cinema Royal*, more given to Kung Fu and Asian romances. More of an arts cinema is the smaller *Salle de 7ème Art* on Ave. Allal Ben Abdallah; advance booking advisable.

Culture The *Théâtre National Mohammed V* on Rue Cairo (south of Bd. Hassan II – see map) puts on a range of concerts (Arabic and Western classical music) and films.

Embassies/Consulates include: **Britain**, 17 Bd. Tour Hassan (☎07/72.09.05 or 07/73.14.03); **Canada**, 13 Zankat Joafar Essadik (☎07/77.13.75); **Denmark**, 4 Rue de Khemisset (☎07/73.25.31); **Netherlands**, 40 Rue de Tunis (☎07/73.35.12); **Norway**, 13 Zankat Joafar

NORTH AND WEST AFRICAN VISAS

The following North and West African nations have consulates, with visa issuing facilities, in Rabat:

Algeria, 10 Zankat Azrou (☎07/76.50.92; Mon–Fri 9.30am–2.30pm). If you turn up at 8.30am, you should be able to collect it the same day; requires four passport photographs; fee is about 60dh but varies by nationality.

Côte d'Ivoire, BP 192, 21 Zankat Teddis (☎07/76.31.51).

Guinea, 15 Rue Hamza, Agdal (☎07/73.27.06). Doesn't usually issue visas unless you are flying direct to Guinea.

Mauritania, 9 Rue Taza, by Tour Hassan (☎07/75.68.17). Rules change almost daily – at time of writing they don't issue visas for overland travel.

Mali, 58 Cité Olm, Soussi, behind Hôtel Hyatt Regency. Visas issued the same day; requires two passport photos; fee is 240dh.

Nigeria, 70 Av. Omar Ibn al-Khattab, Agdal (☎07/77.18.56). Visas issued next day; requires three photos; fee varies with nationality.

Senegal. Visas are issued only at their **Casablanca consulate**: near the *Hôtel Almohades* (☎02/75.41.71; 9am–3pm; 3 photos; 100dh; issued the same day).

Tunisia, 6 Av. de Fes (☎07/72.56.44). Visas issued on the spot; 40dh for a month.

The **French Consulate** at 3 Rue Sahnoun (☎07/77.78.22) issues visas for most of the other West African states, other than Sierra Leone, for which visas are issued by the **UK Consulate**, 17 Bd. Tour Hassan (☎07/72.09.05).

Essadik (☎07/77.13.75); **Sweden**, 150 Av. John Kennedy (☎07/75.44.40); **USA**, 2 Av. de Marrakesh – near the far end of Av. Allal Ben Abdallah (☎07/76.22.65). Standard hours are 8.30–11.30am, Mon–Fri, though you can phone at any time in an emergency. **Irish** citizens are represented by the British Consulate; **Australians** by the Canadians. See box above for **African consulates**.

Galleries Unusually for Morocco, Rabat has a number of worthwhile art galleries, showing works by contemporary artists. *L'Atelier*, 16 Rue Annaba, is the major dealer; try also *Galerie Marsam*, 6 Rue Oskofiah; and *Galerie Le Mamoir*, 7 Rue Baitlahm.

Golf The *Royal Dar es Salaam* golfcourse, on the outskirts of Rabat, is the country's finest – featuring two 18-hole and one 9-hole course designed by Robert Trent-Jones.

Hiking maps Topographic maps of the main hiking areas in the Middle and High Atlas are sold, on production of a passport, at the **Division de la Cartographie**, Ministère de l'Agriculture et de la Réforme Agraire (MARA), 31 Av. Moulay Hassan.

Libraries/cultural associations The *British Council*, 36 Rue Tanja (☎07/76.08.36; marked on our map) operates a small library, with UK papers available for browsing, and puts on various films and events in English. It is also a possible source of information if you want to stay on in Morocco and teach English; open Mon–Fri 9.30am–noon and 2.30–5.45; closed Mon am. The *George Washington Library*, 35 Av. de Fes, has American newspapers. The *American Women's Association Library*, 22 bis Al-Jazair (Mon/Tues 10am–noon, Tue 5.45–7.15pm, Thurs/Fri 11am–1pm, Sat 2–4pm) has a one-for-one paperback exchange, open to all. These libraries can also put you in touch with people if you want to take **lessons in Moroccan Arabic**.

Police The main office is in Rue Soekarno, a couple of blocks from Av. Mohammed V; a central police post is manned at Bab Djedid. In emergency ☎19.

Post office The **PTT Centrale** (open 24hr for phones) is halfway down Av. Mohammed V; its poste restante section is across the road from the main building. The PTT also has a small **philatelic museum**, with displays and sales of Moroccan stamps.

Religious services There is a **synagogue**, with services in Hebrew, on Bd. Moulay Ismail, near Place du Mellah; a **Catholic church** on Place Al Katidraliya, Rue Al Farhat (off Av. Mohammed V); and a **Protestant church** on the corner of Av. Allal Benzerte, off Av. Mohammed V (Sunday service at 11am).

Supermarkets One of the best shops for provisions (including beer and wine) is Maxi Marché on Rue Baghdad, a sidestreet just to the south of the train station.

Tourist offices The **ONMT**, 22 Av. Alger (☎07/77.51.71) is open Mon–Fri June–Sept 9am–3pm; winter 8.30am–noon & 2.30–6.30pm. There is also a rather skeletal **Syndicat d'Initiative** on Rue Patrice Lumumba (opposite the *Grand Hôtel*).

Note: **Telecontact**, *a new annual directory, provides "yellow pages"-style listings and phone numbers for businesses and services in the Rabat/Casablanca region. It is available from news stands or bookshops, price 50dh.*

Salé

Although it is now essentially a suburb of Rabat, **SALÉ** was the pre-eminent of the two right through the Middle Ages, from the decline of the Almohads to the an uneasy alliance in the pirate republic of Bou Regreg. Under the Merenids, in particular, it was a port of some stature, and endowed as such, the most notable survival of these times being its superb **Medersa Bou Inan** – a monument to rival the best of those of Rabat.

In this century, following the French creation of a capital in Rabat, and the emergence of Casablanca as Morocco's great port, Salé passed into a backwater role. It today looks and feels very distinct from Rabat. The spread of a Ville Nouvelle outside its walls has been restricted to a small area round the bus station and the north gates, while the *souks* and life within its medieval limits remain surprisingly traditional. It is a likeable, unpretentious sort of place, and well worth the trip across the estuary.

Access and orientation

From Rabat you can cross the river to Salé by **rowing boat** (see the map), or take a **bus** (#6 or #12) from Bd. Hassan II. The boats charge two dirhams per person and drop you close to the Salé beach; from here it's a steep walk up to **Bab Bou Haja**, one of the main town gates. Both buses drop you at an open terminal just outside the town's principal gate, **Bab Mrisa**.

Salé has a basic and somewhat shadeless **campsite**, *Camping de Salé*, at its beach, and a small, primitive **hotel**, the *Saadiens* (⓪) on Place du Marché. But unless you want to use the campsite as a base for Rabat, there seems little reason to stay. In the evenings, you can eat reasonably at one of the many workers' **cafés** along Rue Kechachin, but the streets empty even earlier than Rabat's.

The Medina

The most interesting point to enter Salé's Medina is through **Bab Mrisa**, just south of the bus terminal. The gate's name – "of the small harbour" – recalls the marine arsenal which used to be sited within the walls, and explains the gate's unusual height. A channel running here from the Bou Regreg has long silted up, but in medieval times it allowed merchant ships to sail right into town, a device that must have been useful during the years of the pirate republic. Robinson

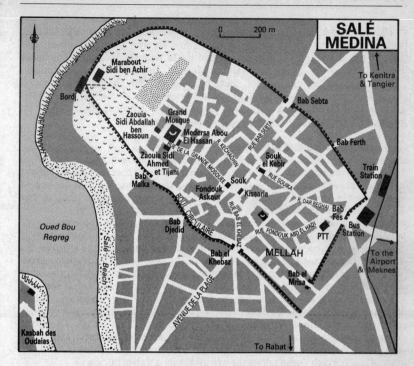

Crusoe was brought into captivity through this gate in Defoe's novel. The gate itself is a very early Merenid structure of the 1270s, its design and motifs (palmettes enclosed by floral decoration; bands of Kufic inscription and *darj w ktarf*, etc) still inherently Almohad in tone.

The souks

Inside Bab Mrisa you'll find yourself in a small square, at the bottom of the old **Mellah** (Jewish) quarter. Turning to the left and continuing close to the walls, you come out after around 350m at another gate, **Bab Bou Haja**, beside a small park. If you want to explore the *souks* – the route outlined below – take the road along the left-hand side of the park. If not, continue on just inside the walls to a long open area; as this starts to narrow into a lane (about 40m further down) veer to your right into the town. This should bring you out more or less at the **Grand Mosque,** opposite which is the **Medersa of Abou El Hassan.**

The park-side street from Bab Bou Haja is **Rue Bab El Khabaz** (Street of the Bakers' Gate), a busy little lane which emerges at the heart of the **souks** by a small **kissaria** (covered market) devoted mainly to textiles. Most of the alleys here are grouped round specific crafts, a particular speciality being the pattern-weave mats produced for the sides and floors of mosques – to be found in the **Souk El Merzouk.** There is also a wool *souk*, the **Souk El Ghezel**, while wood, leather, iron ware, carpets and household items are to be found in the **Souk El Kebir** – the grand *souk*.

Close by the *kissaria* is a fourteenth-century hospice, the **Fondouk Askour**, with a notable gateway (built by Abou Inan – see the Medersa below), and beyond this the Medina's main street, **Rue de la Grande Mosque** leads uphill through the middle of town to the Grand Mosque. This is the simplest approach, but you can take in more of the *souks* by following **Rue Kechachin**, parallel. Along here are located the carpenters and stone-carvers, as well as other craftsmen. In **Rue Haddadin**, a fairly major intersection which leads off to its right up towards Bab Sebta, you'll come upon gold- and coppersmiths.

The Grand Mosque and Medersa

As far as buildings go, the **Grand Mosque** marks the most interesting part of town, its surrounding lanes fronting a concentration of aristocratic mansions and religious *zaouia* foundations. Almohad in origin, the mosque is one of the largest and earliest in Morocco, though what you can see as a non-Muslim (the gateway and minaret) are recent additions.

You can, however, visit its **Medersa** (10dh admission; ask in shops nearby for a guide to open it), opposite the mosque's monumental, stepped main entrance. Salé's main monument and recently restored, it was founded in 1341 by Sultan Abou El Hassan (see Chellah, in Rabat), and is thus more or less contemporary with the Bou Inania *medersas* in Meknes and Fes. Like them, it follows the basic Merenid plan of a central courtyard opening onto a prayer hall, with a series of cells for the students – for whom these "university halls" were endowed – round its upper floors. If this is the first example you've seen, it will come as a surprise after the sparse Almohad economy of the monuments in Rabat. The great Merenid *medersas* are all intensely decorated – in carved wood, stucco and *zellij* – and this is no exception. As you stand within the entrance gate, there is hardly an inch of space which doesn't draw the eye away into a web of intricacy.

What is remarkable, though, despite a certain heaviness which the great Merenid *medersas* manage to avoid, is the way in which each aspect of the work-

---

OULJA: COMPLEXE DES POTIERS

On the Salé side of the estuary, 2km out from the town, the suburb of **Oulja** houses one of Morocco's finest potteries. It has been open only since 1989, established around a rich vein of clay, so its techniques and kilns are modern. For instance, while just three out of the 180 kilns at Safi (Morocco's largest potting town) are fired by gas or electricity, here the ratio is almost exactly the reverse, with just a few specialist kilns using tamarisk wood fuel. But the most important difference is in its quality. While the Safi output often seems tired and routine, at Oulja there is some lovely, wonderfully imaginative stuff being produced.

Visitors are made welcome at the twenty-odd potteries on the complex and you could pick interesting producers at random. Good ones, however, include:

Poterie Demnate (#12). The patron, Bennami Abdelaziz came here after working in Demnate. Wares are enhanced by striking hand-painted flowers.

Poterie Hariky (#10). Superb Islamic designs.

Poterie Tarfaya (#9). Traditional tea sets and mugs – and a flourishing line in patriotic wall plates of Hassan II.

Oulja can be reached by grand taxi from Rabat or Salé. If you want a taxi back, arrange for it to return; otherwise you'll have to walk.

manship succeeds in forging a unity with the others, echoing and repeating the standard patterns in endless variations. The patterns, for the most part, derive from Almohad models, with their stylised geometric and floral motifs, but in the latter there is a much more naturalistic, less abstracted approach. There is also a new stress on calligraphy, with monumental inscriptions carved in great bands on the dark cedarwood and incorporated within the stucco and *zellij*. Almost invariably these are in the elaborate cursive script, and they are generally passages from the Koran. There are occasional poems, however, such as the beautiful foundation inscription, set in marble against a green background, on the rear wall of the court, which begins:

Look at my admirable portal!
Rejoice in my chosen company,
In the remarkable style of my construction
And my marvellous interior!
The workers here have accomplished an artful
Creation with the beauty of youth. . . .

(Translation from Richard B. Parker, *Islamic Monuments in Morocco*).

The *medersa* is only sporadically visited and you'll probably have it to yourself (except for the sparrows and the caretaker) – a quiet, meditative place. Close to its entrance there is a stairway up to the old, windowless cells of the students and to the **roof**, where, looking out across the river to Rabat, you sense the enormity of the Hassan Tower.

Zaouias, moussems and marabouts

Round the Grand Mosque, and over to the northwest, are a trio of interesting buildings. Entrance to all of them is forbidden to non-Muslims, however, as is the rather scruffy cemetery area.

The first of the trio is the **Zaouia Sidi Ahmed El Tijani**, whose elaborate portal faces the Grand Mosque and Medersa. *Zaouias* are a mix of shrine and charitable establishment, maintained by their followers, who once or more each year hold a *moussem*, a pilgrimage-festival, in the saint-founder's honour.

The most important of Salé's *moussems* is that of its patron saint, **Sidi Abdallah Ben Hassoun**, whose **zaouia** stands at the end of the Rue de la Grande Mosquée, a few steps before the cemetery. The saint, who for Muslim travellers plays a role similar to St Christopher, lived in Salé during the sixteenth century, though the origins and significance of his *moussem* are unclear. Taking place each year on the eve of *Mouloud* – the Prophet's birthday – it involves a spectacular procession through the streets of the town with local boatmen, dressed in corsair costumes, carrying huge and elaborate wax lanterns mounted on giant poles. It is by all acounts a lively occasion, much of which can be witnessed away from the forbidden precincts.

At the far end of the cemetery is a third revered site, the white *koubba* and associated buildings of the **Marabout of Sidi Ben Achir**. Sometimes known as "Al Tabib" (The Doctor), Ben Achir was a fourteenth-century ascetic from Andalusia. His shrine, said to have the ability to attract shipwrecks and quell storms – good pirate virtues – reputedly effects cures for blindness, paralysis and madness. Enclosed by nineteenth-century pilgrim lodgings, it, too, has a considerable annual *moussem* on the eve of Mouloud.

South towards Casablanca

It's a little over an hour by *grand taxi* from Rabat to Casa (under an hour by express train) and, if you're making a quick tour of Morocco, there's little to delay your progress. The landscape, wooded in parts, is a low, flat plain, punctuated inland by a series of scruffy light industrial towns.

On the coast, things are slightly more promising: **Mohammedia** has a fine beach and great restaurants, and is, with the smaller resorts of **Temara** and **Skhirat**, a popular seaside escape for the affluent of Rabat and Casablanca. For visitors, however, there's a lot more to get excited about on the coast south from Casa towards Agadir.

Rabat to Mohammedia

Temara Plage, some 14km to the south of Rabat, is (along with Plage des Nations, see p.236), the capital's closest beach resort. If you are planning a day trip, you could take a *grand taxi* direct to the beach from Rabat (around 20 min), or local bus #17 to **Temara Ville** (4km inland); both leave Rabat from Av. Hassan II.

If you're driving, the **coast road** is preferable. Leaving Rabat, take Bd. Misr alongside the Medina wall, then bear left onto Av. Al Moukaouma and its continuation Av. Sidi Mohammed Ben Abdallah. The route is built up almost the whole way from Rabat to Temara. Along the way, you pass by the **National Zoo**; a vast **Complexe Olympique**, built for the 1983 Mediterranean games; and a small but impressive **royal palace** belonging to the heir of Hassan II, Sidi Mohammed.

Temara Zoo
Temara Zoo (open 9.30am–dusk) is an unexpected delight. Most "zoos" in Morocco are scrubby little enclosures with a few sad-looking Barbary apes. This one, however, is positively palatial, as you might expect from what was formerly King Hassan's private menagerie. Amid the imaginatively laid-out grounds there are lions, elephants, gazelles, jackals, desert foxes, giraffes and monkeys; there is a lake, too, with pelicans and wading birds.

Temara Ville and Plage
TEMARA VILLE has an old **Kasbah**, dating from Moulay Ismail's reign, which is now home to the Royal Cavalry School, and a pleasant, Spanish-owned **hotel**, the *Auberge le Provençal* (☎07/74.11.11; ③), which is noted for excellent but rather pricey meals.

At **TEMARA PLAGE** there are several sandy strips, plus a cluster of discos that provide a summer alternative to the lack of action in Rabat. Few people stay here overnight, other than the well-heeled of Rabat, who maintain summer villas. However, if for some reason you want a beach base for Rabat, there's a **campsite** and two **hotels**, *La Felouque* (☎07/74.45.59; ③) and, behind it, the basic *Hôtel Casino* (⑪); the *Felouque* has a swimming pool and a well-regarded **restaurant**, *Les Sables d'Or*. Another good restaurant is the *San Francisco*, built by a Moroccan returned from thirty years in California, and decorated with a full-size Ford Mustang bursting through the bar mirror.

Ech Chiana

ECH CHIANA (also known as Rose Marie Plage) is 9km south from Temara and a slightly plusher resort, with a luxury beachside **hotel**, the *La Kasbah* (☎07/74.91.16; ④), that is very popular with French package tourists. A little back from the beach there is also a modest **auberge**, *Les Cambusias* (☎07/74.91.49; ④), which does good meals and has a **campsite**. A second campsite is attached to another restaurant-bar, *Plage Johara* (☎07/74.92.51).

Skhirat Plage

The **Royal Palace** at **SKHIRAT PLAGE** was the site of a notorious coup attempt by senior Moroccan generals during King Hassan's birthday celebrations in July 1971. The coup was mounted using a force of Berber cadets, who took over the palace, imprisoned the king and massacred a number of his guests. It came within hours of being successful, being thwarted by the apparently accidental shooting of the cadets' leader, General Mohammed Medbuh, and by the strength of personality of Hassan, who re-asserted control over his captors. Among the guests who survived, incidentally, was Malcolm Forbes (see p.73).

The palace still stands, though it fell from royal favour, and there are, as you would expect, a good many luxurious French-style villas – some old, some new, many unfinished. There are two **hotels**: the *Auberge Potinière* (summer only; ②), and, to the south of the main resort, with its own private beach, the *Hôtel Amphitrite* (☎07/74.22.20; ③).

Getting to the resort by public transport, take any of the slow **trains** on the Rabat–Casa line to SKHIRAT VILLE, a small (and uninteresting) farming town, on the hillside, a couple of kilometres up from the beach.

Bouznika and Mansouria

If you have transport, there are a couple of further turn-offs to beaches, prior to Mohammedia. The beaches here are less developed, indeed isolated, and in places reached only by sandy tracks from the main road. At **BOUZNIKA PLAGE** and **DAHOMEY PLAGE** there are primitive summer **campsites**.

Further south, **MANSOURIA** has two more campsites, the *Oubaha* (pretty awful) and *Mimosa* (not much better), and there are a couple of others at the hamlet of **PORT BLONDIN**, at the mouth of the Oued Nefifikh, and the beginning of the Mohammedia sands. The latter also has a **hotel-restaurant**, *La Madrague* (☎03/32.20.20; ②), with a disco in summer, in a strange old building.

Mohammedia

The port of **MOHAMMEDIA** has a dual identity. As the site of Morocco's main oil refineries, and the base of its petrochemical industry, it is an important industrial and commercial city, with a population of some 130,000. Yet it is also a big-name resort – a holiday playground for Casablanca – with one of the best beaches on the Atlantic, a racecourse, a state-of-the-art golf course (King Hassan has a little palace by the links), and the new *Ibn Batouta* yacht marina. These two faces of the city – tourism and industry – are kept quite distinct, with the latter contained in a zone to the west of the city centre and beach.

In summer, the city's population is given a huge boost by Moroccan tourists, mainly from Casa, who camp by the beach in what is called *Mohammedia-Est*: a

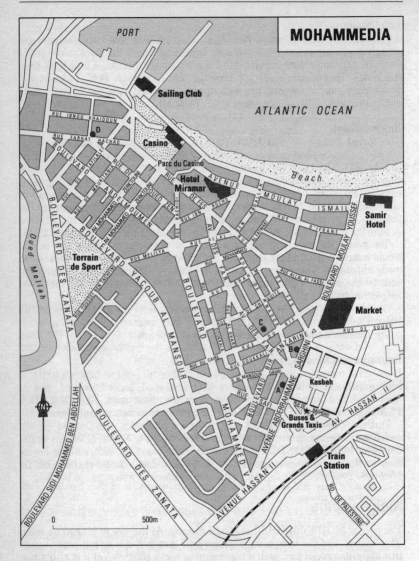

MOHAMMEDIA

PORT

ATLANTIC OCEAN

Sailing Club

RUE IBNOU KHAIDOUN

D

RUE FARHAT HACHAD

Casino

BOULEVARD ABDELMOUMEN

Parc du Casino

Beach

AVENUE

Hotel
Miramar

MOULAY

ISMAIL

Samir
Hotel

BOULEVARD MOULAY YOUSSEF

BOULEVARD YACOUB AL MANSOUR

Terrain
de Sport

BOULEVARD DES ZANATA

Oued Mellah

MOHAMMED

BOULEVARD

Market

RUE DE SOUSS

C

B

Kasbah

A

Buses &
Grands Taxis

N

BOULEVARD SIDI MOHAMMED BEN ABDELLAH

BOULEVARD MOHAMMED V

AVENUE ABDERRAHMANE

RUE SAFI

AV. HASSAN II

BOULEVARD DES ZANATA

AVENUE HASSAN II

Train
Station

BD. DE PALESTINE

0   500m

sequence of tented villages that stretch north towards Port Blondin and
Mansouria. For foreign visitors, there is perhaps less to tempt a stay. Despite a
long history as a trading port – it was known as Fedala prior to Mohammed V's
inauguration of the oil refinery in 1960 – the city has little to speak of in the way
of monuments of "old Morocco". Yet Mohammedia makes a very pleasant stop
over, with its friendly, easygoing atmosphere, and a fine selection of restaurants.
If you are flying in or out of Casablanca, you could do a lot worse than spend a

first or last night here. In July, it may be worth a special trip, for the week-long **Mohammedia Festival**, which encompasses all kinds of cultural activities, craft exhibitions, a fantasia, cycling races and a marathon.

Orientation and accommodation

Orientation is not difficult as "downtown" Mohammedia is quite a small town. Facing the **train station** is a small **Kasbah/Medina** area, built in a period of Portuguese occupation and still preserving their gateways. To the west of the Kasbah, a sequence of boulevards lead down to the beach. **Buses** and **grands taxis** operate beside a small park on Rue de Baghdad, just in front of the train station; local bus #1 runs from here, too, down to the beach.

There are six **hotels**:

Hôtel Castel [A], Av. Abderrahmane Serghini (☎03/32.41.07). The closest hotel to the train station and the cheapest rooms in town. Simple, with cold showers only, but okay. ①

Hôtel Annasr [B], corner of Bd. Moulay Youssef/Av. Abderrahmane Serghini (☎03/32.23.73). Clean rooms with cold showers; above a popular café. ①

Hôtel Argana [C], Av. des F.A.R. (☎03/32.03.08). Good value, with hot showers, and a café-restaurant on the ground floor. Worth booking. ①

Hôtel La Falaise [D], Av. Farhat Hachad (☎03/32.48.28). French-run hotel, closer to the beach. Reasonable rooms off a central courtyard, behind a café/snack bar. ①

Hôtel Samir [labelled], Bd. Moulay Youssef (☎03/31.07.07). A friendly, fairly smart beach-side hotel, with swimming pool and tennis court. ④

Hôtel Miramar [labelled], Rue de Fes (☎03/32.20.21). Upmarket *Meridien* chain hotel, with international facilities, set in its own little park. ⑤

The closest **campsite** is *Camping International Loran* (☎03/32.29.57), 2km south of town; it is a reasonable place. Others to the south are detailed in the previous section on the coast from Rabat to Mohammedia.

Restaurants and nightlife

For its size, Mohammedia's choice of **restaurants** is impressive. Pick from:

Restaurant La Friture, 1 Rue Ibn Toumert. Fried fish and salad, beer or wine, served beside a soothing fountain. Moderate.

Restaurant Sans Pareil, Rue Farhat Hachad – near the *Hôtel La Falaise*. French cuisine, seafood and paella. Moderate.

Restaurant au Bec Fin, Rue Cheikh Chouaib Doukali. A tiny but highly recommended restaurant. Moderate.

Restaurant du Parc, Rue de Fes, near the Parc du Casino and *Ranch Club*. Excellent, with fish specialities. Moderate.

Chaplin's, 8 Rue du Rif. A good choice near the Kasbah, run by a Moroccan family returned from Canada. Copious portions. Moderate.

Restaurant des Sports, Av. Farhat Hachad – near the *Hôtel La Falaise*. (☎03/32.35.32; closed Mon). The owners trained at Cornell University and it shows. Excellent seafood. Moderate to expensive.

Restaurant du Port, 1 Rue du Port (☎03/32.24.66). Previously known as *Chez Iréne*, this is the town's best-known restaurant, renowned for its charcoal grills, served in a flower-strewn garden. Moderate to expensive.

Mohammedia has a few **bars** additional to the restaurants and hotels: the *Ranch Club*, for instance, on Rue de Fes, and there is a **disco-club** at the *Hôtel-Restaurant Madrague* at Port Blondin (see p.261). The town's **Casino** is permanently closed.

Casablanca (Casa, Dar El Baida)

The principal city of Morocco, and capital in all but administration, **CASABLANCA** (*Dar El Baida* in its literal Arabic form) is now the largest port of the Maghreb – busier even than Marseilles, the city on which it was modelled by the French. Its development, from a town of 20,000 in 1906, has been astonishingly rapid and quite ruthlessly deliberate. When the French landed their forces here in 1907 (and established their Protectorate five years later), it was Fes which was Morocco's commercial centre, and Tangier was its main port. Had Tangier not been in international hands, this probably would have remained the case. Instead, the demands of an independent colonial administration forced the French to seek an entirely new base. Casa, at the heart of *Maroc Utile*, the country's most fertile zone and centre of its mineral deposits, was a natural choice.

Superficially, Casa is today much like any other large southern European city: a familiarity which makes it fairly easy to get your bearings and a revelation as you begin to understand something of its life. Arriving here from the south, or even from Fes or Tangier, most of the preconceptions you've been travelling round with will be happily shattered by the city's cosmopolitan beach clubs or by the almost total absence of the veil. These European images shield, however, what is still substantially a "first-generation" city – it still attracts considerable immigration from the countryside – and one which inevitably has some of Morocco's most intense social problems.

Alongside its show of wealth and its prestige developments – most notably the vast **Grande Mosquée Hassan II**, raised by public subscription on a promontory looking out to the Atlantic – the city has had since its formation a reputation for extreme poverty, prostitution, *bidonvilles* (shantytowns) and social unrest. The *bidonville* problem resulted partly from the sheer extent of population increases – which exceeded one million in the 1960s – and partly because few of the earlier migrants intended to stay permanently. Most of them sent back their earnings to their families in the country, intending to rejoin them permanently as soon as they had raised sufficient funds for a business at home.

The pattern is now much more towards permanent settlement, and this, together with a strict control of migration and a limited number of self-help programmes, has eased and cleared many of the worst slums. Also, *bidonville* dwellers have been accorded increasing respect during recent years. They cannot be evicted if they have lived in a property over two years, and after ten years they acquire title to the land and building, which can be used as collateral at the bank for loans. The dread of every *bidonville* family is to be evicted and put in a high-rise block, which is regarded as the lowest of the low on the housing ladder.

The problem of a concentrated urban poor, however, is more enduring and represents, as it did for the French, an intermittent threat to government stability. Casa, through the 1940s and 1950s, was the main centre of anti-French rioting, and it was the city's working class, too, which formed the base of Ben Barka's Socialist Party. There have been strikes here sporadically since independence, and on several occasions, most violently in the food strikes of 1982, they have precipitated rioting. Whether Casa's development can be sustained, and the lot of its new migrants improved, must decide much of Morocco's future.

NEW NAMES AND NEW AVENUES

Place Mohammed V/Place des Nations Unies
The names of these squares are a source of great confusion. In 1991, Hassan II
declared that the old Place des Nations Unies (around which are grouped the city's
main public buildings – the PTT, Tribunal, Prefecture, etc) should henceforth be
known as Place Mohammed V. This for a while seemed to create two Place
Mohammed Vs, as the square below the Medina already bore that name. However,
it appears that the latter is now in turn renamed Place des Nations Unies.

Note also that, as elsewhere in Morocco, many of the **old French street names**
are being revised to bear Moroccan and Arab names. These include:

Rue Branly – Rue Sharif Amzian
Rue Claude – Rue Mohammed El Quorri
Rue Colbert – Rue Chaouia
Rue Foucauld – Rue Araibi Jilali
Rue de l'Horloge – Rue Allal Ben Abdallah

Grande Mosquée–Grand Théâtre Axis
Further map confusion is likely to be caused through the 1990s by the **remodelling
of avenues** to create a ceremonial approach from what is now the **Place des
Nations Unies** to the **Grande Mosquée Hassan II**. The planned route – the so-
called *Grande Mosquée–Grand Théâtre axis*. It will necessitate a fair amount of
demolition southwest of the Old Medina.

Orientation

Casa is a large city by any standards and it can be a bewildering place in which to
arrive, especially if you come in on one of the trains that terminate at the main
Gare des Voyageurs (2km from the centre) rather than continuing on to the
better-situated **Gare du Port** (See "Points of Arrival", following).

Once you're in the city centre, however, orientation is relatively
straightforward. The city centre is focused on a large public square, **Place
Mohammed V** (but note box above), and most of the places to stay, to eat, or (in
a rather limited way) see, are located in and around the avenues that radiate from
it. A few blocks to the north, still partially walled, is the **Old Medina**, which was
all there was of Casablanca until around 1907. Much further out to the south is
the **Habous** quarter – the **New Medina**, created by the French, and to the west,
along the corniche past the Grande Mosquée Hassan II, lies the beach suburb of
Aïn Diab.

Our **map** on the next page covers the city centre, but not Habous and Aïn Diab;
to see how these relate, take a look at the map in the Casablanca *ONMT* pamphlet.
Along with other information, this is available at the city's **ONMT** office, at 55 Rue
Omar Slaoui , or the **Syndicat d'Initiative** at 98 Bd. Mohammed V.

Accommodation

Although there is a large number of hotels in Casa, they operate at near capacity
for much of the year. If at all possible, phone ahead for a room, or at least arrive
fairly early in the day.

Grand Mosque
Hassan II

To El Hank
& Aïn Diab

BOUL SID MOHAMMED DEN ABDALLAH

BOULEVARD SOUR DJEDID

BOULEVARD MOULAY YOUSSEF

RUE JULES MAURAN

RUE DE GOULMINA

BOULEVARD ZIRAOUI

OLD MEDINA

Chleuh
Mosque

Youth
Hostel

Grand
Mosque

Bab Djedid

BD MOHAMMED

RUE DE GOULMINA

RUE DES ANGLAIS

E
D
H
A
C
AVENUE
M

Bus to
Aïn Diab

AVENUE DES F.A.R.

PLACE DES
NATIONS
UNIES

PLACE OUED
EL MAKHAZINE

A

RF ET M GUEDJ

B

BOULEVARD D'ANFA

BOULEVARD ZIRAOUI

PLACE DE
LA FRATERNITÉ

P

PLACE
D'AKNO

O

RUE DE PARIS

BOUL HASSAN

BOULEVARD MOULAY YOUSSEF

PTT

PLACE
MOHAMMED
V

Cathédrale du
Sacré Coeur

Tribunal

Prefecture

French
Consul

BOUL MOULAY YOUSSEF

BD. A. REITZER

RUE RAHA

Parc de la
Ligue Arabe

ONMT

BOULEVARD MOHAMMED ZERKTOUNI

To Nôtre Dame
de Lourdes

CASABLANCA

0   300m

N

Gare
du Port

Centre
2000

To Mohammedia

BOULEVARD MOULAY ABDERRAHMAN

Tour Atlas

DES FORCES

CTM

PLACE
ALLAUA

ARMÉES ROYALES (F.A.R.)

PLACE
MIRABEAU

RUE PASTEUR

RUE

PASTEUR

Grands Taxis
to Rabat

Marché
Central

PLACE
N. PAQUET

BOULEVARD

MOHAMMED

PLACE EL
YASSIR

BOULEVARD

EMILE ZOLA

PLACE DU
20 AOÛT

RUE OULED ZIANE

BD EMILE ZOLA

PLACE DE
LA VICTOIRE

RUE KHOURIBGA

BOULEVARD ABDELLAH BEN YACINE

PLACE
SEMARD

BOUL D'OUJDA

Gare des
Voyageurs

BOULEVARD IBN TACHFINE

ROUTE DES OULED ZIANE

RUE DE LIBOURNE

RUE DE LA RESISTANCE

BOUL DE LA

NEW MEDINA

To Rabat

To Gare
du Habbous

POINTS OF ARRIVAL

BY TRAIN

Most of the **trains** from Marrakesh run to both stations, allowing you to stay on until the **Gare du Port**, 150m from Place des Nations Unies. From Rabat (and Fes/Tangier), however, trains sometimes terminate at the **Gare des Voyageurs**, at the far end of Bd. Mohammed V. From here, if you're quick and very determined, you might just get a place on bus #30, which runs into town from the square in front of the station; otherwise, reckon on a twenty-minute walk or a *petit taxi* ride. Bd. Mohammed V runs straight ahead from the square in front of the station, curving slightly to the left as you come to the next main square (Place Albert 1er).

BY BUS

Bus stations are more central and straightforward. All the *CTM* buses arrive at the *CTM Gare Routière* on Rue Léon l'Africain (off Av. des F.A.R.). Private line buses use a terminal south of the Place de la Victoire.

BY GRAND TAXI

Grands taxis usually stop just behind the *CTM Gare Routière* (see buses, above), by the *Hôtel Safir*.

BY AIR

Coming from the **Aéroport Mohammed V**, used by all international and most domestic flights, there is now a train service to Casablanca, calling at both the Voyageurs (20 min) and Port (30 min) stations; it runs roughly every hour from 8.30am to 10.20pm and costs 35dh. There is also a shuttle bus between the airport and the CTM Gare Routière. For flights at odd hours you would need to charter a *grand taxi*, which should be around 200dh, from behind the CTM (see above).

DRIVING

Traffic is a nightmare in Casa: if you can avoid driving, try to do so. If you have a car, the larger hotels at Aïn Diab offer more security than those in the city centre.

CITY BUSES AND PETITS TAXIS

Getting round within the city, **petits taxis** are easy to find along the main avenues and are invariably metered – as long as the meter is switched on you will rarely pay more than 6dh per taxi for a trip round town. For Aïn Diab the fare is currently 18dh (4dh extra if you get the driver to detour en route round the new Grande Mosquée Hassan II). There is a 20 percent surcharge at night.

You are unlikely to need to make use of **city bus** services, other than those from the airport or Gare des Voyageurs (see above), and, if headed for the seaside, the #9 service from Bd. de Paris to Aïn Diab. They get very crowded at rush hours.

City centre

All of the recommendations below are in the main, central area of the city. No hotels in the Old Medina have been included, as most overcharge for miserable rooms; in the "new city", by contrast, many of the cheaper classified places are quite stylish Art Deco buildings. As usual, listings are in ascending order of price.
Auberge de Jeunesse/Youth Hostel [labelled], 6 Place Amiral Philibert (☎02/22.05.51). A friendly, airy place, nicely sited just inside the Medina, and well maintained. To reach it from Gare du Port, walk up Bd. Houphouet Boigny, then turn right along Bd. des Almohades and take the second opening in the Medina walls: the hostel is on your right, at the near side of a small square. IYHF card not required.

Hôtel Mon Rêve [K], 7 Rue Chaouia (☎02/31.14.39). A good option in a promising area for cheap hotels (the two listings below are close by). Hot showers on a communal landing. ⓾

Hôtel Kon-Tiki [J], 88 Rue Allal Ben Abdallah (☎02/31.49.27). Not quite so good. ⓾

Hôtel Volubilis [O], 20/22 Rue Abdelkrim Diouri (☎02/20.77.89). Fair value. ⓾

Hôtel du Perigord [G], 56 Rue Araibi Jilali (☎02/22.10.85). Quite pleasant, with a little café at street level; arguably the best of the unclassified hotels. ⓾

Hôtel Terminus [T], 184 Bd. Ba Hamad (☎02/24.00.25). Close to the Gare des Voyageurs, so useful if you arrive late or plan to leave early, and can't afford the *Moussafir* (see below). Decent rooms with hot showers on the corridor. ⓾

France Hôtel [M], 18 Rue Mohammed El Qorri (☎02/22.18.19). Reasonable rooms, again with hot showers on the corridor. ⓾

Hôtel Colbert [N], 38 Rue Chaouia (☎02/31.42.41). Useful location if you arrive by bus – it's just round the corner from the CTM. A bit gloomy but cleanish rooms, with baths and (sometimes) hot water. ⓾

Hôtel Rialto [L], 9 Rue Mohammed El Qorri (☎02/27.51.22). A good, safe bet, with a hammam opposite. ①

Hôtel de Foucauld [H], 52 Rue Araibi Jilali (☎02/22.26.66). Not bad. ①

Touring Hôtel [I], 87 Rue Allal Ben Abdallah (☎02/31.02.16). A good looking Art Deco hotel but at present is a bit of a roach trap – and very much a last resort. ①

Hôtel Guynemer [R], 2 Rue Mohammed Belloul (☎02/27.57.64). Pleasant, clean rooms in an attractive, "seen-better-days" hotel. ①

Majestic Hôtel [Q], 55 Bd. Lalla Yacout (☎02/31.09.51). Another old hotel, with a bit of style; rooms at the front are pretty noisy. ②

Hôtel du Centre [F], 1 Rue Sidi Belyout/corner Av. des F.A.R. (☎02/31.24.48). Another in similar vein to the above; used to be called the *Georges V*. ②

Hôtel Excelsior [C], 2 Rue El Amraoui Brahim, off Place des Nations Unies (☎02/20.02.63). This was the city's "Grand Hotel" until the 1960s, when the big chains moved in. It is highly recommended. ②

Hôtel Windsor [A], 93 Place Oued El Makhazine (☎02/20.03.52). Another nice old hotel; large rooms with showers/bathrooms. Unfortunately, it may disappear, as it seems to be on the proposed theatre and metro station site in the remodelling scheme ③

HOTEL PRICE CODES AND STAR–RATINGS

As of 1993, hotels are no longer obliged to levy set maximum rates, according to their official star-ratings, as had long been the custom. However, **prices** still broadly follow the star-rating system, and this is the basis of our own **hotel price codes** set out below and keyed throughout the guide.

Our code	Official classification	Single room price	Double room price
⓾	Unclassified	25–60dh	40–100dh
①	1*A/1*B	60–105dh	100–125dh
②	2*B/2*A	105–145dh	125–175dh
③	3*B/3*A	145–225dh	175–275dh
④	4*B/4*A	225–400dh	275–500dh
⑤	5*luxury	Upwards of 400dh	Upwards of 500dh

TELEPHONE CODES

All telephone numbers in the Greater Casablanca area are prefixed 02. When making a call within the region you omit this prefix. For more explanation of phone codes and making calls within (or to) Morocco, see p.37–38.

Hôtel de Paris [P], 2 Rue Sharif Amzian (☎02/27.38.71). This recently dropped the prefix "grand" from its name, while refurbishing the rooms. Pleasant nonetheless. ③

Hôtel Plaza [D], 18 Bd. Houphouet Boigny (☎02/22.02.26). An old hotel that is just beginning to fade; good rooms and facilities, still, and well priced for its class. ③

Moussafir Hôtel [S], Bd. Ba Hamad (☎02/40.19.84). The latest addition to a chain of tasteful hotels, built by the train stations of major cities. Right by the Gare des Voyageurs. ③

Hôtel Basma [B], 35 Av. Moulay Hassan I, just off Place des Nations Unies (☎02/22.33.23). A new business hotel. ④

Hôtel Toubkal [E], 9 Rue Sidi Belyout (☎02/31.14.14). And yet another. ④

Aïn Diab

The seaside suburb of Aïn Diab provides an alternative base if you can afford any of the trio of hotels below; all are comfortable business-class places, close by the beach. There are also a few unclassified hotels in the area but these cater exclusively for Moroccan guests, and tourists are unlikely to find rooms on offer.

Hôtel Bellerive, 38 Bd. de la Corniche (☎02/39.13.57). ③

Hôtel Karam, Bd. de la Corniche (☎02/39.13.51). ④

Hôtel Tarik, 41 Bd. de la Corniche (☎02/39.13.64). ④

Camping

Camping Oasis, Av. Jean Mermoz, Beausejour (☎02/25.33.67). This is the nearest site, 8km out on the P8 road to El Jadida. It is a reasonable site, frequented mainly by campervans. If driving, follow Bd. Brahim Roudani out from the centre: this straight road becomes Route d'El Jadida and then Av. Jean Mermoz. Bus #31 runs past the site.

For details of **other accessible campsites**, see the previous section on the Mohammedia coast, or the section following Casa, on the route to Azzemmour.

The City

Travel guides used to declare, with some amazement, that Casa had not a single "real" monument. Given the scale and success of the 1930s **Art Deco** landmarks of the city centre – including the ensemble of public buildings on **Place Mohammed V** designed by the French architect d'Henri Prost – this was never quite true. However, the city did undoubtedly lack any one single, great building: a position that, in part, may have prompted King Hassan II's decision to construct here a mosque, the **Grande Mosquée Hassan II**, on a truly epic scale. Set beside the sea, out on the road to Aïn Diab, this is nearing completion – and, if curiosity leads no further in this city, it must be seen.

The Grande Mosquée Hassan II

Work on the huge complex of the **Grande Mosquée Hassan II** was launched in 1980 and the mosque will be inaugurated in 1994. The whole complex, however, and the remodelling of the avenues leading towards it from Place des Nations Unies, is unlikely to be complete much before the millennium. Raised on a rocky platform reclaimed from the ocean, it represents the present monarch's most ambitious building project and will surely be his legacy to Moroccan architecture. Although non-Muslims may not visit the mosque – like all other Moroccan religious buildings – anyone may visit the cultural centre developing round it, and ride the lift to the top of the 200m-high minaret.

Designed by the French architect, Michel Pinseau, the mosque-complex is a phenomenal undertaking. Looking out towards it from the city centre, its huge size tricks you into thinking it is far nearer than it is. Its minaret is actually two hundred metres high, making it by far the tallest structure in the country – as well as the tallest minaret in the world; future plans include mounting a laser on its summit to project beams towards Mecca. The mosque itself provides space for 20,000 worshippers within, where a glass floor reveals the ocean below, and a further 80,000 in its courtyard. Statisticians note that it is thus second only to Mecca in the mosque-size league – and that St Peter's in Rome could fit comfortably inside. Eventually, the mosque will incorporate a Koranic school and *medersa*, and form the centre of a cultural complex including a library and museum.

The facts of construction are startling, too. During the early 1990s, when the mosque was being readied for opening, 1400 men worked by day and a further 1100 by night. Most were master-craftsmen, working marble from Agadir, cedar from the Middle Atlas, granite from Tafraoute, and (the only import) glass from Murano near Venice. Equally extraordinary is its cost – which is reckoned to have exceeded £500m/$750m – and the fact that this was raised entirely by public subscription. Press reports outside Morocco have alleged resentment of an over-enthusiastic sponsoring operation which generated donations through non-voluntary deductions from wages, as well as door to door collections – including approaches to expatriate workers from Germany to Saudi Arabia. However, in Morocco there is a genuine pride in the project, and pictures of the mosque (in effect, illustrated receipts, showing a donation) are displayed in homes and cafés throughout the nation. The mosque had a knock-on effect on the economy, too; at one stage the level of donations was so high that it temporarily reduced Morocco's money supply and brought down inflation.

That the mosque bears King Hassan's name has inspired rumours that it is designed in part as his mausoleum, along the lines of that of his father, Mohammed V, in Rabat. But it is important to add that in addition to his secular position, Hassan is also "Commander of the Faithful", the spiritual leader of Moroccan Muslims. And the building's site, in addition to reflecting Hassan's stated intent to "give the city a heart", is designed to illustrate the Koranic saying, "Allah has his throne on the water".

Mauresque: Place Mohammed V and around

The French city centre and its formal colonial buildings already seem to belong to a different and distant age. Grouped round **Place Mohammed V** (the former Place des Nations Unies), they served as models for administrative architecture throughout Morocco, and to an extent still do. Their style, heavily influenced by Art Deco, is known as *Mauresque* – a French idealisation and "improvement" on Moorish design. The effect of the central ensemble is actually very impressive, the only feature out of place being a clocktower in the *préfecture* – an irresistible French colonial addition. Three times a week the central fountain is lit from within by changing coloured lights, to taped music.

Other impressive Mauresque and Art Deco buildings are to be seen along Boulevard Mohammed V, including a couple of the older hotels. They are beginning to be appreciated by the local authorities and there are, apparently, plans to establish an Art Deco historic district. Trademarks of the style on these private buildings are wrought-iron windows, staircases and balconies, and floral, animal and geometric designs on stuccoed pediments and friezes.

The Cathedral and Quartier Habous

More European in style, though again adopting traditional Moroccan forms, is the old **Cathedral of Sacre Cœur** at the far end of the **Parc de la Ligue Arabe**. Converted for use a school, it is a wonderfully balanced and airy design, paying genuine homage to its Moroccan setting.

About a kilometre to the south, at the end of Av. Mers Sultan, is the **New Medina** – or **Quartier Habous** – which displays a somewhat more bizarre extension of *Mauresque*. Built in the 1930s as a response to the first *bidonville* crisis, it it still looks like a film-set with its idealised French version of domestic Moroccan architecture. The streets, laid out in neat little rows, now have a somewhat twee, shopping-centre feel to them – not at all Moroccan even with the years. What's most unreal, however, is the neighbourhood mosque, flanked by a tidy stretch of green just as though it were a provincial French church.

The Old Medina and the port

The **Old Medina**, lapsing into dilapidation above the port, is largely the product of the late nineteenth century, when Casa began its modest growth as a commercial centre. Before that, it was little more than a group of village huts, half-heartedly settled by local tribes after the site was abandoned by the Portuguese in 1755. *Casa Branca*, the town the Portuguese founded here in the fifteenth century, had been virtually levelled by the great earthquake of that year (which also destroyed Lisbon). Only its name ("The White House"; *Casablanca* in Spanish; *Dar El Baida* in Arabic) survives.

Now relatively underpopulated, the Medina has a slightly disreputable, if also fairly affluent, air. It is said to be the place to go to look for any stolen goods you might want to buy back – a character well in keeping with many of the stalls. There's nothing sinister though, and it can be an excellent source for cheap snacks and general goods. A single main street, **Rue Djemaa ech Chleuh**, edges its way right through the quarter, past most of the market stalls and the principal mosque from which it takes its name. The **walls** on the west side of the Medina are being restored, as part of the approach to the Grande Mosquée Hassan II.

While in the Medina area, you might also spend some time at the **Centre 2000** complex, by the Gare du Port. Built in the mid-1980s, it encompasses twenty or so shops and five restaurants (see listings, p.274). All in all, it's quite an eye-opener into modern Casa life.

Aïn Diab: the beach

You can get out to the beach suburb of **Aïn Diab** by bus (#9 from Bd. de Paris; see our map), by *petit taxi* (easily engaged around Place des Nations Unies) or on foot. The beach starts around 3km out from the port and Old Medina, past the Grande Mosquée Hassan II, and continues for about the same distance.

A beach right within Casa may not sound alluring – and it's certainly not the cleanest and clearest stretch of the country's waters. But Aïn Diab's big attraction is not so much the sea – in whose shallow waters Moroccans gather in phalanx formations, wary of the currents – as the **beach clubs** along its front. Each of these has one or more pools, usually filled with filtered seawater, a restaurant and a couple of snack bars; in the fancier ones there'll also be additional sports facilities like tennis or volleyball and perhaps even a disco. The novelty of coming upon this in a Moroccan city is quite amazing, and it's a strange sight to see

YOU MUST REMEMBER THIS . . .

Probably the best-known fact about Casablanca is that it wasn't the location for the movie – all of which was shot in Hollywood. In fact, Warner Bros, upset by the Marx Brothers filming *A Night in Casablanca*, attempted to copyright the very name Casablanca – which could have been inconvenient for the city.

The film of course owes its enduring success to H. Bogart, I. Bergman and Sam's songs, but at the time of its release it received a major publicity boost by the appearance of Casablanca and Morocco in the news. As the film was being completed, in November 1942, the Allies launched **Operation Torch**, landing 25,000 troops on the coast north and south of Casablanca, at Kenitra, Mohammedia and Safi. The troops were commanded by General Eisenhower and consisted principally of Americans, whom Roosevelt believed were less likely than the British to be fired on by the Vichy French government in Morocco. An infinitely more fortunate coincidence, however, took place in the week of the film's première in Los Angeles in January 1943. Churchill and Roosevelt had arranged an Allied Leaders' summit, and the newsreels revealed its location: the **Casablanca Conference**, held in a hotel (long since gone) in the affluent suburb of Anfa, out beyond Aïn Diab.

Such events – and the movie – are not, it has to be said, evoked by modern-day Casa. Film buffs with a strong sense of irony, however, might check out **Rick's Bar**, in the *Hôtel Hyatt Regency* on Place des Nations Unies (open from 10pm), where the waiters ask for your (very expensive!) drinks orders dressed in trench-coats and fedoras. And for a glimpse of True Brit Ex-Pat life, as it used to be lived, there is always the **Churchill Club** on Rue Pessac in Aïn Diab. Established in 1922, as the "British Bank Club", its one condition of membership is that "the English language only should be spoken on the premises".

women veiled from head to toe looking down onto the cosmopolitan intensity unfolding beneath them.

The prices and quality of the **beach clubs** vary enormously and it's worth wandering round a while to check out what's available. Most locals have annual membership and for outsiders a day or weekend ticket can work out surprisingly expensive (£5–10 a day). But there's quite often one place which has thrown its doors open for free in an attempt to boost its café business. *Piscine Éden Roc,* the first you encounter coming from the port, is often among the cheapest, though it's a little dull and away from the centre. If you're taking a *petit taxi*, ask to be let off a kilometre or so further down the corniche (coast road), at one of the group of clubs near *Le Lido* or *Kon Tiki*.

Out beyond Aïn Diab, along the corniche, is the suburb of **Anfa**, where the city's wealthy have their villas, and companies their corporate headquarters – including the striking **OCP** (*Office Chérifien des Phosphates*) shiny black block.

Restaurants, bars and nightlife

Casa has the reputation of being the best place to eat in Morocco, and if you can afford the fancier restaurant prices, this is certainly true. There are fine seafood restaurants along the corniche at Aïn Diab and the bays beyond, and some stylish, old French colonial ones round the central boulevards. On a budget, too, there's little problem in finding good-value meals or snacks.

For **nightlife**, Aïn Diab, again, is the main location.

Restaurants

Good restaurants in three areas – **downtown Casa**, inside the **Centre 2000** (the shopping complex by the port) and around the **Corniche/Aïn Diab** – are suggested below. In addition, there are inexpensive hole-in-the-wall eateries in the **Old Medina**, and if you're putting together a picnic, the **Marché Central** (6am–2pm) on Rue Chaouia groans under the weight of the freshest and best produce in Morocco.

DOWNTOWN: AROUND THE MAIN BOULEVARDS

Restaurant de l'Étoile Marocaine, 107 Rue Allal Ben Abdallah. Slightly more ambitious, with specialities like *pastilla* and *mechoui*, and a good atmosphere. Unlicensed. Cheap.

Le Caféteria, corner of Rue Abdelkrim Diouri and Rue Chaouia. Casablanca version of an American drugstore; popular with the city's youth. Unlicensed. Cheap to moderate.

Café Intissar, 14 Rue Chaouia. Excellent-value dishes – with an ever-reliable *plat du jour* – served up by a young enthusiastic team. Unlicensed. Cheap to moderate.

Le Buffet, 99 Bd. Mohammed V. Quick and bright, and very popular. Good value *menu du jour*. Unlicensed. Cheap to moderate.

Au Restaurant des Fleurs, 42 Av. des F.A.R. The snackbar downstairs is good for breakfast; upstairs, there is a more formal restaurant serving French and Moroccan dishes. Cheap to moderate.

Restaurant Le Cardinal, 11 Bd. Mohammed V. Traditional French restaurant on the first floor. Moderate.

Restaurant La Corrida, 59 Rue Gay Lussac, near the PTT. Informal *tapas*-style Spanish restaurant run by a Spanish-French couple. Moderate.

Cintra, 84 Rue Allal Ben Abdallah. Piano-bar restaurant with good French menu. Moderate.

Restaurant au Petit Poucet, 86 Bd. Mohammed V. A slice of old Casablanca style, this French restaurant is dressed up like a 1920s Parisian salon (which is really what it was). It was here that the French aviator and writer Saint-Exupéry used to recuperate between his mail-flights south to the Sahara. You come for the decor rather than the food – which is okay but nothing more. Prices are moderate and there is a (much cheaper) snack bar next door.

Al Mounia, 95 Rue du Prince Moulay Abdallah. Traditional Moroccan cuisine served in a salon or out in the garden. You can eat well for 150dh. Moderate to expensive.

Le Marignan, 69 Rue Mohammed Smiha, corner of Bd. Mohammed V, in basement. Excellent Korean food, cooked at the tables. Moderate to expensive.

Taverne du Dauphin, 75 Bd. Houphouet Boigny (☎02/22.12.00). Long-established and very popular fish restaurant. You may need to queue. Moderate to expensive.

CENTRE 2000

There are five restaurants in this shopping complex, which is doen by the Gare du Port; all of them are pretty good.

Le Chalutier (☎03/20.34.55; closed Sun). A busy Spanish-run fish restaurant. Moderate.

Le Mekong (☎03/27.65.36; closed Mon). Asiatic, mainly Chinese, cuisine. Moderate.

La Gondole (☎03/20.74.88). Pizzas and crepes. Gets crowded. Cheap to moderate.

La Tajine (☎03/27.64.00). Well-prepared Moroccan specialities. Moderate to expensive.

Le Retro 1900 (☎03/20.58.28; closed Sun). The most upmarket, serving nouvelle cuisine-type dishes to a largely business clientele. Expensive.

ON THE COAST

Listings below are from east to west along the Corniche to Aïn Diab and beyond.

Le Cabestan, El Hank (☎03/39.11.90; closed Sun). French cuisine, supervised by a highly competent patronne. Nice views of the El Hank lighthouse. Moderate to expensive.

La Mer, El Hank (☎03/36.33.15). Almost next door to *Le Cabestan*; specialises in seafood and fish. Expensive.

Orient Express, 41 Bd. de la Corniche (☎03/36.70.73). An eccentric restaurant, alongside the *Hôtel Tarik*, in a coach from the Orient Express. Fun and above average food. Moderate.

Notre Alsace, 59 Bd. de la Corniche (☎03/36.71.91). A very pleasant bar-restaurant-brasserie; also has a few rooms to let. Moderate.

Restaurant La Mamma, corner of Bd. de la Corniche and Bd. de Biarritz (☎03/39.15.58). A wide range of pasta and standard Italian dishes. Moderate.

Restaurant Sijilmassa, Bd. de Biarritz (☎03/36.13.50). Classic Moroccan dishes, including *pastilla*, served in gardens overlooking the sea. Fantastic view. Moderate.

A Ma Bretagne, Sidi Abderrahmane, 2km west of Aïn Diab (☎03/36.21.12; closed Sun and throughout Aug). French gastronomes visit Casablanca purely to eat at this restaurant, which is run by André Halbert, one of just three *Maître Cuisiniers de France* working in Africa and recipient of an award for the best French cooking in the continent. Specialities include *huîtres au Champagne* and *salade de l'océan au foie gras*; the site is delightful, close to the little island *marabout* of Sidi Abderrahmane (see p.277). Very expensive.

Ice cream and patisseries

Casa has a reputation for its **ice cream parlours** and **patisseries**, too.

Oliver's, Av. Hassan II; **L'Igloo,** Bd. du Janvier (south of Place Mohammed V). The two best ice cream parlours in the city.

Gâteaux Bennis, 2 Rue Fkih El Gabbas. A rival in the Quartier Habous.

Bars and nightclubs

Casa has a surprisingly elusive **nightlife**, at least in the centre, where the clubs tend to be 1960s-themepark-stripjoints. More happens out at Aïn Diab, though none are much recommended to Western women out for a hassle-free drink. Hotel bars provide a fallback – see hotel listings on p.269.

CENTRAL CASA

Au Petit Poucet, 86 Bd. Mohammed V. A bar attached to the famous restaurant; one of the more pleasant downtown serious drinking holes.

American Bar, 49 Bd. Houphouet Boigny. Similar, if perhaps noisier.

Don Quichote, 6 Bd. Houphouet Boigny. A real late-night dive, where you'll likely meet some Casa low-life.

La Fontaine, 133 Bd. Houphouet Boigny. Worse still: an ill-lit strip joint, with a band, belly dancing, and obligatory drinks for the women bar-staff.

Hôtel Safir, Av. des F.A.R. The hotel has an expensive, very swish (and also pretty tasteful) bar – as well as a disco. Relaxed – especially by comparison with all the above . . .

ON THE COAST

Le Balcon 33, 33 Bd. de la Corniche. Lively regular disco.

Le Tube, Bd. de la Corniche. Another popular disco.

Palm Beach Club, Aïn Diab. If you want to live a little more dangerously, try this beerhall, with its belly dancers, heavy-drinking crowd and police on the door to prevent trouble.

Directory

Airline offices include: *Royal Air Maroc,* 44 Av. des F.A.R. (☎02/31.11.57); *Air France,* Av. des F.A.R. (☎02/29.30.30); *British Airways,* c/o *Menara Tours,* Tour Atlas (6th floor), 57 Place Zellaqa (☎02/30.76.07).

American Express c/o *Voyages Schwarz,* 102 Rue Prince Moulay Abdallah (☎02/27.31.33); open Mon–Fri 8.30am–noon & 2.30–6.30pm, Sat 8.30am–noon .

Banks *SGMB,* 84 Bd. Mohammed V; *Crédit du Maroc,* 48–58 Bd. Mohammed V; many others along the same boulevard. Most of the larger hotels will change money outside banking hours. Central ones include the *Hôtel Safir* at 160 Av. des F.A.R. and the *Hyatt Regency* on Place des Nations Unies.

Books/Newspapers For English-language **books** try *English Forum,* 27 Rue Mouftaker Abdelkader, or the *American Language Centre Bookstore,* 1 Place de la Fraternité (just off Bd. Moulay Youssef), both of which have a good range of paperbacks and fair sections on Morocco. *Librairie Farairie,* 43 Rue Araibi Jilali, and *Librairie Nationale,* 2 Av. de Mers Sultan, are also good for a browse. British **newspapers** and the *International Herald Tribune* are available from stands around Place des Nations Unies (and in the *Hyatt Regency* hotel on the square) and at the Gare du Port.

Car hire *Telecontact* (see note at the end of this Directory) lists 65 car hire firms in Casa. Competition is stiff and deals are generally the best in the country, if you spend a while phoning around, or call in at the offices grouped along the Av. des F.A.R. A shortlist might include: *Afric Cars,* 33 Rue Omar Slaoui (☎02/24.21.81); *Avis,* 19 Av. des F.A.R. (☎02/31.24.24); *Budget,* 50 Av. des F.A.R. (☎02/31.40.27); *Europ-Car/InterRent,* 144 Av. des F.A.R. (☎02/31.37.37); *Goldcar,* 5 Av. des F.A.R. (☎02/20.25.10); *Hertz,* 25 Rue Araibi Jilali (☎02/31.22.23); *Tourist Cars,* 53 Rue Allal Ben Abdallah (☎02/31.00.05).

Car repairs Garages include *Renault-Maroc* on Place de Bandoeng (just off our map, below Place Paquet). For information and addresses, contact the *Touring Club du Maroc* (3 Av. des F.A.R.) or *R.A.C. du Maroc* (3 Rue Lemercier).

Consulates There are far fewer consuls than in Rabat. They include: **Britain,** 60 Bd. d'Anfa (☎02/22.16.53); **US,** 8 Bd. Moulay Youssef (☎02/22.41.49); **Denmark,** 12 Rue Champigny (☎02/30.02.11); **Netherlands,** Place du 16 Novembre (☎02/22.17.12).

Cultural events/films Listings are to be found in the free weekly magazine *7 Jours à Casa* (from the tourist offices and major hotels).

Ferry agent *Comanav Voyages,* 43 Av. des F.A.R. (☎02/31.20.50), will give details and sell tickets for most ferry departures from Morocco.

Hammams Every neighbourhood has several; the best is reputed to be *Hay Ali* in the Maarif area – ask a *petit taxi* to take you there.

Medical aid Dial ☎15 for emergency services. Addresses of doctors from the larger hotels, or from the *Croissant Rouge* (Cité Djemaa, 44 Av. E.; ☎02/34.09.14). All-night *pharmacie* is open between Place des Nations Unies and Place Mohammed V.

Police Phone ☎19. Main station is on Bd. Brahim Roudani.

Post office The main *PTT* (for phones/poste restante) is in Place Mohammed V (Mon–Thur 8.30am–12.15pm, Fri 8.30–11.30am).

Shops *Alpha 55,* Av. de Mers Sultan, is a useful department store, with a good, 7th-floor restaurant. Along with the *Centre 2000,* by the port, it can be useful for stocking up on supplies before heading south.

Sports Casa is the best place in Morocco to see Moroccan football; matches are played at the Marcel Cédan stadium (check the local press for details). The city also boasts a racecourse, the Hippodrome, at Anfa (active some Sundays) and, beside it, an 18-hole golfcourse. There is another golfcourse at Mohammedia, to the north.

Tourist Offices Most helpful is the *ONMT,* 55 Rue Omar Slaoui (☎02/27.11.77). The *Syndicat d'Initiative,* 98 Bd. Mohammed V, doesn't seem to have anything to offer.

Tours If you want to book onto a tour of Morocco, *KTI Voyages,* based in Casa, are a very reliable operator, used by British companies like Hayes & Jarvis and Kuoni; their head office is at 432 Rue Mustafa El Maani (☎02/27.14.04). *Mehari Tours,* 14 Rue Taha Houcine (formerly Rue Galilee; ☎02/20.02.70) offer river-rafting, trekking, riding and mountain bike tours in the High Atlas.

Note: *Telecontact, a new annual directory, provides "yellow pages"-style listings and phone numbers for businesses and services in the Casablanca/Rabat region. It is available from news stands and bookshops, price 50dh.*

MOVING ON FROM CASA

Moving on from Casa, *CTM* run **buses** to just about everywhere, including El Jadida, Agadir, Tiznit and various European destinations; tickets and times from the terminal on Rue Léon l'Africain (see map). If you are heading south for Essaouira, the best service is the *CTM* "Mumtaz Express", which leaves at 4.30pm, arriving 10pm at Essaouira; most other services run via El Jadida. In Casa, negotiate at the main stand for Rabat taxis (see above).

For Rabat, Tangier, Meknes, Fes or Marrakesh, you'll probably want to go by **train**. Check times in advance at the *Gare du Port*, and for convenience try to find one that's leaving from this station rather than from the *Gare des Voyageurs*.

CASA TO MARRAKESH

The road and railway speed south across the plains from Casa to Marrakesh – and few people think of stopping along the way. To the east lies the phosphate-mining region, the Plateau des Phosphates, while along the road you pass scarcely more than a handful of local market centres for the (initially quite fertile) agricultural villages, watered by Morocco's greatest river, the Oum er Rbia.

If you are driving, the one detour to consider is to the **Kasbah de Boulaouane**, 50km west of the region's main town, Settat. The Kasbah was one of Moulay Ismail's grandest and most strategic, protected on three sides by a loop in the Oum er Rbia. It has a well, preserved gateway and, within, remains of a palace, vaulted underground chambers and a hammam.

SETTAT itself is a sizeable town – with a population of 150,00 and a single classi-fied **hotel**, the *M'Zamza* (☎03/40.23.66; ②), 1km out on the Casa road.

South to El Jadida

Buses and trains cover the ninety-odd kilometres from **Casablanca to El Jadida** on swift inland routes, of no great interest save for the town of **Azemmour**, an old Portuguese fortress-town at the estuary of the Oum er Rbia – Morocco's greatest river. Using public transport, Azemmour is easiest visited as an excursion from El Jadida, which is only 16km distant.

If you have transport of your own, the old **S130 road** is an enjoyable alterna-tive, trailing the coast the whole way from Casa to Azzemmour. As you clear the urban area, the beaches are increasingly enticing and, as yet, virtually undevel-oped. There is a **campsite** at Temaris Plage, 20km south of Casa.

Sidi Abderrahmane

En route to Azemmour, the most attractive spot is the beach facing the pictu-resque little island **Marabout of Sidi Abderrahmane**, 10km from central Casa, in the first bay that you come to after passing through Aïn Diab. The island itself is a tiny outcrop of rock, under fifty metres from the shore, from which it is possible to walk across at low tide. Non-Muslims, however, may not set foot upon the shrine, which is entirely occupied by the *marabout* – or pilgrim centre – laid out around the shrine of Sidi Abderrahmane, a Muslim Sufi from Baghdad. The pilgrims are, for the most part, the mentally ill and their families, for whom the saint has supposedly curative powers.

Nearby, overlooking the beach, is *A Ma Bretagne* (see p.278), the finest – and most expensive – **restaurant** in the Casablanca area.

Azemmour

AZEMMOUR has an oddly remote history and feel, considering its strategic site on the great Oum er Rbia River. It has long been outside the mainstream of events. When the Portuguese controlled El Jadida, Safi and Essaouira, they stayed here for under thirty years; later, when the European traders moved in on this coast, the town remained a "closed" port. Little bothered by the French, it remains today very much a backwater and sees possibly fewer tourists than any other Moroccan coastal town.

A short visit, nonetheless, is worthwhile, and the town is easily reached by **bus** or **grand taxi** from El Jadida. It's on the train line, too, though the station is 2km out of town, on the far side of the P8. In town, getting your bearings is pretty straightforward. Buses and *grands taxis* stop on Av. Mohammed V, the main thoroughfare of the new town, where drivers will also emerge. At the street's end is a garden square, the Place du Souk, with the **Medina** straight ahead. If you want to stay, there's a choice of three basic **hotels**, the best of which is the *Hôtel de la Victorie* at 308 Av. Mohammed V (☎03/34.71.57; ①). There are also several cafés in town, and a summer restaurant down at the beach (see below).

The Medina

The Portuguese remained in Azemmour long enough to build a circuit of walls, which are stacked directly above the banks of the river and dramatically extended by the white, cubist line of the **Medina**. The best view of all this – and it is impressive – is from across the river, on the way out of town towards Casablanca. To look round the town, however, make your way down from the bus station to the main (landward) side of the ramparts.

At the far corner are the former **Kasbah** and **Mellah** quarters, now largely in ruins – Azemmour's once substantial Jewish population left in 1960 – but safe enough to visit. If you wait around, the local *gardien* will probably arrive, open things up and show you round; if he doesn't turn up, you might find him by asking at the cafés or *syndicat*. Once inside the ruins, you can follow the parapet wall round the ramparts, with views of the river and the gardens, including henna orchards, along its edge. You'll also be shown **Dar El Baroud** (The House of Powder), with its ruined Gothic window, and, nearby, the old town **synagogue**.

It might not sound like much, and you'll have to negotiate the final tip, but all in all it's an interesting and enjoyable break from El Jadida, and easily combined with a swim.

The beach – and birds

The river currents at Azemmour are notoriously dangerous, but there's a nice stretch of **beach** half an hour's walk through the eucalyptus trees above the town. If you go by road, it's signposted to the "Balneaire du Haouzia", a small, private complex of cafés and cabins occupying part of the sands. A three-storey **restaurant**, *La Perle*, recently opened here and looks full of promise.

For **birdwatchers**, the scrub dunes around the mouth of the river should prove rewarding territory – with the possibility of sighting the rare slender-billed curlew in autumn or winter.

Golf and Mehioula

The coast between Azemmour and El Jadida is showing signs of development, the most ambitious of which is the **Royal Golf d'El Jadida**, an eighteen-hole golf course beside the sea, designed by the American Cabell B. Robinson. The links are due to open, along with a five-star hotel and villa complex, in 1994.

If you want a break from the coast, a possible excursion is to **Mehioula**, 14km from Azemmour on the S1318. The road follows the southern banks of the Oum er Rbia through groves of oranges to a gorge. There's a small hotel here, famous in French days, though firmly closed at present.

El Jadida (Mazagan)

The most popular and developed of the "central" Atlantic resorts, **EL JADIDA** is a stylish and beautiful town, retaining the lanes and ramparts of an old Portuguese Medina. Known as *Mazagan* under the Portuguese, it was renamed *El Jadida* – "The New" – after being resettled, partly with Jews from Azemmour, by the nineteenth-century Sultan Abd er Rahman. Under the French, it grew into a quite sizeable administrative centre and a popular beach resort.

Today it's the beach that is undeniably the focal point. Moroccans from Casablanca and Marrakesh, even Tangier or Fes, come here in droves in summer, and, alongside this cosmopolitan mix, there's an unusual feeling of openness. The bars are crowded (a rare feature in itself), there's an almost frenetic evening promenade and – as at Casa – Moroccan women are visible and active participants.

Orientation and accommodation

Orientation is straightforward, with the old **Portuguese Medina**, walled and looking out over the port, and the **Ville Nouvelle** spreading to its south along the seafront. By bus, you will almost certainly arrive at the **bus station** at the southern end of town (bottom-centre on our map overpage), from where it's a twenty-minute walk to the Medina or to most hotels. Coming by train (there is one daily service to and from Rabat/Casa) you arrive at a station 1500m out of town along the Safi road; *petits taxis* are usually available. In summer, leaving El Jadida, bus tickets for Marrakesh or Casablanca should be bought a day ahead.

In summer you'd also be well advised to make a **hotel** booking – rooms can be very hard to find. In fact, at all times you may prefer to make some phone calls before pacing the streets, as the town extends for some distance along the seafront. If you have problems, the very helpful **ONMT** office on Av. Ibn Khaldoun (☎03/34.27.24), may have some ideas; there are flats and villas for rent, if you are staying for a week or more.

HOTELS

Hôtel de France/Hôtel Maghreb [D], 12/16 Rue Lescoul (☎03/34.21.81). This is in reality one hotel – though with two stairways and names. It is old and roomy, with great views of the sea, hot showers on the landing, and very cheap. Highly recommended. ①

Hôtel El Jadida [A], 77 Av. Zerktouni (☎03/34.01.78). Very basic, with cold showers only, and distinctly low standards of cleanliness. Not at all recommended. ①

Hôtel de Port [E], 56 Bd. El Mohit (☎03/34.27.01). A fallback, if needs be. ①

Hôtel Moderne [F], 21 Av. Hassan II (☎03/34.31.33). Very much a family hotel, with a small garden. Hot showers on the corridor. ①

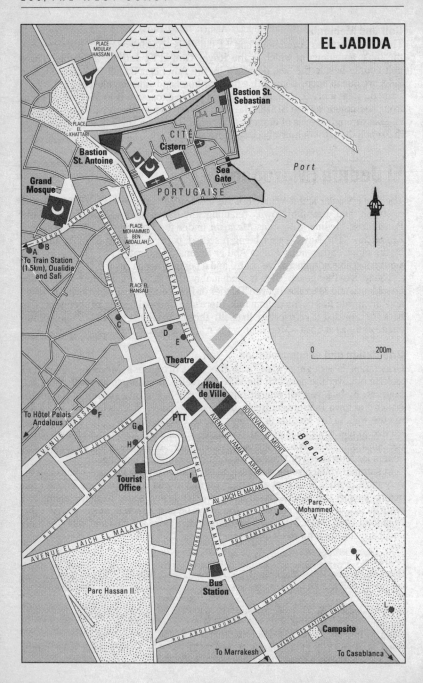

EL JADIDA

PLACE MOULAY HASSAN

Bastion St. Sebastian

RUE AHRIR

PLACE EL KHATTABI

CITÉ

Cistern

Bastion St. Antoine

PORTUGAISE

Sea Gate

Port

Grand Mosque

AVENUE FAKHROUNI

PLACE MOHAMMED BEN ABDALLAH

A
B

To Train Station (1.5km), Oualidia and Safi

RUE M.Z. TAHIR

PLACE EL HANSALI

BOULEVARD DE SUEZ

C

200m

D
E

Theatre

Hôtel de Ville

To Hôtel Palais Andalous

AVENUE HASSAN II

F

RUE JULES VERNE

AV. EL MHATTI

PTT

RUE GRABETTI

G

AVENUE EL JAMIA EL ARABI

BOULEVARD EL MOHIT

H

Beach

Tourist Office

AVENUE

RUE MOHAMMED

I

AV. JAICH EL MALAKI

AVENUE

AVENUE HASSAN II

RUE JULES VERNE

RUE CARPOZEN

J

Parc Mohammed V

RUE DENENORVAL

RUE MOHAMMED V

AVENUE EL JAICH EL MALAKI

K

Parc Hassan II

RUE GEORGES

RUE EL MOKHTAR

Bus Station

RUE ABDELMOUMEN

AVENUE DES NATIONS UNIES

L

Campsite

To Marrakesh

To Casablanca

Hôtel Bordeaux [C], 47 Rue Moulay Ahmed Tahiri (☎03/34.23.56). An old hotel – the oldest in town, so they claim – attractively refurbished. Hot showers on the corridor. ⑩

Hôtel de la Plage [J], Av. Al Jamia Al Arabi (☎03/34.26.48). Formerly a one-star hotel, this recently slipped to become unclassified. It's clean enough, though, and friendly, despite the rather grim bar on the ground floor. ⑩

Hôtel Royal [I], 108 Av. Mohammed V (☎03/34.28.39). A bit pricier but large, airy rooms with generally functional showers, a garden and bar. ⑩

Hôtel Bruxelles [G], 40 Av. Ibn Khaldoun (☎03/34.20.72). Pleasant, clean rooms – with balconies at the front; next to the *Royal*, despite the address. ①

Hôtel Suisse [B], 145 Av. Zerktouni (☎03/34.28.16). Similar to the above, in a useful central location, with an adjoining restaurant. ①

Hôtel de Provence [H], 42 Av. Fqih Mohammed Errafi (☎03/34.23.47). Popular British-run hotel: clean and central, with a good restaurant, a garden for breakfast, and covered parking nearby (10dh for 24hr). The best budget choice, so be sure to reserve ahead. ②

Hôtel Palais Andalous [off map], Rue de la Nouie (☎03/34.39.06). Converted 1930s palace with a touch of fantasy and an excellent bar. It's a bit tricky to find: ask for l'Hôpital Mohammed V, which is opposite. Very good value out of season. ③

Hôtel Mara [K], Av. Al Jamiaa Al Arabi (☎03/34.41.70). An elegant-looking, Art Deco hotel that has developed a rather seedy reputation of late. Has a swimming pool and bar. ④

Hôtel-Club Salam [L], Av. Al Jamia Al Arabi (☎03/34.37.37). Modern package hotel on the beach, with tennis courts and swimming pool. Not as good as most *Salam* hotels. ④

CAMPING

Camping International, Av. des Nations Unies (☎03/34.27.55). A well-equipped, if slightly expensive site with a pool, bar and restaurant. Ten minutes' walk south of the bus station.

Camping Sidi Bouzid, 5km south of town on the Safi road. A pleasant beachside campsite. Local bus #2 runs to the resort from Place Mohammed Ben Abdallah.

The town and beaches

El Jadida's **Medina** is the most European-looking in Morocco: a quiet, walled and bastioned seaside village, with a handful of churches scattered on its lanes. It was founded by the Portuguese in 1513 – and retained by them until 1769 – and it is still popularly known as the **Cité Portugaise**. The Moors who settled here after the Portuguese withdrawal tended to live outside the walls. Budgett Meakin, writing in the 1890s, found an "extensive native settlement of beehive huts, or *nouallahs*" spreading back from the harbour, while European merchants had re-established themselves in the "clean, prosperous and well-lighted streets" of the Medina. As in all the "open ports" on this coast, there was also an important Jewish community handling the trade with Marrakesh; uniquely, old Mazagan had no separate Jewish quarter, or *Mellah*.

The Cité Portugaise

The **Cité Portugaise** is steadily being restored, and a walk round its newly spruced-up ramparts is not to be missed. Nor, above all, is a visit to the beautiful old **Portuguese Cistern** (Mon–Fri 8am–noon & 2–6pm; 10dh), a subterranean vault that mirrors its roof and pillars in a shallow film of water covering the floor. The cistern is entered midway along the Medina's main street, on the left walking down, opposite a small souvenir shop. It was used to startling effect in Orson Welles's great film of *Othello* (see p.294); he staged a riot here, provoked by Iago to discredit Cassio, and filmed it from within and above.

If you continue up the street from the cistern, you'll come to the old **Porte de la Mer**, a sea gate opening onto the port. The churches and chapels, long converted to secular use, are generally closed; the **Grand Mosque** here was once a lighthouse – and looks like it.

The beaches

El Jadida's town **beach** spreads north from the *cité* and port, well beyond the length of the town. It's a popular strip, though from time to time polluted by the ships in port. If it doesn't look too good, or you feel like a change, take a *petit taxi* 3km south along the coastal road past the **Phare Sidi Ouafi** (lighthouse), a broader strip of sand where dozens of Moroccan families set up tents for the summer. Good swimming is to be had and there are makeshift beach cafés.

Plage Sidi Bouzid, 2km further south, is more developed, flanked by some fancy villas, a chic restaurant-bar, *Le Requin Bleu*, renowned for its fish; the less expensive Restaurant Beausejour; and a summer **campsite**. The beach can be reached on bus #2 from Place Mohammed Ben Abdullah, or by *grand taxi*.

Practicalities

For its size, El Jadida is well served by **restaurants**, and has most other facilities you might want to make use of.

Restaurants

Restaurant Cherazad, 38 Place El Hansali. Good Moroccan dishes in a central location; much better than the other Cherazad restaurant in town! Cheap to moderate.

Rotisserie La Broche, 46 Place El Hansali. In keen competition with the Cherazad, so again good value. Cheap to moderate.

Restaurant Tchikito, Rue Mohammed Smiha, off Place El Hansali. A great little fish restaurant, with generous helpings and Koranic decorations. Unlicensed, of course. Moderate.

Hôtel-Restaurant du Provence, 42 Av. Fqih Mohammed Errafi. Well-prepared, French-inspired meals, open to non-residents, and licensed. Moderate.

Restaurant El Khaïma, Av. des Nations Unies, opposite the campsite. Good-value Moroccan and Italian dishes, prepared by an Italian chef. Moderate.

Restaurant Le Tit, 2 Av. Al Jamia El Arabi, by the PTT. Classy cooking and good service. Moderate.

Restaurant Clair du Lune, 1km from the centre, past Parc Mohammed V, on the road towards Casablanca. A good new enterprise, with a café and pizzeria on the ground floor and a restaurant above, looking out to sea. Moderate.

Bars

Bars are to be found mainly in the hotels – try the *Hôtel de la Plage* (lively), *de Provence* (pleasant) and *Palais Andalous* (refined); in addition, *Safari Pub*, 6 Av. Fqih Mohammed Errafi, is an easygoing bar with snacks and light meals.

Directory

Banks include *Credit du Maroc*, *BMCI* and *WAFA* on Av. Al Jamia El Arabi, and *BMCE* at 9 Av. Mohammed Rafy.

Cinemas The *Cinema Paris* and *Cinema Rif* are both on Place El Hansali.

Post office The main PTT is on Place Mohammed V.

Souk A Wednesday *souk* takes place by the lighthouse southwest of town.

El Jadida to Safi

Once again, the main road (and express buses) south, from **El Jadida to Safi**, take an inland road, across the plains. The coast road, however, is equally direct, and extremely pleasant, with little development, some lovely stretches of beach, and major **bird habitats** around the low-key resort of **Oualidia**. It's not much frequented by tourists, who seem to visit either El Jadida from Casa or Essaouira from Marrakesh – rarely both.

El Jadida to Oualidia

The main appeal here is **birdwatching**, though there is a minor ancient site at **Moulay Abdallah** and fine beaches once you are beyond Cap Blanc and the industrial **Port de Jorf-Lasar**, terminal for the *OCP* phosphate plants on the plains inland.

Moulay Abdallah and the ruins of Tit
MOULAY ABDALLAH, 11km from El Jadida, is a tiny fishing village, dominated by a large *zaouia* complex and partially enclosed by a circuit of walls in ruins. At the *zaouia* an important **moussem** is held towards the end of August.

The walls span the site of a twelfth-century **ribat**, or fortified monastery, known as **Tit** ("eyes" or "spring" in the local Berber dialect) and built, so it is thought, in preparation for a Norman invasion: a real threat at the time – the Normans having launched attacks on Tunisia – but one which never materialised. Today, there is little to see, though the minaret of the modern **zaouia** (prominent and whitewashed) is Almohad in origin; behind it, up through the graveyard, you can walk to a second, isolated minaret, which is thought to be even older. If it is, then it is perhaps the only one surviving from the Almoravid era – a claim considerably more impressive than its simple, block-like appearance might suggest.

Sidi Abed and Sidi Moussa
The first good beach beyond Cap Blanc is at **SIDI ABED**, a small village with a café-restaurant and a scattering of villas.

The coast hereabouts is an alternation of sandy beach and rocky outcrops, and past **SIDI MOUSSA**, 37km from El Jadida, it's backed by huge dunes, then, towards Oualidia, cut off by a long expanse of salt marshland. From here on south, for the next 70km or so, birdwatchers are in for a treat (see box). Sidi Moussa is attractive to non-twitchers, too, with its estuary-like lagoon, and its beach. It also has a very pleasant **hotel**, the *Villa la Brise* (Sidi Moussa ☎1, via the operator; ②), with French cooking, a bar, and a swimming pool that's sometimes full. It's a popular base for fishing.

South of Sidi Moussa, the roadside is flanked by saltpans and by extensive plastic hothouses, for intensive cultivation of tomatoes and other vegetables. At **SOUK EL DJEMAA**, as the name suggests, there's a **Friday souk**.

Oualidia and beyond

OUALIDIA, 78km from El Jadida, is a stunningly picturesque little resort – a fishing port and lagoon beach, flanked by a seventeenth-century Kasbah and a (now

BIRD HABITATS AROUND OUALIDIA

The 70km of coast between SIDI MOUSSA (36km south of El Jadida) and CAP BEDDOUZA (34km south of Oualidia) is one of the richest **birdlife habitats** in Morocco. The coastal wetlands, sands and saltpans, the jagged reefs, and the lagoons of Sidi Moussa and Oualidia, shelter a huge range of species – flamingoes, avocets, stilts, godwits, storks, waders, terns, egrets, warblers and many small waders. Numerous countryside species come in, too; golden oriole and hoopoe have been recorded, and flocks of shearwaters are often to be seen not far offshore.

The best watching locations are the two **lagoons** and the rocky headland at **Cap Beddouza**.

unused) royal villa, built by Hassan II's father, Mohammed V. It deserves to be better known: the beach is excellent for swimming, surfing and windsurfing, the atmosphere relaxed, and swimming is safe and easy.

Most of the tourists who come here are Moroccan families and they settle into tent-colonies in and around the **campsite**, *Camping Oualidia*, pleasantly laid out in a garden behind the sand dunes. The hotels are all very good, too, and offer seafood meal to residents and non-residents alike. Choices are:

Motel-Restaurant à l'Araigné Gourmande (☎03/34.64.47). Good-value rooms and a wide range of *prix-fixe* menus. ①

Complexe Touristique Chems (☎03/34.64.78). Under the same management as the motel, offering cabins of various sizes, from singles to family bungalows, all with hot showers. It's a bit pricey, quoting half-board only, but the restaurant is pretty good. ③

Auberge de la Lagune (☎03/34.64.77). The oldest hotel-restaurant with wonderful views from its terrace. Service is a bit surly but the seafood menus, including oysters and mussels, are not to be missed. ①

Hôtel Hippocampe (☎03/34.64.99). Rooms off a flower-filled courtyard and a private beach. Used by a surfing travel operator. Half-board only. ②

Inland from Oualidia: Kasbah Gharbia

The Doukkala plains, inland from the El Jadida–Safi coast have long been a fertile and fought-over region, and there are scattered forts and Kasbahs at several villages. One of the most interesting and accessible is at **GHARBIA**, 20km from Oualidia on the S1336 across an undulating limestone plateau. The **Kasbah** here is a vast enclosure, four kilometres long on each side, bastioned at intervals, and with a gate at each point of the compass, giving onto roads to Oualidia, Safi, El Jadida and Marrakesh: a strategic site. Within, a few houses remain in use and there's a large white house in the centre, occupied by the caid in the days of the Protectorate. If you visit – the trip is only really feasible if you have transport – you will be shown round by a charming bunch of locals, intent on pointing out the various features.

Cap Beddouza and Lalla Fatma

Continuing south from Oualidia, the road climbs a little inland and above the sea, which is hidden from view by sand dunes. It's a pretty stretch and the more so as you approach **Cap Beddouza**, where the rocky headland gives way intermittently to sandy beaches, sheltered by cliffs. At the cape there is a lighthouse and an **auberge**, the *Cap El Bedouza* (no phone; ⑩), with a restaurant, bar and basic, rather overpriced cabins.

The best of the cliff-sheltered beaches is known as **Lalla Fatma**, 51km from Oualidia and just 15km short of Safi (with which it's connected by local bus #15). It is totally undeveloped, with nothing more than a **koubba** and in summer a few Moroccan tents, sometimes a café. If you are intending to stay, you'll need your own transport and to take provisions. The beach is a steep two-kilometre descent from the road; camping on the beach, make sure you've pitched your tent far enough back from the tides. There is a **moussem** at the *koubba* on the thirteenth day of Chaâbane (the month before Ramadan).

Finally, beyond Cap Safi, **Sidi Bouzid** is Safi's local beach. Notwithstanding a couple of pleasant restaurants – notably *Le Refuge* – it's nothing very special, though it does have views down to the town, with its port, industry and Medina.

Safi

Flanked by a strip of fertiliser factories, a vast grain silo and sardine-canning plants, **SAFI** is not the prettiest of Moroccan towns. It does, however, provide a glimpse of an active, modern and working community and the old **Medina** in its centre, walled and turreted by the Portuguese, holds a certain interest. The city – it is genuinely so, with a population over 300,000 – also has a strong industrial-artesan tradition, with a whole neighbourhood above the walls still devoted to **pottery workshops**. These have a virtual monopoly on the green, heavily glazed roof tiles used on palaces and mosques, as well as providing Morocco's main pottery exports, in the form of bowls, plates and garden pots.

Orientation and accommodation

Arriving by **bus**, you should find yourself at the new bus station, around 1500m south of the Medina. The **train station** (Safi has twice-daily connections to the Casa–Marrakesh line at Benguerir) is a similar distance.

From either, it's easiest to hire a *petit taxi* or get on a city bus into one of the main squares, **Place de l'Indépendance**, just south of the Medina, or **Place Mohammed V**, recently spruced up with gardens, and flanked by most of the city's major public buildings – the PTT, Municipalité, and so on.

HOTELS

Hôtel Essaouira (☎04/46.48.09), **Hôtel de Paris** (☎04/46.21.49), **Hotel l'Avenir** (☎04/ 46.26.57), Impasse de la Mer [A]. A trio of cheap, unclassified hotels tucked just inside the Medina. The *Avenir* wins hands down, with cold showers in the rooms, hot showers on the corridor, grand views of the sea, and a café downstairs. ⓪

Hôtel Majestic [B], Place de l'Indépendance (☎04/46.31.31). Clean, with cold showers. ⓪

Hôtel l'Océan [D], 5 Rue du R'bat (☎04/46.42.07). Okay, with hot showers on the corridor. ⓪

Hôtel Sevillana [C], 1 Rue Ben Hassan (☎04/46.27.59). Not too bad, with a pleasant terrace. ⓪

Hôtel Les Mimosas [I], Rue Ibn Zeidoun (☎04/62.32.08). A 1970s block. Comfortable enough rooms, though the bar and disco have a rather dubious local reputation. ②

Hôtel Anis [E], Av. du R'bat (☎04/46.30.78). Rooms and apartments, so good for families and/or long stays. ②

Hôtel Assif [H], Av. de la Liberté (☎04/62.23.11). The best mid-range hotel. Light, airy rooms and a good restaurant, not far from Place Mohammed V. ②

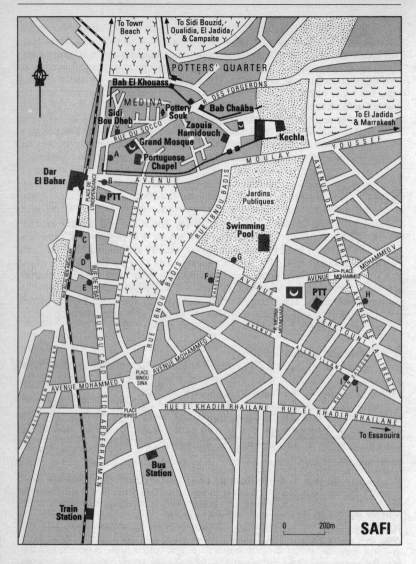

Hôtel Atlantide [F], Rue Chawki (☎04/62.21.60). A pleasant old hotel, if not quite deserving all its stars; has a bar and restaurant. ③

Hôtel Safir [G], Av. Zerktouni (☎04/46.42.99). Good modern hotel with a swimming pool, tennis court, restaurant and bar, and commanding views over the city. ④

CAMPING

Camping International Safi, 2km north of town, signposted to the right of the road to Oualidia. Spacious and well shaded, with a shop, pool and usual facilities. It is 1km from here to the beach at Sidi Bouzid.

The town

The main interest in Safi is in its **Medina**, the adjoining **Dar El Bahar** fort, and the **potters' quarter**, on the hill north of the **Medina**. Further out, on the Oualidia road, is the main industrial quarter and the new port.

Dar El Bahar, Kechla and the Medina

The **Dar El Bahar**, or Château de la Mer (Mon–Fri 9am–noon & 2–4pm; 10dh), is the main remnant of Safi's brief Portuguese occupation (1508–41). Sited on the waterfront, above the old port, it was built – in the Manueline style of the day – as the governor's residence, and saw subsequent use as a fortress and prison. Within, you can see the old prison cells at the foot of a spiral staircase to the ramparts, where a line of Dutch and Spanish cannon is ranged pointing out to sea.

The old Medina walls climb north, enclosing the Medina, to link with another and larger fortress known as **Kechla** – again, Portuguese in origin, and housing the town's modern prison until 1990. It is now a museum (same hours as above), with a half-hearted collection of local ceramics and, of rather more interest, further cannon (British this time), garden courtyards and Portuguese coats-of-arms.

In the **Medina** proper, there is one further relic of the Portuguese, the **Chapelle Portugaise**. This was the choir of their cathedral – left uncompleted on their withdrawal – and again has Manueline motifs. It is most easily found if you enter the quarter from Av. Moulay Youssef. Moving round from here, you reach the Rue du Socco – the main street – which leads uphill past a series of **souks**, food and domestic-goods markets, to the old city gate of Bab Chaaba and the potteries. En route, the **Souk de Poterie** is of most interest, and if you are looking to buy goods, you are likely to find better pieces here than in the potters' quarter itself; Serghini Ahmed's shop (#7) is especially good.

Although non-Muslims are forbidden entry, it is worth recording two important Sufi shrines in the Medina: the **Marabout Sidi Bou Dheb** (at the bottom end of Rue du Socco) and the **Zaouia of Hamdouchia** (near the Kechla). Sidi Bou Dheb is perhaps the best known Sufi saint in Morocco and both his *marabout* and the Hamdouchia *zaouia* host **moussems** (held in May in recent years) attended by their respective brotherhoods; these feature music, dervish-type dancing and, often, trance self-mutilation with hatchets and knives. Heady stuff.

Quartier des Potiers

The **Quartier des Potiers** sprawls above the Medina and is impossible to miss, with its dozens of whitewashed beehive-kilns and chimneys, merging into the cemeteries beyond. The processes here remain traditional – electricity and gas have made scarcely an inroad on the tamarisk-fired kilns – and the quarter is worth at least the time it takes to wander up. The colour dyes, however, and the garish designs are hardly comparable to the beautiful old pieces that can be seen around the country's crafts museums. Indeed, you are as likely to see U-bends for toilets being fired, as anything else.

Practicalities

Safi has a fair selection of restaurants, plus all the usual city facilities, grouped round the Place Mohammed V, Place de l'Indépendance (the PTT is here) and Place Ibnou Sina (where you'll find most of the banks).

Cafés and restaurants

Café M'Zoughan, Place de l'Indépendance. Café-patisserie, good for breakfast.

Le Poulet d'Or, 65 Av. Mohammed V. Well-prepared Moroccan standards. Cheap.

Café-Restaurant El Bahia, Place de l'Indépendance. Café downstairs and restaurant above, with more fancy Moroccan dishes. Moderate.

Restaurant Calypso, Place de l'Indépendance. Reasonable menu du jour, served inside or out in the garden behind. Moderate.

Restaurant de Safi, 3 Rue de la Maraine, off Place de l'Indépendance. Grills. Moderate.

All the classified hotels (see pp.285–86) also have restaurants.

Beaches

The coast immediately south of Safi is heavily polluted and industrialised, and for a beach escape you'll want to head north. Local buses #10/15 run to Lalla Fatima and Cap Beddouza (see p.284) from the Place de l'Indépendance. In summer there are also local buses to Souira Kedima (see below).

Safi to Essaouria: Kasbah Hamidouch

Travelling by bus, you have no option but to take the inland P8, if heading south from **Safi to Essaouria**. With your own transport, you could follow the minor road S6531/6537, which runs, past an industrial strip, to **Souira Kedima**, around 30km south of Safi. This is a fine beach fronted by a rather bleak holiday-bungalow complex, used by people from Safi and Marrakesh on their summer holidays; nearby is an old Portuguese fortress known as **Agouz**.

A little beyond Souria Kedima, a brand new bridge allows you to cross the Oued Tensift (the Michelin map has a "G" for ford at this point) to reach, along a stretch of good but sandy piste, the large and isolated fortress of **Kasbah Hamidouch**. This was built by the ever-industrious Moulay Ismail to control the mouth of the Tensift – one of the most active Moroccan rivers, which here finishes its course from Marrakesh. You can reach its ramparts across the fields.

South of the Kasbah, a **new road** – unmarked on the Michelin map – heads off along the coast towards Essaouria via **Cap Hadid**. At last look it was incomplete, so you may find yourself doing some backtracking to regain the old S6611.

Essaouira (Mogador)

ESSAOUIRA is Morocco's most likeable resort: an eighteenth-century town, enclosed by almost Gothic battlements, facing a cluster of rocky offshore islands, and trailed by vast expanse of empty sands and dunes. Its whitewashed and blue-shuttered houses and colonnades, its wood workshops and art galleries, its boat-builders and sardine fishermen: all provide a colourful and very pleasant back-drop to the beach. The life of the resort, too, is easy and uncomplicated, and very much in the image of the predominantly youthful Europeans and Marrakchis who come here on holiday; unlike Agadir, few of the visitors who stay here are on package tours.

Many of the foreign tourists are drawn by the wind, which can be a bit remorseless for sunbathing but creates much sought-after waves for **surfing** and **windsurfing**. In recent years, Essaouria has gained quite a reputation in this respect, promoting itself as "Windy City, Afrika" and hosting national and international surfing contests. This burgeoning popularity is, inevitably, changing the town's character, with villas springing up along the corniche, but as yet it's very far from spoilt, and remains a thoroughly enjoyable base to rest up after the big-city tensions of Casa or Marrakesh.

Some history

With its dramatic sea bastions and fortifications, Essaouira seems a lot older than it is. Although a series of forts had been built here from the fifteenth century on, it was only in the 1760s that the town, then known as **Mogador**, was established and the present circuit of walls constructed. This work was on the orders of the Sultan **Sidi Mohammed Ben Abdallah**, and carried out by a French captive architect, Theodore Cornut, which explains the town's unique blend of Moroccan Medina and French grid layout.

The sultan's original intention was to provide a military port, as Agadir was in revolt at the time and Sultan Mohammed Ben Abdallah needed a local base. It lent itself superbly to the purpose, as its series of forts ensured complete protection for the bay. Soon, however, commercial concerns gained pre-eminence. During the nineteenth century, Mogador was the only Moroccan port south of Tangier that was open to European trade, and it prospered greatly on the privelege. Drawn by protected trade status, and a harbour free from customs duties, British merchants settled in the Kasbah quarter, and a large Jewish community in the Mellah, within the northeast ramparts.

Decline later set in during the French Protectorate, with their promotion of Casablanca, and was accelerated, after independence, by the exodus of the Jewish community. These days, however, the town is very much back on its feet, as a fishing port and market town, and especially with the recent impetus of tourism.

Orientation and accommodation

Still largely contained within its ramparts, Essaouira is a simple place to get to grips with. At the north end of town is the **Bab Doukkala**; at the south is the town's pedestrianised main square, **Place Prince Moulay El Hassan**, and the fishing **harbour**. Between them run two main parallel streets: **Av. de l'Istiqlal/ Av. Mohammed Zerktouni** and **Rue Sidi Mohammed Ben Abdallah**.

Points of arrival

Buses (both *CTM* and private lines) arrive at a new bus station, inconveniently sited on the outskirts of the town, about 2km (ten minutes' walk) north of Bab Doukkala in the Quartier Industrielle. It is unsignposted and reached along a very ill-lit and in parts unmetalled road, past a shanty-town quarter. Especially at night, it's well worth taking a *petit taxi* into or out from town; the charge is around 6dh (8dh at night).

Grands taxis also operate from the bus station, though they will normally drop arrivals at Bab Doukkala or Place Prince Moulay El Hassan. There is a **petit taxi rank** by the clocktower east of Place Prince Moulay El Hassan.

If you are driving, it's worth making use of the **car parking** space, manned round the clock (5dh for 24hr), south of Place Prince Moulay Hassan.

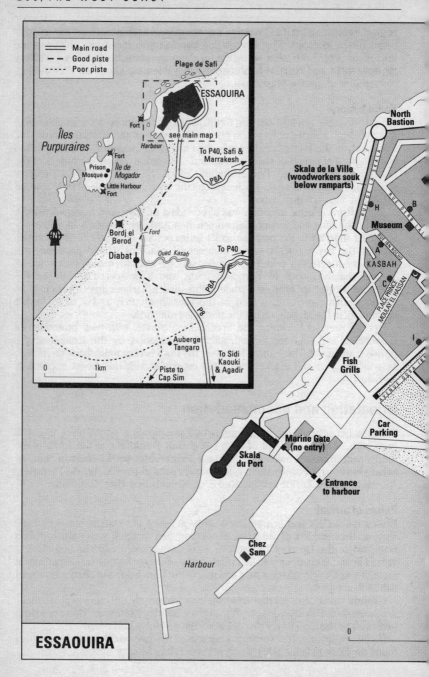

Main road
Good piste
Poor piste

Plage de Safi

ESSAOUIRA

see main map

Îles Purpuraires

Fort

Harbour

To P40, Safi & Marrakesh

P8A

Prison

Île de Mogador

Mosque

Little Harbour

Fort

Fort

N

Bordj el Berod

Ford

Diabat

Oued Kasab

To P40

P8A

P8

Auberge Tangaro

To Sidi Kaouki & Agadir

Piste to Cap Sim

0   1km

North Bastion

Skala de la Ville (woodworkers souk below ramparts)

H

B

Museum

A

KASBAH

C

PLACE PRINCE MOULAY EL HASSAN

I

Fish Grills

Car Parking

Marine Gate (no entry)

Skala du Port

Entrance to harbour

Chez Sam

Harbour

ESSAOUIRA

0

0

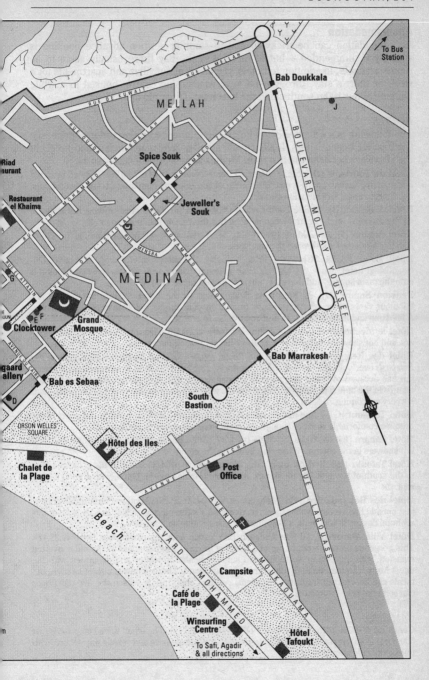

To Bus Station

Bab Doukkala

J

MELLAH

Riad
aurant

Spice Souk

Restaurant
el Khaima

Jeweller's
Souk

MEDINA

G

Grand
Mosque

E F
Clocktower

gaard
allery

Bab es Sebaa

D

Bab Marrakesh

South
Bastion

ORSON WELLES
SQUARE

Hôtel des Iles

Chalet de
la Plage

Post
Office

Beach

BOULEVARD MOHAMMED

Campsite

Café de
la Plage

Winsurfing
Centre

Hôtel
Tafoukt

To Safi, Agadir
& all directions

RUE EL MELLAH
RUE DE KUWAIT
RUE IBNOU TOFAIL
AVENUE MOHAMMED
AVENUE MOHAMMED ZERKTOUNI
RUE EL HANSA
RUE EL AMRANI EL BRIHI

BOULEVARD MOULAY YOUSSEF

AVENUE LALLA AICHA
AVENUE SIDI MOHAMMED BEN ABDALLAH
AVENUE EL MOUKAOUAMA
RUE AGOUASS

Accommodation

Accommodation can be tricky to find in summer – when advance booking is strongly recommended – but at the end of the day there usually seem to be rooms available. In addition to hotels, you can rent out villas and apartments for a week or more's stay, through the local windsurfing centre, housed in a white building about 100m south along the beach from the Café de la Plage.

HOTELS

The following is a selective list of hotels, in roughly ascending order of price; see the map for keyed letters. If all are full, a half-dozen basic, unclassified hotels in the alleyways between the two main Medina streets provide last resorts.

Hôtel du Tourisme [D], Rue Mohammed Ben Messaoud (☎04/47.20.75). Located in an old house in the Kasbah quarter, near the southeast corner of the ramparts; decent, clean rooms, but charges extra for cold showers. ⓪

Hôtel Majestic [B], 40 Rue Derb Laalouj (☎04/47.24.98). Good clean rooms, hot showers on the corridors, and a central location mean that this fills up fast in summer. ⓪

Hôtel Argana [J], Av. 2 Mars (☎04/47.29.75). A reasonable, fairly new hotel, just north of Bab Doukkala; hot showers on the corridors. ⓪

Hôtel Beau Rivage [C], Place Prince Moulay Hassan (☎04/47.29.25). Attractive, old-established hotel, above the *Café de France*. Rooms (some with private showers) look out onto the main square, and there's a "terrasse panoramique", too. ⓪

Pension Smara [H], 26 Rue de la Skala – next to the *Cinema Skala* (☎04/47.23.34). Fabulous views of the sea and ramparts from many of its rooms; hot showers on the corridor. A bit damp and musty, but clean and good value. ⓪

Hôtel le Mechouar [F], Av. Okba Ibn Nafi (☎04/47.20.18). Pleasant rooms with cold showers, and hot showers on the corridor; also a decent restaurant. ①

Hôtel des Remparts [A], 18 Rue Ibn Rochd (☎04/47.25.08). As the name suggests, the *Remparts* overlooks the sea walls. A three-storey, courtyard building, it was once quite grand, but has decayed over the years and is a touch seedy, with everything at times just a little damp. On the plus side, it has a rooftop terrace where you can sunbathe out of the wind – and it's very welcoming. ①

Hôtel Tafraout [G], 7 Rue de Marrakech (☎04/47.29.02). Modern hotel in the heart of the Medina; comfortable rooms – though make sure you get one with windows. ①

Hôtel Sahara [E], Av. Okba Ibn Nafia (☎04/47.22.92). Big rooms around a central well, and hot showers in the rooms – if the plumbing is in the mood. ①

Hôtel Tafoukt [labelled off map], Bd. Mohammed V (☎04/47.25.04). This is located 1km to the south of town, facing the beach. It's a comfortable modern block, with a good restaurant. ③

Hôtel des Iles [labelled], Bd. Mohammed V (☎04/47.23.29). Another comfortable choice, just outside the Medina, with chalet rooms round a swimming pool. Not exactly state-of-the-art hotel design (it was built in 1940) but has a bar and restaurant. ④

Hôtel Villa Maroc [I], 10 Rue Abdallah Ben Yassin near the clocktower (☎04/47.31.47). This gorgeous hotel is straight out of a *World of Interiors* magazine feature: an old converted mansion, with a dozen or so rooms and suites – heated in winter and decorated with the finest Moroccan materials – grouped round a courtyard. There is no restaurant as such, but meals can be ordered from the (excellent) resident chef. In low season the five-star prices can sometimes be negotiated. ④

CAMPING

Camping d'Essaouira, Bd. Mohammed V (☎04/47.38.17). The small town campsite is just 300m out from the walls, past the *Hôtel des Iles*. It is inexpensive and reasonably secure, with toilets and cold showers.

The town

There are few formal "sights" in Essaouria, but it's a great place just to walk around, exploring the **ramparts**, the **harbour** and the **souks** – above all the **thuya wood workshops** – or wandering along the immense wind-swept **beach**.

The Skala de la Ville, thuya wood workshops and galleries

The ramparts are the obvious place to start a tour of Essaouira. If you head north along the lane at the end of Place Prince Moulay El Hassan, you can gain access to the **Skala de la Ville**, the great sea bastion which runs along the northern cliffs. Along the top of it are a collection of European cannon, presented to Sultan Sidi Mohammed Ben Abdallah by ambitious nineteenth-century merchants, and at its end is the circular **North Bastion**, with panoramic views across the Medina, Kasbah and Mellah quarters, and out to sea.

Along the Rue de Skala, built into the ramparts, are a group of **marquetry and wood-carving workshops**, long established in Essaouira. These artesans produce amazingly painstaking and beautiful marquetry work from the local **thuya** (or *thuja*, or *arar* in Arabic), a mahogany-like hardwood from a local coniferous tree, from which they adapt both the trunk and the roots (or *loupe*). With total justice, they claim that their produce is the best in the country. If you see good examples elsewhere they've probably come from here, and if you're thinking of buying – boxes and chess sets are for sale, as well as traditional furniture – this is the best place to do it.

The quality of the marquetry and carving is so high that it seems invidious to pick out individual workshops from the forty or so along the Skala. However, there are certain outlets elsewhere in the town that are worth looking up. These include: **Afalkay Art**, 9 Place Prince Moulay El Hassan; **Jamal Hajhouj**, 7 Place Chefchaouni (located in an old Jewish home, and with perhaps the ultimate thuya artefact – an inlaid lavatory seat); and the **Galerie d'Art Frederic Damgaard** on Av. Oqba Ibn Nafia (daily 9am–1pm & 3–8pm). The latter is actually more a gallery for paintings than thuya creations, regularly exhibiting twenty or so locally based artists. However, it is run by a Danish furniture designer, who uses the traditional thuya techniques in a highly imaginative modern context – and these pieces are well worth seeing.

Also of interest for the local craft content is the **Musée Sidi Mohammed Ben Abdallah** (8.30am–noon & 2.30–6pm; closed Tues) on Rue Derb Laâlouj. This again features excellent displays of marquetry, past and present, as well as more standard handicrafts collections. It is housed in a nineteenth-century mansion on the road running down from the ramparts to Av. de l'Istiqlal. At the time of writing it was closed for renovation.

Spice and jewellery souks and the Mellah

The town's **other souks** spread around and to the south of two arcades, on either side of Rue Mohammed Zerktouni, and up towards the Mellah. Worth particular attention are the **Marché d'Épices** (spice market) and **Souk des Bijoutiers** (jewellers' market). Stallholders in the spice *souk* will extol the virtues of their wares, including exotic remedies for baldness, infertility and so on.

The jewellery business was one of the traditional trades of Essaouira's Jewish community, who have long since deserted the **Mellah**, in the northwest corner of

ORSON WELLES' OTHELLO

Orson Welles filmed much of his **Othello** in Essaouira, returning the Moor (played by Welles himself) to his homeland. The film opens with a tremendous panning shot of the Essaouira ramparts, where Welles placed a scene-setting "punishment" of Iago, suspended above the sea and rocks in a metal cage. Later locations included a local hammam for the murder of Rodrigo – the costumes Welles had ordered from Jewish tailors in the Mellah were not ready, so he had to shoot a scene with minimal clothing – and the Portuguese cistern in El Jadida (see p.281).

The film was something of a personal crusade for Welles, who financed it himself, leaving the cast at intervals to try and borrow money off friends in Italy and France. During the course of the filming, he got through at least four – and perhaps six – Desdemonas, beginning with his fiancé Lea Padovani, until she soured relations by beginning an affair with one of the crew. In the end they were all dubbed, as indeed were many other of the characters – Welles performing most himself.

On its release in 1952, *Othello* was panned by the critics, and at Welles's death it was the only one of his dozen films to which he owned the rights. Forty years on, however, it was restored by his daughter for its anniversary, and shown at film festivals worldwide, and to huge acclaim. Even Essaouira had an open-air showing, in the presence of King Hassan's heir, Sidi Mohammed; this event was accompanied by the official naming of a park area on the front **Orson Welles' Square**, complete with a thuya wood memorial made by Samir Mustapha of the *Hôtel des Remparts*.

the ramparts. A gloomy-looking part of the town, it was locked at night up until the end of the nineteenth century. At the time, Essaouira's Jewish community numbered around 4000, including several families who were to make their mark in the world; the father of British Prime Minister **Benjamin Disraeli** was born here, as was the philanthropist **Moses Montefiore**. The quarter is now noticeably in decay, with many of its houses deserted and in a dangerous condition.

The port

At some point, perhaps around lunchtime or early evening, make your way down to the **harbour,** where fresh sardines (and all variety of other fish) are cooked on the quays. There is also an impressive sea bastion here, the **Skala du Port**, and in addition to the fishing activities – Essaouria is the country's third fishing port, after Agadir and Safi – a busy boatbuilding and repairs industry. Almost all the local craft, even the biggest fishing vessels, are still almost entirely wooden.

The port is entered by a small gate to the left of its main **Marine Gate**.

The beach

Essaouira has beaches to north and south. The **northern** one, known as the Plage de Safi, is good in hot weather and with a calm sea but unattractive and dangerous if the winds are up.

The **southern beach** extends for miles from the town, often backed by dunes, out towards Cap Sim. On its early reaches, the main activity, as ever in Morocco, is football. There's virtually always a game in progress and at weekends a full-scale local league, with a dozen matches side by side and kick-offs timed by the tides. If you're a player, you'll be encouraged to join in, but the weekend games are fun just to watch, and on occasions half the town seems to turn out.

Walking further along the beach, past the pitches and the crowds, you pass the riverbed of the **Oued Kasab**, and then the ruins of an old fort and royal summer pavilion known as the **Bordj El Berod**, half buried in the sand and part submerged at high tide. This was the inspiration for Jimi Hendrix's song *Castles in the Sand*; the guitarist once spent a long, drug-happy summer in the town, as hotel-keepers still like to remind their clients (all claim to have let rooms to the man). The fort is an excellent viewing spot for the Iles Purpuraires, offshore, and their birdlife (see box overleaf). A little further south, inland through the scrub, is the little Berber village of **Diabat**. This was once a legendary hippie hangout, and mythology again suggests that Jimi Hendrix spent time in the colony. These days, it has reverted to an ordinary Berber farming village – a ragged sort of place which (since a police crackdown in the early 1970s) is no longer permitted to rent rooms.

Practicalities

With its fishing fleet and market, Essaouira offers a good range of cafés and restaurants. It also has most services you might need during a stay, including post, phones, banks, etc.

Cafés and restaurants

For an informal lunch, or early evening meal, you can do no better than eat at the line of **grills down at the port**, an Essaouira institution, and cooking fish as fresh as it is possible to be; prices are highly negotiable. Also quite pleasant, if you want to eat Moroccan style, are a series of **"Berber Cafés"**, off to the right (if you're walking up from the harbour) of the Avenue Zerktouni *souks.* Amounting to little more than a street of tiny rooms covered with matting, these serve soup, tea and a variety of *tajines* – or anything you present to be cooked. Some of them are a bit of a tourist trap (and a few are haunted by hustlers peddling dope), but they are frequented also by local fishermen and workers.

Among the **more mainstream restaurants**, pick from:

Café-Restaurant Essalam, Place Prince Moulay El Hassan. Sympathetic management and the best-value set meals in town. Highly recommended.

Chez Sefrani, corner of Rue Sidi Mohammed Ben Abdallah and Rue Zayane. A good, cheap place where a lot of Moroccans eat. It looks like a typical hole-in-the-wall but a door by the counter leads to a massive complex of rooms and alcoves – including a room reserved for women. Most dishes are pretty good and all the food is fresh daily, as the patron, Mustapha, gives away anything unsold to the poor.

Restaurant Miami, 107 Rue du Mellah. New restaurant in the heart of the Medina, with a good set menu. To find it, follow Rue Sidi Mohammed Ben Abdallah to its (north) end, then carry on uphill and look for the signpost.

Chez Toufik, just off the clocktower square. Well-prepared Moroccan dishes, traditional setting and a folk singer most evenings.

Restaurant El Minzah, 3 Av. Oqba Ibn Nafia. Dependable restaurant in a charming 1920s building. Set menus and *à la carte*. Moroccan dishes.

Café-Restaurant Bab Laâchour, Place Prince Moulay El Hassan. A café, favoured by locals, downstairs, with a more tourist-orientated restaurant on the floor above. Excellent.

Restaurant El Khaima, Rue Laâlouj/Place El Khaima. Rather overpriced meals served amid extravagant draperies. The restaurant is, however, licensed and stays open late.

Chalet de la Plage, Bd. Mohammed V – on the seafront, just above the high-tide mark. A well-established seafood restaurant and bar. Both the food and views justify the (slightly) higher than usual prices.

THE ILE DE MOGADOR AND ELEONORA'S FALCON

Out across the bay from Essaouira lie the **Iles Purpuraires**, named from the dyes for purple imperial cloth that the Romans once produced here. The largest of the islands, known as the **Ile de Mogador**, is flanked on either side by a fort which, together with the fort on the islet just off the town harbour, and the Borj El Berod on the beach, covers all possible approaches to the bay. It also has a small harbour, a mosque and a prison (used for political exiles in past centuries but long closed).

It is of most interest these days, however, as a nature reserve, for this is the only non-Mediterranean breeding site of **Eleonora's falcon** – Morocco's most dramatic birds. They are not hard to see, with binoculars, from the beach. The best time is the early evening half-light, when you might spot as many as two or three dozen of these magnificent birds, gliding in low over the sea to hawk for insects. The falcons are summer visitors to Morocco, staying between May and October before making the long return journey south to Madagascar for the winter. The nearby river course also has many **waders** and **egrets** and occasional rarities such as gull-billed tern and Mediterranean gull.

The island has no inhabitants, save for a *gardien* who keeps an eye on the falcons. If you want to visit – and this is strongly discouraged when the birds are resident – you'll have to get a *permit d'autorisation* from the Province office and then negotiate for a boat ride. Don't pay for the ride until you've been collected and returned to the town!

Chez Sam/Restaurant du Port, at the end of the harbour. Another fine seafood restaurant and bar, serving huge portions of fish and (at a price) lobster. A bit unpredictable – as is the service – but good when it's good.

And for breakfast or tea:

Chez Driss, 10 Rue Hajjali – off the top end of Place Prince Moulay El Hassan. The town's most popular meetingplace, good for breakfast, coffee and pastries.

Opera Pâtisserie, Place Prince Moulay El Hassan. New, rather glitzy snack bar.

Bars

You can get a beer or a bottle of wine at *Chez Sam's* or the *Chalet de la Plage*, though both prefer customers to take a meal, and at the *Café Mogador* on the seafront. Alternatives are basically down to the hotels *Tafoukt* and *des Iles*; at the latter, Moroccans gather to drink beer and play chess and draughts.

If you want to buy your own beer or wine, at very much lower prices, there are a number of small supermarkets.

Directory

On the practical front, **Jack's Kiosk** on Place Prince Moulay El Hassan (☎04/47.25.38 or 04/47.39.01) is invaluable. It is really more shop than kiosk, selling English books and newspapers (second-hand books upstairs) and tourist goods, and operating a small travel agency – running local trips, reconfirming flights, etc – and an international phone and fax centre. It is run by Jack Oswald, who, despite his name, is Swiss.

Banks There are four banks in or near Place Prince Moulay El Hassan: a *BMCE*, *BCM*, *Banque Populaire* and *Credit du Maroc*.

Festivals A dozen or so local *moussems*, fairs and festivals are held between March and October. The main event is the *Festival d'Essaouira* in July.

Horseriding The *Club Équestre Sidi Mgdoul*, out of town on the Marrakesh road, hires out horses for riders of all levels of experience.

Post office The PTT is just outside the ramparts on Av. Lalla Aicha; it is open 8am-6pm daily; the phone section is a lot less reliable than *Jack's Kiosk* (see above).

Shops See the section on thuya wood artesans on p.293.

Tourist office Oddly, considering this is the main tourist resort between Tangier and Agadir, there is no tourist office. *Jack's Kiosk* – see above – is the best source of local information.

Transport Leaving Essaouira for **Marrakesh**, there is a non-stop bus which leaves from the Hôtel des Iles – rather than the out-of-town bus station – and arrives in Marrakesh at the train station; tickets for this should be bought from the hotel the day before; departures are currently at 6.30am, arriving at Marrakesh at 8.45am, in time for the 9.08am train to Casa, Rabat and Tangier; coming the other way, it leaves Marrakesh at 1pm, arriving at Essaouira at 3.30pm. The best buses direct to **Casablanca** are the *CTM* "Mumtaz Express" (leaves Essaouira bus station daily at 11pm, arriving Casa at 5am) and the night *Pullman du Sud*; they cost around 10dh more than other departures – money that you will, in any case, save on baggage loading.

South to Agadir

The main road south from Essaouira to Agadir (P8) runs inland for the first 100km or so, with just the occasional piste leading down to a beach or fishing hamlet scattered along the rugged, cliff-lined coast. Along this stretch there is just one resort, Sidi Kaouki, which has the reputation of being Morocco's best windsurfing beach.

The region **inland** is known as the **Haha**, populated by Tashelhaït-speaking Berbers, and actually the westernmost range of the High Atlas. Its slopes are covered in **argan trees**, which are often to be seen with a goat halfway up, nibbling away at the fruit. A handful of very rough pistes head into the hills, struggling over the mountains to meet the Tizi Machou road from Marrakesh to Agadir.

Sidi Kaouki and Cap Sim

The most direct route south from Essaouira (see inset map on p.290) is the piste, with a ford (by a derelict bridge) over the river to **Diabat**; this reaches the P8 in around 10km. If your vehicle isn't up to this road, the alternative is a long looping detour along the P8A to a junction with the P40 to Marrakesh.

Around a kilometre south of the junction of the piste and P8A/P8 a track is signposted to the right to the *Auberge Tangaro* (☎04/47.37.35; ①), a rather chic, Italian-owned place that provides a tempting alternative to staying in Essaouira, if you have transport of your own. Little used except at weekends, when groups of French and German windsurfers arrive from Casablanca and Marrakesh, the *auberge* has a number of **chalet rooms**, and it serves excellent meals. Next door is a small, rather primitive **campsite**. The beach is a half-hour hike.

Back on the P8, a further 7km brings you to a newish sideroad signposted to **SIDI KAOUKI**. The beach here attracts **windsurfers** virtually year round, and looks set for more mainstream development, with a new hotel currently under construction. At present there is just a beach-café, *Chez Omar*, and a luxurious little ten-room **auberge**, *La Residence Kaouki Beach* (⑤), which is run by the Villa Maroc in Essaouira (bookings through them). The latter has a fine restaurant, open to non-residents in the evening.

A little to the north of the beach is the original **Marabout of Sidi Kaouki**, which has a reputation for curing sterility in women, and beyond that is **Cap Sim**, backed by long expanses of dunes. There are usually a couple of camels here, whose *mahouts* offer rides to tourists.

On towards Agadir

The piste south of Sidi Kaouki, marked on the Michelin map, requires a four-wheel-drive vehicle, but back on the inland P8 there is little of interest. **SIMMOU** is a tiny roadside stop with a filling station and a couple of café-restaurants; to the east, one of the better roads leads into the hills to SOUK TNINE IMI N TLIT, where a large **Monday souk** takes place. **TAMANAR** has a petrol station and a reasonable roadside **hotel-restaurant**, the *Étoile du Sud* (①).

Fifteen kilometres south of Tamanar, a well-surfaced road cuts down to the coast at **POINTE IMESSOUANE**, a picturesque little harbour with a few fishermen's cottages. Just to the east is a bay and beach known as **Imoucha**, which, like Sidi Kaouki, is popular with **windsurfers** – and, to a lesser degree, surfers.

A few kilometres beyond the roadside settlement of **TAMRI** (117km), the road rejoins the coast, passing a lagoon, which might detain birdwatchers, and the fishing village of TARHAZOUTE (see Chapter Seven) before the final run to Agadir. Honey and bananas are on sale by the roadside, the latter to boost your sense of arrival in the south.

travel details

Trains

Rabat–Casablanca More or less hourly departures (50min–1hr 30min). Most run to/from *Casa-Port*, though a few exclusively to/from *Voyageurs*.

Casablanca–Tangier Four daily, via Rabat, Mohammedia, Salé, Kenitra, Asilah and Tangier.

  7.15am Casa–Port, arrives Rabat (8.15am), Asilah (12.13pm) and Tangier (1.15pm).

  12.45pm Casa-Voyageurs, arrives Rabat (2.03pm), Sidi Slimane (4.18pm: change for Asilah/Tangier, 6.59pm/7.55pm).

  3.15pm Casa-Voyageurs, arrives Rabat (6.12pm: change for Asilah/Tangier, 10.42pm/11.26pm).

  11.10pm Casa-Voyageurs, arrives Rabat (12.08am), Asilah (4.43am), Tangier (5.37am).

Casablanca–Fes/Meknes Five daily, via Rabat, Salé and Kenitra; all from **Casa-Voyageurs**.

  6am, arrives Rabat (7.18am), Meknes (10.36am) and Fes (11.33am).

  12.45pm, arrives Rabat (2.03pm), Meknes (5.38pm) and Fes (6.40pm).

  5.15pm, arrives Rabat (6.12pm), Meknes (4.09pm) and Fes (5.16pm).

  10.05pm, arrives Rabat (11.17pm), Meknes (2.30am) and Fes (3.34am).

Rabat/Casablanca–Marrakesh Seven daily in 4–6hr (from Rabat), 5hr–7hr 30min (from Casablanca). Departures from Rabat/Casa-Voyageurs at: 4.18am/5.25am (arrives Marrakesh 8.54am), 5.18am/7.54am (11.31am), 8.45am/9.39am (12.43pm), 11.03am/12.08pm (3.13pm), 2.34pm/17.16pm (9.09pm), 6.19pm/7.13pm (10.17pm) and 10.52pm/1.23am (changing at Casa, 5.16am).

Rabat–El Jadida One daily known as the "Doukkala" (7.15pm from Rabat Ville/8.07pm from Casa-Voyageurs, arrives Azemmour 9.11pm, El Jadida 9.26pm; in the other direction, leaves El Jadida 8.15am, arriving Azemmour 8.27, Casa-Voyaguers 9.31am, Rabat Ville 10.23am).

Rabat–Safi Two daily (8.45am/6.22pm from Rabat Ville/9.39am/7.16pm from Casa-Voyageurs, arrives Safi 2pm/11.17pm; in the other direction, leaves Safi 5.45am/8.05am).

Buses

From Rabat Tangier (2 daily; 5hr); Larache (4: 3hr 30min); Salé (frequent; 15min); Casablanca (10; 1hr 40min); Meknes (3; 4hr); Fes (6; 5hr 30min).

From Casa Services to all major (and most minor) towns in Morocco, including Tangier (2 daily; 6hr 30min); Rabat (10; 1hr 40min); El Jadida (3; 2hr); Essaouira (3; 5–7hr; best is the *SATAS*); Agadir (1; 10hr); Marrakesh (3; 4hr).

From El Jadida Casablanca (3 daily; 2hr 30min); Rabat (2; 4hr); Oualidia (daily; 1hr 30min).

From Safi Oualidia/El Jadida (3 daily; 1hr 25min/ 2hr 30min).

From Essaouira Agadir (6 daily; 3hr 30min); Safi (2; 6hr); El Jadida (2; 8hr); Casablanca (4; 5–9hr); Tiznit (1; 7hr). **Note**: Most Essaouira–Marrakesh services (6 daily; 3hr) are non-*CTM* buses.

Grands Taxis

Rabat–Casablanca Regular route, 1hr 20min.

From El Jadida Negotiable to Casablanca.

Flights

Rabat/Casa Mohammed V Airport: International flights to London, Paris and most major destinations. Domestic flights to all major cities in Morocco.

CHAPTER FIVE

MARRAKESH AND THE HIGH ATLAS

Marrakesh – "Morocco City", as the early travellers called it – has always been something of a pleasure city, a marketplace where the southern tribesmen and Berber villagers bring in their goods, spend their money and find entertainment. For tourists it's an enduring fantasy – a city of immense beauty, low, pink and tentlike before a great shaft of

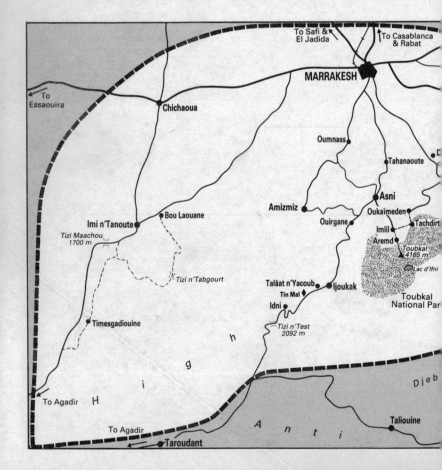

mountains – and immediately exciting. At the heart of it all is a square, **Djemaa el Fna**, really no more than an open space in the centre of the city, but the stage for a long-established ritual in which shifting circles of onlookers gather round groups of acrobats, drummers, pipe musicians, dancers, storytellers and comedians. However many times you return there, it remains compelling. So, too, do the city's architectural attractions: the immense, still basins of the **Agdal** and **Menara** parks, the delicate Granada-style carving of the **Saadian Tombs** and, above all, the **Koutoubia Minaret**, the most perfect Islamic monument in North Africa.

Some fifty kilometres south of Marrakesh rise the **High Atlas**, the grandest Moroccan mountain range. Its foothills and the lush summer pleasureground of **Ourika Valley** can be reached in just an hour by bus or *grand taxi*, and, within the space of a morning, you can leave the city and get up to the **hiking trailheads** of **Asni**, **Imlil** or **Ijoukak**. From here, a network of trails – mulepaths, ridgewalks and climbing routes – radiate across the valleys and mountains, including a trail up North Africa's highest peak, **Djebel Toubkal**.

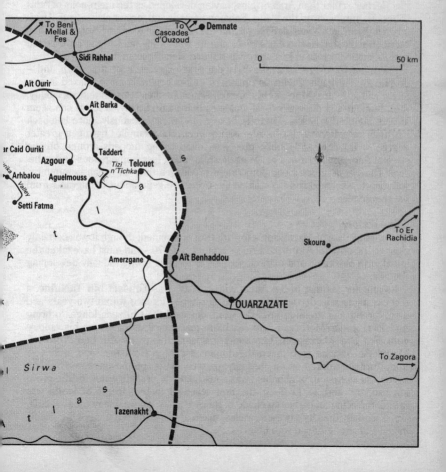

Marrakesh (Marrakech)

Unlike Fes, for so long its rival as the nation's capital, **MARRAKESH** exists very much in the present. Its population is rising, it has a thriving industrial area and it remains the most important market and administrative centre of southern Morocco. None of this is to suggest a bland prosperity – there is heavy unemployment here, as throughout the country, and intense poverty, too – but travelling through it leaves you with a vivid impression of life and activity. And for once this doesn't apply exclusively to the new city, **Gueliz**; the **Medina**, substantially in ruins at the beginning of this century, was rebuilt and expanded during the years of French rule and retains no less significant a role in the modern city.

The Koutoubia excepted, Marrakesh is not a place of great monuments. Its beauty and attraction lie in the general atmosphere and spectacular location – with the magnificent peaks of the Atlas rising right up behind the city, towering through the haze. The feel, as much as anything, is a product of this. Marrakesh has **Berber** rather than Arab origins, having developed as the metropolis of Atlas tribes, Mahgrebis from the plains, Saharan nomads and former slaves from Africa beyond the desert – Sudan, Senegal and the ancient kingdom of Timbuktu. All of these strands shaped the city's *souks* and its way of life, and in the crowds and performers in Djemaa el Fna, they can still occasionally seem distinct.

For most travellers, Marrakesh is the first experience of the south and – despite the inevitable guides and hustlers – of its generally more relaxed atmosphere and attitudes. **Marrakchis** are renowned for their warmth and sociability, their humour and directness – all qualities that (superficially, at least) can seem absent among the Fassis. There is, at any rate, a conspicuously more laid-back feel than anywhere in the north, with women, for example, having a greater degree of freedom and public presence, often riding mopeds around on the streets. And compared to Fes, Marrakesh is much less homogenous and cohesive. The city is more a conglomeration of villages than an urban community, with quarters formed and maintained by successive generations of migrants from the countryside.

Some history

The original date of Marrakesh's **foundation** is disputed, though it was certainly close to the onset of **Almoravid** rule – around 1062–70 – and must have taken the initial form of a camp and market, a *ksour*, or fortified town gradually developing round it.

Its founder (as that of the Almoravid dynasty) was **Youssef bin Tachfine**, a restless military leader who conquered northern Morocco within two years and then, turning his attention towards Spain, defeated the Christian kings, to bring Andalusia under Moroccan rule. Tachfine maintained as bases for his empire both Fes and Marrakesh, but under his son, the pious **Ali ben Youssef**, Marrakesh became very much the dominant centre. Craftsmen and architects from Còrdoba worked on the new city: palaces, baths and mosques were built; a subterranean system of channels was constructed to provide water for the growing palmery; and, in 1126–27, the first seven-kilometre **circuit of walls** was raised, replacing an earlier stockade of thorn bushes. These, many times rebuilt, are essentially the city's present walls – made of *tabia*, the red mud of the plains, mixed and strengthened with lime.

Of the rest of the Almoravid's building works, there remains hardly a trace. The dynasty that replaced them – the orthodox and reforming **Almohads** – sacked the city for three days after taking possession of it in 1147. Once again, though, Marrakesh was adopted as the empire's pre-eminent capital, its domain stretching as far as Tripolitania (modern Libya) in the wake of phenomenal early conquests.

With the accession to the throne in 1184 of **Yacoub el Mansour**, the third Almohad sultan, the city entered its greatest period. Under this prolific builder, *kissarias* were constructed for the sale and storage of Italian and oriental cloth, a new Kasbah was begun, and a succession of poets and scholars arrived at the court – among them Averroes, the most distinguished of Arabic medieval philosophers. Mansour's reign also saw the construction of the great **Koutoubia Mosque** and minaret.

It is astonishing, though, to think that this whole period of Almoravid and Almohad rule – so crucial to the rise of both the city and the nation – lasted barely two centuries. By the 1220s, the empire was beginning to fragment amid a series of factional civil wars, and Marrakesh fell into the familiar pattern of pillage, ruination and rebuilding. It revived for a time to form the basis of an independent **Merenid** kingdom (1374–86) but overall it gave way to Fes until the emergence of the Saadians in the early sixteenth century.

Taking Marrakesh, then devastated by famine, in 1521, and Fes in 1546, the **Saadians** provided a last burst of imperial splendour. Their first sultans regained the Atlantic coast, which had been extensively colonised by the Portuguese; **Ahmed el Mansour**, the great figure of the dynasty, led a conquest of Timbuktu, seizing control of the most lucrative caravan routes in Africa. The **El Badi Palace** – Marrakesh's largest and greatest building project – was constructed from the proceeds of this new wealth, though it again fell victim to dynastic rivalry and, apart from its mausoleum (the **Saadian Tombs**), was reduced to ruins by Moulay Ismail.

Subsequent history under the **Alaouites** – the dynasty perpetuated today by King Hassan – is for the most part less distinguished. Marrakesh remained an imperial capital, and the need to maintain a southern base against the tribes ensured the regular, alternating residence of its sultans. But from the seventeenth to the nineteenth century, it shrank back from its medieval walls and lost much of its former trade. A British traveller's description of the city at the turn of the century as "a squalid, straggling, mazy kind of open cesspool about the size of Paris" is probably not inaccurate, though for the last decades prior to the Protectorate, it enjoyed a return to favour with the Shereefian court. **Moulay Hasan** (1873–94) and **Moulay Abd el Aziz** (1894–1908) both ran their governments from here in a bizarre closing epoch of the old ways, accompanied by a final bout of frantic palace building.

On the arrival of **the French**, Marrakesh gave rise to a short-lived pretender, the religious leader El Hiba, but for most of the colonial period it was run as a virtual fiefdom of its pasha, **T'hami el Glaoui** – the most powerful, autocratic and extraordinary character of his age (see p.321 and pp.363–64).

Since **independence**, the city has undergone considerable change, with rural emigration from the Atlas and beyond, new methods of cultivation in the plains and the development of a sizeable tourist industry. All of these factors combine to make modern Marrakesh the country's largest trading base and population centre (1,425,000 at the last estimate) after Casablanca.

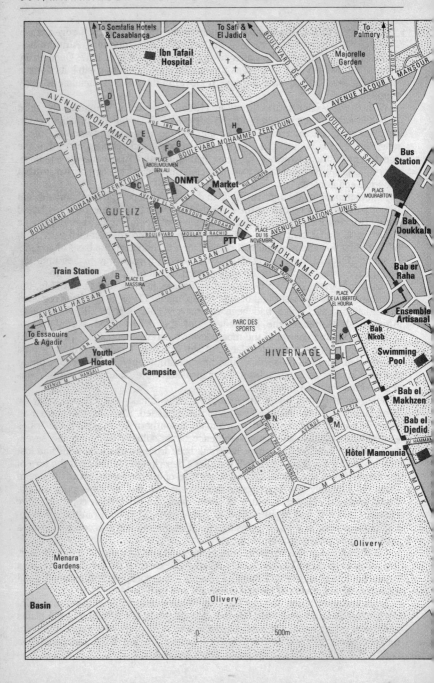

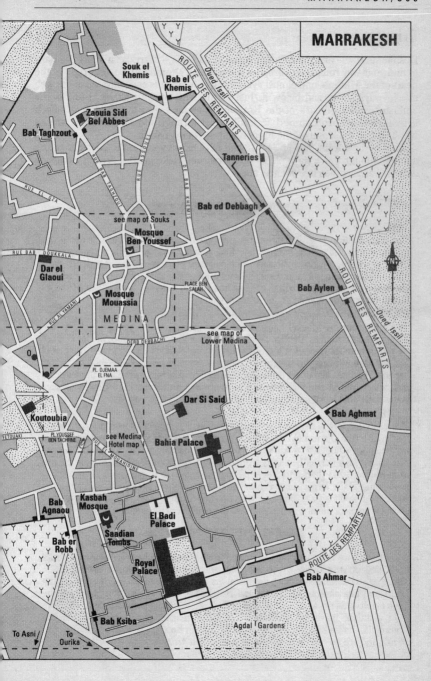

MARRAKESH

Souk el Khemis

Bab el Khemis

ROUTE DES REMPARTS

Oued Issil

Zaouia Sidi Bel Abbes

Bab Taghzout

Tanneries

Bab ed Debbagh

see map of Souks

Mosque Ben Youssef

RUE RAB DOUKKALA

Dar el Glaoui

PLACE BEN SALAH

Bab Aylen

Mosque Mouassia

MEDINA

see map of Lower Medina

DERB DEBBACHI

O

P

PL. DJEMAA EL FNA

Dar Si Said

Bab Aghmat

FETOUAKI

Koutoubia

PL. YOUSSEF BEN TACHFINE

see Medina Hotel map

Bahia Palace

Bab Agnaou

Kasbah Mosque

El Badi Palace

Bab er Robb

Saadian Tombs

Royal Palace

Bab Ahmar

ROUTE DES REMPARTS

Bab Ksiba

To Asni

To Ourika

Agdal Gardens

Oued Issil

ROUTE DES REMPARTS

Orientation

Despite its size – and the tortuous maze of its *souks* – Marrakesh is not too hard to find your way round. The broad, open space of **Djemaa el Fna** lies right at the heart of the **Medina**, and almost everything of interest is concentrated in the web of alleyways above and below it. Just to the west of the Djemaa el Fna is the unmistakeable landmark of the **Koutoubia** minaret – in the shadow of which begins **Avenue Mohammed V**, leading out through the Medina walls at Bab Nkob and up the length of the French-built new city, **Gueliz**.

Only in the **souks** (see pp.314–18 and 327) might you want to consider taking a guide, though you'll have plenty of offers; motorbike guides, driving alongside new arrivals, are also in evidence, alas.

POINTS OF ARRIVAL

BY TRAIN

The **train station** is at the edge of the new town, Gueliz. Keep your wits about you as you emerge, or you'll immediately find yourself engaged with a guide or taxi driver. A regular *petit taxi* (beware unofficial taxis) is a good idea in general, since it's quite a walk to hotels in Gueliz – and a long way to hotels in the Medina; the taxi fare should be no more than 10dh to the Medina, less to hotels in Gueliz. The #3 and #8 buses run from the station to the Djemaa el Fna.

BY BUS

The **gare routière** (for all long-distance bus services) is located just outside the walls of the Medina by Bab Doukkala. You can walk into the centre of Gueliz from here in around ten minutes by following Av. des Nations Unies; to the Djemaa el Fna it's around twenty to twenty-five minutes, most easily accomplished by following the Medina walls down to Av. Mohammed V. Alternatively, catch the #3 or #8 bus, which run in one direction to the Koutoubia, in the other to Gueliz; or save yourself trouble by taking a *petit taxi* (about 10dh).

BY AIR

The city's **airport** is 5km to the southwest. The #11 bus is supposed to run every half hour to the Djemaa el Fna, but it is very erratic. *Petits taxis* or *grands taxis* are a better option, though you will need your wits about you to pay a reasonable fare. The *grands taxis* currently display a price of 50dh (day) and 60dh (night) for the trip from the airport to Gueliz; try not to pay a lot more.

Arriving at the airport on a Friday afternoon, or after about 6pm any day of the week, you won't always find the **bureau de change** open; taxis, however, will accept pounds or dollars, at more or less the equivalent dirham rate.

CITY TRANSPORT

It is a fairly long walk between Gueliz and the Medina, but there are plenty of **petits taxis** and **grands taxis**, which will take you between the two for around 10dh. There are taxi ranks at most intersections in Gueliz and in the Medina at the Djemaa el Fna and outside the Grand Hôtel Tazi. **Bus #1** also runs between the main Gueliz squares and the Koutoubia/Place de Foucauld in the Medina.

In addition, there are **calèches**, horse-drawn cabs which line up near the Koutoubia, the Badi Palace and some of the fancier hotels. These can take up to five people and are no more expensive for locals than *petits taxis*; as a tourist, however, be sure to fix the price before setting out, particularly if you want a tour of the town.

Accommodation

As usual, there is a choice between staying in the Medina or the Ville Nouvelle quarters, Gueliz and Hivernage, or, out on the Casablanca road, Semlalia.

The **Medina**, as usual, has the main concentration of cheap, unclassified hotels, most of which are quite pleasant (though they can be freezing in winter), and a few excellent classified hotels on its periphery. Given the attractions of the Djemaa el Fna and the *souks*, they have to be the first choice.

The main advantages of **Gueliz** hotels are their convenience if you are arriving late at night, particularly at the train station, and, in the more upmarket choices, the presence of a swimming pool. Hotels in **Hivernage** and **Semlalia** are all upmarket, modern buildings, consistently comfortable and sometimes with quite

Note that very few of the *petits taxis* are metered (or admit to a working meter); you either have to fix a price in advance, haggle on arrival, or just decide on what you're paying and hand it over at the end of the trip; the standard fare is 10dh, or 15dh in the evening (a negotiable concept!). *Grands taxis* and *calèches* have by law to display standard prices for specified trips; all these prices are per trip and not per person, as drivers often claim.

BIKES, MOPEDS AND CHARTERING TAXIS

For exploring the more scattered city sights – the Agdal and Menara gardens, for example, or the palmery – the ideal transport is a **bike**. You can rent bikes by the hour or day (40–70dh) from outlets round Rue Bab Agnaou, just south of the Djemaa el Fna, and from outside several of the hotels, including: *Hôtel Foucauld* in the Medina (which also has mountain bikes); *Hôtel Agdal* in Gueliz; and hotels *Toubkal, Siaha Safir, Andalous; El Borj* in Hivernage; and *Hôtel Sahara* in Semlalia. A few garage and car rental outlets along Av. Mohammed V also rent out bikes and **mopeds** (*motos*); *Peugeot* at 225 Av. Mohammed V rents both.

Alternatively, **grands taxis** can be chartered by the day for around 150dh, which works out very reasonable if you split it between four people (the taxis take a maximum six passengers – but four is comfortable). Negotiate at the ranks in Djemaa el Fna or by the PTT in Gueliz.

LOCAL BUS ROUTES

The following buses leave from Rue Moulay Ismail, south of the Djemaa el Fna:

#1 to Gueliz, along Av. Mohammed V.

#2 to Riad el Arous and Bab Doukkala (for the bus station).

#3 to Douar Laskar by Av. Mohammed V/Av. Hassan II, via the train station and passing close to the campsite and youth hostel.

#4 to Daoudiar (a northern suburb), by Av. Mohammed V/Av. d'El Jadida, passing close to the Jardin Majorelle.

#8 to Douar Laskar by Av. Mohammed V/Av. Moulay el Hassan, via the train station and close to the campsite and youth hostel.

#10 to Bd. de Safi, by Bab Doukkala, via the bus station.

#11 to the airport by Av. Menara.

#14 to the train station.

For details on transport out of Marrakesh, and buses to local destinations like Asni or Ourika, see "Leaving Marrakesh" at the end of the city account.

wonderful pools. Semlalia, however, is a bit remote, and Hivernage, while not too far from the Djemaa el Fna, again lacks any city-life of its own.

Advance bookings for hotels are a wise idea, especially for the classified places in the Medina. The worst times are the **Easter** and **Christmas/New Year** holiday periods, when you may arrive and find virtually every decent hotel full to capacity – often with the entourage who travel with King Hassan, who likes to stay in Marrakesh, particularly over the New Year period.

Gueliz/Hivernage/ Semlalia hotels

This is a selection of the better value and best hotels in these areas; Gueliz/Hivernage/Medina periphery ones are keyed on the main map on pp. 304–5.

GUELIZ

Hôtel Farouk [B], 66 Av. Hassan II (☎04/43.19.89). An excellent, recently modernised hotel, that's again very convenient for the train station. ⑩

Hôtel Franco-Belge [F], 62 Bd. Mohammed Zerktouni (☎04/44.84.72). Old hotel built for officers during the Protectorate. The best rooms are off the patio; those on the street are noisy. ①

Hôtel des Voyageurs [G], 40 Bd. Mohammed Zerktouni (☎04/44.72.18). Another old, respectable hotel; unexciting but inexpensive. ①

Hôtel Oasis [E], 50 Av. Mohammed V (☎04/44.71.79). Comfortable rooms, clean and well run. Also has a bar and good-value restaurant. ①

Hôtel Koutoubia [I], 51 Av. El Mansour Eddahbi (☎04/43.09.21). Vaguely stylish, set amid gardens of mimosas and orange trees, and with a friendly and enthusiastic porter. Also has a swimming pool that's sometimes full, and a secure garage. ②

Hôtel Ibn Batouta [J], Av. Yacoub El Marini (☎04/43.41.45). Newish hotel with good rooms, a bar and restaurant. ②

Hôtel Moussafir [A], Av. Hassan II/Place de la Gare (☎04/43.59.29). Tasteful new hotel by the train station, with pool, bar and restaurant; part of the dependable *Moussafir* chain. ③

Hôtel Agdal [C], 1 Bd. Mohammed Zerktouni (☎04/43.36.70). Another good new hotel – and one of the best in Gueliz; pool, bar and restaurant. ④

HOTEL PRICE CODES AND STAR–RATINGS

Hotels are no longer obliged to levy set maximum rates, according to their official star-ratings, as had long been the custom. However, **prices** still broadly follow the star-rating system, and this is the basis of our own **hotel price codes** set out below and keyed throughout the guide.

Our code	Official classification	Single room price	Double room price
⑩	Unclassified	25–60dh	40–100dh
①	1*A/1*B	60–105dh	100–125dh
②	2*B/2*A	105–145dh	125–175dh
③	3*B/3*A	145–225dh	175–275dh
④	4*B/4*A	225–400dh	275–500dh
⑤	5*luxury	Upwards of 400dh	Upwards of 500dh

TELEPHONE CODES

All telephone numbers in the Marrakesh region are prefixed 04. When making a call within the region you omit this prefix. For more explanation of phone codes and making calls within (or to) Morocco, see p.37.

Residence el Hamra [D], 26 Av. Mohammed V (☎04/43.06.30); **Residence les Palmiers [H]**, 96 Bd. Mohammed Zerktouni (☎04/44.75.04). Self-catering apartments for 250dh and up. Not terribly exciting, but might suit families. ④

HIVERNAGE

Hôtel Yasmine [K], corner of Bd. El Yarmouk/Rue Boualaka (☎04/44.61.42). A new and very attractive hotel, only 500m from the Djemaa el Fna, and with a garden, bar, tennis court and swimming pool, plus parking space. ②

Hôtel Imilchil [L], Av. Echouhada (☎04/44.76.53). One of the cheapest hotels in town with a reliably full, if small, swimming pool; again not too far from the Medina. ③

Hôtel Siaha Safir [N], Av. du President Kennedy, Hivernage (☎04/44.89.52). A good hotel, with its own hammam, as well as a fine pool – and not that expensive for its classification. ④

Hôtel Es Saadi [M], Av. Qadissia (☎04/44.88.11). The most elegant hotel in Hivernage, with a beautiful garden and prices half the *Mamounia*, at around £80/$120 for a double. ⑤

HIVERNAGE/MEDINA PERIPHERY

Hôtel Islane [P], 279 Av. Mohammed V (☎04/44.00.81). Opened in 1990, this hotel faces the Koutoubia head-on. It's a bit noisy from the traffic, but comfortable and fine value. ②

Hôtel les Almoravides [O], Arset Djenan Lakhdor (☎04/44.51.42). Average modern hotel, behind the Hôtel de Ville and Ensemble Artisanal. Swimming pool, bar and restaurant. ④

Hôtel La Mamounia [labelled], Av. Bab Jdid (☎04/44.89.81). Set within its own palace grounds, this is – alongside the *Palais Jamai* in Fes – the most beautiful hotel in Morocco. It is also the most expensive, with doubles from 2500dh if you book independently. Room prices drop a bit during the low season, or if you book as part of a holiday package – but they are still pretty astronomical. For a description of the gardens, see p.331–32. ⑤

SEMLALIA

Hôtel le Tichka [off map], 4km out of town on the Route de Casablanca (☎04/44.87.10). State-of-the-art hotel, with fine architecture, a walled garden and swimming pool, and excellent restaurant. The best choice in Semlalia at around £70/$100 a night for a double. ④

Youth hostel

Auberge de Jeunesse/Youth Hostel [labelled on main map], Rue el Jahid (☎04/43.28.31). Quiet, clean and friendly, and a useful first-night standby if you arrive late by train – it's just five minutes' walk from the station (and its buses to the Medina). Open noon–2pm & 6–10pm (winter) 6pm–midnight (summer); IYHF cards compulsory.

Campsite

Camping Municipal [labelled on main map], Av. de France (☎04/43.17.07). A couple of blocks south of Av. Hassan II, so just a five-minute walk if you arrive at the train station; bus #3 or #8 runs from outside, at the corner of Av. de France/Av. Hassan II, to the Djemaa el Fna. A rather bare and unshaded site, with poor facilities for the (relatively high) price: just a café-bar-restaurant and small swimming pool (not always full). However, it's a good point of contact if you want to join up with others heading south, or get info from others on their way back. Open all year.

Medina hotels

Most of the Medina hotels are grouped about a compact, easily walkable area just south of the Djemaa el Fna (see map and key overpage). With six exceptions, which should definitely be booked in advance, they are unclassified. All of the better ones are recommended below; you may strike lucky at others, though some are distinctly miserable and overpriced.

UNCLASSIFIED

Prices in the **unclassified hotels** vary quite considerably, though less from hotel to hotel as from room to room, depending on the size and number of beds. At time of writing, prices start at around 40dh for a small single, 60dh for a double, 80dh for a room with three beds. Bargaining is sometimes possible.

Hôtel Afriquia (☎04/44.24.03). Decent rooms off a pleasant courtyard with orange trees. ⑩

Hôtel El Atlal (☎04/44.51.29). Small, busy, friendly and secure. ⑩

Hôtel Cecil (☎04/44.24.03). Okay, if you need a fallback. ⑩

Hôtel Challa (☎04/44.29.77). A nice building and one of the best cheapies in the quarter. ⑩

Hôtel Charaf, 21 Rue Bani Marine (☎04/42.70.89). Look for the sign, high on a sidewall. ⑩

Hôtel Eddakhla (☎04/42.23.59). Again, reasonable. ⑩

Hôtel Essaouira. A very pleasant, friendly place with rooftop views; next door to the *Hôtel Medina* (below), so they make a good pair to try. ⑩

Hôtel de France, 197 Rue Zitoun el Kedim (☎04/44.30.67). Not to be confused with the dire *Hôtel du Café de France* on the Djemâa el Fna, this is one of the best of the cheapies, secure and recently modernised. It also changes cash and travellers' cheques. ⑩

Hôtel la Gazelle, 12 Rue Bani Marine (☎04/44.11.12). A new hotel with bright, airy rooms, and hot showers, on a street with a row of outdoor foodstalls. ⑩

Hôtel Hillal. Okay. ⑩

Hôtel de la Jeunesse (☎04/44.36.31). *Not* the youth hostel – see preceding Gueliz listings above – but okay. ⑩

Hôtel Medina. A real gem – small, clean, family-run and friendly; good value, too, with hot showers included. Also offers very cheap roof space if you have a sleeping bag. ⑩

Hôtel Nouzha. Clean if basic, and a bit noisy with a questionable taste for 1970s rock on its tape system. ⑩

Hôtel Smara (☎04/44.55.68). Okay; not to be confused with the *Hôtel Smara* in Gueliz. ⑩

Hôtel Souria. Deservedly popular hotel – perhaps the best in these listings – run by a grand old *patronnne* who is selective about her guests and imposes an 11pm curfew. Beware, though, that children are not made welcome. ⑩

Hôtel Zagora. Noisy but good.⑩

Hotels not greatly recommended at time of writing include: *Hôtel des Amis*; *Hôtel Central*; *Hôtel du Café de France*; *Hôtel Mabrouk*; *Hôtel Mauretania*; *Hôtel de la Paix*; *Hôtel Sahara*; *Hôtel de Tourisme*; *Hôtel el Ward*.

CLASSIFIED

Hôtel CTM, Place Djemaa el Fna (☎04/44.23.35). Located above the old bus station. Decent-sized rooms, as clean and as cheap as many of the unclassified places; cold showers. Also has a useful underground garage, if you have a car to look after. ①

Hôtel Oukaïmeden, Place Djemaa el Fna (☎04/44.10.38). Newly refurbished hotel on the north side of the square – just off the top of our map. ①

Hôtel Gallia, Rue de la Recette (☎04/44.59.13). A pleasant building in a quiet cul-de-sac. Airy and spotless rooms off two tiled courtyards. Central heating in winter, air conditioning in summer, and hot water at most times. Highly recommended. ②

Hôtel Ali, Rue Moulay Ismail (☎04/44.49.79). Popular small hotel whose rooms have reliable en suite showers, and heating in winter; rooftop sun terrace, too, and good inexpensive Moroccan meals in the restaurant. The hotel is used as a pick-up point for various trekking groups heading to the High Atlas and so a good source of information. ②

Hôtel Ichbilia, 1 Rue Bani Marine (☎04/43.49.47). A new hotel with comfortable rooms off a courtyard and gallery. ②

Hôtel Minaret, 10 Rue du Dispensaire. Another newish, small hotel, in the street behind the *Hôtel Tazi*; recommended. ②

Hôtel de Foucauld, Av. El Mouahidine (☎04/44.54.99). Rooms are on the small side and there are problems with the water supply, but this is a generally reliable choice, with friendly staff, bicycles for rent, and a licensed restaurant; some High Atlas guides hang out here, too. It offers especially good value if you have a group of three or four to share a room. ②

Grand Hôtel Tazi, corner of Rue Bab Agnaou/Av. Hoummam el Fetouaki (☎04/44.27.87). A grand hotel in the old style, that has seen better days. Pleasant nonetheless, and little more expensive than the *Foucauld* for larger rooms, with hot showers, heating in winter, a garage to the rear, a rooftop bar, and a little swimming pool. When busy, they may insist on guests taking half-board. ②

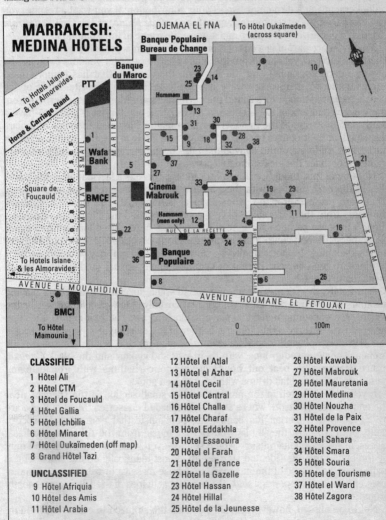

CLASSIFIED

1 Hôtel Ali
2 Hôtel CTM
3 Hôtel de Foucauld
4 Hôtel Gallia
5 Hôtel Ichbilia
6 Hôtel Minaret
7 Hôtel Oukaïmeden (off map)
8 Grand Hôtel Tazi

UNCLASSIFIED

9 Hôtel Afriquia
10 Hôtel des Amis
11 Hôtel Arabia

12 Hôtel el Atlal
13 Hôtel el Azhar
14 Hôtel Cecil
15 Hôtel Central
16 Hôtel Challa
17 Hôtel Charaf
18 Hôtel Eddakhla
19 Hôtel Essaouira
20 Hôtel el Farah
21 Hôtel de France
22 Hôtel la Gazelle
23 Hôtel Hassan
24 Hôtel Hillal
25 Hôtel de la Jeunesse

26 Hôtel Kawabib
27 Hôtel Mabrouk
28 Hôtel Mauretania
29 Hôtel Medina
30 Hôtel Nouzha
31 Hôtel de la Paix
32 Hôtel Provence
33 Hôtel Sahara
34 Hôtel Smara
35 Hôtel Souria
36 Hôtel de Tourisme
37 Hôtel el Ward
38 Hôtel Zagora

Note: This map is intended just for reference and not all hotels included are recommended.

The Djemaa el Fna and Koutoubia

There's nowhere in North Africa like **Djemaa el Fna** – no place that so effortlessly involves you and keeps you coming back. By day it's basically a market, with a few snake charmers and an occasional troupe of acrobats. In the evening it becomes a whole carnival of musicians, clowns and street entertainers. When you arrive in Marrakesh, and after you've found a room, come out here and you'll soon be immersed in the ritual: wandering round, squatting amid the circles of onlookers, giving a dirham or two as your contribution. If you want a respite, you can move over to the rooftop terraces of the *Café de France* or the *Café-Restaurant Argana* to gaze over the sqaure and admire the frame of the Koutoubia.

What you are part of is a strange process. Tourism is probably now vital to the Djemaa's survival, yet apart from the snake charmers, water vendors (who live by posing for photographs) and the hustlers, there's little that has compromised itself for the West. In many ways it actually seems the opposite. Most of the people gathered into circles round the performers are Moroccans – Berbers from the villages and lots of kids. There is no way that any tourist is going to have a tooth pulled by one of the dentists here, no matter how neat the piles of molars displayed on their square of carpet. Nor are you likely to use the scribes or street barbers or understand the convoluted tales of the storytellers, round whom are gathered perhaps the most animated crowds in the square.

Nothing of this, though, matters very much. There is a fascination in the remedies of the herb doctors, with their bizarre concoctions spread out before them. There are **performers,** too, whose appeal is universal. The square's acrobats, itinerants from the Tazeroualt, have for years supplied the European circuses – though they are perhaps never so spectacular as here, thrust forward into multiple somersaults and contortions in the late afternoon heat. There are child boxers and sad-looking trained monkeys, clowns and Chleuh boy dancers – their routines, to the climactic jarring of cymbals, totally sexual (and traditionally an invitation to clients).

And finally, the Djemaa's enduring sound – the dozens of **musicians** playing all kinds of instruments. Late at night, when only a few people are left in the square, you encounter individual players, plucking away at their *ginbris,* the skin-covered two- or three-string guitars. Earlier in the evening, there are full groups: the *Aissaoua*, playing oboe-like *ghaitahs* next to the snake charmers; the Andalusian-influenced groups, with their *ouds* and violins; and the black *Gnaoua*, trance-healers who beat out hour-long hypnotic rhythms with iron clanging hammers and pound tall drums with long curved sticks.

If you get interested in the music there's a small section in the Djemaa, near the entrance to the *souks,* where stalls sell recorded **cassettes**. Most of these are by Egyptian or Algerian Raï bands, the pop music that dominates Moroccan radio, but if you ask they'll play you Berber music from the Atlas, classic Fassi pieces, or even Gnaoua music – which sounds even stranger on tape, cut off only by the end of the one side and starting off almost identically on the other. These stalls apart, and those of the nut roasters, whose massive braziers line the immediate entrance to the potters' *souk,* the **market** activities of the Djemaa are mostly pretty mundane.

Not to be missed, however, even if you lack the stomach to eat at any of them, are the rows of makeshift **restaurants** that come into their own towards early evening. Lit by enormous lanterns, their tables piled high with massive bowls of

---

DJEMAA EL FNA: SECURITY

As a foreigner in the Djemaa el Fna, you can feel something of an interloper – your presence accepted, though not wholly welcomed. Entering into the spectacle down below, it's best to go denuded of the usual tourist trappings – watches, belt-wallets, etc; **pickpockets** do very well out of the square. Beware, also, of being duped by women selling "silver" jewellery; if you decline to buy, they may give you a "present" – and as you move on, large male friends will arrive to accuse you of stealing the trinket. An additional problem are **glue-sniffing kids**, who hang out in the square and can be extremely aggressive in asking for money. The **area round the Koutoubia** also has a bad reputation after dark. Take care.

---

cooked food, each vendor extols his own range of specialities. If you're wary, head for the orange vendors near the *Hôtel CTM*, or go for a handful of cactus fruit, peeled in a couple of seconds at the stalls nearby. For details on more substantial eating in the Djemaa el Fna and elsewhere, see p.332.

Nobody is entirely sure when or how Djemaa el Fna came into being – nor even what its name means. The usual translation is "assembly of the dead", a suitably epic title that seems to refer to the public display here of the heads of rebels and criminals. This is certainly possible, since the Djemaa was a place of execution well into the last century; the phrase, though, might only mean "the mosque of nothing" (*djemaa* means both "mosque" and "assembly" – interchangeable terms in Islamic society), recalling an abandoned Saadian plan to build a new grand mosque on this site. Whichever is the case, as an open area between the original Kasbah and the *souks,* the *place* has probably played its present role since the city's earliest days. It has often been the focal point for rioting – even within the last decade – and every few years there are plans to close it down and to move its activities outside the city walls. This, in fact, happened after independence in 1956, when the new "modernist" government built a corn market (which still stands) on part of the square and tried to turn the rest into a car park. The plan, however, lasted for only a year. Tourism was falling off and it was clearly an unpopular move – it took away one of the people's basic psychological needs, as well as eliminating a perhaps necessary expression of the past.

The Koutoubia

The absence of any architectural feature in the Djemaa – which even today seems like a haphazard clearing – serves to emphasise the drama of the **Koutoubia Minaret**, the focus of any approach to the city. Nearly seventy metres high and visible for miles on a clear morning, this is the oldest of the three great Almohad dynasty towers (the others remaining are in Rabat and Seville) and the most complete. Its proportions – a 1:5 ratio of width to height – established the classic Moroccan design. Its scale, rising from the low city buildings and the plains to the north, is extraordinary, and the more so the longer you stay and the more familiar its sight becomes.

Completed by Sultan Yacoub el Mansour (1184–99), work on the minaret probably began shortly after the Almohad conquest of the city, around 1150. It displays many of the features that were to become widespread in Moroccan architecture – the wide band of ceramic inlay near the top, the pyramid-shaped, castellated *merlons* rising above it, the use of *darj w ktarf* and other motifs – and it also established the alternation of patterning on different faces. Here, the top floor is similar on each of the sides but the lower two are almost eccentric in their variety; the most interesting is perhaps the middle niche on the southeast face, a semicircle of small lobed arches, which was to become the dominant decorative feature of Almohad gates.

If you look hard, you will notice that at around this point, the stones of the main body of the tower become slightly smaller. This seems odd today but originally the whole minaret would have been covered with plaster and its tiers of decoration painted. To see just how much this can change the whole effect – and, to most tastes, lessen much of its beauty – take a look at the Kasbah mosque (by the Saadian Tombs) which has been carefully but completely restored in this manner.

There have been plans over the years to do the same with the Koutoubia and the local press have recently been running a number of articles on various schemes, possibly involving a restoration of the whole mosque area. At present, however, the only parts of the structure that have been renovated are the three gilt balls made of copper at the summit. These are the subject of numerous legends, mostly of supernatural interventions to keep away the thieves. They are thought originally to have been made of gold and were possibly the gift of the wife of Yacoub el Mansour, presented as a penance for breaking her fast for three hours during Ramadan.

The souks and northern Medina

It is spicy in the souks, and cool and colourful. The smell, always pleasant, changes gradually with the nature of the merchandise. There are no names or signs; there is no glass . . . . You find everything – but you always find it many times over.

Elias Canetti: *The Voices of Marrakesh*

The **souks** of Marrakesh sprawl immediately north of Djemaa el Fna. They seem vast the first time you venture in, and almost impossible to navigate, though, in fact, the area that they cover is pretty compact. A long, covered street, **Rue Souk Smarine**, runs for half their length and then splits into two lanes – **Souk el Attarin** and **Souk el Kebir**. Off these are virtually all the individual *souks:* alleys and small squares devoted to specific crafts, where you can often watch part of the production process. At the top of the main area of *souks*, too, you can visit the Saadian **Ben Youssef Medersa** – the most important monument in the northern half of the Medina and arguably the finest building in the city after the Koutoubia Minaret.

If you are staying for some days, you'll probably return often to the *souks* – and this is a good way of taking them in, singling out a couple of specific crafts or products to see, rather than being swamped by the whole. To come to grips with the general layout, though, you might find it useful to walk round the whole area once with a **guide** (see below). Despite the pressure of offers in the Djemaa, don't feel that one is essential, but until the hustlers begin to recognise you (seeing that you've been in the *souks* before), they'll probably follow you in; if and when this happens, try to be easygoing, polite and confident – the qualities that force most hustlers to look elsewhere.

The most interesting **times** to visit are in early morning (between 5 and 8am if you can make it) and late afternoon, at around 4 to 5pm, when some of the *souks* auction off goods to local traders. Later in the evening, most of the stalls are closed, but you can wander unharassed to take a look at the elaborate decoration of their doorways and arches; those stalls that stay open, until 7 or 8pm, are often more amenable to bargaining at the end of the day.

Towards Ben Youssef: the main souks

On the corner of Djemaa el Fna itself there is a small potters' *souk,* but the main market area begins a little further beyond this. Its **entrance** is initially confusing. Standing at the *Café de France* (and facing the mosque opposite), look across the street and you'll see the *Café el Fath* and, beside it, a building with the sign "Tailleur de la Place" – the lane sandwiched in between them will bring you out at the beginning of Rue Souk Smarine.

SOUK SMARINE AND THE RAHBA KEDIMA

Busy and crowded, **Souk Smarine** is an important thoroughfare, traditionally dominated by the sale of textiles. Today, classier tourist "bazaars" are moving in, with *American Express* signs displayed in the windows, but there are still dozens of shops in the arcades selling and tailoring traditional shirts and caftans. Along its whole course, the street is covered by a broad, iron trellis that restricts the sun to shafts of light; it replaces the old rush (*smar*) roofing, which along with many of the *souks*' more beautiful features was destroyed by a fire in the 1960s.

Just before the fork at its end, Souk Smarine narrows and you can get a glimpse through the passageways to its right of the **Rahba Kedima**, a small and fairly ramshackle square with a few vegetable stalls set up in the middle of it. Immediately to the right, as you go in, is **Souk Larzal**, a wool market feverishly active in the dawn hours, but closed for most of the rest of the day. Alongside it, easily distinguished by smell alone, is **Souk Btana,** which deals with whole sheepskins – the pelts laid out to dry and be displayed on the roof. You can walk up here and take a look at how the skins are treated.

The most interesting aspect of Rahba Kedima, however, are the **apothecary stalls** grouped round the near corner of the square. These sell all the standard traditional cosmetics – earthenware saucers of cochineal (*kashiniah*) for rouge, powdered *kohl* or antimony for darkening the edges of the eyes, *henna* (the only cosmetic unmarried women are supposed to use) and the sticks of *suak* (walnut root or bark) with which you see Moroccans cleaning their teeth.

In addition to such essentials, the stalls also sell the herbal and animal ingredients that are still in widespread use for manipulation, or spellbinding. There are roots and tablets used as aphrodisiacs, and there are stranger and more specialised goods – dried pieces of lizard and stork, fragments of beaks, talons and gazelle horns. Magic, white and black, has always been very much a part of Moroccan life, and there are dozens of stories relating to its effects.

LA CRIÉE BERBÈRE

At the end of Rahba Kedima, a passageway to the left gives access to another, smaller square – a bustling, carpet-draped area known as **la Criée Berbère** (the Berber auctions)

It was here that the old **slave auctions** were held, just before sunset every Wednesday, Thursday and Friday, until the French occupied the city in 1912. They were conducted, according to Budgett Meakin's account in 1900, "precisely as those of cows and mules, often on the same spot by the same men . . . with the human chattels being personally examined in the most disgusting manner, and

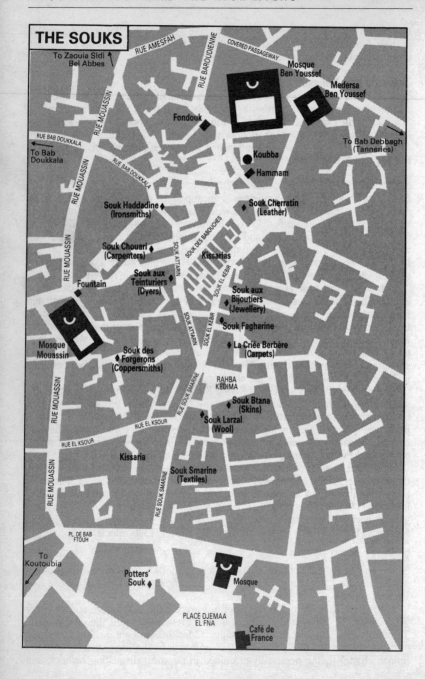

THE SOUKS

RUE AMESFAH

RUE BAROUDIENNE

COVERED PASSAGEWAY

To Zaouia Sidi
Bel Abbes

Mosque
Ben Youssef

Medersa
Ben Youssef

RUE MOUASSIN

Fondouk

RUE BAB DOUKKALA

To Bab
Doukkala

RUE BAB DOUKKALA

Koubba

Hammam

To Bab Debbagh
(Tanneries)

Souk Haddadine
(Ironsmiths)

Souk Cherratin
(Leather)

SOUK DES BABOUCHES

Souk Chouari
(Carpenters)

SOUK ATTARIN

Kissarias

SOUK EL KEBIR

Souk aux
Teinturiers
(Dyers)

Souk aux
Bijoutiers
(Jewellery)

Fountain

SOUK ATTARIN

SOUK EL KEBIR

Souk Fagharine

La Criée Berbère
(Carpets)

Mosque
Mouassin

Souk des
Forgerons
(Coppersmiths)

RUE SOUK SMARINE

RAHBA
KEDIMA

Souk Btana
(Skins)

RUE MOUASSIN

Souk Larzal
(Wool)

RUE EL KSOUR

RUE EL KSOUR

Kissaria

RUE MOUASSIN

SOUK SMARINE

Souk Smarine
(Textiles)

RUE SOUK SMARINE

PL. DE BAB
FTOUH

To
Koutoubia

Potters'
Souk

Mosque

PLACE DJEMAA
EL FNA

Café de
France

Like Fes, Marrakesh can be an expensive place to **buy craft goods** – though if you have anything to barter (designer T-shirts, trainers, rock music cassettes, etc), you'll find people eager enough to arrange an exchange. Before setting out into the *souks* in search of rugs, blankets, or whatever, check out the classic designs in the **Dar Si Said** museum and take a look at the more or less fixed prices in the well-run **Ensemble Artesenal** (daily 8.30am–1pm & 2.30–7pm), just inside the ramparts on Av. Mohammed V.

Official **guides** (50dh for a half day) can be arranged at the *ONMT* or SI tourist office or large hotels; unofficial ones in Djemaa el Fna and almost anywhere you're seen looking perplexed. Some of the latter can be fine, others a struggle, as you are escorted into shop after shop; fix a price in advance. A favourite recommendation of the hustlers is the so-called Berber market – "only today", they'll tell you, with great urgency. In fact, all the main **souks** are open every day, though they're quiet on Friday mornings. Even the big Souk el Khemis (the Thursday Market, held outside Bab Debbagh) now operates most days of the week.

paraded in lots by the auctioneers, who shout their attractions and the bids". Most had been kidnapped and brought in by the caravans from Guinea and Sudan; Meakin saw two small boys sold for £5 apiece, an eight-year-old girl for £3 and 10 shillings and a "stalwart negro" went for £14; a beauty, he was told, might exceptionally fetch £130 to £150.

These days, **rugs and carpets** are about the only things sold in the square, and if you have a good deal of time and willpower you could spend the best part of a day here while endless (and often identical) stacks are unfolded and displayed before you. Some of the most interesting are the Berber rugs from the High Atlas – bright, geometric designs that look very different after being laid out on the roof and bleached by the sun. The dark, often black, backgrounds usually signify rugs from the Glaoua country, up towards Telouet; the reddish-backed carpets are from Chichaoua, a small village on the way to Essaouira, and are also pretty common. There is usually a small **auction** in the *criée* at around 4pm – an interesting sight with the auctioneers wandering round the square shouting out the latest bids, but it's not the best place to buy a rug – it's devoted mainly to heavy, brown woollen *djellabas*.

AROUND THE KISSARIAS

Cutting back to **Souk el Kebir**, which by now has taken over from the Smarine, you emerge at the **kissarias**, the covered markets at the heart of the *souks*. The goods here, apart from the many and sometimes imaginative *couvertures* (blankets), aren't that interesting; the *kissarias* traditionally sell the more expensive products, which today means a sad predominance of Western designs and imports. Off to their right, at the bottom end of the *kissarias*, is **Souk des Bijoutiers**, a modest jewellers' lane, which is much less varied than the one established in the Mellah (see "The Lower Medina") by Jewish craftsmen. At the top end is a convoluted web of alleys that comprise the **Souk Cherratin**, essentially a leather workers' *souk* (with dozens of purse makers and sandal cobblers), though it's interspersed with smaller alleys and *souks* of carpenters, sieve makers and even a few tourist shops. If you bear left through this area and then turn right, you should arrive at the open space in front of the Mosque Ben Youssef; the *medersa* (see the section overleaf) is off to its right.

THE DYERS' SOUK AND A LOOP BACK TO THE DJEMAA EL FNA

Had you earlier taken the left fork along **Souk el Attarin** – the spice and perfume *souk* – you would have come out on the other side of the **kissarias** and the long lane of the **Souk des Babouches** (slipper makers).

The main attraction in this area is the little **Souk des Teinturiers** – the dyers' *souk*. To reach it, turn left along the first alley you come to after the Souk des Babouches. Working your way down this lane (which comes out in a square by the Mouassin Mosque), look to your right and you'll see the entrance to the *souk* about halfway down – its lanes rhythmically flash with bright skeins of wool, hung from above. If you have trouble finding it, just follow the first tour group you see.

There is a reasonably straightforward alternative route back to Djemaa el Fna from here, following the main street down to the **Mouassin Mosque** (which is almost entirely concealed from public view, built at an angle to the square beside it) and then turning left on to Rue Mouassin. As you approach the mosque, the street widens very slightly opposite an elaborate triple-bayed **fountain**. Built in the mid-sixteenth century by the prolific Saadian builder, Abdallah el-Ghalib, this is one of many such fountains in Marrakesh with a basin for humans set next to two larger troughs for animals; its installation was a pious act, directly sanctioned by the Koran in its charitable provision of water for men and beasts.

Below the Mouassin Mosque is an area of coppersmiths, **Souk des Forgerons**. Above it sprawls the main section of **carpenters'** workshops – with their beautiful smell of cedar – and beyond them a small *souk* for **oils** (**Souk des Huivres**) and the **Souk Haddadine** of blacksmiths and metalworkers – whose sounds you'll hear long before arriving.

The Ben Youssef Medersa

One of the largest buildings in the Medina, and preceded by a rare open space, the **Ben Youssef Mosque** is quite easy to locate. Its **medersa** – the old student annexe, and their home until they had learnt the Koran by rote – stands off a side street just to the east, distinguishable by a series of small, grilled windows. The entrance porch is a short way down the side street, covering the whole lane at this point. Recently restored, it is open from 8am to noon and 2.30 to 5.45pm, except on Mondays and Friday mornings; admission is the standard 10dh.

Like most of the Fes *medersas* (see p.189 for a description of their development and function), the Ben Youssef was a Merenid foundation, established by Sultan Abou el Hassan in the fourteenth century. It was, however, almost completely rebuilt under the Saadians, and it is this dynasty's intricate, Andalusian-influenced art that has left its mark. As with the slightly later Saadian Tombs, no surface is left undecorated, and the overall quality of its craftsmanship, whether in carved wood, stuccowork or *zellij*, is startling. That this was possible in sixteenth-century Marrakesh, after a period in which the city was reduced to near ruin and the country to tribal anarchy, is remarkable. Revealingly, parts have exact parallels in the Alhambra Palace in Granada, and it seems likely that Muslim Spanish architects were employed in its construction.

Inside the *medersa*, you reach the main court by means of a long outer **corridor** and a small entry **vestibule**. To the side of this are stairs to **student cells**, arranged round smaller internal courtyards on the upper floors, an **ablutions hall** and **latrine**. Until very recently, a remarkable tenth-century Ommayad marble basin – decorated with eagles and griffins – completed the ensemble, though it has now been removed to the Dar Si Said museum.

The **central courtyard**, weathered almost flat on its most exposed side, is unusually large. Along two sides run wide, sturdy, columned arcades, which were probably used to supplement the space for teaching in the neighbouring mosque. Above them are some of the windows of the **dormitory quarters**, from which you can get an interesting perspective – and attempt to fathom how over eight hundred students were once housed in the building.

At its far end, the court opens onto a **prayer hall,** where the decoration, mellowed on the outside with the city's familiar pink tone, is at its best preserved and most elaborate. Notable here, as in the court's cedar carving, is a predominance of pinecone and palm motifs; around the *mihrab* (the horseshoe-arched prayer niche) they've been applied so as to give the frieze a highly three-dimensional appearance. This is rare in Moorish stuccowork, though the inscriptions themselves, picked out in the curling, vegetative arabesques, are from familiar Koranic texts. The most common, as in all Moroccan stucco and *zellij* decoration, is the ceremonial *bismillah* invocation: "In the name of Allah, the Compassionate, the Merciful . . . ".

The Almoravid Koubba

Even though it is signposted opposite the entrance to the Ben Youssef *medersa*, the **Almoravid Koubba** is easy to pass by – a small, two-storey kiosk, which at first seems little more than a grey dome and a handful of variously shaped doors and windows. Look closer, though, and you may begin to understand its significance and even fascination. For this is the only intact surviving Almoravid building, and it is at the root of all Moroccan architecture. The motifs you've just seen in the *medersa* – the pinecones, palms and acanthus leaves – were all carved here for the first time. The windows on each of the different sides became the classic shapes of Almohad and Merenid design – as did the *merlons*, the Christmas tree-like battlements; the complex "ribs" on the outside of the dome; and the dome's interior support, a sophisticated device of a square and star-shaped octagon, which is itself repeated at each of its corners. Once you see all this, you're only a step away from the eulogies of Islamic art historians who sense in this building, which was probably a small ablutions annexe to the original Ben Youssef Mosque, a powerful and novel expression of form.

Excavated only in 1952 – having been covered over amid the many rebuildings of the Ben Youssef *medersa* – the *koubba* lies just to the south of the present (mainly nineteenth-century) Ben Youssef Mosque. It is mostly below today's ground level, though standing with your back to the mosque you can make out the top of its dome behind the long, low brick wall. There is an entrance gate down a few steps, opposite the Ben Youssef Mosque, where a *gardien* will emerge to escort you round and sell you a ticket (10dh), and may also show you the huge, old water conduits nearby, which brought water from the Atlas.

If the *koubba* is closed, you can get almost as good a view from the roof of a very ancient (but still active) hammam down to the right; the attendants will give you access for a small tip.

The tanneries and northern gates

The main *souks* – and the tourist route – stop abruptly at the Ben Youssef *medersa*. Above them, in all directions, you'll find yourself in the ordinary **residential quarters** of the Medina. There are few particular "sights" to be found here, but if you've got the time, there's an interest of its own in following the crowds, and a relief in getting away from the central shopping district of Marrakesh, where you are expected to come in, look round and buy.

Probably the most interesting targets are **Bab Debbagh** and **Souk el Khemis**. From Ben Youssef you can reach these quite easily: it's about a fifteen-minute walk to the first, another fifteen to twenty minutes round the ramparts to the second. As you pass the entrance porch to the *medersa*, you'll quickly reach a fork in the side street. To the left, a covered passageway leads around behind the mosque to join Rue Amesfah (see below). Head instead to your right, and then keep going as straight as possible until you emerge at the ramparts by Bab Debbagh; on the way you'll cross a small square and intersection, **Place el Moukef**, where a busy and sizeable lane goes off to the left – a more direct approach to Bab el Khemis.

BAB DEBBAGH AND THE TANNERIES

Bab Debbagh is supposedly Almoravid in design, though over the years it must have been almost totally rebuilt. Passing through the gate, you become aware of its very real defensive purpose: three internal rooms are placed in such a manner as to force anyone attempting to storm it to make several turns. The leather goods shop, on the right hand side of Bab Debbagh, gives good views from its roof (for a small fee) over the quarter.

Looking down, you have an excellent view over the **tanneries**, built here at the edge of the city for access to water (the summer-dry Oued Issil runs just outside the walls) and for the obvious reason of the smell. If you want to take a closer look at the processes (see p.197), come in the morning, when the co-operatives are at work; any of the kids standing around will take you in. As at Fes, a tour is an ambivalent experience. There's a beauty about the proceedings but the traditional dyes have been in large part replaced by modern chemicals, which cause sciatica, malignant melanoma and other internal cancers.

BAB EL KHEMIS

Following the road from Bab Debbagh, outside the ramparts, is the simplest approach to **Bab el Khemis** (Gate of the Thursday Market) another recon-structed Almoravid gate, built at an angle in the walls. The **Thursday market** now seems to take place more or less daily, around 400m to the north, above a cemetery and *marabout's* tomb. It is really a local produce market, though odd handicraft items do occasionally surface.

North of the Ben Youssef Mosque

The area immediately **north of the Ben Youssef Mosque** is cut by two main streets: Rue Assouel (which leads up to Bab el Khemis) and Rue Bab Taghzout, which runs up to the gate of the same name and to the Zaouia of Sidi Bel Abbes. These were, with Bab Doukkala, the principal approaches to the city until the present century and along them you find many of the old **fondouks** used for stor-age and lodging by merchants visiting the *souks*.

One of these *fondouks* is sited just south of the mosque and a whole series can be found along Rue Amesfah – the continuation of Baroudienne – to the north and west. Most are still used in some commercial capacity, as workshops or ware-houses, and the doors to their courtyards often stand open. Some date from Saadian times and have fine details of wood carving or stuccowork. If you are interested, nobody seems to mind if you wander in.

THE ZAOUIA OF SIDI BEL ABBES

Rue Amesfah runs for around 150m north of the intersection with Rue Baroudienne before reaching the junction of Rue Assouel (to the east) and **Rue Bab Taghzout** (to the west). Following Rue Bab Taghzout, you pass another *fondouk*, opposite a small recessed fountain known as **Chrob ou Chouf** ("drink and admire"), and, around 500m further down, the old city gate of **Bab Taghzout**. This marked the limits of the original Almoravid Medina, and continued to do so into the eighteenth century, when Sultan Mohammed Abdallah extended the walls to enclose the quarter and the **Zaouia of Sidi Bel Abbes**.

Sidi Bel Abbes, a twelfth-century *marabout* and a prolific performer of miracles, is the most important of Marrakesh's seven saints, and his **zaouia**, a kind of monastic cult centre, has traditionally wielded very great influence and power, often at odds with that of the sultan and providing a refuge for political dissidents.

The present buildings, which are strictly forbidden to non-Muslims, date largely from a reconstruction by Moulay Ismail, an act that was probably inspired more by political motivation than piety. You can see something of the complex and its activities from outside the official boundary – do not, however, try to pass through the long central corridor. The *zaouia* still owns much of the quarter to the north and continues its educational and charitable work, distributing food each evening to the blind.

There is a smaller, though again significant, **zaouia** dedicated to **Sidi Slimane**, a Saadian *marabout,* a couple of blocks to the southwest.

WEST TO BAB DOUKKALA: DAR EL GLAOUI

A third alternative from Ben Youssef is to head west **towards Bab Doukkala.** This route, once you've found your way down through Souk Haddadine to **Rue Bab Doukkala,** is a sizeable thoroughfare and very straightforward to follow. Midway, you pass the **Dar el Glaoui**, the old palace of the Pasha of Marrakesh (see box below) and a place of legendary exoticism throughout the first half of this century. Part of it is nowadays occupied by the Ministry of Culture; visitors are allowed in, at the discretion of the caretaker, but there's little to see. The main section of the palace remains private.

EL GLAOUI: THE PASHA OF MARRAKESH

El Glaoui, the famous Pasha of Marrakesh during the French Protectorate, was the last of the great southern tribal leaders, an active and shrewd supporter of colonial rule and a personal friend of Winston Churchill. Cruel and magnificent in equal measure – see p.364 – he was also one of the most spectacular partygivers around – in an age where rivals were not lacking. At the extraordinary *difas* or banquets held at his Marrakesh palace, the Dar el Glaoui, "nothing", as Gavin Maxwell wrote, "was impossible" – hashish and opium were freely available for the Europeans and Americans to experiment with, and "to his guests T'hami gave, literally, whatever they wanted, whether it might be a diamond ring, a present of money in gold, or a Berber girl or boy from the High Atlas".

Not surprisingly, there was little enthusiasm for showing off the palace since El Glaoui's death in 1956, an event that led to a mob looting the palace, destroying its fittings and even the cars in the garages, and then lynching whomever of the Pasha's henchmen they could find. However, passions have burnt out over the years, and the family has been rehabilitated – one of Thami's sons, Glaoui Abdelssadak, is high up in the Moroccan civil service and vice president of Gulf Oil.

The Lower Medina: palaces, Saadian Tombs and Mellah

Staying in Marrakesh even for a few days, you begin to sense the different appearance and life of its various Medina quarters, and nowhere more so than in the shift from north to south, from the area above Djemaa el Fna to the area below it. At the base here (a kind of stem to the mushroom shape of the city walls) is **Dar el Makhzen**, the royal palace. To its west stretches the old inner citadel of the **Kasbah**; to the east, the **Mellah**, once the largest Jewish ghetto in Morocco; while rambling above it are a series of mansions and palaces built for the nineteenth-century elite.

All in all, it's an interesting area to wander round, though you inevitably spend time trying to figure out the sudden and apparently arbitrary appearance of

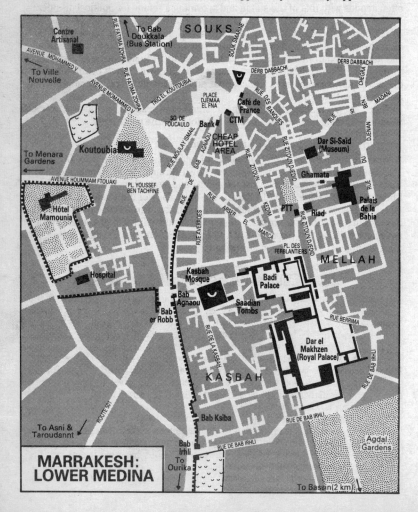

MARRAKESH:
LOWER MEDINA

ramparts and enclosures. And there are two obvious focal points, not to be missed: the **Saadian Tombs**, preserved in the shadow of the Kasbah mosque, and **El Badi**, the ruined palace of Ahmed el Mansour.

The Saadian Tombs

Sealed up by Moulay Ismail after he had destroyed the adjoining Badi Palace, the **Saadian Tombs** lay half-ruined and half-forgotten at the beginning of this century. In 1917, however, they were rediscovered on a French aerial map and a passageway was built to give access from the side of the Kasbah mosque. Restored, they are today the city's main "sight" – overlavish, maybe, in their exhaustive decoration, but dazzling nonetheless. Friday mornings excepted, they are open daily from around 9am to noon and 2.30 to 6pm; go late afternoon, if possible. As a national monument, admission is the usual 10dh; there is no longer, however, a compulsory guided tour – you are left to look round on your own or even just to sit and gaze. A quiet, high-walled enclosure, shaded with shrubs and palms and dotted with bright *zellij*-covered tombs, it seems as much a pleasure garden as a cemetery.

Some form of burial ground behind the royal palace probably predated the Saadian period, though the earliest of the tombs here dates from 1557, and all the principal structures were built by Sultan Ahmed el Mansour. This makes them virtual contemporaries of the Ben Youssef Medersa – with which there are obvious parallels – and allows a revealing insight into just how rich and extravagant the El Badi must once have been. Their escape from Moulay Ismail's systematic plundering was probably due to superstition – Ismail had to content himself with blocking all but an obscure entrance from the Kasbah mosque. Despite this, a few prominent *Marrakchis* continued to be buried in the mausoleums; the last, in 1792, was the "mad sultan", Moulay Yazid, whose 22-month reign was probably the most violent, vicious and sadistic in the nation's history.

THE MAUSOLEUMS

There are two main **mausoleums** in the enclosure. The finest is on the left as you come in – a beautiful group of three rooms, built to house El Mansour's own tomb and completed within his lifetime. Continuing round from the courtyard entrance, the first hall is a **prayer oratory**, a room probably not intended for burial, though now almost littered with the thin marble stones of Saadian princes. It is here that Moulay Yazid was laid out, perhaps in purposeful obscurity, certainly in ironic contrast to the cursive inscription round the band of black and white *zellij*: "And the works of peace they have accomplished", it reads amid the interlocking circles, "will make them enter the holy gardens."

Architecturally, the most important feature of this mausoleum is the *mihrab*, its pointed horseshoe arch supported by an incredibly delicate arrangement of columns. Opposite this is another elaborate arch, leading to the domed **central chamber** and **El Mansour's tomb**, which you can glimpse through the next door in the court. The tomb, slightly larger than those surrounding it, lies right in the middle, flanked on either side by those of the sultan's sons and successors. The room itself is spectacular, faint light filtering onto the tombs from an interior lantern in a tremendous vaulted roof, the *zellij* full of colour and motion and the undefined richness of a third chamber almost hidden from view. Throughout, there are echoes of the Alhambra in Granada, built two centuries previously, and from which its style is clearly derived.

The **other mausoleum**, older and less impressive, was built by Ahmed in place of an existing pavilion above the tombs of his mother, Lalla Messaouda, and of Mohammed esh Sheikh, the founder of the Saadian dynasty. It is again a series of three rooms, though two are hardly more than loggias. Messaouda's tomb is the niche below the dome in the outer chamber. Mohammed esh Sheikh is buried in the inner one – or at least his torso is, since he was murdered in the Atlas by Turkish mercenaries, who salted his head and took it back for public display on the walls of Istanbul.

Outside, **round the garden and courtyard**, are scattered the tombs of over a hundred more Saadian princes and members of the royal household. Like the privileged 66 given space within the mausoleums, their gravestones are brilliantly tiled and often elaborately inscribed. The most usual inscription reads quite simply:

> *There is no God but God.*
> *Muhammad is God's envoy.*
> *Praise Be to God.*
> *The occupant of this tomb died on . . . .*

But there are others – epitaphs and extracts from the Koran – that seem to express the turbulence of the age to a greater degree, which, with Ahmed's death in 1603, was to disintegrate into nearly seventy years of constant civil war. "Every soul shall know death", reads one tombstone; "Death will find you wherever you are, even in fortified towers", another. And, carved in gypsum on the walls, there is a poem:

> *O mausoleum, built out of mercy, thou whose*
> *walls are the shadow of heaven.*
> *The breath of asceticism is wafted from thy tombs*
> *like a fragrance.*
> *Through thy death*
> *the light of faith has been dimmed,*
> *the seven spheres are fraught with darkness*
> *and the columns of glory*
> *broken with pain.*

ACCESS

Getting to the Saadian Tombs, the simplest route from Djemaa el Fna is to follow **Rue Bab Agnaou** outside the ramparts. At its end you come to a small square flanked by two gates. Directly ahead is **Bab er Robb** – outside of which the *grands taxis* and private-line buses leave for Ourika and other local destinations. To the left, somewhat battered and eroded, is the city's only survivng Almohad gateway, **Bab Agnaou** (Gate of the Gnaoua [the blacks]). This is an impressive structure, smaller than the monumental gates of Rabat, but sharing much of their force and apparent simplicity. Notice how the semicircular frieze above its arch creates a strong, three-dimensional effect without any actual depth of carving. At the time of its construction, it was the only stone building in Marrakesh apart from the Koutoubia Minaret.

Passing through the gate, the **Kasbah mosque** is in front of you: its minaret looks gaudy and modern but is, in fact, contemporary with both the Koutoubia and Hassan towers – it was restored to its exact original state in the 1960s. The narrow passageway to the Saadian Tombs is well signposted, at the near right-hand corner of the mosque.

El Badi Palace

To reach the ruins of the **El Badi Palace** – which seems originally to have sprawled across the whole area east of the Kasbah mosque – you have to back-track slightly from the Saadian Tombs. At Bab Agnaou, follow the ramparts up again, this time taking the road just inside them, until you come to a reasonably sized street on your right (just before the walls temporarily give out). Turn into this street, keep more or less straight, and in about 550m, you'll emerge at **Place des Ferblantiers** – a major intersection. On the south side of the *place* is a gate known as **Bab Berrima**, which opens onto a long rectangular enclosure, flanked on either side by walls; go through it, and on your right you'll come to the Badi's entrance. Hours are generally 9am to noon and 2.30 to 6.30pm; admission 10dh; a guided tour is touted but far from essential.

THE INCOMPARABLE PALACE

Though substantially in ruins, and reduced throughout to its red *pisé* walls, enough remains of **El Badi** to suggest that its name – "The Incomparable" – was not entirely immodest. It took the sultan Moulay Ismail over ten years of system-atic work to strip the palace of everything moveable or of value, and even so, there's a lingering sense of luxury and grandeur. The scale, with its sunken gardens and vast, ninety-metre-long pool, is certainly unrivalled, and the odd traces of *zellij* and plaster still left evoke a decor that was probably as rich as that of the Saadian Tombs.

What you see today is essentially the ceremonial part of **the palace complex**, planned on a grand scale for the reception of ambassadors, and not meant for everyday living. It seems likely that El Mansour and the multiple members of his court each had private palaces – smaller, though built to a similar ground plan – to the west and south, covering much of the area occupied today by the Dar el Makhzen, the present Royal Palace.

The **entrance** in current use was probably not the main approach. Going through, you find yourself at the side of a **mosque**, like everything else within

---

AHMED EL MANSOUR

The Badi palace was begun shortly after Ahmed el Mansour's accession, its initial finance came from the enormous ransom paid out by the Portuguese after the Battle of the Three Kings at Ksar el Kebir. Fought in the summer of 1578, this was one of the most disastrous battles in Christian medieval history; ostensibly in support of a rival Saadian claimant, but to all intents a Portuguese crusade, it was led by the king, Dom Sebastião, and supported by almost his entire nobility. Few escaped death or Moorish capture. Sebastião himself was killed, as were both the Saadian claimant and the ruling sultan.

As a result, Ahmed – dubbed *El Mansour* (The Victorious) – came to the throne, undisputed and commanding immediate wealth. He reigned for 25 years, trading in sugar and slaves with Britain, Spain and Italy; seized the gold route across the Sahara with the resultant capture of Timbuktu, which earned him the additional epithet *El Eddahbi* (The Golden); and maintained peace in Morocco through a loose confederation of tribes. It was the most prosperous period in the country's history since the time of the Almohads – a cultural and political renaissance reflected in the coining of a new title, the Shereefian Empire, the country's official name until independence in 1956.

THE MARRAKESH FESTIVAL

Marrakesh utilises the Badi Palace – and other venues in the city – for an annual two-week **Festival National des Art Populaires**. This is the country's biggest and best folklore and music festival, and is held in September. If you are interested in Moroccan music, it would be worth planning your trip around it – were you to be able to establish the precise dates, which vary year by year.

The festival comprises a series of totally authentic and unusual performances, with groups of musicians and dancers coming in from all regions of Morocco. A typical programme will span the range of Moroccan music – from the Gnaoua drummers and the panpipers of Jajouka, to Berber *ahouaches* from the Atlas and southern oases, to classical Andalusian music from Fes.

The shows are held each evening from around 9pm to midnight (tickets are 50dh); before they start, towards sunset, there is a **fantasia** at Bab el Djedid – a spectacle by any standard, with dozens of Berber horsemen firing their guns in the air at full gallop.

this complex, of enormous height. To the rear extends the great **central court**, over 130m long and nearly as wide, and constructed on a substructure of vaults in order to allow the circulation of water through the pools and gardens. When the pools are filled – as during the June folklore festival which takes place here – they are an incredibly majestic sight, especially the main one, with an island that was originally surmounted by an elaborate double fountain.

On each side of the pools were summer pavilions, traces of which survive. The most prominent is at the far end, a monumental hall that was used by the sultan on occasions of state and known as the **Koubba el Hamsiniya** (The Fifty Pavilion), for the number of its columns. Strangely enough, their size and splendour were documented by an observer far removed from the Arab chroniclers who extolled their beauty. The French philosopher Montaigne, while travelling through Italy, saw craftsmen preparing the columns – "each of an extreme height . . . for the king of Fes and Barbary".

South of the courtyard are ruins of the palace **stables,** and beyond them, leading towards the intriguing walls of the present royal palace, a series of **dungeons**, used into the present century as a state prison. You can explore part of these and could easily spend a whole afternoon wandering round the various inner courts above, with their fragments of marble and *zellij* and their water conduits for the fountains and hammams. Like the Saadian Tombs, the Badi inspired contemporary poets, and there is an account, too, by the chronicler El Ifrani, of its construction:

> *El Mansour made workmen come from all the different countries . . . .He paid for the marble sent from Italy in sugar, pound for pound awarded his workers very generously . . . and paid attention even to the entertainment of their children, so that the artisans might devote themselves entirely to their work without being distracted by any other preoccupation.*

If this is even half true, there could be no greater contrast with the next great Moroccan builder, and dismantler of the palace, Moulay Ismail, whose workmen were instead beaten up, starved and abused, and then buried in the walls where they fell. But sixteenth-century crèches aside, the most enduring account of the palace concerns its state opening, a fabulous occasion attended by ambassadors from several European powers and by all the sheikhs and *caids* of the kingdom. Surveying the effect, Ahmed turned to his court jester for an opinion on the new palace. "Sidi," the man replied, "this will make a magnificent ruin."

The Mellah

It was in 1558 – five years before Ahmed's accession – that the city's **Mellah**, the separate Jewish quarter, was created. There is no exact record of why this was done at this particular time. Possibly it was the result of a pogrom, with the sultan moving the Jews to his protected Kasbah – and they, in turn, forming a useful buffer zone (and scapegoat) between his palace and the populace in times of social unrest. But, as likely as not, it was simply brought about to make taxation easier. The Jews of Marrakesh were an important financial resource – they controlled most of the Saadian sugar trade, and comprised practically all of the city's bankers, metalworkers, jewellers and tailors. In the sixteenth century, at least, their quarter was almost a town in itself, supervised by rabbis, and with its own *souks,* gardens, fountains and synagogues.

The present Mellah, much smaller in extent, is now almost entirely Muslim – most of the *Marrakchi* Jews left long ago for Casablanca (where some 6000 still live) or emigrated to France or Israel. The few who remain, outwardly distinguishable only by the men's small black skullcaps, are mostly poor or old or both. Their quarter, however, is immediately distinct: its houses are taller than elsewhere, the streets are more enclosed, and even the shop cubicles are smaller. Until the Protectorate, Jews were not permitted to own land or property – nor even to ride or walk, except barefoot – outside the Mellah; a situation that was greatly exploited by their landlords, who resisted all attempts to expand the walls. Today its air of neglect and poverty – since this is not a prized neighbourhood in which to live – is probably less than at any time during the past three centuries.

AROUND THE QUARTER

The main entrance, in what is still a largely walled district, is at **Place des Ferblantiers**. This square, formerly called Place du Mellah, was itself part of the old Jewish *souk*, and an archway (to your right, standing at Bab Berrima) leads into it. Near the upper end is a **jewellers' souk**, one of the traditional Jewish trades now more or less taken over by Muslim craftsmen; further down are some good spice and textile *souks*. Right at the centre – and situated very much as the goal of a maze – is a small square with a fountain in the middle, **Place Souweka**. You will almost certainly find yourself back here if you wander round for a short while and manage to avoid the blind alleys.

To the east, some 200m away, is the old Jewish **cemetery**, the *Mihaara*. Closer by (and you'll need to enlist a guide to find them) are a number of **synagogues** (*s'noga*). Even when they were in active use, many were as much private houses as they were temples – " . . . serving also as places in which to eat, sleep and to kill chickens" according to Budgett Meakin – and most of them today remain lived in. One of the larger ones, attached to a kind of hostel financed by American Jews, can usually be visited, as (depending on who your guide knows) can a couple of other ones.

North of the Mellah: Palais El Bahia

Heading north from the Mellah – back towards Djemaa el Fna – there are three direct and fairly simple routes. To the left of Place des Ferblantiers, **Avenue**

Hoummam el Ftouaki will bring you out by the Koutoubia. Above the *place*, two parallel streets, **Rue Zitoun el Kedim** and **Zitoun el Djedid** lead up to the Djemaa itself.

El Kedim is basically a shopping street, lined with grocers, barbershops and, at the upper end, a couple of hammams (open all day; one each for men and women). El Djedid is more residential, and it is here that you find the concentration of **palaces and mansions** built in those strange, closing decades of the last century, and the first few years of our own, when the sultans Moulay Hassan and Moulay Abd el Aziz held court in the city.

By far the most ambitious and costly of these was the **Palais El Bahia**, residence of the grand vizier, Si Ahmed Ben Moussa. Shrewd, wilful and cruel, as was the tradition of his age, Bou Ahmed (as he was better known) was a black slave who rose to hold massive power in the Shereefian kingdom and, for the last six years of his life, exercised virtually autocratic control. He was first chamberlain to Moulay Hassan, whose death while returning home from a *harka* he was able to conceal until the proclamation of Abd el Aziz in Rabat (see "Writers on Morocco", in *Contexts*, for the dramatic account). Under Abd el Aziz (who was just twelve when he acceded to the throne), Bou Ahmed usurped the position of vizier from the ill-fated Jamai brothers (see Fes), and then proceeded to rule.

He began building the Bahia in 1894, later enlarging it by acquiring the surrounding land and property. He died in 1900. The name of the building means "The Effulgence" or "Brilliance", but after the **guided tour** round various sections of the rambling palace courts and apartments you might feel this to be a somewhat tall claim. There is reasonable craftsmanship in the main **reception halls**, and a pleasant arrangement of rooms in the **harem quarter,** but for the most part it is all fabulously vulgar and hasn't aged too well. Perhaps this is the main reason for a visit: you come away realising just how much mastery and sophistication went into the Saadian *medersa* and tombs, and how corrupted and dull these traditions had become.

But there is also a certain pathos to the empty, echoing chambers – and the inevitable passing of Bou Ahmed's influence and glory. Walter Harris, who knew the vizier, described his demise and the clearing of his palace in *Morocco That Was*, published just twenty years after the events, by which time Bou Ahmed's name had already become "only a memory of the past":

> *For several days as the Vizier lay expiring, guards were stationed outside his palace waiting in silence for the end. And then one morning the wail of the women within the house told that death had come. Every gateway of the great building was seized, and no one was allowed to enter or come out, while within there was pandemonium. His slaves pillaged wherever they could lay their hands. His women fought and stole to get possesion of the jewels. Safes were broken open, documents and title-deeds were extracted, precious stones were torn from their settings, the more easily to be concealed, and even murder took place . . . . A few days later nothing remained but the great building – all the rest had disappeared into space. His family were driven out to starvation and ruin, and his vast properties passed into the possession of the State. It was the custom of the country.*

ACCESS

For some years during the Protectorate, the palace was used to house the Resident-General, and it is still called into use when the royal family is in the city. This is usually during the winter months, at which times there is no public admission. Its normal **opening hours** are daily from 9am to noon and 2.30 to 5.30pm; the guided tour is compulsory and you are expected to tip 5 to 10dh.

Finding your way to the palace is easy enough: from Rue Zitoun follow the signs to *Palais Gharnata*, keeping straight when they suddenly direct you to the right under an arch. The **Gharnata**, and the nearby **Riad**, "palaces" are among a number of mansions in this part of the city that have been converted into "Tourist Spectacle" restaurants. All of them are expensive – and the shows hideously inauthentic – but it's worth looking into one or two of them during the day, just to see the turn-of-the-century decor.

Dar Si Said Museum

Also worth your while on this route is the **Dar Si Said**, a smaller version of the Bahia, built by a brother of Bou Ahmed, who, being something of a simpleton, nonetheless gained the post of royal chamberlain. It's a pleasurable building, with beautiful pooled courtyards, scented with lemons, palms and flowers, and it houses an impressive **Museum of Moroccan Arts**.

This is particularly strong on its collections of southern **Berber jewellery and weapons** – large, boldly designed objects of great beauty. There are also fine displays of eighteenth- and nineteenth-century **wood carving** from the Glaoui Kasbahs, **modern Berber rug** and a curious group of traditional **wedding chairs** – once widely used for carrying the bride, veiled and hidden, to her new home – and **fairground swings,** used at *moussems* until the 1940s.

Historically, the museum's most important exhibit, recently brought here from the Ben Youssef *medersa*, is a marble **basin**, rectangular in shape and decorated along one side with what seem to be heraldic eagles and griffins. An inscription amid the floral decorations records its origin in tenth-century Córdoba, then the centre of the western Muslim world; the Ommayad caliphs, for whom it was constructed, had few reservations about representational art. What is surprising is that it was brought over to Morocco by the highly puritan Almoravid sultan Ali Ben Youssef and, placed in his mosque, was left untouched by the dynasty's equally iconoclastic successors, the Almohads.

Dar Si Said is a block to the west of Rue Zitoun el Djedid (turn right opposite a mosque, around halfway down); summer admission hours are 9am to noon and 4 to 7pm, winter 9am to noon and 2.30 to 6pm, closed Tuesday; 10dh admission.

Maison Tiskiwin

A further, superb collection of Moroccan art and artefacts is housed in the **Maison Tiskiwin**, which lies between the Bahia and Dar Si Said palaces at 8 Rue de la Bahia. It is not easy to find: start out from the Bahia car park and look out for the name in wrought iron, above a heavy wooden door. It is open officially from 8.30am to 1pm, though a tap on the door in the afternoon might be rewarded if one of the assistants is around.

Behind the wooden door is a beautiful town house, built at the turn of the century in Spanish-Moroccan style, and furnished from the collection of a Dutch anthropologist, Bert Flint, who has been resident in Morocco since the 1950s. Each of the rooms features carpets, fabrics, clothes and jewellery from a different region or town – Tangier, Chaouen, the Rif, Meknes, Fes, Middle Atlas, Khenifra, Beni Mellal and Azilal – and backed by informative notes (in French).

Flint's collection of southern and Saharan exhibits are displayed in Agadir.

The gardens

With summer temperatures of 90 to 100°F – and peaks well above that – it seems best to devote at least the middle of a Marrakesh day to total inactivity. If you want to do this in style, it means finding your way to a garden. There are two – **Agdal** and **Menara** – designed for just this purpose. Each begins near the edge of the Medina, rambles through acres of orchards and olive groves and has, near its centre, an immense, lake-size pool of water. This is all – they are not flower gardens, but, cool and completely still, they seem both satisfying and luxurious, and in perfect contrast to the close city streets. Other, smaller gardens of note include the gorgeous **Jardin Majorelle**, which should on no account be missed, and those of the fabled **Hôtel La Mamounia**.

With the exception of the Hôtel Mamounia, you will want **transport** to get to any of these gardens – either a *petit taxi* or *calèche*. If you are considering a *calèche* trip at any stage, the Agdal or Menara are as perfect destinations as any. Alternatively, to take in both gardens and tour the ramparts and palmery, you could hire a **bike** or *grand taxi* for the day.

Note that the Agdal gardens are sometimes only open on Friday and Saturday; if possible, check before setting out.

Jardin Agdal

The **Agdal** is a confusingly large expanse – some three kilometres in extent and with half a dozen smaller irrigation pools in addition to its *grand bassin*. Beginning just south of the Mellah and Royal Palace, it is a logical continuation of a tour of the Lower Medina. Take the road outside the ramparts below Bab Agnaou/Bab er Robb, and then turn left as you are about to leave the city at Bab Irhli; this route will take you through a *mechouar* (parade ground) by the Royal Palace and to the corner gate of the garden. The garden is often closed during the winter months, if the king is in residence in Marrakesh.

The garden is watered by an incredible system of wells and underground channels that go as far as the base of the Atlas in the Ourika Valley and that date, in part, from the earliest founding of the city. Over the centuries, the channels have at times fallen into disrepair and the gardens been abandoned, but the present nineteenth-century layout probably differs little from any of its predecessors. It is surrounded by walls, with gates at each of the near corners, while inside, the orange, fig, lemon, apricot and pomegranate orchards are divided into square, irrigated plots by endless raised walkways and broad avenues of olive trees.

If you walk out here, it is around 4km from Djemaa el Fna, and a further 2km of unsignposted paths to the main series of pools at its heart. The largest of these is the **Sahraj el Hana** (Tank of Health), which was probably dug by the Almohads and is flanked by a ramshackle old *menzeh*, or summer pavilion, where the last few precolonial sultans held picnics and boating parties. You can climb up on its roof for a fabulous view over the park and across to the Koutoubia and Atlas, and if the caretaker's around, you'll be shown the steam-powered launch which capsized in 1873, bringing Sultan Sidi Mohammed to his death – or, as his epitaph rather more elegantly put it, he "departed this life, in a water tank, in the hope of something better to come".

Nowadays, probably the most dangerous thing you could do here would be to swim in the algae-ridden waters, though the kids do it and it does look unbelievably tempting. It's perhaps better just to pick up some food beforehand – and perhaps a bottle of wine from the Gueliz – and spread out a picnic in local fashion on the paved, shaded pathway round the water's edge.

Jardin Menara

The **Menara** is in a similar vein to the Agdal, though it is has just the one central basin, and it is more olive grove than orchard, with lines of trees rather than groves and walks. It is also much more visited: a popular picnic spot for local families, as well as tourists drawn by its postcard image *bassin* and *menzeh*, with its backdrop of the High Atlas mountains. If you just want to gaze upon one of these still sheets of water, then come out here; it's a lot easier to get to than the Agdal (and a cheaper ride, too). The garden couldn't be simpler to find: just follow Av. de la Menara from Bab Djedid, by the *Hôtel La Mamounia*. In summer, it has several drinks stalls.

Like the Agdal, the Menara was restored and its pavilions rebuilt in the mid-nineteenth century. The poolside *menzeh* (5dh admission) is said to have replaced an original Saadian structure.

Jardin Majorelle

The subtropical **Jardin Majorelle** (or Jardin Bou Saf) is one of the most delightful spots in Marrakesh: a small, meticulously planned botanical garden, created from the 1920s on by the French painter, Jacques Majorelle (1886–1962). Now superbly mature, it is owned and splendidly maintained by fashion designer Yves Saint Laurent, and is open daily to visitors (8am–noon & 2–5pm winter, 8am–noon & 3–7pm summer; 15dh; no children allowed). The entrance is on a small side street off the jacaranda-lined Av. Yacoub el Mansour.

The garden – twelve acres in extent – has an amazing feeling of tranquillity, an atmosphere enhanced by the verdant groves of bamboo, dwarf palm and agave, and the various lily-covered pools. Its keynote colour, used as a wash on the walls, is a striking mauvish-blue – the colour of French workmen's overalls, so Majorelle claimed, though it seems to have improved in the Moroccan light. This brilliantly offsets both the plants – multicoloured bougainvillea, rows of bright orange nasturtiums and pink geraniums – and also the strong colours of the pergolas and concrete paths – pinks, lemon-yellows and apple-greens that look straight out of Yves Saint Laurent's collections. The garden's enduring sound is the chatter of the common bulbuls, flitting among the leaves of the date palms. The pools also attract bird residents such as turtle doves and house buntings.

In the artist's former **studio**, a **Museum of Islamic Arts** (a further 15dh; closed Mon) exhibits Saint Laurent's fine personal collection of North African carpets, pottery and furniture. (Saint Laurent was himself born in Algeria). It also has one room devoted to Jacques Majorelle's paintings – mainly of interest for placing the local scenes (fifty years ago), which include the Kasbah of Aït Benhaddou, near Ouarzazate (see pp.380–81).

Hôtel La Mamounia

Finally – and much closer – you might consider spending an hour or two looking round the gardens of the luxurious **Hôtel La Mamounia**. Walled from the outside world, yet only five minutes' walk from the Djemaa, these were once royal grounds, laid out by the Saadians with a succession of pavilions. Today they're slightly Europeanised in style but have retained the traditional elements of shrubs and walkways.

For the cost of a drink or some tea on the terrace – the latter not cripplingly exorbitant – you can sit and admire the surroundings. Be prepared, though, to resist the swimming pool, since it is strictly reserved for residents, and dress up: visitors are not allowed in wearing shorts or jeans.

If you ask at the desk, and the staff aren't too busy, someone may be prepared to give you a quick tour of the old part of the hotel – where the **Winston Churchill suite** is preserved as visited by its namesake. There are editions of Churchill's books on the shelves, a truly sultan-like bed (and smaller sleeping quarters for his manservant) and photographs of him painting in the gardens. Churchill was a frequent visitor to Marrakesh from the 1930s to the 1950s, and the Mamounia, so it is said, was his favourite hotel in the world.

Even though the hotel has been rebuilt and enlarged since Churchill's day, it's not hard to understand the lasting appeal. Decoratively, it is of most interest for the 1920s Art Deco touches of **Jacques Majorelle** (see p.331), and their enhancements, in 1986, by King Hassan's then-favourite designer, **André Paccard**. The collective result is a splendid fantasy of **public rooms** – including a **casino**, where you might want to gamble your all on the prospect of a stay.

Eating, drinking and nightlife

Marrakesh **restaurant** options break down less rigidly than usual between Ville Nouvelle (Gueliz) and the Medina.

Gueliz, naturally enough, is where you'll find French-style cafés and restaurants and virtually all of the city's bars; and an evening here offers perhaps better opportunity to start up conversations with ordinary Moroccans.

In the **Medina**, however, there's plenty of choice for meals, including the spectacle of the Djemaa el Fna food stalls, a number of good, inexpensive café-restaurants, plus a half-dozen upmarket palace-restaurants where you can dine out in style on the very best traditional Moroccan cuisine.

Medina cafés and restaurants

Recommendations for the Medina span the range: from 20dh to 750dh a head; from a bench in the Djemaa el Fna to the most sumptuous palace decor. Only the places listed under "Moderate" or "Expensive" are licensed to sell alcohol. Be wary of palace-restaurants that aren't listed below; they tend to be geared towards tour groups, with kitsch belly-dancing entertainment, and uninteresting food.

CHEAP
Djemaa el Fna foodstalls. Even if you don't eat at one of them, at some stage you should at least wander down the makeshift lane of food stalls at the north end of the Djemaa el Fna. They look great in the evening, lit by lanterns, and have boundless variety. To partake, just take a seat on one of the benches, ask the price of a plate of food and order all you like; if you want a soft drink or mineral water, the owners will send a boy to get it for you. Guides often suggest that the stalls aren't very healthy, but, as the cooking is so visible, standards of cleanliness are doubtless higher than in many hidden kitchens.

Chez Chegrouni, Djemaa el Fna. A bit more formal: this is an unsigned place, with a small terrace, next to the *Café Montréal* – about ten metres north of the *Café de France*. It's clean, reliable and relaxed, serving excellent *kefta* and *brochettes*, and fresh yoghurt.

Rue Bani Marine, just south of the Djemaa el Fna. This street has about ten excellent-value café-restaurants, which are very popular with locals – recommendation enough. A good one is *Les Poulets de l'Atlas*, on the corner of Rue el Mouahidine.

Mik Mak, Place Foucauld, by *Hôtel Ali*. A central patisserie, for breakfasts and pastries.
Sandwich aux Quatre Palmiers, Av. Mohammed V, facing the Koutoubia. Another fine breakfast spot, with tables under the palms.

MODERATE

Hôtel Ali, Rue Moulay Ismail. Justifiably popular restaurant, with a marvellous-value buffet every evening, featuring salads, *harira*, *couscous* and a dozen *tajines*. There's a great resident musician and meals are on the roof terrace in summer.

Pizzeria Venetia, on the roof of *Hôtel Islane*, opposite the Koutoubia on Av. Mohammed V. American-style pizza joint; serves beer and wine.

Restaurant Argana, Place Djemaa el Fna. This is possibly the best Djemaa el Fna vantage point – opposite the *Banque de Maroc* – and it's worth queueing for a table for this alone. Regular French-Moroccan food at around 70dh.

Hôtel du Café de France, Place Djemaa el Fna. Another superb viewpoint. The hotel itself is wretched but the restaurant – and café – are both pretty good, and fun.

Hôtel-Restaurant Foucauld, Place de Foucauld/Av. el Mouahidine. Quality can be patchy, but on good days this is worth the prices (80–100dh a head) for its palace-type salon, low-key musicians and generous portions of *pastilla*, soups, pâté and vegetables.

Grand Hôtel Tazi, Rue Bab Agnaou. The *Foucauld*'s sister hotel, the *Tazi*, just down the road, has a couple of restaurants – one on the roof in summer – with similar prices and menus. It's also good for breakfast and has the nearest **bar** to the Djemaa el Fna.

Palais Gharnatta, 5 Derb el Arsa, Riad Zitoun Djedid – near Palais el Bahia. Lavish Granada-style salon. Caters for tour groups but also welcomes individuals.

Dar Hadj Idder, 1 Derb el Hajra, Derb Dabachi – off Djemaa el Fna, leaving the square between the Pharmacie Menara and mosque (☎04/44.53.75). The original building and garden were a gift from El Glaoui, Pasha of Marrakesh, to Hadj Idder, his chamberlain. Traditional feasts – from 100dh – but you must book in advance. Moderate to expensive.

EXPENSIVE

Restaurant Marrakechi, 52 Rue des Banques, Place Djemaa el Fna – on the corner of the street just north of the *Café de France* (☎04/42.33.77). A sumptuous new restaurant high up above the square. Imperial but intimate decor, impeccable service and indescribably delicious *pastilla*. Around 180dh a head for a blowout meal.

Restaurant Relais Al Baraka, 1 Djemaa el Fna, by the Commisariat de Police (☎04/44.23.41). French-Moroccan restaurant in a beautiful fountain courtyard; around 350dh a head – and no credit cards accepted.

Restaurant Yacout, 79 Sidi Ahmed Soussi (☎04/31.01.04). Another gorgeous old palace, in the heart of the Medina: you must book ahead, stating a time, and take a *petit taxi*, which will be met by a guide for the last stretch on foot. French-Moroccan cooking of a very high order. Five-course meals are served round an Andalusian courtyard with pool, and there's a terrace with views over the Medina for coffee. Around 350dh a head.

La Maison Arabe, 5 Derb Ferrane, opposite the Bab Doukkala mosque (☎04/42.26.04). This has, for twenty years or so, been regarded as Morocco's finest restaurant, though *Yacout* (above) is challenging its reputation of late. Once again, tables must be booked ahead (and the menu discussed). It is very expensive: do not expect change from 500dh a head.

Le Restaurant Marocain, in the *Hôtel La Mamounia* (☎04/44.89.81). The *Maison Arabe*'s other great rival, which it perhaps equals in quality, and certainly beats in price at around 750dh a head!

Gueliz restaurants

Although Gueliz is not so picturesque a setting for a meal, it would be a mistake to dismiss it entirely as modern and French. It is, after all, the city's main centre and its restaurants are mostly very good value; the pricier ones are licensed.

CHEAP

Café Siroua, 20 Bd. Mohammed Zerktouni. A small, friendly café, open long hours. Good for breakfast.

Café Agdal, 86 Av. Mohammed V, facing *Hôtel Amalay*. Again good for breakfast and snacks; open to midnight.

Restaurant Snack Chawarma, 23 Rue Mauritania. Another decent snackbar.

Hôtel Renaissance, 89 Av. Mohammed V/Place Abdelmoumen Ben Ali. The hotel is closed but there is access, by lift, to a terrace-café on the sixth floor. Also a ground-floor **bar**.

La Petite Auberge, 149 Rue Mohammed el Beqal, opposite *Hôtel Tachfine*. A lively and friendly brasserie, popular with locals; also a back **bar**.

Hôtel Hoaz, 66 Av. Hassan II. You can eat well for as little as 40dh.

MODERATE TO EXPENSIVE

Restaurant Crêperie du Harti, corner of Yacoub el Marini /Place du 16 Novembre, facing the PTT. Pleasant and good value.

Hôtel Oasis, 50 Av. Mohammed V. Good value four-course meals around 60dh. Licensed.

Brasserie du Régent, 34 Av. Mohammed V. Similar fare and prices; evenings only. Also has a fairly serious **bar**.

Brasserie du Petit Poucet, corner of Av. Mohammed V/Rue Mohammed el Bequal. An old restaurant that was once the best in Gueliz. It's fallen a long way since, but retains a little style and serves reasonable French food.

Restaurant Cantanzaro, Rue Tarik Ibn Ziad – behind the Marché Central. A small French-run trattoria, with superb pizzas, pasta and salad, plus reasonably priced wine and beer.

Captain Zara, Rue Souraya. Another French-run Italian restaurant, popular with Moroccans.

Restaurant Chez Jack'Line, 63 Av. Mohammed V, near Place Abdelmoumen Ben Ali. French, Italian and Moroccan dishes, directed by the formidable Jack'Line Pinguet; she says you can eat well for 60dh and splendidly for 100dh.

Restaurant le Jacaranda, 32 Bd. Mohammed Zerktouni/corner of Place Abdelmoumen Ben Ali. Explicitly and convincingly French restaurant, with similar prices to the above. Open fireplace in winter. Closed Tues and midday Weds.

Bagatelle Restaurant, 101 Rue Yougouslavie. Pleasant place – and in summer you can eat in the garden. Closed Wed and Sept.

Restaurant le Dragon d'Or, 10 bis Bd. Mohammed Zerktouni. Vietnamese cuisine. Open daily lunchtime and evenings.

Rotisserie du Café de la Paix, 68 Rue Yougouslavie. Established in 1949, this still offers fine French and Moroccan dishes, served in a salon with a roaring fire in winter, in a shaded garden in summer. A little more expensive than the preceding, at around 120dh a head.

Complexe Jet d'Eau, Place de la Liberté. A new complex with a 24-hour snackbar, a *restaurant gastronomique* (open from 7pm; closed Mon), and a disco, *Le Star's House*.

Palais des Congrès, Av. de France, north of Place de la Marche Verte. The city's most prestigious new building complex includes a five-star hotel, luxurious conference facilities, five bars, two nightclubs and no less than seven restaurants. Expensive.

Bars and nightlife

Entertainment and nightlife in the **Medina** revolve around Djemaa el Fna and its cafés, though sometimes there might be a music group playing in an enclosure behind the Koutoubia on Av. Mohammed V. The only bars in easy reach are in the hotels *Tazi* and *Foucauld* (on the roof), or, for those on expense accounts, the *Mamounia*; see hotel listings for addresses.

In **Gueliz**, there's more variety. Some of the hotels have **discos**, and many have **bars**, in which you are more likely to have Moroccans for company. (Be aware, though, that outside of the hotels, most bars are male preserves).

GUELIZ BARS

Hôtel Amalay, 87 Av. Mohammed V. Fairly relaxed.

Hôtel Oasis, 50 Av. Mohammed V – entered by a door beside the hotel.

La Renaissance, Av. Mohammed V. Ground-floor bar still functioning within the *Hôtel Renaissance* – though the latter is currently closed.

Brasserie du Petit Poucet, corner of Av. Mohammed V/Rue Mohammed el Bequal.

Babylone Club, 75 Bd. El Mansour Eddahbi.

Café-Bar de l'Escale, Rue Mauretania.

Brasserie du Regent, 34 Av. Mohammed V.

Café Oued el Had, 100 Av. Casablanca – a *petit taxi* ride to the outskirts of town. A complex of three bars – the best of them upstairs. Open to 2am.

CASINO

Grand Casino Hôtel La Mamounia, Av. Bab Djedid. Total Unreality, just five minutes' walk from the Djemaa el Fna, but quite fun – and not necessarily that expensive, with low minimum bets on roulette, plus rows of slot machines in the foyer. You are required to dress up a bit: jackets for men, no jeans, etc. Open from 8pm.

Directory

Airlines *RAM*, 211 Av. Mohammed V (☎04/43.09.39). *GB Airways* are represented by Menara Tours (see Travel agencies, below). For **airport information** ☎04/44.03.38.

American Express c/o *Voyages Schwarz*, Rue Mauritania – off Av. Mohammed V, Gueliz (☎04/43.33.21 and 43.30.22); open for transactions Mon–Fri 9am–12.30pm and 3–4.30pm, and until 7pm for mail.

Animal welfare *SPANA* are represented by the Centre Hospitalier pour les Animaux, Daoudiat (☎04/43.31.10).

Banks As in other Moroccan cities, the *BMCE* is the best bet for exchange – accepting VISA/Mastercard, travellers' cheques, Eurocheques and most currencies; it has branches in both the Medina (Place Foucauld – back entrance for exchange) and Gueliz (144 Bd. Mohammed V), open for exchange 8am–8pm every day. *Banque Populaire* have a useful bureau de change on Rue Bab Agnaou, just south of the Djemaa el Fna (see map on p.311), which is open Mon–Sat 9am–noon & 4–7pm. Most of the four- and five-star hotels also offer bureau de change facilities to non-residents.

Bookshops *American Bookstore*, 3 Impasse du Moulin, off Bd. Zerktouni (open Mon & Sat 9am–noon, Mon–Fri 2.30–6.30pm), does English-language books.

Car hire Marrakesh rates are generally the most competitive after Casablanca. The best value deals are usually from local agencies, which include: *Badia*, corner of Av. Mohammed V/Rue Oum er Rbia (☎04/43.56.92; recommended); *Basma*, 3 Av. Yacoub el Marini (☎04/43.29.36); *Concorde Cars*, 154 Av. Mohammed V (☎04/44.61.29 or 43.11.16); and *Sud Cars*, Shell-Atlas filling station, Route de Casablanca (☎04/43.66.77). National/international agencies include: *Avis*, 137 Bd. Mohammed V (☎04/43.37.27); *Budget*, 159 Av. Mohammed V (☎04/43.46.04); *EuropCar/InterRent*, 63 Bd. Mohammed Zerktouni (☎04/43.12.28); *Golden Tours*, 113 Av. Abdelkrim El Kattabi (☎04/43.52.57); *Hertz*, 154 Av. Mohammed V (☎04/43.46.80); and *Tourist Cars*, 64 Bd. Zerktouni (☎04/43.15.30). *Menara Tours* (see Travel agencies, below) can offer a range of deals from local companies.

Car repairs The garage beside the *Hôtel Tazi* in Rue Bab Agnaou (☎04/42.23.39) fixes Renaults, and should be able to direct you elsewhere for spares of the makes they don't stock. *Ourika* at 66 Av. Mohammed V, Gueliz (☎04/43.01.55), deals with Fiats, Hondas, Toyotas and BMWs. Parts are available in Gueliz from the *Centre Européan de l'Automobile* (18 Bd. Moulay Rachid; ☎04/43.15.30) and *Union Pièces Autos* (18 Bd. Mansour Eddahbi; ☎04/43.17.90)

Dentist Dr Bennani, 112 Av. Mohammed V, first floor, opposite the *ONMT* office (☎04/43.11.45), is recommended; he speaks some English.

LEAVING MARRAKESH

LONG-DISTANCE BUSES

Buses to all long-distance destinations leave from the main terminal at **Bab Doukkala**. Buy tickets a day in advance – or turn up early – for the more popular destinations such as Fes, El Jadida, Taroudannt or Zagora. Recommended lines/departures, at time of writing, include:

Taroudannt (over the Tizi n'Test route) *SATAS* bus at 5am.
Zagora *CTM* at 7am (arrives 4.30pm).
Ouarzazate (over the Tizi n'Tichka) *CTM* at 5.30am, 7.30am, 11am and 5.30pm.
Fes *CTM* at 6.30am and 9pm.
Agadir *CTM* at 8am and 6.30pm.
Tafraoute (via Agadir)

Bear in mind, that *CTM* and all the private companies have their own individual ticket windows – choices can be more extensive than at first appears. **CTM** also have an office on Bd. Mohammed Zerktouni in Gueliz, near the ONMT office, where you can buy tickets, and where some of the buses make a secondary call.

Note that for **Essaouira**, the best bus is run by *ONCF* (see "Trains" below).

LOCAL BUSES

Buses to local destinations, including **Ourika**, **Asni** (the trailhead for Djebel Toubkal), and **Moulay Brahim**, leave from just outside Bab er Robb. (Some buses also run to Asni from the Bab Doukkala bus station, from 10am–7pm).

GRANDS TAXIS

Grands taxis can also be useful for getting to Ourika or to Asni – negotiate for these by Bab er Robb (12.5dh is the local rate for a place to Asni). Taxis run less frequently to other destinations but you could try asking some of the drivers at the stands in Djemaa el Fna and by Bab er Raha (between Av. Mohammed V and Bab Doukkala). Essaouira and Agadir (see "Trains", below) are both possible, too.

TRAINS

Flying aside, trains are the quickest and most comfortable way of getting to Casa and Rabat. If you're heading back to Tangier it's possible to do the trip in one, most easily by booking (in advance) a *couchette* on the night train (depart 7.40pm, arrive Tangier 5.50am in theory, around 7am in practice); this must be done on the morning of the day of travel.

The train company, *ONCF*, also run **express buses**, leaving from the train station, to Essaouira (1pm), Agadir (12.58pm, 10.37pm), and Laayoune (10.37pm), though they only sell tickets if there is space after the allocation for train passengers from Casablanca/Rabat. *Grands taxis* are generally on hand to pick up the overflow at these times and are good value, a place to Agadir costing around 80dh.

FLIGHTS

Royal Air Maroc operates domestic flights to Casa (with onward connections to Tangier and Fes), and to Ouarzazate (taking just 25–30 minutes). GB Airways fly weekly to Gibraltar. See "Directory" for addresses/phone numbers.

HITCHING

The campsite can be a good place to arrange lifts, or find people to share the cost of hiring a car or buying petrol. There are always people setting out for Ouarzazate and the southern Kasbah/oasis routes.

Doctor Dr Perez, 169 Av. Mohammed V (☎04/43.10.30) is English speaking and reliable. Also see Pharmacists, below.

Ferry tickets *Comanav Voyages,* 149 Av. Mohammed V (☎04/43.02.65); cash only.

Festivals Local *moussems* include: Setti Fatma (Ourika; mid-Aug; see p.341); Sidi Bouatmane (near Amizmiz; Sept); and Moulay Brahim (near Asni; two weeks after the Mouloud; see p.343).

Food shopping Putting together a picnic lunch, or supplies for the Atlas, the *marché municipal,* in the arcade off the middle of Av. Mohammed V, in Gueliz, is convenient.

Golf The city's international-standard, 18-hole *Royal Golf* is sited 4km out from the centre on the P31 (Tizi n'Tichka) road. It is open to non-members. Green fees are around £20/$30.

Markets The most interesting **weekly souks** in the Marrakesh region include: Asni (Sat); the Toubkal trailhead (see p.349); Amizmiz (Tues, see p.357); and Aït Ourir (Tues), on the road to Ouarzazate (see p.365).

Newspapers *The International Herald Tribune, Time, Newsweek,* etc, plus British newspapers, are available from the newsstands along Av. Mohammed V in Gueliz and in the fancy hotels – notably the *Mamounia.*

Pharmacies There are several in Gueliz along Av. Mohammed V, including a good one just off Place de la Liberté, which has a doctor on call. In the Medina, try *Pharmacie Menara* on the Djemaa el Fna, or the outlets on Rue Bab Agnaou.

Post office The main *PTT,* which receives all **Poste Restante** mail, is on Place 16 Novembre, midway down Av. Mohammed V in Gueliz; it is open Mon–Sat 8am–2pm. The **telephone** section, with its own entrance, stays open until 9pm, and operators will (eventually) place a call for you. There is also a separate office, round the side, for sending parcels. The Medina *PTT* in Place Djemaa el Fna stays open until 7pm; here you can phone direct.

Swimming pools There's a large municipal pool on Rue Abou el Abbes Sebti – the first main road to the left off Av. Mohammed V as you walk past the Koutoubia towards Gueliz; it's very popular and 99-percent male. Some hotels (notably, not the *Mamounia*) allow non-residents to use their pools if you have a meal, and a few allow non-residents to swim for a fee – usefully, if you're staying in the Medina, the *Hôtel Tazi* (a short walk from the Djemaa el Fna).

Tourist offices Both the *ONMT* and *Syndicat d'Initiative* are on Av. Mohammed V – the first is on Place Abd el Moumen Benali, the second is a little way up towards the Medina, at no. 170. Both open daily 8.30am–noon & 3–6pm; the SI is closed Saturday afternoons and Sundays.

Travel agencies *Menara Tours,* 41 Rue de Yougoslavie, near the ONMT office in Gueliz (☎04/44.66.54), are agents for *British Airways* and *GB Airways.* They also hire cars, and run good tours of the south, if you feel like an easier option.

THE HIGH ATLAS MOUNTAINS

The **High Atlas**, North Africa's greatest mountain range, is arguably the most intriguing and most beautiful region of Morocco. A historical and physical barrier between the northern plains and the pre-Sahara, its Berber-populated valleys feel – and are – very remote from the country's mainstream or urban life. For visitors, it is, above all, **trekking** country, with walks to suit all levels of ability and commitment, from casual day-hikes to week-long expedition routes combining a series of peaks (*djebels*) and passes (*tizis* or *cols*). **Mountain-biking**, too, is increasingly popular, on the dirt tracks (*pistes*) and mule paths, while at Ouirgane you can hire **horses** for a ride in the hills.

Despite the forbidding appearance of its peaks, the mountains are surprisingly populated, with their slopes dropping away to valleys and streams, with small Berber villages terraced into their sides. At many of the villages – particularly

---

WINTER TRAVEL IN THE HIGH ATLAS

Note that the High Atlas are subject to snow from November to the end of February, and even the major Tizi n'Tichka pass can be closed for periods of a day or more. Flash floods, too, can present problems, when the snows melt in February–March. If you get caught by the snow, the easiest route from Marrakesh to the south is road 6543 to Agadir, then the P32 through Taroudannt and Taliouine.

For information on trekking seasons – and winter routes above the snow line are a serious endeavour here – see the "Trekking Practicalities" box, on pp.346–47.

---

round the hiking centre of **Djebel Toubkal** (Morocco's highest peak) – *gîte* accommodation is offered in local houses, and there is an established infrastructure of guides and mules for trekking. It must be stressed, though, that part of the attraction of Atlas trekking is that it remains so undeveloped in comparison with, say, the Pyrenees or Alps. The network of walking paths is there because it remains in everyday use, and you experience real mountain life.

Routes and passes

The **Djebel Toubkal** massif provides the focus for most trekking expeditions. It can be reached easily from Marrakesh by taking a bus or taxi to **Asni** – just over an hour's journey – and from there on to the trailhead at **Imlil**. The region can also be approached from **Ouirgane** or **Ijoukak**, a little further south, or, more energetically, from the **Ourika Valley** – a summer playground for the city – or the ski resort of **Oukaïmeden**.

Asni, Ouirgane and Ijoukak all lie on the dramatic **Tizi n'Test** road, which runs over the the highest Atlas pass to connect Marrakesh with Taroudannt: an adrenalin-plugged switchback of almost continuous hairpin curves to be driven with care. As well as its trekking possibilities, the route has an easily accessible historic attraction in the ruins of the twelfth-century mosque of **Tin Mal**, the base from which the Almohads swept down to reconquer Spain.

Moving east is the **Tizi n'Tichka**, which cuts across to Ouarzazate and today bears most of the traffic across the Atlas. This was built to replace the old caravan route to Tafilalt, which was controlled over the last century and for much of the present by the legendary Glaoui family, "the Lords of the Atlas". Their Kasbah, a bizarre cluster of crumbling towers and kitschy-looking 1930s reception halls, is still to be seen at **Telouet**, just an hour from the main road.

The third main Atlas pass, the **Tizi Maachou**, has less drama, unless you leave the main road behind to get into the hills for some trekking in the Western Atlas, the least-known part of the range. For most travellers it simply offers a fast and convenient approach to Agadir.

The Ourika Valley and Oukaïmeden

The **Ourika Valley** is a pleasant prelude to the Atlas – and a fine escape from the summer heat of Marrakesh, as it's treated by the young *Marrakchis*, who ride out on their mopeds to lie around beside the streams and waterfalls. At the end of the road through the valley – and the place to head for – is **Setti Fatma**, which holds one of the country's biggest *moussems* (festivals) in mid-August.

Poised above Ourika to the west is the ski resort of **Oukaïmeden**.

Getting to the Ourika Valley

Access by public transport is simple. **Grands taxis**, **buses** and a fast **minibus** service leave Marrakesh's Bab er Robb regularly through the morning, from around 6am to noon, returning in the late afternoon/early evening. Alternatively, you could hire a car or moped to explore the valley.

Setti Fatma (67km from Marrakesh) is about two hours by bus or taxi. Make sure that your transport is headed there, or at least to **Asgaour** (63km), the last village before Setti Fatma, and doesn't drop you at the near end of the valley at **Dar Caid Ouriki** (33km) or **Arhbalou** (50km): wait until you get one going the whole way. Returning to Marrakesh, you might have to walk up to Asgaour to pick up a bus or taxi.

The valley: Setti Fatma

The road through the Ourika Valley is reliable enough in summer. In spring, however, you should expect to have some trouble from flooding towards the end of the valley; the road is often impassable at IRHEF, where a tributary of the Ourika regularly washes away the bridge/ford. If you camp in winter or early spring, be very aware of the possibility of flash floods and always pitch your tent on high ground, avoiding any spot where water can lie or that might become a course for the torrents when they descend.

Dar Caid Ouriki and Arhbalou

The valley really begins at **SOUK TNINE DE L'OURIKA** (30km from Marrakesh), a small roadside village, which, as its name proclaims, hosts a Monday **souk** – an excursion offered by many of the tour hotels in Marrakesh. Just beyond it, across the river, is **DAR CAID OURIKI**, with a *zaouia* set back in the rocks, near the ruins of an old caidal **Kasbah**.

Beyond here, scattered at intervals over the next forty kilometres, are a series of tiny hamlets, interspersed by a few summer homes and the occasional hotel or café-restaurant. The one sizeable settlement is **ARHBALOU** (43km from Marrakesh), where most of the local people on the bus or in taxis will get off. The village has a new "palace-restaurant", *Le Lion d'Ourika* (☎04/44.53.22), which has plans to open as a hotel, as well as basic rooms to let in the village; good walking in the surrounding hills; and the possibility of some serious trekking in Djebel Yagour (see below). A road west into the mountains leads to the trekking trail-head and ski resort of Oukaïmeden (see p.341).

Moving on through the valley **towards Setti Fatma**, there is an **antiques/ crafts shop**, *Le Musée d'Arhbalou*, 4km south of Arhbalou, which often has interesting stock, and a further 2km on, there are pleasant rooms at the *Hôtel Amnougar* (☎04/44.53.28; ③).

Setti Fatma

SETTI FATMA is the most compelling Ourika destination. Around a kilometre before you arrive, the road comes to an end – it is washed away each year – and taxis drop off their passengers beside a stream of clear, icy water. Only four-wheel-drive vehicles can reach the village itself, which, with its grassy terraces, feels like a real oasis as you arrive from the dry plains around Marrakesh.

In the rocky foothills above the village are a series of six (at times, seven) **waterfalls**. To reach them, you first have to cross the stream, by whatever bridge

HIGH ATLAS BERBERS

Until recent decades, the **High Atlas** region – and its **Berber** inhabitants – was almost completely isolated. When the French began their "pacification" in the 1920s, the way of life here was essentially feudal, based upon the control of the three main passes (*tizis*) by a trio of "clan" families, "the Lords of the Atlas". Even after the French negotiated the co-operation of these warrior chiefs, it was not until the spring of 1933 – 21 years after the establishment of the Protectorate – that they were able to subdue them and control their tribal land, and only then with the co-operation of the main feudal chief, **T'hami el Glaoui**, who continued to control the region as Pasha of Marrakesh (see p.321 and 389).

These days, the region is under official government control through a system of local *caids*, but in many villages the role of the state remains largely irrelevant, and if you go trekking you soon become aware of the mountains' highly distinctive culture and traditions. The longest established inhabitants of Morocco, the Atlas Berbers never adopted a totally orthodox version of Islam (see *Contexts*) and the Arabic language has, even today, made little impression on their indigenous **Tachelhaït** dialects. Their **music** and *ahouache* dances (in which women and men join together in broad circles) are unique, too, as is the village architecture, with stone or clay houses tiered on the rocky slopes, craggy fortified **agadirs** (collective granaries), and **Kasbahs**, which continued to serve as feudal castles of sorts for the community's defence right into the present century.

Berber **women** in the Atlas are unveiled and have a much higher profile than their rural counterparts in the plains and the north. They perform virtually all the heavy labour – working in the fields, herding and grazing cattle and goats and carrying vast loads of brushwood and provisions. Whether they have any greater status or power within the family and village, however, is questionable. The men retain the "important" tasks of buying and selling goods and the evening/night-time irrigation of the crops, and do all the building and craftwork.

As an outsider, you'll be constantly surprised by the friendliness and openness of the Berbers, and by their amazing capacity for languages – there's scarcely a village where you won't find someone who speaks French or English, or both. The only areas where you may feel exploited – and pestered by kids – are the main trekking circuits around Djebel Toubkal, where tourism has become an all-important source of income. Even the hustling, however, is gentler than in the cities – and, given the harshness of life up here, its presence is hardly surprising.

has been thrown up after the last floods; near the beginning of the climb are several cafés, where you can order a *tajine* for your return. The first waterfall is a fairly straightforward clamber over the rocks, flanked by another café, the *Immouzer*. The higher ones are a lot more strenuous, and quite tricky when descending, requiring a head for heights and solid footwear. Returning, from the first of the falls you can loop back to Setti Fatma via the village's twin, ZAOUIA MOHAMMED, a few hundred metres further down the valley.

Setti Fatma has several **accommodation** options. Best are those at the new *Hôtel Tafoukt* (with en suite shower and toilet; ①), at the beginning of the village, or the rooms at the *Café-Restaurant Asgaour* (⑩) in the village, which are a little more basic but spotless and overlooking the river; the *Asgaour* patron, Chebob Lahcen, also cooks excellent meals. The *Café des Cascades* (the first on the route to the falls) also has decent if basic rooms, and the *Café Atlas*, at the north end of the village, has roof space. By contrast, the *Hôtel Azrou* (⑩) isn't too clean or committed, while the *Hôtel La Chaumière* (⑪), signposted 2km back towards Arhbalou, is closed at present.

The **Setti Fatma Moussem** – one of the three most important festivals in the country – takes place for four days around the middle of August, centred on the **Koubba of Setti Fatma**, a little upstream from the Café des Cascades. Entry to the *koubba* is forbidden to non-Muslims, but the festival itself is as much a fair and market as religious festival and well worth trying to coincide with on your travels.

Treks from Setti Fatma

Ourika cuts right into the **High Atlas**, whose peaks begin to dominate as soon as you leave Marrakesh. At Setti Fatma they rise on three sides to 3658m: a startling backdrop which, to the southwest, takes in the main **trekking/climbing zone of Toubkal**. The usual approach to this is from Asni – see pp.346–49 – but it is possible to set out from Setti Fatma, or from Oukaïmeden (see overleaf).

If you are thinking of approaching Toubkal from Setti Fatma, the best route is to trek via **Timichi** to **Oukaïmeden** and take the trail from there to Tachdirt. It is around six hours' walk from Setti Fatma to Timichi (see p.354), and a similar figure on to Oukaïmeden (see below), including a steep ascent up the Tizi n'Atlar (3100m).The two-to-three-day trek direct from **Timichi to Tachdirt** is a lot easier in the opposite direction – and is so described on p.354.

Other adventurous treks from Setti Fatma could include the **Djebel Yagour**, with its many prehistoric rock carvings; the Djebel Tougledn (4064m; involving a night's camp); a longer excursion to **Miltsen**, via Ambougi and Turcht; or a traverse of the **Zat Valley** to emerge just beneath Taddert on the Tizi n'Tichka road. This latter route takes three days' trekking and you need to carry all your food for the journey; the trailhead is a few kilometres north of Setti Fatma.

For all of these trips, a **guide** would be useful. It's possible to arrange one – and mules – at the *Café Azagza*; ask for Houssein Izahan.

Oukaïmeden

The village and ski centre of **OUKAÏMEDEN** is a much easier trekking base from which to set out towards Toubkal – and a good target in its own right, even if you don't have anything that ambitious in mind. "Ouka", as it's known, is reached via a good modern road which veers off from Ourika just before Arhbalou. There are regular **grands taxis** going up from Marrakesh in the winter for the skiers; at other times, you might have to charter a taxi for *la course*, and – beware – you may find the resort virtually closed. The resort has a 10dh entrance fee.

Accommodation

Finding a place to stay is easy enough, so long as the resort is open: if you're depending on it, call ahead. There are numerous **hotels**, including the excellent *Chalet-Hôtel Chez Juju* (☎04/45.90.05; ②), which has rooms and cheaper dormitory accommodation, as well as solid French food and a bar.

The *Club Alpine Chalet* is open only for *CAF* and affiliated Alpine Club members only; it is well equipped, with a bar and restaurant.

HIGH ATLAS WILDLIFE

The High Atlas has unique flora and fauna, which are accessible even to the most reluctant rambler if you base yourself at **Oukaïmeden**, **Imlil** or **Ouirgane**.

The spring bloom on the lower slopes comprises aromatic thyme and thorny caper, interspersed with golden spreads of broom. Higher slopes are covered by more resilient species, such as the blue tussocks of hedgehog broom. The passes ring to the chorus of the painted frog and the North African race of the green toad during their spring breeding seasons, while some species of reptile have become adapted to the specific environment of the stony walls that form the towns and villages of the Atlas mountains, such as the **Moorish gecko**. **Butterflies** which brave these heights include the Moroccan copper and desert orange tip. Other inhabitants range from the almost-invisible praying mantis to the scampering ground squirrel and rare elephant shrew.

Birds to be found among the sparse vegetation include Moussier's redstart and the crimson-winged finch, which prefers the grassy slopes where it feeds in flocks; both birds are unique to North African mountains. The rocky outcrops provide shelter for both chough and alpine chough, the mountain rivers are frequented by dippers who swim underwater in their search for food. Overhead, darting Lanner falcon or flocks of brilliantly coloured bee-eater add to the feeling of abundance which permeates the slopes of the High Atlas. In the cultivated valleys look out for the magpie which, uniquely, has a sky-blue eye mark; there are, too, storks galore. Other High Atlas birds, as the snow melts, include shore larks, rock bunting, alpine accentor, redstarts and wheatears. The wet meadows produce a fantastic spread of hooped-petticoat daffodils, *romulea* and other bulbs.

Rock carvings

Even if you don't stay at the chalet, you might still want to drop in and check the *CAF* diagram describing the whereabouts of the many **prehistoric rock carvings** cut into the sides of the mountain and plateau. Some of the drawings, depicting animals, weapons and geometric designs, are within a twenty-minute walk from the chalet. Hiring a guide is useful.

Skiing

Ouka has the best skiing in Morocco – on the slopes of Djebel Oukaïmeden – and up until the war it could boast the highest ski lift in the world, which remains impressive at 3273m. It gives access to good piste and off-piste skiing, too, with several nursery and intermediate runs on the lower slopes.

Snowfall and snow cover can be erratic, but February to April is fairly reliable. Slopes are sometimes icy early and wet by afternoon, but not having to queue in the mornings lets you get in plenty of sport. Equipment can be hired from several shops next to *Chez Juju* (one at a reasonable 100dh a day), ski-passes cost just 30dh, and lessons are available from local instructors. Several other summits are accessible for ski-mountaineering sorties from here as well, and cross-country enthusiasts often ski across to Tachdirt.

Oukaïmeden to Tachdirt

For casual walkers, the trails from Oukaïmeden are strictly summer only: routes can be heavily snow-covered even fairly late in spring. However, weather conditions allowing, the **trail to Tachdirt** (3hr) is pretty clear and easygoing. It begins a short distance beyond the *teleski* (ski lift), veering off to the right of the dirt road that continues for a while beyond this point. The pass, Tizi n'Edaï, is reached in about two hours; on the descent, the trail divides in two, either of which branch will lead you down into Tachdirt. For more details of this route, described in reverse, and routes on from Tachdirt, see p.353.

The Djebel Toubkal Massif

The **Toubkal Massif**, a more or less roadless area enclosing the High Atlas's highest peaks, is the goal of almost everyone who goes trekking in Morocco. It is easy to get to from Marrakesh – Asni, the "first base", is just over an hour by bus or, simpler, by *grand taxi* (from Bab er Robb) – and its main routes are reasonably well charted. Walking even fairly short distances, you feel very much a visitor in a rigidly individual world. The villages look amazing, their houses stacked one on top of another in apparently organic growth from the rocks, and, corny as it might sound before you arrive, absolutely nothing rivals the costumes of the Berber women, which seem to be routinely composed of ten or twenty different and brilliant-coloured strips of material.

From late spring to late autumn (see note on "Seasons" in the box on p.346), the region's trails are accessible for anyone reasonably fit. Mule tracks round the mountain valleys are well contoured and kept in excellent condition, the main ridges of the range are usually quite broad, and there's a network of village *gîtes* and refuge huts.

In summer, **Djebel Toubkal**, the highest peak in North Africa, is walkable right up to the summit; if you're pushed for time, you could trek it, and be back in Marrakesh, in three days – though at the risk of altitude sickness. Further away, and much less visited, is **Lac d'Ifni**, tucked in a hollow in the mountains, while infinite variations on **longer treks** could lead you into the mountains for a week, two weeks, or more. For anyone really short on time, or who feels unable to tackle an ascent of Toubkal, it's possible to get a genuine taste of the mountains by spending a day or two exploring the beautiful valleys between **Imlil and Aremd**, or between **Asni and Tachdirt**, or those around Ouirgane or Ijoukak, a little further south along the Tizi n'Test road.

After spending time in the Djebel Toubkal region, most people either return to Marrakesh or continue **along the Tizi n'Test road** towards Ouarzazate.

Moulay Brahim

MOULAY BRAHIM is a picturesque village, just off the main Marrakesh–Asni road and dominating the gorges leading up from the plains. The **Kik Plateau** and its escarpment, which runs above the main road towards Ouirgane, is rich botanically and offers perhaps the best panorama of the Atlas mountains. It can be reached from the top end of the town, on a piste past marble quarries (see box on p.348).

The village is a popular weekend spot for *Marrakchis* and an alternative base for a first night in the Atlas, with several small **hotels** (all ①) and **cafés**, and regular **buses** and **taxis** to/from Asni/Marrakesh. It hosts a large **moussem** two weeks after the Mouloud.

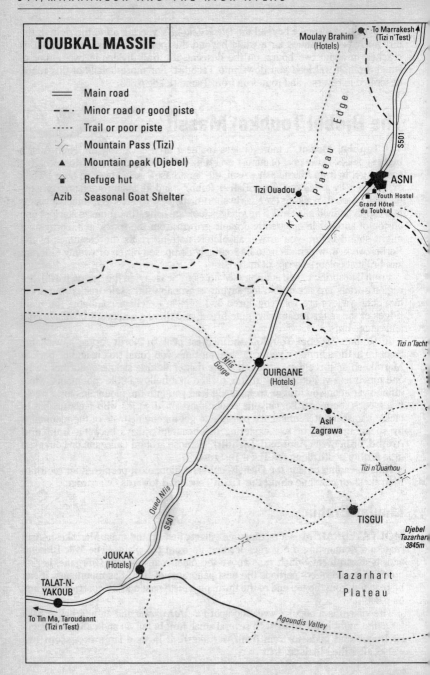

TOUBKAL MASSIF

═══ Main road

▬ ▬ Minor road or good piste

········ Trail or poor piste

⤙ Mountain Pass (Tizi)

▲ Mountain peak (Djebel)

🏠 Refuge hut

Azib Seasonal Goat Shelter

Moulay Brahim
(Hotels)

To Marrakesh
(Tizi n'Test)

Plateau Edge

Kik

S501

ASNI

Youth Hostel
Grand Hôtel
du Toubkal

Tizi Ouadou

Nfis Gorge

Tizi n'Tacht

OUIRGANE
(Hotels)

Asif
Zagrawa

Tizi n'Ouarhou

Oued Nfis

S501

TISGUI

Djebel
Tazarhart
3845m

JOUKAK
(Hotels)

Tazarhart
Plateau

TALAT-N-
YAKOUB

To Tin Ma, Taroudannt
(Tizi n'Test)

Agoundis Valley

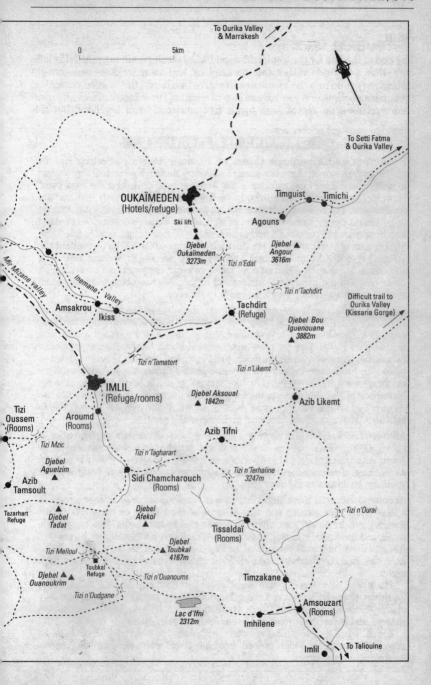

To Ourika Valley
& Marrakesh

0   5km

To Setti Fatma
& Ourika Valley

OUKAÏMEDEN
(Hotels/refuge)

Ski lift

Timguist   Timichi

Agouns

*Djebel
Oukaïmeden
3273m*   *Tizi n'Edaï*

*Djebel
Angour ▲
3616m*

Tizi n'Tachdirt

Mtn Mizane valley

Inemane   Valley

Amsakrou

Ikiss

Tachdirt
(Refuge)

Difficult trail to
Ourika Valley
(Kissaria Gorge)

*Djebel Bou
Iguenouane
▲ 3882m*

Tizi n'Tamatert

Tizi n'Likemt

IMLIL
(Refuge/rooms)

*Djebel Aksoual
▲ 1842m*

Azib Likemt

**Tizi
Oussem**
(Rooms)

Aroumd
(Rooms)

Azib Tifni

Tizi Mzic

Tizi n'Tagharart

*Tizi n'Terhaline
3247m*

*Djebel
Aguelzim ▲*

Sidi Chamcharouch
(Rooms)

**Azib
Tamsoult**

Tizi n'Ourai

*Tazarhart
Refuge*

*Djebel
Tadat ▲*

*Djebel
Afekoï ▲*

Tissaldaï
(Rooms)

Tizi Melloul

*Djebel
Toubkal
4167m ▲*

Toubkal
Refuge   *Tizi n'Ouanoums*

Timzakane

*Djebel ▲ ▲
Ouanoukrim*

Tizi n'Oudgane

*Lac d'Ifni
2312m*

Amsouzart
(Rooms)

Imhilene

Imlil   To Taliouine

Asni

The end of the line for the Toubkal bus and Marrakesh *grands taxis*, **ASNI** is little more than a roadside village and marketplace, and many trekkers pass straight through to get up into the mountains. If you're in a hurry, this is good reasoning, though it's no disaster if you have to stay overnight. The village can feel a bit over-commercialised on arrival, with locals hawking meals and jewellery. But this

---

TREKKING PRACTICALITIES

Equipment and experience Unless you're undertaking a particularly long or ambitious trek – or are here in winter conditions – there are no technical problems to hold anyone back from trekking in the Toubkal area, or making the peak itself. However, the mountain needs to be taken seriously and taken slowly until you are acclimatised. You really should have decent **footwear and clothing** – it's possible to be caught out by summer storms as well as bad winter conditions – and must also be prepared to camp out if neccessary, as the Toubkal refuge is often full.

The main physical problems are the high altitudes (3000–3700m throughout the Toubkal region), the midday heat and the tiring process of walking over long sections of loose *scree* – the mass of small volcanic chippings and stones which cover much of the mountains' surface. All of these can combine to make casual ascents an unhappy and perhaps foolhardy experience.

Seasons Toubkal is usually under snow from November until mid-June. If you have some experience of winter trekking and conditions, it is feasible to climb the peak, and trek the low-level routes, year round, though for Toubkal you may need to wait around a couple of days for clear weather, and it can be wise to use crampons (which can usually be rented in Imlil). For beginners, trekking is better limited to below the snow line. And only those with winter climbing experience should try anything more ambitious than Toubkal, or going much beyond hut level, from November to May; ice axe, crampons, good rain gear and winter competence are required, as several fatalities have recently shown. Full rivers and flash floods in February–March can pose additional problems to the snow.

Altitude Toubkal is 4167m above sea level and much of the surrounding region is above 3000m, so it's possible that you might get altitude sickness and/or head-aches. Aspirins can help, but just sucking on a sweet or swallowing often is as good as anything. If you experience more than slight breathlessness and really feel like vomiting, go down straight away.

Accommodation At most Atlas villages, it is usually possible to arrange a room in a local house; just turn up and ask. At some of the villages on more established routes, there are official *gîtes*, often the homes of mountain guides, who can provide mules and assistance – as well as food, showers, toilets and sometimes hammams. All *gîtes* have to be of recognised quality for inclusion in the ONMT *GTAM* pamphlet (see "Guidebooks", below). Most charge around 20dh per person for a night.

There are also three *refuge* **huts**, Toubkal (formerly known as Neltner), Tazarhart (formerly known as Lepiney) and Tachdirrt, run by the *Club Alpin*; they charge 30dh per person for a bed; Toubkal is often fully booked – especially at Easter – and is always crowded in March/April and July/August.

If you are doing anything remotely ambitious, however, you'll need to be prepared to camp, for which you will need a tent and warm sleeping bag – nights are cold, even in summer.

doesn't last long, and between buses the village drifts back to its usual farming existence. The most interesting time to be here before heading on to Toubkal is for the **Saturday souk**, when the enclosure behind the row of shop cubicles is filled with produce and livestock stalls, plus the odd storyteller or entertainer. An advantage of arriving on Saturday morning (or Friday night) is that you can stock up with cheap supplies, before heading into the mountains. With time to spare, there are many local walks in the fruit-growing areas around (see box below).

Guides and mules Guides can be engaged at Imlil and at a number of the larger villages in the Toubkal region; mules, too, can be hired, usually in association with a guide or porter. Rates are around 150dh a day for a guide, 70dh for a mule. One mule can usually be shared among several people – and if you're setting out from Imlil, say, for Lac d'Ifni, or the Toubkal or Tazarhart refuges, it can be a worthwhile investment. Two extras are to be added to the price – a fee to the car park supervisor in Imlil and a tip to the porter at the end. (Payment to all parties, incidentally, is best made at the end of a trip.) Note that guides are very reluctant – and reasonably so – to work during the month of **Ramadan** (see *Basics*).

Water There are *Giardia* bacteria in many of the streams and rivers downriver from human habitation – including the Toubkal trailhead, Imlil. Purification tablets are advisable, as, of course, is boiling the water.

Clothes Even in the summer months you'll need a warm sweater or jacket and preferably a windbreaker, but tents at this time aren't necessary if you have a good sleeping bag and bivibag/groundsheet. Hiking boots are ideal – you can get by with a decent pair of trainers or jogging shoes, but certainly not sandals. Some kind of hat is essential and sunglasses are helpful.

Other things worth bringing You can buy food in Asni, Imlil and some of the other villages – or negotiate meals – though it gets increasingly expensive the higher and the more remote you get. Taking along a variety of canned food, plus tea or coffee, from Marrakesh is a good idea. A quart bottle of water is enough because you can refill it regularly; water purification tablets are worthwhile on longer trips, as are stomach pills and insect repellent. Children are constantly asking you for *cigarettes, bon-bons* and *cadeaux* – but it's perhaps better for everyone if you don't give in, and limit gifts to those who offer genuine assistance. A worthwhile contribution trekkers can make to the local economy is to trade or give away some of your gear – always welcomed by the guides, who need it.

Guidebooks/information There are almost limitless Atlas hiking routes, only a selection of which are detailed in these pages. For other ideas, either engage a guide at Imlil, or invest in the Atlas Mountain trekking guidebooks by Robin Collomb (West Col), Karl Smith (Cicerone Press) and Michael Peyron (West Col); you may well find one or other of these books on sale at Imlil. The booklet *La Grande Traversée des Atlas Marocains*, published by the ONMT, is also very useful, listing all the qualified guides, *muletiers* and *gîtes*, along with their tarifs.

Maps Survey-type maps are best obtained in advance – see p.19 – though at Imlil you can usually obtain the 1:50,000 and/or 1:100,000 government-survey sheets covering the Toubkal area. They can also be consulted in the *refuges*.

Ski-touring The Toubkal Massif is popular with ski-mountaineering groups from February to April. Most of the *tizis* (cols), and Djebel Toubkal, can be ascended, and a *Haute Route* linking the huts is possible. The Toubkal refuge can get pretty crowded at these times, and the Tachdirt refuge (or, for a serious approach in winter, Tazarart refuge) can make better bases.

WALKS AROUND ASNI AND MOULAY BRAHIM

The Kik plateau

The forested slopes above Asni and Moulay Brahim are dominated by a rocky scarp which is the edge of the hidden limestone **Kik plateau**. In spring a walk up here is a delight, with a marvellous spread of alpine flowers and incomparable views. To get the best from it, set off early in the day and carry water; six to eight hours' walking will bring you over the plateau and onto Moulay Brahim or Ouirgane.

Leaving Asni, walk up the Test road to where it swings out of sight (past the red conical hill). Just past a souvenir stall a mule track breaks off and can be seen rising up the hillside. Take this, then fork right to gain the first pass. Turn right again, through fields, and you eventually join the plateau edge, which you can follow to **Moulay Brahim**; leave the crest to join a piste down to the left, which passes big marble quarries just before the village (see p.343). You can also cut down to Asni by leaving the route midway along.

An alternative day's trek on the plateau is to make for **Ouirgane**, further south on the Tizi n'Test road (see p.357). On the rise to the plateau keep on, forking left, to the pass/village of TIZI OUADU and then follow the dip where a rough piste crosses. Take this down to the road at TIZI OUZLA and follow the road down, with salt mines apparent below. Turn off right to work through paths to join the Nfis River and follow this to Ouirgane.

Valley approaches

The valleys between Asni/Ouirgane and Imlil (Mizane), Tachdirt (Imenane) and Tizi Oussem (Azzaden) offer fine walks, which you might do to acclimatise yourself prior to tackling Toubkal or other mountains. They are all much easier-going if you walk them downhill – back to Asni/Ouirgane. To do so, you could easily take a taxi to the trailheads and walk back from there.

Imlil to Asni. This is a pleasant half-day walk. From Imlil, walk back down the road, then, after about an hour, swap over to the old mule track on the east side of the valley. Take this path up thereafter to a pass and along the trackless crest to the prow that looks to Asni and back to the hills. Descend from here and follow down along the east side of the valley to Asni.

Tachdirt to Asni. There is a long but straightforward trail from Tachdirt downvalley to Asni, taking around seven to nine hours. It's an enjoyable route, through a fine valley with no road or electricity – a good (and neglected) exit from the mountains. You could also do this route from Imlil, heading off towards the trail at the Tizi n'Tamatert (1hr from Imlil), then dropping down to the bottom of the valley at Tinhourine. If you want to camp out a night, en route, there are possible places to pitch a tent below Ikiss or Arg. There are also rooms and soft drinks available at Ikiss and Amsakrou.

Rooms, meals and transport

There are two accommodation options, both of which will store luggage if you want to go off trekking unencumbered:

Auberge de Jeunesse/Youth Hostel, at the far end of the village. Open all year and to all comers, with slightly higher charges for non-IYHF members. There are no cooking facilities and you'll need your own sleeping bag, though blankets can be hired; the location by the river can be very cold in winter.

Grand Hôtel du Toubkal, on the roadside (no phone). A last chance of luxury before the mountains, this has a bar, swimming pool (filled from June to September) and is beautifully decorated and offers magnificent balcony views.

or **meals**, most of the café-stalls will fix you a *tajine* or *harira*, and the Grand Hôtel has a pretty good French-Moroccan menu.

Getting from Asni **to Imlil** is pretty straightforward, with pick-ups (*camionettes*) and taxis shuttling back and forth along the 17km of road, along with larger lorries on Saturdays for the *souk*. The most regular departures from Asni are in the afternoon, from Imlil are in the morning. Both pick-ups and taxis normally wait until they fill their passenger quota, though the latter can be chartered; a place is currently 15dh for tourists.

Buses from Asni run to Marrakesh, Moulay Brahim or Ijoukak and – at around 6am – over the Tizi n'Test to Taroudannt (see p.449). A place in a **grand taxi** can be negotiated to Marrakesh (12.5dh), Moulay Brahim (3dh) or Ouirgane (12dh). Buses and taxis leave from the *souk* entrance area.

Imlil

The trip from Asni to **IMLIL** is a beautiful and a startling transition. Almost as soon as it leaves Asni, the road begins to climb, while below it the brilliant and fertile valley of the Oued Rhirhaia unfolds before you, and small villages crowd into the rocky slopes above. At Imlil the air feels quite different – silent and rarefied at 1740m – and paths and streams head off in all directions.

If you want to make an early start for the Toubkal (Neltner) hut and the ascent of Toubkal, the village is a better trailhead than Asni.

Accommodation

Imlil comprises a small cluster of houses, along with many provisions shops, a CAF *refuge* and several cafés. There is a fair choice of accommodation.

CAF Refuge. Old-established French Alpine Club *refuge*. It provides bunk beds, camping mattresses and blankets, as well as kitchen and washing facilities and luggage storage; rates are 20dh for a dormitory bed (15dh with IYHF card; 10dh with Alpine Club membership). Open all year round.

Hôtel-Café Soleil, on the square by the river; **Hôtel-Café Aksoual**, facing the *refuge*. Both offer decent rooms and the former does superb *tajines*. ①

Hôtel Étoile de Toubkal. As fancy as Imlil gets – and expensive. ②

Gîtes. Several houses offer rooms. Among the best are those offered by the guide Aït Idir Mohammed (contact him at the shop behind the concrete route indicator) at his house in an eyrie overlooking Imlil; he will take care of your baggage while you go trekking.

Alternatively, you might decide to press on and stay the night in Aroumd (see below).

Trekking resources and guides

A first stop in Imlil should be the "**Shopping Centre**", run by Lahcen Esquary, an experienced Atlas guide who speaks English well and has years of experience in organising trekking expeditions. Above the *Shopping Centre*, the *Ribat Tours* agency also organises activities. Both shop and agency sell maps and guides. Also helpful is the *Hôtel-Café Soleil* owner, Aziam Brahim, who works for part of the year for a French trekking company, and his brother Ibelaid Brahim. Other sources of **information** in Imlil are the steady flow of trekkers passing through and the CAF *refuge*, its noticeboard, book and *gardiens* (wardens).

Lahcen Esquary, Aziam and Ibelaid Brahim and Aït Idir Mohammed, are the most experienced of the **qualified guides** listed on the noticeboard in the square, all of whom can arrange treks, ascents, mules, camping, guides, *gardiens* for your baggage and food; note that the rates displayed on the noticeboard are long out of date (see box on p.346).

Imlil to Djebel Toubkal

Most trekkers leaving Imlil are en route for the ascent of Djebel Toubkal – a walk rather than a climb, after the snows have cleared, but a serious business nonetheless (see box on p.353). The route to the ascent trailhead, however, is fairly straightforward – and enjoyable in its own right, following the Mizane Valley to the village of **Aroumd** (4km from Imlil – 1hr–1hr 30mins) and thence through the hamlet of **Sidi Chamarouch** to the **Toubkal (Neltner) Refuge** (3200m; 12km from Imlil – 5–6hr in all), at the foot of Toubkal.

If you start out late in the day, Aroumd can be a useful first base – and it is quieter and in many ways preferable to Imlil. However, most trekkers set out early to mid-morning from Imlil to stay the night at the Toubkal refuge, starting out at first light the next morning for Toubkal in order to get the clearest possible panorama from its heights. Afternoons can be cloudy.

Imlil to Aroumd

To **walk from Imlil to Aroumd**, you basically follow the course of the Mizane River. On the west side there's a well-defined mule track that zigzags above the river for about 2km before dropping to the floor of the valley, just before a crossing point to Aroumd; there is also a new, more circuitous piste, driveable in a reasonably hardy vehicle. Over on the east bank, there's a rough path – around the same distance but slightly harder to follow.

AROUMD (aka AROUND, AREMD) is the largest village of the Mizane Valley, an extraordinary-looking place, built on a spur of loose rock above the valley at 1840m (6040ft). The site resembles nothing so much as a landslide but it also commands one of the most fertile stretches of the Atlas. Terraced fields of corn, potatoes, onions, barley and various kinds of fruit line the valley sides and there is some grazing, too; the village streets are often blocked by goats or cattle – and permanently covered in animal excrement and flies.

This notwithstanding, Aroumd is very much on the trekking circuit. A British trekking company maintains a base in the village and there is a now a café and **guesthouse/campsite** by the river, and quite a number of **rooms** for rent in the village houses. The local **organiser for guides and mules** is Brahim Aït el Kadi, who arranges treks for the British company. He rents out rooms (and will prepare meals) in his house, and can often rent crampons in winter.

Alternatively, it's possible to **camp** slightly upstream: you should ask permission first and, as is usual, pay a small fee – a compensation for nonproduction of crops, since every available bit of land in this valley is cultivated. There is as yet only one shop in Aroumd – despite a population of five hundred – so if you lack the energy to arrange a meal, take along food from Asni or Imlil.

Aroumd to Sidi Chamarouch and Toubkal refuge

From Aroumd, the **Toubkal trail** follows the east (ie the Aroumd) side of the Mizane, climbing and zigzagging round the hard, grey rocks, high above the river. At intervals some of the larger rocks have been marked with red dots to reassure you that you are on the right track. If you have been following the main

mule trail on the west side of the valley from Imlil to Aroumd, you can join t
Toubkal trail without going into Aroumd – it crosses over and merges with
section from Aroumd a short distance after you pass the village to your left.

The river is crossed once more, 1hr 30min to 2hr further down, just befor
arrive at the village of **SIDI CHAMAROUCH**. Set beside a small waterfall,
an anarchic cluster of houses, all built one into another. Its seasonal population o
ten or twelve run soft drinks/grocery shops for tourist trekkers and for
Moroccan pilgrims, who come to the village's *marabout* shrine – sited across the
gorge from the village and reached by a modern concrete bridge which
non-Muslims are strictly forbidden to cross. The shrine is probably a survival of a
very ancient nature cult – in these parts often thinly veiled by the trappings of
Islam. (On the approach to the village you might have noticed a tree, sacred to
local tradition, where the Berbers hang strips of cloth and make piles of stones.)
Camping below the village, beside the stream, is possible. **Rooms** are also
available.

Beyond Sidi Chamarouch, the Toubkal trail climbs steeply in zigzags and
then traverses the flank of the valley well above the Mizane. (The water from the
river is not safe to drink untreated until you get above the Toubkal hut, though
the smaller streams and springs by the path are said to be safe.) The trail,
however, is pretty clear the whole way to the **Toubkal Refuge**, which, at 3207m,
marks the spring snow line.

The Toubkal Refuge

Even in mid-August it gets pretty cold up at the **Toubkal Refuge** (formerly *Refuge
Neltner*) once the sun has disappeared behind the ridge. You will probably,
therefore, want to take advantage of its shelter. The hut is open all year and
charges 30dh per person for a bed (22.50dh with IYHF card; 10dh with Alpine
Club membership). The *gardien* is usually prepared to cook meat or vegetable
tajine for guests (about 25dh per person), though beware that the hut can be very
busy – and crowded. It is badly in need of extension.

Another reason for staying at the *refuge* is that the area around is covered in
rubbish (human waste, too), so if you plan on **camping** nearby, you'll want to go
some way upstream or use the meadows a bit down from the hut.

Climbing Toubkal

At the *refuge* you're almost bound to meet people who have just come down from
Djebel Toubkal – and you should certainly take advantage of them (and/or the
refuge gardien) for a description of the routes and the current state of the South
Cirque trail to the summit. The initial path from the *refuge*, especially, can be easy
to miss, and it's not that easy to find the route down. If you don't feel too confident about it, take a guide: they are usually available at the *refuge*.

THE SOUTH CIRQUE

The **South Cirque** (*Ikkibi Sud*) is the most popular and straightforward ascent
and, depending on your fitness, should take between 2hr 30min and 3hr 30min
hours (2–2hr 30min coming down). It is not a well-defined route, with paths going
off all over the place, but with reasonable instructions on the spot, it's easy
enough to follow without a guide. More of a problem – and something you should
be careful about at any time of the year – is finding the right track down. It is easy
to find yourself in fields of loose scree.

The trail actually begins just below the Toubkal hut, dropping down to cross the stream and then climbing over a short stretch of grass and rock to reach the first of Toubkal's innumerable fields of boulders and scree. These – often needing three steps to gain one – are the most tiring (and humiliating) features of the trek up, and gruelling for inexperienced walkers. The summit, a triangular plateau of stones marked by a tripod, is eventually reached after a lot of zigzagging through a gap in the ridge. It should be reiterated that in winter even this ascent is a snow climb; not for walkers.

THE NORTH AND SOUTHWEST CIRQUES

Robin Collomb, in his *Atlas Mountains* guide, recommends the **North Cirque** (*Ikkibi Nord*) as an alternative -- though longer (4hr 30min) and more ambitious – ascent. It's a bad way down, however, virtually guaranteeing periods of sliding and scraping down the scree.

The **southwest/west cirque**, a third possible approach, is for experienced rock climbers only.

The Toubkal refuge to Lac d'Ifni and beyond

Lac d'Ifni is one of the largest mountain lakes in the Atlas – and the only one of any size in the Toubkal region. From the *refuge* it's about 4–5hrs trek, again involving long, tedious stretches over loose rock and scree, and with odd stretches of snow remaining into July. On the way back, the scree scrambling is even more pronounced. To make the trip worthwhile, take along enough food for a couple of days' camping; there are no facilities en route.

Toubkal to Lac d'Ifni

The **Lac d'Ifni trail** begins at the Toubkal hut, climbing up a rough, stony slope and then winding round to the head of the Mizane Valley towards the imposing *tizi* (or pass) of **Tizi n'Ouanoums**. The pass is reached in about an hour and the path is reasonably easy to follow. There is just one vague division, a little before the ascent of the pass, where a path veers off to the right along the final stretch of the Mizane. The trail up the pass itself is a good, gravel path, zigzagging continually until you reach the summit (3664m), a narrow platform between two shafts of rock.

The views from the summit here are superb, taking in the whole route that you've covered and, in the distance to the south, the hazy green outline of the lake (which disappears from view as you descend). At this point the hard work seems over – but this is a totally false impression! The path down the valley to Lac d'Ifni is slow, steep progress, the scree slopes are apparently endless, and the lake doesn't come back into sight until you are almost there. It is, in fact, virtually enclosed by the mountains, and by what look like demolished hills – great heaps of rubble and boulders.

Lac d'Ifni is a fine sight, with its only human habitations a few shepherds' huts, and the only sound that of water idly lapping on the shore; it is exceptionally deep – up to 50m over much of its area. It makes a poor campsite, however, with scrubby terraces, somewhat fly-ridden by day, and no drinking water source (the lake waters are polluted). You can camp much more enjoyably by carrying on for another hour until you reach the first patches of irrigated valley, high above the village of Imhilene.

CLIMBING TOUBKAL AND OTHER SUMMITS

Toubkal and the other major summits should always be treated as serious efforts. In winter they are only for properly equipped and experienced mountaineers and strictly out-of-bounds for walkers. Even in late spring, if the icy snow has lingered on, they may need ice axe and crampons to justify proceeding. There have been fatalities among inexperienced, ill-equipped walkers going out onto steep snow and slipping, so this is not an alarmist warning. If in doubt, turn back. There are trained guides at Imlil who can hire equipment and lead ascents; do not use casual "guides" encountered along the way, who will often not know the route themselves.

All this area up behind Toubkal – Lac d'Ifni and beyond – needs to be treated as a proper expedition, too, and hiring a **local guide** is strongly recommended.

On from Lac d'Ifni: a loop to Imlil or Tachdirt

Most people return from Lac d'Ifni to the Toubkal *refuge* by the same route but it's quite feasible to make a longer, anticlockwise, loop towards **Imlil** or **Tachdirt**.

LAC D'IFNI TO SIDI CHAMAROUCH
From the lake, you can strike east to the valley above IMHILENE, and beyond it to the Kasbah-like village of AMSOUZART, reached in around three hours. There is a café/campsite here and *gîte* accommodation and meals at Omar's house; ask for him at the café or shop, which is your last chance of supplies on this route.

At Amsouzart, the path to the north follows the west bank for the river, reaching the village of TISSALDAÏ in about four hours; camping is possible in the valley above. From here, it is at least four hours of strenuous trekking to get up the **Tizi n'Terhaline** (3247m). It is worth all the effort, as you descend into a beautiful valley. After about two hours' walking from the pass, you will reach AZIB TIFNI, a collection of shepherds' huts, none more than a metre high.

You can then follow the valley west over another high pass, **Tizi n'Tagharat** to descend steeply to Sidi Chamarouch.

THE LOOP TO TACHDIRT
An alternative route from AZIB TIFNI (above) is to follow the valley to the east, into one of the magnificent gorges of this region. Crossing the first pass, you can camp easily near AZIB LIKEMT (2hr from Azib Tifni), beyond which another more demanding pass, the high **Tizi n'Likemt** (3555m) leads to Tachdirt. From the beginning of October, these *azibs* are empty as the valley becomes completely cut off in winter.

The country east of Azib Likemt is wild in the extreme (too hard even for mules!), so it is inadvisable to try and reach the Ourika Valley that way.

Tachdirt and beyond

Tachdirt (3000m), 8km east of Imlil, is an alternative and in many ways more attractive base for trekking expeditions. As at Imlil, there is a CAF *refuge*, and a fine range of local treks and onward routes. But despite its comparatively easy access – a pleasant mule track up the valley over Tizi n'Tamatert (more direct than the tortuously winding piste) – the village sees only a handful of the trekkers who make it up to Toubkal.

You can walk the **mulepath from Imlil** in three to four hours, or on Saturdays there is a Berber **lorry** (for the Asni *souk*) along the piste. There are as yet no shops in the village (though soft drinks are sold), so take along your own food. The **CAF refuge** (20dh a bed; cooking facilities and some supplies available through the *gardien*) is just above the trail on the left-hand side as you enter the village; it's kept locked, but the *gardien*, Mohammed, should soon appear. He can arrange a guide and mules. There is also a gîte in the village.

Tachdirt to Setti Fatma

This is one of the more obvious routes for anyone contemplating anything beyond a simple daytrip into the hills. Taken at a reasonably human pace, the route can be accomplished in two days' walking from Tachdirt – one if you're fit. There is a well-defined trail all the way, used by locals (who take mules along the whole length), so no particular skills are demanded beyond general fitness. However, several sections are quite exposed. You need a reasonable head for heights.

You'll probably want to carry some food supplies with you. However, meals are offered at the village of Timichi, so cooking gear and provisions are not essential. If you are carrying gear, you might want to hire mules at Tachdirt.

TACHDIRT TO TIMICHI

Tachdirt to Timichi is a superb day's walk. The first three hours or so are spent climbing up to the Tizi n'Tachedirt (3616m), with ever more spectacular views. The character of the valley changes abruptly after the pass, green terraced fields giving way to rough and craggy mountain slopes. The path down is one of the more exposed sections of the route. As you approach Timichi the valley again becomes more green and vegetated.

There are six villages in the valley and this can be a little confusing. Local children, however, will soon be able to show you the correct path to **TIMICHI** and its **gîte**. The gîte is a welcoming place, with a very helpful *gardien*, who offers a tempting range of meals. If you arrive reasonably early in the day, you can make a loop round the hill, exploring all six valley villages, in around three to four hours.

TIMICHI TO SETTI FATMA

Timichi to Setti Fatma is another beautiful trek, taking about half a day. The path becomes steadily wider and more used as you approach Setti Fatma, but it is clear enough along the whole course. At first you follow the river fairly closely but, at a very impressive village perched on a huge rock buttress, you climb upward, to about 1000 or 1500ft above the riverbed. There is little water available on the path for several miles, and potential campsites are limited to small, flat bivvying sites. The path is good but appears perched on the side of the extremely steep valley: care must be taken, as, if you fell, you would only bounce a few times before arriving at the river far below. The path finally zigzags down into the Ourika Valley about 2km north of Setti Fatma.

Tachdirt to Oukaïmeden

This is a fairly straightforward route – a three- to four-hour walk over a reasonable mule track by way of the 2960m Tizi n'Edaï; the Angour ridge lies off to the east along the first part of the trek (see below).

> ### THE WONDER WALK: TOUBKAL TO TICHKA
>
> A few of the trekking companies have started marketing what Hamish Brown describes as "the wonder walk": a two-week trek from **Toubkal to the Tichka plateau**, north of Taroudannt, following the Oued Nfis Valley. The Tichka plateau section of this route is detailed on p.368. Details of the approach from Taroudannt (from which direction the trek is perhaps best made) are given on p.449.

The Angour ridge

Hiking along the ridge of Angour is pretty demanding, taking a full day from Tachdirt and (if the weather turns on you) demanding a night's bivouac. It requires basic climbing skills.

From Tachdirt, the trail zigzags up the lefthand side of the **Imenane Valley** up towards **Tizi n'Tachdirt** (which remains visible the whole way). At the pass (a three-and-a-half-hour steep walk, taking you up to 3616m), a path climbs due north up a rough, grassy slope, to break through crags onto the sloping **plateau**, which can be followed to the **summit of Angour**. This plateau is an unusual feature on a peak with such dramatic cliffs. It is split by a valley. With care, you can follow a ridge down from here to **Tizi n'Edaï** (to pick up the Oukaïmeden trail), or break away straight down to Tachdirt. A guide would be useful.

Tachdirt to Imlil via Tizi n'Aguensioual

Less ambitious, but still demanding a lot of care on the loose, steep scree paths, is an alternative route back from **Tachdirt to Imlil** by way of **Tizi n'Aguensioual**. This takes you first by a tricky-surfaced path to the hamlets of TINERHOURHINE (1hr) and IKISS (15min further down; soft drinks/rooms). From Ikiss a good path (ask someone to point it out) leads up to the Aguensioual pass; over the other side, it's another stony scramble down to the village of AGUENSIOUAL, from where you can follow the Asni road back up to Imlil.

West of Imlil: Tizi Oussem and the Tazarhart refuge

The area west of Imlil and the Djebel Toubkal trail offers a good acclimatisation trek to **Tizi Oussem**, harder treks to the south to the **Tazarhart refuge** (accessible also, from the Toubkal *refuge*), and the possibility of one- or two-day treks **out to Ouirgane or Ijoukak** on the Tizi n'Test road, or back to the Asni–Imlil road at **Tamadout**.

Tizi Oussem and on to Ouirgane

The village of **TIZI OUSSEM** is in the next valley west of Imlil and is reached in about four hours over the Tizi Mzic; the track is not that easy to find, so ask for initial directions. The most interesting section is the path down from the pass to the village. If you are heading for the Tazarhart *refuge*, another path from the pass follows round the hillside to Azib Tamsoult, and then to the gorge for the Tazarhart hut. The valley itself offers a long day's trek **down to Ouirgane** on the Tizi n'Test road. At its foot it becomes a road, but this wanders off to the right and you should abandon it in order to go left and, with luck, arrive at the *Au Sanglier Qui Fume* (see Ouirgane). Experienced walkers can make a two-day expedition to reach **Ijoukak**, with one camp/bivouac en route.

The route to Ouirgane keeps to the west side of the valley. Perhaps even more spectacular is to keep to the east side, crossing, eventually, the Tizi n'Tacht, angle down on a piste, then on by mule tracks to the Asni–Imlil road at **Tamadout**. This trek, in spring, is hard to equal, with green fields, blossoms and snow mountains beyond.

The Tazarhart refuge and around

Some 6hr 30min to 7hr 30min from Imlil, the **Tazarhart refuge** (formerly known as the *Refuge Lepiney*) is essentially a rock-climbing base, above all for the fine cliffs of **Tazaghârt**. You (or a porter) may have to go down to the village to get the hut *gardien*, Omar Abdallah, who is also a very good (and extremely pleasant) guide; he can arrange a room in the village, too, if you prefer. Details of a number of climbs from the *refuge* are given in the Collomb guide, but be warned that in winter they require crampons and ice axes – and climbing experience; there was a fatal accident here in 1989, involving an organised trekking party.

Tizi Melloul (3–4hr from the Tazarhart refuge) allows trekking access to Tazarghârt (3843m), an extraordinary plateau and fine vantage point. You can also cross Tizi Melloul and, with one camp or bivouac, walk **down the Agoundis Valley to Ijoukak**.

Tizi n'Test: Ijoukak, Ouirgane and Tin Mal

The **Tizi n'Test**, the road that extends beyond Asni to Taroudannt and Taliouine, is unbelievably impressive. Cutting right through the heart of the Atlas, it was blasted out of the mountains by the French from 1926 to 1932 – the first modern route to link Marrakesh with the Souss plain and the desert, and an extraordinary feat of pioneer-spirit engineering. Until then, it had been considered impracticable without local protection and knowledge: an important pass for trade and for the control and subjugation of the south, but one that few sultans were able to make their own.

Through much of the last century – and the beginning of the twentieth – the pass was the personal fief of the **Goundafi** clan, whose huge Kasbahs still dominate many of the crags and strategic turns along the way. Much earlier it had served as the refuge and power base of the Almohads, and it was from the holy city of **Tin Mal**, up towards the pass, that they launched their attack on the Almoravid dynasty. As remote and evocative a mountain stronghold as could be imagined, Tin Mal is an excursion well worth making for the chance to see the carefully restored ruins of the twelfth-century mosque, a building close in spirit to the Koutoubia, and for once accessible to non-Muslims.

Practicalities

If you are setting out by **bus from Marrakesh,** you should have four choices, leaving at either 5am (sometimes 6am), 2pm or 6pm. The 5am/6am bus is the only direct one to Taroudannt (7hr 30min), but the others go as far as Ijoukak (4hr); the 2pm bus stops there, and the 6pm one goes on to Taliouine (arriving, after a scary night descent, at around 1–2am). It's important to turn up at least half an hour early if you want tickets on the morning bus. If you're **coming from Asni**, you can pick up any of these buses a little over an hour after they leave Marrakesh.

For anyone **driving**, some experience of mountain roads is essential. The route is well contoured and paved, but between the pass and the intersection with the P32, the Taliouine–Taroudannt road, it is extremely narrow (one and half times a car's width) with almost continuous hairpin bends and blind corners. Since you can actually see for some distance ahead, this isn't as dangerous as it sounds – but you still need a lot of confidence and have to watch out for suicidal local drivers bearing down on you without any intention of stopping or slowing down. Bus and lorry drivers are, fortunately, more considerate. If you are driving a hire car, which is liable to overheat, try to avoid driving the route at midday in the summer months.

From November to the end of April, the pass is occasionally blocked with **snow**. When this occurs, a sign is put up on the roadside at the point where the Asni–Test road leaves Marrakesh and on the roadside past Tahanoute.

The road to the pass and beyond

Heading out on the dawn bus from Marrakesh, you have the least interesting part of the Taroudannt journey to catch up on lost sleep. The landscape over the first couple of hours – before you come to the village of Ouirgane and the beginning of the **Oued Nfis gorges** – is fairly monotonous.

Ouirgane and the Nfis gorges

OUIRGANE is a tiny place, long touted by French guidebooks as a beautiful valley and *étape gastronomique*. In the early hours of an Atlas morning, coming from Marrakesh, this might not be much of an attraction, but after trekking around Toubkal, it is a wonderful place – with a dash of luxury – to lie around and recover. It is also a very pleasant base in itself for day walks, mountain bike forays or horse riding. It hosts a Thursday *souk*.

There are two **hotels**, both with swimming pools. The big one, *Résidence la Roseraie* (☎4 through the operator; ④), is a grand 4*A place, with sauna, tennis and prices to match. It also offers horse riding: 250dh for a half day, 3500dh for a week's package, including two nights at the hotel. A lot cheaper, and equally pleasant, is *Au Sanglier Qui Fume* (☎9 through the operator; ③). Run by the idiosyncratic Mme Thevenin, this has a series of cool chalet-type rooms, scattered round a garden. Half pension is sometimes required, which is no hardship, since the cooking is usually very good. Mules for local treks can be arranged at the *Sanglier*. There are also simple, pleasant rooms at the *Café Badaoui*..

Trekking up behind Ouirgane, one rewarding route is to head for **Tizi Ouadou** and the **Kik plateau** – and then down to Asni and back by taxi. Rather more ambitiously, you could strike northwest to Amizmiz, by way of the Nfis gorges.

OUIRGANE TO AMIZMIZ: THE NFIS GORGES

From Ouirgane, a seven-hour walk by the **Nfis gorges** leads to **AMIZMIZ**, which has regular bus and *grand taxi* connections with Marrakesh along the S507 (to/from the Bab er Robb). It is also the site of a long-established **Tuesday souk**, one of the largest Berber markets south of the Atlas, and not on the tourist trail. The town itself comprises several quite distinct quarters – including a *zaouia*, Kasbah and former Mellah – separated by a small ravine. **Accommodation** is available at the basic (but licensed) *Hôtel du France*.

Ijoukak

Moving on, the best base for a stay in the Tizi n'Test area is **IJOUKAK**. The village has a few basic shops and four small **cafés**. The furthest south of these serves excellent *tajines* and rents out rooms (no sheets, only blankets); it also operates a hammam, which may be welcome after a few days of trekking. It's also possible to camp, though the riverbed is pretty rocky. *Guide Collomb* indicates a CAF-supervised hut at Ijoukak, but it is actually the state forestry house and does not welcome guests.

Walking out from Ijoukak, you can easily explore Tin Mal and Talaat n'Yacoub (see overpage) or try some more prolonged **trekking in the Nfis and Agoundis valleys** – see below. The Agoundis can also be enjoyable just as a day's wandering, if you have nothing more ambitious in mind.

TREKKING AROUND IJOUKAK

Ijoukak gives access to some of the most enjoyable trekking in the High Atlas – all much less developed than the main Toubkal area. Starting from the village, you can trek east up the **Agoundis Valley towards Toubkal**, or west up the long **Ogdemt Valley**. The region to the **west of the Tizi n'Test road** is wilder still; for details – in reverse – of the trek to Afensou and Imi n'Tanoute (on the Marrakesh–Agadir road), see the "Western High Atlas" section at the end of this chapter.

The **survey map** for the area (if you can get hold of it) is *Tizi n'Test* (1.100,000).

AGOUNDIS VALLEY
East from Ijoukak winds the **Agoundis River Valley**. It offers alternative access to Toubkal, but is seldom used. To reach the Toubkal *refuge* would take two days of serious trekking. However, if "peak bagging" is not part of your plan, you could still enjoy a day's trek or an overnight trip up this way.

From Ijoukak walk back down the road towards Marrakesh until you cross the river (200m). A dirt road leads off to your right. A small sign there warns you not to fish for trout in the river. This road continues along the valley for about 10km. It's used by lorries hauling ore from the mines. If you're in a hurry, you could hitch a lift; otherwise, the walk is a pleasant one. There are several villages strung out along the valley making use of the year-round water to farm small patches in the river bottom and on the terraced hillsides. About 2km down the road there is a small square hut below the road on the right. It's a **watermill** which is fascinating to watch if you happen to catch someone inside. Another 3km further and you'll pass an abandoned **rock-crushing factory**, its huge tin and timber structure half falling down. In the house just beyond it, to the west, Ibrahim and Abdallah Jhouliyine offer rooms and meals. Just beyond is the village of **TAGHBART**.

The road splits after 8km, the right fork descending to the river, crossing and continuing on into the mountains to the south. Take the left fork (get off the lorry if you've hitched this far) and follow it as it curves round to the left, to the northeast. At the curve is another village, **EL MAKHZEN**. The road has now been extended a couple of kilometres to **TIJRHICHT**. Along this last section is an ingeniously constructed irrigation ditch hugging the cliffside beneath the road. Here the road ends and a mule trail begins. If you've hitched up here, it probably will have taken you no more than half an hour; on foot it's about two to three hours.

The **trail towards Toubkal refuge** begins to climb into a narrowing limestone gorge with the river a great distance below. Tiny Berber villages are perched on rocky outcrops every 2–3km. Good views in both directions. Toubkal finally appears, rising above the upper reaches of the valley.

Idni and the pass

Until the death of its *patronne*, Mme Giplou, the *Hôtel Alpina* made **IDNI**, just below the pass, an even better place than Ijoukak in which to stop over. Sadly, the hotel seems shut for good now; a loss to the whole neighbourhood and to the buses, which used to break the journey here. Due to the *Alpina's* reputation, however, a number of travellers do still turn up in Idni (many, alas, guided by previous editions of this guide) and the *Café Igdet* across from the hotel has very basic rooms (with bed mats), as well as preparing hot meals and tea. It can get very cold up here at night (there's no electricity), but it's not a disastrous option.

The **Tizi n'Test** (2093m) lies 18km south of Idni. There's a **café-restaurant**, the *Cassecroute*, just to the south of the pass, where you can normally get buses either to drop you off or pick you up. Walk back along the road a kilometre from

---

At **AÏT YOUB** (8km from the end of the road), you will have reached the last and highest cultivated areas (1900m). *Guide Collomb* estimates 3hr 30min to arrive this far, with the help of the occasional lift. Figure on six to eight hours' walking, depending on your fitness.

Toubkal refuge and **Djebel Toubkal** are another long day's trek from here. It's possible to hire a mule and a muleteer, who acts as a guide simply because he knows the way. However, this is not as straightforward and organised as in more frequented places like Imlil. This far into the mountains it is unlikely that you will find anyone who speaks English, but with simple French or Arabic phrases you should be understood.

If you wish to continue on foot alone, *Guide Collomb* is helpful from here. Keep in mind that snow can impede your crossing the pass until midsummer. In any case, you'll need to stay overnight in Aït Youb. Camping should be no problem. It's usually best to ask permission for politeness' sake. When you ask, be prepared for an offer of hospitality and a night's stay in the village. You're in no way imposing by accepting it, but it is understood in all but a few cases that you'll offer something in return when you leave. It will customarily be turned down at least once but usually accepted with persistence on your part.

OUGDEMT VALLEY

West from Ijoukak and the Agoundis Valley lies the **Ougdemt**, a long, pleasant valley filled with Berber villages surrounded by walnut groves.

A dirt road for lorries now stretches for several kilometres up the valley from **MZOUZITE** (3km beyond Tin Mal and 8km from Ijoukak). Beyond this, a trail continues winding up along the river to **ARG** at the head of the valley (6–7hr walking). From Arg you could go for **Djebel Erdouz** (3579m) to the north of Tizi n'Tighfist (2895m), or the higher **Djebel Igdat** to the south (3616m), by way of Tizi n'Oumslama. Both are fairly straightforward when following the mule paths to the passes and can be reached in five to six hours from Arg. Be sure to take your own water in summer as the lower elevations can be dry.

For the very adventurous, a further expedition could be undertaken **all the way to the Tichka plateau** – summer grazing pastures at the headwaters of the Nfis River – and across the other side to the Marrakesh–Agadir road. This would take at least six days from the Tizi n'Test road and require you to carry provisions (and water in summer) for several days at a time.

For a detailed route description, see M. Peyron's *Great Atlas Traverse*. A brief summary of this trail, taken from the opposite direction, follows in the "Western High Atlas" section on p.367.

here and you'll find a track leading straight up to the pass – which itself is dark and restricted – towards a platform mounted by a TV relay station. The views down to the Souss Valley and back towards Toubkal can be stunning.

Over the pass, the **descent towards Taroudannt/Taliouine** is hideously dramatic: a drop of some 1600m in little over 30km. Throughout, there are stark, fabulous vistas of the peaks, and occasionally, hundreds of feet below, a mountain valley and cluster of villages. Taroudannt is reached in around 2hr 30min to 3hr on the descent, Taliouine in a little more; coming up, needless to say, it all takes a good deal longer. For details on Taroudannt and Taliouine, see Chapter Seven.

Tin Mal

The **Tin Mal Mosque**, quite apart from its historic and architectural importance, is a beautiful ruin – isolated above a sudden flash of river valley, with stack upon stack of pink Atlas peaks towering beyond its arches. It has recently been restored anr re-opened and is a highly worthwhile stop if you're driving the Tizi n'Test. If you're staying at Ijoukak, it's an easy eight-kilometre walk, passing en route the old Goundafi Kasbah in Talaat n' Yacoub (see overpage).

The mosque is set a little way above the modern village of TIN MAL (or IFOURIREN) and reached by wandering uphill, across a roadbridge. It is kept locked, but the *gardien* will soon spot you, open it up and let you look round undisturbed (10dh admission – and a tip is expected by the *gardien*). It is used by villages for the Friday service and closed to non-Muslims on that day.

Some history

Tin Mal's site seems now so remote that it is difficult to imagine a town ever existing in this valley. In some form, though, it did. It was here that **Ibn Toumert** and his lieutenant, **Abd el Moumen**, preached to the Berber tribes and welded them into the **Almohad** (or "unitarian") movement; here that they set out on the campaigns which culminated in the conquest of all Morocco and of southern Spain; and here, too, a century and a half later, that they made their last stand against the incoming Merenid dynasty.

This history – so decisive in the development of the medieval Shereefian empire – is outlined in "The Historical Framework" in *Contexts*. More particular to Tin Mal are the circumstances of Ibn Toumert's arrival and the appeal of his puritan, reforming teaching to the local tribes.

Known to his followers as the *Mahdi* – "The Chosen One", whose coming is prophesied in the Koran – Toumert was himself born in the High Atlas, a member of the Berber-speaking Masmouda tribe, who held the desert-born Almoravids, the ruling dynasty, in traditional contempt. He was an accomplished theologian and studied at the centres of eastern Islam, a period in which he formulated the strict Almohad doctrines, based on the assertion of the unity of God and on a verse of the Koran in which Muhammad set out the role of religious reform: "to reprove what is disapproved and enjoy what is good". For Toumert, Almoravid Morocco contained much to disapprove of and, returning from the East with a small group of disciples, he began to preach against all manifestations of luxury – above all, wine and performance of music – and against women mixing in male society.

In 1121, Toumert and his group arrived in Marrakesh, the Almoravid capital, where they began to provoke the sultan. Ironically, this was not an easy task – Ali

Ben Youssef, one of the most pious rulers in Moroccan history, accepted many of Toumert's charges and forgave his insults. It was only in 1124, when the reformer struck Ali's sister from her horse for riding unveiled (as was desert tradition), that the Almohads were finally banished from the city and took refuge in the mountain stronghold of Tin Mal.

From the beginning in this exiled residence, Ibn Toumert and Abd el Moumen set out to mould the Atlas Berbers into a religious and military force. They taught prayers in Arabic by giving each follower as his name a word from the Koran and then lining them all up to recite it. They also stressed the significance of the "second coming" and Toumert's role as *Mahdi*. But more significant, perhaps, was the savage military emphasis of the new order. Hesitant tribes were branded "hypocrites" and massacred – most notoriously in the Forty-Day Purge of the mountains – and within eight years none remained outside Almohad control. In the 1130s, after Ibn Toumert had died, Abd el Moumen began to attack and "convert" the plains. In 1145, he was able to take Fes and, in 1149, just 25 years after the march of exile, his armies entered and sacked Marrakesh.

The mosque
The **Tin Mal Mosque** was built by Abd el Moumen around 1153–54, partly as a memorial and cult centre for Ibn Toumert and partly as his own family mausoleum. Obviously fortified, it probably served also as a section of the town's defences, since in the early period of Almohad rule, Tin Mal was entrusted with the state treasury. Today, it is the only part of the fortifications – indeed, of the entire Almohad city – that you can make out with any clarity. The rest was sacked and largely destroyed in the Merenid conquest of 1276 – a curiously late event, since all of the main Moroccan cities had already been in the new dynasty's hands for some thirty years.

That Tin Mal remained standing for that long, and that its mosque was maintained, says a lot about the power Toumert's teaching must have continued to exercise over the local Berbers. Even two centuries later the historian Ibn Khaldun found Koranic readers employed at the tombs, and when the French began restoration in the 1930s they found the site littered with the shrines of *marabouts*.

Architecturally, Tin Mal presents a unique opportunity for non-Muslims to take a look at the interior of a traditional Almohad mosque. It is roofless, for the most part, and two of the corner pavilion towers have disappeared, but the *mihrab* (or prayer niche) and the complex pattern of internal arches are substantially intact.

The arrangement is in a classic Almohad design – the T-shaped plan with a central aisle leading towards the *mihrab* – and is virtually identical to that of the Koutoubia in Marrakesh, more or less its contemporary. The one element of eccentricity is in the placing of the **minaret** (which you can climb for a view of the general layout) over the *mihrab*: a weakness of engineering design that meant it could never have been much taller than it is today.

In terms of decoration, the most striking feature is the variety and intricacy of the **arches** – above all those leading into the *mihrab*, which have been sculpted with a stalactite vaulting. In the **corner domes** and the **mihrab vault,** this technique is extended with impressive effect. Elsewhere, and on the face of the *mihrab*, it is the slightly austere geometric patterns and familiar motifs (the palmette, rosette, scallop, etc), of Almohad decorative gates that are predominant.

The Goundafi Kasbahs

The **Goundafi Kasbahs** don't really compare with Tin Mal – nor with the Glaoui Kasbah in Telouet (detailed in the following Tizi n'Tichka section). But, as so often in Morocco, they provide an extraordinary assertion of just how recent is the country's feudal past. Despite their medieval appearance, the buildings are all nineteenth- or even twentieth-century creations.

Talâat n'Yacoub

The more important of the Kasbahs is the former Goundafi stronghold and head-quarters in the village of TALÂAT N'YACOUB. Coming from Ijoukak, this is reached off to the right of the main road, down a very French-looking, tree-lined country lane; it is 6km south of Ijoukak, 3km north of Tin Mal.

The **Kasbah**, decaying, partially ruined and probably pretty unsafe, lies at the far end of the village. Nobody seems to mind if you take a look inside, though you need to avoid the dogs near its entrance. The inner part of the palace-fortress, though blackened from a fire, is reasonably complete and retains traces of its decoration.

It is difficult to establish the exact facts with these old tribal Kasbahs, but it seems that it was constructed late in the nineteenth century for the next-to-last Goundafi chieftain. A feudal warrior in the old tradition, he was constantly at war with the sultan during the 1860s and 1870s, and a bitter rival of the neighbouring Glaoui clan. His son, Tayeb el Goundafi, also spent most of his life in tribal campaigning, though he finally threw in his lot with Sultan Moulay Hassan, and later with the French. At the turn of the century, he could still raise some 5000 armed tribesmen within a day or two's notice, but his power and fief eventually collapsed in 1924 – the result of El Glaoui's manoeuvring. The Kasbah here in Talâat must have already been in decay then; today, it seems no more linked to the village than any castle in Europe.

An interesting mountain **souk** takes place in the village on Wednesdays.

Tagoundaft

Another dramatic-looking Goundafi Kasbah is to be seen to the left of the road, a couple of kilometres south of Tin Mal. This one, **Tagoundaft**, is set on a hilltop, and is now privately owned. It is well preserved – as indeed it should be, having been constructed only in 1907.

Telouet and the Tizi n'Tichka

The **Tizi n'Tichka** – the direct route from Marrakesh to Ouarzazate – is not so remote or spectacular as the Test pass. As an important military (and tourist) approach to the south, the road is modern, well constructed and comparatively fast. At Telouet, however, only a short distance off the modern highway, such mundane current roles are underpinned by an earlier political history, scarcely three decades old and unimaginably bizarre. For this pass and the mountains to the east of it were the stamping ground of the extraordinary Glaoui brothers, the greatest and the most ambitious of all the Berber tribal leaders. Their Kasbah-headquarters, a vast complex of buildings abandoned only in 1956, are a reward-ing detour (44km from the main road).

For trekkers, bikers or four-wheel-drivers, Telouet has an additional and powerful attraction, offering an alternative and superb approach to the south, following the old tribal **pass over the Atlas to Aït Benhaddou**.

Telouet: the Glaoui Kasbah

The **Glaoui Kasbah** at TELOUET is one of the most extraordinary sights of the Atlas – fast crumbling into the dark red earth, but visitable, and offering a peculiar glimpse of the style and melodrama of recent Moroccan political government and power. The village itself is tiny, though it holds a small **souk** on Thursdays and has a **café**, which serves meals. There is also a basic **auberge**, run by Ahmed Boukhsas, the guardian at the Kasbah.

The Glaoui: some background

The extent and speed of **Madani** (1866–1918) and **T'Hami** (1879–1956) **el Glaoui's** rise to power is remarkable enough. In the mid-nineteenth century, their family were simply local clan leaders, controlling an important Atlas pass – a long-established trade route from Marrakesh to the Drâa and Dades valleys – but lacking influence outside of it. Their entrance into national politics began dramatically in 1893. In that year's terrible winter, **Sultan Moulay Hassan**, on returning from a disastrous *harka* (subjugation/burning raid) of the Tafilalt region, found himself at the mercy of the brothers for food, shelter and safe passage. With shrewd political judgement, they rode out to meet the sultan, feting him with every detail of protocol and, miraculously, producing enough food to feed the entire 3000-strong force for the duration of their stay.

The extravagance was well rewarded. By the time Moulay Hassan began his return to Marrakesh, he had given *caid*-ship of all the lands between the High Atlas and the Sahara to the Glaouis and, most important of all, saw fit to abandon vast amounts of the royal armoury (including the first cannon to be seen in the Atlas) in Telouet. By 1901, the brothers had eliminated all opposition in the region, and when **the French** arrived in Morocco in 1912, the Glaouis were able to dictate the form of government for virtually all the south, putting down the attempted nationalist rebellion of El Hiba, pledging loyalty throughout World War I, and having themselves appointed **pashas of Marrakesh**, with their family becoming *caids* in all the main Atlas and desert cities. The French were content to concur, arming them, as Gavin Maxwell wrote, "to rule as despots, [and] perpetuating the corruption and oppression that the Europeans had nominally come to purge".

The strange events of this age – and the legendary personal style of T'Hami el Glaoui – are beautifully evoked in Gavin Maxwell's *Lords of the Atlas*, the brooding romanticism of which almost compels a visit to Telouet:

> *At an altitude of more than 8,000 feet in the High Atlas, [the castle] and its scattered predecessors occupy the corner of a desert plateau, circled by the giant peaks of the Central Massif . . . . When in the spring the snows begin to thaw and the river below the castle, the Oued Mellah, becomes a torrent of ice-grey and white, the mountains reveal their fantastic colours, each distinct and contrasting with its neighbour. The hues are for the most part the range of colours to be found upon fan shells – reds, vivid pinks, violets, yellows, but among these are peaks of cold mineral green or of dull blue. Nearer at hand, where the Oued Mellah turns to flow though the Valley of Salt, a cluster of ghostly spires, hundreds of feet high and*

needle-pointed at their summits, cluster below the face of a precipice; vultures wheel and turn upon the air currents between them . . . .

Even in this setting the castle does not seem insignificant. It is neither beautiful nor gracious, but its sheer size, as if in competition with the scale of the mountains, compels attention as much as the fact that its pretension somehow falls short of the ridiculous. The castle, or Kasbah, of Telouet is a tower of tragedy that leaves no room for laughter.

And that's about how it is. If you've read the book, or if you've just picked up on the fascination, it's certainly a journey worth making, though it has to be said that there's little of aesthetic value, many of the rooms have fallen into complete ruin (restoration is "planned"), and without a car, it can be a tricky and time-consuming trip. Nevertheless, even after thirty years of decay, there's still vast drama in this weird and remote eyrie, and in the painted salon walls, often roofless and open to the wind.

The Kasbah

Once at Telouet, make your way to the second **Kasbah** on the hillside – beyond a desolate and total ruin which is all that remains of the original castle built by Madani and his father in the mid-nineteenth century. The castle-palace above is almost entirely T'Hami's creation, and it is here that the road stops, before massive double doors and a rubble-strewn courtyard.

Wait a while and you'll be joined by a caretaker-guide (tours 20dh per group), necessary in this case since the building is an unbelievable labyrinth of locked doors and connecting passages, which, so it is said, no single person ever completely knew their way round. Sadly, these days you're shown only the main halls and reception rooms. You can ask to see more – the harem, the kitchens, the cinema – but the usual reply is "*dangereux*", and so it most likely is: if you climb up to the roof (this is generally allowed) you can look down upon some of the courts and chambers, the bright *zellij* and stucco enclosing great gaping holes in the stone and plaster.

The **reception rooms** – "the outward and visible signs of ultimate physical ambition", in Maxwell's phrase – at least give a sense of the quantity and style of the decoration, still in progress when the Glaouis died and the old regime came to a sudden halt. They have delicate iron window grilles and fine carved ceilings, though the overall result is once again the late nineteenth- and early twentieth-century combination of sensitive imitation of the past and out-and-out vulgarity. There is a tremendous scale of affectation, too, perfectly demonstrated by the use of green Salé tiles for the roof – usually reserved for mosques and royal palaces.

The really enduring impression, though, is the wonder of how and why it ever came to be built at all, since, wrote Gavin Maxwell :

It was not a medieval survival, as are the few European castles still occupied by the descendants of feudal barons, but a deliberate recreation of the Middle Ages, with all their blatant extremes of beauty and ugliness, good and evil, elegance and violence, power and fear – by those who had full access to the inventions of contemporary science. No part of the Kasbah is more than a hundred years old; no part of its ruined predecessors goes back further than another fifty. Part of the castle is built of stone, distinguishing it sharply from the other Kasbahs that are made of pisé or sun-dried mud, for no matter to what heights of beauty or fantasy these might aspire, they are all, in the final analysis, soluble in water.

Approaches to Telouet: Irherm, Taddert and Aït Ourir

Getting to Telouet is easy enough if you have transport: it is a straightforward 21km drive from the Tizi n'Tichka (P31) road, along the paved 6802. On **public transport**, you can take the bus along the Tizi n'Tichka to the Telouet road junction, where there is often a taxi waiting for passengers. Alternatively, you could get off the bus either at Irherm (which has *grands taxis* to Telouet) or to Taddert (which is a closer point to hitch – but has no taxis). Getting back to the Tichka – and on to Marrakesh or Ouarzazate – from Telouet should be less of a problem, as there is usually a trickle of tourist traffic.

Irherm and Taddert
IRHERM, 10km beyond the Tichka mountain pass, has a small basic **hotel** and bar, *Chez Mimi* – a reasonable place to stay if you get stuck. **TADDERT**, on the Marrakesh side of the pass, has a dishevelled, rather gloomy old **auberge**, *Les Noyers* (☎3 through operator; ⑩), though with some compensation in its views and the region's beautiful mountain stream, holm oaks and walnut trees. There's a pleasant half-hour walk to the village of TAMGUEMEMT, above the stream.

Aït Ourir
An alternative stopping point, if you are following the Tichka north from Ouarzazate and don't want to carry on to Marrakesh, is **AÏT OURIR**. On the main road, just outside the village, is an attractive **hotel**, *Le Coq Hardi* (☎156 through operator; ①), with a bar, restaurant, swimming pool and garden; it's used by tour groups, so book ahead for a room. The *Hermitage*, next door, has closed.

Telouet to Aït Benhaddou

If you have four-wheel drive, or a mountain bike, or want a good two-day walk, it is possible to head south from Telouet along the 6803 road to Aït Benhaddou. This is surfaced as far as Anemiter but pretty rough beyond there, and it requires fording at four points – most precariously just north of Aït Benhaddou, where a bridge collapsed in the 1989 floods and has not (at time of writing) been repaired. It is a great route, through some of the most beautiful countryside in the High Atlas.

Before the construction of the Tichka road, this pass was in fact the main route over the Atlas. It was only the presence in the Telouet Kasbah of T'Hami's xenophobic and intransigent cousin, Hammou ("The Vulture"), that caused the French to construct a road along the more difficult route to the west.

Anemiter and beyond
There are *camionettes* from Telouet to **ANEMITER** (12km), one of the largest and best-preserved fortified villages in Morocco, and with a welcoming **gîte**. This is run by Elyazid Mohammed, who is a mountain guide and will take groups (or, at a price, individuals) on one- to five-day **trekking tours** into the Atlas hereabouts. He speaks French and some English.

South of Anemiter the trails and dirt roads take over for the 35km to Aït Benhaddou. The route is perhaps best of all for walkers, offering tranquillity and unparalleled views of green valleys, a river that splashes down the whole course and remarkable turquoise scree slopes amid the high, parched hillsides. Despite the absence of settlements on most of the maps, much of the **valley's northern**

reaches are scattered liberally with communities, all making abundant use of the narrow but fertile valley plain. This unveils a wealth of dark red and crumbling **Kasbahs**, collections of homes grouped among patchworks of wheatfields and hay, terraced orchards, olive trees, date palms and figs – and everywhere children calling to each other from the fields, the river or the roadside.

South to Tamdaght and Aït Benhaddou
There are occasional truck-taxis (*camionettes*) south of Anemiter, along the piste, but it would be best to accept that you'll walk most of the way to Tamdaght, where the tarmac resumes; it takes around ten hours.

Leaving Anemiter, the main mule track clings to the valley side, alternately climbing and descending, but with a general downhill trend as you make your way south. After three kilometres you encounter the first **ford**; it is high enough upstream to be easily crossed, though probably impassable for cars outside the summer months. Beyond here the piste follows the left bank of the river to the hamlet of ASSAKO (two and a half hour's walk from Anemiter), where it climbs to the left round some spectacular gorges and then drops steeply.

Walkers should aim to get beyond this exposed high ground before camping. At TOURHAT, around six or seven hours from Anemiter, you might be able to find a room in a village home. Another three hours south of Tourhat, the trail brings you to **TAMDAGHT**, a scattered collection of buildings with a classic **Kasbah**. This was used as a setting for an *MGM* epic, and retains some of its authentic Hollywood decor, along with ancient and rickety storks' nests on the battlements.

From **Tamdaght to Aït Benhaddou** the road is again paved to AÏT BENHADDOU (see p.380), where there are cafés and three simple hotels where you can pick up a taxi (or usually hitch a lift) on to Ouarzazate.

Marrakesh To Agadir: the Tizi Maachou

The direct route from **Marrakesh to Agadir** – the **Imi n'Tanoute**, or **Tizi Maachou**, pass – is, in itself, the least spectacular of the Atlas roads. If you are in a hurry to get south, however, it is a reasonably fast trip (4hr drive to Agadir) and when the Test and Tichka passes are closed through snow, it normally remains open. Convenience aside, **trekkers** have the most reason for taking this road, for the access from Chichaoua, midway along the road, to the **Western High Atlas**.

Trekking in the Western High Atlas

Exploring this region of the Atlas, you move well away from the usual tourist routes, miles away from any organised refuge, and pass through Berber villages which see scarcely a tourist from one year to the next. You'll need to carry provisions, and be prepared to camp or possibly stay in a Berber village home if you get the invitation – as you almost certainly will. Sanitation is poor in the villages and it's not a bad idea to bring water purification tablets if you plan to take water from mountain streams – unless you're higher than all habitation. Eating and drinking in mountain village homes, though, is surprisingly safe as the food (mainly *tajines*) is cooked slowly and the drink is invariably mint tea.

Getting into the mountains, there are approaches from both north and south: **Imi n'Tanoute** and **Timesgadiouine**, on the main Marrakesh–Agadir bus route (north) and **Taroudannt–Ouled Behril** (south). From the north approaches, rides on trucks bound for mines or markets at trailheads have to be used; from the south, *camionettes* ply up daily to Imoulas, the Medlawa Valley, Tigouga, etc. Tali Abd el Aziz, who runs *Tigouga Adventures* in Taroudannt (see p.449), has full details on the southern approaches mentioned below.

The *IGN* 1:100,000 maps for the area are *Tizi n'Test* and *Igli*.

Chichaoua and the pass

Leaving Marrakesh, the buses normally follow the Essaouira road (P10) as far as **CHICHAOUA**, a small village and administrative centre with several cafés and **hotels** (all ⑩), and a makeshift campsite, with no facilities or security. The village is set at the entrance to the mountains, and is famed in a small way for its carpets. Brightly coloured and often using stylised animal forms, they are sold at the local **Centre Coopératif** and also at the **Thursday market**. The village is the most pleasant stop along the road to break your journey. Beyond Chichaoua, the **road to Essaouira** continues across the drab Chiadma plains. SIDI MOKHTAR, 25km on from Chichaoua, has a **Wednesday souk** with an attractive array of carpets.

For **Agadir**, you begin a slow climb towards **IMI N'TANOUTE**, another administrative centre, with a **Monday souk**, and then cut through the last outlying peaks of the High Atlas. Imi n'Tanoute is of little interest, though if you need to stay before setting out on a trek (see below), there are **rooms** at a couple of the cafés, and provisions. A few kilometres further along the Agadir road, the phrase "Allah – Nation – King" (Alla–al-Watan–al-Malik) is picked out in painted stone letters, over 50ft high, on the hillside. Beyond it is the pass, **Tizi Maachou**, at 1700m. Over it, along the roadside, you often have locals selling bottles of golden argan oil (see p.440), which makes a change from fossils. Slowly, the road descends to the fertile Souss Valley, with its intensive greenhouse cultivation. If you are planning to trek into the Atlas from TIMESGADIOUINE (see p.369), make sure you get dropped at the turnoff, 50km south of Imi n'Tanoute.

Imi n'Tanoute to the Tizi n'Test

A dirt road leads up into the mountains from **Imi n'Tanoute to Afensou**. There's a Thursday market about 17km along the road, at SOUK EL KHEMIS, and so your best chance is to hitch up on a Wednesday with one of the lorries. This trip takes several hours, so don't arrive late in Imi n'Tanoute or you might get stranded. The road (possible for ordinary passenger cars) crosses the **Tizi**

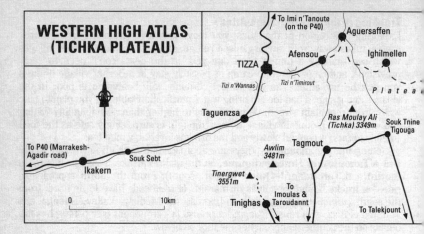

n'Tabghourt pass at 2666m, from where you have an excellent panorama of the entire area, which includes some peaks reaching 3350m.

At **AFENSOU** you are as close as you'll get by road to the centre of the Western High Atlas region. From here you can trek in either direction – east towards Ijoukak or west towards the Marrakesh–Agadir road at Timesgadiouine. Or perhaps just wander round the valleys and peaks at random. It's a somewhat complex system of intervening ridges, so you'll probably need the survey map.

Afensou to Ijoukak

To reach **Ijoukak** and the Tizi n'Test road, trek north from Afensou 4km up the Sembal River to AGUERSAFFEN. Here you turn east-southeast to follow the long **Gourioun River valley** to the **Tichka plateau**, via the **Tizi n' Ouzdim** (or Asdim; 2842m), a trek requiring a whole day. (Snow makes access difficult until late spring.) Cross the plateau – where you'll see shepherds, sheep and their shelters (*azib* on the map) in summer – following the **Nfis River** (see Ijoukak) as it winds through the gorges of the Tiziatin Forest which might force the odd detour. Continue east down the river valley through villages and the shade of walnut trees which reappear after the Tichka plateau. At the village of IMLIL (not to be confused with the Toubkal trekking trailhead) is a shrine to Ibn Toumert, the founder of the Almohad dynasty.

A two-day trek from the plateau will take you to **SOUK SEBT TANAMMERT**. From this Saturday market, a lorry road climbs up to the Test road, not far from the pass itself. You can hitch out here or continue trekking for two more days to MZOUZITE, near Tin Mal: one day north to ARG via Tizi n'Aghbar (2653m) and Tizi n'Tiddi (2744m), and the second day east along the long Ogdemt Valley to Mzouzite, as described under the Tizi n'Test section (see p.359). An excellent trail also descends the Oued Nfis Valley from Souk Sebt, going through beautiful gorges and forested countryside. What the trekking expert Hamish Brown describes as a "Wonder Walk" has been worked out linking the Tichka plateau to Djebel Toubkal, using guides/mules from Taroudannt and Imlil for successive sections. Details are available from *Atlas Maps* (see p.19), or from *Tigouga Adventures* in Taroudannt (see p.449).

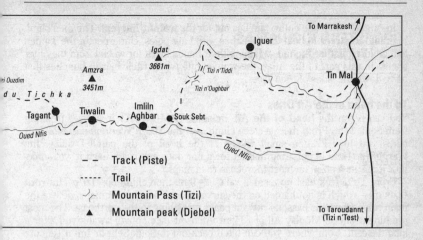

- – – Track (Piste)
- ----- Trail
- ⋎ Mountain Pass (Tizi)
- ▲ Mountain peak (Djebel)

West and a little south from Afensou lie two parallel valleys which culminate at Souk Sebt Talmakent. The more scenic of the two, **Assif n'Aït Driss**, is described below.

Timesgadiouine and the Aït Driss

The second access point to the mountains along the Marrakesh–Agadir road is **TIMESGADIOUINE**, about 50km south of Imi n'Tanoute. ARGANA looks a more plausible point on the map, but the road is no longer used. A small sign around 15km north of Argana indicates Timesgadiouine: get off the bus here, where you'll see a dirt road, a small building and perhaps a few people who, like yourself, are waiting for lifts – nothing else identifies this as an entrance to the mountains. The actual village is 3–4km along the dirt road.

Souk Sebt

Your hitching destination is **SOUK SEBT TALMAKENT**. Lorries will be driving up on Friday afternoon for the Saturday *souk*, but others go up during the week to a mine above AFENSOU and they all pass through Souk Sebt. Be prepared for a wait and a long dusty ride. If you ride up on Friday afternoon, you can camp overnight. Basic food items can be bought here. There are no cafés and no rooms, although the government workers posted to this nowhere place might offer you a room in their offices.

The Aït Driss

The **Aït Driss River** winds its way just below Souk Sebt. It's a pretty valley that narrows to a gorge for a kilometre or two before spreading out and filling up with walnut trees and Berber villages. As you trek up, several other tributaries come down on your right from the main ridge. The two most conspicuous peaks, **Tinerghwet** (3551m) and **Awlim** (3482m), are the same two you can see from Taroudannt, which lies in the Souss plain on their far side. Turn up any of these tributaries for an interesting day's trek. For camping, you're better off in the Aït Driss Valley, where the ground is flatter.

In August you'll see entire families out for the **walnut harvest**. The men climb high into the trees to beat the branches with long poles. Underneath, the women and children gather the nuts, staining their hands black for weeks from the outer shells. In this part of the Atlas, the women often wear their hair in bunches that hang down the sides of their faces.

To the head of the Aït Driss

You can reach the **head of the Aït Driss** at TAMJLOCHT in a day's trekking from Souk Sebt. From there a steep climb over the **Tizi n'Wannas** pass (2367m) takes you to TIZZA, a small village at the head of the parallel valley, the Warguiwn. Tizza is not a big market town nor does any road reach it, yet somehow it merits a place on most Moroccan road maps.

From Tizza trek east up a small valley 2–3km, then climb up **Tizi n'Timirout** (2280m) – which is not named on the survey map. There's a dramatic view of the main ridge from this pass, its rugged peaks stretching to the northeast. The most prominent one is Moulay Ali at 3349m. Afensou (see above) awaits you after a long descent, from where you can hitch back out to Souk Sebt or Imi n'Tanoute or continue on across to the Tizi n'Test road.

Southern approach to the Tichka plateau

In the last few years the potential for mountain exploration in the Western High Atlas has been realised by both local and international trekking companies. The previously mentioned *Tigouga Adventures*, based in Taroudannt, can pass on information and/or organise everything for those wanting to visit the "lost world" of the Tichka plateau and the beautiful valleys leading up to the heights, and British trekking companies, also run spring treks in the region. Going it your own way, *camionettes* from Taroudannt and Ouled Behril ply up to **Imoulas**, **Tagmout** and **Souk Tnine Tigouga**, from whence mule trails lead over the crests. The main routes are outlined below.

Imoulas

IMOULAS is the main town of the foothills, with a Sunday *souk*. From here a piste extends for about 6km northwest to TINIGHAS, whence there is a dramatic route through a gorge to high *azibs* and a hard ascent to **Djebel Tinerghwet** (3551m), the highest peak in the area, and **Awlim** (3481m). East of Awlim extends the **"Ridge of a Hundred Peaks"**, running on to the distant Tichka plateau.

Tagmout

You can stay in a delightful old house at **TAGMOUT**, before following the mule track north, up the stunning **Medlawa Valley**, to the Tichka plateau.

Souk Tnine Tigouga

As the name suggests, **SOUK TNINE TIGOUGA** has a **Monday souk**, the easiest time to get a lift up (or out of) here. Mule tracks north of the village offer a more direct approach to the Tichka plateau, and lead over to Aguersaffen (see p.368).

travel details

Trains

Marrakesh–Casablanca (4 daily; currently at 1.20am, 7.25am, 9.00am and 5.27pm; 4hr).

Marrakesh–Fes via Casablanca) (3 daily; 8–11hr).

Marrakesh–Tangier (2 daily; currently 1.20am and 5.25pm; 15hr 30min).

Marrakesh–Safi (1 daily; 3hr 40min; but this is essentially a phosphate/freight train).

Buses

From Marrakesh Asni (8 daily; 1hr 30min); Taroudannt (2 at dawn; 8hr 30min); Taliouine (1; 7–8hr); Ouarzazate (4; 4–5hr)*; Zagora (2; 9–11hr)*; Agadir (1; 3hr 45min); Inezgane (4; 3hr 30min – change for Agadir); Essaouira (6; 3hr–4hr 30min); Safi (4; 3hr 30min); El Jadida (9; 3hr 30min); Casablanca (hourly; 4hr); Rabat (8 daily; 5hr 30min); Fes (3; 11hr); Beni Mellal (9; 3hr); Azrou (4; 5hr 30min) Demnate (4; 3hr).

The most comfortable is the 10am bus operated by Ligne du Zagora.

Grands Taxis

From Marrakesh Frequent and useful services to the Ourika Valley, Asni and Amizmiz; less frequent departures to Agadir (3hr); negotiable elsewhere, though no other standard runs.

Flights

From Marrakesh Daily (except Tuesdays) to Casablanca with connections on to Tangier. International flights via Tangier or Casablanca.

CHAPTER SIX

THE GREAT SOUTHERN OASIS ROUTES

Immediately when you arrive in the Sahara, for the first or the tenth time, you notice the stillness. An incredible, absolute silence prevails outside the towns; and within, even in busy places like the markets, there is a hushed quality in the air, as if the quiet were a constant force which, resenting the intrusion of sound, minimizes and disperses it straightaway. Then there is the sky, compared to which all other skies seem faint-hearted efforts. Solid and luminous, it is always the focal point of the landscape. At sunset, the precise, curved shadow of the earth rises into it swiftly from the horizon, cutting it into light section and dark section. When all daylight has gone, and the space is thick with stars, it is still of an intense and burning blue, darkest directly overhead and paling toward the earth, so that the night never really grows dark.

Paul Bowles: *The Baptism of Solitude*

The **Moroccan Pre-Sahara** begins as soon as you cross the Atlas to the south. It is not sand for the most part – more a wasteland of rock and scrub – but it is powerfully impressive. The quote from Paul Bowles may sound over the top, but staying at Figuig or Merzouga, or just stopping in the desert between towns, somehow has this effect.

There is, too, an irresistible sense of wonder as you catch a first glimpse of the great river valleys – the **Drâa**, **Dadès**, **Todra**, **Ziz** and **Tafilalt**. Long belts of date palm oases, scattered with the fabulous mud architecture of Kasbahs and fortified *ksour* villages, these are the old caravan routes that reached back to Marrakesh and Fes and out across the Sahara to Timbuktu, Niger and old Sudan, carrying gold, slaves and salt well into the nineteenth century. They are beautiful routes even today, tamed by modern roads and with the oases in decline – and if you're travelling in Morocco for any length of time, this is the part to head for. The simplest circuits – **Marrakesh–Zagora–Marrakesh**, or **Marrakesh–Tinerhir–Midelt** – can be covered in around five days, though to do them any degree of justice you need a lot longer.

The **southern oases** were long a mainstay of the precolonial economy. Their wealth, and the arrival of tribes from the desert, provided the impetus for two of the great royal dynasties: the Saadians (1154–1669) from the Drâa Valley, and the present ruling family, the Alaouites (1669–) from the Tafilalt. By the nineteenth century, however, the advance of the Sahara and the uncertain upkeep of the

SOUTHERN PRACTICALITIES

BUSES, TRUCKS AND TAXIS

All the main road routes in this chapter are covered by ordinary **buses**, and often *grands taxis*, too. On many of the others, local **Berber trucks** (*camionettes*) or **landrover and transit taxis** (detailed in the text) run a similar service, charging standard fares for their trips, which are usually timed to coincide with the network of *souks* or markets in villages en route.

The lorries cover a number of adventurous desert pistes – such as the direct desert route from Zagora to Rissani – some of which are also practicable by car. If you plan to **drive** on these, however, or on the very rough roads over the Atlas behind the Dadès or Todra gorges (which again can be covered by rides in Berber lorries), you'll need to be decently equipped and able to do basic mechanical repairs.

CAR HIRE AND MAINTENANCE

Travelling by bus in the desert, in summer, the main disadvantage is the sheer physical exhaustion involved: most trips tend to begin at dawn to avoid the worst of the heat, and for the rest of the day it can be difficult to summon up the energy to do anything. If you can afford to **hire a car** – even for just two or three days – you'll be able to to take in a lot more, with a lot less frustration, in a reasonably short period of time. There are numerous rental outlets in Ouarzazate, most of which allow you to return their vehicles to Marrakesh, Casablanca or Fes.

Filling stations can be found along all the main routes, but they're not exactly plentiful. Fill the tank whenever and wherever you have the opportunity. It's wise to carry **water**, too, in case of overheating, and, above all, be sure you've got a good **spare tyre** – punctures tend to be frequent on all southern roads. As throughout the country, however, local **mechanics** are excellent (Er Rachidia has an especially good reputation) and most minor problems can be quickly dealt with.

HEALTH

Rivers in the south are reputed to contain bilharzia, a parasite that can enter your body through the soles of your feet. Even when walking by streams in the oases, take care to avoid contact.

CLIMATE AND SEASONS

Temperatures can climb well above 120°F (50°C) in midsummer and you'll find the middle of the day is best spent being totally inactive. If you have the option, spring is by far the most enjoyable time to travel – particularly if you're heading for Zagora (reckoned to be the hottest town in the country), Rissani-Merzouga, or Figuig. Autumn, with the date harvests, is also good. In winter, the days remain hot, though it can get fairly cool at night, and further south into the desert, it can actually freeze. Some kind of hat or cap, and sunglasses, are pretty much essential.

Spring floods The Drâa, in particular, is subject to spring floods, as the snow melts in the Atlas and forges the river currents. Passes across the Atlas at this time, and even trips such as Ouarzazate to Aït Benhaddou, can be difficult or impossible.

TELEPHONE CODES

Telephone numbers in **Ouarzazate, Zagora and Tinerhir** regions are prefixed 04; **Er Rachidia/Erfoud** numbers are prefixed 05; **Figuig** numbers are prefixed 06. When making a call within a region you omit the prefix. For more explanation of phone codes and making calls within (or to) Morocco, see p.37.

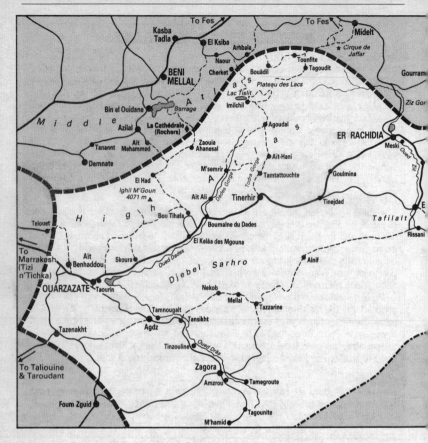

water channels had reduced life to bare subsistence even in the most fertile strips. Under the French, with the creation of modern industry in the north and the exploitation of phosphates and minerals, they became less and less significant, while the old caravan routes were dealt a final death blow by the closure of the Algerian border after independence. The pattern of the last two decades has been one of steady emigration to the northern cities.

Today, there are a few urban centres in the south – **Ouarzazate**, **Erfoud** and **Er Rachidia** are the largest – but these seem only to underline the end of an age. Although the date harvests in late October can still give employment to the *ksour* communities and tourism itself brings in a little money, the rest of the year sees only the modest production of a handful of crops – henna, barley, citrus fruits and roses (developed by the French around El Kelâa des Mgouna for the production of *attar* and rose-water, in the spring).

In recent years, making the situation even more critical, the seasonal rains have frequently failed, and perhaps as much as half the male population of the *ksour* now seeks work in the north for at least part of the year.

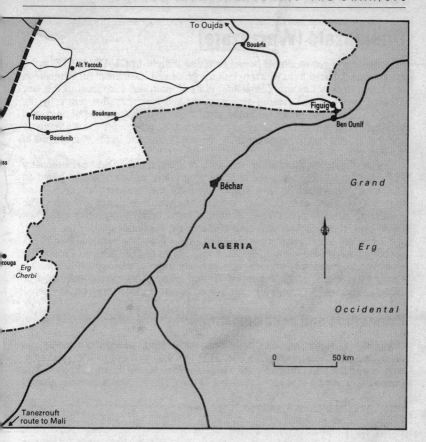

OUARZAZATE AND THE DRÂA

Ouarzazate – easily reached from Marrakesh (6hr by bus) or Taroudannt (6–7hr via Taliouine) – is the standard starting point and crossroads of the south. East of the town stretches the Dadès River, the "Valley of the Thousand Kasbahs", as the ONMT promotes it. To the south, on the other side of a tremendous ridge of the Anti-Atlas, begins the **Drâa Valley** – 125km of date palm oases, which eventually merge into the Sahara near the village of M'hamid.

It is possible to complete a circuit through and out from the Drâa, heading from the valley's main town, **Zagora**, across piste roads west through Foum Zguid to the Anti-Atlas, or east into the **Djebel Sarhro** (a winter/spring trekking centre – see pp.395–98 for details), or across to Rissani in the Tafilalt. However, most visitors content themselves with a return trip along the main **P31** between Ouarzazate and Zagora: a great route, taking you well south of anywhere in the Tafilalt, and flanked by an amazing series of turreted and cream-pink-coloured *ksour*.

Ouarzazate (Warzazate)

At some stage, you're almost bound to spend a night in **OUARZAZATE** and it can be a useful base from which to visit the *ksour* and Kasbahs of Aït Benhaddou or Skoura. It is not exactly compelling in itself, however. Like most of the new Saharan towns, it was created as a garrison and administrative centre by the French and remains pretty much the same today: a deliberate line of functional buildings, together with an array of modern hotels, set along the main highway and lent an odd sort of permanence by the use of concrete in place of the *pisé* of the *ksour*.

During the 1980s, Ouarzazate was a bit of a boomtown. The tourist industry embarked on a wildly optimistic building programme of luxury hotels, based on Ouarzazate's marketability as a staging point for the "Saharan Adventure", and the town was given an additional boost from the attentions of movie makers. The region first came to prominence in the film world nearly thirty years ago, when David Lean shot *Lawrence of Arabia* at nearby Aït Benhaddou and in the Tafilalt, but in the last decade, numerous directors – most famously Bernardo Bertolucci, shooting Paul Bowles's novel, *The Sheltering Sky* – used the town as a base. The Gulf War interruption to tourism, however, and the recessionary 1990s have left Ouarzazate with a rather depressed air and many of its hotels unfinished or vacant. The town is certainly at a crossroads, but the traffic, at present, isn't here.

Orientation and accommodation

Orientation is simply a matter of getting your bearings along the highway and main road, **Av. Mohammed V**. The **CTM** bus station more or less marks the centre, with the **PTT** alongside, and a **tourist office** across the road. **Private line buses** use a station a block to the west of the *CTM*, off the main road; **grands**

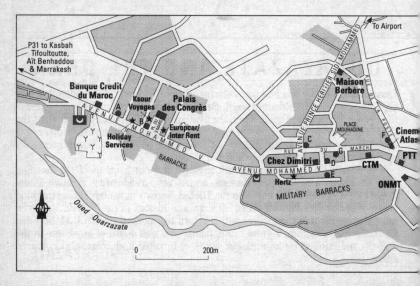

taxis operate out of the central Place Mouhadine; and at the east end of Av. Mohammed V is the town's main sight, Kasbah Taorirt.

Ouarzazate's **airport** is just 1km north of town, served by local taxis.

Accommodation

Finding a hotel room should present few problems. Most of the cheaper and unclassified places are grouped in the centre of town, near the bus stations; the more upmarket ones are mainly set back on the plateau to the north. The listings below are selective and, as usual, in ascending order of price.

Hôtel Royal [D], 24 Av. Mohammed V (☎04/88.24.75). The town's best cheapie, renovated not long ago, and with hot showers in each room; it's much better than the *Essalam* **[E]**, opposite, or the *Hôtel Atlas* **[C]** at 13 Rue du Marché. All are ①

Hôtel Saghro (☎04/88.43.05) and **Hôtel de la Vallée** (☎04/88.26.68). A pair of cheap hotels, located about a kilometre south of town, on the Zagora road. ①

Hôtel Es Saada [F], 12 Rue de la Poste (no phone). Recently refurbished and good value. ①

Hôtel Amlal [G], 24 Rue du Marché (☎04/88.46.00). Brand new hotel with sparkling showers, toilets and everything else. Highly recommended. ①

Hôtel La Gazelle [A], Av. Mohammed V (☎04/88.21.51). The rooms could do with a splash of paint, but they're off an attractive garden courtyard that's full of birdlife; there's also a swimming pool, plus a bar and restaurant, both popular with locals. ②

Hôtel Residence el Warda [B], Place du 3 Mars (☎04/88.20.43). Modern, well-equipped studios and apartments. Convenient location and excellent value. ②

Hôtel Tichka Salam [J], Av. Mohammed V, midway between the centre of town and the Kasbah Taorirt (☎04/88.22.06). Very comfortable and excellent value – it has lost a star in the wake of grander neighbours – with a reliable swimming pool. ③

Hôtel Azghor [H], Bd. Prince Moulay Rachid (☎04/88.26.12). Old established "Grand Hôtel du Sud", with fabulous views to the south and a good-sized swimming pool. ④

Hôtel Belère [I], Bd. Prince Moulay Rachid (☎04/88.28.03). A modern, slightly fancier neighbour, again with a fine pool. ④

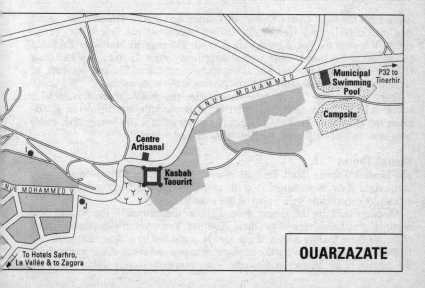

HOTEL PRICE CODES AND STAR-RATINGS

Hotels are no longer obliged to levy set maximum rates, according to their official star-ratings, as had long been the custom. However, **prices** still broadly follow the star-rating system, and this is the basis of our own **hotel price codes** set out below and keyed throughout the guide.

Our code	Official classification	Single room price	Double room price
⑩	Unclassified	25–60dh	40–100dh
①	1*A/1*B	60–105dh	100–125dh
②	2*B/2*A	105–145dh	125–175dh
③	3*B/3*A	145–225dh	175–275dh
④	4*B/4*A	225–400dh	275–500dh
⑤	5*luxury	Upwards of 400dh	Upwards of 500dh

OUT OF TOWN

Kasbah Tifoultoutte, 5km out, on the P31 (☎04/88.46.36). This is a former Glaoui Kasbah, which in the 1960s was converted to a hotel for the cast of *Lawrence of Arabia*. Today it functions mainly as a "traditional-entertainment annexe" for the various hotel tour groups. However, it has a fabulous site (and wonderful views from the roof), and the French *patronne* rents a couple of rooms, which are overpriced but have considerable atmosphere. ②

CAMPSITE

Camping Municipal, 4km east of the centre, just past the Kasbah Taorirt (☎04/88.46.36). A well-maintained site – it wasn't always so – alongside the municipal swimming pool. Meals are available – ordered in advance – at a tent restaurant .

The town and Kasbah Taorirt

Aside from the local Glaoui Kasbah of **Taorirt**, and that of **Tifoultoutte** on the ring road outside town (see hotels, above), Ouarzazate has little in the way of sights. If it's not too hot, a good walk is to the **Barrage El Mansour Eddahbi** (northeast of the town), quite a sight after heavy rains. If you follow the bank round to the east of the lake you come to the semi-ruined **Tazrout Kasbah**, or "Kasbah des Cigognes", with its storks nesting in the battlements.

There is little else in – or to – Ouarzazate, and really the most interesting option is to get out for the day, either to Aït Benhaddou (see below) or a little along the Dadès to Skoura – a beautiful and rambling oasis (see p.391), easily accessible as a day trip using the Boumalne/Tinerhir buses.

Kasbah Taorirt

The **Kasbah Taorirt** (Mon–Fri 8.30am–noon & 3–6pm, Sat 8.30am–noon) stands to the right of Av. Mohammed V, at the east (Tinerhir direction) end of town. It's a dusty, twenty-minute walk from the bus station.

Although built by the Glaoui (see p.321 for background), the Kasbah was never an actual residence of its chiefs. However, located at this strategic junction of the southern trading routes, it was always controlled by a close relative. In the 1930s, when the Glaoui were the undisputed masters of the south, it was perhaps the largest of all Moroccan Kasbahs – an enormous family domain housing numerous sons and cousins of the dynasty, along with several hundred of their servants and labourers, builders and craftsmen, even semi-itinerant Jewish tailors and moneylenders.

Since then, and especially since being taken over by the government after independence, the Kasbah has fallen into drastic decline. Parts of the structure have simply disappeared, washed away by heavy rains; others are completely unsafe; and it is only a small section of the original, a kind of village within the Kasbah, that remains occupied today. That part is towards the rear of the rambling complex of rooms, courtyards and alleyways. What you are shown is just the main reception courtyard and a handful of principal rooms, very lavishly decorated but not especially significant or representative of the old order of things. With an eye, perhaps, to tourist demands, they have become known as "the harem".

Crafts

Opposite the Kasbah is a **Centre Artesanal/Coopérative des Tapis** (Mon–Fri 8.30am–noon & 1–6pm, Sat 8.30am–noon). Stone carving, pottery and the geometrically patterned, silky woollen carpets of the region's Ouzguita Berbers are all produced, displayed and sold here. Newly opened, on the road to the airport, is a branch of the excellent *Maison Berbère* chain, selling high quality carpets and rugs.

Practicalities

Ouarzazate's "Gateway of the South" status ensures a good range of tourist facilities, from banks to car rental.

Cafés and restaurants

There are reasonable but pricey **restaurants** at all the large hotels, a good, modest one at the *Hôtel La Gazelle*, and cheap **café-grills** grouped round the bus station and along the nearby Rue du Marché. Some recommendations you might want to try:

Restaurant Es-Salaam, Av. Prince Heritier Sidi Mohammed. An excellent, inexpensive restaurant, unconnected with the (not very good) hotel next door.

Restaurant Waha, Av. Prince Heritier Sidi Mohammed. Reliable and modestly priced. The patron also owns a restaurant at the oasis village of Finnt, 10km south of town, along a piste off the Zagora road, if you fancy an excursion.

Glacier 3 Mars, 7 Place du 3 Mars. Cheap café-brasserie, popular with locals.

Restaurant Chez Dimitri, Av. Mohammed V. A Foreign Legion-era bar-brasserie, which serves inexpensive *Flag* Specials and pasta dishes. Patronised by local sand expatriates. Good value.

Directory

Airport The *Aeroport Taorirt* is 1km north of town, and served by *petits taxis*. There are direct flights to Agadir, Casablanca, Marrakesh and Paris. *RAM* have a new office near *Chez Dimitri* on Av. Mohammed V.

Banks All the banks are on the north side of Av. Mohammed V. They include (moving west to east): *Crédit du Maroc*, *Wafa Bank*, *BMCE*, *BCM* and *Banque Populaire*.

Beer and wine Alcohol becomes more and more scarce as you head south. The grocery across the street from *Chez Dimitri* sells discreet, newspaper-wrapped bottles.

Bicycles – including mountain bikes – can be hired out from *Ksour Voyages*, 11 Place du 3 Mars.

Buses There are CTM services, leaving from their station near the ONMT office, to Marrakesh (8.30am, 11am & noon) and Zagora (noon). From the private-lines terminal at Place du 3 Mars, SATAS run to Marrakesh (9am), while other companies leave for Zagora at 3.30am and 7am, and east along the Dadès; to the west, two daily buses (8am & 3.30pm) complete the marathon haul to Taliouine, Taroudannt and Inezgane (local connections to Agadir).

Car hire Companies include: *Budget*, in the *Residence el Warda*, Av. Mohammed V (☎04/88.28.92); *Dani Car*, Place du 3 Mars (☎04/88.30.63); *Europcar/InterRent* (☎04/88.20.35); *Hertz*, Place du 3 Mars (☎04/88.20.84); *Holiday Services*, next to *Hôtel la Gazelle*, Av. Mohammed V (☎04/88.29.97; specialises in landrovers).

Cinema *Cinéma Atlas*, Rue de la Poste, next to *Hôtel Es Saada*.

Grands taxis leave from the Place Mouhadine on regular runs along the Dadès to Boumalne (30dh a place; connections on towards Tinerhir and Er Rachidia), and can be negotiated for Marrakesh or Zagora.

Post office The *PTT* on Av. Mohammed V has poste restante facilities, plus a direct-dialling international phone section; it is open Mon–Sat 8.30am–noon & 2.30–6pm.

Tourist office The helpful *ONMT* are just across from the PTT on Av. Mohammed V.

Aït Benhaddou

The first thing you hear from the guides on arrival at **AÏT BENHADDOU** is a list of its movie credits. This is a feature of much of the Moroccan south – where landscapes are routinely fantastic and cheap, exotic-looking extras are in plentiful supply – but, even so, the Benhaddou Kasbahs have a definite edge over the competition. *Lawrence* was filmed here, of course; Orson Welles used it as a location for *Sodom and Gomorrah*; and for *Jesus of Nazareth*, the whole lower part of the village was rebuilt. In recent years, more controlled restoration has been carried out under UNESCO auspices.

Aït Benhaddou is not really the place to catch a glimpse of fading Kasbah life but it is one of the most spectacular sights of the Atlas, piled upon a dark shaft of rock above a shallow, reed-strewn river. The Kasbahs are among the most elaborately decorated and best preserved; they are less fortified than is usually the case along the Drâa or the Dadès, but, towered and crenellated, and with high, sheer walls of dark red *pisé*, they must have been near impregnable in this remote, hillside site.

As ever, it's impossible to determine exactly how old the Kasbahs are, though there seem to have been buildings here since at least the sixteenth century. The importance of the site, which commands the area for miles around, was its position on the route from Marrakesh through Telouet to Ouarzazate and the south: a significance that disappeared with the creation of the new French road over the Tichka pass, which has led to severe depopulation over the last thirty years. There are now only half a dozen families living in the Kasbahs, earning a sparse living from the valley's agriculture and rather more from the steady trickle of tourists.

When you reach the "new village", on the west bank of the river, the road comes to an end. There's a café here and usually a few guides around, who will escort you across the river (in winter you have to wade across, though it is usually only knee-deep) up to the Kasbahs. They are bisected by an incredibly confusing network of lanes, so a guide is useful – and if you ask, it should be possible to see one or two Kasbah interiors. At the top of the hill are the ruins of a vast and imposing **agadir**, or fortified granary.

KSOUR AND KASBAHS

Ksour (*ksar* in the singular), or Kasbahs, are to be found throughout the southern valleys and, to an extent, in the Atlas. They are essentially fortified tribal villages, massive but transitory structures, built in the absence of other available materials out of the mud-clay *pisé* of the riverbanks and lasting only as long as the seasonal rains allow. A unique and probably indigenous development of the Berber populations, they are often monumental in design and fabulously decorated, with bold geometric patterns incised or painted on the exterior walls and slanted towers.

The **Kasbah**, in its southern form, is similar to the *ksar*, though instead of sheltering a mixed village community, it is traditionally the domain of a single family and its dependants. **Agadirs** and **tighremts**, also variants of the *ksar* structure, used to serve as a combination of tribal fortress and communal granary or storehouse in the villages.

The Dadès Kasbahs

Ksour line the route more or less continuously from Agdz to Zagora; most of the larger and older ones are grouped a little way from the road, up above the terraces of date palms. Few that are still in use can be more than a hundred years old, though you frequently see the ruins and walls of earlier *ksour* abandoned just a short distance from their modern counterparts. Most are populated by **Berbers**, but there are also Arab villages here, and even a few scattered communities of **Jews**, still living in their Mellahs. All of the southern valleys, too, have groups of **Haratin**, blacks descended from the west Sudanese slaves brought into Morocco along these caravan routes. Inevitably, these populations have mixed to some extent – and the Jews here are almost certainly converted Berbers – though it is interesting to see just how distinct many of the *ksour* still appear, both in their architecture and customs. There is, for example, a great difference from one village to the next as regards women's costumes, above all in the wearing and extent of veils.

Visiting the region, bear in mind that all of the Drâa **ksour** and **Kasbahs** tend to be further from the road than they look: it's possible to walk for several hours without reaching the edge of the oasis and the upper terraced levels.

Practicalities

The "new village" has three rival **auberges**, catering mainly for tour group lunches but offering basic meals in the evening, and a handful of rooms. *La Kasbah* (Aït Benhaddou ☎2, through the operator; ①), poised on a terrace above the village, is a good place with a *patron*, Mohammed Tibou, who is a friendly source of information; *Al Baraka* (Aït Benhaddou ☎5, through the operator; ①) is the road into the village; lastly, there's the new *Auberge El Ouidane* (⑩), very clean and reasonably priced, and with beautiful views across the river.

Getting to Aït Benhaddou is simple enough by car. Leaving Ouarzazate on the P31 (Tizi n'Tichka) road, you turn right after 18km – along a new, surfaced road (the old piste road runs 4km north). Without a car, the best solution is to get together with others and charter a *grand taxi* from Ouarzazate. Otherwise, you'll need to get a bus to the turn-off and walk from there; coming back, if you don't get a lift from fellow visitors, you would have to try and flag down one of the Marrakesh–Ouarzazate buses (which may not be inclined to stop).

If you're into trekking, mountain biking, or very rough piste-driving, the **jeep track** beyond Aït Benhaddou continues to **Tamdaght**, and from there mule paths climb over the old pass to **Telouet** (see p.365).

South to Zagora: the Drâa oases

The road from **Ouarzazate to Zagora** is wide and well maintained, though it does seem to take its toll of tyres. As in the rest of the south, if you're driving make sure you have a good spare and the tools to change it with. If you're on the bus, get yourself a seat on the left hand side, for the most spectacular views.

Although Zagora is the ostensible goal and destination, the valley is the real attraction. Driving the route, try to resist the impulse to burn down to the desert, and take the opportunity to walk out to one or another of the *ksour* or Kasbahs. Using local transport, you might consider hiring a *grand taxi* for the day – or half-day – from Ouarzazate, stopping to explore some of the Kasbahs en route; if you intend to do this, however, be very clear to the driver about your plans.

The lake and over the Tizi n'Tinififft

The route begins unpromisingly: the course of the Drâa lies initially some way to the east and the road runs across bleak, stony flatlands of semi-desert. After 15km a side road, the P31F, leads down to the El **Mansour Eddahbi dam and reservoir** – which you can see from part of Ouarzazate. In 1989 freak rains flooded the reservoir and the Drâa, for the first time in recent memory, ran its course to the sea beyond Tan Tan.

On the main road, the first interest comes just beyond AÏT SAOUN, one of the few roadside villages along this stretch, where a dramatic change takes place. Leaving the plains behind, the road climbs, twists and turns its way up into the mountains, before breaking through the scarp at the pass of **Tizi n'Tinififft** (1660m). From the summit of the pass there are fine views to the north, with the main Atlas mountains framing the horizon.

The pass is just 4km beyond Aït Saoun. Beyond it the road swings down through a landscape of layered strata, until finally, some 20km from the pass, you catch a first glimpse of the valley and the oases – a thick line of palms reaching out into the haze – and the first sign of the Drâa Kasbahs, rising as if from the land where the green gives way to desert.

Agdz and beyond

You descend into the Drâa Valley at **AGDZ** (68km from Ouarzazate – pronounced Ag–a–dèz), a stopping point for many of the buses and a minor administrative centre for the region. The village consists of just one long street, blood-red coloured, save for the columns of its arcade of shops, picked out in flashes of white and blue. Many of these sell carpets and pottery – and in the few minutes before the bus leaves, prices can drop surprisingly.

It is worth staying longer, however, for just to the north of the village begins a beautiful **palmery**. If the river here is low enough (take care to avoid the bilharzia-infested water) you can get across to view a few **Kasbahs** on the far side, in the shadow of **Djebel Kissane**, an outcrop of the Djebel Sarhro.

If you stop here – in either direction – it is unlikely that you'll get a place back on the Zagora/Ouarzazate bus; however, there are **grands taxis** (to either destination), which, like the buses, leave from from the "Grande Place", and it is possible to stay, too. The village has a trio of **hotels** which could provide an attractive and low-key introduction to the valley. The *Hôtel du Drâa* (Agdz ☎24 through the operator; ①) and *Hôtel des Palmiers* (①) are both clean and adequate, just off the "Grande Place"; the former, given advance warning, will arrange expeditions and picnics. By the ceremonial archway to the town is the *Hôtel Kissane* (Agdz ☎44 through the operator; ③), a new and very pleasant place with obliging staff, a panoramic café and a good salon **restaurant**. The *Hôtel Drâa* also has a restaurant and the *Restaurant Nadhah*, near the *Hôtel des Palmiers*, does inexpensive grills.

There is also a **campsite**, *Camping Kasbah de la Palmeraie* (Agdz ☎80 through the operator), 2km out of town, adjoining an old Glaoui Kasbah (Dar El Glaoui); this again has a few rooms

Tamnougalt and Timiderte
The *ksour* at **TAMNOUGALT** – off to the left of the road, about 6km past Agdz – are perhaps the most dramatic and extravagant of any in the Drâa. A wild cluster of buildings, each is fabulously decorated with pockmarked walls and tapering towers. The village was once the capital of the region, and its assembly of families (the *djemaa*) administered what was virtually an independent republic. It is populated by a Berber tribe, the Mezguita.

A further 8km south is the more palace-like Glaoui Kasbah of **TIMIDERTE**, built by Brahim, the eldest son of the one-time Pasha of Marrakesh, T'hami el Glaoui (see p.321). A kilometre to the south, across stepping stones in the river, is another superb Kasbah, the **Aït Hammousaid**. There are also said to be rock carvings 7km to the west of Timiderte.

Tinzouline
Another striking group of *ksour*, dominated by a beautiful and imposing caid's Kasbah, stands back from the road at **TINZOULINE**, 57km beyond Timiderte (30km north of Zagora). There is a large and very worthwhile **Monday souk** held here and, if you're travelling by bus, the village is one of the better places to break the journey for a while.

Zagora

ZAGORA at first sight seems unpromising: a single street with a group of modern administrative buildings and hotels. Two things, however, redeem it. The first is its location: this is the most productive stretch of the Drâa – indeed, of all the southern valleys – and you only have to walk a mile or so out of the town (actually little more than a village) to find yourself amid the palms and oasis cultivation. The second is its distinct air of unreality. Directly behind the town rises a bizarre Hollywood-sunset mountain, and at the end of the main street is a mock-serious roadsign to Timbuktu ("*52 jours*" – by camel – if the border were open).

Another draw for Zagora is its festivals. The Drâa's big event, the **Moussem of Moulay Abdelkader Jilali**, is celebrated over the Mouloud here, and, like other national festivals such as the **Fête du Trône**, is always entertaining.

Orientation and accommodation
Though it can seem a bit hustley on arrival, and in summer the heat and dryness of the air are totally staggering, Zagora is a pretty easy place to get orientated –

with almost everything of note along the main drag, **Bd. Mohammed V**, or lower **Av. Hassan II**. Across the river, to the south, is the palmery and village of **Amazrou**, a good option for an alternative base, with a couple of hotels and a campsite.

HOTELS

Hôtel des Amis, Bd. Mohammed V (no phone). The cheapest rooms in Zagora, and in summer the hotel rents out (slightly cooler) space on its *terrasse*. No hot water. ⓪

Hôtel Oued Drâa, Bd. Mohammed V (☎04/84.72.10). A little more expensive and a fair bit more comfortable. Very welcoming and clean, with (some) hot showers. ⓪

Hôtel de la Palmeraie, Bd. Mohammed V (☎04/84.70.08). A popular and noisy hotel, with a variety of rooms and prices, plus a Berber tent out the back serving generous meals, and a lively bar (open to 9pm). The hotel also runs tours into the desert "on the backs of camels, with nights under the stars or in tents, eating bread cooked by nomads on the sand" for a half-day, a day, or a week. ①

Hôtel Kasbah Asmaa, Amazrou (☎04/84.72.41). A very welcoming Kasbah-style hotel, set in a beautiful garden, across the river, on the edge of the Amazrou palmery; there is a swimming pool and an excellent "salon" restaurant. Again, camel trips are on offer. ②

Hôtel La Fibule, Amazrou (☎04/84.73.18). Again set in palmery gardens, this offers a choice of accommodation. Originally it was a small restaurant with a dozen rooms round a rooftop terrace; these remain as the "Hotel Kebir", with amazing decor and moderate prices. Adjacent is the "Hotel Ksar", with more comfortable and pricier en suite rooms. In summer there is also tented accommodation in the gardens. The hotel has a swimming pool and restaurant, hires out bikes, and arranges camel rides and 4x4 expeditions. ②–③

Hôtel Tinsouline, Bd. Mohammed V (☎04/84.72.52). Zagora's original "grand hotel" has fallen on slightly hard times and dropped a star, making it pretty good value. It has a swimming pool, restaurant and bar. ③

Hôtel Pullman Reda, on the road between Zagora and Amazrou (☎04/84.72.49). A new tour-group hotel which has the edge on facilities over the *Tinsouline*, a good pool, but not much character. ④

CAMPSITES

Camping Sindibad, Av. Hassan II – five minutes' walk from the town centre. A pleasant site, with lots of shade, decent facilities, a café and a swimming pool (unpredictable!). Also has some rooms, though these are a bit noisy, as the proprietor is a big fan of AC/DC . . .

Camping de la Montagne, 2km along a track from the Zagora–Amazrou road. This is a fine site if you have transport: a little oasis of palms, eucalyptus and tamarisk trees, in the shadow of the sugarloaf Djebel Zagora mountain. It offers running water, cold drinks, meals (cooked to order), and a swimming pool, and has very friendly people in charge. The campsite is also home to a couple of camel owners, who arrange rides to the Djebel Zagora.

TINFOU/TAMEGROUTE: A NIGHT IN THE DESERT

An alternative to staying in Zagora is to head south and stay at one of two hotels poised at the edge of sand dunes, on the road to Mhamid. The first of these is the *Hôtel Riad Dar Naciri* at the village of Tamegroute (19km); the second, at a spot marked simply "▲ Dunes" on the Michelin map, is the little *Auberge Repos du Sable de Tinfou*, one of the most enjoyable small hotels in Morocco.

For details of both, see the section "South of Zagora: Tamegroute and Mhamid". If you don't have a car, it's possible to charter a *grand taxi* to either hotel, though even with haggling it'll be expensive unless you can get a group together.

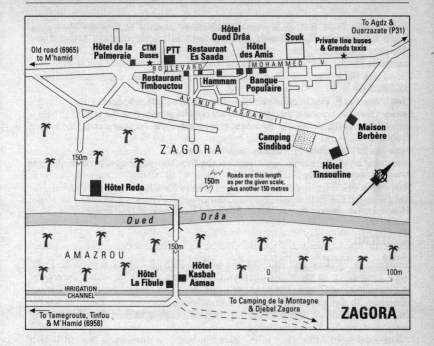

To Agdz &
Ouarzazate (P31)

Old road (6965)
to M'hamid

**Hôtel de la
Palmeraie**   **CTM
Buses**   **PTT**   **Restaurant
Es Saada**

**Hôtel
Oued Drâa**

**Hôtel
des Amis**

Souk

**Private line buses
& Grands taxis**

B O U L E V A R D   M O H A M M E D   V

**Restaurant
Timbouctou**   **Hammam**   **Banque
Populaire**

A V E N U E   H A S S A N   II

**Maison
Berbère**

Z A G O R A

**Camping
Sindibad**

150m

**Hôtel
Tinsouline**

M	Roads are this length
150m	as per the given scale,
M	plus another 150 metres

Hôtel Reda

O u e d   D r â a

150m

A M A Z R O U

**Hôtel
La Fibule**

**Hôtel
Kasbah
Asmaa**

0   100m

IRRIGATION
CHANNEL

To Camping de la Montagne
& Djebel Zagora

ZAGORA

To Tamegroute, Tinfou
& M'Hamid (6958)

Food

There are **meals** to be had at most of the hotels and the campsites. The *Kasbah Asmaa* and *La Fibule* are especially good, and the restaurant at the *Tinsouline* offers a touch of class, if you feel like splashing out. In addition, the *Restaurant Timbouctou* and *Restaurant Es Saada*, both on Av. Mohammed V, do inexpensive Moroccan staples, and are as popular with locals as tourists.

The **dates** of the Zagora oasis are some of the finest in Morocco and stallholders at the market sell dozens of varieties: among them, the sweet *boufeggou*, which will last for up to four years if stored properly; the small, black *bousthami*; and the light, olive-coloured *bouzekri*. There is a date co-operative on the north side of town, which you can visit for a tasting of the varieties.

Directory

Banks The only one is the *Banque Populaire*, midway down Bd. Mohammed V.

Bikes – new mountain ones – are available for hire at the *Hôtel La Fibule*; they are a good way to explore the palmery and Kasbahs of Amazrou; rates are negotiable.

Buses *CTM* departures are from their office on Bd. Mohammed V; private lines leave from the *gare routière/grand taxi* park further along the street. For Ouarzazate, the most convenient departure is the CTM at 7am; there are two private-line departures later in the day. For details of the more challenging routes east and west, see below.

Camel trips There are three camel owners in Zagora, based at the *Hôtel La Fibule*, *Hôtel Kasbah Asmaa* and *Camping de la Montagne* (see opposite). All offer standard trips at the same prices: for an hour, an afternoon or morning (including lunch), or a full day (with three meals). They are open to negotiation for longer trips.

Grands taxis There are regular runs to Ouarzazate, from the rank by the bus station. *Grands taxis* can also be negotiated for a trip south to Tamnegroute and M'hamid (see opposite).

Hammam There is a steambath for men and women alongside the *Hôtel Oued Drâa*.

Petrol/gas There is an *Agip* filling station by the Banque Populaire, and a *Mobil* one by the exit from town on the Agdz/Ouarzazate road.

Post office The *PTT* on Bd. Mohammed V offers poste restante and phones.

Shops There is a branch of the *Maison Berbère* carpet/crafts shop on Av. Hassan II. This is one of the best-quality outlets in the south, with other branches at Ouarzazate, Tinerhir and Rissani.

Souk Markets take place on Wednesdays and Sundays.

Swimming pool There is no public pool but the *Hôtel Tinsouline* allows non-residents to swim for a steep 50dh a day.

Tours Most of the hotels offer tours or expeditions to Kasbahs in the Drâa Valley and/or into the desert: it's worth shopping around, and comparing prices. Camel rides – or longer expeditions – are offered by the *Hôtel La Fibule* and *Camping de la Montagne*.

Amazrou

Amazrou is a village and palmery just to the south of Zagora, across the Drâa, and a great place to spend the afternoon, wandering (or biking – see "Directory" on preceding page) amid the shade of its gardens and *ksour*. The village is, inevitably, wise to the ways of tourism – children try to drag you into their houses for tea and will hassle you to adopt them as guides – but for all that, the oasis life and cultivation are still fairly unaffected.

The local sight, which any of the kids will lead you towards, is the old Jewish Kasbah, **La Kasbah des Juifs**. The Jewish community here were active in the silver jewellery trade – a craft continued by Muslim Berbers after their exodus. It's possible to visit some of the workshops.

Djebel Zagora

Across the valley from Zagora are two **mountains**. Djebel Zagora is strictly speaking the bulky one, with a military post on top, but the name is also used for the smaller, sugarloaf hill above *Camping de la Montagne*.

Watching the sunset from the slopes of the mountain is something of a tradition. Take the road out to the *Hôtel La Fibule/Hôtel Kasbah Asmaa*, then turn left almost at once at the river to follow the road/irrigation channel to *Camping de la Montagne*. Here, swing right on the rough track which leads to a pass between the two peaks, then bends back, rising across the hillside to make an elbow bend on a spur. This is the popular viewpoint – and just feasible by car. The views are startling: you look out across the palmery to further *ksour*, to the Djebel Sarhro (see pp.395–98), and even to a stretch of sand dunes to the south.

There are ruins a little downhill of an eleventh-century Almoravid fort, built as an outpost against the powerful rulers of Tafilalt. The road subsequently goes on to the military fort on the summit (entry forbidden) but the view gains little; from the spur a footpath runs across and down the hillside and can be followed back down to the road just opposite *La Fibule*.

On foot you can climb the mountain more directly on an old zigzag footpath up from near the *Hôtel Kasbah Asmaa*.

South to M'hamid

The **Zagora oasis** stretches for some 30km south of the town, when the Drâa disappears for a while, to resurface in a final fertile belt before the desert. You can follow this route all the way down: the road (6958/6965/6954) is paved over the full 98km from **Zagora to M'hamid**, and with a car it's an enticing option. If you don't have transport, it's all a bit of an effort; there are buses to both Tamegroute and M'hamid, but times (evening departure to Tamegroute) are inconvenient unless you plan to stay overnight at Tamegroute or Tinfou – both of which are attractive options, with possibilities for expeditions. It is also possible to charter a *grand taxi*, which would not be too expensive if you can find a group to share costs, and limit your sights to **Tamegroute** and the **sand dunes** near Tinfou.

To visit M'hamid, it is no longer necessary to get authorisation or to take a guide, as it was in the past, since the region no longer has any military significance, with Polisario contained way to the south. Note that there are no filling stations in M'hamid or Tamegroute, or on the route, so fill your tank in Zagora before setting out.

Tamegroute and Tinfou

Tamegroute (19km from Zagora) is reached by a good asphalt road (6958) down the left bank of the Drâa, just past the *Hôtel La Fibule*. Take care that you get onto this, and not the old road (6965) to M'hamid on the right bank of the river. **Tinfou** lies 10km on from Tamegroute at a point marked on the Michelin map as: ▲ **Dunes**.

Tamegroute

TAMEGROUTE is an interesting and unusual village. It is essentially a group of *ksour* and Kasbahs, wedged tightly together and divided by low, covered passageways; it also has a small potters' co-operative and a Saturday *souk*. Most notably, however, it is home to an ancient and highly prestigious *zaouia*, which was a seat of learning from the eleventh century and, from the seventeenth century, the base of the Naciri Brotherhood. Founded by Abou Abdallah Mohammed Ben Naceur, this exercised great influence over the Drâa tribes until recent decades. Its sheikhs (or holy leaders) were known as the "peacemakers of the desert" and it was they who settled disputes among the *ksour* and among the caravan traders converging on Zagora from the Sudan. They were missionaries, too, and as late as the 1750s sent envoys to preach to and convert the wilder, animist-minded Berber tribes of the Atlas and Rif.

Arriving in the village, you'll likely be "adopted" by a guide and taken off to see the **Zaouia Naciri**, which stands just to the left of the main road (coming from Zagora), before the *Hôtel Riad Dar Naciri*, also on the left. The *zaouia* consists of a *marabout* (the tomb of Naceur, closed to non-Muslims), a *medersa* (theological college – still used by up to 400 students, preparing for university) and a library, which welcomes non-Muslim visitors (closed at lunchtime; donation expected). The sanctuary, as for centuries past, is a refuge for the sick and mentally ill, whom you'll see sitting round in the courtyard; they come in the hope of miraculous cures and/or to be supported by the charity of the brotherhood and other benevolent visitors.

The **library** was once the richest in Morocco, containing 40,000 volumes. Most have been dispersed to Koranic schools round the country, but Tamegroute preserves a number of very early editions of the Koran printed on gazelle hide, and some interesting books, including a thirteenth-century algebra primer featuring Western Arabic numerals, which, although subsequently dropped in the Arab world, formed the basis of the West's numbers, through the influence of the universities of Moorish Spain.

The village **hotel**, the *Riad Dar Naciri* (☎6 through the operator; ⑩), is an attractive place, run by a very friendly extended family. It has an old *ksar* section, with eighteen rooms, most en-suite, and a fine restaurant. They also offer trips out to the sand dunes, and camping in the desert.

Tinfou: dunes and a great auberge

The little *Auberge Repos du Sable* (a phone is said to be on the way, *insh'allah*; ⑩) is sited at the tiny hamlet of **TINFOU**, at the edge of an impressive line of sand dunes – a good substitute for Merzouga if you want to see a real Moroccan sand desert. It is a delightful place: an ancient Kasbah building, with a medieval room key system, a wonderfully ramshackle pool, a private hammam, and fine food. It is inexpensive (90dh for a double), and on summer nights you can move your mattress into the courtyard for the cool and the stars.

What makes the *auberge* special, however, is the Farouj family who run it. The parents, Hassan and Fatima, are both artists, who have exhibited widely in Morocco and Europe; every inch of the walls is decorated with their output (and it is for sale at distinctly non-gallery prices). One of their sons, Mourad, manages the *auberge*, while a second son, Majid, is a camel driver, and arranges trips out to the sand dunes; he is, in the words of one of our correspondents, "a bit crazy – but his trips are a lot of fun".

If you want to book a stay at Tinfou, the full postal address is: Hôtel Auberge Repos du Sable de Tinfou (Chez El Farouj), BP, 6 Tamegroute, Zagora.

Tinfou to M'hamid

About 4km south of Tinfou, you cross the Oued Drâa, and shortly after that join the old road from Zagora to M'hamid (6965). Ahead of you, apparently blocking the route, rises the great mass of the **Djebel Bani** (1095m), through which the road winds up and over a high-level pass. Once across, you enter a picturesque stretch of palmery; signs direct you into this to the *Bivouac Ait Isfoul* and *Auberge Ait Isfoul* – a pair of tourist enterprises which at present are closed.

TAGOUNITE (74km from Zagora) has a **Thursday souk**, and a **café-restaurant**, the *Es Saada*, with six **rooms**, or space on its terrace, if you want to stay overnight. A piste to the west – suitable for 4x4 vehicles only – leads off to Foum Zguid (see Chapter Seven).

Continuing south, the road crosses another pass of the Djebel Bani, the **Tizi Beni Slimane**, to reach the last fertile belt of the Drâa, the **M'hamid el Gouzlane** – Plain of the Gazelles. A few kilometres on, at the palmery/village of **OULAD DRISS**, the Drâa turns sharply towards the west and the Atlantic; there are some well-preserved *ksour* to explore here, and a small **campsite**. A signpost, echoing that of Zagora, tells you that it is *50 jours à Timbuktu*; the two days' camel ride thus far from from Zagora takes around an hour and a half today by car – though only a little further south of here a camel would come into its own.

On the final approach to M'hamid, sand has often drifted across the road, despite being lined with woven palm-leaf shields.

M'hamid

M'HAMID itself is just a small administrative centre, the end rather than climax of this trip. It was once an important market place for nomadic and trans-Saharan trade, but of this role only a rather mundane **Monday souk** remains; certainly, there is no sign of any camel traders or Blue Men, as the tourist literature suggests. Of rather more interest, however, are the sand dunes about 4km away from the village, and the *ksour* of old M'hamid – the village (across the Drâa) that existed prior to the Polisario attack.

Guides can be arranged – together with camel or mule if you want – through the *Hôtel Sahara* (①); this is a fairly primitive place (there is no electricity or running water in the village) but the **rooms** are clean, well blanketed and cheap, and a café behind serves decent **meals**. Across the riverbed, along an avenue of tamarisk shrubs, alternative accommodation is offered at the *Auberge El Khaima*; it again has inexpensive rooms, plus couches in a Berber tent, or **camping**.

The **bus** back from M'hamid to Zagora leaves before dawn.

Desert pistes east and west from Zagora

Most people return from Zagora to Ouarzazate, which is the only road covered by bus and asphalt road, and in some ways the most interesting route, allowing you to continue east along the Dadès Valley towards Boumalne and the Dadès Gorge and then to Tinerhir and the Todra Gorge.

For the desert-minded, however, there are adventurous piste alternatives **east to Rissani** or **west to Foum Zguid** (and beyond to Tata). The Rissani route is possible by landrover taxi, and the Foum Zguid route by lorry or landrover taxi, if you coincide with the markets. With your own vehicle, you'll need a fair amount of confidence in desert driving and orientation skills over the uncertain and rough tracks.

East: Zagora to Rissani

The long route east from **Zagora to Rissani**, in the Tafilalt, is covered by **landrover taxi** each Wednesday (and sometimes on Saturdays). Departure from Zagora is normally at some point between noon and 2pm, from the small *souk* across the road from the *Hôtel Palmeraie*. Ask your hotel to try and reserve a seat for you (around 150dh) and/or arrive early in the day to book a place; take along food and water. You should be dropped at Rissani (outside the *Hôtel El Filalia*) in around nine to ten hours. The taxi heads back to Zagora next day.

The usual route is to backtrack along the Drâa to **Tansikht**, before heading east on a semi-tarmac road to Nkob, where piste takes over for the section through Tazzarine towards Alnif and Rissani; all in all this is around 240km, of which 130km is still piste (though there is a programme to surface the whole route). The more direct route from Zagora, over the **Tizi n'Tafilalt**, has partially disappeared and is very hard to follow; if in doubt, follow the telegraph poles.

Midway along the main route is **TAZZARINE**, which has a fairly large **café-hotel**, the *Bougaffer*(ⓦ). Travellers driving their own vehicles, and the occasional "expedition tour" group, in four-wheel-drive lorries, stop for a night either here or in **ALNIF** (67km further east), a small oasis with a couple of basic **café-hotels**. Rissani is 100km beyond Alnif, along a largely-surfaced road over flattish valleys framed by the mountains of the Djebel Ougnat.

Our **map of the Djebel Sarhro** on p.396 shows these routes, and the accompanying section gives a few details on **trekking possibilities** in the region.

West to Foum Zguid

West from Zagora the maps indicate a road **direct to Foum Zguid**: a route which extends beyond to Tata and from there on towards Tiznit or Taroudannt. After almost two decades of military restriction, this route has recently been opened to tourists; most hire cars should be able to withstand the road surface.

On market days (Sunday and Wednesday), a *camionette* (lorry) taxi leaves the *souk* in Zagora, again around noon to 2pm, arriving in Foum Zguid towards nightfall. Like the Rissani run, it's a bumpy, crowded ride and you should take along food and drink; a *place* is about 40dh. In **FOUM ZGUID**, which has a Thursday souk and a café with **rooms**, you can pick up a *camionette* taxi on Mondays and Thursdays to Tata (see Chapter Seven); there are also buses (Tues, Thurs & Sat) to Tazenakht (change for Taroudannt/Agadir; see below) and Ouarzazate.

Agdz to the Taliouine road

Finally, and again to the west, there is a piste from **Agdz to Tazenakht**, on the road to Taliouine. This is a route basically for piste enthusiasts – it won't save any time over driving to Tazenakht via Ouarzazate – but it is fairly practicable for cars (Renault 4s should be okay), if at times difficult to follow. It is completed by a paved section, from the cobalt mines at ARHBAR to the S510 Foum Zguid road.

The main settlement en route is AÏT SMEGANE-N-EL GRARA, which has a café; the first available petrol is at TAZENAKHT, which has a **hotel** and some worthwhile carpet shops (see also more detailed entry on p.452).

THE DADÈS AND TODRA

The **Dadès**, rambling east from Ouarzazate, is the harshest and most desolate of the southern valleys. Along much of its length, the river is barely visible above ground, and the road and plain are hemmed in between the parallel ranges of the High Atlas and Djebel Sarhro – broken, black-red volcanic rock and limestone pinnacles. This makes the oases, when they appear, all the more astonishing, and there are two here – **Skoura** and **Tinerhir** – that are among the richest and most beautiful in the country. Each lies along the main bus route from Ouarzazate to Er Rachidia, offering an easy and excellent opportunity for a close look at a working oasis and, in Skoura, a startling range of Kasbahs.

Impressive though these are, however, it is the two gorges that cut out from the valley into the High Atlas that steal the show. The **Dadès** itself forms the first gorge, carving up a fertile strip of land behind Boumalne du Dadès. To its east is the **Todra Gorge**, a classic, narrowing shaft of high rock walls, which you can trail by car or transit lorry from Tinerhir right into the heart of the Atlas. If you're happy with the isolation and uncertainties of the **pistes beyond**, it is possible, too, to continue across the mountains – a wonderful trip which emerges in the Middle Atlas, near Beni Mellal on the road from Marrakesh to Fes.

To the south of the Dadès, the **Djebel Sarhro** also offers exciting options, either trekking on foot, or exploring its network of rough piste roads in a 4x4 vehicle. Tours and treks can be arranged through British trekking companies (see *Basics*) or in the "trailhead towns" of El Kelâa, Boumalne and Tinerhir.

The Skoura oasis

The **Skoura oasis** begins quite suddenly, around 30km out from Ouarzazate, along a tributary of the Drâa, the **Oued Amerhidl**. It is an extraordinary sight even from the road, which for the most part follows along its edge – a very extensive, very dense palmery, with an incredibly confusing network of tracks winding across fords and through the trees to scattered groups of *ksour* and Kasbahs.

SKOURA village, which lies just off the main road, at the east end of the oasis, consists of little more than a *souk* and a small group of administrative buildings, where buses stop. You'll probably want the services of a guide to explore some of the Kasbahs, and possibly visit one or two that are still inhabited. If you plan to stay, there is a basic **hotel**, the *Nakhil* (⑩), a rather flyblown place, with intermittent running water. Food is available here or at a couple of café-restaurants; there is a **Monday souk**.

Kasbahs in the Skoura oasis

The Skoura oasis comprises a thin line of irrigated, fertile palmery, with dry rocky slopes to either side. Animals are not permitted to graze in the precious, cultivated area and so are kept just on the dry side of the line; to feed them, women constantly struggle up from the valley with huge loads of greenery – a characteristic sight here and throughout the southern valleys.

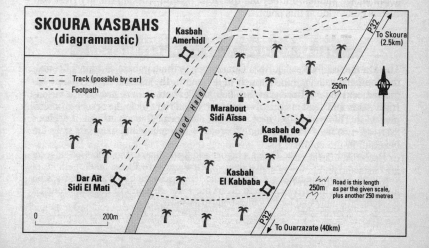

SKOURA KASBAHS
(diagrammatic)

Kasbah Amerhidl
To Skoura (2.5km)

– – – Track (possible by car)
----- Footpath

Oued Haïbi

Marabout Sidi Aïssa

250m

Kasbah de Ben Moro

Dar Aït Sidi El Mati

Kasbah El Kabbaba

Road is this length as per the given scale, plus another 250 metres
250m

0   200m

To Ouarzazate (40km)

SOUTH WEST OF SKOURA

The best point to stop and explore the Skoura oasis is 2.5km before you arrive at the village proper, coming from Ouarzazate (see sketch-map on previous page). Here, by the roadside, is a ruinous Kasbah, with a more recent single-storey building alongside it; tour buses are sometimes parked beside it. This is the **Kasbah de Ben Moro**, which dates from the seventeenth century, and is said to have been built by a Spanish sheikh expelled from Andalusia. It nowadays belongs to the family of Sabir Mohammed, which lived in the old Kasbah until 1970 and now inhabit the house beside it; they use the old part for storage and animals. Mohammed, if at home, will show visitors round, pointing out the living quarters on the first floor, the mill, and kitchens, and he will also guide you through the palmery, along a maze of paths and irrigation channels.

The palmery is one of the lushest in Morocco, full of almond, olive and fig trees, vines and date palms, with alfalfa grass planted below for animal feed. Following the paths behind the Kasbah de Ben Moro, you pass the small white **Marabout of Sidi Aïssa** (Jesus in his Arabised form), and then the (usually dry) riverbed of the Oued Amerhidl. Straight across is the **Kasbah Amerhidl**, the grandest and most extravagantly decorated in the oasis, and again seventeenth century in origin.

Kasbah Amerhidl can also be reached by car, from a turning further along the Skoura road. If you come this way, you'll be surrounded by any number of boys as soon as you stop, and you really have no option but to pay one to watch your car and another to be your guide.

Beyond Kasbah Amerhidl, a track heads off southwest to another impressive-looking Kasbah, the **Dar Aït Sidi El Mati**, and from here it's possible to complete a circuit on foot back to the P32, emerging by the ruinous **Kasbah El Kabbaba**.

NORTH OF SKOURA

There are further impressive Kasbahs to the north of Skoura village, but they are harder to find, and taking a guide along would be invaluable (Mohammed from the Kasbah Ben Moro would be a good choice). To find them, drive through Skoura village and leave it beyond the *Hôtel Nakhil*, crossing the dry river bed – which is quite wide at this point.

KASBAH MAINTENANCE AND DESTRUCTION

Many of the Skoura Kasbahs date, at least in part, from the seventeenth and eighteenth centuries, though the majority here – and throughout the Dadès oases – are much more modern. Dozens of the older fortifications were destroyed in a vicious tribal war in 1893, and many that survived were pulled down in the French "pacification" of the 1920s and 30s. Once a Kasbah has been left unmaintained, it declines very fast – twenty years is enough to produce a ruinous state, if the *pisé* walls are not renewed.

The Kasbah walls in the Dadès – higher and flatter than in the Drâa – often seem unscaleable, but in the course of a siege or war there were always other methods of conquest. A favourite means of attack in the 1890s, according to Walter Harris, who journeyed here in disguise, was to divert the water channels of the oasis round a Kasbah and simply wait for its foundations to dissolve.

After about 4km, and still well within the palmery, you should come to a pair of Kasbahs, **Dar Aït Sous** and **Dar Lahsoune**; the former, small but once very grand, is in a ruinous state, used only for animals; the latter, once a Glaoui residence, is state-owned, and private. A further 2km drive – and directions from locals – takes you to the magnificent **Kasbah Aït Ben Abou**, which is second in Skoura only to Kasbah Amerhidl. It lies on well-farmed land and is still inhabited.

Finally, on the edge of the palmery, you might follow the trail to the imposing **Marabout Sidi M'Barek ou Ali**. A high wall, broken only by a door, encloses the *marabout*, which doubles as a grain store – a powerful twofold protection on both spiritual and military levels.

El Kelâa des Mgouna

Travelling through the Dadès in spring, you'll find Skoura's fields delineated by the bloom of thousands of small, pink Persian roses – cultivated as hedgerows dividing the plots. At **EL KELÂA DES MGOUNA** (also spelt QALAT MGOUNA), 50km east across another shaft of semi-desert plateau, there are still more, along with an immense kasbah-like **rose-water factory**, *Capp et Florale*, where the *eau de rose* is distilled. In late May (sometimes early June), a **rose festival** is held in the village to celebrate the new year's crops: a good time to visit, with villagers coming down from the mountains for the market, music and dancing.

The rest of the year, El Kelâa's single, rambling street is less impressive. There's a **Wednesday souk**, worth breaking your journey for, but little else of interest beyond the locked and deserted ruins of a **Glaoui Kasbah**, on a spur above the river. The local shops are always full of *eau de rose*, though, and the factory can be visited, too, for a look at – and an overpowering smell of – the distillation process. A second factory, *Aromag*, 13km out along the Tinerhir road, can also be visited; it is run by a French company, based – of course – at Grasse.

Practicalities

The town has a single **bank** (*Banque Populaire*, as usual in the south) and two **hotels**. The cheap option, inconspicuously signposted on the main street, is the *Hôtel du Grand Atlas* (☎04/88.38.37; ⑩), a pleasant little place, with a hammam (free) and restaurant. It is run by Aaddi Lahcen and his son, Aaddi Hassan, who can put you in touch, if you wish, with guides for trekking in the Djebel Sarhro (see p.395) and Djebel Mgoun.

The other hotel, up by the Kasbah, is *Les Roses de Dadès* (☎04/88.38.07; ④), an old "Grand Hôtel du Sud", but without much character; it does, however, have a swimming pool, and a **riding stable**, offering treks to local Kasbahs and into the Djebel Sarhro (see p.395–98).

Vallée des Roses

If you have transport, this "secret valley" of the **Asif M'Goun**, north of El Kelâa, would make a good one-day excursion, or a detour en route to Boumalne. The valley begins due north of the town and is trailed by the minor road 6903 to TOURBIST and BOU THARAR, where the 6904 leads south back to EL GOUMT on the main P32 road; both should be practicable with a Renault 4. In spring, the route is lined by thousands of roses, and there is a notable Kasbah at Bou Tharar.

Boumalne du Dadès

BOUMALNE DU DADÈS is a more interesting stop than El Kelâa. It is again well poised for exploration of the Djebel Sarhro, and is the gateway to the Dadès Gorge. In addition, it has some charm of its own, with a pleasant site on a plateau above the Dadès, and a number of small, pleasant and reasonably priced hotels.

Arriving from the Ouarzazate side, you reach a small colonnaded square, with a covered market, *grand taxi* and bus stop, a couple of cafés and the old *Hôtel Adrar*. Uphill from here, on the plateau, are further hotels and facilities, including a PTT but no bank. Two **shops** here – the *Artisanale de Boumalne* and *Maison Aït Atta* – are worth looking round for a good range of carpets and carvings, on sale without great pressure. **Grands taxis** make regular runs to Ouarzazate and Tinerhir. For Msemrir and the Dadès Gorge, you can usually get a landrover taxi, transit or lorry; a regular transit/minibus leaves for Msemrir daily between noon and 2pm, returning at dawn the next morning.

The **hotels**, as usual in ascending order of price, are:

Hôtel Adrar (☎04/83.43.55). A good little hotel, handy for the buses and taxis, and with a terrace café-restaurant to sit and watch the day unfold. ⑩

Hôtel Salam. Up on the scarp, with (limited) views of the valley. Modern and reasonable, with showers on the corridor, and central heating in winter. ⑪

Hôtel Vallée des Oiseaux (☎04/83.41.38). A motel-style place offering a choice of cheap rooms without showers, and better ones, with. ①

Hôtel Chems (☎04/83.00.41). An attractive hotel, with a good restaurant and energetic proprietor. Hot showers in all the rooms. ①

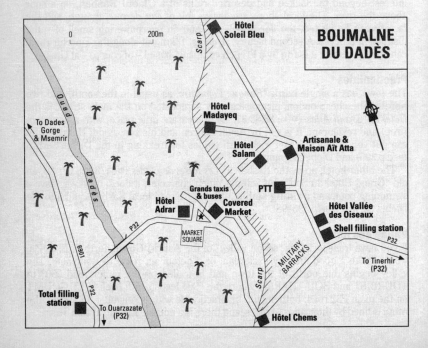

HAMMADA BIRDS AND THE VALLÉE DES OISEAUX

Boumalne offers some exceptional birdwatching possibilities – as can be seen from the logbook at the *Hôtel Soleil Bleu* (see below). To the south of the town are particularly abundant and accessible areas of **hammada** or desert fringe, and a grassy valley. The hammada provides an austere environment, whose dry, sunny conditions are ideal for cold-blooded reptiles and are frequented by Montpelier snake, Atlas agama and fringe-toed lizard. The **grassy plains** provide food for small herds of Edmi gazelle and Addax antelope and shelter for a variety of specialist bird species such as **cream-coloured courser, red-rumped wheatear** and **thick-billed lark**. Predatory **lanner falcon** and **long-legged buzzard** patrol the skies and the rare and elusive **Houbara bustard** makes an occasional appearance.

The most rewarding birding trip in the region is to the so-called **Vallée des Oiseaux**, which heads off the 6907 from Boumalne to Iknioune in the Djebel Sarhro, and heads off towards Tagdilt; it is marked by a line of green (picturesque) shading on the Michelin map. At Tagdilt, they make traditional pottery.

Hôtel Soleil Bleu (☎04/34.41.63). Reached along a piste, 300m beyond the *Hôtel Madayeq*, this has stunning views of the valley, and good, simple rooms with hot showers. It is run by Najim Lachen, who maintains a logbook for **birdwatchers**, with whom the hotel is popular. He also arranges tours and treks, locally for the day to the Vallée des Oiseaux and other promising locations (see box above), or further afield – including an epic trek over the High Atlas to Azilal. ①

Hôtel Madayeq (☎04/83.40.31). PLM chain hotel with four-star facilities (swimming pool, bar and restaurant) and views; from the outside it looks like a drunken Kasbah, made up of huge up-ended bricks. ④

An ambitious tourist complex, **Kasbah Tizarounc**, is planned alongside the Hôtel Chems, sharing its stunning views. It is scheduled to open in 1994.

All these hotels have **restaurants** – a few hours' notice may be required for meals – and, for simple Moroccan fare, the *Café Atlas*, on the market square, does an excellent *tajine*.

The Djebel Sarhro

The **Djebel Sarhro** (or Saghro) lies south of the road from Ouarzazate to Tinerhir and east of that from Ouarzazate to Zagora. It is a bleak but starkly beautiful jumble of volcanic peaks, quite unlike the High Atlas or Anti-Atlas, and punctuated by gorges, ruined Kasbahs, occasional villages, and the black tents of the semi-nomadic **Aït Atta** tribe. Fiercely independent through the centuries, and never subdued by any sultan, they were the last bulwark of resistance against the French, making their final stand on the slopes of Djebel Bou Gafer in 1933 (see box p.398).

Until recently, the Djebel Sarhro had seen few visitors but it is becoming better known and more accessible through **trekking** operators like *Explore* and *Exodus* (see p.6). They operate here from October to March, when the High Atlas is too cold and snow-covered for walking; in the summer, Sarhro itself is impracticable, being too hot and exposed, and with water, always scarce, almost impossible to find. Independent exploration of the range is possible by **car** (all roads on our map are passable by Renault 4 in reasonable weather) or, if you choose, on foot.

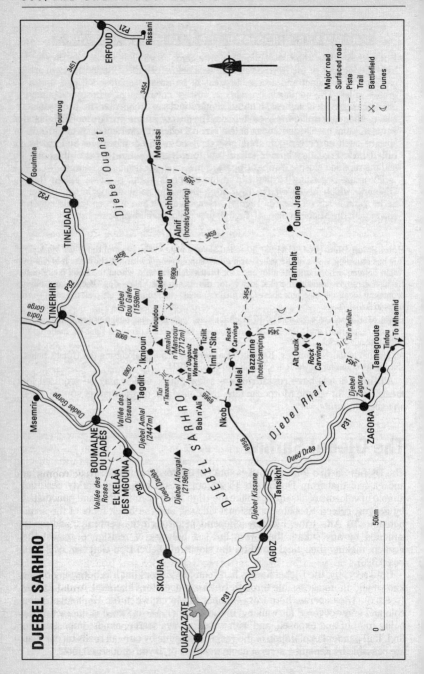

DJEBEL SARHRO

Major road
Surfaced road
Piste
Trail
Battlefield
Dunes

P21
ERFOUD
Rissani
3451
Touroug
3454
Goulmina
Mesissi
P32
Djebel Ougnat
3456
Achbarou
Alnif (hotels/camping)
Oum Jrane
TINEJDAD
3459
3458
Tarhbalt
TINERHIR
P32
6908
Kadem
3454
Djebel Bou Gafer (1598m)
Moudou
6069
6909
Iknioun
Amalou n Mansour (2712m)
Tizlit
Imi n'Site
Rock Carvings
Todra Gorge
3454
Tizi n Tafilalt
Tamegroute
To Mhamid
Tinfou
Tagdilt
Tizi n Tiazzert
Imi n Ougouiz Waterfalls
Tazzarine (hotel/camping)
Ait Ouzik
Rock Carvings
3454
Msemrir
Vallée des Oiseaux
8807
Djebel Amlal (2447m)
Mellal
6569
Djebel Rhart
ZAGORA
BOUMALNE DU DADES
Dades Gorge
Bab n'Ali
Nkob
P31
Djebel Zagora
Vallée des Roses
EL KELÂA DES MGOUNA
DJEBEL SARHRO
6958
Djebel Afougal (2196m)
Oued Drâa
P32
Oued Dades
Tansikht
Djebel Kissane
AGDZ
SKOURA
P31
50km
OUARZAZATE
0

If trekking, you are strongly advised to carry the appropriate **maps** and to use a **guide**. Locally, guides (and mules) are available through the *Hôtel du Grand Atlas* in El Kelâa des Mgouna, the *Hôtel Soleil Bleu* in Boumalne du Dadès, and the *Hôtel de l'Avenir* in Tinerhir; the latter also runs **landrover tours**.

Treks

When planning a trek, bear in mind the harshness of the terrain and the considerable distances involved. Given ten days, you could set out from El Kelâa des Mgouna, explore the area west of the **Tizi n'Tazazert** and loop back to El Kelâa or Boumalne. Alternatively, in about the same time, you could travel by local transport from Boumalne du Dadès or Tinerhir to **Iknioun** and then walk south, by **Djebel Bou Gafer**, to **Imi n'Site** and **Nkob**, taking transport from there either back to Boumalne or Tinerhir or across to Tansikht on the Ouarzazate–Zagora road. You could also do this in the opposite direction from the Drâa Valley.

Iknioun to Nekob

The easiest access to the range for **trekkers** is a transit taxi from Boumalne to **IKNIOUN**; this runs most days, but Wednesday, after the Boumalne *souk* is most reliable. There are rooms in Iknion, if you wish to stay. Alternatively, you can ask to be dropped at the junction of the piste 7km before Iknioun; (there is a large sign here, so you shouldn't miss it), which you could follow in two or three days' **walk to Nkob** (35km). The people at the village 1km along the Nkob road will provide rooms for a first night's stop, though walkers should be prepared to camp, beyond here. The Nkob *souk* is on a Sunday, so if you walk slowly, you can pick up a ride on the Saturday.

Following this route – which is practicable with a four-wheel-drive vehicle – it takes about an hour to a junction (at 2014m) to Tiouft: turn left here and climb steadily for an hour to a faux col, and then across an easy plateau for half an hour to the true col, **Tizi n'Tazazert** (2283m). From here, it's downhill, through rocky scenery, with table-top mesas and volcanic cones visible to the west; as you descend, there are traces of underground water, with palm trees in gullies, and camels grazing almost to the winter snowline.

The piste zigzags down for two hours, with a lot of shortcuts for walkers. The piste runs due south down the main valley to Nkob, but if you have energy, there's an interesting excursion off to the west, up a side valley, to the striking **mountain "gate" of Bab n'Ali**. At **NKOB** there is a café with basic **rooms**, and transits run to the main road at **TANSIKHT**, on the Drâa.

Other routes

In addition to the **north–south route over** the **Tizi n'Tazazert** to Tansikht, it is possible to drive over a much lower pass, the **Tizi n'Tafilalt**, to Zagora. The **east–west routes** between **Tansikht** and **Rissani** (in Tafilalt) are well established and are described at the end of the Drâa section (see p.389).

From these roads, there are astonishing views of the surrounding mountains, of which the most notable are **Djebel Afougal** (2196m), **Djebel Amlal** (2447m) and, the highest, **Amalou n'Mansour** (2712m). All of them are climbed by one or other of the trek operators. **Djebel Bou Gafer** (1598m) is lower and less remarkable but its history adds interest; it can be approached on foot from MOUDOU or KADEM, though either way a guide is again advisable and you may need to camp overnight to make the most of a visit to the battlefield.

THE BATTLE FOR BOU GAFER

For three centuries or more, the **Aït Atta** tribe were the great warriors of the south, dominating the Djebel Sarhro and its eastern extension, the Djebel Ougnat. At the turn of the century, the British journalist Walter Harris reported seeing the young men at Touroug, one of their tribal strongholds, practising running with galloping horses, holding onto their tails – a breakneck skill which enabled those on foot to travel as fast as the riders.

As guerrilla fighters, the Aït Atta resisted the French occupation from the outset. Led by **Hassou Ba Salem**, they finally retreated, at the beginning of 1933, to the rocky stronghold of the **Djebel Bou Gafer**, a chaos of gorges and pinnacles. Estimates vary, but the Aït Atta had at least a thousand fighting men, who, together with their families, totalled around 7,000 people, accompanied by their flocks. They faced vastly superior French forces. Ali, the son of Hassou Ba Salem, says that, according to his father, these included 83,000 troops and four aircraft squadrons.

The French first attacked the stronghold on 21 February and, after that, there were almost daily attacks on the ground and from the air. Many died on both sides but the Aït Atta did not surrender for over a month, by which time they were reduced to half their strength. The victors, moving in on 25 March, occupied, according to one of them, "an indescribable charnel house".

Hassou Ba Salem's conditions on surrender included a promise that the Aït Atta could maintain their tribal structures and customs, particularly insofar as law and order were concerned, and that they would not be "ruled" by the infamous T'Hami el Glaoui (see p.321), the Pasha of Marrakesh, whom they regarded as a traitor to their homeland. The French were content to accept, the battle meaning that their "pacification" was virtually complete, and giving them access to the valuable silver and copper mines at Moudou.

Hassou Ba Salem died in 1960 and was buried at Tagia, his birthplace, 5km from Tinerhir. Ali, his son, succeeded him as leader of the tribe, and took part in the 1975 Green March into the Western Sahara (see p.502). He died in 1992 and is also buried at Tagia. As for the battlefield itself, local guides will show you the sites, including ruins of the fortress. It is still littered with spent bullets, which are covered – and coloured in spring – by clumps of thyme, rock roses and broom.

Other attractions – less demanding – include the **Imi n'Ougoulz waterfalls** and **prehistoric rock carvings** near Mellal and Nkob (local guides are essential). Much more accessible is the **Vallée des Oiseaux**, off the Boumalne–Iknioun road (see wildlife box on p.395).

The Dadès Gorge

The **Dadès Gorge**, with its high cliffs of limestone and weirdly shaped erosions – begins almost as soon as you leave the P32 and head north of Boumalne on the road signposted "Mserhir" (Msemrir). Most travellers cover the first 25km or so by car or taxi, then turn back.

If you're equipped for an expedition route, however, or prepared to hitch (very sporadic) rides on local trucks, you can **loop over to the Todra Gorge** or continue up into (and across) the High Atlas. Alternatively, from Boumalne, a couple of days' walking along the gorge will reward you with superb scenery, and plenty of Kasbahs and *pisé* architecture to admire; there are rooms in several of the villages en route to Msemrir. The gorge is accessible by local transport from Boumalne, with Peugeot taxis, transit vans and Berber lorries (*camionettes*) leaving from the market square for Aït Ali (25km), Msemrir (63km), or occasionally to Atlas villages beyond. Returning to Boumalne, a transit/minibus leaves Msemrir daily at 4am.

See the map "Over the Atlas: Beyond Todra and Dades" on p.408 for routes.

Into the gorge: Boumalne to Msemir

For the first 15–20km, the **Dadès Gorge** is pretty wide and the valley carved out of it is green and well populated. There are *ksour* and Kasbahs clustered all along this stretch, many of them flanked now by more modern-looking houses, but usually retaining the decorative imagination of the traditional architecture.

Boumalne to Aït Oudinar

Just a couple of kilometres along the road (6901) into the gorge from Boumalne, you pass an old **Glaoui Kasbah**, strategically sited as always to control all passage. Three kilometres further in, where the road begins to turn into a hairpin corniche, there is a superb group of **ksour** at **AÏT ARBI**, built against a fabulous volcanic twist of the rocks. The Kasbahs seem like natural extensions of their setting – tinged with the colour of the earth and fabulously varied, ranging from bleak lime-white to dark reds and greenish blacks.

Some 10km on from here is a region known as **Tamnalt**, which is also known by the locals as the "Hills of Human Bodies" after its strange formations (which in fact mostly look like feet). You enter this region over a little pass, flanked by the *Café-Restaurant Meguirne*. The views make this a fine place to stop for lunch (as tour groups do) and it also has four basic and very cheap **rooms** for rent. A kilometre north, there are further rooms – slightly pricier but clean and quite reasonable – at the *Hôtel-Restaurant Kasba* (⑩), which again caters for tour-groups by day, laying on "Berber Weddings" in its courtyard.

On from here, the valley is less fertile and the hills lower. The road continues surfaced past the hamlet of AÏT ALI (23km from Boumalne) to a spot known as **Aït Oudinar**, where a bridge spans the river, and the gorge narrows quite dramatically. The *Auberge Gorges du Dadès* (⑩), by the bridge, is an attractive place to stay, offering a choice between cheap and basic **rooms**, or pricier ones with en suite hot showers, or **camping**; it also serves meals, and arranges **mule trips** with a guide (100dh a day).

Aït Oudinar to Msemrir

The road north of Aït Oudinar continues in bone-shaking fashion, and in a hire car you may decide to go no further. About 6km north of the bridge, however, there are three little **hotels** at one of the most spectacular stretches of the gorge – another very narrow section, full of hairpin bends. The hotels – *Auberge des Peupliers*, *Auberge Tisadrine* and *Hotel la Kasbah de la Vallée* (all ⑩) – again have a choice of basic and fancier en suite rooms.

At **AÏT HAMMOU**, 5km further on, at the north end of the gorge, there is also the basic (no electricity and an outside toilet) *Café-Hôtel Taghia* (⑩), with numerous **rooms** and a terrace. Walking from here, you can scramble up the hill east to a cave with stalactites, or go north to a small but impressive gorge, with views down over the Dadès Gorge.

The road gets worse still beyond here, and in spring is likely to be impassable due to flooding. At other times of year, however, you can drive to Msemrir – 63km, all in all, from Boumalne. Four kilometres before you reach Msemrir, a piste leads off to the left to the Vallée d'Oussikis – well worth a side trip if you have the time (and a sturdy vehicle).

On from Msemrir

At **MSEMRIR** there is another café with **rooms**, and a choice of piste routes: west to join the Todra Gorge at Tamtatouchte, or north across the High Atlas. People drive Renault 4s across both these routes in summer, but they are not really suitable transport – and will break rental conditions; these roads are really best left for lorries or landrovers with four-wheel drive – hairpin bends are routine and broken axles are not uncommon.

Over the Atlas

Heading over the High Atlas, the most direct route is to join the road from Todra at Agoudal: 60km or so of very rough driving, over the **Tizi n'Ouano**. Details of the route beyond (and an account of travel through these villages by Berber *camionettes*) is included in the Todra Gorge section (see p.406).

If you are looking for local transport, you may strike lucky with a lorry from Msemrir to Agoudal, but the route isn't driven nearly as regularly as that from Todra, so be prepared for a long wait at the Msemrir café.

Across to Tamtatoucht

If you are intent on **crossing to the Todra Gorges** to Tamtatoucht, there is virtually no chance of a local lorry, though you might just find a lift with fellow tourists. It should be added, too, that, if you are driving, you'd find it considerably easier to go in the other direction. Coming from the Dadès it's a long, uphill trek, and the seventy-odd kilometres of piste can take a full day to travel.

If you're determined, this is the route (with distances from Msemrir in brackets): leave Msemrir; ignore piste left to Imilchil (1km); ignore another piste to left (3km); pass over Tizi n'Uguert Zegzaoun, 2639m (16km); ignore piste to left (17km); ignore another little piste to left near end of descent (19km); another small pass with panoramic views (34km); ignore another piste left to Imilchil (38km); turn right just before the ravine (42km); reach Tamtatoucht (46km).

Tinerhir (Tinghir)

While **TINERHIR** again is pre-eminently a base – this time for the trip up into the **Todra Gorge** – it is a much more interesting town than other administrative centres along this route. Just east of the modern town is the Tinerhir **palmery**, which feels a world apart, with its groups of *ksour* built at intervals into the rocky hills above, while to the northeast is the Todra **palmery**, a prelude to the gorge. When passing through, don't be in too much of a hurry to catch the first lorry up to the Todra Gorge – these palmeries are major attractions in themselves.

The palmeries seem all the more special after the **journey from Boumalne**: a bleak drive across desolate plains, interrupted by the sudden oases of IMITER (with several fine Kasbahs) and TIMADRIOUINE. The **Djebel Sarhro** (see

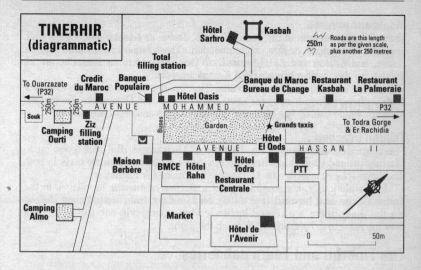

p.395–98) looms to the south for the latter part of the trip, dry barren outlines of mountains, like something from the Central Asia steppes; the drama of this part of the range was another big backdrop in David Lean's *Lawrence of Arabia*.

Orientation and accommodation

Orientation is pretty straightforward. The **buses** and **grands taxis** (standard runs to Boumalne/Er Rachidia) both stop at the arcaded **Place Principale**, and round the square are most of the town's other facilities – hotels, cafés, a couple of **banks** and a **PTT**. To the north is yet another **Glaoui Kasbah** – one of the grandest and most ornamental in the south, though very ruinous.

Accommodation is rarely a problem, with six hotels and two campsites:

Hôtel Oasis, Av. Mohammed V (no phone). Basic and a bit dilapidated. ①

Hôtel Raha, 8 Av. Hassan II (☎04/83.43.79). Another basic hotel – and again not great. ①

Hôtel El Qods, Av. Hassan II (no phone). Much better and only marginally more expensive, this is a new, small hotel with reliable hot showers, and a fine restaurant. ①

Hôtel Todra, Av. Hassan II (☎04/83.42.49). A rambling old building with kitsch decor (created by the Jewish former owner), reasonable en suite rooms, a restaurant and bar. ②

Hôtel de l'Avenir, near the central market (☎04/83.46.04). An excellent new hotel, well furnished, and run by a Spaniard, Roger Mimó, who is quite an authority on the mountains hereabouts. He offers landrover tours, can arrange trekking guides, and will give up-to-date advice if you are planning your own trip. He also has bicycles for hire for exploring the Tinerhir/Todra oases. Reservations highly recommended. ②

Hôtel Saghro, by the Kasbah (☎04/83.41.81). The town's "luxury" hotel has a swimming pool and pleasant views, but it's not the best choice in the south to splash out on. ④

CAMPSITES

Camping Ourti, Av. Mohammed V (☎04/83.32.05). A new site, enthusiastically managed and with a good range of facilities – including hot showers and a swimming pool. Also has a few bungalows, which sleep up to three people.

Camping Almo, off Av. Mohammed V (☎04/83.43.14). Another good site, longer established, and so with a little more shade. Hot showers, a small shop, and a swimming pool.

Meals and carpets

There are **restaurants** at the hotels *El Qods*, *Todra*, *de l'Avenir* and *Saghro* – all, save the overpriced *Saghro*, recommended. The restaurants *Central*, in the centre, and *Kasbah* and *La Palmeraie*, on the road out to Er Rachidia, are all good, too – the (relatively upmarket) *Kasbah*, especially.

If you're interested in buying **crafts**, Tinerhir has a branch of the excellent *Maison Berbère* chain (run by the same family as those in Ouarzazate, Zagora and Rissani), which usually has high-quality rugs, carpets and especially silver.

Tinerhir transport

There are regular **buses** from Tinerhir to Ouarzazate (the 6am goes on to Marrakesh) and Er Rachidia from the Place Principale, and **grands taxis** in both directions (places available for Ourzazate/Boumalne/Er Rachidia).

More ambitiously, it's possible to get a Berber *camionette* to villages in the **Todra Gorge and beyond** (see p.405); on Mondays, from around noon (following the *souk*), there are several lorries leaving – including one that goes right over the Atlas to Arbala, driving through the night.

The Tinerhir and Todra palmeries

There are **palmeries** to the southeast and northeast of Tinerhir, lining both sides of the Todra River. To get something of an overview, the *Hôtel Saghro* has the town's best mirador. To explore, you're best off hiring a **bike** from Roger Mimó at the Hôtel de l'Avenir, and discussing a route with him; the map opposite was based upon his sketches. Alternatively, you could hire a mule – and arrange a guide – in one of the oasis villages.

The oasis follows the usual pattern in these valleys: date palms at the edge, terraces of olive, pomegranate, almond and fruit trees further in, with grain and vegetable crops planted beneath them. The **ksour** each originally controlled one section of the oasis, and there were frequent disputes over territory and, above all, over access to the mountain streams for each *ksour*'s network of water channels. Even in this century, the fortifications were built in earnest, and, as Walter Harris wrote (melodramatically, but probably with little exaggeration): "The whole life was one of warfare and gloom. Every tribe had its enemies, every family had its blood feuds, and every man his would-be murderer."

The map opposite indicates other good viewing points, or **miradors**, along with the most picturesque villages – many of which have **ksour and Kasbahs** with extraordinarily complex patterns incised on the walls. Some include former Jewish quarters – Mellahs – though today the populations are almost entirely Berber and Muslim, mainly from the Aït Atta tribe (see p.398).

TODRA WILDLIFE AND BIRDS

The **Todra Gorge** offers excellent wildlife opportunities. Along the **riverbeds** are colonies of marsh frog and green toad, while the rocky slopes provide shelter for small numbers of ground squirrel. The **scrubby areas** ring to the calls of common bulbul and the **rocky outcrops** provide occasional glimpses of black wheatear, blue rock thrush and rock dove. There are also good numbers of pale crag martin wheeling overhead and soaring above the gorge crest and, if you strike lucky, it is possible to observe the pair of **Bonelli's eagles** which nest in the gorge.

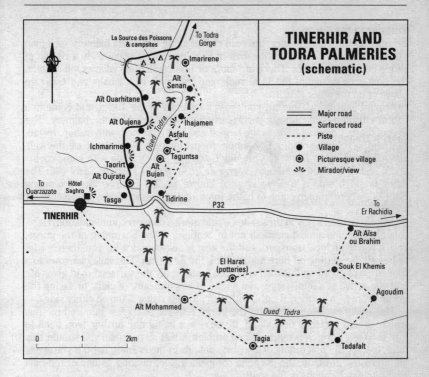

South of Tinerhir there are potteries at **El Harat**, while at nearby **Tagia** are the tombs of the Aït Atta's chiefs, Hassan Ba Salam, and his son, Ali Ba Salam (see p.398). For more on the **Todra palmery** – and approach to the gorge – see below.

The Todra Gorge

Whatever else you do in the south, at least spend a night at the **Todra Gorge** (also spelt Todhra or Toughda). You don't need your own transport, nor any great expeditionary zeal, to get up there, and yet it seems totally remote from the routes through the main valleys – very still, very quiet and magnificent in the fading evening light. The highest, narrowest and most spectacular part of the gorge is only 15km from Tinerhir, and there are three small hotels at its mouth where you can get a room or sleep on the terrace or roof. Beyond here, the road turns into a piste and you're into true isolation: a route you can take all the way over the Atlas, if you can time your visit to fit in with the schedules of Berber lorries or, if driving yourself, you have considerable confidence and a very reliable and sturdy car.

From Tinerhir, the mouth of the gorge (15km) can be reached either by Peugeot **grand taxi** or **transit van**: both leave regularly through the day and charge around 6dh a place. Returning to Tinerhir, you stand a better chance of a taxi if you walk back down to the last village before the gorge; alternatively, it's usually pretty simple to get a lift back with other tourists.

Tinerhir to the gorge

En route to the gorge proper, the road climbs along the Todra palmery (see map on previous page), a last, fertile shaft of land, narrowing at points to a ribbon of palms between the cliffs. There are more or less continuous villages, all of them the pink-grey colour of the local rock, and the ruins of Kasbahs and *ksour* up above or on the other side.

Around 9km from Tinerhir, you cross a tributary of the Todra, and come to a trio of **campsites**, flanking a particularly luxuriant stretch of the palmery. The first of these, *Camping Atlas*, is the largest and best equipped, with a shop, restaurant and, across the road, a few simple rooms for rent. Next along are the well-shaded *Camping du Lac* (aka *Camping Garden of Eden*), again with some rooms and a restaurant, and *Camping/Auberge de la Source des Possions Sacré* (⑩). The latter is set beside a freshwater pool known as "**La Source des Poissons Sacrés**", where women come to bathe (on three successive Fridays) as a cure for sterility.

Anywhere else, a stay at these sites would merit a major recommendation. Here, though, it seems almost churlish not to continue to the beginning of the gorge, and, if you're on local transport, and the heat is not too much for you, there's a lot to be said for getting off here and walking the final 6km. The valley narrows to a thin stripe of green on this final approach, until finally the surfaced road gives out and you arrive at a mini-gorge, and a kind of amphitheatre of cliffs, prefacing the **gorge** proper – a wonderful sight, with canyon walls rising 300m on either side.

This really enclosed section of the gorge runs for just a few hundred metres, which should certainly be walked, if you're not going any further (you need to ford the river – which is not usually a problem). If at all possible, you should stay here, too, for the real drama of the place unfolds in the evening light. If you are at all interested in **birds**, the gorge is compelling, too, ranking as one of the best birdwatching locations in the south.

Staying at the mouth of the gorge

Just before the mini-gorge, at the end of the surfaced road, is the *Hôtel El Mansour* (no phone; ⑩) an attractively ramshackle place, with a pair of palm trees growing out through the roof, excellent and copious meals, and a choice of sleeping in rooms, on the roof (the best option in summer) or on couches downstairs.

A couple of hundred metres round the corner, in the throat of the gorge itself, are two more hotels, the *des Roches* (no phone; ⑩) and *Yasmina* (☎04/83.30.13; ③), both established in the 1930s. These are slightly fancier places, with restaurants (and bars) catering for the half-dozen tour groups shuttled up each day, and mules available for trips up the gorge. Both have excellent food – the set lunches are a bargain – and a choice of accommodation, including modern en suite rooms, or cheaper beds in the salon or tent dining rooms, or out on the terrace.

All three of these hotels are very friendly and relaxed – and all are very cold in winter, when the sun leaves the gorge early in the afternoon. If you wanted to camp, you would do better walking four or five kilometres up the gorge, to reach a more open section; there are plenty of good spots to put up a tent by the river.

Climbing

The Todra Gorge is increasingly being recognised for its climbing potential. There are now many bolted routes, French Grade 5 and above. The *Hôtel El Mansour* keeps an excellent French topo-guide for reference.

Beyond Todra: over the Atlas

It is possible to continue on piste routes beyond the Todra Gorge to **Tamtatoucht**, and from there across the High and Middle Atlas ranges, to emerge on either the P24 (Azrou–Beni Mellal), or the P21 (Midelt–Er Rachidia). In between, you are travelling on isolated and at times very rough tracks, for which four-wheel-drive vehicles (or mountain bikes) are highly desirable, though people make it across in Renaults or Citroens in summer. If you don't have transport, you can travel on a succession of **Berber lorry-taxis** (*camionettes*), timed to coincide with local village *souks*. The attractions of this journey are considerable, offering a real experience of Berber mountain life – the villagers are generally very open and friendly – and some of the most exciting scenery in Morocco, with a succession of fabulous passes, mountains, rivers and gorges.

It is also possible to cross from the Todra Gorge to the **Dadès Gorge**, on a rough piste from Tamtatoucht (see below).

Some practicalities

There are no **banks** between Tinerhir and Khenifra/Kasba Tadla/Rich, so you'll need to have enough cash for the journey. Don't underestimate the expense of buying **food** in the mountains (30–100 percent above normal rates), nor the prices charged for rides in the **Berber lorries**; as a very general guideline, reckon on about 20dh for every 50km. There are police stations at Aït Hani and Imilchil if you need serious help or advice on the state of the pistes.

Setting out on the **lorries** from Todra, the managers of the hotels at the mouth of the gorge usually have an idea of when the next *camionette* will pass through – and they will help arrange your first ride. Promising days to start out are **Wednesday** (to coincide with Aït Hani's Thursday *souk*) and **Friday** (for Imilchil's Saturday *souk*), but it is all a bit pot luck, and you should be prepared for the odd day's wait in a village for a ride, or to walk one or other of the stages of the route. Eventually, everyone seems to get across to **Arhbala** or **Naour** (where there are buses down to Kasba Tadla/Khenifra) or to **Rich** (on the Midelt–Er Rachidia road and bus route); heading for Rich, the most used route is the 3443 from Bouzmou.

Travelling from the **north or east**, the same pattern applies, with lorries up from Arhbala/Rich for the Imilchil *souk*, and down to Todra/Tinerhir after it.

Driving, it would be unwise to attempt the route, without a four-wheel-drive vehicle outside the midsummer period of **June to September**.

Some routes

The road up the Todra Gorge (from the hotels) is the worst section of the route, the track comprising little more than the stones of the river path. After 17km, you reach **TAMTATOUCHT**, quite a sizeable village, with several basic **hotels** and café-restaurants. Beyond this point, the road improves considerably, though it is still unsurfaced and slow, difficult mountain driving.

It's at Tamtatouchte that anyone intent on **crossing over to the Dadès Gorge** (see p.399) should turn off to the west, on the piste 3444 to MSEMRIR; lifts are most unlikely, so it's basically an option for drivers. Leaving Tamtatouchte, head left just before the ravine (2km); ignore the piste off to Imilchil on your right (8km); go over a small, panoramic pass (12km); begin an ascent to the main col, ignoring a piste to the right (27km); ignore another piste to the right (29km);

BY BERBER TAXIS ACROSS THE ATLAS

Dan Richardson and Jill Denton set out from the Todra Gorge to cross the Atlas on Berber lorries. They travelled in midsummer, along with a Belgian who had a useful smattering of Arabic phrases; they themselves had reasonable French. Their account was included in former editions of this guide for a flavour of the route, and is reprinted again, though one correspondent notes that it "over-emphasises the difficulty of the crossing, which is very well used by local people".

As we clambered into the back of the lorry the hotel owner tried to dissuade us. "You don't want to go there . . . This lorry's only going as far as Aït Hani – it's a horrible place . . . ". But after fourteen hours waiting on the porch of the Hôtel El Mansour for a lift we weren't going to be deterred. Whatever was up there in the mountains – the maps were enticingly vague – we meant to find out.

The lorry bumped and strained along the unpaved track, swathed in choking dust, and climbed steadily up out of the Todra Gorge. As the sun fell, the stars gradually emerged until the bowl of the sky sparkled with dozens of constellations and shooting stars. After four hours, we reached a vast plateau and the gates of **Aït Hani**, incongruously manned by an armed soldier. Inside the village – a jumbled blur of mud huts and towers – there was a lengthy discussion on what to do with the *Nazarenes* (Christians). Finally, a man offered us his stable, outside the village. Despite our misgivings, he did us proud, bringing rugs for the floor and reappearing the next morning with mint tea, bread, and his wife, who was entranced by our foreign appearance. We found *her* looks fascinating, too – a tattooed chin, luminous eyes and a bizarre dress resembling a huge tinfoil doily shot with pale blue threads.

It was only in the daylight that we understood the previous day's warnings. The mountain, plateau and buildings were uniformly barren and colourless, except for a few tiny plots of withered vegetables. People peered at us from courtyards and from behind grilled windows, ignoring our tentative greetings, and our host of the night before led us to a low mud building bearing (in English) the name of "The Modern Coffee House". This title, we later learned, had been bestowed by a lone Englishman who had been marooned for four days in the village. We were luckier – we only had to wait for two.

Once the sun was up, swarms of flies would lift off from piles of dung and come to crawl all over us. The heat kept everyone indoors and there was little to do but drink mint tea and gaze at the decor of the coffee house: sooty mud walls, pastel colours and a collage of sardine cans, postcards and Koranic inscriptions. The proprietor was a diminutive, dessicated ancient who vastly enjoyed our plight and told us that the next lorry wasn't due "for some time, if Allah wills it", and in the meantime, wouldn't we like some food, which he could procure with great difficulty? Naturally, the prices were astronomical, though we couldn't really blame him, for in a village where agriculture had almost collapsed due to years of drought, and most of the young men had fled, we represented a veritable goldmine.

When we eventually left Aït Hani, it was in a subdued state – obvious enough to the lorry driver, too, for he demanded an enormous price for the ride to Imilchil, which, stupidly, we paid. A cardinal rule of this kind of travel is to pay only on arrival at your destination, as the Berbers do themselves, and it was all too predictable when, five hours later, the driver pulled into a village some 50km short of our destination and announced he was going no further. Our protests were useless – the man shrugged, pretended to speak no French, and smirked at the other passengers. Then, inspired, the Belgian we were travelling with quoted a Koranic phrase equivalent to "by their deeds shall ye know them", adding, for good measure, that the driver's behaviour was "not beautiful" (*hyrba*) in the sight of Allah. The effect was miraculous. The driver shrivelled with humiliation and returned half the money to us. In a more cheerful mood, we surveyed the village of Bouzmou, found an excellent teahouse on the roadside, and a cheerful lad to show us around.

Bouzmou was delightful: domed, honey-coloured houses, lofty trees, a gushing spring and a football match with fifty participants stirring up the dust in the *place*. Enchanting little girls with hennaed hair and huge earrings, torn between fear and the desire to touch us, scurried back and forth, clinging to each other and shrieking with laughter. The women were straightforward and curious to talk to us, a rarity in Morocco – even in the more "open" communities of Berber villages. Jill was swiftly "adopted", lent a shawl, and her eyebrows and cheeks hennaed. It was proposed that the women tattoo her as well, though the needle was like a cobbler's awl and caked with grime.

Later, we were all directed to a small square where a rain dance was just beginning. Villagers formed circles around the dancers, beating tom-toms and uttering shrill cries. Once we were discovered, they demanded that we join in. Despite the clouds of dust, the noise and the heat, we gave a good ten-minute performance, hoping foolishly that the rain would fall and make us village heroes (it didn't).

Next morning – a Monday – nomads came in for the *souk* with their sheep herds roped neck to neck, to buy clothing, salt and tinware. Among the curiosities on sale were white rocks, which if burned "would reveal in the fire the face of your secret enemy", and smooth, sweet-smelling stones to be used as an "aftershave".

We had to leave Bouzmou that afternoon, for our money was low and all the lorries were departing, laden with sheep and people. Our own – and we counted – held some thirty sheep on the upper deck, an unknown number on the lower, and 28 Berbers balanced on the rails and luggage racks. In the scorching heat, at an average speed of 20km an hour, we spent the next six hours ascending tortuous roads, circumventing precipices, and seeming to *accelerate* as we approached blind corners. At every bend, the sheep bleated with fear and pissed and crapped over everyone's feet and luggage, while above them a Berber periodically unwrapped from the folds of his *djellabah* a hunk of fresh mutton, which he prodded appreciatively.

At some point in the journey, we passed through the village of **Imilchil**, and skirted one of the azure, salt-rimmed lakes on the **Plateau des Lacs**. We saw black nomad tents pegged in the wilderness, the occasional camel, and dozens of donkeys laden down with firewood from the distant forests. At a crossroads, around 15km from Arhbala, we got down from the sheep lorry and picked up another – this time comparatively luxurious with its freight of rough-cut stones.

Arhbala, a small town surrounded by soft mountains and oak and cedar forests, seemed almost metropolitan with its semi-paved streets, electric lighting and double row of shops and cafés. There was no bus to Khenifra, where we hoped to change money, until 3am but, as is common in Morocco, we were "adopted" and taken home to be fed. The meal – *couscous* specially prepared in our honour – was delicious and our host and two older, male companions were hospitable. It left a sour taste, though, as the light bulb in the kitchen was brought out to give us extra light, leaving the man's wife and daughters (who had prepared the meal but not appeared) to crouch over the remains of the meal in the dark.

Around one o'clock, we left for the bus, crawled onto the seats and tried to sleep. Arguments blew around us, but the journey was straightforward and, after the mountains, routine and anticlimactic. At **Khenifra** we were back on the main road to Fes and all that civilisation had to offer: croissants, squat toilets and banks.

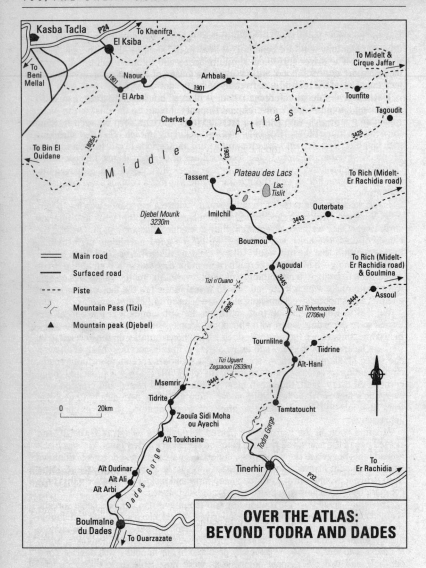

Kasba Tadla

To Khenifra

El Ksiba

To Beni Mellal

Naour

El Arba

Arhbala

To Midelt & Cirque Jaffar

Tounfite

Tagoudit

Cherket

Middle Atlas

To Bin El Ouidane

Tassent

Plateau des Lacs

Lac Tislit

To Rich (Midelt-Er Rachidia road)

Djebel Mourik 3230m

Imilchil

Outerbate

Bouzmou

Agoudal

To Rich (Midelt-Er Rachidia road) & Goulmina

Tizi n'Ouano

Tizi Tirherhouzine (2706m)

Assoul

Tournlilne

Tiidrine

Aït-Hani

| Main road |
| Surfaced road |
| Piste |
| Mountain Pass (Tizi) |
| Mountain peak (Djebel) |

Tizi Uguert Zegzaoun (2639m)

Msemrir

Tidrite

Zaouïa Sidi Moha ou Ayachi

Tamtatoucht

0   20km

Aït Toukhsine

Todra Gorge

Aït Oudinar
Aït Ali
Aït Arbi

Dades Gorge

Tinerhir

To Er Rachidia

P32

Boulmalne du Dades

To Ouarzazate

**OVER THE ATLAS:
BEYOND TODRA AND DADES**

cross the 2639m Tizi Uguert Zegzaoun (30km); ignore another piste to the right (43km); ignore the road on the right that leads to Agoudal/Imilchil (45km); reach Msemrir (46km).

Continuing north from Tamtatoucht into the High Atlas, you need to head towards **AÏT HANI**, another large village, almost the size of Tamtatouchte. It's just off the main route, and if you're driving you can keep going, turning after the town, rather than into it. On the outskirts, as you approach from the south, there is a police/military post, café and store; there's no regular accommodation (but see the account on p.406–7). This region is generally high and barren landscape – the locals travel amazing distances each day to collect wood for fuel. (A poor and little-used piste leads east from Aït Hani towards Goulmina/Rich).

North of Aït Hani there is a stiff climb up to 2700m at **Tizi Tirherhouzine**, then down to **AGOUDAL**. This is a friendly village, and though there is no official hotel, you'll probably be offered a room. It is in a less harsh setting, too, better irrigated, and people seem more relaxed than at Aït Hani.

There is the chance of a room at **BOUZMOU**, too, the next village on, where you might also pick up a *camionette* along piste 3443 to Rich on the Midelt–Er Radchidia road. This is the most commonly used (and best condition) route east from the Imilchil road and sees a lot more traffic than pistes 3444 or 34425.

The road north improves greatly from Agoudal on, passing beyond Bouzmou through a fertile region to **IMILCHIL** (45km from Agoudal). This beautiful village, with a fine caidal Kasbah, is for most people the highlight of the route. It is famed for its **September moussem** – the so-called *Marriage Market of Aït Haddidou*. The *moussem*, once a genuine tribal function, is now somewhat corrupted by tourism (groups are shuttled up from Marrakesh), but it's a lively, extravagant occasion all the same. Imilchil has a couple of small **hotels** and café-restaurants. It also has several resident guides; Bassou Chabout (postal address: 51930 Imilchil Centre, Province d'Er Rachidia) is reliable and qualified.

To the east of Imilchil is the so-called **Plateau des Lacs** – flanked by the twin mountain lakes of **Isli** and **Tislit**. Some groups go up here to camp, but it's not especially compelling. The route north of Imilchil to Arhbala, by contract, runs through spectacular scenery, with steep drops off the road side, constant climbs and descents, and a slow move into forestation. This section has few settlements – and certainly nowhere the size of Imilchil.

A paved road starts a few miles after **CHERKET**. At **ARHBALA** (see p.225), there is a very basic hotel near the marketplace (Wednesday *souk*), and a daily bus on to El Ksiba (see Chapter Three), where you can pick up connections to Khenifra and Beni Mellal.

Tinerhir to Er Rachidia and Erfoud

East from Tinerhir, there is little to delay your progress to **Erfoud/Er Rachidia** and the Tafilalt. The more attractive route is the minor road (3451) from **Tinejdad to Erfoud**; the **Er Rachidia road** (P32) is a fast but dull highway; neither presents any problems for drivers, though be sure to have water and a spare tyre for the 3451, which sees little traffic.

Using local transport, you can get buses or *grands taxis* along the P32 to Er Rachidia; the taxis involve changes at **Tinejdad** (buses and taxis leave from the east end of the town) and **Goulmima**. Alternatively, a private-line bus leaves Tinejdad (from the square used by the *grands taxis*, on the main road) daily at 9.30am along the 3451 **to Erfoud and Rissani**, arriving at Rissani about four hours later; to make the connection, get a *grand taxi* from Tinerhir to Tinejdad.

To Er Rachidia via Goulmima

This is a straightforward and largely barren route, broken only by the oases of Tinejdad and Goulmima.

GOULMIMA (or Goulmina) a long, straggling palmery, is made up of some twenty or so scattered **ksour**. If you have transport, and are interested in exploring, ask directions along the complex network of tracks to the *ksour* known as **Gheris de Charis**, the grandest in the palmery.

Modern Goulmima, beside the highway, is signalled by the usual "triumphal" entrance and exit arches of the south, and has little more within. There is, however, a *Banque Populaire*, and a small **hotel-restaurant**, the *Gheris* (☎05/ 78.31.67; ①). (*Camping Tamarisk*, signposted at this *ksar*, has been closed for some years). **Buses** leave from the street to the left of the eastern archway exit (coming from Tinerhir), **grands taxis** from further up this street.

To Erfoud via Tinejdad

This alternative route – **direct to Erfoud** – is, in parts, eerily impressive. It is paved all the way to Erfoud, though sections are sometimes covered over with sand, the result of small, spiralling sandstorms that can suddenly blow across the region and, for twenty or thirty seconds, cut visibility to zero.

The road branches off from the P32 to Er Rachidia at **TINEJDAD** and follows much of the course of this oasis – a lush strip populated by the Aït Atta tribe, traditional warriors of the south who used to control land and exact tribute as far afield as the Drâa (see p.382). There are some impressive Kasbahs – ask directions to the **Kasbah Asrir** – and, in the modern, one-street village, numerous cafés, and a couple of filling stations. The *Hôtel Tizgui* was closed at last report, but there are rooms at the *Café-Restaurant Al Fath*. You leave the oasis at **MELLAB**, which has another fine **ksar**, and from then on it's more or less continuous desert *hammada* until the beginning of the vast palmery of **EL DJORF** – the Tafilalt's largest *ksar* (6000 population) – on the approach to Erfoud. There are a few cafés in the modern village, a post office and a filling station, but no hotel.

Beside the road, over much of the distance from Mellab to Erfoud, the land is pockmarked by strange, volcanic-shaped humps – actually man-made entries to the old underground **irrigation channels** or *khettara*. Another curiosity, notable here and elsewhere along the oasis routes, are the Berber **cemeteries** walled off from the desert at the edge of the *ksour*. These consist of long fields of pointed stones thrust into the ground (but otherwise unidentified), a wholly practical measure to prevent jackals from unearthing bodies – and in so doing, frustrating their entry to paradise.

ER RACHIDIA, THE ZIZ VALLEY AND THE TAFILALT

The great date-palm oases of the **Oued Ziz** and **Tafilalt** come as near as anywhere in Morocco to fulfilling Western fantasies about the Sahara. They do so by occupying the last desert stretches of the **Ziz** Valley: a route shot through with lush and amazingly cinematic scenes, from its fertile beginnings at the *Source Bleu* (springwater pool) and the oasis meeting point of **Meski**, to an eventual climax amid the rolling sand dunes of **Merzouga**. Along the way, once again, are an impressive succession of *ksour*, and an extraordinarily rich palmery – historically the most important territory this side of the Atlas.

Strictly speaking, the Tafilalt (or Tafilalet) comprises the oases south of **Erfoud**, its principal town and gateway. Nowadays, however, the provinical capital is the French-built garrison town and administrative centre of **Er Rachidia**. If you're making a circuit of the south, you will pass through here, from or en route to Midelt – a journey through the great canyon of the **Ziz Gorges** (see p.223). Er Rachidia is also a crossroads for the route east to Figuig and Algeria (see p.422).

Er Rachidia, Meski and the Ziz Valley

ER RACHIDIA was established by the French as a regional capital – when it was known as *Ksar es Souk*, after their Foreign Legion fort. Today, it represents more than anywhere else the new face of the Moroccan south: a shift away from the old desert markets and trading routes to a modern urban centre. The town's role as a military outpost, originally against tribal dissidence, particularly from the Aït Atta (see p.398), was maintained after independence by the threat of territorial claims from Algeria, and there is still a significant garrison here, even though Morocco's military problems are now hundreds of miles distant, in the Western Sahara.

The town is, in fact, quite a pleasant and relaxed place to stay, with an air of relative prosperity, and a large student population, at the lycée and colleges. In the evenings, the streets come alive, with groups strolling along the main street and packing into the cafés.

Orientation, rooms and food

Er Rachidia has a functional grid lay-out, with most facilities (banks, cafés and restaurants, a covered market and tourist office) strung along the highway/main street – **Av. Moulay Ali Cherif**. This runs all the way through town, between the standard pair of ceremonial arches, turning into **Av. El Massira** after crossing the bridge over the Oued Ziz.

All **buses** arrive at the main bus station, on the Place Principale, just south of Av. Moulay Ali Cherif. **Grands taxis** leave both from here and from Place Hassan II to the north: check on your destination before setting out with baggage.

HOTELS
There is a good range of **hotels** in town. If you want to **camp**, however, it's best to press on to the highly enticing *Source Bleu* at Meski, 18km south (see following section); the Er Rachidia *Camping Municipal*, signposted just across the bridge, has no facilities.

Hôtel Zitoun [D], 25 Place Hassan II (☎05/57.24.49). Basic rooms, with cold showers on the corridor. ①

Hôtel Royal [C], 8 Rue Mohammed Zerktouni (☎05/57.30.68). Slightly preferable but signposted in Arabic only, as is the nearby *Hôtel Marhaba* – which is dire. ①

Hôtel Renaissance [A], 19 Rue Moulay Youssef (☎05/57.26.33). This is very much the best cheap choice, offering clean, simple rooms, some with showers (steaming hot!), and a decent restaurant. ①

Hôtel Meski [off map], Av. Moulay Ali Cherif (☎05/57.20.65). A pleasant old hotel with a swimming pool, a restaurant and a non-alcoholic bar; it is 400m out of town, on the right as you come in from Midelt or Goulmima. ②

Hôtel de l'Oasis [B], Rue Sidi Bou Abdallah (☎05/57.25.19). A fine central hotel, well-managed by a charming Moroccan woman, and with a restaurant and bar. ②

Hôtel Rissani [E], Av. El Massira (☎05/57.21.86). A typical PLM chain hotel, just across the bridge. Nothing special but there's a good-sized pool. ①

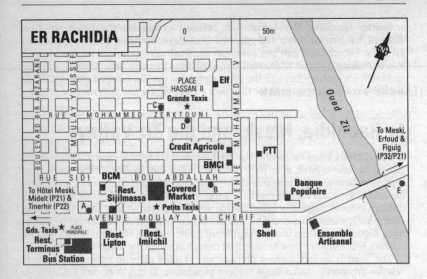

RESTAURANTS

You can eat well at the hotels *Renaissance*, *Meski*, *Oasis* and *Rissani*. Alternatively, there are any number of cafés and restaurants, of which the following, all on Av. Moulay Ali Cherif, are recommended:

Restaurant Imilchil. Excellent food and an attractive setting, with a terrace and garden.

Café Jour et Nuit. Just the one dish – but it's very good: marinated brochettes with a delicious tomato relish.

Restaurant Terminus. Handy for the bus station and reasonable value.

Restaurant Sijilmassa. Again a decent choice near the bus station.

Restaurant Lipton. Another reasonable choice, good for breakfast.

Directory

Banks There are four banks – *Banque Populaire*, *Crédit Agricole*, *BMCI* and *BMC* – all shown on the map. If you're going on to Figuig and Algeria you'll need to change travellers' cheques here.

Buses leave at least four times a day for Erfoud/Rissani, and a similar number head north to Midelt and Fes or Meknes, via the dramatic Ziz Gorge. The *CTM* bus to Ouarzazate goes on to Marrakesh. Note that the only bus to Figuig leaves at 5am (passing the turnoff for Meski about 25 minutes later – where you could flag it down).

Car repairs/spare parts There is a Renault agent by the *Elf* garage on Place Hassan II, which carries a large supply of parts and will order others efficiently from Fes.

Filling stations *Shell* and *Elf* filling stations are shown on the map. There is also a *Ziz* station on the Midelt road, and a *Somepi* station on the Erfoud road.

Grands taxis It is usually no problem to get a seat in a *grand taxi* to Erfoud or, paying the same price, to the Meski turning; these leave from opposite the bus station, as do grands taxis to Tinerhir. *Grands taxis* from Place Hassan II run to other destinations.

Petits taxis leave from outside the covered market on Av. Moulay Ali Cherif.

Post office The *PTT* on Av. Mohammed V – see map – has all usual services.

Shops There is a rather dismal *Ensemble Artisanal* on Av. Moulay Ali Cherif, and, for provisions, a covered market.

Tourist office The *Syndicat d'Initiative* on Av. Moulay Ali Cherif is very closed. However, there's a helpful *Délégation du Tourisme*, alongside the *Hôtel Meski*, if you want detailed information or guidance on anything in the province.

Tours The *Hôtel Renaissance* offers landrover expeditions.

Meski: the Source Bleu

The small palm grove of **MESKI** centres on a natural springwater pool – the famous **source bleue**, created by the French Foreign Legion and long a postcard image of the south and favourite camping site for travellers. It is set on the riverbank, opposite a huge ruined *ksar*, and with several of the springs channelled into a **swimming pool**, it is as romantic a campsite as any you're likely to find.

In recent years, the **campsite** was poorly maintained but its management seems to have got a grip on the place and it is, once again, highly recommended. The pool is enticing again (it is moving springwater, so said to be safe from bilharzia); the toilets are also flushed by springwater; and the camping areas are shaded by bamboo, palms and tamarisks. The site is inexpensive, too, charging just 7dh per person, 10dh per car, or 20dh for a campervan. A café-restaurant is open sporadically, but meals are usually available, given a little notice.

The *source* is somewhat insignificantly signposted, to the right of the Erfoud road, 18km south of Er Rachidia. Coming by bus, ask to get out by the turnoff: from here it's only 400m down to the pool and campsite. **Going on** to Erfoud or back to Er Rachidia from Meski can be tricky, since most of the buses pass by full and don't stop. However, this is an easy place to hitch a lift from other tourists.

If it's not midsummer, you might also consider walking part of the way south from Meski. A superb four-hour **trek** downstream along the Oued Ziz will bring you to **Oulad Aïssa**, a *ksar* with fabulous views over the upper Tafilalt.

South from Meski: the Ziz palmery

Heading south from Meski, **towards Erfoud**, the road (P21) trails the final section of the **Oued Ziz**: make sure you travel this in daylight, for it's one of the most pleasing of all the southern routes: a dry red belt of desert just beyond Meski, and then, suddenly, a drop into the valley and the great **Tizimi palmery** – a prelude of the Tafilalt, leading into Erfoud. Away from the road, **ksour** are almost continuous – glimpsed through the trees and the high walls enclosing gardens and plots of farming land.

If you want to stop and take a closer look at the *ksour*, **AOUFOUSS**, midway to Erfoud, and the site of a **Thursday souk**, is perhaps the most accessible. **MAADID**, too, off to the left of the road as you approach Erfoud, is interesting – a really massive **ksar**, which is considered to be the start of the Tafilalt proper.

Erfoud

ERFOUD, like Er Rachidia, is largely a French-built administrative centre, and its desultory frontier-town atmosphere fulfils little of the promise of the Tafilalt. Arriving from Er Rachidia, however, you get a first, powerful sense of proximity to the desert, with frequent sandblasts ripping through the streets, and total darkness in the event of a (not uncommon) electrical black-out. This desert position is

THE TAFILALT: PAST AND PRESENT

The Tafilalt was for centuries the Moroccan terminus of the **caravan routes** – the famous **Salt Road** to the south– across the Sahara to West Africa, by way of Timbuktu. Merchants travelling south carried with them weapons, cloth and spices, part of which they traded en route at Taghaza (in modern-day Mali) for local **salt**, the most-sought after commodity in West Africa. They would continue south and then make the return trip from the old Kingdom of Ghana, to the west of Timbuktu, loaded with **gold** (one ounce of gold was exchanged for one pound of salt at the beginning of the nineteenth century) and, until European colonists brought an end to the trade, with **slaves**.

These were long journeys: Taghaza was twenty days by camel from Tafilalt, Timbuktu sixty, and merchants might be away for up to a year if they made a circuit via southern Libya (where slaves were still sold until the Italian occupation in 1911). They also, of course, brought an unusual degree of contact with other cultures, which ensured the Tafilalt a reputation as one of the most unstable parts of the Moroccan empire, frequently riven by religious dissent and separatism.

The separatism had a long history, dating back to the eighth century, when the region prospered as the independent kingdom of **Sijilmassa** (see p.421); the dissent began when the *Filalis* – as Tafilalt's predominantly Berber population is known – adopted the **Kharijisite heresy**, a movement which used a Berber version of the Koran (orthodox Islam forbids any translation of God's direct Arabic revelation to Muhammad). Then in the fifteenth century it again emerged as a source of trouble, fostering the Marabout uprising that toppled the Saadian dynasty.

It is with the establishment of the **Alaouite** (or, after their birthplace, *Filali*) dynasty that the Tafilalt is most closely associated. Mounted from a *zaouia* in Rissani, by Moulay Rachid, and secured by his successor, Moualy Ismail, this is the dynasty which still holds power in Morocco, through Hassan II, the fourteenth sultan in the line. The Alaouites were also the source of the wealth of many of the old Kasbahs and *ksour*, from the time of Moulay Ismail, through to this century, the sultans exiled princes and unruly relatives out here to the edge of the desert.

Tafilalt today – and Bayoud disease

The region was a major centre of resistance to the French, who were limited to their garrison at Erfoud and an outpost of the Foreign Legion at Ouled Zohra until 1931. Today, however, deprived of its contacts to the south, it is something of a backwater, with a population estimated at around 80,000 and declining, as the effects of drought and Bayoud disease have taken hold on the palms. Most of the population are small-hold farmers, with thirty or so palms for each family, from which they could hope to produce around a thousand kilos of dates in a reasonable year. With the market price of dates around 6dh a kilo there are no fortunes to be made.

It is reckoned that two-thirds of Morocaan palmeries are infected with **Bayoud disease**. First detected in the Drâa at the beginning of this century, this is a kind of fungus, which is spread from root to root and possibly by transmission of spores. Palms die within a year of an attack, creating a secondary problem by leaving a gap in the wedge of trees, which allows the winds to blow through. The disease cannot be treated economically – the most that farmers can do is to isolate trees by digging a ditch round them – and the only real hope seems to lie in the development of resistant species of palms. Moroccan and French scientists, in collaboration with the *Total* oil company, are at present working on new methods of propagation and cross-breeding. A resistant species has already, in fact, been developed in France, but there's one problem: the dates, so far, taste awful . . .

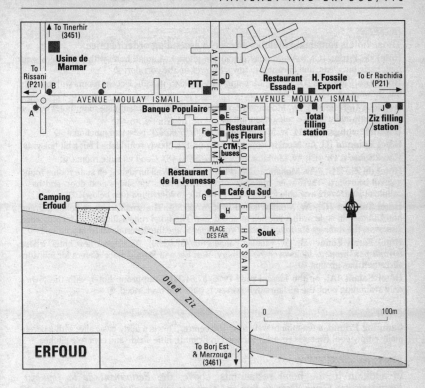

best appreciated from the vantage point of the **Borj Est**, the hill-fort 3km across the river, from where you can get a glimpse of the sands to the south; the fort itself is still used by the military but you can drive up to the walls by car or *petit taxi*.

Views apart, for most travellers Erfoud functions very much as a staging post for the sand dunes near **Merzouga**, and/or the last oasis village of **Rissani**. Its only other point of interest is the local marble industry, which produces a unique polished black marble, shot through with fossilised shells. These rather funerary-like pieces are to be seen throughout the town – including just about every hotel reception desk and bar top – and at a pair of marble works, the *Usine de Marmar*, on the Tinerhir road, and the more central *H. Fossile Export* on Av. Moulay Ismail (see map). Both of these plants have showrooms (and will send and insure their wares home, if you want). The *Marmar* sometimes has impressive exhibits by a German sculptor, Fred Jansen, and his *Ars Natura* group, which bring the fossils alive in an almost 3–D way.

Accommodation

Erfoud has an impressive range of hotels, at all price levels, although its finest – the old Kasbah-like *Grand Hotel du Sud/Sijilmassa* – has departed from the lists of late and been converted into a residence for King Hassan II (his first in the province).

HOTELS

Those hotels remaining include, as ever in ascending order of price:

Hôtel de l'Atlas [C], 5 Av. Moulay Ismail (no phone). A small hotel with a simple restaurant; basic but clean, and cheapest in town. Shower on the corridor. ①

Hôtel Les Palmiers [G], 36 Av. Mohammed V (☎05/57.60.33). Decent rooms with en suite hot showers. ①

Hôtel La Gazelle [D], Av. Mohammed V (☎05/57.60.28). Pleasant nine-room hotel with en suite rooms and a terrace café-restaurant. ①

Hôtel Merzouga [F], 114 Av. Mohammed V (☎05/57.65.32). New and functional. ①

Hôtel Essaada [I], Av. Moulay Ismail (☎05/57.63.17). Newly refurbished but a bit noisy. ①

Hôtel Sable d'Or [E], Av. Mohammed V (☎05/57.63.48). Good en suite rooms. ①

Hôtel de Ziz [H], 3 Av. Mohammed V (☎05/57.61.45). Well-furnished en suite rooms round a small courtyard. The owner, quite an entrepreneur, runs the shops next door, and has a couple of landrovers available for the sunrise shuttle to Merzouga (see below). ②

Hôtel Tafilalet [G], Av. Moulay Ismail (☎05/57.65.35). The small frontage belies a grand hotel, in the old style, with a flourish of new decor. The hotel runs a shuttle to Merzouga and also owns the *Auberge Merzouga* there, if you prefer to see the desert dawn from your bed. ③

Hôtel Farah Zouar [B], Av. Moulay Ismail (☎05/57.62.30). An elegant new hotel, whose *terrasse panoramique* looks over the palmery, Borj Est and Royal Palace. Caters for individuals rather than groups. ③

Hôtel Salam [A], on the Rissani road (☎05/57.64.24). Tour-group hotel, with the town's only swimming pool; the restaurant, however, is poor and overpriced. ④

CAMPING

Camping Erfoud, a ten-minute walk from the centre. This is a fairly basic site, with a perennially empty pool (water is severely rationed in Erfoud), little shade and concrete pitches.

RESTAURANTS

In addition to the hotel restaurants, above, the *Restaurant de la Jeunesse*, *Restaurant les Fleurs*, *Café du Sud* and *Café des Dunes*, all on Av. Mohammed V, do good, modestly priced meals. The *Café des Dunes* is especially good.

Directory

Bank There is a branch of the *Banque Populaire* (see map).

Buses *CTM* buses leave from Av. Mohammed V (see map); others from the Place des F.A.R. There is a daily private-line service to Tinejdad, which allows you to make a connection to Tinerhir, avoiding the need to backtrack via Er Rachidia.

Car repairs Try Madkouri Abid at 114 Av. Mohammed V, next door to the *Hôtel Merzouga*.

Petrol/gas There are *Total* and *Ziz* filling stations on the Er Rachidia road.

Post office The *PTT* has poste restante and other standard services.

The dunes of Merzouga

The **Erg Chebbi**, the sand dunes at **Merzouga**, are one of the great sights of Morocco. They are reached most directly along the 3461 road south of Erfoud, which is surfaced for the first 16km, then gives way to 35km of piste. It is along this road that the landrover tours are offered by the *Hôtel de Ziz* and *Hôtel Tafilalet*, to catch sunrise at the dunes. If you can't afford these, it may be possible to join up with other tourists doing the trip – try asking round at the *Hôtel Salam* or *Hôtel Tafilalet*, either the night before or at dawn. You can, alternatively, reach Merzouga by way of **Rissani** – or complete a circuit by travelling back this way –

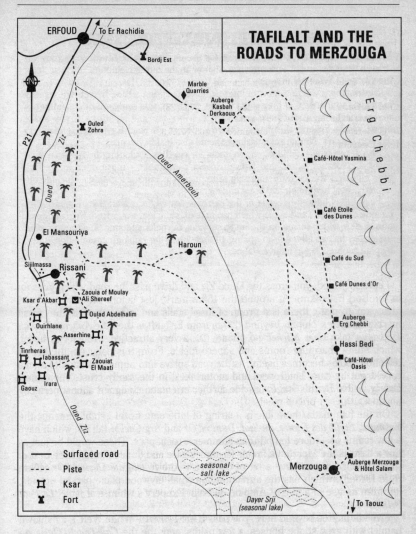

TAFILALT AND THE ROADS TO MERZOUGA

ERFOUD
To Er Rachidia
Bordj Est
Marble Quarries
Auberge Kasbah Derkaoua
Erg Chebbi
Café-Hôtel Yasmina
Ouled Zohra
Oued Amerbouh
Café Etoile des Dunes
El Mansouriya
Haroun
Café du Sud
Café Dunes d'Or
Sijilmassa
Rissani
Auberge Erg Chebbi
Ksar d'Akbar
Zaouia of Moulay Ali Shereef
Hassi Bedi
Café-Hôtel Oasis
Oulad Abdelhalim
Ouirhlane
Asserhine
Tinrheras
Tabassant
Zaouiat El Maati
Irara
Gaouz

Surfaced road
Piste
Ksar
Fort

seasonal salt lake
Merzouga
Auberge Merzouga & Hôtel Salam
Dayer Srji (seasonal lake)
To Taouz

though be prepared for the local hustlers. The Merzouga–Rissani route is covered in a southeast to northwest direction on p.419; it is covered by local transit and landrover taxis.

Erfoud to Merzouga

The road from Erfoud to Merzouga is practicable by Renault 4. It takes around an hour and a quarter, and is reasonably easy to follow, with a line of telephone poles running parallel almost the whole way. A guide isn't necessary, though, if you're travelling alone, an extra person to push, when you get stuck in the sandy tracks, would be wise.

DESERT WILDLIFE AND THE LAKE

Merzouga makes an excellent centre for the exploration of Morocco's sandy (or "true") desert, whose flora and fauna show ingenious adaptations to these least hospitable of living conditions.

Birdwatchers will find most of interest. In early spring a lake, **Dayet Srji**, usually forms just to the west of Merzouga village, and it attracts scores of pink flamingoes – a wonderful sight out here in the wilds. More unusual sightings, if you strike lucky, might include the desert sparrow, desert warbler, Egyptian nightjar and Arabian bustard. Numerous migrants should also be in evidence.

The desert is also an ideal environment for **reptiles**, including the Algerian sand lizard and Berber skink, and typical **desert mammals** – more often located by their giveaway tracks in the morning sand than by nocturnal sightings – include the jerboa, desert hedgehog and fennec (desert fox).

Plant life is limited because of the extreme scarcity of water; the only survivors include the lichens and algae which can take up sufficient water from the condensation of dew which forms on the undersurfaces of rocks and stones, although even the desert has an all-too-brief **spring bloom** when the rains do come – dominated by pink asphodels and mauve statice.

Leaving Erfoud, you cross the Oued Ziz and drive past the road which goes up to the Borj Est (3km). At around the 15km mark, just before the surfaced road gives way to piste, there is a group of fossil stalls and, off to the left, the "fossil marble" quarries. Not far beyond (23km from Erfoud) is the little *Auberge Kasbah Derkaoua* (aka *Chez Michel*; no phone; ②), a very attractive, French-run **hotel**, which offers charming rooms and superb meals. From this point on, the line of telephone poles becomes useful, as the road splays into numerous parallel tracks carved out by cars, landrovers and motorbikes, in the sandy crust. The dunes, clearly visible by this stage, provide further orientation, aligned almost perfectly north–south.

On the hammada/dune line is a string of little **café-hotel** establishments: the *Yasmina*, *Étoile des Dunes*, *du Sud*, *Dunes d'Or* and *Erg Chebbi* (all ①), which have a few rooms or – more tempting in summer – roof space. These would be just as fine a base as the Merzouga hotels for the sunrise and dunes. Perhaps the best of them, if you'd rather have a bit of comfort, is the *Hôtel-Café Dunes d'Or* (40km from Erfoud), which has the attraction of a small plywood plane parked outside, left from its use in a film of Antoine de Saint-Exupéry's whimsical fable, *Le Petit Prince*.

Five kilometres beyond here, you pass HASSI BEDI ("White Well"), a flyblown hamlet with grey adobe houses, a few palms, and, the the the *Café-Hôtel l'Oasis*, an enjoyable little *auberge* run by Obana Ahmed Ifrere, who offers inexpensive rooms and courtyard beds. He will guide you round the oasis and out to the dunes, and can arrange camel rides by the day or hour.

Three kilometres beyond this, you reach the *Auberge Merzouga* (see below), and a kilometre beyond that, the village of Merzouga.

Merzouga

Merzouga itself is no great shakes, but if you want to stay, there are half a dozen **café-hotels** scattered in and round the village and out by the dunes. All of them are pretty basic, with no electricity and outside toilers and showers.

At the **foot of the dunes** are the *Auberge Merzouga* (⑩), well run, with a choice of rooms or sleeping space on its *terrasse*, and, next door, the *Hôtel Salam* (⑩) and *Hôtel Atlas-Sahara* (⑩). In the **village**, the new *Auberge de Touareg* (⑩) is a reasonable choice – basic but clean, and with good (if slow) meals. In addition, there are the *Hôtel des Palmiers* (⑩), which offers cheap couch space; the hostel-like *Auberge La Grand Dune* (⑩), basic but very friendly, with one large room divided by curtains; and the similar *Café des Amis* (⑩). If you've got a sleeping bag, bedding down on the dunes is perhaps best of all – and in summer, when even roofspace can be taken by mid-afternoon, it may be your only choice.

The **dune** by the *Auberge Merzouga* is said to be the highest in Morocco – and, so locals would have it, the world. It is undeniably impressive and it may look familiar, for it was used in a Renault advert, with a car driving down its slope. Cars, incidentally, seem to have an uncontrollable passion for dunes, for Merzouga is a post in the North African Rally (held in June/July); the drivers' stickers add a slightly surreal tone to the village. A more appropriate transport on the dunes is demonstrated by local kids, who sandsurf on plastic bags down the slopes of an evening.

Two local **camel drivers** will arrange trips of anything from a couple of hours' climb up the dunes to two or three days' trekking. Contact either Hassan at the *Hôtel Atlas-Sahara*, or Mohammed at the *Auberge de Touareg*. Two hours at sunset is plenty, if you want a taste of the dunes and minimal saddle-soreness. The prices are highly negotiable: 75dh per person is perhaps about right for a two-hour ride.

Merzouga to Rissani

Heading for Rissani, **landrover taxis** leave around 7am; **lorries** at a similar time on the morning after a *souk*. The route is not that easy to follow, and if you are driving, it would be wise to join a party with one of these vehicles, or arrange a local guide; as with the Erfoud route, you will certainly need two or more people to push the car when you get stuck in the sand. More seriously, if you were caught in high winds you could easily get lost in a sandstorm, and recent rains would present problems to all but four-wheel-drive vehicles. Assuming you're not stuck or lost too often, or too long, the trip should take around two hours.

The route (or a route) is essentially this: leave Merzouga past the post office (on your left); keep the telephone poles on your right for a while; follow the pistes off to the left; skirt the (dry) salt lake and you'll eventually hit asphalt road somewhere in Rissani's palmery – bear left to reach Rissani.

Rissani

RISSANI stands at the last visible point of the Ziz River; beyond it, steadily encroaching on the present town and its ancient *ksour* ruins, begins the desert. From the eighth to the fourteenth centuries, this was the site of the first independent kingdom of the south, Sijilmassa (see box overleaf). It was the first capital of the Tafilalt, and served as the last stop on the great caravan routes south. The British journalist Walter Harris reported thriving gold and slave auctions in Rissani as late as the 1890s.

Rissani has a special place in modern Moroccan lore. It was from the *zaouia* here – which is still an important national shrine – that the ruling **Alaouite dynasty** launched its bid for power, conquering first the oases of the south, then the vital Taza Gap, before triumphing finally in Fes and Marrakesh.

The market

A quarter of Rissani's population live in a large seventeenth-century **ksar**, in addition to which there is just the Place al Massira and one street, lined by the usual administrative buildings. It's a quiet place, which comes to life three times a week for the **souk** – held on Sunday, Tuesday and Thursday.

The market is more for locals than tourists, though it often turns up a good selection of local Berber jewellery – including the crude, almost iconographic designs of the desert. Some of the basic products (dried fruits, farming implements and so on) are interestingly distinct from those of the richer north. Don't expect camels, as some guides promise: apart from the caravans, these were never very common in Tafilalt, the Berbers preferring more economical mules. They are still very much in evidence.

Two permanent **craft shops** might also draw you into an hour or two's browsing: the *Maison Touareg* and the *Maison Berbère* – the latter part of a southern chain that has a reputation for quality rugs and carpets.

Ksour around Rissani

Rissani's older monuments are well into the process of erosion – both through crumbling material and the slow progress of the sands. **Sijilmassa**, whose ruins were clearly visible at the beginning of this century, has more or less vanished – though see the box opposite. The various Kasbahs and reminders of the Alaouite presence are also mostly in some stage of decay, though there is just enough remaining to warrant a battle with the morning heat.

From the administrative street/bus terminal you can head towards a collection of *ksour* on the signposted "Circuit Touristique". The first you encounter, about 2.5km to the southeast, houses the **Zaouia of Moulay Ali Shereef**, the original Alaouite stronghold and mausoleum of the dynasty's founder. Many times rebuilt – the last following floods in 1955 – the shrine is forbidden to non-Muslims.

Beside it, dominating this group of buildings, is the nineteenth-century **Ksar d'Akbar**, an awesomely grandiose ruin which was once a palace in exile, housing the unwanted members of the Alaouite family and the wives of the dead sultans. Most of the structure, which still bears considerable traces of its former decoration, dates from the beginning of the nineteenth century. A third royal *ksar*, the **Ksar Oualad Abdelhalim**, stands around 1500m further down the road. Notable for its huge ramparts and the elaborate decorative effects of its blind arches and unplastered brick patterning, this is one of the few really impressive imperial buildings completed in this century. It was constructed around 1900 for Sultan Moulay Hassan's elder brother, whom he had appointed governor of the Tafilalt.

You can complete the circuit by passing a further group of *ksour* – **Asserehine**, **Zaouiet El Maati**, **Irara**, **Gaouz**, **Tabassant**, **Tinrheras** and **Ouirhlane** – and then looping back into town past a section of **Sijilmassa**. Tinrheras, a ruined *ksar* on a knoll, has fine views over Tafilalt.

Practicalities

Rissani offers a choice of two hotels, both of which have restaurants. The *Hôtel El Filalia* (☎05/57.50.96; ⑩) has the cheaper rooms, and rents out space on its roof terrace. Better quality and better value is the *Hôtel Sijilmassa* (☎05/57.50.42; ⑩), which is new and enthusiastic. There is also a **bank** (*Banque Populaire*), **post office**, several **filling stations**, and a men's **hammam**.

SIJILMASSA: THE BERBER KINGDOM

Sijilmassa was founded in 757 by Berber dissidents, who had broken away from orthodox Islam, and for five centuries, until its collapse under civil unrest in 1393, it dominated southern Morocco.The early dominance and wealth of Sijilmassa was due to the fertility of the **oasis** south of Erfoud. These are watered by parallel rivers, the Oued Rheris and Oued Ziz, which led to its description as the "Mesopotamia of Morocco". Harvests were further improved by diverting the Ziz, just south of modern Erfoud, to the west of its natural channel, thus bringing it closer to the Rheris and raising the water table. Such natural wealth was reinforced by Sijilmassa's trading role on the **Salt Road** to West Africa (see box on p.414), which persisted until the west coast of Africa was opened up to sea trade, particularly by the Portuguese, in the fifteenth century. Coins from Sijilmassa, in this period, have been found as far as Aqaba, Jordan.

Historians disagree about the extent and pattern of Sijilmassa at its height. Some see it as a divided city, comprising several dispersed *ksour*, much as it was after the civil war at the end of the fourteenth century. Others view it as a single, elongated city, spread along the banks of the rivers: 14km from end to end, or half a day's walk.

There is still a gate to be seen on the east side of the Oued Ziz, at the ancient city's northern extremity, just south of El Mansouriya. This is known locally as the **Bab Errih** and may date from the Merenid period (1248–1465), although it has certainly undergone restoration since then. The Alaouites, who brought Sijilmassa to renewed prominence as the provincial capital of the Tafilalt in the seventeenth century, did a major restoration of the garrison. The southernmost point of the ancient city was near the *ksar* of Gaouz, on the "Circuit Touristique".

The (mainly Alaouite) central area is under excavation by a joint team from the Moroccan Institute of Archaeology and the Middle Tennessee State University, under the direction of Dr Ronald Messier. The most accessible and visible remains are to be found a little to the west of Rissani, on the east bank of the Oued Ziz, and within the right angle formed by the north–south main road (P21) as it turns east into Rissani. Here can be traced the walls of a mosque with an early *mihrab* facing south, an adjoining *Medersa* and the walls of the citadel with towers on the length by the river. In Rissani, there is a small museum and study centre where you may get help to explore the site. *With thanks to Dr Ron Messier.*

Leaving town, you can get landrover or transit taxis to **Merzouga**, or, on market days, lorries (*camionettes*), laden to the hilt with Berbers (see p.419 for the route); travelling by taxi, it's best to specify a particular hotel in Merzouga, or you may be dropped at one of the *auberges* north of the village (not that this is necessarily a bad thing). To secure a ride in one of the *camionettes*, head down the main street, past the bank and taxi stand, to the filling station and *Café Panorama*.

Heading **west**, the 10am bus to **Er Rachidia** connects with the 1pm bus to Tinerhir (arriving around 4.30pm) and Ouarzazate. *Grands taxis* also run direct from Rissani to **Tinerhir** (45dh).

An alternative route out from Rissani is the **piste west to Zagora, via Alnif**. This is detailed in reverse on p.389 and is possible in a Renault 4 or, if you can coincide with the market days, by a local landrover taxi. The taxi usually leaves the *Hôtel El Filalia* on Thursdays and Sundays, after the Rissani market, arriving in Zagora around ten hours later; it's possible to arrange a place through the hotel.

OUT EAST TO FIGUIG

The eight- to ten-hour desert journey from **Er Rachidia to Figuig** (pronounced F'geeg) is one of the most exhilarating and spectacular that you can make, certainly among those accessible to travellers without landrovers and proper expeditionary planning. It is startlingly isolated, almost throughout its 393km length, and physically extraordinary: the real outlands of Morocco, dominated by huge empty landscapes and blank red mountains.

What little there is in the way of human presence is a series of struggling mining villages and military outposts, ranging from the desolate, tiny mud hut-type constructions of MENGOUB to the prosperous administrative and garrison centre of **BOUARFA** – a friendly place, which has two basic hotels and where you'll probably have to change buses. The real focus of the region, though, is **Figuig** itself – a great medieval date palm oasis, in the bowl of the mountains and right on the border with Algeria.

If you want to continue on **into Algeria**, the border crossing here is open and functional. Staying in Morocco, you can head north from **Figuig to Oujda** (7hr by bus) and the Mediterranean coast.

The Figuig oasis

The southern oases are traditionally measured by the number of their palms, rather than in terms of area or population. **FIGUIG**, with something like 200,000 trees, has always been one of the largest – an importance further enhanced by its strategic border position. At least twice it has been lost by Morocco – in the seventeenth-century wars, and again at the end of Moulay Ismail's reign – and as recently as 1975 there was fighting in the streets here between Moroccan and Algerian troops.

Orientation, hotels, food and transport

The oasis has even less of an administrative town than usual, still basically consisting of its seven distinct *ksour* villages – which in the past feuded almost continuously over water and grazing rights. These days it is a very relaxed place and, since tourists are no particular currency, entirely hassle-free.

Orientation is relatively simple, with almost everything on the road by which you enter the town. The *Hôtel Meliasse*, the first landmark, is on the right, above the Shell service station. Buses sometimes stop here – there is no bus terminal as such in Figuig – and then again outside the *Hôtel Sahara*. Beyond lie various shops and cafés, and a bank. Beyond here, a left fork leads to a police post, past the *Café Oasis*, and into a garden part of town, which ends at the army barracks. The road turns left, then right, runs along a short length of dual carriageway and finally reaches the *Hôtel/Camping Diamant Vert*.

ACCOMMODATION

Hôtel Meliasse. Very basic and with a mercenary manager who doesn't appear to employ any cleaners. Not recommended! ①

Hôtel Sahara. Somewhat better and cleaner (despite a blind owner), with balconies and a touch of sunlight in the rooms; there is a hammam next door. ①

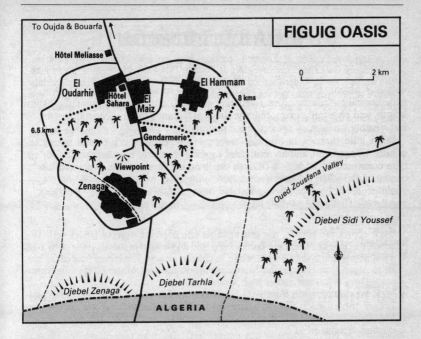

Hôtel/Camping Diamant Vert (☎06/69.90.30). The best choice – and a rather wonderful place to stay, with very pleasant staff. It has a few clean if austere rooms and also offers garden camping, a swimming pool, and a café (soft drinks only; no food) with superb views over the southern portion of the oasis. ⑩

FOOD

Café El Fath. This will make an evening meal on request – and for breakfast, delicious doughnuts are available from a stall nearby.

Café Oasis. Just the one dish – meat and vegetable *tajine*, to order – but it's tasty and filling. Also has a pool table, where you can join the local soldiers whiling away the evening.

BUSES

The ticket office for **buses** north from Figuig is to be found by walking north from the *Hôtel Sahara* and turning left at the fountain/junction. The office is to the right, under the arcades.

The 6am departure goes direct to Oujda with a breakfast stop at Bouarfa. Heading for Er Rachidia, there are just two buses a day from Bouarfa (at 8am and 2pm); catch the 5am bus from Figuig if you want to avoid a long wait.

Exploring the ksour

Figuig's **ksour** are signposted off the main road and are spread out round the base of the hill – each enclosing its own palmery within high turreted walls. Although sporadically organised into a loose confederation, they were until this century fiercely independent – and their relations with each other were peppered with long and bitter blood feuds and, above all, disputes over the limited water

CROSSING INTO ALGERIA

Crossing into Algeria at Figuig is routine, with no restrictions on "pedestrian" passengers (as existed until recently at Oujda). However, there are a few formalities worth knowing before setting off. First of all, before leaving the Figuig administrative centre, you must get your passport stamped at the **police post** (*sûreté*). This must be done on the same day you cross the border – effectively ruling out an early start, since the police post opens at 8am (and closes at 3pm).

Next, drive, walk or hitch the 3km to the **border crossing** – a Beau Geste type of place with some palms and two tents – where you need to get more stamps on both the Moroccan and Algerian sides (open till dusk; closed at lunchtime – for up to three hours!). There is a customs check on the Algerian side, which can take a while if the officers decide to do a search; they may well, as they don't have a lot else to do. If you are driving, you will have to obtain (compulsory) insurance – currently 60 dinars for twenty days.

Beni Ounif

Once across the border, you can head for the Algerian town of **BENI OUNIF**, another 3km walk. There are **banks** here, and if you want to move on the same day it's vital to get into town early enough to change money. The banks (closed, as are all in Algeria, on Fridays and Saturdays) are in the area to the right of the main road. There is just one, rather basic, **hotel**.

Buses going north from Beni Ounif stop by the yellow taxi stand; at around 1.30pm, there's a departure to Saïda, which arrives in the evening (connections on from there to Algiers). There are also **trains** heading north, with early morning and evening departures.

supply. Their strange, archaic shape – with watchtowers rising above the snaking *feggaguir* (or irrigation channels) – evolved as much from this internal tension as from any need to protect themselves from the nomadic tribes of the desert. Likewise, within each of the *ksour*, the elaborate tunnel-like networks of alleys are deliberate (and successful) attempts to prevent any sudden or easy progress.

Your best chance of getting an overview of it all is to head for the **platforme**, poised above the *ksar* of Zenaga. The view from here spans a large part of the palmery and its pink-tinged *ksour*, and you can gaze at the weird, multicoloured layers of the enclosing mountains. If you can find the energy – Figuig in summer feels a little like sitting inside a fan-heater – head down into **Zenaga**, the largest and richest of the seven villages. Going to your left, you should reach its centre, more developed than most in this area, with a couple of cubicle shops and a café in addition to a mosque. For a look at the other *ksour*, it is possible to loop to the right of the main administrative road, past El Maiz to El Hammam el Foukanni.

El Maiz is the prettiest of the *ksour*, with small vaulted lanes and houses with broad verandas pointing south. In **El Hammam**, as the name suggests, there is a hot spring, used by the people for their ablutions. Anyone offering their services as a guide will take you to it. Back on the other side of the administrative road is the **Ksar El-Oudarhir**, which also has some natural springs (one hot, one salty), as well as terraces similar to the ones in El Maiz.

All of the *ksour* have exclusively Berber populations, though up until the 1950s and 1960s there was also a considerable Jewish population. Until the beginning of the twentieth century, Figuig was also the final Moroccan staging point on the overland journey to Mecca.

Figuig to Oujda

Unless you have a strange fascination for (very) small town life, there is really nowhere else on this eastern plateau between Figuig and Oujda which offers very much temptation. **TENDRARA** (Tuesday market) and **AÏT BENIMATHAR** both have basic café-hotels, if you decide to stay overnight. Aït Benimathar is the better choice – a quiet little **hot water oasis**, full of tortoises and snakes. Even if you don't want to stay, it's not a bad place to spend the middle of an afternoon, which you can do by taking the early morning bus from Figuig, then catching a later one for the final 50km to Oujda.

To the west of Bouarfa, the towns are all fairly bleak. If you're into piste driving, there are said to be troglodyte (cave) dwellings up in the hills behind BOUDENIB, towards GOUMARRA.

travel details

Buses

From Ouarzazate Marrakesh (4 daily; 6hr); Zagora (3; 5hr 30min); Tailiouine/Taroudannt (2; 3hr 30 min/5hr); Tinerhir (3; 5hr).

From Zagora Ouarzazate (4 daily; 4–5hr)*; Marrakesh (2 daily; 9–11hr)*.

From Tinerhir Er Rachidia (2 daily; 3hr); Ouarzazate (3; 5hr).

From Er Rachidia Erfoud/Rissani (4 daily; 1hr 30 min/3hr); Tinerhir (2; 3hr); Figuig (1 daily via Bouarfa, currently at 5am; 10hr); Midelt (5; 3hr 30 min); Fes (3; 8hr 30min); Meknes (1; 8hr).

From Erfoud Rissani (4 daily; 1hr 30min); Er Rachidia (4; 1hr 30min); Fes (daily; 11hr).

From Rissani Tinejdad/Goulmina (daily; 3hr 30 min/4hr).

From Figuig Oujda (4 daily; 7hr); Er Rachidia (via Bouarfa; 1 daily; 10hr).

Grands Taxis

From Ouarzazate Regularly to Zagora (3hr). Negotiable for Skoura (1hr) and Aït Benhaddou (1hr 45min, but expensive private trip).

From Zagora Regularly to Ouarzazate (3hr); lorries to Rissani (10hr) and Foum Zguid (8hr).

From Boumalne Landrover taxi at least daily to Msemrir (3hr). Regular run to Tinerhir (50min).

From Tinerhir Regular runs to Boumalne (50 min) and Tinejdad (1hr; from there on to Er Rachidia).

From Er Rachidia Fairly frequent runs to Erfoud (along the route you can negotiate a ticket to Meski) and to Tinejdad (2hr).

From Erfoud Fairly frequent runs to Rissani (1hr 30min) and Erfoud (2hr). Landrover trips direct to Merzouga (1hr; relatively expensive).

Trains

There is a night train from Bouarfa to Oujda (8hr), but this carries mainly freight, and is a distinctly eccentric alternative to the bus from Figuig.

CHAPTER SEVEN

AGADIR, THE ANTI-ATLAS AND THE DEEP SOUTH

Flying to southern Morocco, your destination is most likely to be **Agadir**, which was rebuilt specifically as a tourist resort following its destruction by an earthquake in 1960 and is today something of a showpiece for the "new nation". It is unlikely, though, that you'll want to stay here for long. Agadir has been too deliberately developed – its image is as a winter holiday spot for Europeans – and besides the beach and package tour hotels, there is not much life to be found, and no hint of any local, Moroccan culture.

Fortunately, the rest of **the coast** is altogether different. Just north of Agadir is a series of small fishing villages and cove-beaches without a hotel in sight, while a short way inland is **"Paradise Valley"**, a beautiful and exotic palm gorge, from which a mountain road trails up to the seasonal waterfalls of **Immouzer des Ida Outananem** – a superb one- or two-day trip. To the south of Agadir, the beaches are again very sporadically developed, ranging from solitary campsites at **Sidi Rbat** – one of Morocco's best locations for birdwatching – and **Sidi Moussa d'Aglou**, down to the old port of **Sidi Ifni** – only relinquished by Spain in 1969 and full of splendid Art Deco colonial architecture.

Inland and to the south of Agadir are the **Souss** and the **Anti-Atlas**, easy-going regions whose Chleuh Berber populations share the distinction of having together cornered the country's grocery trade. **Taroudannt**, capital of the fertile Souss plain, has massive walls, animated *souks* and good hotels – a natural place to stay on your way to Marrakesh (which can be reached over the spectacular Tizi n'Test pass) or Ouarzazate. Further south, into the Anti-Atlas mountains, **Tafraoute** and its valley are even more compelling – the stone-built villages and villas set amid a stunning landscape of pink granite and vast rock formations.

For those with more time, a number of adventurous piste and desert trips can be made in the region. One of the best is the **Tata loop**, a surfaced but little-travelled road across the southern Anti-Atlas to the pre-Sahara, comprising a string of true desert **oases**. The route is most easily covered from Tiznit, but it is feasible to do it east to west from Taroudannt. It's well off the usual (or even unusual) tourist trails and is highly recommended.

The **Deep South**, beyond Goulimine and down into the **Western Sahara**, has become more stable in recent years, as the Moroccan army has effectively contained its Polisario adversaries in the war over the former colonial zone of Spanish Sahara. There are now virtually no restrictions on travelling down the coast through Tan Tan and Laayoune, though at present the border with Mauritania is closed. For visitors, the main appeal lies in the experience of travel in the desert, and in the great distances covered. **Goulimine**, the most accessible "desert town", is promoted for its camel market – the traditional meeting place of

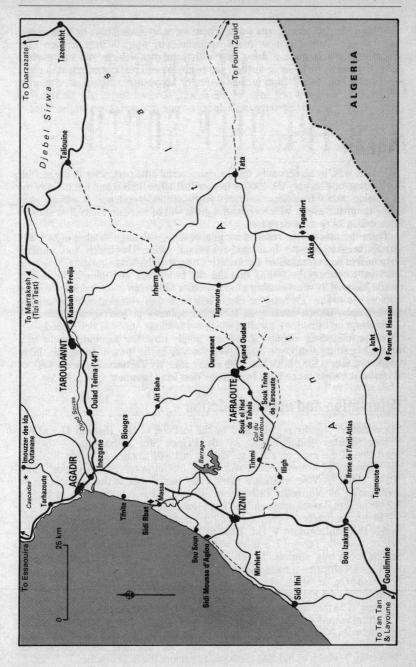

the "Blue Men" (Touareg tribesmen, whose faces are tinged blue by their masks and robes) – but it is now more frequented by tourists than anyone else. Nonetheless, it is quite a drive, and with your own vehicle you can explore several oases nearby. Going further, you begin to need real commitment to reach towns like **Tan Tan**, 125km further south, or **Laayoune**, reached after another 260km. You do get a real taste of the desert, however, especially on the road between Tarfaya and Laayoune, with dunes on one side and ocean on the other.

Agadir

AGADIR was, by all accounts, quite a characterful little port, prior to the terrible earthquake of February 29, 1960: a tremor that killed 15,000 and left most of the remaining 50,000 homeless. Just four years into independence, it was an especially traumatic event, which created a great will to recreate a city that showed Morocco in its best, modern face.

Three decades on, the result is not unappealing, with large swathes of park and garden breaking up the hotel and residential zones. The beach, too, remains magnificent and untramelled by Spanish Costa-style high-rise building. However, it's hard to escape the feeling that the city lacks soul, and though the lack of bustle has novelty value coming from any other Moroccan town, it doesn't exactly compel you to stay. Perhaps the city is best treated as a staging post – or a place to rest up – before moving on to livelier spheres in Marrakesh, Essaouira, Taroudannt or Tafraoute – for all of which destinations Agadir is well placed.

In the immediate vicinity, if you are simply travelling through Agadir as a means of getting south, you might prefer to stay in the town of **Inezgane**, 13km southwest (see p.438); if it's beachlife you're after, try **Tarhazoute** (see p.439); or if you want a night in the hills, **Immouzer des Ida Outanane** (see p.441).

Orientation and accommodation

"Downtown" Agadir is delineated by the junction of **Bd. Hassan II** and **Av. Prince Moulay Abdallah** with **Av. du Prince Sidi Mohammed** – the left-hand side of the inset on our map. Rebuilt in 1960s "modernist" style, it has all the trappings of a town centre, with office blocks, a tourist office, post office (PTT), Hôtel de Ville, municipal market and banks. Just to the northeast is an area known as **Nouvelle Talborjt**, where there is a concentration of budget hotels, local café-restaurants and the main (long-distance) **bus station**.

The fancier hotels are grouped along the main avenues running parallel to the beach: **Bd. Mohammed V**, **Bd. Hassan II** and **Bd. du 20 Aout**. To the southeast of Nouvelle Talborjt is a more working-class residential area and the **Place Salam local bus station**. To the northeast is a hilly, grassed area known as **Ancienne Talborjt** – a memorial to the earthquake, under which lie the remains of the old Medina, which were bulldozed for fear of typhoid breaking out. Further north, still, is the old **Kasbah**, and beyond it, the new industrial port and suburb of **Anzar**. A further industrial zone spreads south towards Inezgane.

Getting round Agadir, you might want to make use of *petits taxis*, as it's a fair walk between Nouvelle Talborjt and the beach, for instance, and a long haul up to the Kasbah. Alternatively, you can hire mopeds and motorbikes (see "Directory"), which would also allow you to explore the local beaches.

POINTS OF ARRIVAL – AND MOVING ON

BY AIR

Agadir's new **airport, Al Massira**, is 25km east of the city. It is well equipped, though the banks and car hire offices are open only during normal office hours and are closed on Sundays. Taxis, however, will accept foreign currency, or you can change money at one of the Agadir hotels before paying them.

Holiday companies run their own buses to meet flights and shuttle passengers to their hotels, and if you've bought a flight-only deal it's worth tagging along with fellow passengers if you want to get into Agadir. If you don't get one of these, airport officials will direct you to the **grands taxis** outside, which charge a standard 100dh fare, for up to six people (arrange to share *inside* the terminal), to Agadir.

Alternatives are to catch the hourly **coach** which runs between the airport and Agadir (12dh fare; it runs to/from the *Dôme* café – see map inset – via the *Hôtel Kamal*), or to travel on **local buses via Inezgane** (13km southeast of Agadir; see p.438). To get to Inezgane catch the brown #22 bus (every 20min from 6.30am–6pm; 3dh) from outside the airport building; once there, pick up local bus #5 or #6 to Agadir (Place Salam – aka Place de l'Abattoir – terminal; bottom right of our map; 1.6dh) or get a place in a *grand taxi*.

Heading for the airport from Agadir, you can use the above services (the last bus from Inezgane leaves at 7pm) or ask your hotel to arrange a taxi. The airport stays open all night, though the café and restaurant are closed from around 7pm.

Driving from the airport, you are well positioned for a first night at Agadir (half an hour's drive), Taroudannt (45mins), or even Marrakesh (about 4hr). Driving **to the airport** from Agadir, you have a choice of routes. The easiest is to leave Agadir by way of Aït Melloul and the Taroudannt (P32) road, turning left at the signposted junction. Alternatively, you can approach from the north, leaving Agadir on the Marrakesh (P40) road, then turning off (right) at Tikitouen.

ARRIVING BY BUS OR GRAND TAXI

All buses that run direct to or from Agadir operate from the **Talborjt bus station** (gare routière) behind Place Lahcen Tamri (see map inset overpage).

If you're coming in by **bus** from the south, you might be dropped in **Inezgane**, 13km southeast (see p.438). Getting into Agadir from here, take local buses #5 or #6, which will drop you at the **Place Salam** (aka Place de l'Abattoir) terminal. **Grands taxis** between Inezgane and Agadir (5dh a place) also run to the Place Salam/Place de l'Abattoir.

LEAVING AGADIR BY BUS OR GRAND TAXI

Leaving Agadir, the best services are operated by *ONCF* (the train company; ticket office at 10 Rue des Orangiers), *CTM* and *SATAS*, though you may need to use other private lines for a few minor destinations, or go via Inezgane. The main services, all from the Talborjt terminal, include:

ONCF: Marrakesh (6am, 9.30am & 1.30pm: 4hr express service); Goulimine/ Tan Tan/Laayoune/Dakhla (8pm; arrives Laayoune 8am).

CTM: Marrakesh (3pm & 6pm); Taroudannt (5.30am); Essaouira (7.30am); Tiznit (3.30am, 6.30am & 12.30pm); Casablanca (9.30pm & 10pm).

SATAS: Tiznit (6am, 7.30am, 1.30pm & 2pm); Taroudannt (6am, 9.45am, 2.30pm & 5.30pm); Tafraoute (1.30pm); Goulimine/Tan Tan (6am & 2pm); Essaouira (6.30am, 10.30am & 2.30pm); Casablanca (6.30am, 9.30pm & 10.30pm).

Agadir's **grands taxis** (from Place Salam) do routine shuttles to **Inezgane** (5dh a place), from where you can make connections to Taroudannt, Taliouine, Tiznit, etc.

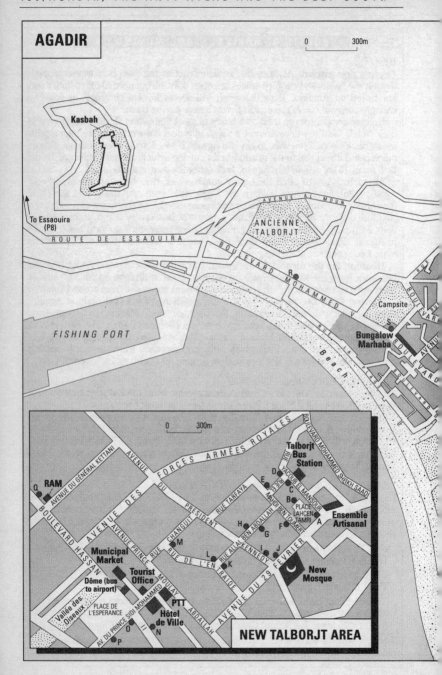

AGADIR

0   300m

Kasbah

To Essaouira
(P8)

ROUTE DE ESSAOUIRA

AVENUE AL MOUN

ANCIENNE
TALBORJT

BOULEVARD MOHAMMED V

R

FISHING PORT

Campsite

S

Bungalow
Marhaba

NEW TALBORJT AREA

0   300m

FORCES ARMÉES ROYALES

BOULEVARD MOHAMMED SHAKH SAADI

Talborjt
Bus
Station

AVENUE DU GENERAL KETTANI

AVENUE DES

AVENUE DU PRESIDENT

RUE TARFAYA

RUE JACOUB EL MANSOUR

Q RAM

D

E

C

B

PLACE
LAHCEN
TAMRI

A

Ensemble
Artisanal

BOULEVARD HASSAN

AVENUE PRINCE

RUE CHANGUIT

M

H

G

F

RUE ALAL BEN ABDALLAH

RUE ALAL KENNEDY

I

J

L

K

AVENUE DU 29 FEVRIER

Municipal
Market

Dôme (bus
to airport)

Tourist
Office

RUE DE L'EN RAIDE

RUE MOULAY MOHAMMED

New
Mosque

Vallée des
Oiseaux

PLACE DE
L'ESPERANCE

RUE SIDI MOHAMMED

PTT

Hôtel
de Ville

AVENUE DU 29 ABDALLAH

AV. DU PRINCE SIDI

Q

I

N

P

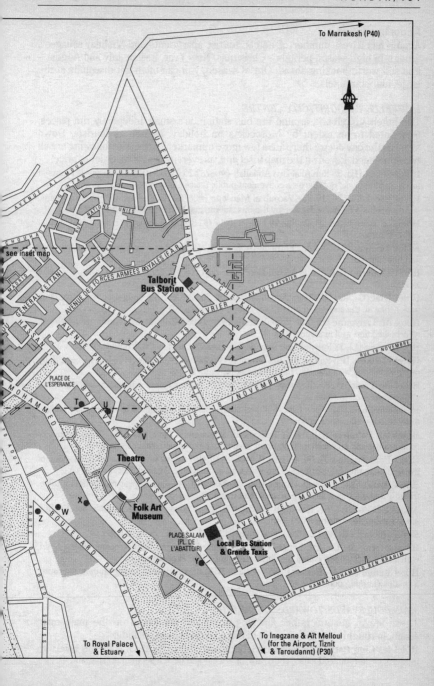

To Marrakesh (P40)

BOULEVARD MOHAMMED

AVENUE AL MOUN

MOKHTAR SOUSSI

NATIONS UNIES

see inset map

RUE DE MARRAKECH

MADRID

CHOUHADA

AVENUE DES FORCES ARMÉES ROYALES (FAR)

GENERAL KETTANI

HASSAN

AVENUE DU 29 FEVRIER

CHEIKH SAADI

AV. DU 29 FEVRIER

Talborjt Bus Station

AVENUE PRINCE MOULAY ABDALLAH

AVENUE DU 29 FEVRIER

PLACE DE L'ESPERANCE

MOHAMMED V

RUE DE LA TOUR

RUE 18 NOVEMBRE

T

U

V

Theatre

HASSAN

RUE 18 / NOVEMBRE

RUE 18 NOVEMBRE

X

W

Z

BOULEVARD DU 20 AOUT

Folk Art Museum

PLACE SALAM (PL. DE L'ABATTOIR)

Local Bus Station & Grands Taxis

Y

AVENUE EL MOUQOWAMA

ROUTE DE L'OUED SOUSS

BOULEVARD MOHAMMED V

RUE CHAIR AL HAMRA MOHAMMED BEN BRAHIM

To Royal Palace & Estuary

To Inegzane & Aït Melloul (for the Airport, Tiznit & Taroudannt) (P30)

Accommodation

Agadir has a vast number of hotels, tourist apartments and "holiday villages", though in high-season periods – Christmas/New Year, Easter, July and August – it is still worth booking ahead. Out of season, you can often get discounts at the large, four-star hotels.

NOUVELLE TALBORJT/CITY CENTRE

The hotels in Talborjt, around the bus station, are small, indepently run places, frequented to an extent by Moroccans on holiday, as well as tourists. Down towards the city centre there are a few more upmarket places. The following are all recommended, keyed on the map inset and, as ever, in ascending order of price:

Hôtel Select [H], 38 Rue Allal Ben Abdallah (☎08/82.26.43). Usually the cheapest rooms in town – a little basic, but there's a convenient public *douche* (showers) alongside. ⑩

Hôtel Excelsior [D], 19 Rue Yacoub el Mansour (☎08/82.10.28). Favoured by Moroccans; fair rooms but a bit noisy, located by the bus station, just beyond a row of grill-cafés. ①

Hôtel Le Tour Eiffel [J], 25 Rue 29 Fevrier (☎08/82.37.12). A pleasant, newish place with a café-restaurant. ①

Hôtel Amenou [A], Rue de l'Entraide (☎08/82.30.26). Another new hotel with smart decor and hot showers. ①

Hôtel Moderne [E], Rue el Mehdi Ben Toumert (☎08/82.33.73). Tucked away in a quiet location. ①

Hôtel Diaf [G], Rue Allal Ben Abdallah (☎08/82.58.52). Reliable budget choice – arguably better than all the above and little (if any) more expensive. ①

Hôtel Aït Laayoune [C], Rue Yacoub El Mansour (☎08/82.43.75). The former *Hôtel Tifawt*, refurbished and well managed. ①

Hôtel Itrane [L], 23 Rue de l'Entraide (☎08/82.14.07). Quiet and welcoming. ①

Hôtel El Bahia [F], Rue Mehdi Ibn Toumert (☎08/82.27.24). A fine little hotel – beautifully modernised and with friendly, English-speaking staff. ②

Hôtel de Paris [I], Av. Kennedy (☎08/82.26.94). Rooms round a fountain courtyard; hot showers are a bit unreliable. ②

Hôtel Sindibad [B], Place Lahcen Tamri (☎08/82.34.77). Comfortable and popular budget hotel with a restaurant and bar. ②

Hôtel les Palmiers [P], Av. du Prince Sidi Mohammed (☎08/84.37.19). Clean, well-kept rooms, a bar and an excellent restaurant; also runs its own car rental company. ②

Hôtel Petit Suede [Q], Bd. Hassan II (☎08/84.07.49). A very pleasant, small hotel – one of the first built after the earthquake, so with a bit of character. Again does car rental. ②

Hôtel Ayour [K], 4 Rue de l'Entraide (☎08/82.49.76). Another decent mid-budget choice; friendly and offering a bit more privacy than usual. ②

Atlantic Hôtel [N], Av. Hassan II (☎08/84.36.61). A good-value, comfortable hotel with a small garden; towards the city centre. ②

Hôtel Talborjt [M], Rue de l'Entraide (☎08/84.18.32). Popular modern hotel. ③

Hôtel Aferni, Av. Général Kettani (☎08/84.07.30). A new and highly recommended hotel, with a pool; located just round the corner from the *Hôtel Petite Suede*. ③

Hôtel Kamal [O], Av. Hassan II (☎08/84.28.17). Rooms and self-catering studios, set round a small swimming pool. ③

MAIN BOULEVARDS/TOWARDS THE BEACH

These are in general rather fancier places, and are keyed on the main map. Again, in roughly ascending order of price, good choices include:

Hôtel les Cinq Parties du Monde [Y], Bd. Hassan II (☎08/84.25.45). A friendly hotel with modern, clean rooms off a tiled courtyard, plus a bar and decent set-menu restaurant. ②

HOTEL PRICE CODES AND STAR-RATINGS

Hotels are no longer obliged to levy set maximum rates, according to their official star-ratings, as had long been the custom. However, **prices** still broadly follow the star-rating system, and this is the basis of our own **hotel price codes** set out below and keyed throughout the guide.

Our code	Official classification	Single room price	Double room price
⓪	Unclassified	25–60dh	40–100dh
①	1*A/1*B	60–105dh	100–125dh
②	2*B/2*A	105–145dh	125–175dh
③	3*B/3*A	145–225dh	175–275dh
④	4*B/4*A	225–400dh	275–500dh
⑤	5*luxury	Upwards of 400dh	Upwards of 500dh

TELEPHONE CODES

All telephone numbers in the Agadir region/Souss/Anti-Atlas/Western Sahara are prefixed 08. When making a call within the region you omit this prefix. For more explanation of phone codes and making calls within (or to) Morocco, see p.37.

Hôtel Aladin [T], Rue de la Jeunesse (☎08/84.32.28). Small hotel in a quiet back street, again with a bar and restaurant. ③

Hôtel Sud Bahia [U], Rue des Administrations Publics (☎08/82.07.82). Large, 1960s-style package tour hotel, with a swimming pool, restaurant, bar and nightclub. ④

Hôtel Miramar [R], Bd. Mohammed V (☎08/84.07.70). This was the only hotel that survived the earthquake. It's a homely, twelve-room place, elegantly redesigned by André Paccard, doyen of the *Hôtel La Mamounia* in Marrakesh and several of King Hassan's palaces. It has a bar and Italian restaurant, but no pool, which makes it fine value. ③

Hôtel Mabrouk [W], Bd. du 20 Août (☎08/84.06.06). Another small hotel, with an attractive garden. ③

Hôtel Adrar [X], Bd. Mohammed V (☎08/84.04.17). Not a very promising building but has a good reputation for service and facilities. ④

Beach Club [off map], Route de l'Oued Souss (☎08/84.43.43). At the southern end of the beach, this is a tasteful new hotel with all facilities. ④

Hôtel Amadil [off map], Route de l'Oued Souss – south of the *Beach Club* (☎08/84.06.20). A huge complex, with a trio of pools and everything from sauna to pétanque; beach-trikes are hired nearby, too. ④

Hôtel Oasis [S], Bd. Mohammed V (☎08/84.33.13). Brand new, Swiss-owned and -run luxury hotel. Very efficient and everything works – as you'd expect. ④

RESIDENCES

At the mid-range of the price scale, studios and apartments are as popular as hotels in Agadir. All have self-catering facilities and several feature fine restaurants; many of them discount prices by 40 percent out of season. Possibilities include:

Farah Studios (☎08/84.39.33), **Hôtel Residence Karam** (☎08/84.42.49), **Studiotel Soraya** (☎08/84.40.58), **Studiotel Afoud** (☎08/84.39.99), all on Rue de la Foire [V], which runs up to Bd. Hassan II just west of the stadium. The *Farah* and *Afoud* have highly regarded Moroccan restaurants. All except the *Farah* have (small) swimming pools.

Résidence Sacha, Place de la Jeunesse (☎08/82.55.68). Just off the town centre in a quiet square. French managed, good-sized studios (some with private gardens), and a small pool.

OUT OF TOWN

There are several hotels off the road south of town towards Inezgane and the airport; they are listed below in order of appearance driving from Agadir. For hotels in Inezgane itself, see p.439.

Hôtel Pyramide, Chemin de l'Oued Souss – 5km from Agadir (☎08/83.47.05). An attractive hotel with a swimming pool and riding stable, where you can hire horses to go trekking along the dunes and over to the bird-rich estuary (see box below). ③

Hôtel-Club Hacienda, Chemin de l'Oued Souss – 6km from Agadir (☎08/83.01.76). A top-category *Village de Vacances* offering golf, swimming, and all the facilities.⑤

Hôtel-Restaurante La Pergola, Route de Inezgane – 8km from Agadir (☎08/83.08.41). Characterful French-run hotel with a restaurant which, when on form, is memorable. ②

Hôtel Provençal, Route de Inezgane – 9km from Agadir (☎08/83.26.12). Another French-run *auberge*, with a decent restaurant, plus a bar and a swimming pool. ③

CAMPING

Camping Agadir [labelled], Bd. Mohammed V (☎08/84.09.81). This is fairly well located, within easy walking distance of the centre and beach, and is reasonably secure, but there's little shade and campervans dominate. It has a snack bar and other facilities. Open all year.

The beach and town

More than most resorts, Agadir's life revolves round its beach, and if you're not into sunbathing you won't want to stay long. If you are booked on a package here, make as many independent excursions as possible – Immouzer, Taroudannt, Tafraoute and Marrakesh are all in easy striking distance using local buses or hiring a car for a couple of days.

Along the beach

Few details are needed on the **beach** itself, which extends an impressive distance to the south of the town, is swept each morning and, being patrolled by mounted police, is almost devoid of hustlers. Along its course are a number of cafés which sell drinks and hire out sunbeds and umbrellas – the *Oasis Bar* is one of the nicest, very clean and with good service. There's also a municipal **swimming**

THE SOUSS ESTUARY: BIRDS AND THE PALACE

For anyone with an interest in **birdwatching**, the **Oued Souss estuary** should prove rewarding. The northern banks of the river have good views of a variety of waders and wildfowl including greater flamingo (most evident in August and September), spoonbill, ruddy shelduck, avocet, greenshank and curlew, while the surrounding scrubby banks also have large numbers of migrant warblers and Barbary partridge.

An additional sight, of a rather different nature, is Hassan II's **Royal Palace**, built in the 1980s in an imaginative blend of traditional and modern forms, which can be glimpsed from the riverbank. It cannot, of course, be visited.

To reach the estuary, you could walk along the beach – if you're energetic – from Agadir. Alternatively, you can go by road, taking the Inezgane road out of town and turning off to the right at the signpost to the **Hôtel Pyramid** (see Agadir hotels – "Out of Town", above). If your main interest is wildlife, you might want to stay out here, as the hotel hires out horses, with which you can trek through the woods, and along the dunes to the estuary.

pool (summer only) at the north end if you don't care for the ocean, which – it should be stressed – has a **very strong Atlantic undertow** and is definitely not suitable for children unless closely supervised.

At the south end of the beach, just beyond the *Hôtel Amadil*, **camel rides** are offered, and **beach-trikes** rented for a ride along the sands, up on the dunes, and over to the estuary (see box below). This is reached past an area known as Founty: quite a pleasant place, where – at present – a hundred or so villas are scattered behind the sand dunes and eucalyptus forest. There are plans to turn this area into a vast new tourist complex, to be known as *Palm Beach*, which will include a pair of Jack Nicklaus-designed golf courses.

To the north of the beach, the **fishing port** is worth a stroll. You can haggle for fish yourself, at very low prices, if you're doing your own cooking, or have it cooked for you at grills down by the entrance to the port. Most of these operate until 11pm in summer, 7pm in winter.

The Valley of the Birds and Folk Art Museum

As a break from the beach, you might wander into the **"Valley of the Birds"**, a dry river valley which runs down from Bd. Hassan II, under Bd. Mohammed V, to Bd. du 20 Août. It's basically a narrow strip of parkland, with a little aviary and zoo, a waterfall and a children's playground: all very pleasant, and the lush vegetation draws a rich variety of birds throughout the year.

A few blocks to the south is an outdoor theatre – built along Roman odeon lines – underneath the south side of which is the new **Agadir Folk Art Museum** (Mon–Sat 9.30am–1pm & 2–6pm; 10dh). This has been set up by Bert Flint, a Dutch anthropologist, and serves as a sister museum to his Maison Tiskiwin in Marrakesh, housing his extensive collections of southern Moroccan crafts and artefacts, with special attention to Saharan nomadic art. The exhibits are superb and – equally compelling – are placed in context, with slides, videos and photographs to illustrate their expression of traditional and contemporary daily life.

Ancienne Talborjt, the Kasbah and some history

The raised plateau of **Ancienne Talborjt** – which entombs the town demolished in the 1960 earthquake – is marked by a small mosque and unfinished memorial garden. Relatives of the 15,000 dead come to this park area to walk, remember and pray: a moving site, after so many years.

For visitors, however, a more tangible sight of old Agadir is the **Kasbah**, on the hill to the north of the port. This is an eight-kilometre trip, and worth making if you have transport, for a marvellous view of Agadir and the coast. You can see the Kasbah quite clearly from Agadir, too – and more particularly a vast "Allah–King–Nation" slogan, picked out in Arabic, in white stones, on the slopes below.

The Kasbah itself, although it survived the quake, is little more than a bare outline of walls and an entrance arch – the latter with an inscription in Dutch and Arabic recording that the Netherlands began trading here in 1746 (capitalising on the rich sugar plantations of the Souss plain). It's not much, but it is one of the few reminders that the city has any past at all, so complete was the destruction of the 1960 earthquake. In fact, Agadir's history closely paralleled that of the other Atlantic ports: colonised first by the Portuguese in the fifteenth century, then, recaptured by the Saadians in the sixteenth, carrying on its trading with intermittent prosperity, overshadowed, more often than not, by the activities of Mogador (Essaouira).

Abroad, up until the earthquake, Agadir's name was known mainly for a crisis in colonial squabblings in 1911. The Germans, protesting against French and British plans to carve up North Africa, sent a gunboat to Agadir, which let loose a few rounds across the bay. Like the Fashoda crisis in Egypt, the event very nearly sent the balloon up to launch World War I.

Eating, drinking and nightlife

For an international resort, Agadir is a bit staid, with little in the way of bars, clubs or discos, outside of the large hotels. However, there are plenty of cafés and restaurants, for all budgets, and including a few "ethnic" choices if you feel like a break from Moroccan or French-style food.

Restaurants

As with hotels, there's a concentration of inexpensive café-restaurants in Nouvelle Talborjt, where you can get regular Moroccan meals at pretty regular Moroccan prices. There are many cafés and mid-price restaurants on or near the beach, too, including two that stay open 24 hours, along with a fair range of more sophisticated places – a few of which almost justify a stopover in themselves.

NOUVELLE TALBORJT/CITY CENTRE

Mille et Une Nuits, Place Lahcen Tamri. Serves a range of Moroccan staples – *couscous*, *tagine*, *brochettes* and *harira*; always fresh, busy and good value. Cheap.

Café-Restaurant Echabab, Place Lahcen Tamri. Usually has a good and inexpensive *plat du jour*. Open to midnight. Cheap.

L'Amirante, 19 Rue des Orangiers. Value for money if you stick to the local dishes – which are in any case better than the international offerings. Moderate.

Ogill, 86 Rue des Oranges. Seafood. Open until midnight. Moderate.

Restaurant Madame Marquez, 84 Rue des Orangiers (☎08/84.15.88). A fine restaurant, that concentrates on fish and seafood dishes, including a great *paella*. Run by a Luxembourg *restauranteure* and her husband, a former top-class boxer from Martinique. Moderate.

Restaurant Caverne, Bd. Hassan II. Friendly and good value. Moderate.

Restaurant l'Étoile de Marrakech, on the ground floor of the *Studiotel Afoud*, Rue de la Foire (☎08/84.39.99). Renowned traditional Moroccan restaurant. Moderate.

Restaurant Darkoum, Av. Général Kettani (☎08/82.26.22). Good local dishes with occasional live music. Open 7.30pm to midnight. Moderate.

La Tonkinoise, ground floor of *Residence Tislit*, next door to *Hôtel Les Palmiers*, Av. du Prince Sidi Mohammed (☎08/82.27.25). Viatnamese cooking – highly recommended. Moderate.

Café-Restaurant Tamount, 47 Av. President Kennedy. Copious helpings of well-prepared Moroccan dishes. Moderate.

MAIN BOULEVARDS/TOWARDS THE BEACH

Restaurant Don Vito, on the beach. Good for pizza and pasta, snacks and soft drinks, though the wall-to-wall Roger Whittaker is a bit much to take. Moderate.

Restaurant du Port, Port d'Agadir – near the campsite. Fish and seafood – as you'd expect from the location inside the fishing port. Take your passport, as you have to go through customs. Open noon–3pm & 7–10pm. Moderate.

Restaurant Jour et Nuit, on the beach; **Restaurant Tente**, "under" the swimming pool. Moroccan and French dishes and snacks. Both are open 24hr. Moderate.

Residence Tafkout, Bd. du 20 Août. This tourist complex has a number of restaurants, with French, Moroccan, Italian and seafood menus. Moderate to expensive.

Le Miramar, in the *Hôtel Miramar,* Bd. Mohammed V (☎08/86.26.73). This is reckoned the city's most chic restaurant – a beautifully decorated place overlooking the fishing port. Fine Italian cooking, particularly fish and seafood. Fairly expensive.

Bars and nightlife

Both the *Jour et Nuit* and *Tente* restaurants (see above) also have bars open 24 hours. Other nightlife options include:

Corniche Restaurant Bar, close by the *Jour et Nuit* (above) on the beachfront. A clear winner for night-time entertainment, hosting some excellent bands led by local musicians.

Disco Tan Tan, in the *Hôtel Almohades.* Perhaps the best of the hotel discos.

Bylbos Disco, in the *Hôtel Les Dunes d'Or.* This can be lively, too, though admission and drinks are expensive.

Directory

Airlines *Royal Air Maroc* have an office on Av. du Général Kettani, opposite the junction with Bd. Hassan II (☎08/84.08.08). They fly from Agadir to Casablanca (daily, Marrakesh (five weekly), Dakhla (three weekly), Laayoune, Fes and Tangier (all twice weekly), and Er Rachidia, Tan Tan and Ouarzazate (weekly). Also international flights to the Canary Islands (twice weekly), London, Milan, Paris, Vienna and Zurich.

American Express c/o *Voyages Schwartz,* Bd. Hassan II (☎08/82.49.48); open Mon–Fri 9am–noon & 3–6pm; closed weekends.

Banks There are over a dozen banks in the downtown area; regular hours are Mon–Fri 8am–noon & 2.30–5pm. *Banque Populaire* on Bd. Hassan II is helpful – and will guide you through the motions of opening an account if you decide to stay on in Morocco; they also have a little bureau de change, next to *Hôtel Kamal* on Bd. Hassan II, which is open on Saturdays. *ABM* on Av. du Prince Sidi Mohammed (opposite the PTT), *BMCE* on Av. du Général Kéttani and *Crédit du Maroc* on Av. des F.A.R. are useful for VISA/Access transactions; the BMCE has the city's only VISA cash dispenser/teller machine. Most large hotels also change money.

Books and newspapers Since the demise of *The Crown English Bookshop* (which was by the Tourist Office – in case it reopens), Agadir has had no English-language bookshop. A small selection of novels and coffee table books on Morocco are sold at Atlas Bureau, 16/20 Av. Prince Moulay Abdallah, and Debit Pilote, 65 Bd. Hassan II. English newspapers and the *International Herald Tribune* are available from kiosks on Av. Hassan II and at the foot of Av. du Prince Sidi Mohammed, and at larger hotels.

Car hire If you're heading for the Anti-Atlas or cutting across to the south, hiring a car from Agadir makes a lot of sense. It's also very competitive, with fifty or so hire companies competing for your custom. Check several before you make a decision, and check that you are being offered an all-inclusive price (insurance, etc), and whether you can return the car to another city, or to Agadir airport.

A good place to start looking is the **Bungalow Marhaba** on Bd. Mohammed (see map), where you'll find *Hertz* (☎08/84.09.39), *Budget* (☎08/84.07.62), *Europcar/InterRent* (☎08/84.03.37) and *Tourist Cars* (☎08/84.02.00), together with the local operators *Weekend Cars* (☎08/84.06.67), *Lotus Cars* (☎08/84.05.88) and *Afric Cars* (☎08/84.09.22; highly recommended by our resident Agadir correspondent). *Avis* (☎08/84.03.45), the only other major company, are on Bd. Hassan II.

Also personally recommended are three other local companies: *Amoudou Cars,* Immeuble Abdou, Av. Hassan II, near *Hôtel Cinq Parties du Monde* (☎08/84.37.72); *Golden Tours,* Bd. Mohammed V (☎08/84.03.62); and *Méditerranée Cars,* Immeuble Dolador, Rue El Massira (☎08/84.19.68).

Car repairs Some recommendations: for Renaults, *Castano,* Rue Kadi Aïad; for Citroëns/Peugeots, *Garage Citroën,* Rue du 3 Mars; for Fiats, *Auto-Hall,* Rue de la Foire. There are many others, doubtless equally good.

Cinemas The town has three: the *Sahara* in Talborjt; the *Salam*, on Place Salam/Place de l'Abattoir; and *Rialto*, the newest, near the municipal market.

Consulates An honorary British consul is based at the *Beach Club* hotel on the beach (☎08/84.43.43); there are also consuls for Norway (☎08/82.34.47) and Sweden (☎08/82.30.48). There is no US, Canadian, Australian or Dutch consular representation.

Ferries For Tangier ferries, book at *COMANAV*, Place Mohammed V (☎08/82.04.52). Note that the ferry from Agadir to Las Palmas (Canary Islands) has been discontinued.

Medical care Most of the big hotels can provide addresses for English-speaking doctors. Current recommendations include: doctors: Dr Martinez Espinoza (☎08/82.06.31) and Dr Tarik Ljubuncic (☎08/84.10.78); and dentists: Dr Noureddine Touhami, Immeuble MZ – Apt. 4 (near the PTT), Av. Prince Moulay Abdallah (☎08/82.04.52). Alternatively, take a taxi to the Polyclinique, which is efficient, or the Clinique Massira, a few blocks down from the PTT on Av. Prince Moulay Abdallah.

Moped/motorbike/bike hire *MotoHire*, near the beach, on Bd. du 20 Août, hires out Yamaha 125s at about 150dh a day (lower rates for the week), well worth considering for trips to Immouzer and beyond. It also has cheaper mopeds (*motos*), intended for local use but practical for shuttling to Banana Village and Tarhazoute. Outlets alongside the hotels *Europa* and *Almohades* also hire motos and bikes.

Post office The main *PTT* is right in the middle of town at the end of Av. Sidi Mohammed; hours are Mon–Fri 9am–noon & 3–6pm, Sat 9am–noon only; the efficient telephone section stays open till 9pm.

Religious services The Église Sainte-Anne celebrates daily mass at 6.30pm and on Sundays at 10am and 7pm; its priests are French, Dutch and Indian.

Shopping For **crafts shopping**, the *Uniprix* shop at the corner of Bd. Hassan II and Av. du Prince Sidi Mohammed and *Sud Galleria*, further along Bd. Hassan II opposite the *Hôtel Karam*, are useful (at least for an initial idea of things), as they sell goods at fixed prices. So, too, does the chaotic *Ensemble Artisanal* (daily 9am–1pm & 3–6pm) on Rue 29 Fevrier, just north of Place Lahcen Tamri. If you buy anything elsewhere in Agadir – rugs, carpets, *babouches*, etc – you will have to do some very heavy bargaining indeed. Better by far, however, would be to visit the *souks* at Taroudannt for the day.

The *Uniprix* shop also sells the cheapest **spirits, beer and wine** (along with general provisions). The best **supermarket** is *Sawma Supermarket*, 1 Rue de Hôtel de Ville, just off Av. Hassan II.

Tourist offices The *ONMT* is on the balcony level of Immeuble A, entered off Av. Sidi Mohammed and the raised walkway opposite the post office. There is a helpful *Syndicat d'Initiative* on Av. Mohammed V (☎08/84.03.07).

Travel agents *Menara Tours*, 341 Av. Hassan II (☎08/93.52.11), are agents for British Airways and offer all usual services, including car hire.

Inezgane

INEZGANE, on the north bank of the Oued Souss, is almost a suburb of Agadir, just 13km distant. The two could hardly be more different, however, for Inezgane is wholly Moroccan, and is a major transport hub for the region – much more so than Agadir – with buses and *grands taxis* going to most southern destinations, including regular departures to Taroudannt*, Essaouira and Marrakesh. Inezgane itself is connected with Agadir by local bus #5 and #6 bus (very frequent) and by frequent *grand taxi* (5dh a place, arriving/leaving Agadir at Place Salam).

*****Grands taxis from Inezgane to Taroudannt**, often cover the route in two stages. The first taxi take you to OULAD TEIMA (or "44" as it's known after the kilometre-marker from Agadir), where your driver will arrange a connection on to Taroudannt.

If you arrive late at Agadir airport, and want to head straight on south, you could do a lot worse than stay here, rather than Agadir; you may be able to negotiate a slightly cheaper taxi from the airport, too. Rooms are usually no problem, with a choice of ten **hotels** on and around the central Place Al Massira, near the bus station. Good choices would be: *Hôtel de Paris*, 30 Bd. Mohammed V (☎08/ 83.05.71; ①; with an inexpensive restaurant); *Hôtel Issafen*, Bd. Moulay Abdallah (☎08/83.04.13; ①; with en suite rooms); or *Hôtel Hagounia*, 9 Av. Mokhtar Soussi (☎08/83.27.83; ②; again with a good inexpensive restaurant).

North of Agadir: the coast to Cap Rhir

Along the **coast north of Agadir**, tourist development rapidly begins to fade, and the beach at **Tarhazoute** (19km from Agadir) belongs to a different world, with entirely local accommodation and not a "proper" hotel in sight. This – and the coast towards Cap Rhir – is popular surfing territory, and Essaouira (see Chapter Four) is of course a major surfing resort. The route is also a good one for birdwatchers – as is the coastline south of Agadir.

Transport is pretty straightforward. From Agadir, city buses #12 and #14 run more or less on the hour up the coast to Tarhazoute, while Essaouira buses take the route beyond, via Cap Rhir. The coast is a good target, too, if you hire mopeds or motorbikes in Agadir.

Agadir to Tarhazoute

The coast road north of Agadir begins unpromisingly, passing through the city's industrial sector, a strip known as CITÉ ANZAR. You can see and smell the petrol, butane, cement and fish, and may wonder why you left Agadir bay.

At 11km from Agadir, however, things improve, as you reach TAMRARHT, which is also spelt TAMRHAKHT but universally known as "**Banana Village**" after its thriving banana grove and roadside stalls. You can eat extremely well at the roadside **café-restaurants** here, which are a weekend favourite of the wealthier Agadiris; the ones to look for are the last three on the left, heading north, or the *Orama Tajine*, on the hill above and just before the village, coming from Agadir. At the north end of the village is "**Banana Beach**", a sandy strip, broken by the Oued Tamraht. To the east, a kilometre before you reach Tamraht proper, a road heads inland through "**Paradise Valley**", a beautiful palm-lined gorge, and up into the mountains to **Immouzer des Ida Outanane** .

Around 2km out of Tamrarht, a prominent rocky headland, **Les Roches du Diable**, is flanked by further good beaches on either side. The southern one is used by fishermen who stay in bamboo huts here in the summer. Shortly beyond here (at the 17km mark from Agadir), a signposted piste leads to a **ranch**, the *Centre de Tourisme Equestre R.E.H.A.*, where you can go **horse trekking** into the mountains; if you are interested, book through one of the larger Agadir hotels.

Tarhazoute

Twenty kilometres from Agadir is the fishing village of **TARHAZOUTE** (or TAGHAGANT, as it appears on some maps), a ramshackle cluster of compact, colour-washed houses. It is flanked on either side – indeed, from way north of

---

ARGAN TREES

One of the stranger sights of the Souss are goats clambering about the trunks of spiny, knotted **argan trees** – a tree, similar to the olive, that is found only in this region. The argan nuts are harvested from late May onwards, depending on the height above sea level, and often have to be recovered from the goat dung (having passed through their gut).

Unappetising though that might sound, **argan oil** has a sweet and rich taste, and is used in many Moroccan dishes and salads, or for dunking bread. It is quite a delicacy, and not easily extracted: whilst one olive tree provides around five litres of olive oil, it takes the nuts from thirty argan trees to make just one litre of argan oil. Plastic bottles of argan oil are commonly sold at the roadside in the Agadir area.

Cap Rhir down to Agadir – by a great swathe of beach, interrupted here and there by headlands and for the most part deserted. Until 1990, the village itself had no electricity (it's still without running water) and inevitably it attracts a rather different clientele from Agadir. Twenty and even ten years ago, it was Morocco's hippy resort *par excellence*, and things haven't changed all that much. International hippydom has been replaced by surfers and young Moroccans – plus an added campervan community of elderly Europeans in the winter – and in summer, the café-managers still belt out non-stop rock music and play cool.

Accommodation is mainly in private rooms, all pretty basic, which give you buckets to fetch water from the spring beside the mosque for washing (there is a hammam – for women until 6pm, men after 6pm – in Tamrahrt/Banana Village). Most people rent rooms by the week and rates are therefore highly negotiable – try 250dh a week for two people. There is also a **campsite**, *Camping Tarhazoute*, set just back from the beach, a bit scruffy, and used mainly by campervans.

For **meals**, *Restaurant Les Sables d'Or*, on the cliff top at the south end of the village, is highly recommended. It's a café and bar, as well, with steps down to the beach. The new *Restaurant La Baraka*, down by the beach, is also pretty good, serving up grilled fish at a very reasonable price.

On to Cap Rhir: beaches and birdwatching

North of Tarhazoute is a beach known, somewhat literally, as **25km–Plage** (its distance from Agadir). This is an attractive spot, defined by a rocky headland, and offering good surfing.

A further 5km brings you to – yes, **30km–Plage**, flanked by smart summer villas, and the little village of AGHOUT. From here on to Cap Rhir, there are many little beaches, with caves on the rocky outcrops. The stretch is also known as **Paradis Plage**, and so marked on some maps. At the spot known as Amesnaz (not a village as such), 33km from Agadir, there's a really superb strand.

Cap Rhir (41km from Agadir) is distinguished by its lighthouse, one of the country's first, built by the French in 1926; the keepers welcome visits – and tips. This area, together with **TAMRI** village and **lagoon**, 3km north, is particularly good for **birdwatching**. A report in *Bird Watching* magazine claimed some notable seabird sightings at the cape in recent years, among them Madeiran and Bulwer's petrels, "though you are more likely to see Cory's or Manx Shearwaters, Gannet and Common Scoter". At the lagoon, Audouin's gulls come in to bathe, and bald ibis are a strong winter possibility. There are a couple of forlorn-looking **cafés** at Tamri for sustenance.

For the continuation of this route along the P8, see p.297, where it is covered in a north–south direction from Essaouira. For much of the distance the road runs some way inland, with just the occasional piste leading down to the sea.

Inland to "Paradise Valley" and Immouzer

The trip up to **Immouzer des Ida Outanane** and its waterfalls – via **"Paradise Valley"**, a beautiful palm-lined gorge – is a superb excursion from Agadir. It is feasible in a day (Immouzer is 62km from Agadir) but much more enjoyable if you stay the night at one or other of the superb *auberges* (30km up the valley or at Immouzer) or take time to explore and camp in the valley.

The road to Immouzer is surfaced the whole way; it leaves the P8 coast road at AORIRE, 11km north of Agadir (make sure you take the right-hand fork in the village – the left-hand one is a dead-end, up a palmery). A daily bus leaves Agadir at 2pm (from the street behind *Hôtel Sindibad* on Place Lahcen Tamri), arriving in Immouzer around 4.30pm; it returns each morning at 8am. Minibus taxis also run to Immouzer for the Thursday market (a trip that can be booked at any Agadir travel agent or through most of the larger hotels).

"Paradise Valley"

"Paradise Valley" begins around 10km east of Aorire, as the road suddenly turns a bend into a deep, palm-lined gorge, with a river snaking along the base. The best stretch starts just after the turnoff for Immouzer. You can hire a mule to explore the valley's numerous Berber villages, and it's a glorious place to **camp**, though in the spring pitch your tent well away from the riverbed in case of flash floods.

Continuing along the "main road" (7002), at around the 30km mark from Tamrarht, you pass a small new **auberge**, the *Hôtel Tifrit* (no phone; ①). Set in a beautiful little palmery, with a river winding through, this is a rival for the famous Immouzer hotel – and about half the price. It is run by a charming family, has a swimming pool and provides fine Moroccan meals.

After a further 20km of winding mountain road, you reach the village of **Immouzer des Ida Outanane**, tucked away in a westerly outcrop of the Atlas.

Immouzer des Ida Outanane

IMMOUZER DES IDA OUTANANE is a minor regional and market centre (of the Ida Outanane, as its full name suggests). The **waterfalls**, for which the village is renowned, roll down from the hills 4km to the northwest: follow the road down through the main square and off to the left. They can be be spectacular in spring, when the waters reach flood levels and almond blossoms are everywhere, but tight control of irrigation reduces the cascade on most occasions to a trickle, with the villagers "turning on" the falls for special events only. However, the petrified canopy of the falls is of interest in its own right, and there's a full **plunge pool**, and also a second waterfall, nearby, which is still allowed to flow its natural course (ask directions to "Le Deuxieme Cascade").

However, what is really appealing here is the overall feel of things. There's a hamlet just across the stream from the falls, and a **café** (*Café de Miel*) with basic food, near which you can camp out in the olive groves. The whole area is perfect for walkers. You can follow any of the paths with enjoyment – a good one, near the village, cuts up across the cliffs to the *Hôtel des Cascades* – or even trek off to the Marrakesh road (see below). The **birdlife** adds an exciting dimension, with birds of prey commonplace; Bonelli's eagle is a good bet, and you might well spot golden eagles or crag martins.

In Immouzer village, there's a **souk** every Thursday. The local speciality is honey, and the bees are said to feed from wild marijuana and other herbs in the mountains.

Staying in Immouzer

The **Hôtel des Cascades** (☎08/83.47.05; ③) is on the edge of Immouzer and signposted from its main square. It is a really delightful place, set amid gardens of vines, apple and olive trees, and hollyhocks, with a huge and placid panorama of the mountains rolling down to the coast, and a spectacular path down to the foot of the falls. The food, too, is memorable and there's a swimming pool (full in summer) and tennis court, and pony-trekking. It is slightly pricey, perhaps, but open to bargaining on its "pension" rates.

If at all possible, book ahead, as the only alternative accommodation are basic rooms at the café just on the right as you enter the village, or at the *Hôtel Tifrit*, 30km distant on the road up from "Paradise Valley" (see above).

East from Immouzer: treks and pistes

A very rough piste road breaks off from the Immouzer–Agadir road, 5km south of Immouzer, and leads to the Agadir–Marrakesh road (P40): it makes a varied and interesting full day's hike and you can catch a bus or taxi back from the S511 to Agadir. The *Hôtel des Cascades* will run walkers to the end of the initial valley (or you could walk there the night before and sleep out on the pass beyond; carry water), from which the road winds up to cross a high limestone plateau. It then drops to circuit a huge hollow in the hills and descends to a (seasonal) river before climbing up to a pass through to the P40.

If you have a sturdy vehicle, there's a better road which runs east through Immouzer village and over to the P40 at ARGANA, by way of ISK. This is a high route – often snowbound in winter and perilous in spring after the thaw – and quite spectacular in parts, blasted out of sheer rock face, before descending amid Martian-red hills.

South of Agadir: the Massa lagoon

Around 40km south of Agadir, the **Massa lagoon** is possibly Morocco's most important **bird habitat** (see box opposite), attracting unusual desert visitors and often packed with flamingoes, avocets and ducks. The immediate area of the lagoon is a protected zone, closed to visitors, but you can get in some rewarding birdwatching if you base yourself at the nearby campsite and chalet complex of **Sidi Rbat**, set beside a long, wild beach and rolling sand dunes. The best **times to visit** are March to April or October to November.

THE MASSA LAGOON: BIRDWATCHING

The protected reserve of **Oued Massa** has perhaps the richest habitat mix in Morocco, drawing in a fabulous array of birds. The **sandbars** are visited in the early morning by flocks of sandgrouse (black-bellied and spotted varieties) and often shelter large numbers of cranes; the **ponds** and **reedbed** margins conceal various waders such as black-tailed godwit, turnstone, dunlin, snipe and little crake; the deeper **open waters** provide feeding grounds for greater flamingo, spoonbill, white stork and black-winged stilt; and overhead the skies are patrolled by marsh harrier and osprey.

The surrounding **scrubby areas** also hold black-headed bush shrike and a variety of nocturnal mammals such as Egyptian mongoose, cape hare and jackal, while the Sidi R'bat *complexe* offers its own wildlife highlights – a local population of Mauritanian toad in the shower block at night and a café terrace from which the most fortunate might observe **bald ibis**, one of the world's rarest birds.

Enthusiasts with transport might also like to follow the Oued Massa inland, 20km to the east, to the **Barrage Youssef Ben Tachfine**, an enormous freshwater reservoir, edged by the Anti-Atlas. Possible sightings include black wheatear and rock dove. By the lake is a car park, where campervans sometimes overnight.

Transport of your own is a considerable advantage for exploring the lagoon area. The best approach from Agadir is to turn west off the P30 Tiznit road at Aït Belfa; from the south you can turn west along the 7053 towards Tassila, shortly after reaching the Oued Massa. Either route will bring you to a T-junction in the centre of MASSA, a long, straggling village with a small **hotel**, the *Tassila* (②), which is sometimes used by birdwatching groups. From here, 8km of sandy road lead alongside the coast and north of the lagoon to a *marabout's* tomb, **Sidi Rbat**, and, nearby, beside the sea, a **campsite/chalet compex**, *La Complexe et Balnéaire Sidi R'bat* (☎ 94 through the operator). This is a rather scruffy site but offers simple cabins round a shaded courtyard or camping for a small charge;' it also has a café and a very poor restaurant.

Without transport, you could charter a taxi in Agadir or Inezgane for the trip to Sidi Rbat; this should cost around 100dh (for up to six people). Alternatively, you could take a local bus/*grand taxi* from Agadir to Inezgane, and a *grand taxi* from there to Massa, and then walk/hitch on from there to Sidi Rbat. On the return journey, try to get a lift with fellow tourists from Sidi Rbat, as few of the taxis stop in Massa on their way north to Agadir.

The **beach** at Sidi Rbat itself can often be misty and overcast – even when Agadir is basking in the sun – but on a clear day, it's as good as anywhere else and the walks, at any rate, are enjoyable.

Tifnite

The stretch of coast south of Agadir, and north of Massa, is virtually undeveloped, once you clear the sprawl at the edge of Inezgane. It is accessible at a couple of points from the P30, but there is little to go out of the way for. **TIFNITE**, the name that appears most prominently on most maps, is a little collection of fishing huts, strange to come upon so close to "international" Agadir. It attracts a few campervan travellers in summer.

Taroudannt

With its majestic, red-ochre circuit of walls, **TAROUDANNT** is one of the most elegant towns in Morocco and an excellent "first base" if you arrive in the country at Agadir. The walls, the *souks* and the stark, often heat-hazed backdrop of the High Atlas to the north, are the town's chief attractions – though none of them is powerful enough to bring in the Agadir tour groups in any great number. It is consequently a very friendly, laid-back sort of place, with all the good-natured bustle of a Berber market town. In addition, the town forms a useful base for trekking into the Western High Atlas or on to the Djebel Sirwa to the east, while for anyone into great road journeys, it stands at the beginning of two superb road routes – north over the Tizi n'Test to Marrakesh (see p.356) and south to the oases of Tata and Foum el Hassan (see pp.455–57).

Taroudannt's position at the head of the fertile Souss Valley has always given it a commercial and political importance – it was often the first major conquest of new imperial dynasties. It never became a "great city", however. Even the Saadians, who made Taroudannt their capital in the sixteenth century (and built most of its circuit of walls), moved on to Marrakesh. The town's present status, as a major market centre, but with a population of only around 30,000, is probably much as it always has been.

Orientation and accommodation

On arrival, the town can seem highly confusing, with ramparts heading off for miles in every direction and large areas of open space and derelict building areas – some due to flash flooding, others under cultivation.

In fact, the central town, with its *souks* and workshops, is quite compact, and within the walled "inner city" there are just two main squares – **Place Assarag** and **Place Talmoklate** – with the **souk** area between them to the north. Place Assarag, with its low arcaded front and its many cafés, is very much the centre of activity. Over to the east is a further walled enclosure, the old **Kasbah** area, in one corner of which is the *Hôtel Palais Salam*. If you arrive by **bus**, most of the *CTM* and *SATAS* services will deposit you at the Place Assarag, other lines at Place Talmoklate, from which *grands taxis* also operate. (See the "Directory" section for details of departures).

Getting round town, there are **petits taxis** (usually to be found in Place Talmoklate) and, with similar tariffs, a few **calèches** – horse-drawn cabs. You can also hire **bikes** (again, see "Directory" for details).

Hotels

All the cheaper **hotels** are on or around Place Assarag or Place Talmoklate, while dotted round town are a few rather fancier places, including a fine splurge, the *Hôtel Palais Salam*.

Recommendations (the seven less salubrious and poor-value hotels on Place Assarag aren't listed) include, in ascending order of price:

Hôtel les Oliviers [F], Av. du Prince Heritier Sidi Mohammed (☎08/85.20.21). Small, pretty basic rooms – but cheap and clean. ①

Hôtel Roudani [C], overlooking Place Assarag (☎08/85.22.19). Marginally better rooms, meals on the square, and a fine rooftop terrace for breakfast. ①

Hôtel Es Sabah [A], Av. Mohammed V – just west of Place Assarag (☎08/85.22.97). Larger rooms and clean enough. ⓪

Hôtel El Warda [G], Place Talmoklate (☎08/85.27.63). Front rooms have balconies over the square and there's a restaurant. Prices highly negotiable. ⓪

Hôtel Mentaga [H], Place Talmoklate (☎08/85.23.83). Four rooms round a landing; unusual for Morocco, it is run by a woman, who was widowed but kept the hotel going. ⓪

Hôtel les Arcades [D], Place Assarag (☎08/85.23.73). Better known for its restaurant, but it has four decent enough rooms and very friendly staff. ⓪

Hôtel Taroudannt [B], Place Assarag (☎08/85.24.16). A Taroudannt institution, this was run by a grand old French *patronne* up until her death in December 1988. It retains her influence (and amazing poster collection) and is well worth the money for its patio garden, cool air and bar. The cooking is excellent, too – both French and Moroccan. ①

Hôtel Saadiens [E], Bordj Oumansour (☎08/85.25.89). A pleasant modern hotel, north of the squares, with a licensed restaurant, a patisserie, hot showers and swimming pool. ②

Hôtel Palais Salam [labelled] (☎08/85.21.30). Located in a nineteenth-century palace, just inside the ramparts, in the Kasbah quarter, this is a beautiful place – though make sure you get the rooms or suites in the towers or garden pavilions, rather than on the new modern floor. There is a small swimming pool, cocktail bar and two excellent restaurants. ④

Hôtel Gazelle d'Or, 2km out of town to the southwest (☎08/85.20.39). This is an extraordinary place, worth seeing even if you have no possibility of staying: a hunting lodge created by a French baron in the 1920s, in a Morocco-meets-Provence style. It was converted to a hotel after the war and guests (mostly well-heeled Brits) stay in bungalows in the lush gardens. Rates are astronomical – quite possibly the highest in North Africa. ⑤

Around the town

Taroudannt's twin attractions are its **ramparts** – best toured by bike – and its **souks**. The latter are not large by Moroccan city standards, but are varied and authentic and much of the work you find here is of outstanding quality. On Thursdays and Sundays there is a **regional souk**, which brings in Chleuh Berbers from the villages to sell farm produce and a few odd pieces of craftwork; this takes place out by the northeast gate, **Bab El Khemis**.

The souks

There are two principal *souks*: the **Souk Arab Artisanal**, immediately east of Place Assarag (and north of Place Talmoklate), and the **Marché Berbère**, south of Place Talmoklate.

The **"Arab" souk** – easiest approached along the lane by the *BMCE* bank (you will probably emerge in Place Talmoklate – it's a tiny area) – is good for rugs, carpets, leather goods and other traditional crafts, but most especially **jewellery**. This comes mainly from the Anti-Atlas villages nowadays, though until the 1960s there was an active artisan quarter here, comprising mainly Jewish craftsmen; little of it is as "antique" as the sellers would have you believe. Some stalls also sell striking limestone **sculptures**, similar to the ones found in the north at Chaouen and an obvious oddity – often figurative in design and more African than Islamic. For good-quality wares, the *Antiquaire Haut Atlas*, run by Licher El Houcine at 36 Souk Smara, is locally recommended.

The **Marché Berbère** is a more everyday *souk*, with spices and vegetables, as well as clothing and pottery, and again jewellery and carpets. It is most easily entered alongside the *Hôtel Mentaga* in Place Talmoklate. Interesting stalls include the *Cadeaux de Taroudannt*, 35 Av. Nasr, run by Benjeddi Ahmed, and

TAROUDANNT

Oued Ouâar

Bab Targhount

Tanneries

Banque Populaire

SGMB

C D

PLACE ASSARAG

Souk Arab Artisanal

A   B

BMCE

G   PLACE TALMOKLATE

F

H

Marché Berbère

To Hôtel Gazelle d'Or (2km)

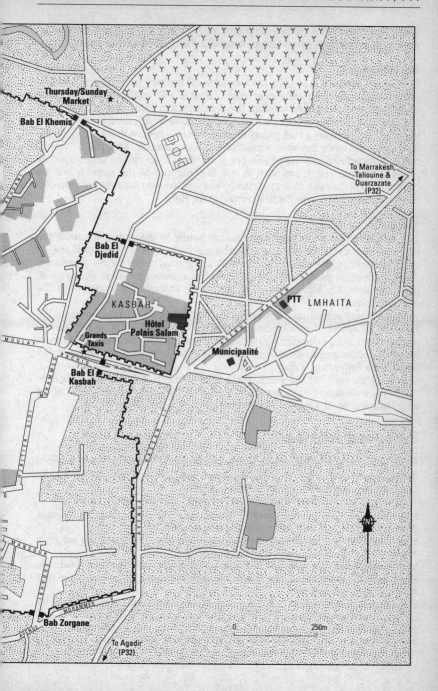

Thursday/Sunday Market ★

Bab El Khemis

To Marrakesh,
Taliouine &
Ouarzazate
(P32)

Bab El
Djedid

KASBAH

Hôtel
Palais Salam

Grands
Taxis

PTT   LMHAITA

Municipalité

Bab El
Kasbah

MOULAY

Bab Zorgane

To Agadir
(P32)

N

0   250m

the hand-embroidered clothes shop next door, which does superb kaftans for women, and *gandoura* (short-sleeve) and *foukia* (long-sleeve) robes for men.

The tanneries

The leather **tanneries**, as ever, are located some distance from the main *souks* – placed outside the town walls on account of their smell – leather is cured in cattle urine or pigeon droppings – and for the proximity to a ready supply of water. In comparison to Marrakesh, or particularly Fes, the tanneries here are very small, but, sadly, they display a rare variety of skins for sale – not just those of the ubiquitous sheep and cows, but silver foxes, racoons and mountain cats as well. Many of these furs are illegal imports into Europe or North America and we urge no participation in the process. If you want to visit the tanneries all the same, follow the continuation of the main street past the *Hôtel Taroudannt* to the ramparts; turn left there and, after 100m, take the first turning to the right.

The walls

The town's various **walls and bastions** can hardly be ignored, and, outside the height of summer, they make an enjoyable circuit to explore. They total around five kilometres in extent and you can walk along stretches of them – sometimes dropping down to the foot of collapsed stretches and always with an eye to avoiding excrement. On balance, it is perhaps more enjoyable to cycle round the outside perimeter.

On your way round, take a good look at the old **Kasbah quarter** round the *Hôtel Palais Salam*. Now a kind of ramshackle village within the town, this was once a winter palace complex for the Saadians and contains the ruins of a fortress built by Moulay Ismail. (Non-residents can use the swimming pool at the *Palais Salam* for a daily fee of 30dh).

Beyond the walls to the south, signs point to the **Hôtel Gazelle d'Or** (see "Hotels"), a pleasant two-kilometre cycle. A mint tea on its terrace is just about affordable and worthwhile for a look at the gardens, especially in spring.

Eating and drinking

Basic but inexpensive **café-restaurants** can be found along the street between the two main squares: you could pick from any one of these hole-in-the-wall stalls, most of which have just a couple of tables outside.

Among places big enough to have a name, and the town's hotels, pick from:

Hôtel Roudani, Place Assarag; **Hôtel El Warda**, Place Talmoklate; **Hôtel les Arcades**, Place Assarag. These all have inexpensive, good-value set meals.

Chez Fouad, Av. Sidi Mohammed – between the two squares. The nearest you will get to fish and chips in the Souss – and very good they are, too.

Hôtel Taroudannt, Place Assarag. Fine French and Moroccan meals – and a bar. Moderate.

Hôtel Saadiens, Bordj Oumansour. Top-floor licensed restaurant, with a view of the High Atlas from its terrace.Moderate.

Hôtel Palais Salam, Kasbah. French and Moroccan restaurants – both superb in the evening (lunches cater for groups), though expensive. Also has a pleasant terrace bar.

Hôtel Gazelle d'Or, 2km out of town. The tented dining room here is quite a sight – and a major extravagance for dinner, when men are required to wear jackets and ties. Lunch by the pool is less costly – and nobody would be likely to object to your swimming afterwards.

TREKKING FROM TAROUDANNT

The **Western High Atlas** – routes across which are covered on pp.368–69 – are easily accessible from Taroudannt, the peaks of Tinergwet (3551m) and Awlim (3481m) west of the **Tichka Plateau** looking temptingly close as you look out to the mountains from a roof terrace at dawn or dusk. One of the very best trekking routes in Morocco – "The Wonder Walk" as it is called by some trekking companies – is to make a two-week trip up to the plateau and on to Djebel Toubkal (see p.355), Morocco's highest peak. The **Djebel Sirwa** (see p.451) is also within easy reach of the town.

If you are interested in a **guided trek**, contact **Tali Abdel Aziz**, who runs *Tigouga Adventures* with his partner, **El Aouad Ali**; they are English-speaking, highly knowledgeable, and have planned out a number of magnificent routes with the Scottish mountain writer, Hamish Brown. Their possible itineraries include the "Wonder Walk" above, though they are happy to take you on one- or two-day treks if you prefer. Aziz provides real experience of Berber life on his treks, living and eating in local houses or camping on the plateau or by the spectacular Nfis River (bread baked on the spot, muleteers singing round a bonfire – it's a world of magic). Independent trekkers, however, can use his services to get established before going on to trek, climb or (increasingly popular on the Tichka Plateau) ski-tour.

Aziz can be contacted at home by phone or in person (40 Derb El Gazara; ☎08/85.35.01), or through the *Hôtel Taroudannt*; if you prefer to make arrangements in advance, his postal address is BP132, Taroudannt, Souss, Morocco. As with all guides, the cost of a trek with Aziz or Ali should be negotiated in advance and preferably confirmed in writing.

Directory

Banks There are four: the *BMCE*, *SGMB* and *Banque Populaire* on Place Assarag, and the *BMC* on Place Talmoklate. All have exchange facilities.

Bicycles can be hired by the hour, half- or full-day from from the *Hôtel Salam* and from a little shop near the *Hôtel Taroudannt*, just off Place Assarag.

Buses Going on from Taroudannt by bus needs a little advance planning as regards routes and terminals (which vary between the Place Assarag and Place Talmoklate). The most reliable services are those operated by *SATAS* (who have an unmarked office in Place Tamoklate) and *CTM* (who have an office in the *Hôtel les Arcades* in Place Assarag); other, smaller private-line services run mainly from Place Talmoklate. *SATAS* departures include: Tata (Place Assarag; Wed & Sat at 8am – tickets when the bus arrives at 7.30am; arrives at 2pm); Tizi n'Test/Marrakesh (Place Assarag; 5am; see p.356 for this route); Agadir (Place Assarag; daily at 5am, 10.30am, 2.30pm & 5.30pm; some go on or make connections to Marrakesh or Casablanca); Talioune/Ouarzazate (Place Talmoklate; 8am & noon; the morning bus continues to Zagora).

Car repairs There's a garage for Citroens and Peugeots just inside Bab Targhount (☎08/85.52.22).

Grands taxis operate out of Place Talmoklate and the area just inside the Bab El Kasbah; they make regular runs to and from Inezgane/Agadir (often with a change of cars midway at Ouled Teima – see p.438), and can be chartered for Taliouine, or at considerable expense, Asni or Marrakesh (over the Tizi n'Test road).

Hammam There is a hammam located 30m behind the *Hôtel Taroudannt* – it is signposted only in Arabic (a green tiled entrance, no. 50, next to a butcher's), so you may need to ask someone. Women can steam from noon to 4pm; men all other hours; 4dh admission (massage extra).

THE OUED SOUSS: BIRDWATCHING

The **Oued Souss** is another key Moroccan bird habitat, with a rich array of winter residents, and a huge range of migrants in the spring.

Using Taroudannt as your base, the bridge or causeway north of **Freija** (see below) would be good points to spend a day birdwatching. Hoopoe, woodchat shrike, orphean, sub-Alpine and Bonelli's warbler, bee-eater and nightingale are all likely sightings in the spring, while stone curlew, great grey shrike and serin are common in winter. Raptors are also likely to be evident: black and black-shouldered kite, griffon vulture and tawny eagle among them. In the evening, you might spot black-bellied sandgrouse and red-necked nightjar (a Souss speciality).

Another site, more scenic and likely to be even more rewarding for birds, is the **Aoulouz Gorge**, 90km east of Taroudannt (just off the P32 Taroudannt–Talioune road). The gorge is home to a small colony of bald ibis; spring migrants include everything from booted eagle and black kite to white stork; and Barbary falcon, Moussier's and black redstart, blue rock thrush and tock bunting all winter here.

Over **Taroudannt** itself, you can usually see little and pallid swift in the evenings, while setin and Spanish swallow are common in scrubby areas.

Around Taroudannt: Freija and Tioute

East of Taroudannt, the oases and Kasbahs of **Freija** and **Tioute** are close enough to explore in a half-day's trip by car (or a day by hired bike). Freija lies 11km east of Taroudannt, on the south bank of the Oued Souss; Tioute is a further 26km.

Birdwatchers may find they don't actually reach either site, due to the attractions of the **Oued Souss** itself (see box above).

Freija

The shortest **route to Freija** is to turn south from the Ouarzazate road (P32) at Aït Yazza, 8km out from Taroudannt. You must then ford the riverbed (this may be impossible in spring if the river is in flood) and follow an abandoned causeway. An alternative, longer route leads from the Agadir road, along the surfaced 7027, though this is more like 20km in all.

FREIJA is interesting for two features. First, it is an ancient, fortified village, standing on a low hill above (and safe from flooding by) the Souss. In the past it was easy to defend; today, it affords sweeping views of the river, the fertile plains beyond, and the High Atlas. Second are the remains of an old **Kasbah**, a little further to the south, alongside the road in from the 7027. Built of *pisé* (mud and gravel), this is now crumbling in parts but the guest section (fronting the road) remains in good condition, and families still occupy the resident wings, along with their domestic animals. If you enter the courtyard and show an interest, you are likely to be invited in to look round.

Tioute

TIOUTE can be reached directly from Freija on the minor 7024 road, or – more easily – by turning right off the 7025 road to Igherm and Tata. Either way, you should arrive at one of the five straggling villages which form Tioute palmery, with a hill before you, capped by a large, stone-built Glaoui **Kasbah**.

A rough track leads up to the Kasbah, which is one of the grandest in the south and still owned by the local caid. It is at present being renovated, possibly for use as a hotel or restaurant, and if the workmen are around you should be able to see part of the interior – including water tanks, a vault (for valuables), a prison (for hostages), and an open space for festivities. Profiled against the first foothills of the Anti-Atlas, it is a highly romantic sight – a location for *Ali Baba and the Forty Thieves*, starring Fernandel and Yul Brynner. Equally impressive are its fabulous views over the luxuriant palmery, with the High Atlas peaks beyond.

Taliouine and the Djebel Sirwa

The roads east from **Taroudant to Taliouine** lack the drama of Tizi n'Test – the classic route from Taroudannt to Marrakesh – but are efficient approaches to the southern oases. There are attractive stretches, too, particularly the Taliouine–Ouarzazate section, which changes gradually to semi-desert and offers views of the weirdly shaped mountains of the Anti-Atlas.

For trekkers, the **Djebel Sirwa** (or Siroua), north of Taliouine, is one of the finest mountain sections of the Anti-Atlas. It is scarcely less impressive than the more established High Atlas trekking areas, and a great deal less frequented.

Taroudannt to Taliouine – and north to Toubkal

The new 7027 road (shown as under construction on the Michelin map) follows the **Oued Souss** from Taroudannt, speeding the approach if you are driving. It meets the P32 just south of the village of **AOULOUZ** and its **gorge** (see box opposite). Aoulouz has a café with a few rooms, and *souks* on Wednesday and Sunday.

To the east of Aoulouz, piste P32b leads to TAÏSSA, at the southern end of the **Assif n'Tifnout** valley, which is trailed north by a rough piste to Amsouzart, just east of **Lac d'Ifni** and **Djebel Toubkal** (see map on p.344). It is possible to drive this in a sturdy vehicle and you can make a two-day tour, returning to Taliouine (or doing it in the opposite direction – see overpage); or to walk it, or take local transport along the stage. From Aoulouz there are fairly frequent shared taxis to ASSARAG, where you'll find rooms, and whence a few hours' walk north will take you to **AMSOUZART** (see p.353) where you can stay at Omar's; from there you can reach **Lac d'Ifni** and Djebel Toubkal.

Buses and *grands taxis* between Taroudannt and Talioune stick to the P32 road, with a major halt (and taxi stage) at **OULED BERHIL**, 35km east of Taroudannt. An old **Kasbah** just outside the village has been turned into a sumptuous restaurant, the *Riad Hida*, with half a dozen rooms if you fancy stopping (☎13 through the operator; ①). The house formerly belonged to a Dane, who scrupulously restored its traditional and highly ornate ceilings and architecture.

Taliouine

TALIOUINE lies at a pass, its land gathered into a bowl, with a scattering of buildings on or above the roadside. More village than town, it is dominated by a magnificent **Kasbah** built by the Glaoui, though in a much-decayed state and used mainly to house farm animals. The best-preserved section of the Kasbah, however, is still inhabited by a few families, who might offer to show you round. The Kasbah's decoration is intricately patterned, its windows moulded with palm fronds (some still showing their original paint), and the towers (climb very much at your own risk) are built round squat, downward-tapering pillars.

With your own vehicle, you can set out from Taroudannt, visit the Kasbah and move on easily enough to Ouarzazate the same day. Relying on public transport, you should reckon on staying, which, in any case, is an attractive proposition. Few tourists do, despite the presence of two **hotels**, and ther are other Kasbahs in the hills round the village, if you have time to explore them.

Taliouine practicalities

Accommodation is a choice between the expensive *Grand Hôtel Ibn Toumert* (☎30 through the operator; ④), right next to the Kasbah, and, 2km east of the village, on the main road, the small *Auberge Souktana* (no phone; ②). The former is nothing very special – at least for the price – but the *Souktana* is a wonderful little place, run by Jadid Ahmed (who is an experienced mountain guide – see below) and his French wife Michelle. In winter, try to turn up early in the day as there are only four rooms; it doesn't matter so much in summer, when you can sleep out on their roof terrace or camp in the garden (at other times it's too cold).

Travelling by bus, ask to be dropped at one or other hotel. If you arrive too late for a room at the *Souktana*, a café on the right of the road (coming from Taroudannt) rents out basic rooms. There is a **hammam** in the village; the *Souktana* will give you directions. A Monday **souk** is held across the valley behind the Kasbah.

Heading on by **bus or taxi** can be frustrating, as many arrive in – and leave – Taliouine full for Taroudannt or Ouarzazate; it pays to go to the main bus stop, as buses can pass the *Souktana* full and then leave half empty from the bus stop; there is an 8am departure for Marrakesh. *Grands taxis* from Taliouine only go as far west as Oulad Behril (80km; change for Taroudannt) and as far east as Tazenakht (84km; change for Ouarzazate; see below).

Tazenakht

TAZENAKHT, at the junction of the Ouarzazate and Foum Zguid roads, has regular buses and *grands taxis* to Ouarzazate, plus buses to Foum Zguid and also to Arhbar (from where you might be able to get a lorry across to Agdz in the Drâa Valley – see p.390). The village has a *Banque Populaire*, a filling station, and **rooms** and meals at the *Hôtel Zenaga* (☎32 through the operator; ⓪), or livelier *Café-Restaurant Étoile* (⓪), both clean enough, though without electricity. Alongside the latter is a large courtyard with a magnificent display of **carpets**, blankets and clothes, including many of the bold geometric designs of the Ouzguita tribe. If you have time on your hands, there is also a carpet co-operative.

The road beyond Tazenakht **to Ouarzazate** is unexciting, running well to the east of Djebel Sirwa.

An approach to Djebel Toubkal

A classic piste route north of Taliouine (piste 6386) skirts the edge of the Djebel Sirwa to reach **Amsouzart**, just east of Lac d'Ifni and Djebel Toubkal. There, you could trek in the Toubkal area, or alternatively make a loop back down to Aoulouz via the Assif n'Tifnout (see previous page). This route is shown on the "Région de Marrakech" inset on the *Michelin* map, and Jadid Ahmed at the *Souktana* has a detailed route-map, as he offers it as a two-day landrover expedition. In summer it is just about practicable in an ordinary car.

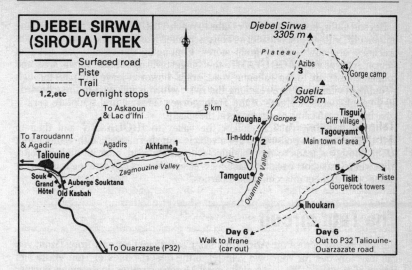

DJEBEL SIRWA (SIROUA) TREK

- Surfaced road
- Piste
- Trail

1,2,etc Overnight stops

0   5 km

To Askaoun & Lac d'Ifni

To Taroudannt & Agadir

Taliouine

Souk, Grand Hôtel, **Auberge Souktana**, Old Kasbah

Agadirs   Akhfame **1**

Zagmouzine Valley

To Ouarzazate (P32)

Djebel Sirwa 3305 m

Plateau

Azibs **3**   Gorge camp **4**

Gueliz 2905 m

Atougha *Gorges*   Ti-n-lddr **2**

Tisgui Cliff village

Tagouyamt Main town of area

Ouamrane Valley

Tamgout   **Tislit 5** Gorge/rock towers   Piste

Ihoukarn

Day 6 Walk to Ifrane (car out)

Day 6 Out to P32 Taliouine–Ouarzazate road

Into the Djebel Sirwa (Siroua)

The **Djebel Sirwa** (or Siroua) is an isolated volcanic peak, rising from a high area (3000m-plus, so take it easy!) to the south of the High Atlas. It offers as good trekking as you can find anywhere – rewarded by magnificent views, great trekking, a cliff village and dramatic gorges. It is best in spring; winter is extremely cold.

A week-long circuit, taking in Sirwa, is outlined on the map above, the numbers being the overnight halts. Mules to carry gear, as well as tent hire, can be arranged by Jadid Ahmed at the *Auberge Souktana* or by Tali Abdel Aziz in Taroudannt (see box on p.449), though neither operate in the Sirwa in winter. Mules would be a worthwhile investment to ensure enjoyment – and accurate navigation. Having Ahmed along, however, is the best guarantee of success; he is a great character, speaks fluent French and English and makes tasty *tajines*.

If you are going it alone, the relevant survey maps are the 1:100,000 *Taliwine* and 1:50,000 *Sirwa*. Jadid Ahmed can show you these, and he dispenses advice whether or not you engage his guiding services.

The circuit

The initial day is a gentle valley ascent along a piste to **AKHFAME** where there are rooms and a Kasbah.The piste actually reaches west of here as far as Atougha but, *souk* days apart, transport can be nil and the walk is a pleasant enough introduction. Beyound Akhfamane the piste climbs over a pass to another valley at **TAMGOUT** and up it to **ATOUGHA,** before contouring round into the upper valley, where you can stay at *azibs* (goat shelters) or bivouac.

Djebel Sirwa (3304m) can itself be climbed from Atougha in five to six hours: a pull up from the southern cirque onto a plateau, crowned with rock towers; the nervous may want to be roped for one section of the final scramble. The sub-peak of **Guliz** is worth ascending, too, and a bivouac in the gorge below is recommended.

Beyond Guliz, keep to the lower paths to reach **TISGUI** and don't fail to visit the unique **cliff village** just outside: its houses, ranked like swallows' nests on a 1000ft precipice, are now used as grain stores. Continuing the circuit, past fields of saffron, you reach **TAGOUYAMT**, the biggest village of the Sirwa area and connected by piste to the Taliouine road. Trails, however, leave it to pass through a couple of villages before reaching the river, which is followed to the extraordinary conglomerate features of the **Tislit gorges**. This natural sculpture park is amazing; you can camp or get rooms at the village.

On the last day, you can follow the valley to **IHOUKARN** and then to **IFRANE**, where it's possible to get a vehicle out; alternatively, a three-hour trek to the southeast leads to the Taliouine–Ouarzazate road, near its highest point, from where transport back to Taliouine is easier. Ahmed can arrange transport at either point to meet unaccompanied parties.

The Tata circuit

Heading **south** across the **Anti-Atlas** from Taroudannt, or east from Tiznit, you can travel by bus (or your own vehicle) to the **desert oases** of **Tata**, **Akka** and **Foum el Hassan**. This is one of the great Moroccan routes, increasingly popular since it was surfaced over the whole course, but with the feel, still, of a desert world apart. The scenery is wild and impressive, with occasional camel herds and lonely, weatherbeaten villages.

Roads and buses

The paved roads along the Taroudannt–Tata–Tiznit circuit are not clearly marked on all maps (the *Michelin* has them right), so are worth setting out here. They are: the 7027/7025 from Taroudannt to Irherm; then the 7085 to Imitek; and finally the 7111, which joins the Akka–Tata road (7084) 5km south of Tata.

By **bus**, the route can be covered in either direction. From **Taroudannt**, *SATAS* buses run to Tata twice a week (Wed/Sun at 8am; 8–10hr), returning on the following mornings. From **Tiznit**, buses leave for Tata daily at 4.30am and at 11am. The 11am bus starts at Agadir, however, and may well be full by the time it reaches Tiznit; if it is, you could probably catch it at BOU IZAKARN (or BOUIZAKARNE), where it lets off passengers, by taking a *grand taxi* there from Tiznit. On weekdays, the Tiznit–Tata buses run via Ifrane de l'Anti-Atlas (see p.459).

Taroudannt to Tata

Leaving the P32 Taroudannt–Taliouine road at the 8km mark, the Tata road skirts through the edge of the oasis of **Freija**, and past the turning to **Tioute** (for both of which, see p.450), before beginning to wind and climb into the stark Anti-Atlas mountains.

At **IRHERM** (or IGHERM; 93km from Taroudannt) there's a **Wednesday souk**, where the bus will stop for a long break. The region is said to be known for its silver daggers and inlaid rifle butts, though more than likely you'll just find an assortment of hand-made copper pots and water urns. Igherm itself, now an administrative centre and with some new buildings to prove it, was a copper town for centuries, carrying on trade with the Saharan caravans. The *souk* apart, it is today a drab, sluggish town – not a place to get caught between buses. If by chance you do find yourself stranded, there are two good **rooms** at the *Café-Restaurant Atlas* on the way into the village from Taroudannt.

For the dedicated driver, pistes lead from Irherm to **Tafraoute** and **Taliouine**. Both are in pretty terrible condition, though the former is being improved. If you want to enquire about trucks along them (or conditions), try the *Café l'Escale* on the town square, where the truck drivers hang out and play cards. The very rough piste 7086 heads due south to Tata, too, though it has seen little traffic since the paving of the 7085.

Leaving Irherm, the paved road (7085) crosses the **Tizi Touzlimt** and then descends to SOUK KHEMIS D'ISSAFEN (Thursday *souk*) and the **Akka Valley**, lined by a palmery over the next thirty kilometres. It's a wonderful trip, with, to the east, the constantly amazing contours of the Anti-Atlas mountains, which twirl and twist from pink to grey-green, their sharply defined bands of rock varying from horizontal to vertical.

At IMITEK, the last oasis before Tata, you must turn left onto the paved 7111 for Tata (35km). The 7085 deteriorates to piste for a 34km stretch to Akka.

Tata

TATA is a small administrative and garrison town, flanking a large oasis. Its tiled and colonnaded streets are laid out in iron-grid style below a steep-sided hill – known as **La Montagne** (and offering a rare overview of the oasis) – and flanked by the equally predictable duo of **Av. des F.A.R.** and **Av. Mohammed V**. It is a leisurely place, with a friendly (if early-to-bed) air, and distinct desert influences in the darker complexion of the people, the black turbans of the men and the colourful sari-like coverings of the women (who wear black in the Anti-Atlas).

Midway along Av. Mohammed V is the main square, **Place Marche Verte**, which **buses** run in and out of: *SATAS* have departures at 3am for Akka/Tiznit/Agadir (arriving 8am/noon) and on Mondays and Thursdays at 6am for Taroudannt (arriving 11am); *Transports Chagiri* have a sporadic night run at 11pm to Taroudannt/Ouarzazate (arriving 5am/10am). Check these times earlier

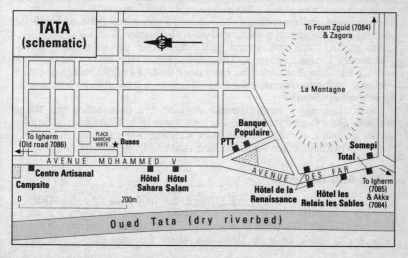

EAST TO THE DRAA: FOUM ZGUID

The route from **Tata to Foum Zguid** and, for the intrepid, beyond to **Zagora** is a much more remote journey than the "Tata loop", and strictly for the committed. At the time of writing, though, it is open and can be travelled without a permit (a situation that could change at any time: check with the police post in Tata).

From **Tata**, occasional lorries cover the 150km of rough *piste* to **Foum Zguid**, a rocky ride and not really practicable with anything less than four-wheel drive. The route runs through a wide valley, following the course of a seasonal river, amid some extremely bleak landscape, which is now and then punctuated by the occasional oasis and *ksar*. There are passport controls at TISSINT (halfway) and again as you approach **FOUM ZGUID**, a tiny place with a café (rooms, but not much to eat) opposite a welcome palmery and some *ksour*.

From **Foum Zguid**, there are *SATAS* **buses** three times a week (Tuesday, Thursday and Saturday at 7am) to **Ouarzazate** – and on to Marrakesh. Alternatively, a ride with a **lorry** along more very rough *piste* will get you to **Zagora** in seven or eight hours. This road, again, is not suitable for light vehicles and the transport is a bit haphazard; it also lacks most of the redeeming features of Tata to Foum, with no oases or villages to break the tedium.

---

in the day and, if possible, book a seat. There are also *grands taxis* (routine to Akka and Tissint – midway to Foum Zguid); trucks also run to Tissint/Foum Zguid, especially on Sunday night and Monday morning for its Monday *souk*.

The town's five **hotels**, in ascending order of price, are:

Unnamed hotel, 44 Place Marche Verte – by the bus station. Not recommended. ①

Hôtel Salam, 41 Av. Mohammed V (no phone). Above a café – the sign is in Arabic only. Rooms are basic and not that clean. ①

Hôtel Sahara, 81 Av. Mohammed V (☎08/80.21.61). Marginally better. ①

Hôtel de la Renaissance, 9 Av. des F.A.R. (☎08/80.20.42). On both sides of the road – an older cheaper section on one side and a new, more comfortable barrack-like block on the other. The restaurant is good – and licensed. ②

Les Relais des Sables, Av. des F.A.R. (☎08/80.23.01). A smart new hotel with comfortable rooms built round a succession of little gardens – and a swimming pool. ③

There is also a small **campsite**, with shade, and for tents, real grass, set beside the municipal swimming pool at the far end of Av. Mohammed V.

For meals, you'll find several **grill-cafés** under the colonnades on Av. Mohammed V, plus a patisserie. The café-restaurant right next to the patisserie serves a fine *tajine*. For something more fancy (and/or a drink), there's no choice – it has to be the **restaurant** at the *Hôtel Renaissance*. If possible, it's best to order a few hours in advance.

Lastly, Tata has a **bank** (*Banque Populaire*), a **post office**, two **filling stations**, and a **Centre Artisanal**. The town's very lively **Thursday** and **Sunday** souks are held at an enclosure – or, more accurately a series of pisé courtyards – known as El Khemis, 6km out on the Akka road (7084); the mainstay is dates.

Akka and its oasis

Continuing along the circuit towards Tiznit, the 7084 passes through **AKKA**, a roadside town with a large and very interesting oasis extending north. It is said to have been one of the northern depots of the ancient caravan routes and still hosts a large weekly **souk**, again on Thursdays, where the oasis dates (Akka means "dates" in the local Berber language) are much in evidence. There is also a smaller local *souk* on Sundays.

Akka's palmery rewards a stay, with sweet spring water, some delightful bathing pools and good walks to see rock paintings and a gorge to the north. Its disadvantage is a poor and unwelcoming **café-hotel**, the *Tamdoult* (①), though it serves good food. A new three-star hotel is said to be under construction in the oasis village of Aït Rahal, to the north, and there is a rough **campsite** a little way along the Foum El Hassan road.

The swimming holes, known as Les Cascades, are really a series of shallow, dammed irrigation pools, enclosed by palms. To reach them on foot, amble through the palmery and gardens in the direction of the gap in the mountains. Leaving Akka, you cross the dry river bed by a concrete

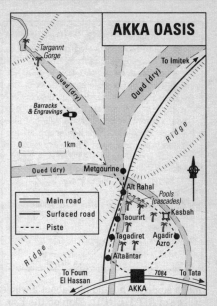

barrage and follow the path through the almost continguous villages of Aït Aäntar, Tagadiret and Taouriret; a road trails the path. The oasis itself is wonderful, with the sound of water and the cooing of nesting partridges. In some parts of it people live in separate houses, enclosed by private plots, in others are clusters of dwellings with open, unwalled groves, criss-crossed by paths and irrigation ditches. Southeast of Aït Rahal is a **Kasbah** and an **agadir** (fortified granary).

A trek of around three hours to the northwest of Aït Rahal should bring you to the **Targannt Gorge**, in which a cluster of oases are tucked between the cliffs. There are ruins of houses, though the place is deserted nowadays, save for the occasional nomadic camel herder. The route is across desert, passable to landrover-type vehicles, though the track is poorly defined. En route (and an aid to navigation) is a small hill on which the French built a barracks. There are **rock engravings** of oxen at the eastern end of the hill – some modern, others perhaps up to two thousand years old. Approaching the gorge, a lone palm tempts you to its mouth. A guide from the village would be helpful, while bringing food and a tent would reward you with a gorgeous camping spot.

There are more **rock carvings**, said to be prehistoric, near the village of OUM EL ALEK (or OUM EL AÄLAGUE), 7km southeast of Akka, off the Tata road.

West to Foum El Hassan – and rock carvings at Aït Herbil

The next major oasis beyond Akka is **FOUM EL HASSAN** (FAM EL HISN on the *Michelin* map), 90km to the west – and 6km off the main road. This is basically a military post on the edge of an oasis. Some fighting with Polisario took place here several years ago, but everything's quiet now; there is, however, passport control. If you need a **room**, the only possibility is at the café on the right-hand side of the square. Besides a couple of shops, there's very little else.

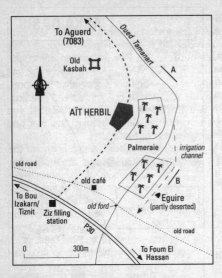

There are countless **prehistoric rock carvings** in this region, and engaging a guide you will probably find his own local favourites. One reader advised heading "for the huge V in the mountains that rise up behind the town. A dirt road follows the valley and, after 4–5km, you should find some carvings. The best require a little climbing to get to, but they are reputedly the finest in Morocco – pictures of elephants and rhinoceros, 15–30cm high, and dating roughly from 2000–500 BC, a time when the Sahara was full of lakes and swamps. Camping is possible here in the valley and preferable to staying in the town."

Our last researcher in the area, it has to be said, was defeated by the track described above but at Tiznit met a student who told him about a whole series of rock carvings near his home village of **AÏT HERBIL**, 2km off the P30, around 15km west of Foum El Hassan. The junction is easy to recognise, as it's immediately opposite a *Ziz* filling station. You can get there by *grand taxi* from Foum El Hassan or Bou Izakarn/Tiznit.

There are two series of rock carvings, marked as "A" and "B" on the sketch-map above, both easily accessible on foot. To **reach "A"** you should walk north-east from the village, across the dry riverbed. On the opposite bank is a steep rock fall, and to the right of a patch of distinctive grey rocks are perhaps as many as a hundred small carvings, depicting gazelles, bison, a giraffe and a bird or two. The rock fall looks recent but clearly, with the carvings all in the same plane, it has not shifted for centuries, even millennia.

To **reach "B"** you must leave the village to the southeast, walking through the palmery, and again across the dry riverbed, to find a concrete irrigation channel which at this point runs high above the level of the river. Before reaching the partly deserted village of Eguire, high on the left, look for carvings on the rocks to the left. There are fewer examples here but they are larger.

West to Bou Izakarn: Amtoudi and Ifrane de l'Anti-Atlas

Beyond Aït Herbil, the P30 continues across a barren patch of hammada to the oasis and roadside village of **TAGHJICHT** (or TARHJIJT). A road north of here leads to Amtoudi (see below), and if you need to stop the night, en route, there is a fine, new **hotel**, the *Taghjijt* (☎08/87.30.53; ②). The vilage has regular *grands taxis* east to Foum El Hassan and west to Bou Izakarn.

At **TIMOULAY**, 26km further west, it is usually possible to get a *grand taxi* to Ifrane de l'Anti-Atlas.You should also be able to get one for the final 14km stretch to **BOU IZAKARN**, a larger village with routine buses and *grands taxis* to Goulimine and Tiznit (for Tafraoute). It, too, has a small **hotel**, the *Anti Atlas* (☎08/87.41.34; ①), though it is best left for emergencies.

Amtoudi (Id Aïssa)

If you have transport, it's worth making an excursion from the Bou Izakarn/ Tiznit road to visit **AMTOUDI** (or ID AÏSSA, as it appears on most maps). This can be reached by either of two roads north of the P30 (at around 55km and 70km from Foum El Hassan); they join at SOUK TNINE D'ADAÏ, where the last 10km of road to Amtoudi become rougher and less distinct. Using local transport, you might be able to negotiate a *grand taxi* at TAGHJICHT, the second junction, especially on a Monday, when there is a market at Souk Tnine d'Adaï. If you intend to stay, be sure to have enough provisions, since Amtoudi has just one small shop and a lunch-only restaurant for visiting tour groups.

The sight that brings tour groups to Amtoudi is its **agadir**, which is one of the most spectacular and best preserved in North Africa. *Agadirs* are collective, fortified storehouses, where grain, dates, gunpowder and other valuables were kept safe from marauding tribes. This one is built impressively on a pinnacle of rock. You can climb (or ride a mule) up a winding track and walk round in the site, providing the *gardien* is there. If by chance you find the place overrun by tourists, you can escape the crowds with a walk down the palm-filled **gorge**; here another imposing but decaying *agadir* is perched on top of the cliff and, after about 3km, you'll come to a spring and waterfall. It is possible to **camp** near the river.

Ifrane de l'Anti-Atlas

IFRANE DE L'ANTI-ATLAS is one of the most rewarding oasis detours along this route – a small Berber town, with three surrounding *douar* (each with its own Kasbah and endless walls), together with an administrative centre containing a pink, fort-like barracks. The place is particularly out of the way and visitors can expect to be the object of attention and followed everywhere by kids. However, there are beautiful walks among the *douar*, springs, and ingenious water channels, and, if you don't have transport, there are basic **rooms** (most with mats rather than beds) at the *Café de la Paix* and *Café de la Poste*. The former is preferable, with a couple of rooms on the roof, looking out across the valley and distant oasis; it is also the best place to eat. A **Sunday souk** serves the surrounding villages.

The **oasis** is the centre of one of the oldest settled regions in Morocco – and one of the last places in the south to convert to Islam. Across the dry riverbed stand the ruins of the old **Jewish Kasbah**, or **Mellah**. Legend holds that Ifrane's Jews settled here in the sixth century BC, fleeing persecution from King Nebuchadnezzar of Babylon; this has yet to be substantiated but it is certain that the Jewish community goes back to pre-Islamic days. It endured up until the 1950s, when, as elsewhere in the south, there was a mass exodus to Israel and, to an extent, Casablanca and Rabat. A Berber family has since moved into one of the inhabitable Kasbahs, and a few of the other buildings remain partially intact; the rest is a mass of crumbling walls. Locals recall their former Jewish neighbours as "good people" who kept mainly to themselves.

Around the next bend in the stony riverbed, and up the hill on the right, lies the Jewish **cemetery**. Broken tombstones, inscribed in Hebrew, lie strewn about. It's said that relatives still come here to visit the graves and burn candles in memory of the deceased. The Muslim past of Ifrane is evident as well, with white-domed tombs of saints and *marabouts* dotting the surrounding countryside.

Tiznit

Despite its solid circuit of walls, TIZNIT was founded as late as 1882, when Sultan Moulay Hassan (Hassan I) was undertaking a *harka* – a subjugation or (literally) "burning" raid – in the Souss and Anti-Atlas. It still seems to signal a shift towards a desert, frontier-town mentality and past: to the west the Chleuh Berbers of the Anti-Atlas suffered their first true occupation only with the bitter French "pacification" of the early 1930s, and Tiznit itself was the base of **El Hiba**, who declared himself sultan here in 1912 after learning of Moulay Hafid's surrender to the French under the Treaty of Fes. The so-called "Blue Sultan" – a name given on account of his blue desert robes – El Hiba led a considerable force of Berbers to Marrakesh, which acknowledged his authority, before advancing on Fes in the spring of 1913. Here they were defeated, though his resistance continued, first in Taroudannt, later into the Anti-Atlas, until his death, near Tafraoute, in 1919.

The town bears the stamp of its military history – huge *pisé* walls, neat administrative streets and a considerable garrison – but it's not a bad staging point if you arrive here too late in the day to continue on to Tafraoute, Sidi Ifni or Tata; the town itself is easily reached by bus from Agadir or *grand taxi* from Inezgane. It also has an exhilarating **beach** at **Sidi Moussa d'Aglou**, 17km distant, where the surf and the fierce Atlantic currents have warded off development.

Orientation, rooms and food

Orientation is simple. There are 5km of walls and eight major gates, of which three are important: **Bab Oulad Jarrar**, **Bab El Aouina** and **Les Trois Portes**. Most of the traffic in and out of the walls passes through these gates, of which the third (as its name suggests) was a French addition.

Arriving from the south or north, **buses** or **grands taxis** will drop you in the **Mechouar** – the old parade ground, now the main square – just inside the town walls. Coming from Tafraoute by taxi, you may be dropped at a roundabout, outside the walls, where the roads also lead to Agadir and Goulimine.

It's around the Mechouar and along the adjacent **Av. 20 Août** that you'll find most of the facilities – banks, the post office, bus offices, a market area and a Centre Artisanal – and all of the cheap **hotels**. A few additional, more upmarket hotels are out by the roundabout. The town **campsite** is just outside Bab Oulad Jarrar; it is secure but unshaded.

Hotels

There are a dozen or more unclassified hotels in the walled city, the best of which are listed below; none can guarantee hot water but in a cul-de-sac off Rue du Bain Maure there is a public showerhouse (*Douche Atlas*). Also listed below are all three classified options. They are, as ever, in ascending order of price:

Hôtel des Amis [C], Mechouar (☎08/86.21.29). Spartan but clean and very cheap, with a roof terrace overlooking the square. ①

Hôtel Sahara [E], Rue de l'Hôpital (☎08/86.24.98). Not so clean but a cheap fallback. ①

Hôtel Atlas [D], Mechouar (☎08/86.20.60). A popular and inexpensive hotel – try to book ahead. Also has a good-value restaurant. ①

Hôtel CTM [F], opposite the *grands taxis* park (☎08/86.22.11). Another good choice, with a café-restaurant on the first floor. ①

Hôtel Al Mourabatine [A], Rue du Bain Maure (no phone). Okay but poorer value. ①

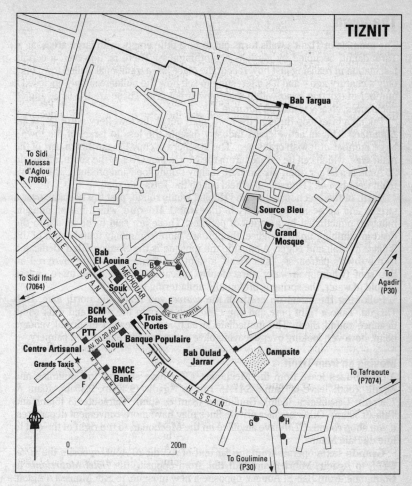

TIZNIT

Bab Targua

To Sidi
Moussa
d'Aglou
(7060)

Source Bleu

Grand
Mosque

To
Agadir
(P30)

Bab
El Aouina

To Sidi Ifni
(7064)

MECHOUAR

Souk

RUE DU BAIN

C B
D A

E

RUE DE L'HÔPITAL

BCM
Bank

Trois
Portes

PTT

AV. DU 20 AOUT

Centre Artisanal

Souk

Banque Populaire

Grands Taxis

Bab Oulad
Jarrar

Campsite

To Tafraoute
(P7074)

BMCE
Bank

F

AVENUE HASSAN II

G H

I

0   200m

To Goulimine
(P30)

Hôtel Belle Vue [B], Rue du Bain Maure (☎08/86.21.09). An old and well-maintained hotel, with a pleasant café. ⑩

Hôtel Mauretanie [I], Rue Bir Anzarane (☎08/86.20.92). Good value, with easy parking, a restaurant and bar, and several cafés and shops nearby. ①

Hôtel de Paris [G], Av. Hassan II (☎08/86.28.65). A new and modestly priced hotel. The restaurant is also popular with locals. ②

Hôtel de Tiznit [H], Rue Bir Anzarane (☎08/86.24.11). A classier alternative, with a bar, nightclub and swimming pool. ③

There is a five-star hotel under construction opposite the *Hôtel de Paris*.

Restaurants

Besides the hotel restaurants above, there are numerous **café-restaurants** in and around the Mechouar, the best of which is the *Bon Acceuil*. Others are to be found outside the walls on Av. Mohammed V and down by the roundabout.

The town

The promise of Tiznit's walls turns out to be a little empty, with large areas, as at Taroudannt, occupied by gardens or nothingness. There is, however, a certain fascination in realising just how recent the place is – a traditional walled town built only a century ago – and it's interesting to see how the builders simply enclosed a number of existing *ksour* within their new street grid. These are the large angled enclosures, clearly visible on our map.

Taking a brief loop through the town, start out at the **jewellery souk** (*Souk des Bijoutiers*), still an active crafts industry despite the loss to Israel of the town's large number of Jewish craftsmen. The jewellers occupy the northerrn part of the main *souk*, which can be entered from the Mechouar. Over to the south, off Av. du 20 Aôut, is a larger **open-air market**, mainly selling food and produce. The town's main weekly *souk* (Thursdays) is held out on the Tafraoute road.

North of the Mechouar, Rue de l'Hôpital winds round, past the hospital, over a stream and up beside a cemetery to the **Grand Mosque**, which has an unusual minaret, punctuated by a series of perches. These are said to be an aid to the dead in climbing up to paradise, though are more commonly found south of the Sahara in Mali and Niger. Alongside the mosque is the **Source Bleu**, dedicated to the town's patroness, Lalla Tiznit, a saint and former prostitute martyred on this spot (whereupon water miraculously appeared). These days, more or less devoid of water, the spring is profoundly unflattering to her.

Following the street on north of the *source*, you reach the north gate, **Bab Targua**. Take a right here and you can climb up onto the walls and walk some distance round them. The immediate stretch is a somewhat mournful vantage point, however, looking over decaying olive groves and an abandoned palmery.

Moving on from Tiznit

All the **buses** leave from the Mechouar. *CTM* have services to Goulimine and Agadir (both leave at 5am); *SATAS* run to Agadir (9.30am, 9.45am, 10am & 7.30pm), Casablanca (8am), Goulimine (8am & 4pm), Tafraoute (3.45pm) and Tata (9.30am). Other smaller private lines may have more convenient departures, if you shop round. *CTM* have an office on the Mechouar, to the right of the exit to Rue du Bain Mauré.

Grands taxis operate from the far end of Av. du 20 Aôut, opposite the *Hôtel CTM*, to Agadir, Mihrleft and Sidi Ifni; from opposite the *Hôtel Mauretanie* to Goulimine; from Bab El Aouina, opposite a new mosque, to Sidi Moussa d'Aglou; and from the roundabout, opposite the *Hôtel Tiznit*, for Tafraoute. In addition to regular grands taxis, there are ten-seater transits and landrovers to Tafraoute, but turn up early in the day to be sure of a place, as the last leaves around 4pm.

Sidi Moussa d'Aglou

The beach at **SIDI MOUSSA D'AGLOU** is 17km from Tiznit, along a barren, scrub-lined road. Getting there on local transport, you'll have to negotiate a *grand taxi* from outside the Mechouar; there is supposed to be a bus as well, but don't count on it. Hitching back into Tiznit, however, shouldn't present a problem.

The **beach**, is well worth the effort – an isolated expanse of sand, with a wild, body-breaking Atlantic surf (and with a dangerous undertow, too, so be careful). There's no village as such at the beach but round the headland to the right (as you face the sea) is a tiny **troglodyte fishing village**, with a hundred or so primitive cave-huts dug into the rocks.

It is possible to stay by the beach. There are fifteen **cabins** to rent at the *Motel d'Aglou*(⑩), to the left of the road as you come down to the beach, and about 1500m further down (along a track away from the beach) is a **campsite** with a café and a further handful of rooms. Except in the middle of summer and around Christmas (when migrant workers back from France come out here to camp with their families), you're likely to be the only people around. The motel, however, has a small **restaurant**.

Tafraoute

Approached by beautiful scenic roads through the Anti-Atlas – either from Tiznit (the best approach) or Agadir – **Tafraoute** is worth all the effort and time it takes to reach. The town is the centre for a group of stone-built villages on the strange, wind-eroded slopes of the **Ameln Valley**, shot through with pink- and mauve-tinged thumbs of granite and enclosed by a jagged panorama of mountains – "like the badlands of South Dakota", as Paul Bowles put it, "writ on a grand scale".

The best time for a visit to Tafraoute is early spring, in order to see the almond trees in full blossom, or in autumn, after the summer heat is subdued. In midsummer it can be stunningly hot here, giving little incentive to spend time wandering round the villages.

The routes from Tiznit and Agadir

Both approaches to Tafraoute are rewarding and, if you're driving, you may well want to take advantage of this by coming in from Tiznit and leaving for Agadir, or vice versa. If you're doing just one, the Tiznit approach has a distinct edge, winding through a succession of gorges and a grand mountain valley.

Buses and **grands taxis** cover the route from Tiznit several times daily. On the Agadir route, there is just one bus each day, starting at Inezgane, and no *grand taxi* run – though you could of course charter a taxi at Agadir or Tafraoute.

Tiznit to Tafraoute

The Tiznit–Tafraoute road (7074) passes a succession of oasis-like villages, almost all of them named after the *souk* that they are host to (see p.45 for the Arabic name-days). In winter and spring the road is sometimes crossed by streams but it is generally passable enough; the drive takes around four hours, but leave plenty of time to see (and navigate) the mountains before dusk.

At **ASSAKA** (15km from Tiznit), a substantial new bridge has been built over the Oued Tazeroualt – the river that causes most difficulty in winter and spring. Around 25km further on, just before Tirhmi, a road heads south into the Anti-Atlas to the **Zaouia of Sidi Ahmed ou Moussa** (11km), which for a while in the seventeenth century controlled its own local state, the Tazeroualt, whose capital was at nearby (and now deserted) **Illigh**. The *zaouia* remains active and hosts a **moussem** during the second or third week of August, which would be worth trying to attend. Sidi Ahmed is the patron of Morocco's acrobats – most of whom come from this region of Morocco – and return to perform.

Just beyond **TIRHMI** (aka TIGHMI; 44km from Tiznit), the road begins its ascent of the **Col du Kerdous** (1100m). At the top of the pass is a **hotel**, the *Kerdous* (☎08/86.20.63; ④), created from an old fortress and recently re-opened after a long restoration. It is worth at least a stop for a tea and breathtaking views.

At the end of the descent is the village of **JEMAA IDA OUSSEMLAL** (64km from Tiznit), which offers basic rooms at the *Hôtel de la Victoire* (①), and the last filling station before Tafraoute. The **road divides** as you enter the village. The left fork, which runs downhill through the village (and past the hotel), is the **"old road"**, which continues to Tafraoute as the 7074 – a picturesque route that drops into the Ameln Valley via Souk ad Tahala (once a Jewish village). The right fork (7146), skirting the village, is a **"new road"** to Tafraoute, via IZERBI, where the Minister of Housing has a Disney-style chateau. It is a longer route but well surfaced, flatter and faster, arriving in Tafraoute through a grand spectacle of mountains and the lunar landscape around Agard Oudad (see p.468).

Agadir/Inezgane to Tafraoute via Aït Baha

The S509 road runs from Agadir to Tafraoute via Aït Baha. It is a bit drab between Agadir and Aït Baha, but the section from there on to Tafraoute is a highly scenic (and slow and winding) mountain ride past a series of fortified Kasbah-villages – **Tioulit** being a spectacular example.

Before then comes **AÏT BAHA**, the largest village en route, and a character-less roadside halt with a small **hotel**, two cafés and very little shade. It hosts a **Wednesday souk**. There is a confusing junction not far before you arrive at Tafraoute: coming from Aït Baha, the road off to the left is to Irherm (a very rough piste once you pass the village of AÏT ABDALLAH), the right to Tafraoute.

The daily **bus service** along this route, resumed after being halted for a number of years, breaks for tea at Aït Baha.

Tafraoute

TAFRAOUTE stands at the edge of a rambling palmery – quite unexpected after a rather barren approach over the last few kilometres from both Tiznit and Agadir. It is a small place, created as an administrative centre by the French, and little expanded since, as *Tafraoutis* prefer to stick to their villages, or at least return to them after working elsewhere or abroad (see box overpage). It is a pleasant place and most visitors, women as well as men, find it one of the most relaxed destinations in Morocco. **Getting around** the Ameln villages, you can use a combination of taxis and walking, or hire **mountain bikes** from an outlet opposite the PTT.

GROUND SQUIRRELS

Along the road from Tiznit to Tafraoute, you will probably notice children holding little furry animals for sale – live, on a piece of string – by the roadside. These are ground squirrels, which are known locally as *anzid* or *sibsib*, and are destined for the *tajine* dish, in which they are considered quite a delicacy. Recognisable by the prominent stripes down their side, and long tails, ground squirrels are common in the tropics but unknown in Europe. In theory, being rodents, they are forbidden fare for Muslims but they have long been ascribed medicinal properties – which makes them licit.

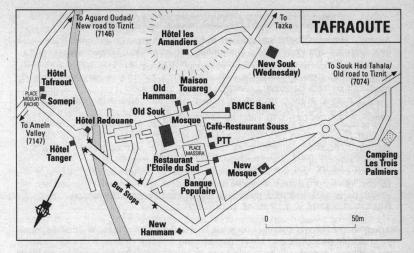

Accommodation and meals

The town has a campsite and four hotels, so it's wise to arrive early or book ahead to be sure of a room.

Hôtel Redouane, by the bridge (☎08/80.00.66). A bit seedy with basic and not very clean rooms at erratic prices. Has a terrace restaurant on the first floor. ⑩

Hôtel Tanger, across the road (☎08/80.00.33). Slightly better rooms, again with a restaurant (quite good), where you can eat outside. ⑩

Hôtel Tafrout, Place Moulay Rachid (☎08/80.01.21). New hotel, by the filling station. Much better than the *Redouane* and *Tanger*, with well-decorated rooms, hot showers on the corridor, and a very welcoming manager. ②

Hôtel Les Amandiers, on the hill above the town – ten minutes' walk (☎08/80.00.08). Kasbah-style building offering comfortable if unexciting rooms, a dull restaurant (cheaper for residents), great views from the terrace, and a bar. A pictorial map on the wall gives a useful impression of the Ameln Valley and environs – though before many changes to the roads. ④

Camping Les Trois Palmiers, ten minutes' walk from the centre. A small, secure and shaded enclosure, with hot showers. Also two bungalots (sic) for rent.

In addition to the hotels, there are a couple of **restaurants** in the town: the *Café-Restaurant Souss*, serving regular Moroccan fare at modest cost, and the *Restaurant l'Étoile du Sud*. The latter is a bit pretentious, with a tent done up for tourists and an embarrassing cabaret of music and belly-dancing, but the food can be worthwhile if you hit a good day and there's a nice indoor salon for winter evenings. The only **bar** is up at the *Hôtel les Amandiers*.

Directory

Banks The *Banque Populaire* is open only on Wednesdays for the town's *souk*, but there's an inconspicuous *BMCE* behind the PTT, with standard opening hours.

Buses generally leave from the "main" street, either side of the bridge over the dry riverbed (see map). One bus a day, operated by *Express* (blue bus), runs to Inezgane, via Aït Baha and Biougra, departing at 1pm. All the other buses go to Tiznit by the "new road" and sometimes beyond to Agadir, Marrakesh and Casablanca.

Hammam There is a new one next to the bakery.

TAFRAOUTE VILLAGE ECONOMICS

Among Tafraouti villages, **emigration** to work in the grocery and hotel trade – all over Morocco and France – is a determining aspect of life. The men always return home to retire, however, building European-looking villas amid the rocks, and most of the younger ones manage to come back for a month's holiday each year – whether it be from Casablanca, Tangier, Paris or Marseilles.

But for much of the year, it is the women who run things in the valley, and the only men to be found are the old, the family-supported or the affluent. It is a system that seems to work well enough: enormously industrious, and very community-minded, the *Tafraoutis* have managed to maintain their villages in spite of adverse economic conditions, importing all their foodstuffs except for a little barley, the famed Tafraouti almonds and the bitter oil of the argan tree.

Oddly enough, this way of life has exact parallels in Tunisia, with the people of Djerba; less surprisingly, both social structures developed through crisis and necessity. Between 1880 and 1882, this whole region was devastated by famine.

Market/shops There is a Wednesday **souk**, held in the centre of town. Worthwhile permanent **crafts shops** include the *Coin des Nomades* and *Artisanat du Coin*, both unpressurised, and *La Maison Touareg*, only marginally more so, for carpets. Tafraoute is well known for its *babouches*, and a narrow street of *cordonniers* sell quality slipperwear just below the Place Marche Verte.

Mountain guides Recommended trekking guides for the region include Ouhammou Mohammed (contact through the reception at *Hôtel Redouane*, where he works from time to time, or through his friend who runs the *Coin des Nomades* shop) and Ouakrim Mohammed (contact through the restaurants or *Hôtel les Amandiers*).

Post Office The *PTT* is open 8.30am–noon & 2–6.30pm); when it is closed, phone calls can be made from the *Hôtel des Amandiers* at 30 percent commission.

Taxis Shared *grands taxis* and landrover taxis tend to disappear as the morning progresses.

The Ameln Valley

You could spend days, if not weeks, wandering round the 26 villages of the **Ameln Valley**. Set against the backdrop of the rocks, they are all beautiful both from afar and close up – with springs, irrigation systems, brightly painted houses, and mosques. On no account, either, should you miss out on a walk to see the **painted rocks** in their albeit faded glory.

Starting out from Tafraoute, **Oumesnat**, 8km to the northeast, is a good first objective, as you can usually get a lift there, or charter a taxi at modest cost; taxis could also be arranged to pick you up from a village at the end of the day. From Oumesnat, you could walk the length of the valley from village to village: the walk to Anemeur, for example, is around 10–12km. More serious walkers might consider making an ascent of the **Djebel El Kest**.

The villages are built on the lower slopes of the Djebel El Kest, between the "spring line" and the valley floor, allowing gravity to take the water through the village and on to the arable land below. Tracks link the villages, following the contour lines – and frequently the irrigation channels – and most are accessible from the road only by crossing an intricate network of these irrigation canals, orchards and allotments. Many of the villages have basic shops where you can buy drinks, if little else.

Oumesnat to Anameur – and a loop back to Tafraoute

OUMESNAT, like most Ameln settlements, emerges out of a startling green and purple rockscape, crouched against the steep rock walls of the valley – on which locals point out the face of a lion. From a distance, its houses, perched on the rocks, seem to have a solidity to them – sensible blocks of stone, often three storeys high, with parallel sets of windows. Close up, they reveal themselves as bizarre constructions, often built on top of older houses deserted when they had become too small or decrepit; a few of them, with rooms jutting out over the cliffs, are held up by enormous stilts and have raised doorways entered by short (and retractable) ladders.

One of the houses, known as **La Maison Traditionelle**, is owned by a blind Berber and his son, who will show visitors round (*gratuité* expected). They give an interesting tour, explaining the domestic equipment – grindstones, water-holders, cooking equipment – and the lay-out of the house with its guest room with separate entrance, animals' quarters, and summer terrace for sleeping out. To get the most from a visit, you may need to engage an interpreter.

From Oumesnat, you can walk through or above a series of villages to **ANAMEUR**, where there is a *source bleu*, or natural springwater pool, a meandering hike of around three hours.

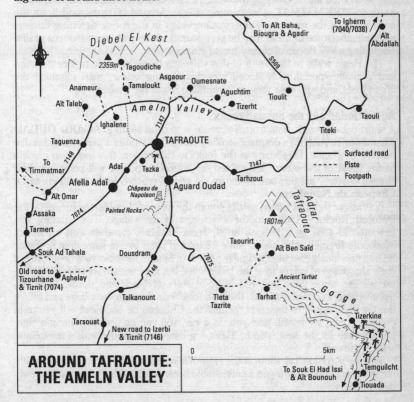

AROUND TAFRAOUTE: THE AMELN VALLEY

The Ameln's highest village, **TAGOUDICHE** (TAGDICHTE on the road sign), where the trail up the **Djebel El Kest** (or Lekst) begins, is accessible by landrover along a rough piste. There is a shop and a floor can usually be found if you want to stay overnight, for an early morning ascent. It is a rough and rocky scramble – there's no actual climbing involved – over a mountain of amethyst quartzite. There is a black igneous dyke below the summit pyramid, and a few goatherd shelters (*azibs*) on the top.

Returning to Tafraoute from the Ameln Valley, you can walk over a pass back from the 7148 road near IGHALENE in around three hours. The path isn't particularly easy to find but it's a lovely walk, taking you past flocks of sheep and goats tended by their child-shepherds. The route begins as a piste (east of the one to Tagoudiche), then you follow a dry riverbed off to the right, up a side-valley, where the zig-zags of an old track can be seen. Cross to go up here – not straight on – and, once over the pass, keep circling left till you can see Tafraoute below.

Tirnmatmat

To the west, the road (7148) along the Ameln Valley crosses an almost imperceptible watershed into a valley to the west. At AÏT OMAR (see map), a piste heads north to **TIRNMATMAT**, a welcoming village. Around 200m beyond it, on the north bank of the river, are numerous **carvings** in the rocks, depicting hunters and animals (some of these may be prehistoric), along with more modern graffiti (including a VW Beetle of clearly recent vintage).

The **ridge walk** to the south of this village is taken by some trekking parties and is really special, with Bonelli's eagles circling below, goats climbing the argan trees, and wild boar (beware!) snuffling round the bushes.

Agard Oudad and the painted rocks

A short but enjoyable walk from Tafraoute is to head south to **AGARD OUDAD** (3km from Tafraoute), a dramatic-looking village built under a particularly bizarre outcrop of granite. Like many of the rocks in this region, this has been given a name. Most of the others are named for animals – people will point out their shapes to you – but this one is known (in good French-colonial tradition) as **Le Chapeau de Napoléon**.

A stranger sight, however, awaits you in the form of "Les Pierres Bleues" – the **Painted Rocks** – 1500m to the southwest of the village. The painting was executed in 1984 by a Belgian artist, **Jean Verame**, together with a team of Moroccan firemen, who hosed some 18 tons of paint over a large area of rocks; he had previously executed a similar project in Sinaï. The rocks have lost some of their sharpness of colour over the last decade but they remain weird and wonderful, all the same: blue and red hills, clusters of black and purple boulders, mesmerising in effect. To reach them on foot, walk through the village and follow the flat piste round to the right, behind the Chapeau de Napoléon – if you're in doubt a young guide will take you. In a car, you can go part way along a sign-posted piste off the new road to Tiznit – a longer 3km route with a ten-minute walk at the end.

Verame stayed in Tafraoute at the *Hôtel Redouane* and the reception will – without great interest! – show you a coffee-table book detailing the project in its newly painted glory.

Tazka

Anther easy walk from Tafraoute is to **TAZKA**, about 2km southwest, where there is a **prehistoric carving** of a gazelle. To get there, follow a path through the palmery, just beyond the *souk* enclosure marked on our Tafraoute map. When you emerge, past the remains of an old Kasbah, you will see on your left the houses of Tazka at the foot of a high granite bluff. Take the lesser path to the right of the bluff and the carvings – a modern one on the rockface and an old one on the tilted surface of a fallen rock – are on your left after around 200m.

A southern circuit from Tafraoute

A beautiful day's outing is to drive southeast from Tafraoute towards **Souk El Had Issi**, a route that takes in some of the most beautiful country of the Anti-Atlas, including a fabulous gorge and palmery. If you have a sturdy vehicle and a taste for bone-shaking pistes, you can make a loop of it, returning to Tafraoute on the "new road" from Tiznit via Izerbi. The route is also offered as a **landrover trip** by the local guide Ouhammou Mohammed (see Tafraoute "Directory"), who has family at Souk El Had Issi; he can also arrange accommodation in the village, if you fancy staying out there for a day or two.

Leaving Tafraoute, follow the "new road" out past Agard Oudad, turning left around 3km south of the village. This road climbs over the hills, with superb panoramas back across Tafraoute and the Ameln Valley, to reach **TLETA TAZRITE** (15km from Tafraoute), which has a *souk* on Friday – not Tuesday as its name implies.

The paved road is quite broken beyond here. Past the modern village of **TARHAT** (TAGHAOUT) you enter a canyon, which the piste follows for the next 46km, and just a little beyond here, high on your left, are the twelfth-century remains of **ancient Tarhat**, a fortified village and agadir perched on the lip of a sheer rock wall. A footpath leads up to it from the modern village.

At **TIZERKINE**, a lovely oasis snaking along the canyon, all semblance of paved road comes to an end. A passable piste continues (be sure to take the right fork, 5km from Tizerkine) to the village of **TEMGUILCHT**, dominated by the very large and impressive **Zaouia Sidi Ahmed ou Mohammed** (no entrance to non-Muslims); on to **SOUK EL HADD ISSI** (SOUK EL HAD ARFALLAH IHRIR on the *Michelin* map), with a Sunday *souk*; then past a fine agadir (5km on); and finally to **AÏT BOUNOUH** at the end of the canyon.

A piste climbs over the hills from Aït Bounouh to bring you out on the **"new road"** from **Tiznit** to **Tafraoute** near IZERBI. At Izerbi, pistes also continue south towards Amtoudi and the Bou Izakarn–Tata road.

Tiznit to Goulimine – and Sidi Ifni

Heading **south from Tiznit to Goulimine**, you have a choice of routes: a fast inland road across scrubby desert via **Bou Izakarn**, or a more circuitous journey along the coast, by way of the splendid old Spanish colonial port of **Sidi Ifni**. Most people will probably choose to do one route down and the other back, which is sound enough. On no account, however, dismiss the Sidi Ifni route as an unneccessary detour: it turns out an unexpected highlight for many visitors.

Tiznit to Sidi Ifni: Mirhleft

The route down the coast from Tiznit to Sidi Ifni passes, around the midway point, the roadside village of **MIRHLEFT**, a friendly, bustling little place, set back a kilometre from a good beach. Buses and *grands taxis* from Tiznit could drop you here – or you could use Sidi Ifni as a base. The beach itself is a beautiful, totally undeveloped curve of sand, with crashing waves and strong currents; inevitably, it attracts surfers and campervans.

The village has several cafés and four basic **hotels**, all without electricity and with scarce water; the best of them is the *Tafkout* (①). Another decent hotel, the *Mirhleft* (①) is a little closer to the beach. For campervans there is an accepted parking area, along a track leading from the waterstand to the beach. There is a Monday *souk*, mainly devoted to second-hand items.

To the south are further **beaches**, of which the best are **Plage du Marabout** (3km from Mirhleft, by a prominent *marabout* tomb) and **Plage Aftas**, which has a little hotel, the *Aftas*, open only in midsummer months.

Sidi Ifni

SIDI IFNI is unique and interesting – uniquely interesting, in fact: a town that was relinquished by Spain only in 1969, after the Moroccan government closed off landward access to the colonial enclave. Twenty-five years on, it still preserves an outpost air and, if the mood takes you, can seem rather wonderful. Built in the 1930s, on a cliff-top site, it is full of sweeping architectural lines and elaborate ironwork: all in all, a bizarre memorial to colonialist purpose (or perhaps the lack of it), and surely the finest and most romantic Art Deco military town ever built. It is a very relaxed place and of late has a rather more prosperous air, with renovation and patches of gardens turning round its old decayed film-set atmosphere. It has easy connections with Tiznit and Goulimine by bus and *grand taxi*.

The town, or more accurately, the site, was Spanish from 1476 to 1524, when the Saadiens threw them out. In 1860, the Treaty of Tetouan – the culmination of Morocco's first military defeat by a European power in 200 years – gave it back to them, though they didn't re-occupy it until 1934, after they (and the French) had "pacified" the interior.

Orientation and accommodation

Approaching Sidi Ifni from Tiznit, you pass through a modern and nondescript Moroccan suburb, then the road swings down, across the Oued Ifni, and into Sidi Ifni proper (stay on the bus!). Once you've arrived town, you should have no problems in orientation: it's a straightforward grid, with steps leading down to the sea.

Finding **accommodation** is easy enough, too, with five hotels, all moderately priced, and a campsite. The choices are:

Hôtel Houria (aka *Hôtel Liberté*), off Av. Mohammed V; **Hôtel Ifni**, Av. Mohammed V. Both of these have small, clean rooms catering mainly for a Moroccan clientele, in for the market. ①

Hôtel Suerte Loca, Rue Moulay Youssef (☎08/87.53.50). A characterful place – the name ("Crazy Luck") and a *bodega*-style bar with table football and pinball reveals its small-town Spanish *fonda* origins – which has been well renovated and is run by a very welcoming (and English-speaking) family. It has cheap rooms in the old Spanish wing, slightly pricier en suite ones in a new wing, and is deservedly popular. There is also a good café-restaurant, local music most nights, and a terrace overlooking the town and sea. ①

To Mirhleft
& Tiznit (7064)

To Abbainou
& Goulimine
(7129)

Hôtel Aït
Ba Hamram

Hôtel
Suerte Loca

Filling Station

Restaurant Atlantic

Grands
Taxis

AVENUE EL

Jardin
Houria

Hammam

RUE MOULAY YOUSSEF

CTM Buses

Hôtel
Houria

AVENUE MOHAMMED

Spanish
Consulate

HOURIA

Law Courts

Hôtel
Bellevue

PLACE
HASSAN
II

Banque
Populaire
& BMCE

Local Buses

Hôtel Ifni
Cinema

AVENUE SIDI MOHAMMED ABDALLAH

AV. SIDI MOHAMMED

Lighthouse

Hôtel
de Ville

Filling
Station

Souk

Post
Office

Police

HASSAN   II

AVENUE

Restaurant
Tamimt

To the
new port
(7014)

Campsite

To the
old port

0   100m

SIDI IFNI

Hôtel Bellevue, just off Place Hassan II (☎08/87.50.72). A fine building, with 1930s neon lights on the walls, and sea views; good value but with a noisy bar and slow restaurant. ①

Hôtel Aït Ba Hamram, Rue de la Plage – at the bottom of the steps (☎08/87.51.73). Another grand building, with marginally better rooms than the *Bellevue*, perhaps, a good restaurant (order in advance – especially fish), and a bar. ①

Camping Sidi Ifni, Av. Sidi Mohammed. A rather spartan site with little shade.

In addition to the hotels, there are just two **restaurants**, the contrast between which could hardly be greater:

Restaurant Atlantic, 1 Av. Houria (☎08/87.50.86). Run by two Germans, this has a most impressive (and somewhat expensive) menu. There are also a few rooms to let (*privat-pension*). Well worth a try.

Restaurant Tamimt, Av. Hassan II. A friendly, local little place, serving grilled chicken and *tajines*. Seats outside.

The Town

It is the Spanish feel – and the **Art Deco architecture** – that is most attractive about Sidi Ifni. The town beach is not that great (Mirhleft, see preceding section, is better) and is in any case prone to long sea mists.

The obvious place to start out is the **Place Hassan II**, whose street signs only partly disguise the change from its previous incarnation as the *Plaza de España*. It stands at the heart of the town and immediately sets a tone for the place. An Andalusian garden and tiled fountain, perfect for the evening *paseo*, flank its centre, while at one end stands a **Spanish consulate** – a building straight out of García Márquez, now it seems, terminally closed – and, at the other, a **church** in Moorish–Art Deco style, now adopted for use as the law courts. All these buildings are in immaculate condition, with their stunning pastel shades picked out. There is also a fine little patisserie on the square, too – good for its wares in this case, rather than architecture.

More Art Deco splendour, however, is to be seen nearby in the tiled **post office** (*CTT* rather than *PTT* – in its Spanish form), whence those mystifying stamps of the 1950s emerged, as any (ex-) collector will recall. And there are a whole sequence of monumental **stairways**, rambling down towards the port and beach, and a magnficent deco **lighthouse**.

To the south of the town is the **old port**, built by the Spanish, and out to sea is an odd little concrete island, connected to the mainland by a sort of cablecar, where ships once used to dock. There's a **new port** further south, with big new sardine- and anchovy- processing factories.

On Sundays a large **souk** – complete with musicians and storytellers – takes place out near the abandoned airfield. Taxis shuttle out from town.

Moving on

CTM **buses** run from the bottom end of Av. Mohammed V; there are departures at 7am and 2pm for Tiznit and Agadir. More local buses, to Goulimine and Tiznit, go from the street one block north of the post office. **Grands taxis** run to Tiznit and Goulimine, leaving from a street in the northwest of the grid (see map).

There is little of note on the route south from Sidi Ifni to Goulimine, though the route itself is a pleasant one, especially in spring, when the slopes are green with a mass of euphorbia.

Tiznit to Goulimine via Bou Izakarn

Moussems apart, it is **the route down** to Goulimine that is the main attraction. It is best taken, at least in one direction, with a detour to Sidi Ifni (see above).

Travelling on the inland route, the only place of any size that you pass is the palmery and village of **BOU IZAKARN** (Friday *souk*), where the road to Ifrane de l'Anti-Atlas and the Tata oasis (see p.455) heads off east into the Anti-Atlas. *Grands taxis* can be negotiated here for Ifrane de l'Anti-Atlas and Amtoudi (see p.459). There is also a basic **hotel**, the *Anti-Atlas* (☎08/87.41.34), on the Goulimine road, which does little to deserve its 1-star status.

Goulimine

GOULIMINE sounds pretty exciting in the brochures: "The Gateway to the Sahara", with its nomadic "blue men" and traditional camel market. The truth, sadly, is considerably more mundane. Though the scenery is indeed impressively bleak, you're still a long way short of seeing any Saharan dunes, and the camel market itself is a rather depressing sham, maintained largely for the tour groups bussed in from Agadir. Even the locals have begun to indulge in theatrical cons, ferrying people out to see "genuine *hommes bleus*" in tents outside town. For a more convincing and exciting sense of the desert, you would do a lot better to make for M'hamid in the Drâa (see p.389) or Merzouga in the Tafilalt (see p.416).

The one time that a visit to Goulimine would be worthwhile in itself is if you could coincide with one of the region's annual **moussems** – when you really are likely to see Touareg nomads. It's difficult to get information about the exact dates of the *moussems* – they vary considerably from year to year – but, in general, there is usually one held in June at Asrir, 10km southeast of Goulimine.

Orientation and practicalities

Goulimine is a fairly standard administrative town but with a distinctly frontier feel to it, and with a couple of small, fairly animated *souks*. At its heart is the **Place Bir Anzarane**, with the main cluster of hotels and café-restaurants to its north.

If you arrive by **bus**, you'll probably be dropped to the north of this area (top of our map), while **grands taxis** run to a square a similar distance to the south.

ACCOMMODATION

Accommodation is very limited and prices at most of the hotels are hiked up every Friday night as tourists come into town for the camel market. All but one are unclassified:

Hôtel l'Ere Nouvelle, Bd. Mohammed V (☎08/87.21.19). Cheapest in town and not too bad, with hot showers on request; also has a modest café-restaurant (order in advance). ①

Hôtel la Jeunesse, Bd. Mohammed V – opposite (☎08/87.22.21). A tolerable second choice, if the above is full. Located up a steep flight of steps. ①

Hôtel Place Bir Anzarane, Place Bir Anzarane (no phone and sign in Arabic only). Okay, again with a café-restaurant. There are no showers but there is a hammam diagonally across the square, between the mosque and PTT. ①

Hôtel Oued Ed Dahabi, Place Bir Anzarene. Not recommended. ①

Hôtel Salam, Route de Tan Tan (☎08/87.87.20.57). You might decide it's worth paying the extra money for a room here at the town's finest hotel. It offers reasonably large rooms round an open patio, a decent restaurant and Goulimine's only bar. The hotel also displays three-dimensional paintings by an excellent local artist, Hamid Kahlaoui. ②

Camping Goulimine. This is not much of an option – stony, exposed, and a walk of about 1200m from Place Hassan II (follow the signs; it's just below the military garrison).

MEALS AND SHOWS

The *Hôtel Salam* has the best **meals**, as well as rooms. Other places worth considering include *Café Marche Verte*, *Le Diamant Bleu* and *Café Jour et Nuit*, up near the PTT; the latter is usually open night and day, as it promises.

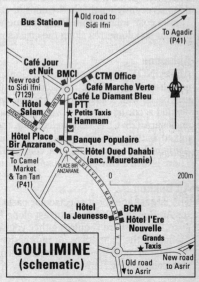

Several of the hotels and cafés put on shows of **Guedra dancing** on Friday and Saturday nights and Saturday lunchtimes. Much has been written about this traditional, seductive women's dance of the desert – performed, from a kneeling position (developed for the low tents) to a slow, repetitive rhythm. The shows, however, are a bit of a travesty.

OTHER PRACTICALITIES
The town has three **banks**: *BCM*, *Banque Populaire* and *BMCI*, all marked on the map. There are also numerous shops, several of which specialise in Saharan "antiques" – mainly carpets and jewellery, but also leather goods, silver ware, knives, stones and old money. Moving on, *CTM* and *SATAS* buses both run from the **bus station**, north of Place Bir Anzarane, though *CTM* tickets can be bought from their booking office by the *Café Marche Verte*.

The "Camel Market"
Goulimine's **Saturday souk** serves a regular local purpose, with all the usual Moroccan goods on sale: grain, vegetables, meat, clothes, silver, jewellery, sheep and goats. What it doesn't have in very great measure are camels, as the beasts have steadily fallen from favour over the years in the wake of lorries and transit vehicles, and the caravan routes, of course, are no more. The few you do see here have either been brought in just for show or to be sold off for meat.

The market is held a kilometre out of town on the road to Tan Tan; it starts around 6am and a couple of hours later the first tourbuses arrive from Agadir.

Around Goulimine: springs, oases and Plage Blanche

There are a couple of good little trips out from Goulimine: to the hot springs of **Abbainou**, 15km northeast, and to the oasis of **Aït Boukha**, 17km southeast; both offer pleasant alternative **accommodation** to a night in Goulimine. So, too, does a recently established campsite at **Fort Bou-Jerif**, an old French Foreign Legion post, inland from **Plage Blanche** – the "White Beach" that stretches for sixty or so kilometres along the coast southwest of Goulimine.

Abbainou
ABBAINOU, 15km northeast of Goulimine, is a relatively easy excursion, with *grands taxis* negotiable and affordable (from the main rank by the *souk*). It is a tiny oasis, with a *koubba* and hot springs, channelled into two bath enclosures – divided according to sex – where you can soak the afternoon away. The women's enclosure (28°C) is very welcoming, though the men's is 10°C hotter! There is mixed bathing in the evenings. If you want to stay, the French-run *Auberge Abainou* has **rooms** round a courtyard, cold showers, a restaurant and a bar. There is also a **campsite**, *Camping Abainou*, and several café-restaurants.

Aït Bekkou
The largest and most spectacular oasis in the Goulimine area is **AÏT BEKKOU** (or Aït Boukka), 10km southeast along the road to ASRIR, then a further 7km on piste. To get there requires either your own transport or chartering a *grand taxi*. Alongside the palmery is an impressive new hotel, the *Tighmert* (☎08/87.30.53; ③), built in mock-Kasbah style and decorated, like the *Hôtel Salam* in Goulimine, with paintings by Hamid Kahlaoui.

Aït Bekkou is a thriving agricultural community, with an especially lush strip of cultivation along a canal, irrigated from the old riverbed and emerging from a flat expanse of sand. You might even see the odd herd of camels being grazed out here. To reach it, head for the thicket of palms about 2km behind the oasis (or pick up a guide on the way).

Fort Bou-Jerif and Plage Blanche

Fort Bou-Jerif is a truely romantic spot, established and run, not perhaps surprisingly, by a young French couple, Guy and Evy Dreumont. It stands beside the Oued Assaka, 13km from the sea, and is marked on the Michelin map by a little fort symbol (with the words *O. Noun* to the left). The route involves 20km of paved road (to Tisséguemane), then 18km of piste, passable by car or campervan; it can, alternatively be approached by landrover along the coast from Sidi Ifni.

If the attractions of staying at an old French Foreign Legion camp in the middle of nowhere are not enough to entice you, then it should be reported that there is good French cooking (camel *tajine*, no less) and that the Dreumonts offer some superb four-wheel-drive excursions in the area, including, of course, trips to the Plage Blanche. They offer rooms as well as camping, power points for caravans, and rows of very clean showers (hot water) and toilets. To book ahead, write to them at: Fort Bou Jerif, BP 504 Guelmin, Morocco.

THE DEEP SOUTH AND WESTERN SAHARA

Few travellers venture south of Goulimine – and on the surface there is little enough to commend the trip. The towns – **Tan Tan**, **Tarfaya**, **Laayoune** and **Dakhla** – are modern administrative centres, with no great intrinsic interest. The route, however, across vast tracts of hammada – bleak, stony desert – is another matter. The odd line of dunes unfolds on the horizon to the east, the ocean parallels much of the road to the west, and there is no mistaking that you have reached the **Sahara** proper. Returning, if you don't fancy a repeat of the journey, there are flights from Ad Dakhla and Laayoune to Agadir, or from Laayoune to the **Canary Islands** (also accessible from Agadir)

An additional point of interest, now that the war with Polisario seems to be on the wane, is the attention being lavished on the region by the Moroccan authorities. The **Western Sahara** (the old Spanish Saharan colony, reclaimed by Morocco with the 1975 Green March) begins just to the south of Tarfaya. **Laayoune**, never greatly regarded by the Spanish, has been transformed into a showcase capital for the new provinces; there are industrial plans, too, for **Tarfaya**; and, with an eye to the traditional nomadic dwellers, the Moroccan authorities have also been assisting in building up the local camel herds.

The region's economic importance was long thought to centre on the phosphate mines at **Boukra**, southeast of Laayoune. However, these have not been greatly productive in recent years, and the deposits are not especially rich by the standards of the Plateau des Phosphates east of Casablanca. In the long term, the rich deep-water fishing grounds offshore are likely to prove a much better earner. This potential is gradually being realised with the construction of a new port at Laayoune, together with industrial plant for fish storage and processing.

Note that throughout the former Spanish colonial zone, **Spanish** remains the dominant **second language**; younger people, officials and administrators, however, will generally speak good French.

Goulimine to Tan Tan

The approach from **Goulimine to Tan Tan** runs along 125km of straight desert road, across a bleak area of scrub and hammada. There are few features to speak of en route: a café and filling station (50km from Goulimine); a small pass (85km); and finally a crossing of the **Oued Drâa** (105km), invariably dry at this point. There is a **police post** here, where non-nationals are obliged to fill in forms about their mother's maiden name, profession, and so on (see box overpage).

In colonial times, the Drâa was the border between the French and Spanish protectorates and a piste heads west to a last French **fort** at its mouth. Somewhat confusingly, although this was the border of the Protectorate, the land to the south was not actually part of the Spanish Saharan colonies: the northernmost of these, Seguiat El Hamra, began just south of Tarfaya, and the southern one south of Boujdour. After independence in 1956, the Spanish gave back to Morocco the strip of territory north of Tarfaya, keeping the two Saharan colonies until November 1975 (see box on p.478).

By public transport, you have a choice of either a **grand taxi** (leaving Goulimine from out on the Tan Tan road, near the camel *souk*) or a **bus** (several daily, including express services from Agadir). There is a **filling station** 50km from Goulimine (75km before Tan Tan).

Tan Tan

Arriving at **TAN TAN**, under an archway of kissing camels, you might just find yourself wondering why. A drab administrative centre, it survives in a low-key way through its status as a duty-free zone (the shops are full of radios and electric razors) and rather more so by its fishing port, which is responsible for a large percentage of Morocco's sardine exports. Its one claim to fame is that it was a departure point for the famous **Green March** (*La Marche Verte* – see p.478), an event you find commemorated on postcards throughout the south.

The town has around 50,000 inhabitants, many of them former nomads, who retain their distinctive pale blue robes. This clothing is much in evidence in the **souks** – the most animated part of a hot, sleepy town – as are a variety of *lithams*, strips of cotton that are wrapped round the head. The latter are a wise investment as sun protection if you are heading further south.

The town
Tan Tan's main street, **Av. Mohammed V**, runs from the archway gently downhill from northeast to southwest. There are buildings along its length, though to the east you can still catch glimpses of a parallel ridge, and to the west, the dry riverbed of the Oued Ben Khlil, which "flows" north to join the Oued Drâa. At the bottom end of Av. Mohammed V, and off it to the west (right) is **Place de la Marche Verte**, with the **bus and grand taxi rank**, and several hotels.

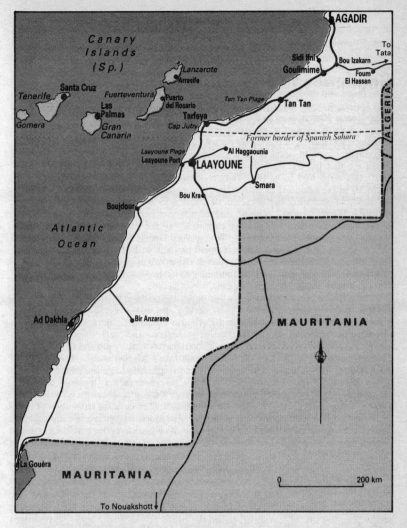

Most of the "official" buildings – the **Municipalité**, **PTT**, **Banque Populaire** – are at the top end of Av. Mohammed V, where a smaller, tree-lined square, referred to locally as **La Poste de la Police**, provides a further focus. **Petits taxis** can be found here, if needed.

There are a number of unclassified **hotels** to choose between on and around Place de la Marche Verte, by far the best of which is the *Hôtel Dakar* (☎08/87.73.08; ⑩). The town also has two classified hotels, the *Hôtel l'Étoile du Sahara*, 17 Rue El Fida (☎08/87.70.85; ①), and the *Hôtel Amgala*, Av. de la Jeunesse (☎08/87.72.97; ①).

THE SAHARAN PROVINCES

Until 1987–88, any trip **south of Tan Tan**, into the **former Spanish Sahara**, involved getting permission from the military authorities. The routes are today open quite routinely – indeed the Moroccan authorities are actively encouraging tourists to explore the region. There is a hotel complex under construction at Tan Tan Plage, and the French *Club Med* is already established at Laayoune.

The Green March, war and political claims

The politics of the area are a highly sensitive matter in Morocco: so much so, that all maps and guides of the country must have the territory included as part of the Moroccan kingdom. Some background to this is included in *Contexts*. The essential facts are that the old Spanish colonies of **Rio de Oro** and **Seguiat El Hamra**, sometimes referred to as the **Western Sahara**, were occupied by Morocco on Spanish withdrawal in 1975. These claims were based on historic Moroccan control of the area, including the presence of a fort said to have been built by Moulay Ismail in the 1670s near Laayoune, and the activities here of Hassan I.

Whatever their legitimacy, King Hassan II enjoyed enormous acclaim with his tactical occupation of the territory – the so-called **Green March** (*La Marche Verte*) of November 1975, when 300,000 unarmed civilians walked across the old frontier and "returned" the territories to the Alaouite Kingdom of Morocco. Territorial counterclaims, however, came almost immediately from Mauritania and from various groups among the indigenous Sahrawis.

Through the next two decades, a war raged on and off in the desert between the Moroccan army and authorities (who occupy and administer the entire former Spanish colony) and Algerian-backed **Polisario** guerrilla fighters, operating from bases round Tindouf, across the border in Algeria. The war, which for a time affected areas within Morocco's "former" boundaries, was, by the end of the 1980s, largely contained by the creation of an extraordinary **"desert wall"** (see *Contexts*). In the meantime Polisario increasingly turned to diplomacy to gather support.

In 1988 a UN-sponsored ceasefire, with a **referendum** on "incorporation" or independence, was accepted in principal by both sides, and it seemed a settlement was at last in sight. However, the years since have seen constant frustration of the UN aims, with arguments over the voting list (and Morocco "returning" Sahrawis to the province) leading to indefinite postponement of the referendum. Military action again resurfaced round the wall. The present position, with UN observers still in place, is a stand-off.

Visiting the provinces

Given the factors above, all travellers are advised to check the most **up-to-date information** before attempting anything too ambitious in the region, and certainly before trying to take any road route into Mauritania (impossible at the time of writing). All the main road signs south of Agadir, however, now give the distances to Laayoune and Dakhla – and even Dakar – and **visiting Laayoune** and **Smara**, at least, is pretty routine, involving nothing more than a sequence of form-filling and routine questions at police posts along the way. The only obstacle here would be for visitors with the occupation "journalist" in their passport: a profession not welcome in the region, unless under the aegis of an official press tour.

A more practical problem, however, is **accommodation**, with UN supervisors occupying virtually all of the better hotels in Laayoune, Boujdour, Dakhla and Smara. It would be wise to phone a few places in these towns in advance of a visit, unless you are prepared to camp.

For a **meal**, there are cafés around Place de la Marche Verte, and a restaurant at the *Hôtel Dakar* (order in advance); the town has no bars. Entertainment is limited to the *Renaissance* **cinema**, between the Poste de la Police and the dry riverbed. It has a café, *Le Glacier*, on its terrace. Moving on, **grands taxis** can be arranged to Laayoune and Goulimine. **Buses** go to Agadir (*CTM* at 7.30am, 10pm & 2am; *SATAS* at 5am & 3pm) and Laayoune (*CTM* at 1.15am & 2am; *SATAS* at 10am).

Tan Tan Plage

TAN TAN PLAGE, 28km from town on the coastal route to Laayoune, has been theoretically earmarked for development as a resort, though in the past ten years the ambitious four-star *Hôtel Ayoub* has failed to get much beyond its foundations. At present, therefore, there is very little to see (a scattering of houses, shops, banks and a couple of mosques), even less to do, and nowhere to stay. There are, however, two **cafés**, the better of which, *Étoile de l'Océan*, does good fish.

The **beach** itself is unenticing – littered with broken glass, not too clean due to the proximity of a large sardine port nearby, and often swamped in seaweed.

A loop through Smara

It is possible to make a loop **from Tan Tan along the new road to Smara**, returning by way of the P44 to Laayoune, and from there across to Tan Tan via Tarfaya – a circuit of some 800km. There are **buses** along each section (though not every day). If you're driving, you will find **filling stations** in Tan Tan, Smara and Laayoune – petrol, incidentally, is subsidised throughout the Western Sahara – so if you embark on the trip be sure to fill up, and to carry good water supplies.

Tan Tan to Smara

The ONMT literature on the Deep South extols the P44 between Tan Tan and Smara as "the new Saharan road". It is indeed impressive, in the sheer absence of habitation and features: there are grand vistas of hills and valleys to the east for the first 20km, then for the next 200km to Smara it is perfectly flat. At 75km from Tan Tan is the route's single roadside hamlet, ABITH (or ABBATIH), where there are a couple of flyblown cafés and a flag pole.

From Abith to Smara there is nothing of interest, although the desert does get perceptibly darker in colour, due to the presence of black basalt.

Smara

SMARA (ES SEMARA) developed as an important caravan route across the Sahara, but today it is basically a military garrison town. The only link with the past are the ruins of the **Grand Mosque of Ma El Aïnin**, the "Blue Sultan", who controlled the region at the turn of the last century. If you do come to the town you should certainly see this – a strange construction of black basalt from the local hills. The "old mosque", marked on our map, is also made of basalt. Another distinctive aspect of the town are the small white eggbox-like domes serving as roofs for the buildings – a device said to keep the interior cooler.

The military presence is very noticeable in Smara and includes both the Moroccan army and the UN, here to supervise the ceasefire and referendum. The difficulties of this are apparent even from a cursory look at Smara, for there is a huge tented city outside the town of former residents of Western Sahara returned from the north; Polisario, inevitably, contest their origins and right to vote.

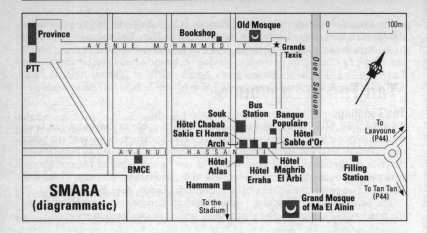

The best of Smara's five **hotels** tend to be block-booked by the UN at present, so don't count on finding anything more than a basic room. The options are:

Hotel Erraha, 16 Av. Hassan II (☎08/89.92.27). A friendly hotel with small rooms, cold showers, and a roof terrace. There are grill-cafés on either side. ①

Hotel Atlas, Av. Hassan II (no phone). Unusually, managed by a woman. No showers but a hammam is close by. ①

Hotel Sable d'Or, Av. Hassan II (no phone). Again basic but adequate. ①

Hotel Chabab Sakia El Hamra, Av. Hassan II (no phone). A little more expensive but worth the extra if you can get a room. The reception is on the first floor, above the *CTM/ONCF* office. ①

Hotel Maghrib El Arbi, Av. Hassan II (no phone). A modern hotel, currently block-booked by the UN, whose vehicles are prominent outside. ①

For **meals**, there are numerous café-restaurants and open-air grill-cafés along Av. Hassan II. The town also has a couple of **banks** (*BMCE* and *Banque Populaire*), a **filling station**, and several garage-workshops for **car repairs**. *CTM* and *ONCF* **buses** run to Tan Tan/Agadir (three times daily) and Laayoune (most days). Check times at the office. Note that the **road east from the town**, towards the Algerian town of TINDOUF (where the Polisario have their main base), is firmly closed.

West to to Laayoune

West from Smara, heading to Laayoune, you pass through slightly more featured landscape than the route from Tan Tan to Smara. For the first 5km the desert remains black-ish, from the basalt, and then, for the next 20km, there are brown, flat-topped hills. The land then levels, as the new road keeps straight, cutting from time to time across stretches of the old piste, which is marked by a line of cairns and poles.

At around 40km from Smara, water pipes are being laid beside the road, leading to the water marked on the Michelin map at **Oumcheggag**: an ancient spring which will not, of course, be renewed. Further on, around 75km from Smara, you become aware of the Boukra/Laayoune conveyor belt snaking its way to the south of the road. This bears phosphates from **BOUKRA**, 30km to the southeast, a mining town with a large garrison. South of Boukra is a restricted military zone.

Eventually the belt and the road from Boukra join the main road, which becomes much better surfaced for a final loop **north to Laayoune**, past the old Spanish fort of DCHIRA (out of bounds to all but the military).

Tan Tan to Laayoune

The route between **Tan Tan Plage and Laayoune** is the most memorable stretch of the journey in the Deep South, cutting as it does between desert and ocean. The coast, somewhat defying expectations, is mainly cliff – the desert dropping directly away to the sea, with only the occasional stretch of beach.

Tan Tan to Tarfaya

Between Tan Tan and Tarfaya there is little more than the roadside settlement of **AKHFENIR** (about 150km south of Tan Tan) with its three cafés and filling station. Just beyond here is a rare stretch of accessible beach, with reputedly wonderful fishing.

TARFAYA is a small town (population 7000) with a fishing port and a large monument to the Green March. It may be in line for greater things if an oil shale development, currently under consideration by Shell, goes ahead, but for the moment it's a quiet place, probably not far different from its years as a staging post for the *Aéropostale Service* – when aviators such as Antoine de Saint-Exupéry used to rest up on their way down to West Africa. The service is commemorated annually in October by a **"Rallye Aérien"**, with small planes flying south from Toulouse to Dakar in Senegal; Tarfaya is a night's stop. Oddly enough, the town was actually founded, at the end of the last century, by a British trader, and was originally known as Port Victoria. During the Spanish occupation, it was known as Villa Bens and served as a very low-key capital for the "Southern Protectorate"; they abandoned it in 1958, leaving a church, a fort (still brooding over the town) and a handful of villas. Today it has been overshadowed by Laayoune, and has just one (unsignposted and unclassified) **hotel**, located opposite the two cafés.

South to Laayoune

South of Tarfaya you cross the old border of Spanish Sahara, and traverse real sand desert – the **Erg Lakhbayta**. The effect, however, is lighter than that implies, for along the way are a series of enormous **lagoons**, their water prevented from reaching the sea by long spits of sand, and **salt pans**, still being worked. These are important migratory sites, which should provide considerable rewards for **birdwatchers**.

Laayoune

With a population of 100,000, **LAAYOUNE** (AL AYOUN) is the largest and the most interesting town of Western Sahara. Its development as a provincial capital is almost immediately obvious – and impressive, as you survey the new 30,000-seat stadium, complete with real grass, maintained for the area's handful of football teams. The city has the highest per capita government spending in Morocco and soldiers, billeted here for the conflict with Polisario, have been employed in many of the projects.

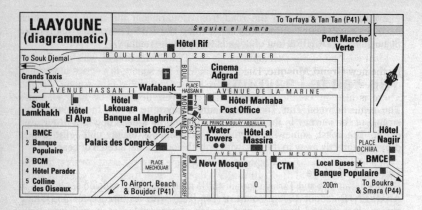

The population growth – from little more than a village when the Moroccans took over – has been aided by massive subsidies, which apply throughout Western Sahara, and by an agreement that settlers should initially pay no taxes. They are a mix of Sahrawis, many of them driven here by the drought of the last few years, and Moroccan immigrants from the north in search of work.

Orientation and accommodation

The first sight of Laayoune, coming from Tarfaya, is across the steep-sided valley of the Seguiat El Hamra, which has been dammed to make another – shallow – lagoon. The old "lower" town, built by the Spanish, lies on the southern slope of the valley, with the new "upper town", developed since the Green March, on the high plateau beyond. The map above is highly diagrammatic.

Laayoune's **hotels** have done good business over the past few years with the UN, who block-book the best, and often spread into others. At the time of writing, it is wise to phone ahead, unless you're happy with basic rooms at the dozen or so unclassified hotels in Souk Djemal. Options are:

Hôtel Sidi Ifni, Hôtel Farah, Hôtel Inezgane, Hôtel Atlas, Hôtel Victoire, Hôtel Sakia El Hamra, all in the Souk Djemal (Jmal). Very basic, very cheap and unused to Westerners. ⑩

Hôtel Rif, just off Bd. 28 Fevrier, overlooking the Seguiat El Hamra. This is much better than the *souk* hotels – a friendly place, recently refurbished. Cheap and excellent value. ⑪

Hôtel Marhaba, Av. de la Marine – opposite the *Cinema Adgrad* (☎08/89.32.49). A good, modest hotel. ①

Hôtel El Alya, 1 Rue Kadi El Ghalaoui (☎08/89.31.33). Very poor, despite the category. ③

Hôtel Lakouara, Av. Hassan II (☎08/89.33.78). Good but block-booked by the UN. ③

Hôtel Nagjir, Place Dchira (☎08/89.41.68). New and very comfortable, with a restaurant, bar and disco (perhaps the only disco in Western Sahara). Not block-booked, but often full. ④

Hôtel Parador, Av. de l'Islam (☎08/89.45.00); **Hôtel al Massira**, 12 Av. de la Mecque (☎08/89.42.25). These hotels are owned by *Club Med*, who also have an annex at Laayoune Plage (see opposite), primarily for sea fishing. These two are UN block-booked at present. ⑤

The four last-named hotels have **restaurants**. Elsewhere, the *Café Tetuan*, 182 Place Dchira, and *Café-Restaurant Snak Fes* (*sic*), 32 Av. Hassan II, serve Moroccan standards, and the *Cremerie Agdaz*, next door to *Snak Fes*, is good for soft drinks and breakfast. Also warmly recommended is *Restaurant Hagounia*, close by the *Hôtel Nagjit*.

The town

Most of the new building is in the upper town; the old Spanish settlement, more dishevelled, lies down below, with its old and disused cathedral.

Most striking of the developments is the **Place Mechouar**, which is flanked by the new **Grand Mosque**. Lining one side of the square is a series of tent-like canopies for shade and at each corner are towers to floodlight the square at night. There is also an ambitious **Palais des Congrès**, designed by King Hassan's then-favourite architect, French-born André Paccard.

Across the way is the new **stadium**, which, if the Moroccans have their way, and FIFA decide to "go for Africa", will be a venue for World Cup football before very long.

In addition to such public statements, there are a few pleasant corners, like the landscaped gardens of the **Colline des Oiseaux**, with their cages of exotic birds – complete with blinds to be drawn down over the cages in the event of sandstorms. Of some interest, too, is the **Complexe Artisanal**, on Av. de la Mecque, where twenty little workshops, capped with white cupolas, provide space for metal, wood and jewellery craftsmen.

Directory

Banks are located at the foot of Bd. Mohammed V, near Place Hassan II. They include: *BMCE, Banque Populaire, BCM, Wafabank* and *Banque Al Maghrib. BMCE* and *Banque Populaire* also have branches in Place Dchira.

Buses *CTM* departures are from outside their office at 20 Av. de la Mecque; they arrive from Agadir/Tan Tan at 10am and return at 3pm. *ONCF* buses go from Av. Oum Saad; they arrive from Agadir/Tan Tan at 1pm and return at 5pm. More "local" buses, for Smara, Tarfaya and Tan Tan, leave from Place Dchira.

Car hire *Agence Massira Travel*, Av. de la Mecque (☎08/89.32.16); *BTS*, Av. de la Mecque (☎08/89.42.24); Ouled Abdallah, Place Dchira (☎08/89.39.11). None of the major operators are represented.

Flights *RAM*, 7 Place Bir Anzarane (☎08/89.40.77), operate flights from the town airport (a short taxi ride east) to Agadir (3 weekly), Casablanca (daily), Dakhla (weekly), Smara (2 weekly), Tan Tan (3 weekly) and Las Palmas (Canary Islands, 4 weekly).

Post office This is still marked in Spanish as the Correos, just up from Av. Hassan II .

Taxis *Grands taxis* leave from Place Lamkhakh; landrover taxis from Av. Mazouir.

Tourist office There may be no tourists in town (our last researcher met just one) but there's a fully fledged *ONMT* office on Av. de l'Islam, opposite the *Parador*. The director speaks Moroccan Arabic and Italian.

Laayoune Plage

LAAYOUNE PLAGE is 20km distant: leave town on the P41 to Boujdor, then, past the airport, turn right off the main road and quickly left at a sign to *Camping Touristique*. At the beach – which is very windy, year round, with big Atlantic breakers – there is a sporadically open café-restaurant. If you want to camp, you'll find the site 2km north on a rough piste; it is a large compound with cold showers, electricity and a little shop, open all year. In July and August, reputedly, it can get very full with Moroccans from Smara and Tan Tan. Nearby, open by arrangement with the *Parador/Club Med* in Laayoune, is the *Club Med* annex for big sea fishing.

South from Laayoune

Depending on the military situation, you might be able to obtain permission to continue **south of Laayoune** down to Dakhla. There is a daily *CTM/ONCF* bus along this route (it starts out from Agadir) and *grand taxi* runs; the bus is often full, so you'll have to push your way on if you want to pick it up en route. The road is reasonably good, though drivers should beware of occasional sand-drifts, and camels grazing by or on the road. Foreigners will need to form-fill at numerous checkpoints along the way.

Lemsid to Dakhla

The first habitation along the road is **LEMSID**, 110km from Laayoune, which, if you're not into travel for travel's sake, is perhaps the place to turn round. There is a small **café-shop** here that provides basic meals for the route's lorry drivers.

South of Lemsid, the sea is guarded by cliffs for most of the way to the fishing port of **BOUJDOR**. The landscape here is a little more mellow, with a long beach to the north. Rocks, however, make the sea dangerous for swimming and surfing. The village itself has a filling station, various cafés and a **hotel**, the *Boughraz* (no water; ⓪); a large tent encampment is on the outskirts. The hotel lobby doubles up as a cinema, which is the main excitement going, though the old Portuguese lighthouse can be visited, if you find yourself stuck for something to do!

South again from Boujdor the road runs inland, rejoining the coast at the tiny settlement of SKAYMAT – less of an oasis than it looks on the map.

Dakhla – and the road to Mauritania

Finally, 322km from Laayoune, you reach the town of **DAKHLA** (or AD DAKHLA) on a long spit of land. This was a Spanish outpost, known as Villa Cisneros in the colonial days, when it served as a minor administrative centre for the Rio de Oro, though the only remains are a church and the odd man hole cover. It remains military in character, and once you have explained your presence, you should be prepared to mix largely with soldiers on leave.

There are half a dozen basic **hotels**, the best of which are the *Hôtel Doubs* (⓪), to the left on entering the town, near a large barracks, and the *Hôtel Bahia* (⓪), close to the bus depot. It's not the most compelling resort, but there are lovely beaches nearby, superb fishing, and there's even a **bar** in town, *Bar Juan*, which conjures up real beers.

To Mauritania

The road **south of Ad Dakhla** is closed to all but military traffic – and Mauritanian visas are not issued in Rabat for this border. For a period in 1992, however, overland groups were taking this route, in convoy with Moroccan military down to LA GOUÈRA, the Moroccan frontier post, and then with Mauritanian troops from NOUADHIBOU.

If you are very committed, it may be worth making enquiries through the overland operators listed on p.7. Individual landrover travellers, however, are unlikely to meet with success. If you have managed to obtain a Mauritanian visa, the procedure, once at Dakhla, is to apply to Caid Jemal, the provincial governor, and he will fax to Rabat for authorisation to provide you with a convoy. This normally takes a couple of days. The route, it scarcely needs to be said, is quite an adventure: 464km of mixed piste and tarmac down to Nouadibhou.

travel details

Buses

From Agadir Essaouira (6 daily; 3hr 30min); Taroudannt (4; 2hr 30min); Tiznit (4; 2hr); Goulimine (2; 4hr 30min); Marrakesh (5; *SATAS/CTM* direct; 4hr); Tata (4am and 7am daily; 9hr); Casablanca (7.30pm; 5hr).

From Inezgane Marrakesh (4 daily; 3hr 30min); Goulimine (5; 4hr 30min); Taroudannt (4; 2hr); Taliouine/Ouarzazate (4; 3hr 30min/5hr).

From Taroudannt Marrakesh via Tizi n'Test (daily at 4am; 8hr 30min); Marrakesh, via Inezgane/Imi n'Tanoute (daily at 5am; 6hr); Taliouine/Ouarzazate (5 daily; 1hr 30min/3hr); Tata (3 a week; 8–10hr).

From Tiznit Tafraoute (4 daily; 3hr 30min–6hr 30min); Goulimine (6; 2hr 30min); Sidi Ifni (2; 2hr 30min); Tata (2; 7hr).

From Tafraoute Agadir (4 daily; 5hr); Tiznit (3; 3hr).

From Goulimine Tan Tan (3 daily; 3hr).

Grands Taxis

From Agadir Shuttle to Inezgane (15min; 2dh); regularly to Oulad Teima* (1hr; connection to Taroudannt).

From Inezgane Regularly to Oulad Teima* (40min; connection to Taroudannt) and Tiznit (1hr 30min).

From Oulad Teima* Regularly to Taroudannt (1hr).

From Taroudannt Linked service, with changes, to Ouled Behril, Aoulouz and Taliouine.

From Tiznit Landrover taxis to Tafraoute (regular departures, not always very easy to get on; they stop around 4pm; 2hr 30min). Regularly to Goulimine (2hr; sometimes with connection at Bou Izarkan).

From Goulimine Regularly to Tan Tan (2hr 30min).

*Oulad Teima is also known as Quarante-Quatre – "44" – as it is 44km from Agadir.

Ferries

From Agadir Weekly car/passenger ferry (Saturday 7pm) to Las Palmas, Canary Islands (arrives Sunday 5pm).

Flights

From Agadir Daily to Casablanca (and from there to Tangier, etc); several times a week to Tan Tan, Laayoune and Las Palmas (Canary Islands); 3 times a week to Ad Dakhla. International flights to London, etc, though tickets are not especially cheap if you buy them at this end.

From Tan Tan Most days to Laayoune.

From Laayoune Most days to Las Palmas (Canary Islands), Tan Tan and Agadir.

From Ad Dhakla 3 times a week to Agadir.

PART THREE

THE

CONTEXTS

THE HISTORICAL FRAMEWORK

Morocco's emergence as a "modern" nation-state is astonishingly recent, dating from the occupation of the country by the French and Spanish at the beginning of this century, and its subsequent independence in 1956. Prior to this, it is best seen as a kind of patchwork of tribes, whose shifting alliances and sporadic bids for power defined both the government and its extent.

With a handful of exceptions, the country's ruling sultans controlled only the plains, the coastal ports and the regions around the imperial capitals of Fes, Marrakesh, Rabat and Meknes. These were known as *Bled el Makhzen* – the governed lands, or, literally, "the Lands of the Storehouse". The rest of the Moroccan territories – the Rif, the three Atlas ranges and the outlying deserts – comprised *Bled es Siba*, "the Lands of the Dissidents". Populated almost exclusively by Berbers, the original (pre-Arab) inhabitants, they were rarely recognised as being anything more than under local tribal authority.

The balance between government control and tribal independence is one of the two enduring themes of Moroccan history. The other is the emergence, expansion and eventual replacement of the various **sultanate dynasties**. These at first seem dauntingly complicated – a succession of short-lived tribal movements and confusingly similar-named sultans – but there are actually just seven main groups.

The first of them, the **Idrissids**, became the model by founding the city of Fes towards the end of the eighth century and bringing a coalition of Berber and Arab forces under a central *makhzen* (government) authority. The last, the **Alaouites**, emerged in the mid-seventeenth century from the great palm oasis of Tafilalt and, continuing with the current king, Hassan II, still hold constitutional power. It is around these groups – together with the medieval dynasties of the **Almoravids, Almohads,** **Merenids, Wattasids** and **Saadians** – that the bulk of the following sections are organised.

PREHISTORY

The first inhabitants of the **Maghreb** – the Arab term for the countries of North Africa – probably occupied the **Sahara**, for thousands of years a great savannah fertile enough to support elephants, zebras and a whole range of other game and wildlife. Little is known about these ancestors of the human species, although it seems likely that there were groups of hunter-and-gatherer hominids here as early as 1,000,000 BC.

Around 15,000 BC there seem to have been **Paleolithic** settlements, and before the Sahara went into decline (from 3000 BC), primitive pastoral and agricultural systems had begun to develop. It is possible, too, to trace the arrival of two independent Stone-Age cultures in the Maghreb: the Neolithic **Capsian Man** (circa 10,000–5000 BC), probably emerging from Egypt, and, slightly later, **Mouillian Man**. From these people, fair-skinned and speaking a remote "Libyan" language, stem the cave and rock drawings of the pre-Sahara and High Atlas, the earliest archaeological sites in Morocco.

PHOENICIANS AND CARTHAGINIANS

The recorded history of the area begins about 1100 BC with a series of trading settlements established by the **Phoenicians**. These were small, isolated colonies, usually built on defensible headlands round the coast, and there was probably little initial contact between them and the inhabitants of the interior, whom they knew as Libyans and Ethiopians – or collectively as *Barbaroi*, or **Berbers**.

As the emphasis shifted away from the Phoenicians themselves, and their African trading routes were taken over by the former colony of **Carthage** (modern Tunis), some of the ports grew into considerable cities, exporting grain and grapes, and minting their own coinage. On the "Moroccan" coast, the most important colonies were at Lixus (near Larache), Tingis (Tangier) and Chellah (near Rabat), but they spread as far east as Melilla; in the south a flourishing dye factory was also maintained on an island off Essaouira.

Officially, the Carthaginian Empire collapsed with its defeat in the **Punic Wars** (196 BC) against Rome, but in these provincial outposts, life seems to have been little affected. If anything, the colonies grew in stature and prosperity, absorbing hundreds of Punic refugees after the Roman sacking of Carthage. It was a first sign of Morocco's intrinsic historic and geographic isolation in what was to become known as *Maghreb el-Aksa* (The Land of the Farthest West). Even after the Romans had annexed and then abandoned the country, Punic was still widely spoken along the coast.

BERBER KINGDOMS AND ROMAN RULE

Prior to total Roman annexation, and the imposition of direct imperial rule in 24 AD, the "civilised" Moroccan territories for a while formed the **Berber kingdom of Mauritania**. This was probably little more than a confederation of local tribes, centred round Volubilis (near Meknes) and Tangier, but it gained a certain influence through alliance and occasional joint rule, with the adjoining Berber state of Numidia (essentially modern Algeria). The most important of the Berber rulers, and the only ones of which any substantial records survive, were **Juba II** (25 BC–23 AD) and his son **Ptolemy**. Both were heavily Romanised: Juba, an Algerian Berber by birth, was brought up and educated in Rome, where he married the daughter of Antony and Cleopatra. His reign, if limited in its extent, seems to have been orderly and prosperous, and under his son the pattern might well have continued. In 42 AD, however, Emperor Caligula summoned Ptolemy to an audience in Lyons and had him assassinated – so the story goes – for appearing in a more brilliant cloak than his own. Whatever the truth, and Rome may just have been eager for direct rule, it proved an inauspicious beginning.

ROMAN RULE

The early years of Rome's new imperial province were taken up with near-constant **rebellions** – the first one alone needing three years and over 20,000 troops to subdue.

Perhaps discouraged by this unexpected resistance, the **Romans** never attempted to colonise Morocco-Mauritania beyond its old limits. The Rif and Atlas mountains were left unpenetrated, and, of the interior, it was only

Volubilis – already a city of sorts, and at the heart of the north's fertile vineyards and grain fields – that was in any way exploited. In this the Romans were establishing an enduring precedent: not just in their failure to subdue *Bled es Siba*, which also defied the later sultans, but also in their treatment of Morocco as a useful "corridor" to the greater agricultural wealth of Algeria, Tunisia and Spain.

When the Roman legions were withdrawn in 253 AD, and the **Vandals** took power in southern Spain, the latter were interested only in taking Tangier and Ceuta for use as staging posts en route to northern Tunisia. Similarly, the **Byzantine General Belisarius,** who defeated the Vandals and laid claim to the Maghreb for Justinian's Eastern Empire, did little more than replace the Ceuta garrison.

It was understandable, of course. Any attempt to control Morocco would need manpower far in excess of these armies, and the only overland route through the country – across the Taza gap – was scarcely practicable even in peacetime. Not until the tenth century, and the great northward expansion of the desert nomads, was Morocco to become a land worthy of substantial exploitation in its own right, and even then only through the unifying and evangelising impetus of Islam.

THE COMING OF ISLAM

The irruption of **Islam** into the world began in 622 AD, when the Prophet Muhammad moved with his followers from Mecca to Medina. Within thirty years they had reached the borders of India, to the east; were threatening Byzantine Constantinople, to the north; and had established themselves in the Maghreb at Kairouan in present-day Tunisia.

After this initial thrust, however, sweeping across the old provinces of the Roman world, the progress of the new religion was temporarily slowed. The Berbers of Algeria – mainly pagan but including communities of Christians and Jews – put up a strong and unusually unified resistance to Arab control. It was only in 680 that the governor of Kairouan, **Oqba Ibn Nafi**, made an initial foray into Morocco, taking in the process the last Byzantine stronghold at Ceuta.

What happened afterwards remains uncertain. There is a story, perhaps apocryphal, that Oqba embarked on a 5000-kilometre **march**

through Morocco, raiding and subjugating all in his path, and preaching Islam all the way to the west – the Atlantic Ocean. But whether this expedition had any real Islamising influence on the Moroccan Berbers is unlikely. Oqba left no garrison forces and was himself killed in Algeria on his return to Kairouan.

Islam may have taken root among some of the tribes. In the early part of the eighth century the new Arab governor of the West, **Moussa Ibn Nasr**, returned to Morocco and managed to establish Arab control (and carry out mass conversions to Islam) in both the northern plains and the pre-Sahara. Like the Romans and Byzantines before him, though, his main thrust was towards **Spain**. In 711, the first Muslim forces crossed over from Tangier to Tarifa and defeated the Visigoths in a single battle; within a decade the Moors had taken control of all but the remote Spanish mountains in northern Asturias; and their advance was only halted at the Pyrenees by the victory of Charles Martel at Poitiers in 732.

The bulk of this invading and occupying force were almost certainly **Berber converts** to Islam, and the sheer scale of their military success must have had enormous influence in turning Morocco itself into a largely Muslim nation. It was not at this stage, however, in any way an Arab one. The extent of the Islamic Empire – from Persia to Morocco, and Ghana to Spain – was simply too great for Arab numbers. Early attempts to impose taxes on the Moroccan Berbers led to a rebellion and, once again outside the political mainstream, the Maghreb fragmented into a series of small, independent **principalities**.

THE IDRISSIDS (8TH–11TH CENTURIES)

This drift found an echo in the wider events of the Muslim world, which was undergoing its first – and most drastic – dissension, with the split into **Sunni** and **Shia** sects. In Damascus the Sunni Abbasid dynasty took power, the Shi'ites dispersing and seeking refuge to both the east and west.

One of them, arriving in Morocco around 787, was **Moulay Idriss**, an evidently charismatic leader and a direct descendant (greatgrandson, in fact) of the Prophet Muhammad. He seems to have been adopted almost at once by the citizens of Volubilis – then still a vaguely

Romanised city – and by the Aouraba Berber tribe. He was to survive for three more years, before being poisoned by order of the Sunni caliph, but in this time he managed to set up the infrastructure of an essentially Arab court and kingdom – the basis of what was to become the Moroccan nation. Its most important feature, enduring to the present with Hassan II, was his being recognised as *Imam*. To the Moroccans this meant that he was both spiritual and political leader, "Commander of the Faithful" in every aspect of their lives.

Despite the brevity of Moulay Idriss's reign, and his sudden death in 791 or 792, his successors, the **Idrissids**, were to become the first recognisable Moroccan dynasty. Moulay Idriss himself left a son, born posthumously to a Berber woman, and in 807, after a period of an apparently orderly regency, **Moulay Idriss II** was declared sultan and *imam*. He ruled for a little over twenty years – something of a golden age for the emerging Moroccan state, with the extension of a central, Arabised authority throughout the north and even to the oases beyond the Atlas.

Idriss's most important achievement, however, was the establishment (if perhaps not the foundation) of the city of **Fes**. Here, he set up the apparatus of court government, and here he also welcomed large contingents of Shi'ite **refugees**. Most prominent among these were groups from Córdoba and Kairouan, then the two great cities of Western Islam. In incorporating them, Fes (and, by extension, Morocco) became increasingly Arabised, and was suddenly transformed into a major centre in its own right. The **Kairaouine University** was established, becoming one of the three most important in Islam (and far ahead of those in Europe); a strong crafts tradition took root; and Fes became a vital link in the trade between Spain and the East, and between the Maghreb and Africa south of the Sahara.

Fes was to remain the major Moroccan city, and the country's Arab spiritual heart, right up until the present century. The Idrissid state, however, fragmented again into **principalities**, most of which returned to their old isolation, until, at the turn of the tenth century, the context began to change. In al-Andalus – the Muslim territories of Spain – the Western Caliphate collapsed and itself splintered into small rival states. Meanwhile in Tunisia, the well-established Fatimid dynasty moved their capital to Egypt, clashed with their nominated governors, the Zirids, and unleashed on them the hostile nomadic tribe of the Banu Hilal.

It was a move which was to have devastating effects on the Maghreb's entire lifestyle and ecological balance, as the **Hilali** nomads swept westwards, destroying all in their path, bringing to ruin the irrigation systems and devastating the agricultural lands with their goats and other flocks. The medieval Maghrebi historian, Ibn Khaldun, described their progress as being like a swarm of locusts: "the very earth seems to have changed its nature", he wrote, "all the lands that the Arabs have conquered in the last few centuries, civilisation and population have departed from them".

THE ALMORAVIDS (1062–1145)

Morocco was to some extent cushioned from the Hilali, and by the time they reached its southern oases (where they settled), the worst was probably over. But with the shattered social order of the Maghreb, and shifting power struggles in Spain, came an obvious vacuum of power.

It was this which created the opportunity for the two great Berber dynasties of the Middle Ages – the **Almoravids** and the **Almohads**. Both were to emerge from the south, and in each case their motivating force was religious, a purifying zeal to **reform** or destroy the decadent ways which had reached Morocco from the wealthy Andalusian Muslims of Spain. The two dynasties together lasted only a century and a half, but in this period Morocco was preeminent in all of Western Islam, maintaining an empire that at its peak stretched right across the Maghreb to Libya, south to Senegal and Ghana and north into Spain. Subsequent history and achievements never matched up to this imperial dream, though even today its memories are part of the Moroccan concept of nation. "**Greater Morocco**", the nationalist goal of the late 1950s, sketched out areas that took in Mauritania, Algeria, Tunisia and Libya, while even the present war in the Sahara looks back to the reality of the medieval empires.

The **Almoravids**, the first of these dynasties, began as a reforming movement among the Sanhaja Berbers in what is now Mauritania. A nomadic desert tribe – similar to the Touaregs who occupy the area today – they had been converted to Islam in the ninth century, but perhaps only to nominal effect. The founders of the movement, a local sheikh who had returned from the pilgrimage to Mecca and a *fakir* from the Souss plain, found widespread abuse of orthodox practice. In particular, they preached against drinking palm wine, playing licentious music and taking more than four wives. It seemed like a message unlikely to captivate an already ascetic, tent-dwelling people, but it rapidly took hold.

Founding a *ribat* – a kind of warrior monastery similar to the European Templar castles, and from which the movement takes its name – they soon gained a following and considerable military force. In 1054, they set out from the *ribat* to spread the message through a *jihad* (holy war), and within four years they had gained control of Ghana to the south. Turning towards Morocco, they established themselves in Marrakesh by 1062, and, under the leadership of **Youssef bin Tachfine**, went on to extend their rule throughout the north of Morocco and, to the east, as far as Algiers.

At no time before had any one leader exercised such strong control over these territories, uniting the tribes for the first time under a single religious doctrine – a simple, rigorous and puritanical form of Sunni orthodoxy. And so it remained, at least as long as the impetus of *jihad* was sustained. In 1085, Youssef undertook his first, and possibly reluctant, expedition to **Spain**, invited by the Muslim princes of **al-Andalus** after the fall of Toledo to the Christians. He crossed over the straits again in 1090, this time to take control of Spain himself. In this he was successful, and before his death in 1107, he had restored Muslim control to Valencia and other territories lost in the first wave of the Christian Reconquest.

The new Spanish territories had two decisive effects. The first was to reorientate Moroccan culture towards the far more sophisticated and affluent Andalusian civilisation; the second to stretch the Almoravid forces too thin. Both were to contribute to the dynasty's decline. Youssef, disgusted by Andalusian decadence, had ruled largely from **Marrakesh**, leaving his governors in Seville and other cities. After his death, the Andalusians proved disinclined to accept these foreign overlords, while the Moroccans themselves became vulnerable to charges of being corrupt and departing from their puritan ideals.

Youssef's son **Ali** was, in fact, extraordinarily pious, but, unprepared for (and not interested in) ceaseless military activity, he was forced to use Christian mercenaries to maintain control. His reign, and that of the Almoravids, was effectively finished by the early 1140s, as a new movement, the Almohads, seized control of the main Moroccan cities one after another.

THE ALMOHADS (1145–1248)

Ironically, the **Almohads** shared much in common with their predecessors. Again, they were forged from the Berber tribes – this time in the High Atlas – and again, they based their bid for power on an intense puritanism. Their founder **Ibn Toumert,** attacked the Almoravids for allowing their women to ride horses (a tradition in the desert), for wearing extravagant clothes, and for being subject to what may have been Andalusian corruptions – the revived use of music and wine.

He also provoked a **theological crisis**, claiming that the Almoravids did not recognise the essential unitary and unknowable nature of God: the basis of Almohad belief, and the source of their name – the "unitarians". Banished from Marrakesh by Ali, Ibn Toumert set up a *ribat* in the Atlas at **Tin Mal**. Here he waged war on local tribes until they would accept his authority, and eventually revealed himself to them as the Mahdi – "the chosen one" and the final prophet promised in the Koran.

Charismatic and brutal in his methods, Toumert was aided by a shrewd assistant and brilliant military leader, **Abd el Moumen**, who took over the movement after his death and extended the radius of their raids. In 1145, he was strong enough to displace the Almoravids from Fes, and two years later he drove them from their stronghold in Marrakesh. With the two cities subdued, he was now effectively sultan.

Resistance subsided and once again a Moroccan dynasty moved **towards Spain** – this time finally secured by the third Almohad

sultan, **Yacoub el Mansour** (The Victorious), who in 1195 defeated the Christians at Alarcos. El Mansour also pushed the frontiers of the empire east to Tripoli, and for the first time, there was one single rule across the entire Maghreb. With the ensuing wealth and prestige, he launched a new building programme – the first and most ambitious in Moroccan history – which included a new capital in Rabat and the magnificent gateways and minarets of Marrakesh and Seville.

Once more, however, imperial expansion precipitated disintegration. In 1212, Yacoub's successor, **Mohammed en Nasr**, attempted to drive the Spanish Christians as far back as the Pyrenees and met with decisive defeat at the battle of **Las Navas de Tolosa**. The balance was changing, and within four decades, only the Kingdom of Granada remained in Spanish Muslim hands. In the Maghreb, meanwhile, the eastern provinces had declared independence from Almohad rule and Morocco itself was returning to the authority of local tribes. In 1248, one of these, the **Merenids** (or Beni Merin), took the northern capital of Fes and turned towards Marrakesh.

THE MERENIDS AND WATTASIDS (1248–1554)

This last (300-year) period of Berber rule in Morocco is very much a tailpiece to the Almoravid and Almohad empires – marked by increasing domestic **instability** and economic stagnation, and signalling also the beginning of Morocco's **isolation** from both the European and Muslim worlds. The Spanish territories were not regained, and Granada, the last Moorish city, fell to Ferdinand and Isabella in 1492. Portuguese sea power saw to it that foreign seaports were established on the Atlantic and Mediterranean coasts. To the east, the rest of the Maghreb fell under Turkish domination, as part of the Ottoman Empire.

In Morocco itself, the main development was a centralised administrative system – the **Makhzen** – which was maintained without tribal support by standing armies of Arab and Christian mercenaries. It is to this age that the real distinction of *Bled el Makhzen* and *Bled es Siba* belongs – the latter coming to mean everything outside the immediate vicinities of the imperial cities.

THE MERENIDS

Perhaps with this background it is not surprising that few of the twenty-one **Merenid sultans** – or their cousins and successors, the Wattasids – made any great impression. The early sultans were occupied mainly with Spain, at first in trying to regain a foothold on the coast, later with shoring up the Kingdom of Granada. There were minor successes in the fourteenth century under the "Black Sultan", **Abou el Hassan**, who for a time occupied Tunis, but he was to die before being able to launch a planned major invasion of al-Andalus, and his son, **Abou Inan**, himself fell victim to the power struggles within the mercenary army.

The thirteenth and fourteenth centuries, however, did leave a considerable **legacy of building**, perhaps in defiance of the lack of political progress (and certainly a product of the move towards government by forced taxation). In 1279, the garrison town of Fes el Djedid was established, to be followed by a series of brilliantly endowed colleges, or *medersas*, which are among the finest surviving Moorish monuments. Culture, too, saw a final flourishing. The historians Ibn Khaldun and Leo Africanus, and the travelling chronicler Ibn Battuta, all studied in Fes under Merenid patronage.

THE WATTASIDS

The **Wattasids**, who usurped Merenid power in 1465, had ruled in effect for 45 years previously as a line of hereditary viziers. They maintained a semblance of control for a little under a century, though the extent of the *Makhzen* lands was by now minimal.

The Portuguese had annexed and colonised the seaports of Tetouan, Ceuta, Tangier, Asilah, Agadir and Safi, while large tracts of the interior lay in the hands of religious warrior brotherhoods, or *marabouts*, on whose alliances the sultans had increasingly to depend.

THE SAADIANS AND CIVIL WAR (1554–1669)

The rise and fall of the **Saadians** was in some respects an abridged version of all of the dynasties that had come before them. They were the most important of the *marabouts* to emerge in the early years of the sixteenth century, rising to power on the strength of their religious positions (they were *Shereefs* – descendants of the Prophet), climaxing in a single, particularly distinguished reign, and declining amid a chaos of political assassinations, bitter factional strife and, in the end, civil war.

As the first Arab dynasty since the Idrissids, they mark the end (to date) of Moroccan Berber rule, though this was probably less significant at the time than the fact that theirs was a government with no tribal basis. The *Makhzen* had to be even further extended than under the Merenids, and Turkish guards – a new point of intrigue – were added to the imperial armies.

Slower to establish themselves than the preceding dynasties, the Saadians began by setting up a small principality in the **Souss**, where they established their first capital in Taroudannt. Normally, this would have formed a regular part of *Bled el Makhzen*, but the absence of government in the south allowed them to extend their power to **Marrakesh** around 1520, with the Wattasids for a time retaining Fes and ruling the north.

In the following decades the Saadians made breakthroughs along the coast, capturing Agadir in 1540 and driving the Portuguese from Safi and Essaouira. When the Wattasids fell into bankruptcy and invited the Turks into Fes, the Saadians were ready to consolidate their power. This proved harder, and more confusing, than anyone might have expected. **Mohammed esh Sheikh**, the first Saadian sultan to control both the southern and northern kingdoms, was himself soon using Turkish troops, and was, in fact, assassinated by a group of them in 1557. His death unleashed an incredibly convoluted sequence of factional murder and power politics, which was only resolved, somewhat fortuitously, by a battle with the Portuguese twenty years later.

THE BATTLE OF THE THREE KINGS

This event, **The Battle of the Three Kings**, was essentially a Portuguese crusade, led by the youthful King Sebastião on the nominal behalf of a deposed Saadian king against his uncle and rival. At the end of the day, all three were to perish on the battlefield, the Portuguese having suffered a crushing defeat, and a little-known Saadian prince emerged as the sole acknowledged ruler of Morocco.

His name was **Ahmed "el Mansour"** (The Victorious, following this momentous victory), and he was easily the most impressive sultan of the dynasty. Not only did he begin his reign clear of the intrigue and rivalry that had dogged his predecessors, but he was immensely wealthy as well. Portuguese ransoms paid for the remnants of their nobility after the battle had been enormous, causing Portugal to go bankrupt – the country, with its remaining Moroccan enclaves, then passed into the control of Habsburg Spain.

Breaking with tradition, Ahmed himself became actively involved in European politics, generally supporting the Protestant north against the Spanish and encouraging Dutch and British trade. Within Morocco he was able to maintain a reasonable level of order and peace, and diverted criticism of his use of Turkish troops (and his own Turkish-educated ways) by embarking on an **invasion of Timbuktu** and the south. This secured control of the Saharan salt mines and the gold and slave routes from Senegal, each sources of phenomenal wealth, which won him the additional epithet of *El Dhahabi* (The Golden One). It also reduced his need to tax Moroccans, which made him a popular man.

CIVIL WAR

Ahmed's death in 1603 caused abrupt and lasting chaos. He left three sons, none of whom could gain authority, and, split by **civil war**, the country once again broke into a number of principalities. A succession of **Saadian rulers** retained power in the Souss and in Marrakesh (where their tombs remain testimony to the opulence and turbulence of the age); another *marabout* force, the **Djila**, gained control of Fes; while around Salé and Rabat arose the bizarre **Republic of the Bou Regreg**.

The Bou Regreg depended almost entirely on **piracy**, a new development in Morocco, though well established along the Mediterranean coasts of Algeria and Tunisia. Its practitioners were the last Moors to be expelled from Spain – mainly from Granada and Badajoz – and they conducted a looting war against primarily Spanish shipping. For a time they met with astounding success, raiding as far away as the Irish coast, dealing in arms with the British and the French, and even accrediting foreign consuls.

MOULAY ISMAIL & THE EARLY ALAOUITES (1665–1822)

Like the Saadians, the **Alaouites** were *Shereefs*, first establishing themselves as religious leaders – this time in Rissani in the **Tafilalt**. The struggle to establish their power also followed a similar pattern, spreading first to Taza and Fes and finally, under Sultan **Moulay Rashid**, reaching Marrakesh in 1669. Rashid, however, was unable to enjoy the fruits of his labour, since he was assassinated in a particularly bloody palace coup in 1672. It was only with Moulay Ismail, the ablest of his rival sons, that an Alaouite leader gained real control over the country.

MOULAY ISMAIL

The reign of **Moulay Ismail**, perhaps the most notorious in all of Morocco's history, stretched over 55 years (1672–1727) and was to be the country's last stab at imperial glory. In Morocco, where his shrine in Meknes is still a place of pilgrimage, he is remembered as a great and just, if unusually ruthless, ruler; to contemporary Europeans – and in subsequent historical accounts – he is noted more for his extravagant cruelty. His rule certainly was tyrannical, with arbitrary killings and an appalling treatment of his slaves, but perhaps it was not much worse than that of the European nations of the day. The seventeenth century was the age of the witch trials in Protestant Europe, and of the Catholic Inquisition.

Nevertheless, Moulay Ismail stands out among the Alaouites because of the grandness of the scale on which he acted. At **Meknes**, which he made his new imperial capital, he garrisoned a permanent army of some 140,000 black troops, a legendary guard he had built up personally through slaving expeditions in Mauritania and the south, as well as by starting a human breeding programme. The army kept order throughout the kingdom – Morocco is today still littered with their Kasbahs – and were able to raise taxes as required. The Bou Regreg pirates, too (the so-called Sallee Rovers), were brought under the control of the state, along with their increasingly lucrative revenues.

With all this, Ismail was able to build a palace in Meknes that was the rival of its contemporary, Versailles, and he negotiated on equal terms with the **Europeans**. Indeed, it was probably the reputation he established for Morocco that allowed the country to remain free for another century and a half before the European colonial powers began carving it up.

SIDI MOHAMMED AND MOULAY SLIMANE

Like all the great, long-reigning Moroccan sultans, Moulay Ismail left innumerable sons and a terminal dispute for the throne, with the powerful standing army supporting and dropping heirs at will.

Remarkably, a capable ruler did emerge fairly soon – Sultan **Sidi Mohammed** – and for a while it appeared that the Shereefian empire was moving back into the mainstream of European and world events. Mohammed retook El Jadida from the Portuguese, founded the port of Essaouira, traded and conducted treaties with the Europeans, and even recognised the **United States of America** – one of the first rulers to do so.

At his death in 1790, however, the state collapsed into civil war, the two capitals of Fes and Marrakesh in turn promoting claimants to the throne. When this period drew to some kind of a close, with **Moulay Slimane** (1792–1822) asserting his authority in both cities, there was little left to govern. The army had dispersed; the *Bled es Siba* reasserted its old limits; and in Europe, with the ending of the Napoleonic wars, Britain, France, Spain and Germany were all looking to establish themselves in Africa.

Moulay Slimane's rule was increasingly isolated from the new realities outside Morocco. An intensely orthodox Muslim, he concentrated the efforts of government on eliminating the power and influence of the Sufi brotherhoods – a power he underestimated. In 1818 the Berber tribes loyal to the Derakaoui brotherhood rebelled and, temporarily, captured the Sultan. Subsequently, the sultans had no choice but to govern with the co-operation of local sheikhs and brotherhood leaders.

Even more serious, at least in its long-term effects, was Moulay Slimane's attitude towards **Europe**, and in particular to Napoleonic France. Exports were banned; European consuls banished to Tangier; and contacts which might have helped maintain Moroccan independence were lost.

MOULAY HASSAN AND EUROPEAN DOMINATION

Once started, the European domination of Moroccan affairs took an inevitable course – with an outdated, medieval form of government, virtual bankruptcy and armies pressganged from the tribes to secure taxes, there was little that could be done to resist it.

The first pressures came from the **French**, who defeated the Ottomans in 1830 and occupied Algiers. Called to defend his fellow Muslims, Sultan **Abd er Rahman** (1822–59) mustered a force but was severely defeated at Isly. In the following reign of **Mohammed III** (1859–73), **Spanish** aspirations were also realised with the occupation of Tetouan – regained by the Moroccans only after the offer to pay the Spanish massive indemnities and provide them with an Atlantic port (which Spain later claimed in Sidi Ifni).

MOULAY HASSAN

Outright occupation and colonisation were by the end of the nineteenth century proving more difficult to justify, but both the French and the Spanish had learned to use every opportunity to step in and "protect" their own nationals. Complaints by Moulay Hassan, the last precolonial sultan to have any real power, actually led to a debate on this issue at the 1880 **Madrid Conference**, but the effect was only to regularise the practice on a wider scale, beginning with the setting up of an "international administration" in Tangier.

Moulay Hassan could, in other circumstances, have proved an effective and possibly inspired sultan. Acceding to the throne in 1873, he embarked on an ambitious series of modernising **reforms**, including attempts to stabilise the currency by minting the *rial* in Paris, to bring in more rational forms of taxation, and to retrain the army under the instruction of Turkish and Egyptian officers. The times, however, were against him. He found the social and monetary reforms obstructed by foreign merchants and local caids, while the European powers forced him to abandon the plans for other Muslim states' involvement in the army.

He played off the Europeans as best he could, employing a British military chief of staff, Caid MacClean, a French military mission and German arms manufacturers. On the frontiers, he built Kasbahs to strengthen the defences at Tiznit, Saïdia and Selouane. But the government had few modern means of raising money to pay for these developments. Moulay Hassan was thrown back on the traditional means of taxation, the *harka*, setting out across the country to subdue the tribes and to collect tribute. In 1894, returning across the Atlas on just such a campaign, he died.

THE LAST SULTANS

The last years of independence under Moulay Hassan's sons, Moulay Abd el Aziz and Moulay Hafid, were increasingly dominated by Europe.

The reign of **Abd el Aziz** (1894–1907), in particular, signalled an end to the possibilities of a modern, independent state raised by his reforming father. The sultan was just a boy of ten at his accession, but for the first six years of his rule the country was kept in at least a semblance of order by his father's vizier, Bou Ahmed. In 1900, however, Bou Ahmed died, and Abd el Aziz was left to govern alone – surrounded by an assembly of Europeans, preying on the remaining wealth of the court.

The first years of Morocco's twentieth-century history were marked by a return to the old ways. In the Atlas mountains, the tribal chiefs established ever-increasing powers, outside the government domain. In the Rif, a pretender to the throne, **Bou Hamra**, led a five-year revolt, coming close to taking control of Fes and the northern seat of government.

European manipulation during this period was remorselessly cynical. In 1904, the French negotiated agreements on "spheres of influence" with the British (who were to hold Egypt and Cyprus), and with the Italians (who got Tripolitana, or Libya). The following year saw the German Kaiser Wilhelm visiting Tangier and swearing to protect Morocco's integrity, but he was later bought off with the chance to "develop" the Congo. France and Spain, meanwhile, had reached a secret arrangement on how they were going to divide Morocco and were simply waiting for the critical moment.

In 1907, the French moved troops into **Oujda**, on the Algerian border and, after a mob attack on French construction workers, into Casablanca. Abd el Aziz was eventually deposed by his brother, Moulay Hafid (1907–12), in a last attempt to resist the European advance. His reign began with a coalition with the principal Atlas chieftain, Madani el Glaoui, and intentions to take military action against

the French. The new sultan, however, was at first preoccupied with putting down the revolt of Bou Hamra – whom he succeeded in capturing in 1909. By this time the moment for defence against European entrenchment, if indeed it had ever been possible, had passed. Claiming to protect their nationals – this time in the mineral mines of the Rif – the Spanish brought over 90,000 men to garrison their established port in Melilla. Colonial occupation, in effect, had begun.

THE TREATY OF FES

Finally, in 1910, the two strands of Moroccan dissidence and European aggression came together. Moulay Hafid was driven into the hands of the French by the appearance of a new pretender in Meknes – one of a number during that period – and, with Berber tribesmen under the walls of his capital in Fes, was forced to accept their terms.

These were ratified and signed as the **Treaty of Fes** in 1912, and gave the French the right to defend Morocco, represent it abroad and conquer the *Bled es Siba*. A similar document was also signed by the Spanish, who were to take control of a strip of territory along the northern coast, with its capital in Tetouan and another thinner strip of land in the south, running eastwards from Tarfaya. In between, with the exception of a small Spanish enclave in Sidi Ifni, was to be French Morocco. A separate agreement gave Spain colonial rights to the Sahara, stretching south from Tarfaya to the borders of French Mauritania. The arbitrary way in which these boundaries were drawn was to have a profound effect on modern Moroccan history. When Moroccan nationalists laid claim to the Sahara in the 1950s – and to large stretches of Mauritania, Algeria and even Mali – they based their case on the obvious artificiality of colonial divisions.

THE FRENCH AND SPANISH PROTECTORATES (1912–56)

The fates of **Spanish and French Morocco** under colonial rule were to be very different. When **France** signed its Protectorate agreement with the sultan in 1912, its sense of **colonial mission** was running high. The colonial lobby in France argued that the colonies were vital not only as markets for French goods and as symbols of France's greatness, but also because they fulfilled France's *"mission civilis-atrice"* – to bring the benefits of French culture and language to all corners of the globe.

There may have been Spaniards who had similar conceptions of their role in North Africa, but reality was very different. **Spain** showed no interest in developing the Sahara until the 1960s; in the north the Spanish saw themselves more as conquerors than colonists. Its government there, described by one contemporary as a mixture of "battlefield, tavern and brothel", did much to provoke the Rif rebellions of the 1920s.

LYAUTEY AND "PACIFICATION"

France's first resident-general in Morocco was **General Hubert Lyautey**, often held up as the ideal of French colonialism with his stated policy: "Do not offend a single tradition, do not change a single habit." Lyautey recommended respect for the terms of the Protectorate agreement, which placed strict limits on French interference in Moroccan affairs. He recognised the existence of a functioning Moroccan bureaucracy based on the sultan's court with which the French could co-operate – a hierarchy of officials, with diplomatic representation abroad, and with its own social institutions.

But there were other forces at work: French soldiers were busy unifying the country, ending tribal rebellion; in their wake came a system of roads and railways that opened the country to further colonial exploitation. For the first time in Moroccan history, the central government exerted permanent control over the mountain regions. The **"pacification"** of the country brought a flood of French settlers and administrators.

In France these developments were presented as echoing the history of the opening up of the American Wild West. Innumerable articles celebrated "the transformation taking place, the stupendous development of Casablanca port, the birth of new towns, the construction of roads and dams . . . The image of the virgin lands in Morocco is contrasted often with metropolitan France, wrapped up in its history and its routines. . . ".

Naturally, the interests of the natives were submerged in this rapid economic development, and the restrictions of the Protectorate agreement were increasingly ignored.

SPAIN AND THE REVOLT IN THE RIF

The early history of the **Spanish zone** was strikingly different. Before 1920 Spanish influence outside the main cities of Ceuta, Melilla and Tetouan was minimal. When the Spanish tried to extend their control into the Rif mountains of the interior, they ran into the fiercely independent Berber tribes of the region.

Normally, the various tribes remained divided, but faced with the Spanish troops they united under the leadership of **Abd el-Krim**, later to become a hero of the Moroccan nationalists. In the summer of 1921, he inflicted a series of crushing defeats on the Spanish army, culminating in the massacre of at least 13,000 soldiers at Annoual. The scale of the defeat, at the hands of tribal fighters armed only with rifles, outraged the Spanish public and worried the French, who had their own Berber tribes to deal with in the Atlas mountains. As the war began to spread into the French zone, the two colonial powers combined to crush the rebellion. It took a combined force of around 360,000 colonial troops to do so.

It was the last of the great tribal rebellions. Abd el-Krim had fought for an independent **Rifian state**. An educated man, he had seen the potential wealth that could result from exploiting the mineral deposits of the Rif. After the rebellion was crushed, the route to Moroccan independence changed from armed revolt to the evolving middle-class resistance to the colonial rulers.

NATIONALISM AND INDEPENDENCE

The French had hoped that by educating a middle-class elite they would find native allies in the task of binding Morocco permanently to France. It had the opposite effect. The educated classes of Rabat and Fes were the first to demand reforms from the French that would give greater rights to the Moroccans. When the government failed to respond, the demand for reforms escalated into demands for total independence.

Religion also played an important part in the development of a nationalist movement. France's first inkling of the depth of nationalist feeling came in 1930, when the colonial government tried to bring in a **Berber dahir** – a law setting up a separate legal system for the Berber areas. This was an obvious breach of the Protectorate agreement, which prevented the French from changing the Islamic nature of government. Popular agitation forced the French to back down.

It was a classic attempt to "divide and rule", and as the nationalists gained strength, the French resorted more and more to threatening to "unleash" the Berber hill tribes against the Arab city dwellers. They hoped that by spreading Christianity and setting up French schools in Berber areas, the tribes would become more "Europeanised" and, as such, useful allies against the Muslim Arabs.

Before World War II, the nationalists were weak and their demands aimed at reforming the existing system, not independence. After riots in 1937, the government was able to round up the entire executive committee of the small nationalist party. In 1943, the party took the name of **Istiqlal** (Independence); the call for complete separation from France grew more insistent. The loyal performance of Moroccan troops during the war had raised hopes of a fairer treatment for nationalist demands, but France continued to ignore Istiqlal, exiling its leaders and banning its publications. But during the postwar period, it was at last developing into a mass party – growing from 10,000 members in 1947 to 100,000 by 1951.

The developments of the 1950s, culminating in Moroccan independence in 1956, bear a striking resemblance to the events in Algeria and Tunisia. The French first underestimated the strength of these independence movements, then tried to resist them and finally had to concede defeat. In Algeria and Tunisia, the Independence parties gained power and consolidated their positions once the French had left. In Morocco, on the other hand, Istiqlal was never uncontested after 1956 and the party soon began to fragment – becoming by the 1970s a marginal force in politics.

The decline and fall of Istiqlal was due mainly to the astute way in which Sultan (later King) **Mohammed V** associated himself with the independence movement. Despite threats from the French government, Mohammed became more and more outspoken in his support for independence, paralysing government operations by refusing to sign legislation. Serious rioting in 1951 persuaded the French to act: after a period of house arrest, the sultan was sent into exile in 1953.

This only increased his popularity. After a brief attempt to rule in alliance with **Thami el-Glaoui**, the Berber pasha of Marrakesh who saw the sultan's absence as an opportunity to expand his power base in the south, the French capitulated in 1955, allowing the sultan to return.

The government in Paris could see no way out of the spiralling violence of the nationalist guerrillas and the counterviolence of the French settlers. Also, perhaps equally significantly, they could not sustain a simultaneous defence of the three North African colonies – and economic interests dictated that they concentrate on holding Algeria. Finally, in 1956, Morocco was given full **independence** by France and Spain.

On independence, Sultan Mohammed V changed his title to that of king – reflecting a move towards a modern constitutional monarchy.

MOHAMMED V

Unlike his ancestors the sultans, **Mohammed V** had inherited a united country with a well-developed industrial sector, an extensive system of irrigation and a network of roads and railways. But years of French administration had left little legacy of trained Moroccan administrators. Nor was there an obvious party base or bureaucracy for the king to operate within.

In 1956, Istiqlal party members held key posts in the first **government**. The regime instituted a series of reforms across the range of social issues. Schools and universities were created, a level of regional government was introduced and ambitious public works schemes launched. There were moves, also, against European "decadence", with a wholesale clean-up of Tangier, and against the unorthodox religious brotherhoods – both long-time targets of the Istiqlal.

Mohammed V, as leader of the Muslim faith in Morocco and the figurehead of independence, commanded huge support and influence in Morocco as a whole. In government, however, he did not perceive the Istiqlal as natural allies. The king bided his time, building links with the army – with the help of Crown Prince Hassan as commander-in-chief – and with the police.

Mohammed's influence upon the army would prove a decisive factor in the Moroccan state withstanding a series of **rebellions** against its authority. The most serious of these were in the Rif, in 1958–59, but there were challenges, too, in the Middle Atlas and Sahara. The king's standing and the army's efficiency stood the test. Crown Prince Hassan, meanwhile, as the army commander, helped to translate internal pressures into renewed nationalism. The army began a quasi-siege in the south, exerting pressure on the Spanish to give up their claims to the port of Sidi Ifni.

In party politics, Mohammed's principal act was to lend his support to the **Mouvement Populaire** (MP), a moderate party set up to represent the Berbers, and for the king a useful counterweight to Istiqlal. In 1959, the strategy paid its first dividend. Istiqlal was seriously weakened by a split which hived off the more left-wing members into a separate party, the **Union Nationale des Forces Populaires** (UNFP) under Mehdi Ben Barka. There had always been a certain tension within Istiqlal between the moderates and those favouring a more radical policy, in association with the unions.

MODERN MOROCCO: HASSAN II (1961–)

The death of Mohammed V in 1961 led to the accession of **King Hassan II**, the current ruling monarch. Today, some thirty years on, his reign represents perhaps the longest period of stability – albeit with a few uncertain periods – in the country's history.

In many respects the nation's **development since independence** has been remarkable. The French had built an administrative capital in Rabat and a relatively sophisticated infrastructure in Casablanca and other economically useful zones, but most other regions were left without adequate roads, health and education facilities or other trappings of a modernising state. In the kingdom's northern and southern extremities, the Spanish colonial rule left even less on which the new state could base its policy of creating viable development. At independence, there were scarcely any doctors or graduates in the Spanish zones.

Despite the poverty still apparent in so much of the country, it should be remembered that in less than three decades much has been done to bring the whole kingdom into the twentieth century. It is an achievement in the face of a

huge **population explosion** which means there are now more than 25 million Moroccans. They form a predominantly youthful population – 40 percent are aged under 14 – and are clamouring for the sort of jobs and education of which their parents and grandparents were routinely deprived.

VALUES AND TRADITIONAL ROLES

While the quest for modernisation has been one theme running through post-independence Morocco, **traditional values** – as they are perceived by the Palace – are another important factor in understanding the contemporary kingdom.

In many respects Hassan is a very modern monarch, regularly pictured playing golf, horse-riding with Ronald Reagan or meeting fellow heads of state. As a power politician he has few peers. But he is also careful to maintain his status as a traditional ruler – one of the very few left in the Afro-Arab world. When in his flowing robes at a state occasion or religious festival, Hassan is the *Amir al-Muminin* (Commander of the Faithful), Morocco's **religious leader** as well as its temporal ruler.

This role is of great political significance as it adds to Hassan's prestige in the country and gives his monarchy the sort of deep-rooted legitimacy so lacking in other developing countries. Presiding over a complex system of traditional loyalties, ethnic and regional divisions, Hassan has used traditions based in the days of the Sultanate to underpin his modern monarchy – and so far they have served him well.

This is one reason why the Palace remains at the centre of the Moroccan political universe and why one word from the king carries more weight than all the debates in a parliamentary session, the decisions of his most powerful ministers or even international opinion. Hassan himself has stated that it would be an abnegation of his religious role as king if he were not to play a central role in government.

Critics, however, say that for the system to evolve Hassan must genuinely devolve power. Through the promotion of local authorities (*collectivités locales*) and a new stratum of regionally based *associations* a limited form of **devolution** is underway. Hassan has even talked of dividing the country along federal lines, with the German *länder* as a model, though he has not yet acted in this direction.

The continued postponement of general elections in the period 1989–93 was explained in part by the political system's inability to develop a new configuration in which the Throne would remain dominant, but with increased input from a wider **body of opinion**. Those pushing to be heard include a growing younger generation of professionals who feel alienated from the traditional political parties, which are still run by men who emerged during the independence struggle and Hassan's first years as monarch. **Riots in Fes** in December 1990 showed that there was a large urban underclass whose voice must also be heard.

The **rise of radical Islam** across the Arab world, and notably in neighbouring Algeria, has not left Morocco unaffected. However, as the country looked forward to general elections in 1993, King Hassan could feel confident in his unique blend of religious authority – moulded by listening carefully to the mosque as well as more Westernised opinion – and the efficiency of his security forces. The security forces monitor dissident sentiment closely, especially in such Islamist recruiting grounds as local mosques, and have undoubtedly played a part in avoiding the emergence of a mass Islamist movement such as the Algerian *Front Islamique du Salut* (FIS).

Islamist sentiments, though, retain the potential to provoke popular rebellions against established regimes throughout the post-communist Arab world, and other challenges must be faced. The political system will have to evolve to meet the demands of a fast-liberalising economy and an increasingly literate, urbanised population. And Hassan, who turned sixty in 1991, must thus retain all his finely developed political faculties to be sure of handing over a peaceful kingdom to **Crown Prince Sidi Mohammed**, his heir apparent.

CONSTITUTION AND ELECTIONS

Domestic politics since independence have centred on a battle of wills between the dominant political forces in the kingdom: the Palace and its allies; a legalised opposition which has at times succumbed to the temptation to enter government; and underground movements such as the Marxist-Leninist Ilal Amam and, more recently, groups of Islamist radicals.

Even before independence, in a 1955 speech, Mohammed V had promised to set up "democratic institutions resulting from the holding of free elections". The country's first **constitution** was not ready until after his death, however. It was only in 1962, under Hassan II, that it was put to, and approved by, a popular referendum.

The constitution was drafted in such a way as to favour the pro-monarchy parties of the centre. In the **1963 elections** that followed, a coalition of loyalist parties, the *Front pour la Défense des Institutions Constitutionelles* (FDIC), won a majority of seats, though with a strong showing still by the Istiqlal, whose powerbase was in Fes and the agricultural belt of the north, and by the UNFP, who held much support in the Souss and in Casablanca.

In the political struggles which followed, an increasingly radicalised UNFP, inspired by Algerian President Ahmed Ben Bella's socialist experiment, and by Nasserism in Egypt, criticised not just the government (which was possible) but also the king (which was not). It was no great surprise when in 1963 the authorities "discovered" a plot against Hassan's life in which UNFP leaders were implicated. There followed the **Ben Barka affair**, one of the most notorious episodes in modern Moroccan (and French) history. Ben Barka, the UNFP leader, seeking exile in France, was assassinated there – an incident whose political ramifications have endured into the 1990s.

The UNFP subsequently split, with the largest element going on to form the *Union Socialiste des Forces Populaires* (USFP), led by Abderrahim Bouabid until his death in 1992. Party politics were not allowed to develop as the opposition would have liked, however. After student riots in Casablanca in 1965, Hassan declared a **state of emergency** and took over the government directly.

The relative ease with which Hassan was able to rule without democratic institutions underlined the weakness of the parties. The Istiqlal was never able to recover from the 1959 split, and as an opposition party its power dwindled even further. The UNFP and the unions were weakened by the arrests of their leaders and by internal divisions over policy. Despite the increasingly strident attacks on what it called a "feudal" and "paternalistic" regime, the UNFP never managed to develop a coherent platform from which it could oppose the king and build real popular support.

The weakness of the parties was further revealed in 1970, when Hassan announced a **new constitution**, to bring an end to emergency rule. Its terms gave the king greater control over parliament than in 1962.

The events of 1971–72, however, were to show the real nature of the threat to the monarchy. In July 1971, a group of soldiers led by an army general broke into the royal palace in Skhirat in an attempt to stage a **coup**; more than 100 people were killed, but in the confusion Hassan escaped. The following year another attempt was launched, as the king's private jet was attacked by fighters of the Moroccan Air Force. Again, he had a very narrow escape – his pilot was able to convince the attacking aircraft by radio that the king had already died. The former interior minister, General Oufkir, seems to have been behind the 1972 coup attempt and it was followed by a major shake-up in the armed forces. Oufkir died soon after; his family remain imprisoned and incommunicado until 1991.

THE GREEN MARCH AND SAHARAN WAR

The king's real problem was to give a sense of destiny to the country, especially to the increasingly disillusioned Moroccan youth, for whom employment opportunities had conspicuously failed to appear. The game of the political parties had proved sterile. What Hassan needed was a cause similar to the struggle for independence that had brought such prestige to his father.

That cause was provided in 1975, when the Spanish finally decided to pull out of their colony in the **Western Sahara**. In the 1950s Istiqlal had laid claim to the Sahara, as well as parts of Mauritania, Algeria and Mali, as part of its quest for a "greater Morocco". By 1975, Hassan had patched up the border dispute with Algeria and recognised the independent government in Mauritania; it turned out this was only a prelude to a more realistic design – Moroccan control of the Western Sahara.

The discovery of **phosphate reserves** in the Sahara during the 1960s brought about Spain's first real attempt to develop its Saharan colony. Before then it had been content merely to garrison the small coastal forts in Dakhla (then known as Villa Cisneros) and La Guera, with occasional forays into the interior to pacify the tribes. With increased investment in the region during the 1960s, the nomads began to settle in the newly created towns along the coast, particularly the new capital in Laayoune. As education became more widespread, the Spanish were confronted with the same problem the French had faced in Morocco thirty years earlier – the **rise of nationalism**.

Pressure began to mount on General Franco's government to decolonise one of the last colonies in Africa. In 1966, he promised the UN that Spain would hold a referendum "as soon as the country was ready for it". Economic interests kept Spain from fulfilling its promise, and in 1969 work began on opening the phosphate mines in Boukra. Meanwhile, the Saharans began to press the case for independence themselves. In 1973, they formed the *Frente Popular para la Liberación de Saguia el-Hamra y Río de Oro*, or **Polisario**, which began guerrilla operations against the Spanish. Polisario gained in strength as Spain began to signal it would pull out of the Sahara and as the threat to Saharan independence from Morocco and Mauritania grew more obvious.

Spanish withdrawal in 1975 coincided with General Franco's final illness. King Hassan timed his move perfectly, sending some 350,000 Moroccan civilians southward on *Al Massira* – the "Green March" or *La Marche Verte* – to the Sahara. Spain could either go to war with Morocco by attacking the advancing Moroccans or take the easy way out and withdraw without holding the promised referendum. Hassan's bluff worked and in November 1975 a secret agreement was reached in Madrid to divide the Spanish Sahara between Morocco and Mauritania as soon as Spanish troops withdrew.

The popular unrest of the 1960s and the coup attempts of 1971–72 were forgotten under a wave of patriotism. Without shedding any blood, Morocco had "recaptured" part of its former empire. But the king had underestimated the native Sahrawis' determination to fight for an independent Sahara, their Saharan Arab Democratic Republic (SADR). Nearly 40,000 of them fled the Moroccan advance, taking refuge in Mauritania and Algeria.

In an unprecedented move, Algeria ceded an area of its territory in the desolate *Hamada* region southeast of **Tindouf** to Polisario. Sahrawi refugees – along with a number of

Moroccan-born dissidents – settled in camps run by Polisario. According to the best estimates there were about 165,000 people living in five tented and increasingly unhygiénic camps by 1989. Polisario, however, had managed to set up schools and hospitals in these most unpromising circumstances – winning many friends abroad in the process, much to Morocco's displeasure.

The camps also formed a base for the movement's government-in-exile, the SADR, and a launch pad a for a classic guerrilla campaign against Morocco and Mauritania, until Sahrawi pressure proved too much for Nouakchott and it withdrew from its alliance with Morocco in 1979. By the early 1980s Polisario had succeeded in closing the territory's mines and had pinned the Moroccan *Forces Armées Royales* (FAR) into an area round the capital, Laayoune, and Dakhla in the south.

The early success of Polisario's campaign said much for the Sahrawi's prowess as desert guerrilla fighters – a fact Morocco's FAR battle-hardened officers now willingly concede, even if the intensely nationalist local press does not. It was equally due to the high level of military support offered by Algeria, which used Polisario as a stick with which to beat Morocco, its perceived rival for regional dominance.

ECONOMIC AND SOCIAL PROBLEMS

At home, the attention and budget demanded by the Saharan war compounded the problems of the economy. By 1981, an estimated 60 percent of the population were living below the poverty level, unemployment ran at approximately 20 percent (40 percent among the young) and perhaps 20 percent of the urban population lived in shantytowns, or *bidonvilles*.

Official figures for **unemployment** and even gross domestic product (GDP) are often very approximate. The young "student" operating as a guide in Fes or Marrakesh may well not appear in national employment figures. The shopkeeper he leads you to could also be in the informal economy, outside the tax net and compass of official data. And despite sometimes strenuous efforts to modernise and rationalise economic behaviour in the 1970s and 1980s, the "**informal sector**" remains enormous – perhaps equal in size to GDP.

Informal economic activity and the family network (for many still the only effective system of social services they know) disguise the real socio-economic position, which bears little relation to the official figures. They have also acted as a safety-valve for an increasingly hard-pressed population. The informal economy also finances some of Morocco's richest citizens, whose huge wealth – reflected in the opulent villas, discreetly hidden in the most upmarket quarters of major cities – may also not appear in official data.

Throughout much of the 1980s, the government, preoccupied by the war, seemed to neglect these pressing **social problems**; indeed, an austerity campaign to please its international creditors, including a wage freeze and a cut in subsidies for basic foodstuffs, appeared to increase the problems even more for the poor. In June 1981 a one-day **protest strike** in Casablanca led to a running battle and at least 100 deaths. Demonstrators were brought to trial and given stiff sentences, as were the UNSP leader Bouabid and fourteen socialist members of parliament.

Local **elections** were held in June 1983, and appeared to be a resounding royalist victory, providing the government with a mandate to continue with its austerity measures. But the opposition parties, including Istiqlal, complained of electoral fraud, and the failure to proceed with parliamentary elections in October showed that all was not well. Using Article 19 of the constitution, Hassan assumed all executive and legislative power, **governing by decree** in the absence of an elected government. It was a brave move on his part. The government was facing bankruptcy and if the IMF was to reschedule Morocco's massive debts, the **austerity campaign** would have to become even harsher. Hassan announced a 12.5 percent cut in government expenditure and massive cuts in subsidies, and then stood alone to face the backlash.

Demonstrations against the cuts began in Marrakesh in early January 1984, and within a week had spread north to Nador and Al Hoceima. Later, **"bread riots"** broke out in Oudja and Tetouan. Clashes with the authorities were inevitable, and by the end of the month between 100 and 600 people had died. Hassan announced on television that further cuts in subsidies would be postponed, but at the same time he condemned extremists on the left and right as being the instigators of the riots and promised the restoration of order. A massive campaign of arrests followed. Over 700 rioters were arrested and sentenced to long prison terms.

THE IMF AND EC

Despite the pessimistic assessments of many analysts, the 1984 bread riots were not repeated later in the decade and the 1980s will be remembered as a period of relative social peace, economic hard times and consolidations in the Western Sahara after several years of setbacks. In September 1984 Hassan went to the polls once more and was rewarded with the re-election of a centrist-royalist coalition. After six months of suspension, **democratic government** had been restored.

Following the mid-1980s economic crisis – which was compounded by a build-up of international debt, contracted in the over-optimistic mood of the previous decade when Morocco hoped that rising phosphate prices (which then did not hold) would do for it what rising oil prices did for the OPEC states – relations with the **IMF** and the World Bank have been a constant factor in Moroccan life. The struggle to mobilise sufficient funds to finance essential imports and schemes in priority sectors like agriculture, power and water is ever present. Without international support, achieving sustainable economic growth would have proved impossible – although Moroccans also place much store in their native entrepreneurial talents. In sectors ranging from vehicle assembly to marketing, Morocco has developed domestic industries to a relatively high level.

Substantial international support remains essential, however, and has forced Morocco to depart from its nineteenth-century image as "the China of the West" and seek closer ties with a wide range of countries. Relations with the IMF, World Bank and bilateral supporters have prompted moves towards liberalising the economy in the period since Morocco's first rescheduling in 1984. In 1989 Hassan called for all non-strategic public companies and holdings to be privatised. A **privatisation** minister was appointed, but like many other policies, privatisation has taken longer to put into effect than its supporters had hoped – and is unlikely to have radical consequences for several years.

Meanwhile, with the king firmly nailing his colours to the mast of economic liberalisation, new efforts were made to encourage foreign investment, in technologically advanced manufacturing industries as well as **textiles** and, an increasingly important earner, **tourism**.

In 1992–93, clear signs emerged that Morocco had overcome its rescheduling problems of the 1980s and was more committed to **economic modernisation** than at any time since the 1960s. This would require a substantial inflow of foreign investment – crucially providing modern management skills, knowhow, technology transfer and access to international markets, as well as capital – and the emergence of a new managerial class independent of the old social loyalties. By 1992, over a thousand foreign companies were operating in the kingdom, with an increasing number targeting their production on exports into the European Community (EC).

Morocco's controversial application to join the **European Community**, made in the 1980s, was rejected. But, given Morocco's economic and strategic potential, Brussels has pushed sometimes unwilling European governments to develop closer relations with the kingdom. In 1992–93 negotiations began between the EC Commission and Rabat to establish the first of a new generation of **free trade agreements** between the Community and southern Mediterranean states.

Greater access to European markets and closer ties with the EC back Morocco's claims to be an ideal base for investment by multinationals and smaller companies on the flank of the Mediterranean – a region now promoting itself as a manufacturing and services centre for Europe's **southern sunbelt**, the projected focus for EC growth over the next few decades. If this strategy succeeds, Morocco hopes to achieve the high levels of economic growth enjoyed by the "new dragons" of the Pacific Rim. At a more sobering level, this is essential if it is to meet the demands of its fast-growing, youthful and increasingly well-educated population.

CALLS FOR CHANGE IN THE 1990s

The opposition, which had been quiet through much of the 1980s, started to reassert itself in the new decade. In May 1990, the **Chamber of Representatives** (parliament) debated the first ever motion of censure against a Moroccan government. The motion, criticising the government's economic management, failed, but it pointed nevertheless to changing attitudes. Traditional opposition parties showed revived enthusiasm for challenging the government – though not the king – with the knowledge that if their opposition fails, younger Moroccans may be tempted to follow Islamist and other illegal political trends. Hassan, for his part, also seems aware of the need for change as the so-called "Saharan consensus", the mood of national unity engendered by the assertion of Moroccan sovereignty over the Western Sahara, threatens to run out of steam.

How far things have changed will be judged when **parliamentary elections** are held. These were constantly delayed from late-1989, when Hassan called a referendum to postpone elections for two years, so as to allow a peace settlement in Western Sahara to be achieved. A massive majority supported him in this, but the conflict with Polisario was not settled, and continues in 1993, despite the arrival of a UN force, MINURSO. At time of writing (summer 1993), elections are on the horizon once more, using revised electoral lists and other polling techniques which might ensure more fairness than in the past.

As the Saharan conflict, too, appears to draw to a close, it is ever clearer that economic and social issues – and demands – will become more pressing on the king's agenda. If the opposition is to exploit this, it must appeal to the majority of younger Moroccans, who have little time for the established parties and trade unions, with their old generation of leaders and network of loyalties. The disappointing performance of Morocco's parliamentarians poses major questions over the future of the existing system.

As the experience of the 1984 rioters – many of whom are still in prison – shows, those who oppose from outside the existing channels can expect severe problems. In some respects Morocco is in advance of changes in other developing countries, with the development of a sometimes critical press and a system which has allowed many former political opponents and prisoners to be reintegrated into daily life and hold responsible jobs. Former student radicals, who may have been impris-

oned and even tortured, now hold positions of responsibility in the local press, universities and even government departments.

However, for those who remain outside the system, life is extremely difficult. Criticism of the kingdom's **human rights** record is widespread and has led to direct conflict with organisations like Amnesty International. Human rights remain a highly sensitive issue, despite some advances. Groups like Amnesty have either chosen to target Morocco for campaigns intended to undermine the state – according to Hassan's most vocal supporters – or provide essential support for oppressed opponents, depending on which side of a very polarised debate one takes.

Despite his officials' tendency to dismiss the reports of human rights groups as troublemaking and foreign interference, Hassan has not been impervious to such criticism. A bad press abroad has the potential to damage international relations, as was the case during the 1990s, when relations with a key ally, France, were hurt by the publication of a highly critical study of Hassan, Gilles Perrault's *Notre Ami le Roi*. In 1992, the kingdom's leading dissident, Abraham Serfaty, was one of many well-known figures in a **release of political prisoners** that included many soldiers held since the 1972 failed coup in a dungeon prison at Tazmamart in the High Atlas.

While leftists made the running in the first three decades of independence, **radical Islam** poses the greatest threat in the 1990s – especially given Hassan's status as *Al Amir al Muminin* (Commander of the Faithful). The largest Islamist group, *Al Adl Wal Ihsan* (Justice and Benevolence), is led by Abdessalam Yassine, who would now be considered a moderate by Middle East standards. Yassine and his followers have often been imprisoned, usually on charges of belonging to an illegal organisation. There have also been incidents involving smaller and violent groups, notably Abdelkarim Mottei's Islamic Youth Society, though their influence should not be overstated, although unprecedented demonstrations against the Gulf War in 1991 saw several thousand Islamists take to the streets. Thus far, however, the threat (Hassan called it a "plague" in a recent interview with the Western media) has been contained, as the authorities have worked hard to restrict any

Islamic movement from developing beyond a series of local, fragmented groups. Apparently, the Islamists can count on little support in the universities and especially the countryside. Thus, although radical Islam could pose a threat to the system, it is unlikely to take the form of events in Algeria or elsewhere. At least for now, the monarchy seems secure – albeit in a fast-changing political environment

NORTH AFRICAN UNITY MOVES

In August 1984 King Hassan made the surprise announcement of a **"Treaty of Union" with Libya**. To the outside world, it seemed a bizarre act for Morocco to associate itself with Colonel Gaddafi, the arch enemy of the United States – which had for a decade been providing aid and military assistance to Morocco.

But Hassan had correctly judged the mood of his people and, in a referendum, the treaty was endorsed almost unanimously. Moroccans were more than happy to show their appreciation for a leading role in moves towards **Maghreb unity**.

The Libyan union reflected an idea deeply rooted in Maghreb history, which gained considerable ground in the late 1980s as North African governments looked for new ways of developing their economies and, above all, new evidence to persuade their youthful populations that development was still achievable in a rapidly changing world. Some kind of **economic co-operation and unity in North Africa** also became a vital concept, as Spain and Portugal entered the European Community, and the traditional North African economic ties – with France long the major trading partner – came under threat.

In June 1988, a **Maghreb Summit** was held in Algiers. Hassan attended with a Moroccan delegation – his first visit to Algeria for two decades – and there was an immediate result in the resumption of full diplomatic ties between Morocco and Algeria, and the opening of the Oujda–Maghnia border to all traffic.

A SAHARAN SETTLEMENT?

The summit, and resumption of relations, have also promoted hopes for a negotiated **settlement to the dispute in the Sahara**. With riots of their own at home in October 1988, which included an attack on Polisario's office in

Algiers, the Algerian government has shown signs of wanting to pull out from the conflict. In any case, over the decade, Morocco had gradually been winning the war. Beginning in 1981, the FAR have built a series of heavily defended **desert walls** that exclude the Polisario from successively larger areas of the desert; by 1985, the phosphate mines were back in use and by 1987, the sixth wall had effectively blocked off Polisario from Mauritania and left only 15 percent of the land area outside Moroccan control. Meanwhile the government was making concerted attempts to win the approval of the Saharan residents, injecting vast sums into creating a model city and capital in **Laayoune**.

Under United Nations auspices, a **ceasefire** was agreed in the spring of 1989. Although it has been somewhat sporadically observed, there has subsequently been no major military conflict. And, under UN auspices, protracted negotiations have continued for a **referendum** to be held among the Sahrawis to determine their future state. In the early stages of negotiation, King Hassan met with a Polisario deputation in Marrakesh, and promised that if the Sahrawis vote for independence, Morocco will be the first nation to open an embassy in Laayoune. Such talk reflected a new confidence in the situation, and a conviction, seemingly shared among all parties, that the conflict has burned itself out.

Nevertheless, four years after the UN announced its ceasefire, the path to a referendum remains blocked, with a 1992 date for the referendum frustrated by quarrels over the voting list, Morocco having enabled thousands of said-to-be-Saharan immigrants to return to the Western Saharan cities. Hassan has also perhaps decided that there is nothing to be gained for Morocco in holding a referendum, at least in the immediate present, and has indicated that he would prefer, first, for international opinion to recognise that the Western Sahara is a part of Morocco. In this assertion, he was given a considerable boost in 1992 by the defection of the Polisario foreign minister, Ibrahim Hakim, who declared that "the vast majority of Western Saharans see their future within the framework of a united and unified Morocco". More ominously, for Polisario hopes, he quoted Algeria's defence minister as saying "You should stop dreaming about a state in the

Sahara, because the establishment of such a state is not in Algeria's interest and is against its wishes". The old backer seemed finally to have turned.

At the time of writing, the UN has once again imposed a deadline – the end of 1993 – for an independent referendum to take place. Crucially, the vote allows them to press ahead with a referendum, even without agreement from Morocco or Polisario, on terms negotiated by former UN Secretary General Javier Perez de Cuellar, and which favour Morocco.

UMA

Wider rapprochement in the Maghreb culminated, in February 1989, at a meeting of the Algerian, Libyan, Mauritanian, Moroccan and Tunisian leaders in Marrakesh to form the long-awaited regional grouping, the **Arab Maghreb Union** – known by its evocative acronym **UMA**, from the French *Union de Maghreb Arabe* – but sounding like the Arabic word *'umma*, or community.

One of the main consequences of the UMA's formation has been an **opening of borders**, to the benefit of travellers, but especially for the millions of North Africans who now go either to shop for scarce goods in neighbouring countries (stimulating the black market throughout the region) or to visit family and friends. Colonisation and the drawing of boundaries divided many thousands of families; rather like the situation in postwar Europe, Maghrebis have often had to struggle to be reunited with their families. If the UMA does nothing else it will have brought North Africans together.

The UMA has raised high hopes – many of which have yet to be achieved. But by bringing countries together and providing forums to discuss economic, political and social co-operation it has radically improved the often troubled relations between North African states. After the Saharan war is finally over, the government will have to offer the population higher living standards and greater opportunities than during the past decade when the Saharan consensus meant a large part of the population making sacrifices for the national good. At least the budgetary strains imposed by the Saharan campaign will be eased, pumping more resources into areas where they are needed. But much will depend on how the Saharan issue is resolved as to the direction Morocco takes in the next decade. And as many young Moroccans will say, much remains to be done to make life a little easier than it is at present.

CHRONOLOGY

10,000–5000 BC	**Capsian** and **Mouillian Man** spread across the Maghreb Neolithic cultures	**Rock carvings** in Oukaïmeden, Foum el Hassan and other less accessible sites
1100 BC	**Phoenician** settlements	Bronze Age. First trading port in **Lixus** (near Larache)
500 BC	**Carthaginians** take over Phoenician settlements and greatly expand them	Remains in Lixus, and in Rabat Archaeological Museum
146 BC	Fall of Carthage at end of the Third Punic War; Roman influence spreads into **Berber kingdoms** of Mauritania-Numidia	Bust of Juba II (Rabat)
27 BC	Direct **Roman** rule under Emperor Caligula	**Volubilis** developed as provincial capital; other minor sites at Lixus and Tangier Mosaics in Tetouan and Rabat museums
253 AD	Roman legions withdrawn	
429	**Vandals** pass through	
535	**Byzantines** occupy Ceuta	

ISLAM

622	Muhammad and followers move from Mecca to Medina and start spread of Islam	
ca. 705	**Moussa Ibn Nasr** establishes Arab rule in north and pre-Sahara, and in 711 leads Berber invasion of Spain	

IDRISSID DYNASTY (788–923)

788	**Moulay Idriss** establishes first Moroccan Arab dynasty	Founding of Moulay Idriss and Fes
807	Moulay Idriss II (807–836)	**Fes** developed with Kairouan and Andalusian refugee quarters, and establishment of Kairaouine Mosque
10th–11th c.	Hilali tribes wreak havoc on Maghrebi infrastructure	

ALMORAVID DYNASTY (1062–1145)

1062	**Youssef bin Tachfine** establishes capital in Marrakesh; first great Berber dynasty	**Koubba** in Marrakesh is only surviving monument, except for walls and possibly a minaret in Tit (near El Jadida)
1090	Almoravid invasion of **Spain**	

ALMOHAD DYNASTY (1147–1248)

1120s	**Ibn Toumert** sets up a *ribat* in Tin Mal in the High Atlas	Ruined mosque of Tin Mal
1145–1147	**Abd el Moumen** takes first Fes and then Marrakesh	Extensive building of walls, gates and **minarets**, including the Koutoubia in Marrakesh
1195	**Yacoub el Mansour** (1184–99) extends rule to Spain, and east to Tripoli	New capital begun in **Rabat**: Hassan Tower, Oudaia Gate
1212	Defeat in Spain at Las Navas de Tolosa	

MERENID DYNASTY (1248–1465)

Abou Youssef Yacoub (1258–86) establishes effective power
Abou el Hassan (1331–51) and **Abou Inan** (1351–58), two of the most successful Merenids, extend rule briefly to Tunis

Portuguese begin attacks on Moroccan coast, taking Ceuta and later other cities

Zaouia and mausoleum in **Chellah** (Rabat); new city (El Djedid) built in **Fes**
Medersas in Fes (Bou Inania, Attarin, etc), Meknes and Salé

Portuguese cistern in El Jadida; walls and remains in Azzemour, Asilah and Safi

WATTASID DYNASTY (1465–1554)

Wattasids – Merenid viziers – usurp power
Fall of **Granada**, last Muslim kingdom in Spain; Jewish and Muslim refugees settle in Morocco over next 100 years or so
Marabouts establish *zaouias*, controlling parts of the country

Chaouen built and **Tetouan** founded again by refugees

SAADIAN DYNASTY (1554–1669)

Mohammed esh Sheikh (d. 1557) founds dynasty in Marrakesh

Battle of Three Kings leads to accession of **Ahmed el Mansour** (1578–1603), who goes on to conquer Timbuktu and the gold and slave routes to the south

Pirate **Republic of Bou Regreg** set up by Andalusian refugees

Saadian Tombs and Ben Youssef *medersa* (Marrakesh); pavilion extensions to Kairaouine Mosque (Fes)
El Badi palace (Marrakesh)

Rabat Medina

ALAOUITE DYNASTY (1669–)

Moulay Ismail imposes the Alaouite dynasty on Morocco

Sidi Mohammed (1757–90)

Moulay Suleiman (1792–1822)

Treaty of Fes brings into being French and Spanish **"Protectorates" (1912–56)**

Riffian revolt under Abd el Krim

T'Hami el Glaoui becomes Pasha of Marrakesh and rules south for French

Nationalist **Istiqlal** party formed in Fes

Independence

Accession of **Hassan II**

Green March into Western Sahara

North African unity moves

New imperial capital in **Meknes** (Ismail's mausoleum, etc); **Kasbahs** and **forts** built; **palaces** in Tangier and Rabat
Ismail and his successors rebuild **grand mosques**, etc, especially in **Marrakesh**, where many later Alaouites make their capital – many of the city's **pavilions** and **gardens** date from the early eighteenth century
Final burst of **palace** building – El Badi (Marrakesh), Palais Jamai (Fes)

European **Villes Nouvelles** built outside the Moroccan Medinas; **"Mauresque"** architecture developed for administrative buildings (best in Casa, Rabat, Tetouan and Sidi Ifni)

Glaoui palaces in Telouet and Marrakesh; **Kasbah** fortresses throughout the south

New royal **palaces** in all major cities – most recently and spectacularly in Agadir

Hassan II Mosque in Casablanca

ISLAM IN MOROCCO

It's difficult to get any grasp of Morocco, and even more so of Moroccan history, without first knowing something of Islam. What follows is a very basic background: some theory, some history and an idea of Morocco's place in the modern Islamic world. For more depth on each of these subjects, see the book listings in the section that follows.

BEGINNINGS: PRACTICE AND BELIEF

Islam was a new religion born of the wreckage of the Greco-Roman world around the south of the Mediterranean. Its founder, a merchant named **Muhammad*** from the wealthy city of Mecca (now in Saudi Arabia), was chosen as God's Prophet: in about 609 AD, he began to receive divine messages which he transcribed directly into the **Koran** (*Qu'ran*), Islam's Bible. This was the same God worshipped by Jews and Christians – Jesus is one of the minor prophets in Islam – but Muslims claim He had been misunderstood by both earlier religions.

The distinctive feature of this new faith was directness – a reaction to the increasing complexity of established religions and an obvious attraction. In Islam there is no intermediary between man and God in the form of an institutionalised priesthood or complicated liturgy; and worship, in the form of prayer, is a direct and personal communication with God. Believers face five essential requirements, the so-called **"Pillars of faith"**: prayer five times daily (*salat*); the pilgrimage (*hadj*) to Mecca; the Ramadan fast (*sanm*); almsgiving (*zakat*); and, most fundamental of all, the acceptance that "There is no God but God and Muhammad is His Prophet" (*shahada*).

---

*"Muhammad" is the standard spelling today of the Prophet's name – and a more accurate transcription from the Arabic. In Morocco there is some cause for confusion in that the name of the former king, *Mohammed* V, is still spelled that way on maps and street signs and in most Western histories.

THE PILLARS OF FAITH

The Pillars of Faith are still central to Muslim life, articulating and informing daily existence. Ritual **prayers** are the most visible. Bearing in mind that the Islamic day begins at sunset, the five daily times are sunset, after dark, dawn, noon and afternoon. Prayers can be performed anywhere, but preferably in a mosque, or in Arabic, a *djemaa*. In the past, and even today in some places, a *muezzin* would climb his minaret each time and summon the faithful.

Nowadays, the call is likely to be less frequent, and prerecorded; even so, this most distinctive of Islamic sounds has a beauty all its own, especially when neighbouring *muezzins* are audible simultaneously. Their message is simplicity itself: "God is most great (*Allah Akhbar*). I testify that there is no God but Allah. I testify that Muhammad is His Prophet. Come to prayer, come to security. God is great." Another phrase is added in the morning: "Prayer is better than sleep".

Prayers are preceded by ritual washing and are recited with the feet bare. Facing Mecca (the direction indicated in a mosque by the *mihrab*), the worshipper recites the Fatina, the first chapter of the Koran: "Praise be to God, Lord of the worlds, the Compassionate, the Merciful, King of the Day of Judgement. Thee do we worship and Thine aid do we seek. Guide us on the straight path, the path of those on whom Thou hast bestowed Thy Grace, not the path of those who incur Thine anger nor of those who go astray." The same words are then repeated twice in the prostrate position, with some interjections of *Allah Akhbar*. It is a highly ritualised procedure, the prostrate position symbolic of the worshipper's role as servant (Islam literally means "obedience"), and the sight of thousands of people going through the same motions simultaneously in a mosque is a powerful one. On Islam's holy day, Friday, all believers are expected to attend prayers in their local grand mosque. Here the whole community comes together in worship led by an *imam*, who may also deliver the *khutba*, or sermon.

Ramadan is the name of the ninth month in the lunar Islamic calendar, the month in which the Koran was revealed to Muhammad. For the whole of the month, believers must obey a rigorous fast (the custom was originally modelled on Jewish and Christian practice), forsaking all forms of consumption between sunrise and sundown; this includes food, drink, cigarettes and any form of sexual contact. Only a few categories of people are exempted: travellers, children, pregnant women and warriors engaged in a *jihad*, or holy war. Given the climates in which many Muslims live, the fast is a formidable undertaking, but in practice it becomes a time of intense celebration.

The pilgrimage, or **hadj**, to Mecca is an annual event, with millions flocking to Muhammad's birthplace from all over the world. Here they go through several days of rituals, the central one being a sevenfold circumambulation of the Kaba, before kissing a black stone set in its wall. Islam requires that all believers go on a *hadj* as often as is practically possible, but for the poor it may well be a once-in-a-lifetime occasion, and is sometimes replaced by a series of visits to lesser, local shrines – in Morocco, for instance, to Fes and Moulay Idriss.

Based on these central articles, the new Islamic faith proved to be inspirational. Muhammad's own Arab nation was soon converted, and the Arabs then proceeded to carry their religion far and wide in an extraordinarily rapid territorial expansion. Many peoples of the Middle East and North Africa, who for centuries had only grudgingly accepted Roman paganism or Christianity, embraced Islam almost immediately.

DEVELOPMENT IN MOROCCO

Islam made a particularly spectacular arrival in Morocco. **Oqba Ibn Nafi**, the crusading general who had already expelled the Byzantines from Tunisia, marked his subjugation of the far west by riding fully armed into the waves of the Atlantic. "O God," he is said to have exclaimed, "I call you to witness that there is no ford here. If there was, I would cross it".

This compulsory appreciation of Morocco's remoteness was prophetic in a way, because over the succeeding centuries Moroccan Islam was to acquire and retain a highly distinctive character. Where mainstream Islamic history is concerned, its development has been relatively straightforward – it was virtually untouched, for instance, by the Sunni–Shia conflict that

split the Muslim world – but the country's unusual geographical and social circumstances have conspired to tip the balance away from official orthodoxy.

Orthodoxy, by its very nature, has to be an urban-based tradition. Learned men – lawyers, Koranic scholars and others – could only congregate in the cities where, gathered together and known collectively as the *ulema*, they regulated the faith. In Islam, this included both law and education. Teaching was at first based entirely in the mosques; later, it was conducted through a system of colleges, or *medersas*, in which students would live while studying at the often adjoining mosque. In most parts of the Islamic world, this very learned and sophisticated urban hierarchy was dominant. But Morocco also developed a powerful tradition of **popular religion**, first manifested in the eighth-century Kharijite rebellion – which effectively divided the country into separate Berber kingdoms – and endures to this day in the mountains and countryside.

MARABOUTS

There are three main strands of this popular religion, all of them deriving from the worship of saints. Everywhere in Morocco, as well as elsewhere in North Africa, the countryside is dotted with small domed **marabouts**: the tombs of holy men, which became centres of worship and pilgrimage. This elevation of individuals goes against strict Islamic teaching, but probably derives from the Berbers' pre-Islamic tendency to focus worship round individual holy men. At its simplest, local level, these saint cults attracted the loyalty of the Moroccan villages and the more remote regions.

More prosperous cults would also endow educational institutions attached to the *marabout*, known as *zaouias*, which provided an alternative to the official education given in urban *medersas*. These inevitably posed a threat to the authority of the urban hierarchy, and as rural cults extended their influence, some became so popular that they endowed their saints with genealogies traced back to the Prophet. The title accorded to these men and their descendents was *shereef*, and many grew into strong political forces. The classic example in Morocco is the tomb of Moulay Idriss, in the eighth century just a local *marabout*, but eventually, as the base of the Idrissid clan, a centre of enormous influence that reached far beyond its rural origins.

Loyalty to a particular family – religiously sanctified, but essentially political – was at the centre of the shereefian movements. In the third strand of popular devotion, the focus was more narrowly religious. Again, the origins lay in small, localised cults of individuals, but these were individuals worshipped for their magical and mystical powers. Taken up and developed by subsequent followers, their rituals became the focal point of **brotherhoods** of initiates.

THE AISSAOUA

Perhaps the most famous Moroccan brotherhood is that of Sidi Mohammed Bin Aissa. Born in Souss in the fifteenth century, he travelled in northern Morocco before settling down as a teacher in Meknes and founding a *zaouia*. His powers of mystical healing became famous there, and he provoked enough official suspicion to be exiled briefly to the desert – where he again revealed his exceptional powers by proving himself immune to scorpions, snakes, live flames and other hostile manifestations. His followers tried to achieve the same state of grace. Six hundred were said to have attained perfection – and during the saint's lifetime, *zaouias* devoted to his teachings were founded in Figuig and elsewhere in the Maghreb.

Bound by its practice of a common source of ritual, the Aissaoua brotherhood made itself notorious with displays of eating scorpions, walking on hot coals and other ecstatic practices designed to bring union with God. It was perhaps the most flamboyant of these brotherhoods, but most at any rate used some kind of dancing or music, and indeed continued to do so well into this century. The more extreme and fanatical of these rites are now outlawed, though the attainment of trance is still an important part of the *moussems*, or festivals, of the various confraternities.

TOWARD CRISIS

With all its different forms, Islam permeated every aspect of the country's pre-twentieth-century life. Unlike Christianity, at least Protestant Christianity, which to some extent has accepted the separation of church and state, Islam sees no such distinction. **Civil law** was provided by the *sharia*, the religious law contained in the Koran, and **intellectual life** by the *msids* (Koranic primary schools where the 6200 verses were learned by heart) and by the great medieval mosque universities, of which the Kairaouine in Fes (together with the Zitoura in Tunis and the Al Azhar in Cairo) was the most important in the Arab world.

The religious basis of Arab study and intellectual life did not prevent its scholars and scientists from producing work that was hundreds of years ahead of contemporary "Dark Age" Europe. The remains of a monumental water clock in Fes and the work of the historian Ibn Khaldun, are just two Moroccan examples. Arab work in developing and transmitting Greco-Roman culture was also vital to the whole development of the European Renaissance. By this time, however, the Islamic world – and isolated Morocco in particular – was beginning to move away from the West. The Crusades had been one enduring influence promoting division. Another was the Islamic authorities themselves, increasingly suspicious (like the Western church) of any challenge and actively discouraging of innovation. At first it did not matter in political terms that Islamic culture became static. But by the end of the eighteenth century, Europe was ready to take advantage. Napoleon's expedition to Egypt in 1798 marked the beginning of a century in which virtually every Islamic country came under the control of a **European power**.

Islam cannot, of course, be held solely responsible for the Muslim world's material decline. But because it influences every part of its believers' lives, and because East–West rivalry had always been viewed in primarily religious terms, the nineteenth and twentieth centuries saw something of a **crisis in religious confidence**. Why had Islam's former power now passed to infidel foreigners?

REACTIONS

Reactions and answers veered between two extremes. There were those who felt that Islam should try to incorporate some of the West's materialism; on the other side, there were movements holding that Islam should turn its back on the West, purify itself of all corrupt additions and thus rediscover its former power. While they were colonies of European powers, however, Muslim nations had little chance of putting any such ideas into effective practice. These could only emerge in the form of co-operation with, or rebellion against, the ruling power. But the postwar era of **decolonisation**, and the simultaneous acquisition through oil of relative economic independence, brought the Islamic world suddenly face to face with the question of its own spiritual identity. How should it deal with Western values and influence, now that it could afford – both politically and economically – almost total rejection? A return to the totality of Islam – **fundamentalism** – is a conscious choice of one consistent spiritual identity, one that is deeply embedded in the consciousness of a culture already unusually aware of tradition. It is also a rejection of the West and its colonial and exploitative values. Traditional Islam, at least in some interpretations, offers a positivist brand of freedom that is clearly opposed to the negative freedoms of Western materialism. The most vehement Islamic fundamentalists are not passive reactionaries dwelling in the past, but young radicals – often students – eager to assert their new-found independence. Islam has in a sense become the "anti-imperialist" religion – think, for example, of the Black Muslim movement in America – and there is frequent confusion and even conflict between secular, left-wing ideals and more purely religious ones.

MODERN MOROCCO

There are two basic reasons why only a few Islamic countries have embraced a rigidly traditional or fundamentalist stance. The first is an ethical one: however undesirable Western materialism may appear, the rejection of all Western values involves rejecting also what the West sees as the "benefits" of development. Perhaps it is begging the question in strictly Islamic terms to say that the emancipation of women, for example, is a "benefit". But the leaders of many countries feel that such steps are both desirable and reconcilable with a more liberal brand of Islam, which will retain its place in the national identity. The other

argument against militant Islam is a more pragmatic, economic one. Morocco is only one of many countries which would suffer severe economic hardship if they cut themselves off from the West: they have to tread a narrow line that allows them to maintain good relations both with the West and with the Islamic world.

ISLAM AND THE STATE

In Morocco today, Islam is the official state religion, and King Hassan's secular status is interwoven with his role as "Commander of the Faithful". Internationally, too, he plays a leading role. Meetings of the Islamic Conference Organisation are frequently held in Morocco and, in one of the most unlikely exchanges, students from Tashkent in the USSR have come to study at Fes University. For all these indications of Islamic solidarity, though, **state policy** remains distinctly moderate – sometimes in the face of extremist pressure.

RURAL RELIGION

Not surprisingly, all of this has had more effect on urban than on rural life – a difference accentuated by the gap between them that has always existed in Morocco. Polarisation in religious attitudes is far greater in the **cities**, where there is inevitably tension between those for and against secularisation. Islamic fundamentalism offers a convenient scapegoat to many Western-orientated governments in the Muslim world, but if its actual strength is sometimes open to doubt, its existence is probably not.

Away from the cities, religious attitudes have changed less over the past two generations. Religious brotherhoods such as the Aissaoua have declined since the beginning of the century, when they were still very powerful, and the influence of mystics generally has fallen. As the official histories put it, popular credulity in Morocco provided an ideal setting for charlatans as well as saviours, and much of this has now passed. All the same, the rhythms of **rural life** still revolve around local *marabouts*, and the annual *moussems*, or festivals-cum-pilgrimages, are still vital and impressive displays.

WILDLIFE

Few countries in the Mediterranean region can match the variety and quality of the wildlife habitats to be found in Morocco. Whether you are an expert botanist, a dedicated birdwatcher or simply a visitor with an interest in a totally different environment, the wildlife experience of your travels should be extremely rewarding.

HABITATS

There are three main **vegetation zones** which can be distinguished as you travel through the country.

● The most northerly and westerly zone – the **Mediterranean** and **northern Atlantic coastal strips** – is typical of the European Med region, encompassing semi-arid pastoral lands of olive groves and cultivated fields.

● Further inland lie the barren **Rif mountains** (the home of *kif* or marijuana plants) and the more fertile **Middle Atlas range**, where the montane flora is dominated by cedar forest which, despite its reduction in more recent times, provides a unique mosaic of forest and grassland. The **High Atlas**, beyond, is more arid but has its own montane flora.

● Finally, there is the most southerly zone of the desert fringe or **Sahel**, a harsh environment characterised by pebbly *hammada*, tussock grass, the occasional acacia tree and a number of sand dunes, or *ergs*.

These zones provide a wide variety of **habitat types**, from coastal cliffs, sand dunes and estuarine marshlands to subalpine forests and grasslands, to the semi-arid and true desert areas of the South. The **climate** is similarly diverse, being warm and humid along the coastal zones, relatively cooler at altitude within the Atlas ranges and distinctly hotter and drier south of the High Atlas, where midday temperatures will often climb higher than 40°C during the summer months. Not surprisingly, the plant and animal life in Morocco is accordingly parochial, species distributions being closely related to the habitat and climate types to which they are specifically adapted.

Many of these habitats are currently under threat from land reclamation, tourist development and the inevitable process of **desertification**, and the resulting habitat loss is endangering the existence of several of the more sensitive species of plants and animals to be found in Morocco. Human persecution of wildlife, however, is limited, as the tribes are largely disarmed and hunting is more the preserve of French tourists.

On the positive side, the *International Committee for Bird Preservation* (I.C.B.P.) and the *Eaux de Forêt* of the Moroccan Agriculture Ministry have been involved in the designation of protected status to several **wetland sites** along the Atlantic coast; at Merdja Zerga and Lac de Sidi Bourhaba, education centres have been set up with resident wardens and interpretive materials. The government has also done some good work on the problems of erosion and desertification and has implemented extensive and impressive schemes of **afforestation and reclamation**.

BIRDS

In addition to a unique range of **resident bird species**, distributed throughout the country on the basis of vegetation and climatic zonation, the periods of late March/April and September/October provide the additional sight of vast **bird migrations**.

Large numbers of birds which have overwintered south of the Sahara migrate northwards in the spring to breed in Europe, completing their return passage through

Morocco in the autumn. Similarly, some of the more familiar northern European species choose Morocco for their overwintering grounds to avoid the harshness of our winter clime. These movements can form a dramatic spectacle in the skies, dense flocks of birds moving in procession through bottleneck areas such as Tangier and Ceuta where sea crossings are at their shortest.

RESIDENT SPECIES

The **resident species** can be subdivided on the basis of their preferred habitat type:

● **Coastal/marine species**. These include the familiar moorhen and less familiar **crested coot**, an incongruous bird which, when breeding, resembles its northern European relation but with an additional pair of bright red knobs on either side of its white facial shield. Other species include the diminutive **little ringed plover** and **rock dove**.

● **South of the High Atlas**. Among these are some of the true desert specialities, such as the **sandgrouse** (spotted, crowned, pin-tailed and black-bellied varieties), **stone curlew**, **cream-coloured courser** and **Houbara bustard** – the latter standing over two feet in height. Other well-represented groups include **wheatears** (4 varieties), **larks** (7 varieties) and **finches**, **buntings**, **warblers**, **corvids** (crow family), **jays**, **magpies**, **choughs** and **ravens**, **tits** (primarily blue, great and coal) and **owls** (barn, eagle, tawny and little). Although many of these species can be found in northern Europe, subtle variations in colour and pattern can be misleading and a closer look is often worthwhile.

Raptors (birds of prey) provide a mouthwatering roll call of resident species, including **red-** and **black-shouldered kite**, **long-legged buzzard**, **Bonelli's**, **golden and tawny eagles**, **Barbary**, **lanner and peregrine falcons** and more familiar **kestrel**.

MIGRANT SPECIES

Migrant species can be subdivided into three categories: summer visitors, winter visitors and passage migrants.

● **Summer visitors**. The number of species visiting Morocco during the summer months may be low but includes some particularly interesting varieties. Among the **marine/**

coastal types are the **manx shearwater**, **Eleonora's falcon** and **bald ibis** – in one of its few remaining breeding colonies in the world.

The **mountain species** include the small **Egyptian vulture** and several of the **hirundines** (swallows and martins) and their close relatives, the **swifts**, such as **little swift**, **red-rumped swallow** and the more familiar **house martin**.

A particularly colourful addition at this time of year in the **Sahel regions** is the **blue-cheeked bee-eater**, a vibrant blend of red, yellow, blue and green, unmistakeable if seen close up.

● **Winter visitors.** The list of winter visitors is more extensive but composed primarily of the marine or coastal/estuarine varieties. The most common of the truly marine (*pelagic*) flocks include **cory's shearwater**, **storm petrel**, **gannet**, **razorbill** and **puffin**. These are often found congregated on the sea surface, along with any combination of **skuas** (great, arctic and pomarine varieties), **terns** (predominantly sandwich) and **gulls** (including black-headed, Mediterranean, little, herring and the rarer Audouin's) flying overhead.

A variety of coastal/estuarine species also arrive during this period, forming large mixed flocks of **grebes** (great-crested, little and black-necked), **avocet**, **cattle egret**, **spoonbill**, **greater flamingo**, and wildfowl such as **shelduck**, **wigeon**, **teal**, **pintail**, **shoveler**, **tufted duck**, **pochard** and **coot**.

Migrant **birds of prey** during the winter months include the **common buzzard** (actually a rarity in Morocco), **dashing merlin** and both **marsh** and **hen harriers**.

● **Passage migrants**. There are many birds which simply pass through Morocco en route to other areas, and are thus known as passage migrants. Well-represented groups include **petrels** (5 varieties) and **terns** (6 varieties) along coastal areas, and **herons** (4 varieties), **bitterns**, **cranes**, **white and black stork** and **crake** (spotted, little, Baillon's and corncrake) in the marshland/estuarine habitats.

Further inland, flocks of multicoloured **roller**, **bee-eater** and **hoopoe** mix with various **larks**, **wagtails** and **warblers** (13 varieties), forming large "windfall" flocks when climatic conditions worsen abruptly. Individual species of note include the aptly named black-winged stilt, an elegant black and white wader, with long, vibrant red legs, often found among the disused saltpans; and the nocturnal nightjars (both common and red-necked), which are most easily seen by the reflection of their eyes in the headlamps of passing cars.

Birds of prey can also form dense passage flocks, often mixed and including large numbers of black kite, short-toed eagle and honey buzzard. Over open water spaces, the majestic osprey may be seen demonstrating its mastery of the art of fishing.

● "Vagrant" species. Finally, Morocco has its share of occasional or "vagrant" species, so classified on the unusual or rare nature of their appearances. These include such exotic varieties as glossy ibis, pale-chanting goshawk, arabian bustard and lappet-faced vulture. Inevitably, they provide few, if any, opportunities for viewing.

FLORA

In the light of its climatic harshness and unreliable rains, the flora of Morocco is remarkably diverse. Plant species have adapted strategies to cope with the Moroccan climate, becoming either specifically adapted to one particular part of the environment (a habitat type), or evolving multiple structural and/or biochemical means of surviving the more demanding seasons. Others have adopted the proverbial "ostrich" philosophy of burying their heads (or rather their seeds in this case) in the sand and waiting for climatic conditions to become favourable – often an extremely patient process!

The type of flowers that you see will obviously depend entirely on where and when you decide to visit. Some parts of the country have very short flowering seasons because of high temperatures or lack of available water, but generally the best times of year for flowering plants are either just before or just after the main temperature extremes of the North African summer.

The best time to visit is spring (late March to mid-May), when most flowers are in bloom. Typical spring flowers include purple barbary nut iris, deep blue germander and the aromatic claret thyme, all of which frequent the slopes of the Atlas ranges. Among the woodland flora at this time of year are the red pheasant's eye, pink virburnum, violet calamint and purple campanula, which form a resplendent carpet beneath the cedar forests. By late spring, huge tracts of the High Atlas slopes are aglow with the golden hues of broom and secluded among the lowland cereal crops, splashes of magenta reveal the presence of wild gladioli.

By midsummer the climate is at its most extreme and the main concern of plants is to avoid desiccation in the hot, arid conditions. Two areas of exception to these conditions are the Atlantic coastal zones, where sea mists produce a slightly more humid environment, and the upper reaches of the Atlas ranges which remain cool and moist at altitude throughout the year. Spring comes later in these loftier places and one can find many of the more familiar garden rock plants, such as the saxifrages and anemones in flower well into late July and August.

Once the hottest part of the summer is past (September onwards), then a second, autumn bloom begins with later varieties such as cyclamens and autumn crocus.

HABITAT VARIETIES

The range of plants you are likely to encounter is similarly influenced by specific habitats:

● Seashores. These include a variety of sand-tolerant species, with their adaptations for coping with water-loss, such as sea holly and sea stocks. The dune areas contrast starkly with the Salicornia-dominated salt marshes – monotonous landscapes broken only by the occasional dead tamarisk tree.

● Arable land. Often dominated by cereal crops – particularly in the more humid Atlantic and Mediterranean coastal belts – or olive and eucalyptus groves, which extend over large areas. The general lack of use of herbicides allows the co-existence of many "wild flowers", especially in the fallow hay meadows which are ablaze with the colours of wild poppy, ox-eye daisy, muscali (borage) and various yellow composites.

● Lowland hills. These form a fascinating mosaic of dense, shrubby species, known as *maquis*, lower-lying, more grazed areas, known as *garrigue*, and more open areas with abundant aromatic herbs and shrubs.

Maquis vegetation is dominated by **cistaceae** (rockroses) and **euphorbiae**, such as **argan**. The lower-lying *garrigue* is more typically composed of aromatic herbs such as **rosemary**, **thyme** and **golden milfoil**. Among these shrubs, within the more open areas, you may find an abundance of other species such as **anemones**, **grape hyacinths** and **orchids**.

The orchids are particularly outstanding, including several of the *Ophrys* group, which use the strategy of insect imitation to entice pollinators and as such have an intricate arrangement of flowers.

● **Mountain slopes**. Flowering later in the year, the slopes of the **Atlas ranges** are dominated by the blue-mauve **pitch trefoil** and golden drifts of **broom**. As you travel south through the Middle Atlas, the verdant **ash**, **oak**, **atlantic cedar** and **juniper forest** dominates the landscape. Watered by the depressions that sweep across from the Atlantic, these slopes form a luxurious spectacle, ablaze with colour in spring.

Among the glades beneath the **giant cedars** of the Middle Atlas, a unique flora may be found, dominated by the vibrant **pink paeony**. Other plants which form this spectacular carpet include **geranium**, **anchusa**, **pink verburnum**, **saffron mulleins**, **mauve cupidanes**, **violet calamint**, **purple campanula**, the diminutive **scarlet dianthus** and a wealth of **golden composites** and **orchids**.

Further south, the **Toubkal National Park** boasts its own varieties and spring bloom; the thyme and thorny caper are interspersed with the blue-mauve **pit trefoil**, **pink convulvulus**, the silver-blue and pinks of everlasting flowers of **cupidane** and **phagnalon** and golden spreads of **broom**. At the highest altitudes, the limestone Atlas slopes form a bleak environment, either covered by winter snows or scorched by the summer sun. However, some species are capable of surviving even under these conditions, the most conspicuous of these being the widespread purple tussocks of the **hedgehog broom**.

● **Steppeland**. South of the Atlas, temperatures rise sharply and the effect on flora is dramatic; the extensive cedar forests and their multicoloured carpets are replaced by sparse grass plains where the horizon is broken only by the occasional stunted **holm oak**, **juniper**

or **acacia**. Commonly known as wattle trees, the acacia were introduced into North Africa from Australia and their large yellow flowers add a welcome splash of colour to this barren landscape. One of the few crop plants grown in this area is the **date palm**, which is particularly resistant to drought. The steppeland is characterised by the presence of **esparto grass**, which exudes toxins to prevent the growth of competing species. These halfa grass plains are only broken by the flowering of **broom** in May. Within rocky outcrops, this spring bloom can become a mini-explosion of colour, blending the hues of **cistus** and **chrysanthemum** with the pink of **rockrose**, yellow of **milfoil** and mauve of **rosemary**.

● **Desert fringe (*hammada*)**. Even the desert areas provide short-lived blooms of colour during the infrequent spring showers; dwarf varieties such as pink **asphodels**, yellow **daisies** and mauve **statice** thrive briefly while conditions are favourable. Under the flat stones of the hammada, colonies of lichens and microscopic algae eke out an existance; their shade tolerance and ability to obtain sufficient water from the occasional condensation which takes place under these stones allows them to survive in this harshest of environs. No matter how inhospitable the environment or extreme the climate appear, somewhere, and somehow, there are plants surviving – if you take time to look for them.

AMPHIBIANS

There are very few remaining amphibians in Morocco – relics of a bygone, more fertile era, now restricted to scarce watery havens. They are more apparent by sound than sight, forming a resonant chorus during the night and early morning. One of the more common varieties is the **green frog**, typically immersed up to its eyes in water, releasing the odd giveaway croak. Another widespread individual, most abundant in the regions round Marrakesh, is the **western marsh frog**.

The toads are represented by the **Berber toad**, another nocturnal baritone, and the **Mauritanian toad** whose large size and characteristic yellow and brown-spotted colouration make it quite unmistakeable.

Some Moroccan amphibians are capable of survival at surprisingly **high altitudes**. The painted frog is a common participant in the chorus that emanates from the *oueds* (river-beds) of the High Atlas, while the wide-ranging whistle of the North African race of the **green toad**, famed for its ability to change its colour with the surrounding environment, can be heard at altitudes in excess of 2000m.

REPTILES

Reptiles are far more widespread in their distribution than their amphibious cousins. Their range extends from the Mediterranean coastal strip – where the few remaining **tortoises** (sadly depleted through "craft items" sold to the tourist trade) are to be seen – to the *hammada* itself.

The forested slopes of the Middle Atlas are frequented by the **blue and green-eyed lizard** and the **chameleon**; the former uses its size and agility to capture its prey, whereas the latter relies on the more subtle strategy of colour co-ordination, stealth and a quicksilver tongue.

Several species have adapted to the specific environment of the stony **walls** that form the towns and villages. The **Spanish wall lizard** is a common basker on domestic walls, as is the **Moorish gecko**.

Further south, the drier, scrub-covered slopes form an ideal habitat for two of Morocco's largest **snakes**. The **horseshoe snake** (which can exceed 2m in length) and **Montpelier snake** hunt by day, feeding on birds and rats. Also found in this harsh environment are the **Atlas agama** and **fringe-toed lizard**.

Finally, there are the **desert "specialists"**, such as the **Algerian sand lizard** and **Berber skink**. The skinks make a fascinating spectacle; commonly known as "sand fish", they inhabit the *ergs* and appear to "swim" through the sand, where their yellow-brown coloration provides the perfect camouflage. Of numerous species of lizard that live in the hammada, the more obvious include the many colours and varieties of the **spiny-tailed lizard** (*dhub* in Arabic), an omnivore feeding on a mixed diet of insects, fruit and young shoots. The one really poisonous species is the **horned viper**, only half a metre in length, which spends the days buried just below the surface of the sand and feeds by night on jerboas and lizards.

MAMMALS

Larger animal life in Morocco is dominated by the extensive nomadic herds of goats, sheep and camel which use the most inaccessible and barren patches of wilderness as seasonal grazing areas.

One of the most impressive of the wild mammals, however, is the **Barbary ape** – in fact not a true ape but a Macaque monkey. These frequent the cedar forests south of Azrou in the Middle Atlas and can be seen on the ground foraging for food in the glades. Other inhabitants of the cedar forest include **wild boar** and **red fox**.

A speciality of the Oued Souss, outside Agadir, is the **common otter**; this is now a rare species in Morocco and can only be seen with considerable patience and some fortune.

The majority of the smaller mammals in Morocco live south of the Atlas ranges in the hammada, where the ever-present problem of water conservation plays a major role in the life-style of its inhabitants. Larger herbivores include the **Edmi gazelle** and the smaller, and rarer, **Addax antelope,** which graze the thorn bushes and dried grasses to obtain their moisture.

Many of the desert varieties reduce the problems of body temperature regulation by adopting a nocturnal lifestyle. Typical exponents of this strategy are the **desert hedgehog** and numerous small rodents such as the **jerboa**. A common predator of the jerboa is the **fennec** (desert fox), whose characteristic large ears are used for both directional hearing (invaluable as a nocturnal hunter) and heat radiation to aid body cooling.

An oddity, found in the Djebel Toubkal area of the High Atlas, is the African **elephant shrew** – a fascinating creature, like a little mouse, with an elephantine trunk.

INSECTS

Insect life is widespread throughout Morocco, its variety of form occupying unique, overlapping roles.

BUTTERFLIES

Most colourful are the butterflies, of which over a hundred species have been recorded, predominantly in the Middle and High Atlas ranges. The most obvious, which can be seen from April onwards, are generally the largest and most colourful, such as the brilliant sulphur **Cleopatra**, **large tortoiseshell** and **cardinal**. Located on the grassy slopes within the ranges are less conspicuous varieties: the **hermit**, **Spanish marbled white**, **fritillaries**, **graylings**, **hairstreaks** and **blues** – such as the small **larquin's** and **false baton**.

Later in the year, from about June onwards, the glades and woodland edges of the Middle Atlas cedar forests provide the perfect habitat for **dark green fritillaries**, while in the higher flowery fields, at altitudes of up to 2000m, **knapweed fritillaries**, **large grizzled** and **Barbary skippers** abound. Particularly attractive is the **Amanda's blue**, found at altitudes in excess of 600m through till midsummer if nectar remains available.

On the rocky slopes of Toubkal National Park, south of Marrakesh, the **Morrocan copper butterfly** may be seen flitting through the thyme. In the higher Atlas gorges (1700m or more), the **desert orange tip** is more prevalent, being found on its larval food plant, the thorny caper. The Atlas also sees one of the world's most extraordinary butterfly migrations, when waves of painted ladies and Bath whites pass through, having crossed the Sahara from West Africa, en route across the Bay of Biscay to the west of England.

OTHER INSECTS

Other common groups include **grasshoppers**, **crickets** and **locusts**. In the High Atlas, **praying mantis** may be seen, such as **eremiaphila**, whose brown coloration provides excellent camouflage.

Beetles are another common group, though they tend to avoid the heat of the day, remaining in their burrows and emerging at night to feed. The **darkling beetles** are particularly abundant and voracious scavengers.

Finally there are **arachnids**, of which there are three major groups in Morocco – scorpions, spiders and camel spiders. **Scorpions** are nocturnal, hiding under suitable covered depressions during the day such as rocks and boulders (or rucksacks and shoes!). Some of the six or so species which may be found in Morocco are poisonous but most are harmless and unlikely to sting unless provoked. The **camel spiders** (or wind-scorpions) are unique. They lack a poisonous tail but possess huge

jaws with which they catch their main source of prey, scorpions.

Spiders are rare in Morocco, only being found in large numbers within the Atlas ranges. Here, it is possible to see several small species of **tarantula** (not the hairy South American variety!) and the white **orb-web spider** *Argiope lobata*, whose coloration acts as a disruptive pattern against pale backgrounds.

A CHECKLIST OF THE MAIN SITES

Features on key Moroccan wildlife, and especially bird, habitats are to be found throughout the guide; the main entries are boxed. They include:

● **NADOR/KARIET ARKMANE/RAS-EL-MA** Salt marshes and coastal sand dunes, good for waders and gulls. ➡ p.134

● **OUED MOULOUYA**. Lagoons and sand spits, with outstanding birds.➡ p.134

● **DJEBEL TAZZEKA NATIONAL PARK** Where the Rif merges with the Middle Atlas: slopes covered in cork oak and woodland; **butterflies** from late May/early June, and **birds** such as the hoopoe. ➡ p.127

● **MERDJA ZERGA** Large wetland area guarantees good **bird** numbers at all times of year, especially **gulls and terns** (including the **Caspian tern**). ➡ p.91

● **LAC DE SIDI BOURHABA** Freshwater lake, with outstanding **birds of prey**. ➡ p.236

● **OUALIDIA** Mix of ragged, rocky coast, sands, lagoon, marshes and salt pans. Good for small waders. ➡ p.284

● **ESSAOUIRA** Coastal dunes, river and offshore islands attract **waders** and **egrets**; also **Eleanora's falcon** between May and October. ➡ p.296

● **AGADIR/OUED SOUSS** Riverbank attracts waders and wildfowl, migrant warblers and Barbary partridge. ➡ p.434

● **OUED MASSA** Important inland lagoon and reserve that is perhaps the country's number one bird habitat. ➡ p.443

● **FES**. Evening roost of egret and alpine swift; **white stork** on rooftop nests of walls. ➡ p.204

● **MARRAKESH: JARDIN MARJORELLE**. Lush garden with turtle doves, house buntingsand common bulbuls. ➡ p.331

● **CEDAR FORESTS SOUTH OF AZROU**
Species include green-eyed lizard and chameleon; **butterflies** from April onwards; **Barbary apes**. Moroccan woodpecker and **booted eagle**. ➡ p.218

● **AGUELMAME AZIGZA** Middle Atlas inland lake and forest: hawfinch, diving duck and marbled teal in autumn/winter. ➡ p.218

● **DAYET AAOUA** Another Middle Atlas lake: flocks of grebes, **crested coot**, grey heron and cattle egret; migrant birds of prey include **red kite**. ➡ p.214

● **DJEBEL TOUBKAL NATIONAL PARK** High Atlas mountains: sights include Moorish gecko, rare butterflies; Moussier's redstart and crimson-winged finch, both unique to North African mountains; hooped-petticoat daffodils, *romulea* and various other bulbs in spring. ➡ p.342

● **TODRA GORGE** Marsh frog and green toad; ground squirrel; common bulbul, black wheatear, blue rock thrush and rock dove. **Bonelli's eagles** nest in the gorge. ➡ p.402

● **BOULMALNE: DESERT HAMMADA** Atlas agama and fringe-toed lizard; specialist bird species such as cream-coloured courser, red-rumped wheatear and thick-billed lark. **Houbara bustard**. ➡ p.395

● **MERZOUGA** Sandy (or "true") desert: all-too-brief **spring bloom** of pink asphodels and mauve statice; Algerian sand lizard and Berber skink; birds include fulvous babbler, blue-cheeked bee-eater, the rare desert sparrow and even Arabian bustard. ➡ p.418

FIELD GUIDES

There is little written specifically about Moroccan wildlife, but some field guides to Mediterranean Europe extend coverage to North Africa, and most are in any case reasonably practicable for the area.

● **General field guides**
Pete Raine *Rough Guide to Mediterranean Wildlife* (Penguin, UK). Includes a detailed chapter on Morocco, plus very readable rundowns on the species.

● **Birds**
P and F Bergier *A Birdwatcher's Guide to Morocco* (Prion Press, UK). An excellent practical guidebook which includes site-maps and species lists.

Heinzel, Fitter and Parslow *The Birds of Britain and Europe with North Africa and the Middle East* (Collins, UK/Stephen Green Press, US).

● **Flowers**
Oleg Polunin and Anthony Huxley *Flowers of the Mediterranean* (Oxford UP, UK/US).

● **Butterflies**
Lionel Higgins and Norman Riley *A Field Guide to the Butterflies of Britain and Europe* (Collins, UK/Stephen Green Press, US).

● **Mammals**
Theodor Haltenorth and Helmut Diller *A Field Guide to the Mammals of Africa* (Collins, UK/ Stephen Green Press, US).

MUSIC

Wherever you go in Morocco you are likely to hear music. It is the basic expression of the country's folk culture – indeed to many of the illiterate countrypeople it is the sole expression – and in its traditions it covers the whole history of the country. There are long and ancient pieces designed for participation by the entire communities of Berber villages; songs and instrumental music brought by the Arabs from the east and Andalusian Spain; and in more recent times, the struggle for independence, too, found celebration in song.

Although the most common musical phenomenon that you will hear is the *muezzin* calling the faithful to prayer, amplified from minarets, most Moroccan music is performed for the sake of entertainment rather than religion. At every weekly *souk*, or market, you will find a band playing in a patch of shade, or a stall blasting out cassettes they have on sale. In the evenings many cafés feature musicians, particularly during the long nights of Ramadan. Television also plays its part, with two weekly programmes devoted to music, and the radio stations, too, broadcast a variety of sounds.

BERBER MUSIC

Berber music is quite distinct from Arab-influenced forms in its rhythms, tunings and sounds. It is an extremely ancient tradition, probably long predating even the arrival of Arabs in Morocco, and has been passed on orally from generation to generation. There are three main categories: village music, ritual music and the music of professional musicians.

Village music is always essentially a collective performance. Men and women of the entire village will assemble on festive occasions to dance and sing together. The best-known dances are the **ahouach**, in the western High Atlas, and the **ahidus**, performed by Chleuh Berbers in the eastern High Atlas. In each, drums (*bendirs*) and flutes are the only instruments used. The dance begins with a chanted prayer, to which the dancers respond in chorus, the men and women gathered in a large ring in the open air, round the musicians. The *ahouach* is normally performed at night in the patio of the Kasbah; the dance is so complicated that the musicians meet to prepare for it in a group called a *laamt* set up specially for the purpose. In the *bumzdi*, a variation on the *ahouach*, one or more soloists perform a series of poetic improvisations.

Ritual music is rarely absent from any rites connected with the agricultural calendar – such as *moussems* (see *Basics*) – or major events in the life of individuals, such as marriage. It may also be called upon to help deal with *djinn*, or evil spirits, or to encourage rainfall. Flutes and drums are usually the sole instruments, along with much rhythmic hand-clapping, although a community may have engaged professional musicians for certain events.

The **professional musicans**, or **imdyazn**, of the Atlas mountains are itinerant, travelling during the summer, usually in groups of four. The leader of the group is called the *amydaz* or poet. He presents his poems, which are usually improvised and give news of national or world affairs, in the village square. The poet may be accompanied by one or two members of the group on drums and *rabab*, a single-string fiddle, and by a fourth player, known as the *bou oughanim*. This latter is the reed player, throwing out melodies on a double clarinet, and also acts as the group's clown. *Imdyazn* are found in many weekly *souks* in the Atlas.

Chleuh professional musicians are known as **rwais**. A *rwai* worthy of the name will not only know all the music for any particular celebration, but also have its own repetoire of songs – again commenting on current events – and be able to improvise. A *rwai* is made up of a single-stringed *rabab*, one or two *lotars* and sometimes a *naquous*. Once the *lotar* has been tuned to the *rabab*, a piece begins with an improvisation on the *rabab* before the main tune, and quickens in pace as it builds towards an abrupt end. One of the most famous *rwai* performers is **Lhaj Aomar Ouahrouch**, who has made numerous recordings.

ANDALOUS MUSIC

Morocco's classical music comes from the **Arab-Andalusian tradition** and is to be found, with variations, throughout the Maghreb. It is thought to have been invented, around a thousand years ago, in Córdoba, in then Moorish Spain, by an outstanding musician called Ziryab from Baghdad. He founded the classical form called *nawba*.

The original 24 **nawba** were suites directly linked to the hours in the day; only four full and seven fragmentary *nawba* have been preserved in the Moroccan tradition. Complete *nawbat*, which can last several hours, are rarely performed in one sitting. Pieces are usually chosen according to the hour of the day or the circumstances. The movements are made up of poems, or *can'a*, set to music, with instrumental introductions. The lyrics usually deal with love, though they are sometimes religious, glorifying the Prophet and divine laws.

When the Arabs were driven out of Spain, which they had known as Al Andalus, the different musical schools were dispersed over the Maghreb. The Valencian school continued in Fes, the Granadan in Tetouan and Chaouen. All have to an extent been influenced by Berber folk music. In fact many groups in northern Morocco play both Andalous music and Berber folk. The three most important **orchestras** are those of: Fes, led by Abdelkrim Rais; Tetouan, led by Abdesadak Chekara; and Rabat, led by Loukili; Chaouen has also produced many great Andalusian musicians.

Orchestras are made up of *rababs* (fiddles), *ouds* (eleven-string fretless lutes), *kamanjehs* (violins) of various pitches, *derbukas* (pottery drums), *tars* and sometimes a *kanum* (zither).

RELIGIOUS MUSIC

As well as the chants of the Koran, which are improvised on a uniform beat, the *adhan*, or call to prayer, and the songs about the life of the Prophet Muhammad, there is another whole range of prayers and ceremonies belonging to the Sufi **brotherhoods**, or *tarikas*, in which music is seen as a means of getting closer to Allah. These include the music used in processions to the tombs of saints during *moussems*.

The aim is for those present to reach a state of mystic ecstasy. In a private, nocturnal ceremony called the *hadra*, the Sufi brothers attain a trance by chanting the name of Allah (*dker*) or dancing in a ring holding hands. The songs and music are irregular in rhythm, quickening towards an abrupt end. Some brotherhoods play for alms in households that want to gain the favour of their patron saint.

GNAOUA

The **Gnaouas** are a religious brotherhood (see "Islam in Morocco") whose members are descendants of slaves brought from the Sudan by the Arabs. They have devotees all over Morocco, though the strongest concentrations are in the south, particularly in Marrakesh.

The brotherhood claim spiritual descent from Bilal, an Ethiopian who was the Prophet's first *muezzin*. Most Gnaoua ceremonies, or *deiceba*, are held to placate spirits, good and evil, which have inhabited a person or place. These rites have their origins in sub-Saharan Africa, and an African influence is evident in the music itself. The principal instrument, the *gimbri*, is a long-necked flute almost identical to instruments found in Mali, Senegal and elsewhere in West Africa, among the Wolof and Mandinka peoples. The other characteristic sound of Gnaoua music is the *garagab*, a pair of metal castanets, which beat out a trance-like rhythm.

Nowadays, Gnaoua music can be heard at festivals and in the entertainment squares in Marrakesh and elsewhere.

THE ARAB TRADITION

The effect of constant wars and changes of ruler has been to prevent **Middle Eastern Arab music** from having as strong an influence as might be expected. One kind of song with close Arab links is the classical *malhum*, which is accompanied on lute, *kamanjeh*, and percussion, always obeying the rules of the Eastern mode system, or *makam*.

The songs are classified according to the structure and metre of their verses, which are reflected in the music. One of the most famous contributors to this genre was the seventeenth-century poet Abdelaziz al Maghrawi. More recently, radio and television have brought *asri*, in which classical and popular, Eastern and European influences are mixed within the basic framework of the Middle Eastern *makam*, with plenty of instrumental improvisation thrown in for good measure. A leading modern exponent of this style is Toulali – or L'Hadj l'Hocine Toulali, to give him his full name.

The popular Arab music known as *sh'sha'abi* follows the same mode system but has a different verse structure. *L'aita*, a variation on this from the plains between the Casablanca coast and the High Atlas mountains, relies for its effect on the interplay of free singing over a rhythmic accompaniment. One star of all these genres is **Abdeslam Cherkaoui** of Fes, who has made several recordings.

CHAABI

Chaabi means "popular" and the music that takes this name started out as street music performed in the squares and *souks*. It can now be heard in cafés, at festivals and at weddings, especially in the summer. At its more basic level, it is played by itinerant musicians, who will turn up at a café (some cafés keep their own instruments for musicans) and play some songs. Songs are usually finished with a *leseb*, which is often twice the speed of the song itself and forms a background for syncopated clapping, shouting and dancing. Early evening during Ramadan is the best time to find music cafés of this kind in full swing.

During the 1970s a more sophisticated version of *chaabi* began to emerge, with groups setting themselves up in competition with the commercial Egyptian and Libyan music which dominated the market (and the radio) at the time. These groups were usually made up of two stringed instruments – a *sentir* (bass *guimbri*) and a lute – and a *bendir* and *darabuka* or *tan-tan* as percussion. As soon as they could afford to, they updated their sound and image with the addition of congas, bouzoukis, banjos and even electric guitars. The *sentir* and *bendir*, however, remain indispensable.

Their music is a fusion of Arab, African and modern Western influences, combining Berber music with elements taken from the Arab *malhum* and Sufi rituals, Gnaoua rhythms and

the image of European groups. Voices play an important part. The whole group sings, either in chorus or backing a lead soloist. The lyrics deal with both love and social issues, sometimes carrying messages which have got their authors into trouble with the authorities. Sometimes there are breaks for speeches.

The three most popular groups of this kind are Jil Jilala, Lem Chaheb and Nass el Ghiwane, all from Casablanca. **Jil Jilala** was formed in 1972 as part of a Milhun theatre group. Its music is based on a Milhun style, using poetry as a reference (and starting) point. More recently they have worked with Gnaoua rhythms. They use a *ghaita* and – rare in these lineups – some Western wind instruments. **Nass el Ghiwane**, the most politicised of the three (and frequently in trouble with the authorities), lays great emphasis on the words of its recitatives, verses and choruses. Its music again combines Sufi and Gnaoua influences.

Lem Chaheb is probably the Moroccan group best known abroad, through its work with the German group Dissidenten, two of whose members play and record with them. It has an excellent lead singer, and the substitution of an electric guitar and congas for the *sentir* and *tan-tan* has enabled it to develop its music further than other groups.

In the 1980s another generation of groups has emerged which combines traditional with modern influences, this time based in Marrakesh but again concentrating on Gnaoua rhythms. The most successful of these is **Muluk el Hwa**, a group of Berbers who used to play in the Djemaa el Fna square. The line-up is entirely acoustic: *bendir, tan-tan, sentir,* bouzouki, *karkabat* and hands.

Nass el Hal, formed in 1986, offers two shows, one using a traditional acoustic line-up with bouzouki and violin, the other with drum kit and electric guitar. Its repertoire includes peasant harvest and hunting dances, and religious dances.

Other groups with recordings to their name include **Izanzaren**, of the Casablanca school, and **Shuka**, who do everything from Andalous to Gnaoua. Capitalising on the success of all these groups and the demand for cassettes, several *sentir* players have also made recordings, with percussion accompaniment. These include Hassan el Gnaoui, L'Gnaoui Mahmoud and company.

FUSION

Morocco is an ideal place for experiment with fusion of all kinds. Such disparate figures as Brian Jones, Robin Williamson and John Renbourn have been attracted by its rhythms, and in 1989 the Rolling Stones returned to record an album, using the **Pan Pipers of Jajouka** (whom Brian Jones had originally recorded).

The most successful group has been the Berlin-based **Dissidenten**. Before their collaboration with Lem Chaheb, they had also worked with Mohammed Zain, a star *nai* (flute) player from Tangier who belongs to a Sufi sect, and the Gnaoua *gimri* players Abdellah el Gourd, Abdelkader Zefzaf and Abdalla Haroch, producing several recordings. The remarkable *oud* player **Hassan Erraji** has been working in Britain, and recently Belgium, with his groups Belcikal and Arabesque Music.

The **Spaniards** have concentrated mainly on Arab-Andalousian music. There have been several notable collaborations between flamenco musicians and Andalous orchestras, such as that of José Heredia Maya and Enrique Morente with the **Tetouan Orchestra**, and Juan Peña Lebrijano with the **Tangier Orchestra**. Muluk el Hwa has also done interesting work with the Spanish group Al Tall on the medieval Valencian music known as "Xarq Al Andalus".

RAÏ

Raï – the word means "opinion" – originated in the western Algerian region around the port of Oran, and in the last years of the 1980s it has been toppling the Egyptian and Libyan stars who once ruled the cassette stores.

It has traditional roots in Bedouin music, with its distinctive refrain (ha-ya-raï), but as a modern phenomenon has more in common with Western music. The backing is now solidly electric, with rhythm guitars, synthesizers and usually a rock drum kit as well as traditional drums. Its lyrics reflect highly contemporary concerns – cars, sex, sometimes alcohol – which have created some friction with the authorities. However, Moroccans have taken easily to the music and there are now up-and-coming Moroccan *raï* stars such as **Cheb Khader** and the mysterious **Chaba Zahouania**. The latter is said to be forbidden

by her family from being photographed for her recordings.

Raï influence is also to be heard in the folk music of the **Oujda** area, the closest Moroccan town to Oran, in artists like **Rachid Briha** and **Hamid M'Rabati**.

Algerian *raï* stars who are popular in Morocco include Cheb Khaled, Cheb Mami and Chaba Fadhela. Cassettes of all these artists are available in the cities.

SEPHARDIC MUSIC

Moroccan Jews, many of whom have now emigrated to Israel, left an important legacy in the north of the country. Their songs and ballads are still in the medieval Spanish, spoken at the time of their expulsion from Spain five centuries ago.

Apart from the narrative ballads, these are mainly songs of courtly love, as well as lullabies and some on biblical themes. They are usually accompanied on a *tar*. The marriage ceremony has also been carefully preserved.

FOLK INSTRUMENTS

Folk instruments are very rudimentary and fairly easy to make, and this, combined with the fact that many music cafés keep their own, allows for a genuinely amateur development. Many of the instruments mentioned below are also to be found under the same or similar names (and with slight variations) in Algeria, Tunisia, Libya and even Egypt.

Morocco has a great many stringed and percussion instruments, mostly fairly basic in design. There are also a few **wind instruments**. The **Arab flute**, known by different tribes as the *nai*, *talawat*, *nira* or *gasba*, is made of a straight piece of cane open at both ends, with no mouthpiece and between five and seven holes, one at the back. It requires a great deal of skill to play it properly, by blowing at a slight angle. The **ghaita** or *rhita*, a type of oboe popular under various names throughout the Muslim world, is a conical pipe made of hardwood, ending in a bell often made of metal. Its double-reeded mouthpiece is encircled by a broad ring on which the player rests his lips in order to produce the circular breathing needed to obtain a continuous note. It has between seven and nine holes, one at the back. The **aghanin** is a double clarinet, identical to the Arab *arghoul*. It consists of two parallel pipes of wood or cane, each with a single-reed mouthpiece, five holes and a horn at the end for amplification. One pipe provides the tune while the other is used for adornments.

The most common **stringed instrument** is the **gimbri**. This is an African lute whose sound box is covered in front by a piece of hide. The rounded, fretless stem has two or three strings. The body of the smaller treble *gimbri* is pearshaped, that of the bass *gimbri* (*hadjouj* or *sentir*) rectangular. The Gnaouas often put a resonator at the end of the stem to produce the buzz typical of Black African music. The *lotar* is another type of lute, used exclusively by the Chleuh Berbers. It has a circular body, also closed with a piece of skin, and three or four strings which are plucked with a plectrum.

The classic Arab lute, the **oud**, is used in classical orchestras and the traditional Arab orchestras known as *takhts*. Its pear-shaped body is covered by a piece of wood with two or three rosette-shaped openings. It has a short, fretless stem and six strings, five double and one single. The most popular stringed instruments played with a bow are the **kamanjeh** and the **rabab**. The former is an Iranian violin which was adopted by the Arabs. Its present Moroccan character owes a lot to the Western violin, though it is held vertically, supported on the knees. The *rabab* is a spike fiddle, rather like a viol. The bottom half of its long, curved body is covered in hide, the top in wood with a rosette-shaped opening. It has two strings.

The Chleuh Berbers use an archaic single-stringed *rabab* with a square stem and sound-box covered entirely in skin. Lastly, there is the **kanum**, a trapezoidal Arab zither with over seventy strings, grouped in threes and plucked with plectra attatched to the fingernails. It is used almost exclusively in classical music.

Rapid hand-clapping and the clashes of bells and cymbals are only part of the vast repertoire of Moroccan **percussion**. Like most Moroccan drums the **darbuka** is made of clay, shaped into a cylinder swelling out slightly at the top. The single skin is beaten with both hands. It is used in both folk and classical music. The **taarija**, a smaller version of the *darbuka*, is held in one hand and beaten with the other. Then there are treble and bass **tan-tan** bongos, and the Moorish **guedra**, a large drum which rests on the ground. There is also a round wooden drum with skins on both sides called a **tabl**, which is beaten with a stick on one side and by hand on the other. This is used only in folk music.

As for **tambourines**, the ever-popular **bendir** is round and wooden, 40 or 50cm across, with two strings stretched under its single skin to produce a buzzing sound. The **tar** is smaller, with two rings of metal discs round the frame and no strings under its skin. The **duff** is a double-sided tambourine, often square in shape, which has to be supported so that it can be beaten with both hands.

Only two percussion instruments are made of metal: **karkabat**, double castanets used by the Gnaouas, and the **nakous**, a small cymbal played with two rods.

WHERE TO BUY INSTRUMENTS

MEKNES

A musical instrument *souk* is under the archway connecting Souk Bezzarin and Rue des Sarraria, on the edge of the Medina – just past Bab el Djedid, if coming from Place el Hedim. Stalls are good value and there is much choice in a small area.

TETOUAN

A couple of good shops to browse and bargain in are to be found in and around the Rue Terrafin and Rue Ahmed Torres area.

FES

Both Talâa Kebira and Talâa Seghira, close to Bab Boujeloud, have stores at intervals. Nearby here, ask for Abdillah Alami in the Kasbah Boujeloud, who sells excellent hand-made drums.

AVERAGE PRICES

Oud (£35–70); *Ghaïta* (£10–18); *Naï* (£3–6); *Bendir* (£3–6); *Tara* (£3–6); *Hadjouj* (£30–50); *Darabouka* (£8–12); *Qasba* (£8–12); *Garageb* (£2–3); *Tan-Tan* (£5–15); *Gimbri* (£15–30).

RECORDINGS

In Morocco, **cassettes** of all kinds are readily available – folk, traditional, modern, and especially those made by the better-known groups – Jil Jilala, Nass el Ghiwane, Lem Chaheb, Muluk el Hwa, Nass el Hal, etc. They cost around 14–17dh (£1–1.50) for a tape – which almost always lasts exactly 46 minutes!

Good choices to start a collection could include:

Nass el Ghiwane (La Voix el Maarif, LVEM 125).

Nass el Ghiwane: Chant d'Espoir (Nassana, EH1264).

Jil Jilala (Disques Gam, GB8788).

Orchestra Fisal (Fourkafane FM14).

Hamïd Zahir (Tichkophone, TCK548).

Records and CDs are much harder to find and better bought in Europe, though there they are limited to ethnic, folk and Andalous music, or fusion with European groups. In the listings below, those with an asterisk are highly recommended; those with two asterisks, you'd be cheating yourself not to enjoy . . .

GENERAL COMPILATIONS

Music of Morocco (Library of Congress). A rare but wonderful compilation by Paul Bowles – available in some record libraries.*

Music of Morocco (Folkways). Another Library of Congress Project, more easily available.

THE MCM PROJECT

The French label *MCM* (Maison de la Culture du Monde) is collaborating with the Moroccan Ministry of Culture to produce a series of CDs and cassettes, covering all Moroccan folk styles. The first of there releases have been:

Orquesta de Fes Nuba Al-Ushashag (6 CDs).

Milhun by various leading singers (3 CDs).

Ghranati The Algerian variant of Andalous, including a banjo as a classical instruemnt (1 CD).

Music of the Rwais Berber music (4 CDs).

BERBER MUSIC

Maroc/1, Musique Tachelhit: Rais Lhaj Aomar Ouahrouch (Ocora).*

Maroc/2, Moyen Atlas, Musique Sacrée et Profane (Ocora).*

Orchestre de Fes, Maroc: Musique Classique Andalou-Maghrebine (Ocora).**

Maroc: Chants et Danses (Le Chant du Monde).

Berberes du Maroc, Ahwach (Le Chant du Monde).*

Maroc Eternel (Arion).

Hmaoui Abd El Hamid, La flûte orientale (Arion).**

The Rwais, Moroccan Berber Musicians from the High Atlas (Lyrichord).*

Songs and Rhythms of Marocco (Albatros).

Muluk el Hwa, Cançons de Jma-el-Fna (Di-fussió Mediterrania).

Master Musicians of Jajouka (Adelphi).

Jilala/Gnaoua: Moroccan Trance Music (Sub Rosa, Austria; CD).*

RELIGIOUS MUSIC

Morocco, Music of Islam & Sufism (BM).

ARABIC TRADITIONS

Abdeslam Cherkaoui, Morocco: Arabic Traditional Music (Unesco collection; Auvidis).*

Hassan Erraji, Moroccan Folk Song (ME).*

Arabic Songs And Dances (Request).

ANDALOUS MUSIC

Ustad Massano Tazi, Musique Classique Andalouse de Fes (Ocora; CD/cassette only).**

Chekara con la Orquesta de Tetuan (Ariola).*

ANDALOUS/FLAMENCO CROSSOVERS

José Heredia Maya y Orquesta Andalusi de Tetuan, Macama Jonda (Ariola).*

Juan Peña "El Lebrijano" and the Orquesta de Tanger, Encuentros (Globestyle).**

FUSION

Hassan Erraji and Arabesque, Nikriz (Sterns).*

Lem Chaheb with Dissidenten, La Chanson Populaire Marocaine (Club du Disque Arabe; CD only, containing their two best Moroccan cassettes).** *Sahara Electrik* (Globestyle).*

Kwaku Baah and Ganoua (Island).

Sidi Seddiki Shouf! (Globestyle). Modern sounds from a London-based expatriate.

SEPHARDIC MUSIC

Judeo-Español Songs from Morocco (Saga).

Sephardic Jews – Ballads, Wedding Songs, Songs, and Dances (Folkways).

MOROCCAN FICTIONS

Storytelling is an age-old Moroccan tradition – and an active one, as any visit to a weekly *souk* will reveal. The American novelist Paul Bowles, a resident in Tangier more or less since the war, became interested in such tales in the early 1950s and began tape recording and transcribing examples told by various Moroccan friends – Ahmed Yacoubi, Larbi Layachi, Abdeslam Boulaich and, in particular, Mohammed Mrabet, with whom he continues to collaborate.

Mrabet's work now amounts to a dozen collections of stories, novels and novellas. The piece included here is in some ways atypical – Mrabet's interests are rooted more in his experience of city life – but it shows his showmanship and masterful handling of a deeply traditional theme of Moroccan storytelling, the casting of spells. Abdeslam Boulaich, better known as a painter, reveals a similar interest in folk humour. Mohammed Chourki, by contrast, is a more literary figure, with a novel and books on Tennessee Williams and Jean Genet to his name. Alone among the three authors here, he wrote his text (in Classical Arabic), with Bowles translating from an oral reading in Maghrebi.

For details of books by these various authors, see the bibliography on p.546.

MOHAMMED MRABET: THE LUTE

A young man named Omar got onto his mare one day and rode over his father's land for many miles, looking for the right place to build a small house of his own. He came to a hill between the forest and the olive groves. This is the spot, he said. Here I can play my lute all day.

Little by little he built a cottage, bringing the materials from his father's house, and doing all the work himself. When it was done he furnished it with everything he needed for the pleasant life he intended to lead. His most important possession was his lute, which he had trained so that when anyone was coming it sounded its strings in warning. Then Omar would look into the opening under the strings and watch the person as he approached.

Outside the house he built an arbor of canes where he could lie back and drink his tea. And he would sit out there in the shade of the arbor with the green trees all around him, smoking kif and drinking tea. At length he would take down his lute and begin to play.

Farther down the valley lived two sisters whose father and mother had died, leaving them alone in a big house. The younger sister was still only a girl, and there was a handsome village lad with whom she was friendly. The older sister, who desired the boy for herself, caught sight of him talking to the girl under a tree. Later she questioned her.

Who was that you were talking to?

The boy from the village.

What did he say to you?

The girl smiled and looked very happy. He said beautiful words and wonderful things. Because I love him and he loves me.

What? cried the woman. And you're not ashamed to say such a thing?

Why should I be? We're going to be married.

The older sister jumped up and rushed out. She began to burn powders and to chant, and it was not long before she burst into the room with a scream and flung a handful of black powder over the girl. At that instant her sister no longer stood in front of her – only a camel, which she chained outside.

A few days later the village boy came to see the younger sister. The woman greeted him from the doorway and invited him into the house. He sat down and looked around, and then through the window he saw the camel.

Why have you got that camel chained to the ground with its legs tied together? he asked her.

She's a bad animal, the woman said. I have to keep her chained up so she won't get into trouble.

Let the poor thing loose so it can graze, he told her. It has no life at all this way. Unfasten the chain and untie the ropes.

No, no. I can't do that.

The boy waited a moment. Then he said: The girl who lives here. Where is she?

That girl? She's getting married tomorrow.

What? he cried. But she was going to marry me!

No. She never mentioned anything about that to me, she told him. Anyway, that's the way it is.

Then she laughed. And what about me? Don't you like me?

Yes, he said. Of course I like you.

Why don't you and I get married, then?

The boy looked at her, and then he looked out at the camel. All right, he said at length. I'll marry you. But only if you set that camel free.

Without saying anything the woman went outside and undid the chain and ropes, and the camel walked away. Then she came in and said she would see him that evening.

As the boy went along the path to the village he came upon the camel waiting for him. He was horrified to hear it speak with the voice of the girl.

Don't trust my sister, it said. You see what she's done to me. I'm the one you were going to marry. Go as far away from here as you can, and stay away. I've got to try and get back my body somehow.

Then the camel walked away, and the boy was too downcast to call after it. He left the village the same afternoon.

One day not long afterward as Omar lay under his arbor on a mat drinking tea, the cords of his lute suddenly sounded. When he peered inside it he saw a camel. He watched it come nearer, and then he hung up the lute and went out into the orchard. The camel walked straight to him and said: Good afternoon.

Omar was startled. You can speak?

I said good afternoon. Yes, I can speak.

I've never seen a talking camel, he said.

But I'm not a camel. That's the trouble. And she told him what her sister had done to her. Then she said: I have a favor to ask of you. Let me stay here with you for a while.

Omar looked thoughtfully at the animal, and said: Ouakha. You can stay with me.

The camel lay down beside the arbor, and Omar began to play the lute. It was the hour when the birds sang and flew from tree to tree. When the birds became quiet, he glanced at the camel and saw that tears were falling from its eyes. He put the lute aside.

The next day as Omar sat in the arbor talking with the camel, he heard the strings of the lute. When he looked inside, he saw a woman walking through the wilderness, over the rocks and between the trees. He watched for a while, but she did not come any closer. Finally she disappeared. He sat down.

Tell me, he said to the camel. What was your sister doing at the moment you felt yourself becoming a camel?

The camel thought for a while. Then it said: She sprinkled some powder over my head, and she had a piece of green cloth in her hand. I saw her fold it three times and then throw it on top of a chest.

I have a friend who might be able to help, Omar told her. He often comes by around this hour.

As they sat there a large crow came flying over the trees, and alighted on the ground beside the arbor. After they had greeted each other, Omar said: You're an expert thief, aren't you?

The crow was embarrassed. It's true I've stolen things. But all that is in the past.

Omar smiled. Good, he said. But you've still got to steal one more time. Do you know Tchar Flanflani?

Yes.

You've got to get into that big house there and look around until you find a green cloth. Don't unfold it. Bring it to me.

Ouakha, said the crow, and it flew off.

They did not have to wait long for it to return, carrying the green cloth in its claws. As Omar took the cloth in his hands and let it unfold, instead of a camel lying on the ground beside the arbor, it was a girl.

He stared at her first in amazement and then with delight, for she was beautiful. Then she jumped up and threw her arms around him, and he embraced her. Together they went into the house.

The following day when the sister looked to see if the green cloth was safe in its place, she did not find it. She searched for it inside the house and out, but without success. As Omar and the girl sat in the shade of the arbor, the strings of the lute began to vibrate. He peered into it and saw the woman walking in the forest.

Here, he said to the girl. Look in here and see if you know who that is.

She looked inside the lute and drew back. It's my sister! she whispered. She's looking for me.

Omar hung up the lute and walked out to the orchard to meet the woman. When he came up to her she looked at him and said: Who are you?

That's what I want to ask you, he said. Who are you and where have you come from and what do you want here? This is my land you're on, and the edge of it is a long way from here.

I'm looking for a camel, she said. A camel I've lost.

I have your camel, he told her.

What! Where is it? What have you done with it?

It's over there, he said, pointing to the arbor where the girl stood. And she came out and walked toward them.

The woman looked at Omar. You won't win! she cried. Then she turned and went back the way she had come.

A few days after this, Omar put the girl onto the mare and rode with her to his father's house, where they celebrated their marriage with a wedding feast that lasted for three days. Then the married couple rode back to the little house. The two were very happy together, and the days passed swiftly.

But one moonlit night as they lay asleep in bed, the lute hanging on the wall twanged its strings. Omar sprang up and put his eye to the hole. A woman dressed all in white walked in the brilliant moonlight. He pulled the lute down and played softly for a while. The next time he looked in, a dense white cloud had formed around the figure of the woman in the orchard, and the cloud was so thick that she could not move one way or the other. Omar hung the lute on the wall and got back into bed.

What was it?

It was your sister. She's down there in the orchard now, dressed all in white. I've got her shut in. She can't go forward or backward.

Let her go! the girl begged him. We mustn't be cruel to her. I can't bear to think of her suffering.

Omar paid no attention to her pleas, but turned over and went to sleep. In the morning after he had bathed and had his breakfast, he sat down under the arbor, smoked a few pipes of kif, and said to the girl: Come here and look.

Inside the lute she saw the swirling cloud among the olive trees. Omar took the lute and played on it for a moment. Then he handed it back, and she looked again. The cloud had disappeared, and the woman stood there shouting up at them from the orchard.

I'll be back! she screamed.

Another night as they slept, the lute again sounded a warning, and Omar seized it and put his eye to the hole. Seeing the woman, he played a loud fast melody for a while. When he peered in the next time, he saw that once again a cloud had formed around the woman, but this time it had risen high into the air with her, where it remained, as still as a rock. He got into bed and said nothing about it.

But the next morning when the girl looked outside she called to Omar. There's something hanging in the air above the orchard!

It's your sister, he said.

Forgive her this time, and she'll never come back to bother us any more, his wife said, and she went on pleading with him.

Your sister will never change, Omar told her. She ought not to be pardoned and turned loose to do harm in the world.

But the girl sobbed and begged him to let her sister down, and finally he got up and plucked on the lute. The cloud slowly settled onto the ground and blew away. This time the woman did not stay to say anything, but ran off as soon as she felt the earth beneath her feet.

When she got back to her house, she shut herself in and fasted for four days. At the end of this time she had a vision of two trees whose trunks stood very close one to the other. She forced herself between them and knew that something great had happened. When she turned, she saw eight strings of gut stretched from a crosspiece between the tree trunks, and she knew that this was the way to get into Omar's house without alerting the lute. From then on she spent all her time preparing the strips of gut and the other things she would need when she found the two trees. When she had everything ready, she began to go regularly to the forest below the little house, in search of the place she had seen in her vision. She found it one night. It was in a dense part of the woods, just below the house. Quickly she squeezed in between the two tree trunks.

The moment she had pushed through, a wall formed around her body and over her head, so that she was encased in a shell of rock between the two trees. The lute by Omar's bed made a loud sound as though it had been hurled to the floor, and then it began to play a strange, halting melody, a thing Omar had never heard it do before. He waited until it had stopped, and then he took it down and looked into it.

Your sister! he cried. There's nothing I can do! She's dying. The lute did it by itself. I didn't touch it.

The girl seized the lute and held it close to her face. Beyond the strings she saw the two trees and the boulder between them. And then through the casing of the stone she saw her sister's face. Her mouth was open and her eyes rolled from side to side as she gasped

Then the wall of stone around her body became smoke and blew away through the trees, and she fell forward onto the ground.

ABDESLAM BOULAICH:
THREE HEKAYAS

Cowardice

A Moslem, a Jew, and a Christian were sitting in a cafe talking about Heaven. They agreed that it was a difficult place to get into, but each one thought he would have a better chance than the others.

You have to have the right clothes, the Christian told them. I always wear a jacket and a tie.

Let's go and see, said the other two.

They started out, and when they got close to Heaven, the Moslem and the Jew stopped walking, and the Christian kept going until he reached the door of Heaven.

Our Lord Solomon, who guards the door, said to him: Where are you going?

Inside, the Nazarene answered.

Who are you?

My name is John.

Stand back, said Our Lord Solomon.

Then the Jew and the Moslem spoke together. The Moslem said: He didn't get in. But we will.

I'll go first, said the Jew.

That's right. You go, the Moslem told him.

So the Jew walked up to the door of Heaven. And Our Lord Solomon said to him: Where are you going?

Inside.

Who are you?

Yaqoub, said the Jew.

Stand back!

The Moslem saw this and said to himself: That's that. Neither one of them got in. Now I'll try.

He walked until he got to the door of Heaven. Then he pulled the hood of his djellaba down over his face. And Our Lord Solomon said to him: Where are you going?

Inside.

Who are you? Our Lord Solomon asked him.

I am the Prophet Mohammed, he said. And he went in. The Jew was watching. He said to himself: If he can get in there, so can I.

And he took a sack and filled it with sticks of wood and slung it over his shoulder. Then he walked up to the door.

Where are you going? asked Our Lord Solomon.

The Jew stuck his foot in the door.

Who are you?

The Prophet Mohammed's manservant, he said. And the Jew went in.

The Christian had been watching. He was afraid to try to get in by lying, and so he went back to his country and told everyone that Heaven did not exist.

Stupidity

In a small mountain village lived a man who could not talk very well because he had no roof to his mouth. When it came time for him to marry, his family chose him a girl who had the same trouble. But since the man had never seen her, nor had the girl seen him, neither one knew how the other one spoke.

The day of the wedding, the man went into the girl's room. The servant brought in the taifor with a pot of couscous on it, and then she went home, leaving the front door unlatched.

The man sat with his hands folded in front of him, and so did the girl. Each one was looking at the other, waiting for the other to speak. She

---

The next morning Omar and his wife went to the spot and found her body lying there between the two arar trees.

We must bury her, said the girl.

Not on my land, Omar told her. On her own land, if you like, but not here.

And each afternoon when he sat with his wife under the arbor playing the lute, the crow came and sat with them, and listened.

1977.

was waiting for the man to say: Eat. And he was waiting for her to say: Eat. He was afraid to speak for fear she would hear his voice and not be able to love him. And the girl was afraid he would hear hers and not want her for a wife. Each one looked at the other, and the door of the house was unlatched.

A beggar was passing through the street, crying: For the love of Allah, a little bread! And no one paid him any attention. When he came to the house of the bridegroom he saw the door ajar, and he pushed it open and walked in. He went through the courtyard and came to the room where the two were sitting. Then he saw the man and the girl looking at one another, with the food in front of them on the taifor, and neither one saying anything. The bridegroom saw the beggar standing there. He wanted to tell him to get out. But he would not speak, and so he shook his head up and down at him. But the beggar thought he meant: Go on and eat. He sat down and began to eat the couscous, and he went on eating until there was only a little left. Then he ate the meat, and when he had finished, he took the bone and hung it around the man's neck on a string, because he thought the man was simple-minded. And he went out.

A dog was running through the street. When it came to the house of the bridegroom it caught the smell of food coming through the open door, and it went into the courtyard. It ran to the door of the room where they were sitting, and went in. The man and the girl sat still and said nothing. The dog put its feet up on the taifor and licked up the rest of the couscous. It was still hungry. Then it saw the bone that hung around the bridegroom's neck, and it seized it between its jaws and tried to run. The man fell over onto the floor, and the dog dragged him to the door. The dog kept pulling, and the man's head hit the wall.

Then the man cried out: Help me untie the string!

The girl heard his words, and she was no longer afraid to speak.

The beggar was right! she said. I can't live with such a man!

But you speak the same way! he cried.

I'm the only one who wouldn't have minded that, she told him. And she went out of the house, and left the man on the floor with the dog pulling at the bone.

Greed

A sickly man who lived in the city married a girl from the country. He was never very hungry, but the girl was healthy and ate a great deal. One day the man went to the market and bought many vegetables and four cow's feet. When he took the food home to his wife, he told her: Make me a stew so I can have it when I come home for lunch.

Yes, she said.

But wait for me, he said. Don't eat anything until I get back.

I won't, she said.

When he had gone she made the stew. And then she waited. He ought to be here soon, she said to herself. He'll be here any minute.

After he had finished working, the man went to a café and began to play cards. He stayed there in the café a long time, and his wife went on waiting. Soon she was very hungry. She took one of the cow's feet out of the stew and ate it. And she said to herself: It doesn't matter. When he comes I'll make up something to tell him.

The man came home and sat down. Where's the stew? he said. You haven't eaten anything, have you?

Not yet, she told him. She brought the stew and began to ladle it out. Then the man noticed that there were only three feet in the pot. He began to shout: And the other foot? Where is it?

I haven't got it, she said. You brought three and I cooked three. I hate cow's feet anyway.

The man was very unhappy. Do you want to kill me? he cried. Bring me the other foot, or I may die right here.

Die, if that's what you want, she told him. Why are you waiting?

The man rolled over onto the floor and began to moan.

Get up! said his wife. But he only told her to fetch the fqih and make him wash him so he could be buried.

When she came in with the fqih, the girl said to her husband again: Get up off the floor!

Have you got the cow's foot? he asked her.

The fqih began to wash him.

Get up! she said. Don't you want to have your burial clothes put on you?

Have you brought the cow's foot?

She did not answer. The people came in and dressed the man in his kfin, ready to be buried. And then they laid him on the litter.

You're off to the cemetery, his wife told him. They carried him through the doorway into the street.

Where's the cow's foot? he cried. His wife shut the door.

The people walked through the streets carrying him on the litter. When they passed in front of the market, the butcher saw the procession. Who's that who has died? he asked. They told him.

And to think that only this morning he was here in my shop, the poor man, and he bought four cow's feet!

When the dead man heard this, he sat up on his litter. How many did you say? he called to the butcher.

Four!

Ah, you see? he said. And my wife told me I'd bought only three.

No. It was four, said the butcher.

The man lay down again. And the men carrying him were talking and did not notice anything. They went on their way to the cemetery. When they got there they lifted him off the litter and started to lower him into the ground. But at that moment he sat up again.

Wait! he told the fqih. I've got three cow's feet at home that I still haven't eaten. It's not good to be hungry when you arrive in Heaven. I'm going to run back and eat them now. If I do get to Heaven then, at least I'll have some food inside me.

The people let go of him, and he ran home. When he went into the house his wife said: You came back? You're still alive?

Give me the three cow's feet, he told her. She gave them to him. He ate one. But then he was no longer hungry, and his wife ate the other two.

1961

MOHAMMED CHOUKRI: THE PROPHET'S SLIPPERS

More pleasure and fantasy. More money, more ways of getting hold of it. I was tired of enjoying myself, and yet I was not satisfied. Fatin walked toward me, white as snow in the blood-red light of the bar. She took one of my notebooks, looked at it, and grinned.

She muttered something unintelligible and moved away again, disappearing among those who were kicking the air. It was three o'clock in the morning, and I was bored and nervous. Om Kalsoum was singing: "Sleep never made life seem too long, nor long waiting shortened life."

A black man appeared, white on black. He took one of my books and began to read aloud: "This total liberty has its tragic and pessimistic side." He put it down. "What's that book about?" he demanded.

"It's about a man who doesn't understand this world," I said. "He hurts himself and everybody who comes near him."

He nodded, lifted his glass, and drank. When he had finished, he said: "You're crazy."

I saw Fatin writing in a notebook. Meanwhile I smoked, drank, and thought about the matter of the slippers. The lights went off. Women cried out. When they came on again,

both men and women murmured. I bought another drink for Khemou, and she gave me a kiss that left a sweet taste in my mouth. Her brown tongue tickled. She was eating chocolate, and her laugh was red in the light from the bar. Khemou walked off and Fatin came up to me. She handed me a slip of blue paper. On it she had written: *Rachid. What do you know about love? You spend more time writing about love than you do making love. The one who has never studied love enjoys it more than the one who knows all about it. Love is not a science. Love is feeling, feeling, feeling.*

Miriam Makeba went into "Malaysia." She has a white voice. I began to write on the same piece of blue paper. *Fatin, you are my red bed, and I'm your black blanket. I'm beginning to see it that way.*

I looked around for Fatin. Her mouth was a wound in her face, and a foreign sailor was sucking on it. She had her right arm around him and was pouring her drink onto the floor with her left hand. Khemou came by and offered me her lips, like a mulberry. I bought her another drink. I was so pleased with the effect of her kiss that I began to think once more about selling the slippers. How much ought I to ask for them? A million francs, the Englishman ought to pay, if he wants the Prophet's slippers. He's an idiot in any case, or he couldn't be taken in by such a tale. But how can I tell just how stupid he is? It was he who first brought it up, the black-market story.

Fatin appeared, black, blonde, white. I handed her the slip of blue paper. She looked at me and smiled. I was thinking that girls like her only made trouble. Her little mouth now looked like a scar that had healed. I thought of the Indian poet Mirzah Asad Allah Ghalef:

> *For those who are thirsty*
> *I am the dry lip.*

She wants a kind of love that will make her unhappy. What I like about her is that she still believes the world ought to be changed.

Khemou and Latifa began to scream at each other like two cats fighting, while Miriam Makeba's white voice continued to sing. Khemou pulled Latifa's black hair, knocked her down, and kicked her face. Latifa screamed and the blood ran from her nose. The colors all came together in my head. Leaving the blue paper with me, Fatin ran to separate the two. I read on it: *You're right. I serve them my flesh, but I don't feel it when they eat me.*

Vigon is singing in his white voice. "Outside the Window." Vigon is singing, and I think of the almond trees in flower, and of snow, which I love.

Khemou and Latifa came out of the rest room. They had made up, like two little girls. They began to laugh and dance as if nothing had happened. I sat there smoking, while in my imagination I attacked each man in the bar whose face I didn't like. A kick for this one, a slap in the face for that one, a punch in the jaw for that one over there. Watching myself do as I pleased with them put me into a better frame of mind.

Tomorrow I'll sell the slippers. Fatin came past again, and I asked her why Khemou and Latifa had been quarreling. She said it was because Khemou had told the man Latifa was drinking with that she had tuberculosis.

Is it true? I asked her.

Yes, she said. But she says she's cured now.

The Englishman and I were at my house, eating couscous. He turned to me and said: "This is the best couscous I've ever tasted."

From time to time he looked toward the corner where my grandmother sat, her head bent over. I told him the couscous had been sent from Mecca. "My aunt sends a lot of it each month."

He looked at me with amazement. "It's fantastic!"

So that he would get the idea, I added: "Everything in the house was brought from Mecca. Even that incense burning is sent each month."

We finished the couscous and started on another dish of meat baked with raisins and hot spices. "It's called *mrozeya*," I told him.

He muttered a few words, and then said: "Ah, nice. Very nice." My grandmother's head was still bent over. I saw that the Englishman was looking at her, sitting there in her white robes. The incense and the silence in the room made her seem more impressive. She was playing her part very well. Our demure little servant brought the tea in a silver teapot. She too was dressed in immaculate white, and she too kept her face hidden. Her fingers were painted with elaborate designs in henna, and her black hair shone above her enormous earrings. She made no false moves. She greeted the Englishman without smiling, as I had instructed her to do. It became her to look grave. I had never seen her so pretty.

The mint tea with ambergris in it seemed to please the Englishman. "Do you like the tea?" I asked him.

"Oh, yes! It's very good!"

There was silence for a while. I thought: The time has come to rub Aladdin's lamp. I got up and went to whisper in my grandmother's ear. I did not even form words; I merely made sounds. She nodded her head slowly, without looking up. Then I lifted the white cushion and removed the piece of gold-embroidered green silk that covered it.

The Englishman looked at the slippers, made colorless by age. His hand slowly advanced to touch the leather. Then he glanced at me, and understood that I did not want him to touch them.

"My God! They're marvelous!"

I covered the slippers as I stood there, in order to let him observe them through the veil of green silk. Slowly and with great care I turned and put the cushion back into its place, as if I were applying a bandage to an injury. He glanced at me, and then stared for a long time in the direction of the slippers. Understanding that it was time to leave, he stood up.

We were sitting at the Café Central. For the third time since we had left the house, he said: "Then it's impossible?"

"A thing like that is so difficult," I said. "I wouldn't know how to do it. It was hard enough to get her to let you even look at them. You can be sure you're the only Christian ever to have seen them. And no other is going to, either."

"I understand," he said. "But perhaps we can come to an agreement."

"I understand too. But what can I do? Those slippers are my grandmother's very life. If she should find them missing, she might lose her mind, or have a heart attack. I'm very fond of her, naturally, and I respect her feelings about the slippers."

"I'll give you time to think about it," he said. "But try and persuade her."

"Yes. But when you think of how hard it was to get her to allow you to look at them, you can see how much harder it would be to persuade her."

"Do what you can," he said.

I said I would. but that I thought it was out of the question. Then I said: "Listen. I have an idea. But only on one condition."

"What's that?"

I hesitated for an instant.

"Tell me. Perhaps we can find a way."

"You'd have to leave Tangier the minute you got the slippers."

"That would be all right," he said, understanding. "It's an excellent tactic."

"And I'd have to get out of Tangier myself and stay somewhere else. And I couldn't come back as long as my grandmother was still alive."

"No."

"I couldn't stay on here once they were gone."

"I quite understand."

"It's those slippers that keep her alive, you might say."

"Yes, yes. How much do you want for them?"

I stared at him, and my voice said: "A million francs."

"Oh!" he cried. "No! That's very high!"

"But you'll have something extremely rare. No museum has anything like them. And I'll regret what I've done for the rest of my life."

"I know, I know. But that's a great deal of money. I'll give you half a million. I can't pay any more than that."

"You'd have to pay more than that," I told him.

"No, no. I can't. I haven't got it."

"You give me your address, and I'll write you from wherever I go, and you can send me the rest later."

We looked at each other for a few seconds. In my mind I was thinking: Go on, say the word, Mister Stewart.

"Very well," he finally said.

Wonderful, Mister Stewart, I thought.

"Where shall we meet tomorrow?" I asked him.

He reflected for a moment, and said: "I'll wait for you in the lobby at the Hotel Minzah."

"No," I said. "Outside the hotel. In the street. And you must have your ticket with you, so you can leave the minute I give you the slippers."

"Of course."

"What time will that be?"

While he hesitated I was thinking: Come on, Mister Stewart. Make up your mind.

"At three o'clock in the afternoon."

I got up, shook hands with him, and said: "Keep it to yourself."

"I shan't breathe a word."

"It's not only my grandmother who's going to be upset, but everybody who knows she has the slippers."

I walked away. A moment later I turned and saw him leaving the café.

I found him waiting for me in front of the hotel. He seemed nervous, and he looked wide-eyed at the bag I was carrying. I saw that he had a packet in his hand. Half a million, I thought. More pleasure, more time to think of other such tricks later. The colors in the bar.

I motioned to him to follow me, and stopped walking only when we were a good distance from the entrance to the hotel. We stood facing one another, and shook hands. He looked down at my bag, and I glanced at the packet he held in his hand.

I opened the bag, and he touched the slippers for a second. Then he took it out of my hands, and I took the packet from him. Pointing to a parked car, he said: "There's the car that's going to take me to the airport."

I thought to myself: And tonight I'll be at the Messalina Bar.

I sat down in the corner the same as

always. I smoked, drank, and bought kisses without haggling over their price. I'm fed up with pleasure. Fed up, but not satisfied. One woman is not enough.

"Khemou's in the hospital," Fatin told me. "And Latifa's at the police station. She got drunk and hit Khemou on the head with a bottle."

I asked Fatin who the girls were who were sitting in the corner opposite me. She said they were both from Dar el Beida. She picked up one of my notebooks and walked away with it. I waved at the younger of the two. She spoke for a while with her friend. And I drank and smoked and waited for the first kiss of a girl I had never yet touched.

She got up and came over, and I saw the small face relax. Her mouth was like a strawberry. She began to sip the drink I bought her. Her lips shone. Her mouth opened inside mine. A strawberry soaked in gin and tonic. Eve eating mulberries. Adam approaches her, but she puts the last berry into her mouth before he can get to her. Then he seizes the last berry from between her teeth. The mulberry showed Eve how to kiss. Adam knows all the names of things, but Eve had to teach him how to kiss.

Two men had begun to fight over one of the girls. The shorter of the two lost his balance. The other kicked until someone seized him from behind.

Fatin put a piece of blue paper in front of me. I was drinking, smoking, and eating mulberries from the new small mouth. I read what was written on the piece of blue paper. *I'm not the same person I was yesterday. I know it but I can't say it clearly. You must try and understand me.*

The new face held up her empty glass. I looked again at the mulberries. The barman was busy drawing squares on a small piece of white paper. "Give her another drink," I told him. The friend who had been sitting with her came over. "Give her a drink too," I said.

I thought: More mulberries and human flesh. More tricks and money. I began to write on Fatin's slip of blue paper: *I must not try to understand you.*

1973

WRITERS ON MOROCCO

As any glimpse at the book listings following will show, there's also a long tradition of writing on Morocco. The pieces that follow – from Budgett Meakin, Walter Harris, Elias Canetti and Paul Bowles – represent the best of the genre and much of its range.

BUDGETT MEAKIN: IN MOORISH GUISE

To those who have not themselves experienced what the attempt to see an eastern country in native guise entails, a few stray notes of what it has been my lot to encounter in seeking for knowledge in this style, will no doubt be of interest. Such an undertaking, like every other style of adventure, has both its advantages and disadvantages. To the student of the people the former are immense, and if he can put up with whatever comes, he will be well repaid for all the trials by the way. In no other manner can a European mix with any freedom with the natives of this country. When once he has discarded the outward distinguishing features of what they consider a hostile infidelity, and has as far as possible adopted their dress and their mode of life, he has spanned one of the great gulfs which have hitherto yawned between them.

Squatted on the floor, one of a circle round a low table on which is a steaming dish into which each plunges his fist in search of dainty morsels, the once distant Moor thaws to an astonishing extent, becoming really friendly and communicative, in a manner totally impossible towards the starchy European who sits uneasily on a chair, conversing with his host at ease on the floor. And when the third cup of tea syrup comes, and each lolls contentedly on the cushions, there is manifested a brotherly feeling not unknown in Western circles under analogous circumstances, here fortunately without a suggestion of anything stronger than "gunpowder".

Yes, this style of thing decidedly has its delights – of which the above must not be taken as the most elevating specimen and many are the pleasant memories which come before me as I mentally review my life "as a Moor". In doing so I seem to be again transported to another world, to live another life, as was my continual feeling at the time. Everything around me was so different, my very actions and thoughts so complete a change from what they were under civilisation, that when the courier brought the periodical budget of letters and papers I felt as one in a dream, even my mother tongue sounding strange after not having heard it so long.

Often I have had to "put up" in strange quarters; sometimes without any quarters at all. I have slept in the mansions of Moorish merchants, and rolled up in my cloak in the street. I have occupied the guest chambers of country governors and sheikhs, and I have passed the night on the wheat in a granary, wondering whether fleas or grains were more numerous. I have been accommodated in the house of a Jewish Rabbi, making a somewhat similar observation, and I have been the guest of a Jewish Consular Agent of a Foreign Power, where the awful stench from the drains was not exceeded by that of the worst hovel I ever entered. I have even succeeded in wooing Morpheus out on the sea-shore, under the lea of a rock, and I have found the debris by the side of a straw rick an excellent couch till it came on to rain. Yet again, I have been one of half a dozen on the floor of a windowless and doorless summer-house in the middle of the rainy season. The tent of the wandering Arab has afforded me shelter, along with calves and chickens and legions of fleas, and I have actually passed the night in a village mosque.

When I set out on my travels in Moorish guise, it was with no thought of penetrating spots so venerated by the Moors that all non-Muslims are excluded, but the idea grew upon me as I journeyed, and the Moors themselves were the cause. This is how it came about. Having become acquainted to some extent with the language and customs of the people during a residence of several years among them as a European, when I travelled – with the view of rendering myself less conspicuous, and mixing more easily with the natives – I adopted their dress and followed their style of life, making, however, no attempt to conceal my nationality. After a while I found that when I went where I was not known, all took me for a Moor till they heard my speech, and recognised the foreign accent and the blunders which no native could make. My Moorish friends would often remark that were it not for this I could enter mosques and saint-houses with impunity.

For convenience' sake I had instructed the one faithful attendant who accompanied me to call me by a Muslim name resembling my own, and I afterwards added a corruption of my surname which sounded well, and soon began to seem quite natural. This prevented the attention of the bystanders being arrested when I was addressed by my man, who was careful also always to refer to me as "Seyyid", Master, a term never applied to Europeans or Jews.

Having got so far, a plan occurred to me to account for my way of speaking. I had seen a lad from Manchester, born there of an English mother, but the son of a Moor, who knew not a word of Arabic when sent to Morocco by his father. Why could I not pass as such a one, who had not yet perfected himself in the Arabic tongue? Happy thought! Was I not born in Europe, and educated there? Of course I was, and here was the whole affair complete. I remember, too, that on one or two occasions I had had quite a difficulty to persuade natives that I was *not* similarly situated to this lad. On the first occasion I was taken by surprise, as one among a party of English people, the only one dressed in Moorish costume, which I thought under those circumstances would deceive no one. When asked whence I came, I replied "England", and was then asked, "Is there a mosque there?" I answered that I was not aware that there was one, but that I knew a project had been set on foot to build one near London. Other questions followed, as to my family and what my father's occupation was, till I was astonished at the enquiry, "Has your father been to Mekka yet?"

"Why, no", I answered, as it dawned upon me what had been my interrogator's idea – "he's not a Muslim!"

"Don't say that!" said the man.

"But we are not", I reiterated, "we are Christians".

It was not as difficult to persuade him that I was not at least a convert to Christianity from Islam, as I should have thought it would have been to persuade him that I was a Muslim. Bearing this in mind, I had no doubt that by simply telling the strict truth about myself, and allowing them to draw their own conclusions, I should generally pass for the son of a Moorish merchant settled in England, and thus it proved. Once, during a day's ride in Moorish dress, I counted the number of people who saluted by the way, and was gratified to find that although on a European saddle this suggested to the thoughtful that my mother must have been a European, and I heard one or two ask my man whether she was a legal wife or a slave! In conversation, however, I was proud and grateful to proclaim myself a Christian and an Englishman. My native dress meant after all no more than European dress does on an Oriental in England: it brought me in touch with the Moors, and it enabled me to pass among them unobserved.

Another striking instance of this occurred in Fez, where, before entering any house, I paid an unintentional visit to the very shrine I wished to see. Outside the gates I had stopped to change my costume, and passing in apart from my faithful Mohammed, after a stroll to about the centre of the city, I asked at a shop the way to a certain house. The owner called a lad who knew the neighbourhood, to whom I explained what I wanted, and off we started. In a few minutes I paused on the threshold of a finely ornamented building, different from any other I had seen. All unsuspicious, I enquired what it was, and learned that we were in a street as sacred as a mosque, and that my guide was taking me a short cut through the sanctuary of Mulai Idrees!

Some days later, lantern and slippers in one hand, and rosary in the other, I entered with the crowd for sunset prayers. Perspiring freely within, but outwardly with the calmest appearance I could muster, I spread my prayer-cloth and went through the motions prescribed by law, making my observations in the pauses, and concluding by a guarded survey of the place. I need hardly say that I breathed with a feeling of relief when I found myself in the pure air again, and felt better after I had had my supper and sat down to commit my notes to paper. In the Karûeeïn I once caught a suspicious stare at my glasses, so, pausing, I returned the stare with a contemptuous indignation that made my critic slink off abashed. There was nothing to do but to "face it out".

From *The Land of the Moors: A Comprehensive Description*, by Budgett Meakin (London, 1901).

WALTER HARRIS: *THE DEATH OF A SULTAN*

In 1893 Mulai Hassen determined to visit the desert regions of Morocco, including far-off Tafilet, the great oasis from which his dynasty had originally sprung, and where, before becoming the ruling branch of the royal family, they had resided ever since their founder, the great-grandson of the Prophet, had settled there, an exile from the East.

Leaving Fez in the summer, the Sultan proceeded south, crossing the Atlas above Kasba-el-Maghzen, and descended to the upper waters of the Wad Ziz. An expedition such as this would have required a system of organisation far in excess of the capabilities of the Moors, great though their resources were. Food was lacking; the desert regions could provide little. The water was bad, the heat very great. Every kind of delay, including rebellion and the consequent punishment of the tribes, hampered the Sultan's movements; and it was only toward winter that he arrived in Tafilet with a fever-stricken army and greatly diminished transport.

Mulai Hassen returned from Tafilet a dying man. The internal complaint from which he was suffering had become acute from the hardships he had undergone, and he was unable to obtain the rest that his state of health required, nor would he place himself under a regimen. For a few months he remained in the southern capital, and in the late spring 1894 set out to suppress a rebellion that had broken out in the Tadla region.

While camping in the enemy country he died. Now, the death of the Sultan under such circumstances was fraught with danger to the State. He was an absolute monarch, and with his disappearance all authority and government lapsed until his successor should have taken up the reins. Again, the expedition was in hostile country, and any inkling of the Sultan's death would have brought the tribes down to pillage and loot the Imperial camp. As long as the Sultan lived, and was present with his expedition, his prestige was sufficient to prevent an attack of the tribes, though even this was not unknown on one or two occasions, and to hold his forces together as a sort of concrete body. But his death, if known, would have meant speedy disorganisation, nor could the troops themselves be trusted not to seize this opportunity to murder and loot.

It was therefore necessary that the Sultan's demise should be kept an absolute secret. He had died in the recesses of his tents, themselves enclosed in a great canvas wall, inside which, except on very special occasions, no one was permitted to penetrate. The knowledge of his death was therefore limited to the personal slaves and to his Chamberlain, Bou Ahmed.

Orders were given that the Sultan would start on his journey at dawn, and before daylight the State palanquin was carried into the Imperial enclosure, the corpse laid within it, and its doors closed and the curtains drawn. At the first pale break of dawn the palanquin was brought out, supported by sturdy mules. Bugles were blown, the band played, and the bowing courtiers and officials poured forth their stentorian cry, "May God protect the life of our Lord". The procession formed up, and, led by flying banners, the dead Sultan set out on his march.

A great distance was covered that day. Only once did the procession stop, when the palanquin was carried into a tent by the roadside, that the Sultan might breakfast. Food was borne in and out; tea, with all the paraphernalia of its brewing, was served: but none but the slaves who knew the secret were permitted to enter. The Chamberlain remained with the corpse, and when a certain time had passed, he emerged to state that His Majesty was rested and had breakfasted, and would proceed on his journey – and once more the procession moved on. Another long march was made to where the great camp was pitched for the night.

The Sultan was tired, the Chamberlain said. He would not come out of his enclosure to transact business as usual in the "Diwan" tent, where he granted audiences. Documents were taken in to the royal quarters by the Chamberlain himself, and, when necessary, they emerged bearing the seal of State, and verbal replies were given to a host of questions.

Then another day of forced marches, for the expedition was still in dangerous country; but Mulai Hassen's death could no longer be concealed. It was summer, and the state of the Sultan's body told its own secret.

Bou Ahmed announced that His Majesty had died two days before, and that by this time his young son, Mulai Abdul Aziz, chosen and nominated by his father, had been proclaimed at Rabat, whither the fleetest of runners had been sent with the news immediately after the death had occurred.

It was a *fait accompli*. The army was now free of the danger of being attacked by the tribes; and the knowledge that the new Sultan was already reigning, and that tranquillity existed elsewhere, deterred the troops from any excesses. Many took the occasion of a certain disorganisation to desert, but so customary was this practice that it attracted little or no attention.

Two days later the body of the dead Sultan, now in a terrible state of decomposition, arrived at Rabat. It must have been a gruesome procession from the description his son Mulai Abdul Aziz gave me: the hurried arrival of the swaying palanquin bearing its terrible burden, five days

dead in the great heat of summer; the escort, who had bound scarves over their faces – but even this precaution could not keep them from constant sickness – and even the mules that bore the palanquin seemed affected by the horrible atmosphere, and tried from time to time to break loose.

No corpse is, by tradition, allowed to enter through the gates into a Moorish city, and even in the case of the Sovereign no exception was made. A hole was excavated in the town wall, through which the procession passed direct into the precincts of the palace, where the burial took place. Immediately after, the wall was restored.

From *Morocco That Was,* by Walter Harris (1921). Reprinted in a paperback edition by Eland Books, London.

ELIAS CANETTI: *THE UNSEEN*

At twilight I went to the great square in the middle of the city, and what I sought there were not its colour and bustle, those I was familiar with, I sought a small, brown bundle on the ground consisting not even of a voice but of a single sound. This was a deep, long-drawn-out, buzzing "e-e-e-e-e-e-e-e". It did not diminish, it did not increase, it just went on and on; beneath all the thousands of calls and cries in the square it was always audible. It was the most unchanging sound in the Djemaa el Fna, remaining the same all evening and from evening to evening.

While still a long way off I was already listening for it. A restlessness drove me there that I cannot satisfactorily explain. I would have gone to the square in any case, there was so much there to attract me; nor did I ever doubt I would find it each time, with all that went with it. Only for this voice, reduced to a single sound, did I feel something akin to fear. It was at the very edge of the living; the life that engendered it consisted of nothing but that sound. Listening greedily, anxiously, I invariably reached a point in my walk, in exactly the same place, where I suddenly

became aware of it like the buzzing of an insect: "e-e-e-e-e-e-e-e".

I felt a mysterious calm spread through my body, and whereas my steps had been hesitant and uncertain hitherto I now, all of a sudden, made determinedly for the sound. I knew where it came from. I knew the small, brown bundle on the ground, of which I had never seen anything more than a piece of dark, coarse cloth. I had never seen the mouth from which the "e-e-e-e-e" issued; nor the eye; nor the cheek; nor any part of the face. I could not have said whether it was the face of a blind man or whether it could see. The brown, soiled cloth was pulled right down over the head like a hood, concealing everything. The creature – as it must have been – squatted on the ground, its back arched under the material. There was not much of the creature there, it seemed slight and feeble, that was all one could conjecture. I had no idea how tall it was because I had never seen it standing. What there was of it on the ground kept so low that one would have stumbled over it quite unsuspectingly, had the sound ever stopped. I never saw it come, I never saw it go; I do not know whether it was brought and put down there or whether it walked there by itself.

The place it had chosen was by no means sheltered. It was the most open part of the square and there was an incessant coming and going on all sides of the little brown heap. On busy evenings it disappeared completely behind people's legs, and although I knew exactly where it was and could always hear the voice I had difficulty in finding it. But then the people dispersed, and it was still in its place when all around it, far and wide, the square was empty. Then it lay there in the darkness like an old and very dirty garment that someone had wanted to get rid of and had surreptitiously dropped in the midst of all the people where no one would notice. Now, however, the people had dispersed and only the bundle lay there. I never waited until it got up or was fetched. I slunk away in the darkness with a choking feeling of helplessness and pride.

The helplessness was in regard to myself. I sensed that I would never do anything to discover the bundle's secret. I had a dread of its shape; and since I could give it no other I left it lying there on the ground. When I was getting close I took care not to bump into it, as if I might hurt or endanger it. It was there every evening, and every evening my heart stood still when I first distinguished the sound, and it stood still again when I caught sight of the bundle. How it got there and how it got away again were matters more sacred to me than my own movements. I never spied on it and I do not know where it disappeared to for the rest of the night and the following day. It was something apart, and perhaps it saw itself as such. I was sometimes tempted to touch the brown hood very lightly with one finger – the creature was bound to notice, and perhaps it had a second sound with which it would have responded. But this temptation always succumbed swiftly to my helplessness.

I have said that another feeling choked me as I slunk away: pride. I was proud of the bundle because it was alive. What it thought to itself as it breathed down there, far below other people, I shall never know. The meaning of its call remained as obscure to me as its whole existence: but it was alive, and every day at the same time, there it was. I never saw it pick up the coins that people threw it; they did not throw many, there were never more than two or three coins lying there. Perhaps it had no arms with which to reach for the coins. Perhaps it had no tongue with which to form the "l" of "Allah" and to it the name of God was abbreviated to "e-e-e-e-e". But it was alive, and with a diligence and persistence that were unparalleled it uttered its one sound, uttered it hour after hour, until it was the only sound in the whole enormous square, the sound that outlived all others.

From *The Voices of Marrakesh*, by Elias Canetti (Marion Boyars, London, 1978); first published in German in 1967.

PAUL BOWLES: POINTS IN TIME, X

The country of the Anjra is almost devoid of paved roads. It is a region of high jagged mountains and wooded valleys, and does not contain a town of any size. During the rainy season there are landslides. Then, until the government sends men to repair the damage, the roads cannot be used. All this is very much on the minds of the people who live in the Anjra, particularly when they are waiting for the highways to be rebuilt so that lorries can move again between the villages. Four or five soldiers had been sent several months earlier to repair the potholes along the road between Ksar es Seghir and Melloussa. Their tent was beside the road, near a curve in the river.

A peasant named Hattash, whose village lay a few miles up the valley, constantly passed by the place on his way to and from Ksar es Seghir. Hattash had no fixed work of any sort, but he kept very busy looking for a chance to pick up a little money one way or another in the market and the cafés. He was the kind of man who prided himself on his cleverness in swindling foreigners, by which he meant men from outside the Anjra. Since his friends shared his dislike of outsiders, they found his exploits amusing, although they were careful to have no dealings with him.

Over the months Hattash had become friendly with the soldiers living in the tent, often stopping to smoke a pipe of kif with them, perhaps squatting down to play a few games of ronda. Thus, when one day the soldiers decided to give a party, it was natural that they should mention it to Hattash, who knew everyone for miles around, and therefore might be able to help them. The soldiers came from the south, and their isolation there by the river kept them from meeting anyone who did not regularly pass their tent.

I can get you whatever you want, Hattash told them. The hens, the vegetables, oil, spices, salad, whatever.

Fine. And we want some girls or boys, they added.

Don't worry about that. You'll have plenty to choose from. What you don't want you can send back.

They discussed the cost of the party for an hour or so, after which the soldiers handed Hattash twenty-five thousand francs. He set off, ostensibly for the market.

Instead of going there, he went to the house of a nearby farmer and bought five of his best hens, with the understanding that if the person for whom he was buying them should not want them, he could return the hens and get his money back.

Soon Hattash was outside the soldiers' tent with the hens. How are they? he said. The men squeezed them and examined them, and pronounced them excellent. Good, said Hattash. I'll take them home now and cook them.

He went back to the farmer with the hens and told him that the buyer had refused them. The farmer shrugged and gave Hattash his money.

This seemed to be the moment to leave Ksar es Seghir, Hattash decided. He stopped at a café and invited everyone there to the soldiers' tent that evening, telling them there would be food, wine and girls. Then he bought bread, cheese and fruit, and began to walk along the trails that would lead him over the mountains to Khemiss dl Anjra.

With the twenty-five thousand francs he was able to live for several weeks there in Khemmiss el Anjra. When he had come to the end of them, he began to think of leaving.

In the market one morning he met Hadj Abdallah, a rich farmer from Farsioua, which was a village only a few miles from his own. Hadj Abdallah, a burly, truculent man, always had eyed Hattash with distrust.

Ah, Hattash! What are you doing up here? It's a while since I've seen you.

And you? said Hattash.

Me? I'm on my way to Tetuan. I'm leaving my mule here and taking the bus.

That's where I'm going, said Hattash.

Well, see you in Tetuan, said Hadj Abdallah, and he turned, unhitched his mule, and rode off.

Khemiss dl Anjra is a very small town, so that it was not difficult for Hattash to follow along at some distance, and see the house where Hadj Abdallah tethered his mule and into which he then disappeared. He walked to the bus station and sat under a tree.

An hour or so later, when the bus was filling up with people, Hadj Abdallah arrived and bought his ticket. Hattash approached him.

Can you lend me a thousand francs? I haven't got enough to buy the ticket.

Hadj Abdallah looked at him. No. I can't, he said. Why don't you stay here? And he went and got into the bus.

Hattash, his eyes very narrow, sat down again under the tree. When the bus had left, and the cloud of smoke and dust had drifted off over the meadows, he walked back to the house where the Hadj had left his mule. She still stood there, so he quietly unhitched her, got astride her, and rode her in the direction of Mgas Tleta. He was still smarting under Hadj Abdallah's insult, and he vowed to give him as much trouble as he could.

Mgas Tleta was a small tchar. He took the mule to the fondaq and left it in charge of the guardian. Being ravenously hungry, he searched in his clothing for a coin or two to buy a piece of bread, and found nothing.

In the road outside the fondaq he caught sight of a peasant carrying a loaf in the hood of his djellaba. Unable to take his eyes from the bread, he walked towards the man and greeted him. Then he asked him if he had work, and was not surprised when the man answered no. He went on, still looking at the bread: If you want to earn a thousand francs, you can take my mule to Mdiq. My father's waiting for her and he'll pay you. Just ask for Si Mohammed Tsuli. Everybody in Mdiq knows him. He always has a lot of men working for him. He'll give you work there too if you want it.

The peasant's eyes lit up. He agreed immediately.

Hattash sighed. It's a long time since I've seen good country bread like that, he said, pointing at the loaf that emerged from the hood of the djellaba. The man took it out and handed it to him. Here. Take it.

In return Hattash presented him with the receipt for the mule. You'll have to pay a hundred francs to get her out of the fondaq, he told him. My father will give it back to you.

That's all right. The man was eager to start out for Mdiq.

Si Mohammed Tsuli. Don't forget.

No, no! Bslemah.

Hattash, well satisfied, watched the man ride off. Then he sat down on a rock and ate the whole loaf of bread. He had no intention of returning home to risk meeting the soldiers or Hadj Abdallah, so he decided to hide himself for a while in Tetuan, where he had friends.

When the peasant arrived at Mdiq the following day, he found that no one could tell him where Si Mohammed Tsuli lived. He wandered back and forth through every street in the town, searching and enquiring. When evening came, he went to the gendarmerie and asked if he might leave the mule there. But they questioned him and accused him of having stolen the animal. His story was ridiculous, they said, and they locked him into a cell.

Not many days later Hadj Abdallah, having finished his business in Tetuan, went back to Khemiss dl Anjra to get his mule and ride her home. When he heard that she had disappeared directly after he had taken the bus, he remembered Hattash, and was certain that he was the culprit. The theft had to be reported in Tetuan, and much against his will he returned there.

Your mule is in Mdiq, the police told him.

Hadj Abdallah took another bus up to Mdiq.

Papers, said the gendarmes. Proof of ownership.

The Hadj had no documents of that sort. They told him to go to Tetouan and apply for the forms.

During the days while he waited for the papers to be drawn up, signed and stamped, Hadj Abdallah grew constantly angrier. He went twice a day to talk with the police. I know who took her! he would shout. I know the son of a whore.

If you ever catch sight of him, hold on to him, they told him. We'll take care of him.

Although Tetuan is a big place with many crowded quarters, the unlikely occurred. In a narrow passageway near the Souq el Fouqi late one evening Hadj Abdallah and Hattash came face to face.

The surprise was so great that Hattash remained frozen to the spot, merely staring into Hadj Abdallah's eyes. Then he heard a grunt of rage, and felt himself seized by the other man's strong arm.

Police! Police! roared Hadj Abdallah. Hattash squirmed, but was unable to free himself.

One policeman arrived, and then another. Hadj Abdallah did not release his grip of Hattash for an instant while he delivered his denunciation. Then with an oath he struck his prisoner, knocking him flat on the sidewalk. Hattash lay there in the dark without moving.

Why did you do that? the policemen cried. Now you're the one who's going to be in trouble.

Hadj Abdallah was already frightened. I know. I ought not to have hit him.

It's very bad, said one policeman, bending over Hattash, who lay completely still. You see, there's blood coming out of his head.

A small crowd was collecting in the passageway.

There were only a few drops of blood, but the policeman had seen Hattash open one eye and had heard him whisper: Listen.

He bent over still further, so that his ear was close to Hattash's lips.

He's got money, Hattash whispered.

The policeman rose and went over to Hadj Abdallah. We'll have to call an ambulance, he said, and you'll have to come to the police station. You had no right to hit him.

At that moment Hattash began to groan.

He's alive, at least! cried Hadj Abdallah. Hamdul'lah!

Then the policemen began to speak with him in low tones, advising him to settle the affair immediately by paying cash to the injured man.

Hadj Abdallah was willing. How much do you think? he whispered.

It's a bad cut he has on his head, the same policeman said, going back to Hattash. Come and look.

Hadj Abdallah remained where he was, and Hattash groaned as the man bent over him again. Then he murmured: Twenty thousand. Five for each of you.

When the policeman rejoined Hadj Abdallah, he told him the amount. You're lucky to be out of it.

Hadj Abdallah gave the money to the policeman, who took it over to Hattash and prodded him. Can you hear me? he shouted.

Ouakha, groaned Hattash.

Here. Take this. He held out the banknotes in such a way that Hadj Abdallah and the crowd watching could see them clearly. Hattash stretched up his hand and took them, slipping them into his pocket.

Hadj Abdallah glared at the crowd and pushed his way through, eager to get away from the spot.

After he had gone, Hattash slowly sat up and rubbed his head. The onlookers still stood there watching. This bothered the two policemen, who were intent on getting their share of the money. The recent disclosures of corruption, however, had made the public all too attentive at such moments. The crowd was waiting to see them speak to Hattash or, if he should move, follow him.

Hattash saw the situation and understood. He rose to his feet and quickly walked up the alley.

The policemen looked at each other, waited for a few seconds, and then began to saunter casually in the same direction. Once they were out of sight of the group of onlookers they hurried along, flashing their lights up each alley in their search. But Hattash knew the quarter as well as they, and got safely to the house of his friends.

He decided, however, that with the two policemen on the lookout for him, Tetuan was no longer the right place for him, and that his own tchar in the Anjra would be preferable.

Once he was back there, he made discreet enquiries about the state of the road to Ksar es Seghir. The repairs were finished, his neighbours told him, and the soldiers had been sent to some other part of the country.

From *Points in Time*, by Paul Bowles (Peter Owen, London, 1982).

ONWARD FROM MOROCCO

Going on overland from Morocco there are two basic options. The most obvious is to take in something of **Spain** and, if you've developed any interest in Moorish art, to visit the three great Andalusian cities of the south – **Granada**, **Córdoba** and **Sevilla**. Each of these boast superb Islamic monuments, which, to be honest, are more spectacular than any in Morocco. Granada has the fabulous fifteenth-century Alhambra palace, home of the last Moorish rulers in al-Andalus; Córdoba has a tenth-century mosque, now the city's cathedral; and Seville has one of Yacoub el Mansour's magnificent Almohad towers, again adapted to Christian use as the local bell tower, or Giralda. For all of this – and a great deal more – *The Rough Guide to Spain* (Rough Guides/Penguin, £8.99) has the requisite details.

The second option, and one that is considerably more ambitious, is to travel "**the Maghreb Circuit**" east from Morocco into **Algeria** and **Tunisia**, where, if you still have the time and energy, you could cross over by ferry to Italy and either loop back to northern Europe (Italian trains are cheap) or take another ferry on from Bari or Brindisi to Greece. Don't be put off by the distances involved in any of this, nor by travellers' tales of Algerian bureaucracy at the border (though these are true enough); it's an exciting, feasible and immensely satisfying trip, and there's an added fascination in that all of this region – from Spain and Morocco up as far as Sicily – comprised the western Arab empire in the early Middle Ages.

Mosques, incidentally, may be visited freely in Algeria and, to an extent, in Tunisia.

ALGERIA

Algeria is much less well known in the West than either Morocco or Tunisia and it has always been the most adventurous part of North Africa to travel through. This it remains – above all in its mind-boggling desert routes.

Algerians themselves are extremely hospitable, and there is none of the hustling that you find in Morocco. If you can speak French, you will be able to communicate with ease – the language of colonial years (150 years here, as opposed to just 50 in Morocco) endures, along with many facets of French culture. Indeed, all European travellers are initially assumed to be French. It tends to be an advantage if you can make it clear that you're not.

Red Tape

Visas are essential for all Europeans (except Scandinavians, Spanish and Swiss) and for North Americans and Australasians. Technically, they should be obtained in your home country – a good idea if you are organised – although it is usually possible to obtain one, within the day, at the Algerian consulate in Rabat (see Rabat "Listings"), or (a much longer process) in Oujda.

While in Algeria you are required to change 1000 dinars (about £70) into Algerian currency at the official rate; you may be asked to do so at the border. This restriction is no longer waived for students, and money cannot be changed back again. The black market is widely used, and if you're staying longer than your officially changed 1000 dinars will last, you will find rates offered up to three times better. The best currency for black market exchange is French francs. However, beware of losing track of what you've declared on your C.D. form and what you have in your pocket.

Borders

There are two **borders** open between Morocco and Algeria – at OUJDA and, 300km to the south, at the desert oasis of FIGUIG. The former used to be closed to "pedestrian traffic" but it is now routinely open, following the improvement in Moroccan–Algerian relations after the 1988 Maghreb Summit.

Routes

The fastest route through Algeria cuts across the big **northern cities** of ORAN, ALGIERS and CONSTANTINE. This is not in itself the most interesting part of the country, though the mountain scenery is often spectacular.

Making relatively short detours the rewards are greater. TIMGAD, almost completely preserved, is one of the most extraordinary Roman towns anywhere; any one of the roads between BATNA and the immense oasis of BISKRA will take you through dramatic canyons; the TURQUOISE COAST, west of Algiers, is a long series of mountainous and isolated coves; and in the mountains by the Moroccan border,

TLEMCEN's Islamic architecture is among the most important and beautiful in North Africa.

If you have time to spare, though, even as little as a week, try to take in at least something of **the south**. The sheer size of the desert regions here is hard to grasp: TAMANRASSET, near the Niger border, for instance, is further from Algiers than London is. Closer, and easily accessible from the north, there are also some of the most spectacular Saharan dunes – stretching between EL OUED, the so-called "City of a Thousand Domes", and the fantastic architecture of GHARDAIA.

Going through the deep south really does feel more like travel than tourism and time and energy are needed to explore the desert pistes. The two really compelling attractions are both mountain ranges: the HOGGAR, rising over 3000m to the north of Tamanrasset, and the TASSILI, some way to the east, with its exceptional prehistoric cave paintings.

Guidebooks

The trip across the Algerian Sahara to West Africa is covered in detail in the *Rough Guide to West Africa* (Rough Guides/Penguin, £12.99). Simon and Jan Glen's *Sahara Handbook* (Lascelles, UK) is also useful for the practicalities of taking a car across the desert. The only guides to Algeria are in French: try a combination of the *Guide Bleu: Algerie* and, for budget practicalities, the *Guide du Routard: Algerie-Tunisie* (both published by Hachette, Paris).

TUNISIA

Crossing from Algeria to Tunisia is normally straightforward, though the number of border posts open varies according to the state of relations between the two countries (which are currently good). The most regular posts are in the north at ANNABA-BABOUCH and SOUK AHRAS-GHARDIMAO (the train crossing), but at the time of this writing you can cross in the south, too, at EL OUED-HAZOUA.

Much more Westernised than either Morocco or Algeria, Tunisia is recognisably Mediterranean in character and a relaxed place to end up after some desert travelling. Its best-known attractions are the long white-sand **beaches** and easy-going resorts, and in a North African context these are perhaps its greatest novelty. But there is considerably more to the country than this – not least its highly individual **desert architecture**, and the Maghreb's most important **Roman sites** – and the accessibility of everything (you can comfortably travel its length in a couple of days) makes it a satisfying place to visit and get to know.

Red Tape

North Americans, Australasians and Benelux nationals need a **visa** to visit Tunisia. This can be obtained in a couple of hours from the Tunisian Consulate in Rabat (see Rabat "Listings"). Other Europeans need no visa.

On to Sicily or beyond

Continuing on from Tunisia, there are regular, year-round **ferries** to the Sicilian ports of PALERMO and TRAPANI, and links from there to Naples, Genoa, Sardinia and Malta. Apart from the last two weeks of August (when all ferries from Tunis are packed with returning migrant workers) it is usually possible to get tickets on these; if you have a car, however, it's essential to make your bookings in advance for travel between July and September.

Guidebook

For a full treatment of the country, *The Rough Guide to Tunisia* (Rough Guides/Penguin, £8.99) seems an obvious choice.

THE CANARY ISLANDS

A last alternative, onward from Morocco, is to head for the **CANARY ISLANDS**, just a few miles offshore from the disputed territory of the former Spanish Sahara. There is a weekly car and passenger ferry from Agadir to Las Palmas (see Agadir "Practicalities") between September and May. Alternatively, you can fly to Las Palmas from Agadir or Laayoune.

BOOKS

Publishers detailed below are in the form "UK Publisher/US Publisher" where two editions exist. Where books are published in one country only, this follows the publisher's name. O/p signifies an out-of-print, but still highly recommended, book. University Press is abbreviated as UP.

The *Maghreb Bookshop*, 45 Burton St, London WC1, UK (☎071/388 1840) supplies new, rare and out-of-print books on all aspects of North Africa, both to callers and by worldwide mail order.

GENERAL/TRAVEL

Margaret and Robin Bidwell (eds), *Morocco: The Traveller's Companion* (IB Tauris, UK). This fills a much-needed slot, with excerpts from key writers of the past five centuries, including many translated by the editors from the French.

Paul Bowles, *Points in Time* (Peter Owen, UK), *Their Heads Are Green* (Abacus/Ecco Press). Novelist, poet and composer Paul Bowles has lived in Tangier most of his life and more or less singlehandedly brought translations of local writers (see "Moroccan Fictions" on pp.527–35) to Western attention. *Points* is a remarkable series of tales and short pieces inspired by episodes and sources from earliest times to the present day; the final piece is excerpted in the "Writers on Morocco" section. *Heads* includes a couple of travel essays on Morocco and a terrific piece on the psychology of desert travel.

Peter Mayne, *A Year in Marrakesh* (Eland Books/Hippocrene Books). Mayne went to Marrakesh in the early 1950s, found a house in an ordinary district of the Medina, and tried to live like a Moroccan. He couldn't, but wrote an unusually perceptive account explaining why.

Elias Canetti, *The Voices of Marrakesh* (Marion Boyars/Farrar Straus and Giroux). Impressions of Marrakesh in the last years of French rule, by the Nobel prize-winning author. The atmosphere of many pieces still holds – see the excerpt printed under "Writers on Morocco".

OLDER ACCOUNTS

Walter Harris, *Morocco That Was* (1921; reprinted by Eland Books/Greenwood). Harris, *Times* correspondent in Tangier from the 1890s until his death in 1933, saw the country at probably the strangest ever stage in its history – the last years of "Old Morocco" in its feudal isolation and the first of French occupation. *Morocco That Was* is a masterpiece – alternately sharp, melodramatic and very funny. It incorporates, to some extent, the anecdotes in his earlier *Land of an African Sultan* (1889, o/p) and *Tafilet* (1895, o/p).

John Drummond Hay, *Western Barbary: its Wild Tribes and Savage Animals* (1846, o/p). The account is more sympathetic (and less wild) than the title suggests: a fine narrative of a journey from Tangier to Larache, during which Hay (the future British Consul in Tangier) is told fabulous tales of local life.

Edmondo de Amicis, *Morocco: Its People and Places* (1882, reprinted by Darf Publishers, London). More intrepid journeying in the Harris mould – illustrated with copious line drawings.

Budgett Meakin, *The Land of the Moors* (1900; reprinted by Darf/State Mutual Book), *The Moors: A Comprehensive Description* (1902, o/p). These wonderful encyclopaedic volumes were the first really detailed books on Morocco and Moroccan life. Many of Meakin's "Comprehensive Descriptions" remain accurate and the sheer breadth of his knowledge – from "Berber Feuds" to "Specimen Recipes" and musical notations of "Calls to Prayer" – is fascinating in itself. Highly recommended library browsing.

Leo Africanus, *History and Description of Africa* (no recent edition but available in major libraries). Written in the mid-sixteenth century, this was the book Meakin himself followed, "astounded at the confirmation [of its accuracy] received from natives of remote and almost inaccessible districts". Leo, who was Moroccan by birth, was captured as a young man by Christian pirates. He subsequently converted and lived in Italy; the book was suggested to him by the Pope, and so there's more than a hint of propaganda about his accounts. (See also Amin Maalouf, under "Fiction".)

OF LESSER INTEREST

R. B. Cunninghame Graham, *Mogreb-el-Acksa: A Journey in Morocco* (1898; reprinted by Marlboro Press, US). And yet more adventuring and anecdotes, most interesting of which is an enforced stay in a caidal Kasbah in the High Atlas (his host did not understand the motive of "curiosity"). The prose, however, is flat.

Wyndham Lewis, *Journey into Barbary* (1932; reprinted by Black Sparrow Press, US). Terrific drawings and an obscure, eccentric and very rambling text.

Edith Wharton, *In Morocco* (1920; reprinted by Century/David & Charles). Wharton dedicated her book to General Lyautey, Consul General of the Protectorate, whose modernising efforts she greatly admired. By no means a classic, it is nonetheless worth reading for glimpses of harem life in the early part of the century.

Nina Epton, *Saints and Sorcerers* (1958, o/p). Highly readable travelogue, concentrating on folk customs and religious sects and confraternities.

Rom Landau, *Morocco: Marrakesh, Fez, Rabat* (1967, o/p). Landau has written numerous books on Morocco, none of them very inspiring. This one's redeeming feature is an excellent series of photographs – including rare pictures of mosque interiors.

Antoine de Saint-Exupéry, *Wind, Sand and Stars* and *Southern Mail* (various editions, some with Flight to Arras and/or Night Flight). Accounts by the French aviator of his postal flights down to West Africa, by way of Cap Juby in the then-Spanish Sahara.

Sylvia Kennedy, *See Ouarzazate and Die* (Abacus/Scribners). An account of visits to Morocco in 1990–91, both before and during the Gulf War. The narrative is hyperbolic and highly critical – Moroccan officials would not be impressed to find the book in your luggage – but it has some good observations nonetheless.

HISTORY

Neville Barbour, *Morocco* (Thames & Hudson/Walker, o/p). A lucid, straightforward account of Morocco from the Phoenicians to "the present day" (1965).

Susan Raven, *Rome in Africa* (Routledge, UK/US). A new and well-illustrated survey of Roman (and Carthaginian) North Africa.

Roger Le Tourneau, *Fez in the Age of the Marinides* (University of Oklahoma Press, US). Interesting if slightly specialist study of the Merenid capital of Morocco. Tourneau's *The Almohad Movement* (Princeton University Press, 1981, o/p) is also extremely good.

Douglas Porch, *The Conquest of Morocco* (Macmillan/Fromm International). Accessible and fascinating account of the extraordinary manoeuvrings and characters of Morocco's turn-of-the-century history.

David Woolman, *Rebels in the Rif* (Stanford University Press, US). Academic but very readable study of the Riffian war in the 1920s and of the tribes' uprising against the Moroccan government in 1956.

Gavin Maxwell, *Lords of the Atlas* (1966, reprinted by Century/David & Charles). Drawing heavily on Walter Harris' accounts of the Moorish court (see above), this is the story of the Glaoui family – literally the "Lords" of the High Atlas, where they exercised almost complete control from the turn of the nineteenth century right through to Moroccan independence in 1956. Not an attractive tale but a compelling one, and superbly told.

Tony Hodges, *Western Sahara: the Roots of a Desert War* (Croom Helm/Chicago Review). The former Spanish colony of Western Sahara-Rio d'Oro is the most contentious issue of modern Moroccan politics: this is the latest, fullest and most interesting book on the subject.

NORTH AFRICA/ARAB WORLD

J.M Abun-Nasr, *History of the Maghreb in the Islamic Period* (Cambridge UP, UK/US). Morocco in the wider context of North Africa by a distinguished Arab historian.

Peter Mansfield, *The Arabs* (Penguin, UK/US). General introduction to the Arab world, from its beginnings through to the 1970s. Short final sections deal with each individual country.

R. Oliver and J. D. Fage, *A History of Africa* (Penguin, UK/US). Morocco within the context of its continent.

ANTHROPOLOGY

Fatima Mernissi, *Beyond the Veil: Male–Female Dynamics in Modern Muslim Society* (Al Saqi Books/Indiana UP). Seminal book by a feminist Moroccan sociologist from the Mohammed V University in Rabat.

Fatima Mernissi, *Doing Daily Battle: Interviews with Moroccan Women* (The Women's Press/Rutgers UP). Eleven women – carpet weavers, rural and factory workers, teachers – talk about all aspects of their lives, from work and housing to marriage. A fascinating insight into a resolutely private world.

Elizabeth Fernea, *A Street in Marrakesh* (Doubleday, US, o/p). Highly readable account of a woman anthropologist's period of study and experiences in Marrakesh.

Elizabeth Fernea and Basima Q. Bezirgan, *Middle Eastern Muslim Women Speak Out* (University of Texas Press, US). Straightforward and accessible social anthropology, including interesting transcriptions of Berber women's songs from the High Atlas.

Ernest Gellner and Charles Micaud (eds), *Arabs and Berbers* (Duckworth/Lexington Press, 1973, o/p). Authoritative collection of anthropological articles on Berbers and tribalism in Morocco. Interesting, if read on a rather selective basis.

Ernest Gellner, *Saints of the Atlas* (University of Chicago Press, US). The bulk of this book is an in-depth study of a group of *zaouia*-villages in the High Atlas, but there are excellent introductory chapters on Morocco's recent past and the concept and origins of Berbers.

Kevin Dwyer, *Moroccan Dialogues: Anthropology in Question* (Waveland Press, US). Fascinating series of recorded conversations with a farmer from a village near Taroudannt, ranging through attitudes to women, religion and village life to popular Moroccan perceptions of the Jews, the French and even the hippies. Well worth a look.

Vincent Crapanzano, *Tuhami: Portrait of a Moroccan* (University of Chicago Press, US). Tuhami is an illiterate Moroccan tilemaker in Meknes: this study is an interesting, if at times slightly impenetrable, mix of ethnography and psychology.

David Seddon, *Moroccan Peasants: A Century of Change in the Eastern Rif* (William Dawson, UK). Covers similar ground to David Woolman (see "History"), though with a more strictly anthropological approach.

Bernard Lewis, *The Jews of Islam* (Routledge/Princeton UP). Morocco had over 30,000 Jews until the mass emigrations to Israel in the 1940s and 1950s. Lewis discusses their position (which was perhaps the most oppressed within the Arab world) and their political and cultural contributions. Disappointingly, he doesn't attempt to cover the period of emigration itself.

Shlomo Deshen, *The Mellah Society: Jewish Community Life in Sherifian Morocco* (University of Chicago Press, US). Academic study of economic activity and political organisation in the Mellahs prior to the Protectorate.

Edward Westermarck, *Ritual and Belief in Morocco* (1926); *Wit and Wisdom in Morocco* (1930). *Ritual* is a seminal work on Morocco and remains a fascinating storehouse of social and anthropological detail. *Wit* is entirely a collection of Moroccan proverbs. Both are well worth the effort to track down in libraries.

ISLAM

The Koran (numerous editions). The Word of God as handed down to the Prophet is the basis of all Islam, so essential reading for anyone interested. The Oxford UP edition is the clearest and liveliest translation.

S. H. Nasr, *Ideas and Realities of Islam* (Collins, UK/US). Probably the clearest and most useful general introduction.

Maxime Rodinson, *Muhammad* (Penguin/Pantheon). Challenging account of the Prophet's life and the immediate impact of his ideology.

ART/ARCHITECTURE

Richard Parker, *A Practical Guide to Islamic Monuments in Morocco* (Baraka Press, Charlottesville, Virginia, US). Exactly what it claims to be – very helpful and well informed, with introductory sections on architectural forms and motifs, and craft traditions. Available at the *American Bookstore* in Rabat.

Titus Burckhardt, *Fes: City of Islam* (Islamic Texts Society, UK); *Moorish Culture in Spain* (o/p). Burckhardt's *Spain* is a superb study of architecture, history, Islamic city-design and the mystical significance of its art – and as such it's entirely relevant to medieval Morocco. *Fes* is worth dipping into, if only for the photos, as the conceptual approach and respect for tradition can be a bit hard going.

Lisl and Landt Dennis, *Living in Morocco* (Thames & Hudson, UK/US). Fabulous picture studies of Moroccan craft and domestic design, both traditional and modern.

Matisse in Morocco (Thames & Hudson, UK/US). A gorgeous book of the paintings and drawings from the artist's stay in 1912–13.

David Talbot Rice, *Islamic Art* (Thames & Hudson, UK/US). Clear, interesting and well-illustrated survey – though only two chapters directly concern Morocco.

Michael Brett, *The Moors* (Orbis, o/p). A fine illustrated survey of the Moorish Empire, well thought out and with an understanding text.

Andre Paccard, *Traditional Islamic Craft in Moroccan Architecture* (Éditions Atelier, France, 2 vols). French coffee-table tome beyond all possible rival. The text is poor, but it is massively illustrated and – uniquely – includes photographs of Moroccan Royal Palaces currently in use.

Jean Besanceon, *Costumes of Morocco* (KPI, UK). Lavish prints, drawn in the 1930s and 1940s when they were still current. Most are now museum pieces.

Salma Damluji, *Zillij: the Art of Moroccan Ceramics* (Garnet, UK). An expensive but beautifully illustrated study.

In addition, a number of large, glossy books on Moroccan jewellery, gardens, paintings, manuscripts, carpets, buildings, etc, usually with French texts, are to be found in most of the larger bookshops in Morocco.

FOOD

Robert Carrier, *Taste of Morocco* (Arrow, UK); **Paula Wolfert**, *Good Food from Morocco* (John Murray, UK). Mouthwatering recipes from the largely domestic canon of Moroccan food. Wolfert's book, originally published in the 1960s, has a more rural emphasis than Carrier's tour of the grand kitchens.

PHOTOGRAPHS

Alan Keohane, *Berbers of the Atlas* (Hamish Hamilton, UK). A marvellous collection of colour photos of daily life in the Atlas.

Owen Logan, *Al Maghrib: Photographs from Morocco* (Polygon, UK). Superb black and white portraits in a beautifully produced monograph.

Shirley Kay, *Morocco* (Quartet, 1984, o/p). Glossy and well-written picture book introduction to the country.

MOROCCAN FICTION

TRANSLATIONS BY PAUL BOWLES

Mohammed Mrabet, *Love with a Few Hairs* (City Lights, US); *The Boy Who Set the Fire & Other Stories* (City Lights, US); *The Lemon* (Peter Owen/City Lights); *M'Hashish* (City Lights, US); *The Chest* (Tombouctou, US); *Marriage With Papers* (Tombouctou, US); *The Big Mirror* (Black Sparrow Press, US); *Harmless Poisons, Blameless Sins* (Black Sparrow Press, US); *The Beach Café and The Voice* (Black Sparrow Press, US); *Look and Move On: An Autobiography* (Peter Owen/Black Sparrow Press).

Mohammed Choukri, *For Bread Alone: An Autobiography* (City Lights, US). Choukri is also author of two brief anecdotal biographies – *Jean Genet in Tangier* (Ecco Press, US) and *Tennessee Williams in Tangier* (Cadmus Editions, US, o/p), also translated by Bowles.

Larbi Layachi, *A Life Full of Holes* (published under the name Driss ben Hamed Charhadi; Grove Press, US). See also "Other Moroccan Fiction", below.

Five Eyes, stories by **Mohammed Mrabet**, **Larbi Layachi**, **Mohammed Choukri**, **Ahmed Yacoubi** and **Abdesiam Boulaich** (Black Sparrow Press, US, o/p).

All of the above are taped and translated from the Maghrebi by **Paul Bowles**. It's hard to generalise about them, except to say that they are mostly "tales" (even the autobiographies, which seem little different from the fiction), share a common fixation with intrigue and unexpected narrative twists, and are often punctuated by episodes of violence. None have particular characterisation, though this hardly seems relevant as they have such a strong, vigorous narrative style – brilliantly matched by Bowles's sharp, economic language.

The **Mrabet** stories – *The Beach Cafe* is perhaps his best – are often *kif*-inspired, and this gives them a slightly paranoid quality, as Mrabet himself explained: "Give me twenty or thirty pipes . . . and an empty room can fill up with wonderful things, or terrible things. And the stories come from these things."

For a taste of the stories, see "Moroccan Fictions" on p.527–35.

OTHER MOROCCAN FICTION

Tahar Ben Jelloun, *The Sand Child* (Quartet/Harcourt Brace). Ben Jelloun, resident in Paris, is Morocco's most acclaimed writer – and in the case of this novel, which won the French Prix Goncourt, the reputation is just. An unusually "fictional" tale, its subject, the Sand Child, is a girl whose father brought her up as a boy. Two other novels by Ben Jelloun are available: *Sacred Night* ((Quartet/Harcourt Brace) and *With Downcast Eyes* (Little, Brown, US).

Anouar Majid, *Si Yussef* (Quarter, UK). An interesting if somewhat tortuous narrative: the author writes as Lamin, a student in Fes, who presents the life story of an old man, born in Tangier in 1908, and his tales of the city.

Larbi Layachi, *Yesterday and Today* (Black Sparrow Press, US), *The Jealous Lover* (Tombouctou, US). The former is a kind of sequel to *Life Full of Holes* (see above), describing in semi-fictionalised form Layachi's time with Paul and Jane Bowles; the latter is more of a novel and rather less successful.

Abdelhak Serhane, *Messaouda* (Carcanet, UK). Adventurous, semi-autobiographical novel about growing up in Azrou during the 1950s. The narrator's development parallels that of his country; his attempts to free himself from the patriarchy and authoritarianism of his father are used as an allegory for the struggle against French colonialism and its aftermath.

Driss Chraibi, *Heirs to the Past* (Heinemann UK/US). Again concerned with the crisis of Moroccans' post-colonial identity, and again semi-autobiographical as the author-narrator (who has lived in France since the war) returns to Morocco for the funeral of his father. Also available – though in rather over-literal and unspirited translation – are two further novels, *The Butts* and *Mother Comes of Age* (Forest Books/Three Continents Press).

Brick Ousaïd, *Mountains Forgotten by God* (Forest Books/Three Continents Press). Autobiographical narrative of an Atlas Berber family, which gives an impressive sense of the harshness of mountain life. As the author describes it, it is "not an exercise in literary style [but] a cry from the bottom of my heart, of despair and revolt".

Margot Badran and Miriam Cooke (eds), *Opening the Gates: A Century of Arab Feminist Writing* (Virago, UK). Includes three Moroccan pieces, including a traditional women's tale, recounted by the Moroccan feminist, Fatima Mernissi.

WESTERN FICTION

PAUL BOWLES

NOVELS: *The Sheltering Sky* (Granada/Ecco Press); *Let It Come Down* (Arrow/Black Sparrow Press); *The Spider's House* (Arena/Black Sparrow Press).

STORIES: *Collected Stories of Paul Bowles 1939–76* (Black Sparrow Press, US) gathers together work from numerous earlier editions. Post-1976 collections include *Midnight Mass* (Peter Owen/Black Sparrow Press), *Call at Corazón* (Peter Owen) and *Unwelcome Words* (Tombouctou, US).

Bowles stands out as the most interesting and the most prolific writer using North African themes – and with Bertolucci's film of *The Sheltering Sky* he has, at last, regained some of the recognition he was due (the novel was a best seller on publication in 1955). Many of his stories are similar in vein to those of Mohammed Mrabet (see above), employing the same sparse forms, bizarre twists and interjections of violence. The novels are something different, exploring both Morocco (or, in *The Sheltering Sky*, Algeria) and the ways in which Europeans and Americans react to and are affected by it.

If you read nothing else on the country, at least get hold of ***The Spider's House*** – one of the best political novels ever written, its backdrop the traditional daily life of Fes, its theme the conflicts and transformation at the last stages of the French occupation of the country.

The last few years have seen a flurry of **biographies and memoirs of Bowles** and his literary friends and acquaintances in **Tangier**:

Ian Finlayson, *Tangier: City of the Dreams* (Collins, UK)). Good on the Moroccans, whom Bowles has translated.

Michelle Green, *The Dream at the End of the World: Paul Bowles and the Literary Renegades of Tangier* (Bloomsbury, UK)). Strong narrative and compulsively peopled: the best read if you're looking for one book on Tangier literary life.

Christopher Sawyer-Lauçanno, *Paul Bowles: An Invisible Spectator* (Paladin/Weidenfeld & Nicholson). A somewhat laborious effort, comparing the episodes of Bowles' life and fiction. The subject clearly loathed the project.

Gary Pulsifer (ed), *Paul Bowles by his Friends* (Peter Owen UK). A fascinating and affectionate selection of reminiscences by a cast of Beats and others who made their way to Bowles's flat in Tangier.

Bowles's autobiography, *Without Stopping* (Macmillan/Ecco Press), is also of interest for its Moroccan episodes (though William Burroughs dubbed it "Without Telling"), as is his more recent *Two Years Beside the Strait/ Days: A Tangier Journal, 1987–89* (Peter Owen/Ecco Press).

OTHER FICTION SET IN MOROCCO

Arturo Barea, *The Forging of a Rebel* (Flamingo, UK reprint, 3 vols, 1988, o/p). Autobiographical trilogy dealing with events of the 1930s. Volume two, *The Track,* concerns the war and colonisation of the Rif, the Spanish entry into Chaouen and life in Tetouan.

William Bayer, *Tangier* (Dutton, US, 1971, o/p). Thinly disguised potboiler set amid the Tangier expat life of the 1960s.

Jane Bowles, *Everything is Nice – Collected Stories* (Virago, 1989). The title story is a perfect evocation of Moroccan life, rendered in the author's unique and idiosyncratic style. Jane Bowles was resident in Morocco on and off, with Paul Bowles, from the 1940s until her tragic death in 1973. Millicent Dillon's biography, *A Little Original Sin: the Life of Jane Bowles* (Virago, £10.95), includes some fascinating material.

Anthony Burgess, *Earthly Powers* (Penguin, UK/US), *Enderby Anthology* (Penguin, UK/US). Sporadic scenes in 1950s-decadent Tangier.

Aldo Busi, *Sodomies in Eleven Point* (Faber, UK/US). A (highly) picaresque tour of Morocco.

Elisa Chimenti, *Tales and Legends of Morocco* (Astor-Honor, US). Travelling in the 1930s and 1940s with her father, personal physician to Sultan Moulay Hassan, Chimenti learned many of these simple, fable-like tales from Berber tribesmen whose guest she was.

Rafael Chirbes, *Mimoun* (Serpent's Tail, UK/ US). Compelling tale of a Spanish teacher, based south of Fes, adrift amid sexual adventures and bizarre local life and antagonisms.

Esther Freud, *Hideous Kinky* (Penguin/ Harcourt Brace). An English hippy takes her two daughters to Marrakesh, where they live simply, as locals. A wonderful narrative – funny, sad, and full of informed insights – told through the persona of the five-year-old.

Brion Gysin, *The Process* (Paladin/Overlook Press). Beat novel by ex-Tangier resident and friend of William Burroughs. Fun, if a little caught in its (zany 1960s) age.

Richard Hughes, *In the Lap of Atlas* (Chatto, UK, o/p). Traditional Moroccan stories – cunning, humorous and ironical – reworked by the author of *A High Wind In Jamaica*. Also includes a narrative of Hughes' visit to Telouet and the Atlas in 1928.

Jane Kramer, *Honor to the Bride Like the Pigeon that Guards its Grain Under the Clove Tree* (Farrar, Straus & Giroux, US, 1970, o/p). Fictional narrative based on the true story of a Berber woman's kidnap in Meknes.

Amin Malouf, *Leo the African* (Quartet, UK). Superb historical novel, recreating the life of Leo Africanus, the fifteenth-century Moorish geographer, in Granada and Fes and on later travels.

Robin Maugham, *The Wrong People* (Gay Men's Press, UK). Gay tragedy, set in Tangier.

Leonora Peets, *Women of Marrakesh* (C.Hurst, UK). Stories of domestic life in the city from the 1930s to 1970 by a long-term Estonian resident.

GLOSSARY OF MOROCCAN TERMS

ADHAN the call to prayer

AGADIR fortified granary

AGDAL garden or park containing a pool

AGUELMANE lake

AÏN spring

AÏT tribe (literally, "sons of"); also BENI

ALAOUITE ruling Moroccan dynasty from the seventeenth century to the present king, Hassan II

ALMOHAD the greatest of the medieval dynasties, ruled Morocco (and much of Spain) from ca.1147 until the rise to power of the Merenids ca.1224

ALMORAVIDS dynasty that preceded the Almohads, from ca. 1060 to ca. 1147

ANDALOUS Muslim Spain (a territory that centred on modern Andalucía)

ARABESQUE geometrical decoration or calligraphy

ASSIF river (often seasonal) in Berber

BAB gate or door

BABOUCHES slippers (usually yellow)

BALI (or **QDIM**) old

BARAKA sancity or blessing, obtained through saints or *marabouts*

BARBARY European term for North Africa in the sixteenth to nineteenth centuries

BENI tribe (as Aït)

BERBERS native inhabitants of Morocco, and still the majority of the population

BLED countryside, or, literally "land"; **BLED ES MAKHZEN** – governed lands; **BLED ES SIBA** – land outside government control

BORDJ fort

CAID district administrator; **CADI** is an Islamic judge

CHLEUH southern Berber from the High or Anti-Atlas or plains

COL mountain pass (French)

DAR house or palace; **DAR EL MAKHZEN**, royal palace

DAYA, DEYET lake

DJEBEL mountain peak or ridge; a **DJEBALI** is someone from the mountains; the **DJEBALA** are the main tribe of the Western Rif

DJEDID, JDID new

DJELLABA wool or cotton hooded outer garment

DJEMAA, JAMAA mosque, or Friday (the main day of worship)

DJINN nature spirits (genies)

ERG sand dune

FAKIR Koranic schoolteacher or lawyer, or just an educated man

FANTASIA display of horsemanship performed at larger festivals or *moussems*

FASSI inhabitant of Fes

FILALI alternative name for the Alaouite dynasty – from the southern Tafilalt region

FONDOUK inn and storehouse, known as a *caravanserai* in the eastern part of the Arab world

GANDOURA man's cotton garment (male equivalent of a kaftan); also known as a FOKIA

GHARB coastal plain between Larache and Kenitra

GNAOUA Moroccan black person, originally from Guinea; also a sect, or brotherhood, who play drum-based trance music

HABBOUS religious foundation or bequest of property for religious charities

HADJ pilgrimage to Mecca

HAMMADA stony desert of the sub-Sahara

HAMMAM Turkish-style steam bath

HARKA "burning" raid undertaken by sultans in order to raise taxes and assert authority

IDRISSID first Arab dynasty of Morocco – named after its founder, Moulay Idriss

IMAM prayer leader and elder of mosque

ISTIQLAL nationalist party founded during the struggle for independence

JOUTIA flea market

KASBAH palace centre and/or fortress of an Arab town; also a feudal family castle in the south. Like the Spanish *alcazar*

KHETTARA underground irrigation canal

KIF hashish, cannabis

KOUBBA dome; small *marabout* tomb

KSAR, KSOUR (pl.) village or tribal stronghold in the south

LALLA "madam"

LITHAM veil

MAGHREB "West" in Arabic, used for Morocco and the North African countries

MAKHZEN government

MARABOUT holy man, and by extension his place of burial. These tombs, usually whitewashed domes, play an important (and heterodox) role in the religion of country areas

MECHOUAR assembly place, court of judgement

MEDERSA student residence and, in part, a teaching annexe, for the old mosque universities

MEDINA literally, "city", now used for the original Arab part of any Moroccan town. The Kasbah is usually a quarter of the Medina

MELLAH Jewish quarter

MERENIDS dynasty from eastern plains who ruled from the thirteenth to fifteenth centuries

MIHRAB niche indicating the direction of Mecca (and for prayer)

MINARET tower attached to a mosque, used for call to prayer

MINZAH pavilion in a (usually palace) garden

MOULAY descendant of the Prophet Muhammad, a claim and title adopted by most Moroccan sultans

MOULOUD festival and birthday of the Prophet

MOUSSEM pilgrimage-festival

MSALLA prayer area

MUEZZIN, MUEDDIN singer who calls the faithful to prayer

NAZARENE, NSRANI Christian

OUED river; can be seasonal or even dry on a permanent basis (a WADI in its Anglicised form).

PISÉ mud and rubble building material

PISTE rough road

PROTECTORATE period of French and Spanish colonial occupation (1912–56)

QAHOUAJI café patron

RAMADAN month of fasting

RAS source or head

RAS EL MA water source

RIBAT monastic fortress

SAADIAN southern dynasty from Drâa Valley, who ruled Morocco during the fifteenth century

SEBGHA lake or lagoon

SEGUIA irrigation canal

SHEIKH leader of religious brotherhood

SHEREEF descendant of the Prophet

SIDI, SI respectful title used for any man, like "Sir" or "Mister"

SOUK market, or market quarter

SUFI religious mystic; philosophy behind most of the religious brotherhoods

TABIA mud building material, as *pisé*

TIGHREMT similar to an *agadir* – fortified Berber home and storage place

TOUAREG nomadic Berber tribesmen of the disputed Western Sahara, fancifully known as "Blue Men" because of the blue dye of their cloaks (which gives a slight tinge to their skin)

TIZI mountain pass; as COL in French

WATTASID fifteenth-century dynasty who replaced their cousins, the Merenids

ZAOUIA sanctuary established around a *marabout's* tomb; seminary-type base for religious brotherhood

ZELLIJ geometrical mosaic tilework

GLOSSARY OF MOROCCAN STREETNAMES

Moroccan streets are often named after well-known historical figures, events and dates, and in recent years there has been a concerted drive to replace the old panoply of French and Spanish colonial names. As they're revealing of Moroccan interests and historical figures, a glossary follows of some of the most common.

Transliteration from Arabic into the Roman alphabet means that there are often many variations of the same name.

ABDELKRIM EL KATTABI Leader of the Rif war against the Spanish. In 1921, his Berber warriors defeated a Spanish army of 60,000 at Annoual. He formed the independent republic of the Rif, but was defeated by Spanish/French forces in 1926.

ALLAL BEN ABDALLAH On 11 September, 1953, he tried to kill Sultan Ibn Aaraf who had been appointed by the French to succeed Mohammed V when he was sent into exile. Allal Ben Abdallah crashed an open car into the royal procession on its way to the mosque in Rabat and attacked the Sultan with a knife.

EL FARABI Born in Farab, now in Uzbekistan, he studied in Baghdad and taught as a 'Sufi' in Aleppo, now in Syria. He lived from 870 to 950 and is one of the greatest Islamic philosophers; he harmonised Greek philosophy and Islamic thinking. He studied Aristotle, and was known as second only to him. Thus, he was known as Al Muallim Al Thani ('the second teacher').

FERHAT HACHAD On 7 and 8 December, 1952, there were massive riots in the streets of Casablanca and hundreds were killed. The overt cause of this was the assassination in Tunis of Ferhat Hachad, a Tunisian trade union leader and Arab nationalist.

HASSAN II The reigning monarch and elder son of Mohammed V, whom he succeeded on **3 March, 1961**. He was born on 9 July, 1929, and his birthday is celebrated every year as Youth Day. He launched the Green March (see on p.556) on **6 November, 1975**.

IBN BATOUTA Born in Tangier (1304), he trained as a lawyer, made the pilgrimage to Mecca and was taken with a desire for further travel. He visited China and India, returning to Fes where he dictated his discoveries to a student. At the time, he was regarded as a romancer, but his reports turned out to be true.

IBN KHALDOUN Arab philosopher and historian, born in Tunis (1322) of an aristocratic family long resident in Muslim Spain, which he visited in 1362. He served as ambassador to Castile, Tamerlaine and the court at Fes. Study of North African history led him to his political theories about the natural life of a dynasty which he argued lasted only four generations.

IBN ROCHD Also known as *Averroes*, another of Islam's greatest philosophers. He was born in Córdoba (1126) and died in Marrakesh (1198). He introduced Christian monks to Aristotle, but worked principally on astronomy, theology, mathematics and, particularly, medicine. Based in Marrakesh, he was doctor to Yacoub El Mansour.

IBN TACHFINE/YOUSSEF IBN TACHFINE A devout Muslim Berber from Adrar, now in Mauritania, and the first Sultan of the Almoravid dynasty. He founded Marrakesh in 1060, captured Fes in 1069, fought against Alphonse IV and ruled Muslim Spain and the Maghreb as far east as Algiers.

IBN TOUMERT/MEHDI IBN TOUMERT Learned theologian, radical reformer and revolutionary leader, known as "The Torch". He was born around 1080, travelled to the Middle East in 1107, returned to Marrakesh in 1121, was expelled from there and took refuge with his warrior monks in the mountain stronghold of Tin Mal in 1124, where he died around 1130. He was believed by his followers to be the *mahdi* – the "sinless one".

IBN ZAIDOUN Leading Andalusian poet of the eleventh century; like others, he followed the traditions of the east.

IBN ZIAD/TARIK BEN ZIAD/ TARIK IBN ZIAD Berber chieftain who led the troops of Moussa Ibn Noussar across the Straits of Gibraltar. He defeated the Visigoths, near Tarifa, in 711, to bring seven centuries of civilisation when the rest of Europe lived in the Dark Ages. He gave his name to Gibraltar – Djebel (mount) Tarik.

EL MANSOUR EDDAHBI The victory over the Portuguese at the Battle of the Three Kings in 1579 gave great prestige to El Mansour Eddahbi who suceeded his brother (who died in the battle). Mansour means "victorious"; Eddahbi means "golden".

MOHAMMED V Born in Fes in 1909, the third son of Sultan Moulay Youssef, he was chosen by the French to succeed his father on **18 November, 1927**. He was unprepared for his role, but gained strength with experience. He supported the joint manifesto of **11 January, 1944**, arguing for independence; he spoke openly for independence in Tangier, then in the International Zone, on **9 April, 1947**, and was deposed by the French on **20 August, 1953**. He returned from exile on **16 November, 1955**, to a hero's welome and secured independence on **2 March, 1956**. He died in 1961 and was succeeded by his elder son, Hassan II.

MOHAMMED BEN ADDALLAH/SIDI MOHAMMED BEN ABDALLAH Grandson of Moulay Ismail, he gained the throne in 1757, and brought some order out of chaos. He established Essaouira in the 1760s, drove the Portuguese from El Jadida, armed the port of Larache and developed Tangier. Finally he contained the Spanish in their enclaves.

MOHAMMED ZERKTOUNI The most famous Moroccan freedom fighter. On 24 December, 1953, in Casablanca's central market he placed a bomb in a shopping basket which killed twenty people and injured twenty-eight. The choice of Christmas Eve was symbolic: Mohammed V had been exiled on 20 August, 1953 – the eve of Aïd El Kebir.

MOKHTAR SOUSSI Poet and nationalist figure during the French occupation. On independence, he became the government minister of *habous* (religious foundations which fund mosques, hospitals and schools). He also wrote a twelve-volume history of the Souss, his native province.

MOULAY ABDALLAH/PRINCE MOULAY ABDALLAH Younger son of Mohammed V. He married a Lebanese princess, Lamia Sohl and often deputised for his brother, Hassan II. He died in 1984.

MOULAY EL CHERIF/MOULAY RACHID First Sultan (1666–1672) of the Alaouite dynasty – originally an Arab family which settled in the

Tafilalt in the twelfth century, where they lived modestly for centuries before seizing power. Er Rachidia (and its main street) are named after Moulay Rachid.

MOULAY HASSAN/HASSAN I The last notable Alaouite Sultan (1873–1894) before the French Protectorate. He strived to damp down European-sponsored rebellion, attempting to reform his army with the help of a Scottish clan chieftain, Caid Harry MacLean. He died suddenly and was succeeded by his son, Abd El Aziz, a profligate dreamer.

MOULAY IDRISS/MOULAY IDRISS I/ MOULAY IDRISS II Father and his posthumous son by a Berber mother. Moulay Idriss I (788–91) founded the first orthodox Muslim dynasty, ruling the northern Maghreb from Tlemcen, now in Algeria, to the Atlantic. After a regency, his son, Moulay Idriss II (804–28), came to the throne; he founded Fes and is regarded as the father of the Moroccan state.

MOULAY ISMAIL The second Sultan of the Alaouite dynasty (1672–1727), but the first to establish complete rule over Morocco. His 55-year reign was one of the longest, and said to be the most brutal, in Moroccan history. He chose, and developed, Meknes as his capital. After his death, his sons fought over the succession and chaos ensued.

MOULAY YOUSSEF Appointed by the French as Sultan (1912–27); he was the father of Mohammed V and grandfather of Hassan II.

MOUSSA IBN NOUSSAR Followed Oqba Ibn Nafi (see below) and converted the Berbers again to Islam. He conquered all the territory as far south as the Tafilalt, and launched Tarik Ibn Zaid across the Straits of Gibralter.

OQBA IBN NAFI Military general and missionary who led the first Arab expedition westwards to convert the Berbers to Islam. He left Arabia in 666; founded Kairouan in present-day Tunisia in 670; and moved on into Morocco, reaching the Atlantic in 682. He was ambushed and killed by Berbers in (present-day) Algeria on his return to the east.

PRINCE HERETIER SIDI MOHAMMED/ PRINCE SIDI MOHAMMED Hassan II's elder son and the heir to the throne, born in Rabat on 21 August, 1963. As his father before him, he is being groomed to rule and is increasingly seen with his younger brother, Prince Sidi

Rachid, attending national and international events with his father.

SALAH EDDINE EL AYOUBI (1137–90) Better known in the West as Salah Al Din or Saladin. He recaptured Jerusalem (then known, in Arabic, as Al Qods) from the Crusaders in 1187.

YACOUB EL MANSOUR/YACOUB MANSAUR AL MOUAHIDI Powerful Sultan (1184–99) who created an empire comprising Muslim Spain and most of North Africa. He won the title "Mansour" (Victorious) when he defeated the Christians under Alfonso VIII of Castile at the battle of Alarcos on 18 July, 1195. He was a generous patron of poets and philosophers.

DATES

Numerous dates, particularly those associated with Mohammed V and Hassan II (see their respective entries), have been commemorated as street names. The most common include:

11 January, 1944 Mohammed V backed the nationalist cause when the Istiqlal party issued its manifesto on 11 January, 1944, demanding, for the first time, not just reform but independence.

29 February, 1960 The Agadir earthquake struck thirteen minutes before midnight, lasting fifteen seconds.

2 March, 1956 France renounced the Protectorate and, in a formal treaty, recognised Moroccan independence. It was the 45th anniversary of the entry of French troops into Fes.

3 March, 1961 Aïd El Arch (Feast of the Throne) is celebrated on the anniversary of the accession of the king. Since Hassan II ascended the throne on 3 March, 1961, Aïd El Arch has been celebrated on that date.

16 August, 1953 Over three days (16–18 August, 1953) there were anti-French riots in Casablanca, Rabat, Marrakesh and Oujda. Over 45 people were killed and more than eighty injured in Oujda alone on 16 August.

20 August, 1953 On this day, the eve of Aïd El Kebir, Mohammed V was deposed by the French and was exiled first in Corsica, then Madagascar. Mayhem followed.

6 November, 1975 The date of the Green March – Al Massira Al Khadra (see below).

16 November, 1955 Mohammed V returned from exile to a hero's welcome. He told crowds around the Rabat Palace that the Protectorate was over and independence would follow.

18 November, 1927/18 November, 1955 Mohammed V ascended the throne on 18 November, 1927 and thus, during his reign, this was celebrated as Aïd El Arch (see 3 March, above). In 1955, it was also celebrated as Independence Day and has been celebrated subsequently as such. The three days (16, 17 & 18 November) are taken as a holiday and are known as *Les Trois Glorieuses*.

EVENTS/ORGANISATIONS

AL JAMIA AL ARABI The Arab League: formed in Egypt in 1945 and moved to Tunisia in 1979 following the Camp David peace accord between Egypt and Israel.

AL MASSIRA AL KHADRA/MARCHE VERTE The Green March into then-Spanish Sahara was led by Ahmed Osman, Prime Minister at the time and brother-in-law to Hassan II. It began on 6 November, 1975, and on 14 November Spain transferred administration of the territory to Morocco and Mauritania.

BIR ANZARANE Town in the western Sahara and site of fierce battle between Moroccan and Polisario forces in 1979.

EL HOURIA Houria means freedom/*liberté*.

FAR/FORCES ARMÉES ROYALES After Mohammed V and Hassan II, the Armed Forces is the most popular name for avenues/ boulevards, and their motto 'God, the Fatherland and the King' is to be found prominently displayed on many a hillside.

ISTIQLAL Istiqlal means **independence** and was adopted as its name by the nationalist party formed in Fes in 1943, with Allal al Fasi as its first president. By 1951, the party had 100,000 members.

OUED EL MAKHAZINE Site of the Battle of the Three Kings (see El Mansour Eddahbi, above). The Portugese found themselves trapped in a fork between the river Loukis and its tributary, the Oued El Makhazine. In European histories it is more often referred to as the battle of Ksar El Kebir.

LANGUAGE

Very few people who come to Morocco learn to speak a word of Arabic, let alone anything of the country's three distinct Berber dialects. This is a pity – you'll be treated in a very different way if you make even a small effort to master basic phrases – though not really surprising. Moroccans are superb linguists: much of the country is bilingual in French, and anyone who has significant dealings with tourists will know some English and maybe half-a-dozen other languages, too.

If you can speak **French,** you'll be able to get by almost anywhere you care to go; it is worth refreshing your knowledge before coming – and, if you're not too confident, bringing a good English–French phrasebook. **Spanish** is also useful, and widely understood in the old Spanish colonial zones around Tetouan and the Rif, and in the Deep South.

MOROCCAN ARABIC

Moroccan Arabic, the country's "official" language, is substantially different from "classical" Arabic, or from the modern Arabic spoken in Egypt and the Gulf States. If you speak any form of Arabic, however, you will be able to make yourself understood. Egyptian Arabic, in particular, is familiar to most Moroccans, through soap operas on TV, and many will adapt their speech accordingly.

Pronunciation

There are no silent letters – you pronounce everything that's written – including double vowels. Letters and syllables in italics should be stressed.
Here are some keys to follow in pronouncing:

kh	like the "ch" in Scottish lo*ch*	ay	as in "say"
gh	like the French "r" (a slight gargling sound)	q	like "k" but further back in throat
ai	as in "eye"	j	like "s" in pleasure

Basics

Yes	*Na'am, Ee*yeh	(Very) good	Mezyena (b*zef*)
No	La	Bad/"ugly"	*Meshee* mezyena/*khai*b
Please	Min*fad*lik/ *A*fek	Beautiful	*Zwe*en/*zwe*ena
Thank you	*Shok*ran/ Baraka*low*fik	Today	Ly*oom*/ lee*oom*
(polite response – *Ble*jmeel)		Tomorrow	*Ghe*dda

Greetings and farewells

Hello	La *bes*	What's yours?	S*mee*tik?
(informal, to one person)		See you later.	N'*shoo*fik min bad
Hello	Sal*am* Wa*lay*koom	. . . God willing	. . . In*shall*ah
(formal, to a group; response – Wa*lay*koom sal*am*)		(response to "In*shall*ah" is In*shall*ah)	
Good morning	Sbah l'*khir*	Good night	Lee*la sai*eeda
Good afternoon	Msa l'*khir*	Good-bye	B*slem*ah
My name is	Ismee. . .	Bon voyage	Treq sa*lama*

Directions, travelling, and accommodation

Where is . . . ?	Feen kayn . . . ?	Here, there	Hnna, Temma
. . . a (good) hotel?	. . . Otel (mizeeyen)	When is the bus/train?	Waqtash l'kar/tren?
. . . a campsite?	. . . Mookhaiyem	First/last/next	Loowel/L'akher/Lee minbad
. . . a restaurant?	. . . Restaurant	Write it (please).	Ktib ha (Afek)
. . . a bank?	. . . Bank	Do you have a room?	Wesh andik wahid beet?
. . . the bus station?	. . . Mahatat d'lkeeran	Can I see it?	Wesh yimkin nshoof?
. . . the train station?	. . . l'Gare	Is there. . . ?	Wesh kayn . . . ?
. . . a toilet?	. . . Vaysay/ W.C.	. . . a (hot) shower?	. . . Doosh (skhoon)
Straight	Neeshan/ tol	. . . a window?	. . . Serjem
(To the) left, right	(Al) Leeser, Leemin	. . . a key?	. . . Saroot
Near, far	Qreeb, Baieed	Can we camp here?	Wesh yimkin nkhaimoo
Junction	Rompwa		hanna

Buying and numbers

How much (is that)?	Bsh hal (hadeek)	I want something. . .	Bgheet shihaja . . .
This isn't good	Hadee meshee mizeeyen	. . . else	. . . okhra
Too expensive	Ghalee bzef	. . . better than this	. . . khir min hadee
. . . (for me)	(aliya)	. . . like this	. . . bhal hadee
Still too expensive	Mazal ghalee bzef	(but)	(walakeen)
Do you have. . . ?	wesh andik. . . ?	. . . larger, smaller	. . . kebira, seghira
Okay	Wakha	. . . cheaper	. . . rkhaysa

1	wahed	12	tinach	40	arbaeen
2	tneen (Classical)	13	teltach	50	khamseen
	jooj (everyday)	14	arbatach	60	setteen
3	tlata	15	khamstach	70	seba'een
4	arba	16	settach	80	tmaneen
5	khamsa	17	sebatach	90	tsa'een
6	setta	18	tmentach	100	mia
7	sebaa	19	tsatach	200	miateen
8	tmenia	20	achreen	300	telt mia
9	tse'ud	21	wahed u achrin	400	arba mia
10	achra	22	tneen u achrin	1000	alef
11	hadach	30	tlateen		

Useful phrases/reactions

I have . . .	Andee . . .	. . . key	. . . saroot
That's all	Sahfee	. . . baggage	. . . baggaj/howayj
I don't have any money	Mandeesh floos	Help!	Ateqq/ Ownee!
		How do you say?	Keef tkooloo?
I've seen it already.	Shift ha baada	Excuse me	Smeh lee
I don't want any.	Mabgheetsh	Sorry, I apologise	Asif
I don't understand.	Mafhemsh	Never mind, so it goes	Maalesh
Do you understand?	Wesh fhemtee?	No problem	Meckee mushkeel
Get lost!	Seer!	Respect yourself	Ihtarim nafsak
Everything's fine.	Koolshee mizeeyen	(a term of admonition)	
Let's go!	Yallah!	Calm down	
Watch out!	Andak/ Balek!	(literally, "lengthen your	Tawil balak
I've lost . . .	Msha leeya . . .	mind")	
. . . passport	. . . passeport	You honour us	Too-shah-rif-na
. . . ticket	. . . beeyay/ warqa	Patience is a virtue	As-sobrmin Allah

BERBER WORDS AND PHRASES IN TASHELHAÏT

There are three **Berber dialects** which encompass roughly geographical areas. They are known by several names, of which these are the most common:

Riffi – The Rif mountains and Northern Morocco
Zaian, Tamazight – The Middle Atlas and Central Morocco
Tashelhaït, Soussi, Chleuh – The High and Anti-Atlas and the South

As the most popular Berber areas for visitors are the High Atlas and South, the following is a very brief guide to **Tashelhaït words and phrases.**

Basics

Yes, no	Eyeh, Oho	Today	Zig sbah
Thank you, please	Barakalaufik	Tomorrow	Ghasad
Good	Eefulkee/Eeshwa	Yesterday	Eegdam
Bad	Khaib	Excuse me	Semhee
		Berbers	Shleuh

Greetings and Farewells (All Arabic greetings understood)

Hello	La bes darik (man)	See you later	Akrawes dah inshallah
(response – *la bes*)	La bes darim (woman)	Goodbye	Akayaoon Arbee
How are you?	Meneek antgeet?	Say hello to your	Sellum flfamilenik
(response – *la bes Imamdulah*)		family	

Directions and names on maps

Where is. . . ?	Mani heela . . . ?	I want to go to . . .	Reeh . . .
. . . the road to . . .	. . . aghares s . . .	(literally, "I want")	
. . . the village . . .	. . . doowar . . .		
. . . the river . . .	. . . aseet . . .	**On survey maps you'll find these names:**	
. . . the mountain . . .	. . . adrar . . .	Mountain	Adrar, Jbel
. . . the pass . . .	. . . tizee . . .	River	Assif, Oued
. . . your house	. . . teegimeenik	Pass (of)	Tizi (n.)
Is it far/close?	Ees yagoog/eeqareb?	Shepherd's hut	Azib
Straight	Neeshan	Hill, small mountain	Aourir
To the right/left	Fofaseenik/fozelmad	Ravine	Talat
Where are you going?	Manee treet? (s.)	Rock	Azrou
	Manee drem? (pl.)	("n" between words indicates the possessive,"of")	

Buying and numbers

1	yen	21	Ashreent d yen d mrawet	A lot/little	Bzef/eemeek
2	seen	22	Ashreent d seen d mrawet	Do you have . . . ?	Ees daroon . . . ?
3	krad	30	Ashreent d mrawet	Is there . . . ?	Ees eela . . . ?
4	koz	40	Snet id ashreent	. . . food	. . . teeremt
5	smoos	50	Snet id ashreent d mrawet	. . . a mule	. . . aserdon
6	sddes	100	Smoost id ashreent/meeya	. . . a place to sleep	. . . kra lblast
7	sa				mahengwen
8	tem	How much is it?	Minshk aysker?	. . . water	. . . amen
9	tza	No good	oor eefulkee		
10	mrawet	Too expensive	Eeghula bzef	**Imperatives you may hear**	
11	yen d mrawet	Come down a little (in price)	Nuqs emeek	Sit	Gawer, Skoos
				Drink	Soo
12	seen d mrawet	Give me . . .	Feeyee . . .	Eat	Shta
		I want . . .	Reeh . . .	Here	Omz
20	Ashreent	Big/Small	Mqorn/Eemzee	(when handing something to someone)	

FRENCH ESSENTIALS

Basics and greetings

Yes/no	Oui/non	Could you?	Pourriez-vous?
Hello, good day	Bonjour	Why?	Pourquoi?
Sorry, excuse me	Pardon	What?	Quoi?
How are you?	Ça va?	Open	Ouvert
Goodbye	Au revoir	Closed	Fermé
Please	S'il vous plaît	Go away!	Va-t-en
Thank you	Merci	Stop messing me about!	Arrête de m'emmerder!
I/you	Je/vous	No confidence!	Pas de confiance!

Directions

Where is the road for . . . ?	Quelle est la route pour . . . ?	Far	Loin
Where is . . . ?	Où est . . . ?	When?	Quand?
Do you have . . . ?	Avez vous . . . ?	At what time?	A quelle heure?
. . . a room?	. . . une chambre?	Write it down, please	Écrivez-le, s'il vous plaît
Here, there	Ici, là	Now	Maintenant
Right	A droite	Later	Plus tard
Left	A gauche	Never	Jamais
Straight on	Tout droit	Today	Aujourd'hui
Near	Proche, près	Tomorrow	Demain
		Yesterday	Hier

Things

Bus	Car, autobus	Key	Clef
Bus station	Gare routière	Roof	Terrasse
Railway	Chemin de fer	Passport	Passeport
Airport	Aéroport	Exchange	Change
Railway station	Gare	Post office	Poste
Ferry	Ferry	Stamps	Timbres
Lorry	Camion	Left luggage	Consigne
Ticket (return)	Billet (de retour)	Visa	Visa
Bank	Banque	Money	Argent

Buying

How much/many?	Combien?	Like this/that	Comme ceci/cela
How much does that cost?	Combien ça coute?	What is it?	Qu'est-ce que c'est?
Too expensive	Trop cher	Enough	Assez
More/less	Plus/moin	Big	Grand
Cheap	Bon marché	Little	Petit

NUMERALS

١	1	١٠	10	١٩	19	٨٠	80
٢	2	١١	11	٢٠	20	٩٠	90
٣	3	١٢	12	٢١	21	١٠٠	100
٤	4	١٣	13	٢٢	22	٢٠٠	200
٥	5	١٤	14	٣٠	30	٣٠٠	300
٦	6	١٥	15	٤٠	40	٤٠٠	400
٧	7	١٦	16	٥٠	50	١٠٠٠	1000
٨	8	١٧	17	٦٠	60		
٩	9	١٨	18	٧٠	70		

ARABIC/BERBER PHRASEBOOKS & LEARNING MATERIALS

Arabic phrasebooks

Moroccan Arabic Phrasebook (Lonely Planet, Australia). The most functional English–Moroccan Arabic phrasebook.

In Moroccan bookshops, you can pick up a *Guide de Conversation/Conversation Guide*, which covers basic phrases of English–French–Moroccan Arabic–Berber.

Arabic coursebooks

Ernest T. Abdel Massih, *An Introduction to Moroccan Arabic* ($18; 3 accompanying tapes, $20); *Advanced Moroccan Arabic* ($15; 4 tapes $32). Both published by University of Michigan Press.

Richard S. Harris and Mohammed Abn Tald, *Basic Course in Moroccan Arabic* (Georgetown UP 1980).

Berber coursebooks

Ernest T. Abdel Massih, *A Course in Spoken Tamazight: Berber Dialects of the Middle Atlas* ($15; 7 tapes $49); *A Reference Grammar of Tamazight, Plus An Introduction to the Berber Language ($15) University of Michigan Press*.

Arabic lessons in Morocco

Contact the *American Language Centre* (head office: 1 Place de la Fraternité, Casablanca).

University of Michigan Publications

For **books** write to The Publications Secretary, Centre for Near Eastern and North African Studies, 144 Lane Hall, University of Michigan, Ann Arbor, Michigan 48109. For **tapes** write to: Michigan Media Resource Centre (Tape Duplication Service), University of Michigan, 400 S. Fourth Street, Ann Arbor, Michigan 48103.

Bookshops

The following bookshops usually have language reference material:

Librairie des Colonnes, Bd. Pasteur, Tangier.

American Language Centre Bookstore, Bd. Moulay Youssef, Casablanca.

American Bookstore, Rue Tanja, Rabat.

The Maghreb Bookshop, 45 Burton St, London WC1, UK .

INDEX

MAP INDEX

DIRECT ORDERS IN THE USA

Title	ISBN	Price
Able to Travel	1858281105	$19.95
Australia	1858280354	$18.95
Berlin	1858280338	$13.99
Brittany & Normandy	1858280192	$14.95
Bulgaria	1858280478	$14.99
Canada	185828001X	$14.95
Crete	1858280494	$14.95
Cyprus	185828032X	$13.99
Czech & Slovak Republics	185828029X	$14.95
Egypt	1858280753	$17.95
England	1858280788	$16.95
Europe	185828077X	$18.95
Florida	1858280109	$14.95
France	1858280508	$16.95
Germany	1858280257	$17.95
Greece	1858280206	$16.95
Guatemala & Belize	1858280451	$14.95
Holland, Belgium & Luxembourg	1858280877	$15.95
Hong Kong & Macau	1858280664	$13.95
Hungary	1858280214	$13.95
Italy	1858280311	$17.95
Kenya	1858280435	$15.95
Mediterranean Wildlife	1858280699	$15.95
Morocco	1858280400	$16.95
Nepal	185828046X	$13.95
New York	1858280583	$13.95
Paris	1858280389	$13.95
Poland	1858280346	$16.95
Portugal	1858280842	$15.95
Prague	185828015X	$14.95
Provence & the Côte d'Azur	1858280230	$14.95
St Petersburg	1858280303	$14.95
San Francisco	1858280826	$13.95
Scandinavia	1858280397	$16.99
Scotland	1858280834	$14.95
Sicily	1858280370	$14.99
Thailand	1858280168	$15.95
Tunisia	1858280656	$15.95
USA	185828080X	$18.95
Venice	1858280362	$13.99
Women Travel	1858280710	$12.95
Zimbabwe & Botswana	1858280419	$16.95

Rough Guides are available from all good bookstores, but can be obtained directly in the USA and Worldwide (except the UK*) from Penguin:

Charge your order by Master Card or Visa (US$15.00 minimum order): call 1-800-255-6476; or send orders, with complete name, address and zip code, and list price, plus $2.00 shipping and handling per order to: Consumer Sales, Penguin USA, PO Box 999 – Dept #17109, Bergenfield, NJ 07621. No COD. Prepay foreign orders by international money order, a cheque drawn on a US bank, or US currency. No postage stamps are accepted. All orders are subject to stock availability at the time they are processed. Refunds will be made for books not available at that time. Please allow a minimum of four weeks for delivery.

The availability and published prices quoted are correct at the time of going to press but are subject to alteration without prior notice. Titles currently not available outside the UK will be available by January 1995. Call to check.

* For UK orders, see separate price list

DIRECT ORDERS IN THE UK

Title	ISBN	Price
Amsterdam	1858280184	£6.99
Australia	1858280354	£12.99
Barcelona & Catalunya	1858280486	£7.99
Berlin	1858280338	£8.99
Brazil	0747101272	£7.95
Brittany & Normandy	1858280192	£7.99
Bulgaria	1858280478	£8.99
California	1858280575	£9.99
Canada	185828001X	£10.99
Crete	1858280494	£6.99
Cyprus	185828032X	£8.99
Czech & Slovak Republics	185828029X	£8.99
Egypt	1858280753	£10.99
England	1858280788	£9.99
Europe	185828077X	£14.99
Florida	1858280109	£8.99
France	1858280508	£9.99
Germany	1858280257	£11.99
Greece	1858280206	£9.99
Guatemala & Belize	1858280451	£9.99
Holland, Belgium & Luxembourg	1858280036	£8.99
Hong Kong & Macau	1858280664	£8.99
Hungary	1858280214	£7.99
Ireland	1858280516	£8.99
Italy	1858280311	£12.99
Kenya	1858280435	£9.99
Mediterranean Wildlife	0747100993	£7.95
Morocco	1858280400	£9.99
Nepal	185828046X	£8.99
New York	1858280583	£8.99
Nothing Ventured	0747102082	£7.99
Paris	1858280389	£7.99
Peru	0747102546	£7.95
Poland	1858280346	£9.99
Portugal	1858280842	£9.99
Prague	185828015X	£7.99
Provence & the Côte d'Azur	1858280230	£8.99
Pyrenees	1858280524	£7.99
St Petersburg	1858280303	£8.99
San Francisco	1858280826	£8.99
Scandinavia	1858280397	£10.99
Scotland	1858280834	£8.99
Sicily	1858280370	£8.99
Spain	1858280079	£8.99
Thailand	1858280168	£8.99
Tunisia	1858280656	£8.99
Turkey	1858280133	£8.99
Tuscany & Umbria	1858280559	£8.99
USA	185828080X	£12.99
Venice	1858280362	£8.99
West Africa	1858280141	£12.99
Women Travel	1858280710	£7.99
Zimbabwe & Botswana	1858280419	£10.99

Rough Guides are available from all good bookstores, but can be obtained directly in the UK* from Penguin by contacting:

Penguin Direct, Penguin Books Ltd, Bath Road, Harmondsworth, West Drayton, Middlesex UB7 0DA; or telephone our credit line on 081-899 4036 (9am–5pm) and ask for Penguin Direct. Visa, Access and Amex accepted. Delivery will normally be within 14 working days. Penguin Direct ordering facilities are only available in the UK.

The availability and published prices quoted are correct at the time of going to press but are subject to alteration without prior notice.

* For USA and international orders, see separate price list

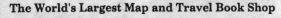
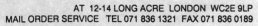

You are
A STUDENT

You travel
THE WORLD

You want
TO SAVE MONEY

Here's how

The International
Student Identity Card

International Student Identity Card
Internationale Studentenausweis/Carte internationale d'étudiant

ISIC

R 2195089

Family name/Name/Nom de famille
Sian
First Name/Vorname/Prénom
Sharoush
Born/Geburtsdatum/Né le
20/8/1973
Nationality/Nationalität/Nationalité
French
Studies/Studienfach, Schule/Etablissement d'enseignement
University of Paris

STUDENT

Available at Student Travel Offices Worldwide.

Entitles you to discounts and special services worldwide.